Vampires
Over the Ages

FIRST EDITION

A Cultural Analysis of Scientific,
Literary, and Cinematic Representations

Edited by
Tomislav Longinovic

Bassim Hamadeh, CEO and Publisher
Michael Simpson, Vice President of Acquisitions
Jamie Giganti, Managing Editor
Jess Busch, Graphic Designer Supervisor
Brian Fahey, Licensing Associate
Kate McKellar, Interior Designer

Copyright © 2014 by Cognella, Inc. All rights reserved. No part of this publication may be reprinted, reproduced, transmitted, or utilized in any form or by any electronic, mechanical, or other means, now known or hereafter invented, including photocopying, microfilming, and recording, or in any information retrieval system without the written permission of Cognella, Inc.

First published in the United States of America in 2014 by Cognella, Inc.

Trademark Notice: Product or corporate names may be trademarks or registered trademarks, and are used only for identification and explanation without intent to infringe.

Printed in the United States of America

ISBN: 978-1-62131-538-4 (pbk) / 978-1-62131-819-4 (br)

Contents

Epigraph ... 1

Critical Essays

The History of the Word *Vampire* ... 5
    Katharina M. Wilson

Forensic Pathology and the European Vampire ... 13
    Paul Barber

East European Vampires ... 37
    Felix Oinas

In Defense of Vampires ... 45
    John V. A. Fine, Jr.

South Slavic Countermeasures Against Vampires ... 53
    Friedrich S. Krauss

Vampurella: Darwin and Count Dracula ... 57
    Charles S. Blinderman

The Taboo Upon the Dead ... 69
    Sigmund Freud

Capital ... 77
    Karl Marx

Introducing the Dracula of Fiction, History, and Folklore ... 81
    Raymond T. McNally and Radu Florescu

The Archbishop's Vampires ... 85
    Francesco Paolo De Ceglia

Absent Presences in Liminal Places: Murnau's Nosferatu and the Otherworld of Stoker's Dracula   105
    Saviour Catania

Dracula Horror Stories of the Fifteenth Century   115
    Raymond T. McNally and Radu Florescu

Dark Shamans: Kanaimà and the Poetics of Violent Death   125
    Neil L. Whitehead

Giving up the Ghost   147
    Nina Auerbach

Hungary and Czecho-Slovakia   161
    Montague Summers

Bram Stoker and the Search for Castle Dracula   189
    Raymond T. McNally and Radu Florescu

The Quick and the Undead: Visual and Political Dynamics in Blood: The Last Vampire   195
    Christopher Bolton

LITERARY REPRESENTATIONS

The Mysterious Stranger   209
    Anonymous

Good Lady Ducayne (1896)   231
    Mary Elizabeth Braddon

Clarimonde   247
    Theophile Gautier

The Family of a Vourdalak   265
    Alexis Tolstoy

Dracula's Guest 279
   Bram Stoker

Varney the Vampyre, or, the Feast of Blood 287
(excerpt) (1845)
   James Malcolm Rymer

Wake Not the Dead 295
   Johann Ludwig Tieck

Murderer the Women's Hope 311
   Oskar Kokoschka

The Ghost Sonata 315
   August Strindberg

For the Blood Is the Life 333
   F. Marion Crawford

Revelations in Black 343
   Carl Jacobi

Luella Miller 355
   Mary E. Wilkins-Freeman

The Girl with the Hungry Eyes 363
   Fritz Leiber

Love-Starved 373
   Charles L. Grant

Shambleau 381
   C. L. Moore

Epigraph

Prejudice in favor of size. Men clearly overestimate everything large and obtrusive. This comes from their conscious or unconscious insight that it is very useful if someone throws all his strength into one area, and makes of himself, so to speak, one monstrous organ. Surely, for man himself, a *uniform* cultivation of his strengths is more useful and beneficial, for every talent is a vampire that sucks blood and strength out of the remaining strengths; and excessive productivity can bring the most gifted man almost to madness. Even within the arts, extreme natures attract notice much too much, but a much lesser culture is also necessary to let itself be captivated by them. Men submit from habit to anything that wants to have power.

— Friedrich Nietzsche, *Human, All Too Human*

Friedrich Nietzsche, "Aphorism 260," *Human, All Too Human*, trans. Helen Zimmern. Copyright in the Public Domain.

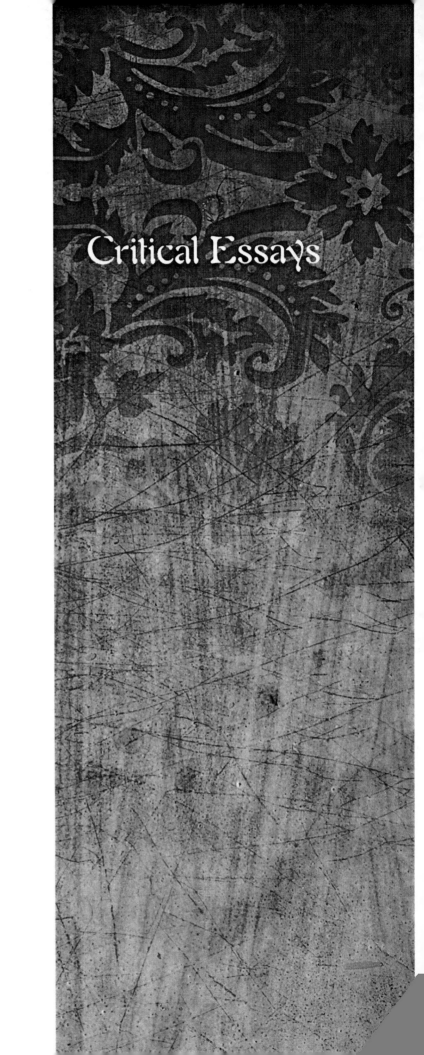
Critical Essays

The History of the Word *Vampire*

Katharina M. Wilson

LIKE THE LEGEND OF the living dead, so the origin of the word *vampire* is clouded in mystery. For most readers and authors alike, the vampire is a dark and ominous creature of the woods of Hungary or Transylvania. His name is often believed to be of the same national origin.[1] However, both linguistic studies concerning the etymology of the term *vampire* and the first recorded occurrences of the word in major European languages indicate that the word is neither Hungarian nor Romanian.

There are four clearly discernible schools of thought on the etymology of *vampire*, advocating Turkish, Greek, Slavic, and Hungarian roots for the term. The four groups are, respectively, chronological and geographic entities: the first group is represented by a nineteenth-century Austrian linguist and his followers; the second consists of scholars who were the German contemporaries of the early eighteenth-century vampire craze; the third comprises recent linguistic authorities; and the last is almost entirely limited to recent English and American writers.

The first group of etymological theorists on the word *vampire* consists of Franz Miklosich and many followers, Montague Summers and Stephan Hock among them, who use him as their authority.[2] Miklosich, a late nineteenth-century Austrian linguist, suggests in his influential work *Etymologie der slavischen Sprachen* that the word *vampire* and its Slavic synonyms *upior, uper,* and *upyr* are all derivatives of the Turkish *uber* (witch).

The second theory subscribes to the classical origins of the term. Summers, for instance, refers to an unidentified authority claiming the Greek verb πι (to drink) as a possible source for *vampire*.[3] Another etymological explanation along this line was proposed by Harenberg in the eighteenth century. S. Hock quotes the German scholar as saying, "Es läst sich vermuten dass das Wort zusammen gesetzet sey aus Bluht draus Vam geworden, und piren, das ist begierig nach einer Sache trachten."[4]

The third theory, which advocates the Slavic origin of the word, has now gained almost universal acceptance, and the root noun underlying the term is considered to be the Serbian word *BAMIIUP*. Kluge, Falk-Torp, the Grimm brothers, Wick, and Vaillant all point to the Serbian origin of the word as do, for example, the *OED* (London, 1903), the German *Brockhaus,* the Spanish *Encyclopedia Universal Illustrada* (Madrid, 1930–33), and the *Swensk Etymologisk Ordbok* (Lund, 1934–54).[5] Vasmer mentions the 1074 *Liber Prophetarum* as a possible source for the term, but this suggestion is refuted by A. Brückner on the grounds that in the *Liber Prophetarum* the word *upir* appears as a proper name.[6] Other sporadic attempts to explain the Slavic etymology of the word include Sobolevskij's theory that *vampire* derives from an old Polish or Polabic root and Maszynski's suggestion that the Serbo-Croatian verb *pirati* (to blow) contains the stem for *vampire*.[7] A. N. Afanas'ev lists several possible theories, among them the Lithuanian *wempti* (to drink).[8]

A quite convincing case for the Bulgarian origin of the word is made by A. Brückner in his 1934 article "Etymologien."[9] He contends the Serbian term *vampir* is only a borrowing from Bulgarian via Greek. Thus, the Serbian *BAMIIUP* appears to have served merely as a transmitter, but is not the root of the term.

The fourth school of writers, notably English and American, contend that the belief in vampires has its roots in ancient superstition but that the word itself is of recent and Hungarian origin. In a recent publication on vampires, for example, Raymond McNally says:

> Linguistic authorities differ over the origin of the word. For example, F. Miklosich, an eminent scholar of Slavic languages, claims that "vampire" derives from uber, the Turkish word for witch. But undoubtedly the source of "vampire" is the Hungarian word vampir.[10]

Similar statements are made by Summers and Wolf, just to name a few.[11] Their speculations, however, seem utterly unfounded, for the first appearance of the word *vampir* in Hungarian postdates the first use of the term in most Western languages by more than a century.

Just as the etymology of *vampire* is subject to controversy, so is the history of the introduction

---

Katharina M. Wilson, "The History of the Word Vampire," *Journal of the History of Ideas*, vol. 46, no. 4, pp. 577–583. Copyright © 1985 by University of Pennsylvania Press. Reprinted with permission.

of the word into the recorded vocabulary of major European languages and literatures, and the way of transmission is not always clear.

In France, according to most dictionaries, the word *vampire* was introduced in 1737 through the *Lettres Juives*, the ninth chapter of which recounts two incidents of vampirism in the village of Kisilova near Graditz.[12] But the *Mercure Galant* reported already in 1693 and 1694 cases of vampirism in Poland and Russia.[13] Also, in 1693 a Polish clergyman asked the Sorbonne how one is to deal with vampires or corpses believed to be vampires. Calmet records that the doctors Fromageau, de Precelles, and Durieroz unanimously condemned the cruel treatment.[14] The term, however, became a household word in French only after Dom Calmet's 1746 publication of his *Dissertations sur les apparitions et sur les revenants et les vampires*.

In French belles lettres the vampire theme appears first as a reaction to the popularity of Polidori's story *The Vampire* and its dramatic versions in England. *The Vampire* was translated into French in 1819 by Henry Faber, and it was followed by more or less obvious imitations and continuations by Cyprien Bernard (1819), Charles Nodier (1820), and others.

The German fortunes of the word are strikingly similar to those in France, even though a cognate of the term *vampire* was already introduced to the German scholarly audience in 1721, when Gabriel Rzazynski published his work *Historia naturalis curiosa regni Poloniae*.[15] Rzazynski recounts several seventeenth-century stories of Polish, Russian, and Lithuanian vampires, which he calls by their Polish name (*upior*). In the vernacular, however, the term first appeared in newspaper reports of the *Wiener Diarium* and other Viennese papers that published, as in France, the results of an official investigation concerning vampirism in the Graditz district which took place in 1725. Some of the pamphlets identified the Serbian district Graditz as a place in Hungary (rather than a province of Hungary); this reference may underlie the popular belief that Hungary is the homeland of vampires. Six years later even greater attention was given to an incident in the winter of 1731–32, when a vampire epidemic was reported in Medvegya, Serbia. The incident involved Arnold Paul, and the case, reported in the *Visum et Repertum* of the investigating commission, was reprinted in Nuremberg in 1732 in the *Commercium litterarium ad rei medicae et scientiae naturalis incrementum institutum*.[16] The official reports were followed in Germany and Austria by a burst of medical and philosophic treatises by anonymous authors and by scholars such as C. F. Demelius (1732), G. Gengell (1732), J. C. Pohlius (1732), J. C. Meinig (1732), J. H. Voigt (1733), J. C. Fritch (1732), J. H. Zopf (1733), J. C. Harenberg(1733), J. C. Stock(1732), and G. B. Bilfinger (1742).[17]

The first use of vampires in German belles lettres occurred in 1748, when August Ossenfelder's poem "Der Vampyr" appeared as the appendix to Christlob Mylius' article about vampires in the *Naturforscher*. The vampire theme received the first truly memorable treatment in 1797, when Goethe composed his "vampirisches Gedicht" entitled "Die Braut von Corinth," but the actual wide-scale popularity of the vampire theme was occasioned, as in France, through the translations and adaptations of Polidori's *The Vampire* in the 1820s.

In England, the term first appeared in the seventeenth century. According to Todd and Skeat, Paul Ricaut (Rycaut) introduced the term in his *State of the Greek and Armenian Churches*, published in 1679.[18] Todd quotes Ricaut as saying: "[The vampire is] ... a pretended demon, said to delight in sucking human blood, and to animate the bodies of dead persons, which when dug up, are said to be found florid and full of blood." The reference, however, is misleading, as Ricaut does not mention vampires by name here; he only describes the phenomenon as a superstition resulting from the reproachable overuse of excommunications in the Greek church. Ten years later, in 1688, the term must have been fairly well known, because Forman, in his *Observations on the Revolution in 1688*, written in the same year and published in 1741, used the term in a footnote metaphorically without attaching any explanation to it. He says:

> Our Merchants, indeed, bring money into their country, but it is said, there

is another Set of Men amongst us who have as great an Address in sending out again to foreign Countries without any Returns for it, which defeats the Industry of the Merchant. These are the Vampires of the Publick, and Riflers of the Kingdom.[19]

The *OED* mistakenly refers to the *Travels of 3 English Gentlemen from Venice to Hamburg, Being the Grand Tour of Germany in the Year 1734,* as the first use of the word in English. The composition of the *Travels* postdates both Ricaut and Forman by half a century, and the work was not published until 1810, when the earl of Oxford's library was printed in the *Harleian Miscellany.* The description of vampires in the *Travels* is nevertheless the first serious English explanation of the phenomenon and will therefore be considered here.

The anonymous author of the *Travels* was a member of the Royal Society and of the University of Oxford, and this description of vampires is contained in the description of Lubiana in the duchy of Carniola, Serbia. Usually, only the first sentence of the two very informative pages dealing with vampires is given, so it will be quoted more fully here. It reads:

> These Vampyres are supposed to be the bodies of decreased persons, animated by evil spirits, which come out of the graves, in the night time, suck the blood of many of the living, and thereby destroy them. Such a notion will, probably, be looked upon as fabulous and exploded, by many people in England; however, it is not only countenanced by Baron Valvasor, and many Carnioleze noblemen, gentlemen, etc., as we were informed, but likewise actually embraced by some writers of good authority. M. Jo. Henr. Zopfius, director of the Gymnasium of Essen, a person of great erudition, has published a dissertation upon them, which is extremely learned and curious, from whence we shall beg leave to transcribe the following paragraph: "The Vampyres, which come out of the graves in the night-time, rush upon people sleeping in their beds, suck out all their blood, and destroy them. They attack men, women, and children, sparing neither age nor sex. The people attacked by them complain of suffocation, and a great interception of spirits; after which, they soon expire. Some of them, asked at the point of death, what is the matter with them, say they suffer in the manner just related from people lately dead, or rather the spectres of those people; upon which, their bodies, from the description given of them, by the sick person, being dug out of the graves, appear in all parts, as the nostrils, cheeks, breast, mouth, etc. turgid and full of blood. Their countenances are fresh and ruddy; and their nails, as well as hair, very much grown. And, though they have been much longer dead than many other bodies, which are perfectly putrified, not the least mark of corruption is visible upon them. Those who are destroyed by them, after their death, become Vampyres; so that, to prevent so spreading an evil, it is found requisite to drive a stake through the dead body, from whence, on this occasion, the blood flows as if the person was alive. Sometimes the body is dug out of the grave, and burnt to ashes; upon which, all disturbances cease. The Hungarians call these spectres Pamgri, and the Serbians Vampyres; but the etymon, or reason of these names, is not known.... These spectres are reported to have infested several districts of Serbia, and the *bannat* of Temeswaer, in the year 1725, and for seven or eight years afterwards, particularly those of Mevedia, or Meadia, and Parakin, near the Morava. In 1732, we had a relation of some of the feats in the neighborhood of Cassovia; and

the publick prints took notice of the tragedies they acted in the bannat of Temeswaer, in the year 1738. Father Gabriel Rzaczynski, in his natural history of the kingdom of Poland, and the great duchy of Lithuania, published at Sendomir, in 1732, affirms, that in Russia, Poland, and the great duchy of Lithuania, dead bodies, actuated by infernal spirits, sometimes enter people's houses in the night, fall upon men, women, and children, and attempt to suffocate them; and that of such diabolical facts his countrymen have several very authentic relations. The Poles call a man's body thus informed Upier, and that of a woman Upierzyca, i.e., a winged or feathered creature; which seems to be deduced from the surprising lightness and activity of these incarnate demons.[20]

The appearance of the *Travels* in the *Harleian Miscellany* was followed by extremely popular works on the vampire theme, such as Byron's "The Giaur," Southey's "Thalaba," and Polidori's *The Vampire*.

In Italy, the Latin use of the word precedes its use in the vernacular. Pope Benedict XIV responded to a question similar to the one asked at the Sorbonne. Unlike the learned doctors, however, Pope Benedict realized that the belief in vampires was firmly rooted in ancient superstition and was not easy to extirpate. He considered the subject in Chapter 4 of the second edition of his work *De Servorum Dei Beatificatione et de Beatorum Canonizatione*, published in Rome in 1749. In the chapter entitled "De vanitate vampyrorum," the pope takes issue with the cruel maltreatment and mutilation of corpses believed to be vampires. In the vernacular, the term *vampiro* first appeared in Davanzati's *Dissertazione sopra i vampiri* in 1789.

In Russian, *vampir* is said to be a recent borrowing from either German or French, while the Russian cognates of *vampire*, *upir* and *upyr*, were shown by Brückner to be of Bulgarian origin.[21] Kayimierz Moszyinsk, on the other hand, argues that the term *upire* has been known for a long time among the East Slavs, for written sources of the years 1047, 1495, 1600 mention the word either as a proper name (of a Novgorodian prince) or as place names.

Finally, in Hungary and Transylvania, the supposed homeland of vampires, the term *vampire* exists only as a neologism and was never as popular as in the West. In Hungarian, the word *vampir* first appeared in 1786 in an article of the *Nyelvtudományi Értekletek*: "Vampirok ... living people."[22] Thus, the term postdates the English and French use by a century and the German use by half a century. According to Benkő Lóránd, the word was introduced in Hungary through the German press.[23] Mór Jókai introduced the term into Hungarian belles lettres in 1874. In Transylvania, on the other hand, the term is even more recent and is included in the *Dictioner de Neologisme*. Nandris points out that "for vampire the Slavs had a word, which does not exist as a loan word in Rumanian, and the Russian word of which is *upyr*."[24] In an article on Romanian vampires, Agnes Murgoci notes several vampire-related superstitions and says, "As regards the names used for vampires, dead and alive, *strigoi* (fem. *strigoica*) is the most common Roumanian term, and *moroii* is perhaps the next most usual."[25] The term *vampire* is little used, but Ms. Murgoci has found a reference to vampires in the *Biserica Orthodoxa Romana*: "The Archbishop Nectarie (1813–19) sent round a circular to his higher clergy (protopopes) exhorting them to find out in what districts it was thought that the dead became vampires."[26]

In sum, the earliest recorded uses of the term *vampire* appear in French, English, and Latin, and they refer to vampirism in Poland, Russia, and Macedonia (southern Yugoslavia). The second and more sweeping introduction of the word occurs in German, French, and English, and records the Serbian vampire epidemic of 1725–32.

Thus, the historical data appear to complement the linguistic studies, for the first occurrences of the term *vampire* in European languages all refer to the Slavic superstitions; the wide dissemination of the term and its extensive use in the vernacular follows the outburst of vampirism in Serbia. Paradoxically, although the superstition of vampirism seems to have developed in eastern Europe, the word *vampire* (for which the Slavic cognate is *upir)*, which is now universally used to describe the phenomenon, seemed to have gained popularity in the West.

Notes

1. A great many of the vampire novels and plays are set either in Hungary or in Transylvania as, for example, Bram Stoker's *Dracula* and Melesville's play *Le Vampire*. I am grateful to Prof. A. O. Aldridge of the University of Illinois for his helpful suggestions.
2. Franz Miklosich, *Etymologischen Wörterbuch der slavischen Sprachen* (Vienna: Wilhelm Braumüller, 1886).
3. Montague Summers, *The Vampire, His Kith and Kin* (London, 1928), 18.
4. Stephan Hock, "Die Vampyrsagen und ihre Verwertung in der deutschen Literatur," in *Forschungen zur neueren Litteraturgeschichte* 17 (1900): 1–133.
5. Kluge, *Etymologisches Wörterbuch der deutschen Sprache* (Berlin, 1975); Falk-Torp, *Norwegisch-Ddnisches etymologisches Wörterbuch,* 12th ed. (Leipzig, 1956); Wick, *Die Slawischen Lehnowörter in der neuhochdeutschen Schriftsprache* (Marburg, 1939).
6. Max Vasmer, *Russisches etymologisches Wörterbuch* (Heidelberg, 1953); and A. Brückner, "Etymologien," *Slavia Casopis pro Slovanskon Filologii*, 13 (1934): 272–280.
7. Quoted from Vasmer, *Russisches Etymologisches Wörterbuch*.
8. A. N. Afanas'ev, "Poetic Views of the Slavs regarding Nature," in *Vampires of the Slavs,* ed. Jan L. Perkowski (Cambridge, Mass., 1976), 164.
9. Brückner refutes earlier and contemporary attempts to assign a Serbian origin to the term, and he proposes that the Bulgarian word *upir* lies at the root of the word *vampir*. He defines *upir* by saying, "Es nannten so Bulgaren die den Alten bekannten Nachtvögel mit ehernem Schnabel welche Schlafenden das Blut aussaugen" (279). He also explains the gradual change in meaning from one mythological monster to another: "… die Nachtvögel sind zu Nachtwandlern, zu Nachtmenschen geworden, die nunmehr aus dem Grabe steigen und vom Blute der lebenden zehren" (279). Incidentally, the Slavic word *strigoi*, which now means "monsters" or "werewolves," originally referred to night-birds that sucked the blood of children as well. Brückner suggests that the term *upir* was borrowed by the Greeks from Bulgarian, just as the Greek word for werewolf, *strigoi*, is also a Bulgarian borrowing, and acquired the nasal "am" in Greek. He says: "Das 'am' vom heutigen Vampir ist somit neugriechisch, der Name selbst bulgarische Benennung der strigae, die sich erst im Christlichen Aberglauben aus Nachtvögeln zu eigenen Vampiren verwandelten …" (279).
10. Raymond I. McNally, *A Clutch of Vampires* (Greenwich: New York Graphic Society, 1974), 10.
11. Summers, *The Vampire,* 18. Leonard Wolf, *The Annotated Dracula* (New York, 1975).
12. Yovanovitch, *La Guzla de Prosper Mérimée* (Paris, 1911), 310.
13. Quoted by Dom Calmet, *Traité sur les apparitions des esprits, et sur les vampires, ou les revanans de Hongrie, de Moravia* (Paris, 1751), Vol. 2, 60: "Ils paroissent depuis midi jusqu'à minuit, et viennent sucer le sang des hommes au des animaux vivans en si grande abondance, que quelquefois il leur sort par la bouches, par le nez et principalement par les oreilles, et que quelquefois le cadavre nage dans son sang répandu dans son cercueil. On dit que le Vampire a une espèce de faim, qui lui fait manger le linge qu'il trouve autour de lui."
14. Ibid, Vol. 2, 65ff.
15. Gabriel Rzazynsky, *Historia naturalis curiosa regni Poloniae* (Sendomir, 1721), is credited by Hock with introducing vampires to the German scholarly audience.
16. Interestingly (at least to readers of Bram Stoker's *Dracula*), Gypsies were used as experts for destroying the Serbian vampires. Prof. Vukanović quoting Rauft says: "In the year 1731 vampires disturbed the village of

Medvedja. The High Command from Belgrade immediately sent a commission of German officers and others to the spot. They excavated the whole cemetery and found that there were really vampires there, and all those dead found to be vampires were decapitated by the Gypsies, their bodies cremated and the ashes thrown into the river Morsira," T. P. Vukanovic, "The Vampire," in *Vampires of the Slavs*, ed. Perkowski, 205.

17. C. F. Demelius, *Philosophischer Versuch, ob nicht die merckwurdige Begebenheit derer Blutsauger in Niederungarn, anno 1732 geschehen, aus denen principiis naturae könne erleuchtet werden* (Vinariensi, 1732); G. Gengell, *Evers Atheism* (quoted by the *Travels of 3 English Gentlemen)*; J. C. Pohlius, *Dissertatio de hominibus post mortem sanguisugis, vulgo sic dictus vampyren* (Leipzig, 1732); J. C. Meinig, *Besondere Nachricht von denen Vampyren oder so genannten Blut-Saugern* (Leipzig, 1732); J. H. Voigt, *Kurtzers Bedencken von denen Acten-Mässigen Relationen wegen derer Vampiren, oder Menschen- und Vieh-Aussaugern* (Leipzig, 1732); J. C. Fritch, *Eines Weimarischen Medici muthmassliche Gedanken von denen Vampyren, oder sog. Blutsangern* (Leipzig, 1732); J. H. Zopf, *Dissert. de. Vampyris Serviensibus* (Duisburg, 1733); J. C. Harenberg, *Vernünftige und Christliche Gedanken über die Vampirs oder Bluhtsaugende Todten* (Wolffenbüttel, 1733); J. C. Stock, *Dissertatio Physica de Cadaveribus Sanguisugia* (Jena, 1732); G. B. Bilfinger, *Elements Physices cum Disquisitione de Vampyris* (Leipzig, 1742).

18. Todd's augmented edition of Dr. Johnson's *English Dictionary* (1827); and W. Skeat's *Etymological Dictionary of the English Language* (1884).

19. Charles Forman, *Observations on the Revolution in 1668* (London, 1741), 11.

20. *Travels of 3 English Gentlemen*, in *Harleian Miscellany* (London, 1810).

21. The recent introduction of the term *vampir* from German or French into Russian is attested by Vasmer (see n. 6 above) and by Preobrazhensky, *Etymological Dictionary of the Russian Language* (New York, 1951).

22. Quoted from Benkö Lóránd et al., *A Magyar Nyelv Történeti Etimologiai Szótará* (Budapest: Akadémiai Kiadó, 1976). The same is said in *Révai Nagy Lexikona*.

23. Ibid.

24. Grigore Nandris, "The Historical Dracula: The Theme of His Legend in the Western and in the Eastern Literatures of Europe," in *Comparative Literature: Matter and Method*, ed. A. O. Aldridge (Urbana, 1969), 124.

25. Agnes Murgoci, "The Vampire in Roumania," in *Folklore* 37 (Dec. 1926): 321. [Ed. note: See also herein, pp. 12–34.]

26. Ibid., 323–324.

Forensic Pathology and the European Vampire

Paul Barber

> If there is in this world a well-attested account, it is that of the vampires. Nothing is lacking: official reports, affidavits of well-known people, of surgeons, of priests, of magistrates; the judicial proof is most complete. And with all that, who is there who believes in vampires?
>
> — *Rousseau,* Lettre à l'Archevèque de Paris[1]

I

The modern reader might assume that the vampires of the eighteenth century were much like the ghosts of today, which exist in a rather murky underworld, far from the haunts of Scientific Method. In actuality, however, as one might gather from Rousseau's remarks, nothing could be further from the truth: a number of "vampires" were actually dissected by surgeons, who compiled a report in which they came to the conclusion that there was in fact something very spooky going on.

Moreover, whatever was happening, it was not only spooky, it was catching: the vampire infected his victims, causing them to become vampires as well, so that the phenomenon tended to occur as an epidemic. In the late seventeenth century, such an epidemic of vampirism occurred in Poland and Russia, and the French *Mercure galant* carried the following account of it:

> They appear from midday to midnight and come to suck the blood of living people and animals in such great abundance that sometimes it comes out of their mouths, their noses, and especially, their ears, and that sometimes the body swims in its blood which has spilled out into its coffin. They say the vampire has a kind of hunger that causes him to eat the cloth he finds around him. This revenant or vampire, or a demon in his form, comes out of his tomb and goes about at night violently embracing and seizing his friends and relatives and sucking their blood until they are weakened and exhausted, and finally causes their death. This persecution does not stop at one person but extends to the last person of the family, at least as long as one does not interrupt its course by cutting off the head or opening the body of the vampire. Then one finds his body, in its coffin, limp, pliable, bloated, and ruddy, even though he may have been dead for a long time. A great quantity of blood pours from his body.[2]

Such accounts became common in the eighteenth century, and the best-attested of them, the *locus classicus* of vampire stories, told of events that occurred in the 1720s, near Belgrade, when a man named Arnold Paole died an accidental death, after which several people died suddenly of what had been traditionally viewed as "vampirism." Forty days after his burial, Paole was exhumed:

> [It was found] that he was complete and incorrupt, also that completely fresh blood had flowed from his eyes, ears, and nose, and the shirt and graveclothes were also bloody. The old nails on his hands and feet, along with the skin, had fallen off, and new ones had grown. Since they could see from this that he was a true vampire, they drove a stake through his heart, according to their customs, whereupon he let out a noticeable groan and bled copiously.[3]

A few years later there was another such outbreak of "vampirism." Among others, the authorities found:

> A woman by the name of Stana, twenty years old, who had died in childbirth three months before, after a three-day sickness, and who had said before her death that she had painted herself with the blood of a vampire

Paul Barber, "Forensic Pathology and the European Vampire," *Journal of Folklore Research*, vol. 24, no. 1, pp. 1-32. Copyright © 1987 by Indiana University Press. Reprinted with permission.

in order to be free of him, wherefore she herself, like her child—which had died right after birth and because of a careless burial had been half-eaten by dogs—must also become vampires. She was whole and undecayed. After the opening of the body a quantity of fresh, extravascular blood was found *in cavitate pectoris*. The *vasa* of the *arteriae* and *venae*, like the *ventriculis cordis*, were not, as is usual, filled with coagulated blood, and the whole *viscera*, that is, the *pulmo, hepar, stomachus, lien et intestina*, were quite fresh as they would be in a completely healthy person.[4]

Clearly these accounts, however well attested—and the people present at Stana's disinterment included "two officers, military representatives from Belgrade, two army surgeons, a drummer boy who carried their cases of instruments, the authorities of the village, the old sexton and his assistants"[5]—contain details that cannot possibly be true and so must be dismissed. It is quite obvious, for example, that a dead body cannot groan, that blood coagulates after death, that a corpse is pale, not flushed, and is subject to rigor mortis, and that decomposition takes place shortly after death, certainly in less time than forty days.

Or do we know these to be "facts"? As we shall see, they do not stand up at all well under scrutiny. In fact, it will be shown here that the closer we look at the descriptions of "vampires" in their graves, the more accurate—as descriptions—these prove to be. Far from being merely fanciful horror stories, the vampire stories prove to be an ingenious and elaborate folk hypothesis that seeks to explain otherwise puzzling phenomena associated with death and decomposition—phenomena that are now well understood. Viewed as a theory, the vampire lore may be—as we now know—quite wrong, but like the Ptolemaic astronomy, it is capable of describing events accurately and has predictive value. In its history, however, it differs from such theories as Ptolemy's in that it was not the creation of a single person and no single Copernicus ever came forth to refute it—that was done piecemeal, over centuries—so that in modern times we no longer even understand how and why it came about.

To complicate the matter further, while modern forensic analysis has brought about an understanding of the phenomena of death and decomposition, this understanding simply has not reached most of us yet. We do not choose to spend a great deal of time thinking about how our bodies will decay after death. Thus it is that we remain convinced that—to give just one particularly dramatic example—a dead body cannot groan, as Arnold Paole's is said to have done; but however persuaded you are of this, you would be well advised not to make any sizable bets on the matter without consulting your local coroner, for he will most certainly tell you otherwise.

In order to understand the vampire lore, then, we will have to unravel two sets of misconceptions: theirs and ours. In attempting to do so we will ask an obvious but neglected question: if bodies do not, in fact, turn into vampires, then what does happen to them? And do the actual events have any relation to those of the folklore?

From time to time scholars have attempted to explain the vampire lore by suggesting that perhaps the bodies were not dead at all, but were those of people buried alive, by accident. That would account for their bleeding, groaning, etc. No one, as far as I can tell, has published a serious study of this view, probably because it flies in the face of all our best evidence: the "vampires" we have the best information on were dug up (like Paole) long after their interment. Consequently, to prove that they were merely in a coma, one would have to prove that human beings can survive deprivation of air, food, and water for weeks and months at a time.

In looking for a simpler explanation, we will proceed as follows:

1. We will summarize the stories about vampires and revenants, using as our data those details that occur again and again in such stories. In the course of our discussion it should become apparent that our informants are themselves all looking at

the same data—dead bodies perform pretty much the same worldwide—but with a wealth of information at their disposal the informants make different choices in identifying the characteristics of their particular native monster.

As we shall see, the vampire and the revenant are identical in their origin: both start out as dead bodies. It is just in the telling that they diverge, and the principal source of their divergence is based on an ingenious interpretation of a striking but quite normal phenomenon associated with death and decomposition (see below, number 4). This is not the reason, however, why I will not concern myself with the much-debated typological distinctions between the vampire, the revenant, and their other relatives: it proves unexpectedly difficult to talk about the genus "revenant" without doing violence, from time to time, to the technical terms for the various species. Consequently, rather than either qualify my terms endlessly or make up a new, all-encompassing term, I shall ask the reader to accept for now the following working definition of a vampire/revenant: "any dead human being who, in folklore, is believed to return to life in corporeal form." I shall use the term *revenant* where possible, as it seems to me the more general term, but where the process of transformation is at issue, I shall use *vampirism* rather than *revenantism*, for reasons that probably need no elaboration.

In the interests of economy, I shall limit the discussion to European vampires and revenants. Actually, however, such creatures occur in folklore throughout the world, as one would expect, and scholars have remarked on the similarity of "vampires" in China to those in Europe.[6]

2. Second, in attempting to understand the folklore of death, we will study what actually happens to a body after death.
3. And finally we will put the two sets of data together—what people knew about vampires and what we now know about dead bodies—and see if they do not in fact correspond remarkably well.

II

The following, then, is a summary of information that has been reported about vampires and revenants:

1. Murder victims,[7] suicides,[8] and victims of plague[9] tend to become revenants. Indeed, revenants cause plague.[10] They were often unpopular people even before their deaths.[11]
2. The earth is disturbed at the revenant's grave, or there are holes in the earth.[12]
3. The body has not decomposed, is bloated, and is flushed and ruddy. "If, after a period of time, it remains incorrupt, exactly as it was buried, or if it appears to be swollen and black in color, having undergone some dreadful change in appearance, suspicions of vampirism are confirmed."[13] (Note that what is being said here is that, if the body has not changed, then it is that of a vampire, whereas if it has changed—then it is that of a vampire.)
4. He may suck blood from his victims, evidence of which is the bloating and the blood at the lips of his body when he is found in his grave.[14]
5. The friends and neighbors of the revenant die after his death.[15]
6. He can be heard in the grave, chewing on his extremities or on the shroud, especially in times of plague.[16]
7. He is most likely to be about in the winter.[17]
8. His body is warm to the touch.[18]
9. He has an evil smell.[19]
10. His body shows no signs of rigor mortis.[20]
11. His hair and nails have continued to grow after death.[21]
12. His principal natural enemies are wolves and dogs.[22]
13. The revenant cannot cross water[23] and must return to his grave by sunrise.[24]
14. Potential revenants may be disposed of in swamps.[25]

15. It takes some time for a person to become a revenant after death. Most accounts mention either nine days[26] or forty days.[27]
16. A revenant can be killed by the following means:

    a. Pierce him with a stake (in different areas, different types of wood are specified).[28] Sometimes a needle is specified.[29]
    b. Cut off his head.[30]
    c. Cut out his heart.[31]
    d. Burn him.[32]
    e. All of the above.[33]

17. A revenant may be kept in his grave by pinning him to his coffin or to the ground in his grave,[34] or by securing the grave with bolts or weighing down the body.[35]
18. Revenants may be controlled by the harnessing of their compulsions, as by scattering poppy or millet or mustard seeds in their graves (they must then gather them up one by one), or by putting a fishing net or a sock into the grave with them (they must unravel these, usually at the rate of one knot per year).[36]
19. Flames shoot out of the mouths of some Slavic vampires.[37]
20. When a revenant is killed in his grave, he is apt to scream or groan and to move suddenly, and fresh blood flows from his wounds.[38]
21. You may protect yourself from a revenant by means of garlic.[39]
22. Vampires and other revenants are frequently described sitting up after death, sometimes in the grave or coffin.[40]
23. Vampirism is a phenomenon of the villages, not of the cities; of the lower classes, not the upper.[41]

One misconception about the folklore of vampires might be noted here. Contrary to popular belief, the species "vampire" is not a native of Hungary, although, as we shall see, Hungary has representatives of the genus. The Western idea that vampires are Hungarian is, however, a rather old tradition itself, dating back to the eighteenth century, when some of the incidents of "vampirism" took place in what was then part of Hungary.[42] This idea was given added force when the makers of the movie version of Bram Stoker's novel chose a Hungarian (Bela Lugosi) to play the part of Count Dracula, a figure derived from Vlad the Impaler, a prince (not a count) of Wallachia (not Transylvania), who has in common with the Hungarians the fact that no tradition of vampirism at all—in folklore at least—attaches to him.[43]

III

As noted, any attempt to make sense out of the folklore of death must begin with considering the facts of death. We shall discuss these under the following categories:

1. Decomposition: characteristics
2. Coagulation and decoagulation of blood
3. Decomposition: duration

Our primary sources will be two standard texts: Glaister and Rentoul's *Medical Jurisprudence and Toxicology,* hereafter to be referred to as "Glaister," and Albert Ponsold's *Lehrbuch der gerichtlichen Medizin.* In addition, I shall cite the views of Dr. Terrence Allen, deputy medical examiner of the Los Angeles Chief Medical Examiner's Office, who answered several questions for which I could not easily get adequate answers from the literature.

1. *Decomposition: characteristics.* Glaister and Ponsold give an exhaustive account of the stages of decomposition, but only a few details are important to our discussion:
   — The face of the body undergoes swelling and discoloration.
   — The abdomen distends because of the gases given off by the microorganisms that cause decomposition.
   — A blood-stained fluid escapes from the mouth and nostrils.
   — The nails are shed and the hair is loosened, while the beard appears to grow (but does not) because the facial skin sinks back.

- The abdominal and thoracic cavities burst open.[44]
2. *Coagulation and decoagulation of blood.* The blood does in fact clot after death, but when the source of oxygen has been cut off very quickly, as when death is sudden, the blood soon liquefies again and remains in that condition.[45]
3. *Decomposition: duration.* In the popular imagination, decomposition is viewed as both a quicker and a more complete process than it necessarily is. In the movies, for example, the decay of a body is typically shown to be complete, with nothing left but bones that remain in anatomically correct relation to one another.

The reality is very different indeed. According to Glaister, "Putrefaction begins at about 50°F, and is most favored by temperatures ranging from 70° to 100°.[46] The temperature of the ground, a few feet below the surface, is normally well below this ideal temperature. European oenologists, in fact, expect the temperature of a wine *cave* to be around 54° Fahrenheit. It will be seen from this that a body will not, in fact, decompose quickly in a grave at all. "It may be accepted as a general principle," says Glaister, "that a body decomposes in air twice as quickly as in water, and eight times as rapidly as in earth."[47]

Moreover, under certain conditions bodies may not decompose at all. Where there are hot, desiccating sands or currents of dry air, mummification may take place.[48] Where there is a superabundance of moisture, little air, and few microorganisms, a process called saponification may take place, which preserves the body indefinitely.[49] The bodies of those who are poisoned tend to resist decay simply because the poison kills the microorganisms that cause decay.[50]

And finally, bodies can be preserved by immersion in acid peat bogs, as is the case with the so-called Bog People, many of whom date from the early Iron Age. According to Christian Fischer:

> The reason for the preservation of the bog bodies (and of other organisms also) lies in the special physical and biochemical makeup of the bog, above all the absence of oxygen and the high antibiotic concentration. The manner in which the body was deposited is also of great importance—for example, placed in the bog in such a way that air was rapidly excluded. It is important not only that the bog water contained a high concentration of antibiotics but also that the weather was cold enough (less than 4°C) to prevent rapid decomposition of the body. If the body had been deposited in warm weather, one can assume that the presence of anaerobic bacteria in the intestinal system would have had a destructive effect on the interior of the corpse before the liquid of the bog could penetrate the body.[51]

In numerous cases such bodies were preserved so well that, in modern times, on their discovery by peat-cutters, their discoverers have gone to the police rather than to an archaeologist, as it was apparent to them that a murder had taken place, and they believed it to have been a recent event, rather than one from two thousand years in the past.

IV

It remains for us to look once again at our information about vampires, this time with an eye to asking ourselves if we cannot now make sense of it, in light of what we know about what actually happens to bodies after death.

1. *Murder victims, suicides, and victims of plague tend to become vampires.* Note that these three categories of the dead have in common that they are inadequately buried, the first two for obvious reasons—murderers tend to give only limited attention to the niceties of funerary procedures, while suicides ignore them completely—the last because, during epidemics, so many people died that burial was often very hasty. The Blums, in fact, quote one informant

who actually defines the Greek *vrykolakas* as an unattended dead body: "These were dead people who had died alone and had no one there to take care of them."[52] And the people of Oldenburg, getting right to the heart of the matter, came to the conclusion that vampirism could occur simply because a body was not buried deeply enough.[53]

This is because what is really happening is not that bodies are turning into revenants, but that they are coming to the attention of a populace that has only a very inadequate understanding of how a body decays. The bodies that are buried well do not draw attention to themselves later, as did, for example, that of the child in the account quoted earlier, which was dug up by dogs "because of a careless burial." Moreover, as Glaister points out, people who die suddenly, in apparent good health, do not decompose as rapidly as those who die after a long illness.[54] It will be seen that murder victims and suicides are especially likely candidates for "vampirism": not only are they not buried properly, but, because of their sudden death, they do not decay quickly.

To these considerations must be added the fact that even normal burials are often not very deep, for reasons that will be immediately clear to anyone who has ever tried to dig a deep hole without the aid of a backhoe. Creighton cites a nineteenth-century account of Bedouin burials that illustrates this problem: "The deceased is buried the same day or on the morrow. They scrape out painfully with a stick and their hands in the hard-burned soil a shallow grave. I have seen their graves in the desert rained by foul hyenas, and their winding-sheets lay half above ground."[55] Where the soil is rocky, shallow burial—or another form of disposal of the corpse—becomes inevitable.[56] And Edmund Schneeweis observes that the Serbo-Croatians generally dig their graves to a depth of one to one-and-a-fifth meters.[57] In view of this, it is no surprise that they have always had more than their share of "vampires."

2. *The earth is disturbed at the grave of the vampire.* If a body is given a shallow burial, then undergoes bloating, the surface of the earth will, in fact, be disturbed. It was once believed that one could detect the presence of a vampire in a grave by attempting to lead a horse across the grave. If the horse balked, the grave contained a vampire.[58] If there is anything at all to this story, it could be that the horse was balking simply because of the looseness of the dirt over the grave, occasioned by the swelling of the corpse, or because it could smell the corpse. The action of predators (see number 13 below) and the settling of the earth would also presumably disturb the surface of the grave.

3. *The body is intact and is bloated, and the face is flushed and ruddy.* If the body is buried, there is nothing surprising about its preservation, since it has been protected from air, moisture, maggots, and warmth, the principal agents of decomposition. But even if it is lying in the open a body will sometimes remain intact for a long time, especially in cold weather.

The bloating occurs because the internal organs, which decompose first, produce gases that then have no escape route. Krauss remarks that the Slavs believed that "ein Vampyr wäre von dem Blute der Menschen, die er ausgesogen, ganz rot und aufgebläht"[59] ("a vampire was all red and swollen from the blood of the people whom he had sucked out"). Here we see that the description (if not the explanation) is accurate enough: a corpse does in fact bloat and change color, and the color may vary considerably, ranging from pale through red to livid and even black. I have in my files, in fact—courtesy of the Los Angeles Medical Examiner's Office—a slide of a decomposing Caucasian corpse that I originally thought to be that of a black man, so darkened was the skin.

Probably one of the things we are seeing in regard to a flushed and ruddy face is what is referred to as postmortem lividity or livor mortis.[60] When death occurs, the oxygen in the blood is used up, whereupon the blood turns dark in color, and because circulation has come to an end, the corpuscles—now dark—are caused by gravity to sink toward whatever is the low side of the body. Since the plasma and corpuscles separate (when the blood liquefies), and since the plasma is lighter than the corpuscles, both in weight and in color, it will be seen that the face of a body may be pale if it is supine, dark if it is prone. If Hans Naumann is right, then, and the "weisse Frau" is to be derived from the characteristic pallor of a (supine) dead body, then it would seem as if his "schwarzer Mann" might have a corresponding origin, except that the figure is a reflex of the appearance of a *prone* body.[61]

That this is possible is suggested by the fact that potential revenants were normally buried face down, so that they would not find their way to the surface.[62] It will be seen that such a burial practice would cause the face of the corpse to discolor—note Krauss's observation above—thereby proving to those who buried it, then dug it up again, that their original presumption was correct, and the corpse really was that of a vampire.[63]

While it is entertaining to speculate on the matter, however, it does not seem to me as if one can hope to prove or disprove Naumann's thesis: the "weisse Frau" and "schwarzer Mann" are strictly in the domain of legend. Unlike the vampires and revenants, they are not exhumed in the form of actual bodies from actual graves. Moreover, the coloration of a dead body is a more complicated matter than is suggested by this very brief analysis, because decomposition also changes the color of the skin.

4. *There is blood at the lips and nose*. Again, this is normal in a decomposing body. It occurs because the lungs, which are rich in blood, deteriorate after death and are under pressure from the bloating of the internal organs. A blood-stained fluid is forced out through the mouth and nose.

It will be seen now why it was believed that the vampire drank blood: here you have a body that is clearly full of something that was not there when you buried it—it is bloated—and there are obvious traces of blood at the lips. Furthermore, the gravesite is disturbed (by the swelling of the body). The villagers, instead of remarking to one another that here is an obvious case of bloating, resulting from the production of gases by microorganisms and accompanied by traces of blood-stained fluid induced by pulmonary edema, conclude that the body has been climbing out of the grave to suck blood, and that is why, when you drive a stake through it to kill it, it proves to be full of blood. (See number 20 below: liquid blood.)

Worldwide, there are some common means of dealing with this phenomenon of bloody fluid escaping from the mouth of the corpse. Frequently the mouth is tied shut, as is done with the elder Bolkonski in *War and Peace*, and in much of Europe this is considered important, since, if it were not done, the body would become a revenant.[64] I have seen Peruvian mummies (in the Ethnographic Museum in Vienna) with wool stuffed into their mouths, and it seems likely that this is done to soak up the liquid. In Australia soft plant fibers are said to be used similarly.[65]

5. *The friends and neighbors of the vampire die after his death*. I suspect that what is important here is not relationship but propinquity. We would say that they all died of the same contagious disease, which the people close to the "vampire" are more likely to catch than those distant from him. Their view is that the vampire must have climbed out of his grave—the earth above the gravesite is disturbed, after all—and attacked his friends and neighbors at night, sucking their blood. It must have happened at night because no one saw him.

6. *He can be heard in the grave, chewing on his extremities or on the shroud*. It will be seen how startled people would be to find that a sound was issuing from a grave, as we all know that the dead are unusually quiet by nature. Nevertheless, dead bodies can make a certain limited number of sounds, and there is considerable reason to believe that the sound described here is that of the body rupturing as the result of the bloating caused by decomposition. This bursting of the body, which can be quite audible, is not necessarily sudden, like that of a balloon being popped; it can be a prolonged event, like the sound of the air escaping from a tire. Some years ago, on a hike in Monterey County, I came upon the body of a Hereford calf that was undergoing this dreadful experience. The pressure of the gases was forcing what is called purge fluid to escape from the body. This was very audible, even from some distance away—indeed, I heard the body before I saw it. The emission of purge fluid, incidentally, would seem to account for

stories of bodies that are heard making noises in the grave, are dug up, and are found to be "lacerated and swimming in blood."[66] It could be, incidentally, that this belief—that the dead can be heard chewing in their graves—reinforced the age-old custom of providing the dead with food and drink.

If the swollen body is punctured, of course, the rupturing is apt to be sudden and dramatic, and this process has been unforgettably chronicled (the body in this case being that of an elephant) by John Taylor in his *African Rifles and Cartridges*.[67] Taylor describes an "immense out-rush of stinking gas and muck." That our vampires perform similarly is suggested by the practice (attested both for Poland and Yugoslavia) of covering them with a hide or cloth or dirt to prevent the blood of the vampire from spurting onto his killers, as this would kill them or cause them to go mad.[68]

The observation that the vampire chewed on his extremities seems to result from the tendency, in wet climates, of the limbs of corpses to lose their flesh while the trunk, perhaps because it is covered with clothing or a shroud, does not appear to have done so. One can observe this in pictures of Tollund Man. Also, Evans remarks that saponification is more likely to take place where the body is covered.[69] I suspect, but cannot think how I can prove it, that the eating of the shroud is simply an interpretation of the effect of capillary attraction on the shroud, as the mouth is emitting fluids. That this is plausible is suggested by the common belief that such eating can be prevented by the simple expedient of keeping the shroud away from the mouth of the revenant.[70]

There are fairly numerous accounts, incidentally, of the bursting of the body of the vampire. Trigg gives one such account:

> Among some gypsies it is believed that a simple curse is sufficient to destroy a troublesome vampire. In one Rumanian gypsy folktale, for example, a vampire is quickly destroyed simply by saying to him, "God send you burst." On hearing this the vampire was so enraged that he literally burst, leaving nothing but a large pool of blood where he had stood.[71]

Here we have two common motifs, the swelling (and subsequent bursting) of the corpse and the suspiciously liquid blood. Murgoci gives another account of a vampire that burst with anger, and Vakarelski observes that Bulgarian vampires, when killed, leave only liquid blood behind.[72]

Finally, the reader may protest that the bursting of the body, being an event of limited duration and taking place under the ground, would presumably not be easily noticed. This is of course true, which is why it is that such things tend to happen during epidemics—that is, when hundreds of people are being buried, and not very deeply at that. It could be that at such times it would be hard *not* to notice such sounds, especially since people would be frequenting the graveyard more than usual. In any case, folklore is rich in accounts of sounds being emitted from graves.[73]

7. *He is most likely to be about in the winter.* Here we must recall that a vampire is characterized, among other things, by his disinclination to decay properly. The decay of the body is of course retarded by low temperatures: note Fischer's remark (in section III above) about how only those bog bodies would have remained intact that were deposited in the bogs in cold weather.[73] In the eighteenth century, when Flückinger's famous *Visum et Repertum* was published, no one seems to have noticed that the vampires of Medvegia were dug up in January! That the bodies had not decayed, which was such a source of astonishment to the doctors who investigated them, can scarcely come as a surprise.

8. *His body is warm, to the touch.* This could be because the process of decomposition generates heat. According to Ponsold it is actually possible for the temperature of the body to *increase* after death, as a result of decomposition.[74] In the eighteenth century the botanist Pitton de Tournefort observed first-hand the dissection of a Greek *vrykolakas* and wrote an account of it in which he describes trying, without success, to explain this phenomenon to the people of

Mykonos. De Tournefort's description of the stench from the body—and he maintains that it was in fact merely a dead body—was sufficiently graphic that his account was thoroughly bowdlerized, both in English and (later) French publications. An accurate version of it can be found in Jan Perkowski's *Vampires of the Slavs*.[75]

According to Dr. Allen, such a rise in temperature would be uncommon: normally the body would be in equilibrium with the ambient temperature. He points out, however, that a body will frequently seem warm because one's hands are cold, which is why modern books on forensic investigation insist that one determine temperature with a thermometer, not by touch.

9. *He has an evil smell.* Surely no comment is necessary by now.

10. *His body shows no signs of rigor mortis.* In fact, rigor mortis is a temporary condition. Glaister discusses in detail the factors that determine its time of onset, length, etc.[76] Incidentally, Aidan Cockburn tells of a Chinese mummy, two thousand years old, of which "the tissues were still elastic and the joints could be bent."[77]

11. *His hair and nails have continued to grow after death.* Sometimes the teeth grow as well, although this is more commonly noted in fictional vampires than in those of folklore. The hair, nails, and teeth do not in fact grow after death: they merely appear to do so as the skin shrinks back. Eventually two other events take place: the nails fall off and a phenomenon known as skin slippage occurs (both these events may be seen in the account of Arnold Paole in section I above).

A recent article in *National Geographic* shows and discusses this phenomenon of the apparent lengthening of the fingernails.[78]

12. *His principal natural enemies are wolves and dogs.* This belief clearly arises out of a misinterpretation of a common phenomenon: the tendency of wolves and dogs to dig up and eat corpses that are not either buried deeply or protected in some way, as by a casket. We have seen how, in the account quoted in section I, the child's body had been half-eaten by dogs, because of a careless burial, and Dr. Allen tells me that it is quite common for animals to dig up bodies that have been buried superficially. They may even carry off parts of the body. Many burial practices can be shown to be attempts to deal with this problem. The Bedouins, for example, have been said to have preferred to bury their dead in rocky areas to that they could cover the graves with stones to protect them from wolves. If the burial was in sand, then brush was used for this purpose.[79]

Some years ago I inadvertently conducted an informal experiment on this issue when I buried the body of a pet chicken in my yard only to discover that (to state the matter within the context of Russian mythology) Mother Earth repeatedly rejected the unclean corpse, until finally I dug a deeper hole, covered the corpse with rocks, filled the hole, and issued a stern warning to my dog. Years later I realized that I had encountered a typical problem of burial and had responded with a typical solution.

Incidentally, one of the lesser-known ecological niches is filled by white wolves that, in certain areas, occupy graveyards and keep down the vampire population.[80] This suggests that when the wolf is found digging up a corpse, and the corpse is found to be undecayed—hence a vampire—then the wolf is seen as an ally of the villagers. This could explain the extremely close relationship between werewolves and vampires: in eastern Europe, the werewolf, after his death, becomes a vampire.[81] The clustering of the three ideas—death, werewolf, and vampire—may occur simply because death produces a corpse which attracts a wolf.

And finally, when wolves or dogs dig up a body, it will be seen that they are far more likely to bring a limb to the surface than the trunk of the body, simply because it is easier to do so. This may account for the fact that the *lugat*, a type of Albanian revenant, which is otherwise invulnerable, is no match for a wolf: "he [the wolf] bites his leg off, whereupon the lugat retreats into his grave and decides to remain quiet from now on."[82] It may also account for the origin of stories in European folklore of how a hand reaches out of the grave. Sometimes the hand is that of a child that struck its mother,[83] or it is that of someone who has brought down a curse upon himself, such as a patricide, a thief, or a perjurer—a group not unlike that of our standard revenants.[84] Here too the curse may be less significant than the inadequate burial. Such stories, however, occur in various degrees of elaboration, and I do not mean to suggest that each of them had its origin in an actual event—only that the event is not as improbable as it must seem at first sight.

13. *The vampire cannot cross water and must return to his grave by sunrise.* Here we must remember three things: (a) the body is not buried very deeply; (b) it has bloated spectacularly (up to nearly twice its original size), filling up with lightweight gases, thereby increasing in buoyancy; and (c) it may well be buried in ground that has a high water table, such as a swamp. It is extremely common for bodies of murder victims to be disposed of in water with enough weight to submerge the body, but not enough to keep it submerged when putrefaction causes it to bloat. According to Dr. Allen, in fact, it is almost impossible to keep a body submerged. He provided me with a photograph of a body that had floated to the surface even though it was weighed down with a piece of cast iron that weighed 145 pounds! The body itself weighed five pounds *less* than the weight that it had carried up to the surface of the water, and we must note that we have no way of knowing what was the upper limit of the lift provided by the bloated body. We know only that it would lift at least 145 pounds (125 when one takes into account the buoyancy of the iron in water).

Here we see yet another reason why it is that the vampire emerges from his grave: his body may simply be more buoyant than its surroundings. It should also be pointed out that, according to Glaister, waterlogged soils tend to retard decomposition.[85] Thus we may imagine the following scenario: if the earth is waterlogged and the body bloats, rising to the surface, the local inhabitants, coming out in the daytime and finding the "vampire," quite intact, at the surface, might conclude that

(a) the vampire did not make it back to his grave by dawn, or
(b) a vampire cannot cross water.

Still another interpretation of the same phenomenon seems to be implied in Murgoci's report that "vampires never drown, they always float on top."[86]

That bodies of suspected revenants frequently ended up in water, incidentally, is well attested. In Russia, for example, where the revenant was believed to be responsible for droughts, the practice arose of digging up the body and throwing it into a lake or stream, apparently on the assumption that, with a sufficiency of water at its disposal, it would leave the clouds alone.[87]

14. *Potential revenants may be disposed of in swamps.* Some light may be thrown on this practice merely by asking about alternatives. Even leaving aside the hydrotropic character of the soul, which is presented as the rationale for numerous funerary procedures,[88] the possibilities are limited by the nature of the problem. If you wish to dispose of a dangerous corpse, you will naturally choose a site that is away from human habitation. You could go into the hills, if there are hills, but it must be remembered that you are obliged to transport a corpse. Such corpses have proved to be preternaturally heavy,[89] unless of course it is merely the fear and trembling of their bearers that makes them seem so.

In any case, it seems likely that you would choose low uninhabitable ground over high uninhabitable ground, unless the death occurred on high ground. When this is the case, as it is with the revenant Glam in *Grettir's Saga*, the body is likely to be covered with rocks or brush to keep it in place.[90] For one thing, there may not be a deep enough soil for burial; for another, it is apt to be rocky soil, which is difficult to dig in.

When a body is disposed of in a swamp, on the other hand, the problems are different. While the depth of soil is likely to be adequate, the high water table might make it impossible to dig a deep hole. And once you know that the body is apt to become a revenant (i.e., bloat and come to the surface), you will be forced to come up with means of preventing this from happening. Some of the more obvious means would be puncturing the corpse (to release the gases), weighing it down with rocks, and holding it down with a latticework of branches.

Fortunately, we are not reduced to mere speculation on this point, for close to two thousand bodies—quite well preserved in many cases—have been dug out of bogs in Europe, many of them held down in just the ways I have described.[91] Some of these were clearly the "bad dead" of their age, people who had died "before their time" and so refused to decompose properly.

15. *Length of time for the transformation to take place.* Both numbers—nine and forty—are simply examples of mythic time, which occurs in standard quantities. One of the German terms for a revenant is *Neuntöter* (ninekiller),[92] and in Swabia it was said that a drowning victim remains underwater for nine days.[93] In the Bible, such things as days in the wilderness and the duration of floods occur in units of forty, and the number has made its way into vampire lore because in the Eastern Orthodox church it was believed that, after death, the soul remains on earth for that length of time. As for the *actual* time required for a body to "become a vampire" (which is to say, become swollen and discolored), that is simply incalculable: there are too many variables.

16. *To kill a vampire, you must pierce him with a stake.* The staking of a vampire makes a certain kind of sense when you consider that what is being "killed" is a bloated corpse. The most direct way of reducing it to what it was is to puncture it.

This puncturing of the body is common even before burial, as a prophylactic measure: "should the devil inflate [the skin of the body], then the air would escape."[94] Other examples of such puncturing are common in the literature.[95]

Frequently sharp objects have been buried with the body in order to puncture it if it should bloat. Richard Beitl, for example, describes sickles being buried with bodies in Transylvania "allegedly in order to prevent the swelling of the body,"[96] and Norbert Reiter says that the Slavs buried bodies with a sickle around the neck of the corpse, "so that the vampire would cut his throat if he left the grave."[97] Perkowski quotes a Romanian informant who says that the sickle must be driven into the corpse's heart,[98] and according to Csiszár, the Hungarians attempted to prevent the bloating of the body by putting iron objects on it: "There are also evil souls of a sort that spoil the corpse. When they creep in, then the stomach bloats and the dead person acquires a smell. [To deal with this] one puts iron implements on the stomach of the dead person."[99] (Note that the stench and bloating are regarded here as something unnatural.) Balassa and Ortutay give a similar report for Hungary, saying that a sickle "is laid on the body to prevent bloating" and adding that such sickles have been found in graves dating back to the ninth century.[100] Tekla Dömötör also remarks that—in Hungary—people laid either a sickle or some other metal object on the dead person "so that the corpse would not bloat," and says that "in reality this occurred so that the dead person would not come back as a revenant."[101] It will be seen that both interpretations are correct, since it is the bloating—and consequent disturbance of the burial site—that is interpreted as the dead person trying to get out of his grave. The sickle is expected to prevent this by puncturing the body. This function of the sickle, incidentally, might cause one to puzzle over a possible relationship to the traditional conception of death as a skeleton carrying a scythe or sickle.[102] Sickles are in fact often found in the presence of skeletons because of the above-mentioned burial practice, and both Burkhart and Schneeweis suggest that one of the Slavic words for vampire *(prikosac)* may be derived from a word for scythe.[103]

In addition to sickles, Schneeweis mentions various iron implements—knives and swords and axes—being used thus. In his opinion, such implements may have been intended "to prevent the return of the soul into the body."[104] Frequently the deterrent effect of these objects has been attributed to the magical quality of iron,[105] and while it is beyond the scope of this article to deal with the subject adequately, I cannot help wondering if the weight and sharpness of iron were not originally the significant characteristics (weight for holding the body down, sharpness for puncturing it), especially since there are common reports of other, nonferrous implements being used in this way. Often, for example, we are told of sharpened stakes that have been driven into graves, so that the body might be punctured if it tries to come to the surface,[106] and Krauss describes both knives and hawthorn stakes being used in this way in Serbia.[107]

Also, in addition to those cases where the sharp object is clearly meant to puncture the body, there are others where its function has apparently been reanalyzed, as when Strackerjan reports that, in Oldenburg, the needle with which the shroud was sewn had to be laid into the coffin—not just any needle would do.[108]

And finally it must be noted that such puncturing of the dead body is as common now as in the past, and for some of the same reasons. In Guyana, for example, after the Jonestown massacre, a doctor was sent in to puncture the bloating corpses so they would not burst.[109] And the practice of embalming, which in the United States dates from the time of the Civil War (because bodies were being brought home by train), may be viewed as a kind of preemptive strike against "vampirism," in that it is intended to prevent all those messy events that are brought about by decomposition.

Embalming, incidentally, might seem to imply a radically different conception of the afterlife than does cremation, since the one method preserves the body while the other destroys it. Looked at another way, however, the two methods have the same function: both render the body inert—unable to develop into something ugly and threatening. Puncturing the body, on the other hand, while it would have an immediate and dramatic effect on the condition of the body, would not end the process of change, which may explain why, so often in the history of vampirism, we find that bodies were dug up repeatedly and each time "killed" in some new way, until eventually—as with de Tournefort's *vrykolakas*—they were cremated.

As for cremation, it proves to be a rather complicated subject, an understanding of which requires some consideration of the physics of combustion. I discuss it in detail in *Vampires, Burial, and Death*.

17. *Keeping the revenant in his grave by pinning the body or weighing it down.* Here again we are seeing methods of dealing with a purely mechanical problem: the tendency of the corpse, having bloated, to disturb the surface of the earth, or even to pop up to the surface if the ground is waterlogged. I have before me a photograph (from the second page of the *Los Angeles Times,* dated 11/1/1985) that shows a coffin floating in a flooded graveyard, in Louisiana. According to the caption, several coffins floated up out of the ground in the floodwaters left by Hurricane Juan. This particular one was tied to a tree by someone who believed, apparently, that a dead body could not only leave the grave under the right conditions, but could not even be counted on to remain in its vicinity. Sealed coffins, like bloated bodies, are remarkably buoyant.

It must come as no surprise to find that we have large quantities of archaeological evidence demonstrating that bodies were in fact frequently pinned or weighed down. Ludwig Pauli describes such burials in detail in his book on Celtic beliefs, and Edmund Schneeweis observes that the gravestone originally was intended to keep the dead person in his grave.[110] Burkhart, incidentally, argues that, of all the methods of laying the dead, the oldest is probably that of *mechanically* holding the body in place.[111] Clearly the reason why this is so is that bodies tend not to stay put, both because of their buoyancy and because they are attacked by animals.

18. *Controlling revenants by means of their compulsions.* The accounts of revenants being obliged to unravel nets appears to be a reinterpretation of a common practice of keeping bodies in their graves by means of nets. Erhard Eylmann, in his *Die Eingeborenen der Kolonie Südaustralien,* gives an account of aborigines wrapping the body in a net "so that the dead person would not leave the grave and do harm to the living."[112] It may be, then, that the original purpose of this practice was forgotten—the net was intended as a mechanical restraint—and a reinterpretation came into being, according to which the net was there to give the revenant something to do. The use of the various grains may have been an extension of the idea of occupying the revenant.

Even in modern times, incidentally, the net is sometimes mentioned merely as a means of keeping a body from becoming a revenant, with no reference to his practice of unravelling the net.[113]

19. *Flames come out of the mouth of the vampire.* As implausible as this seems at first sight, it is actually likely that something of this sort would, in fact, happen when a "vampire" is cremated. This is because the body of the supposed vampire is swollen to bursting with the gases of decomposition, and these gases (mostly methane) are highly flammable. Since the gases are forming interstitially within the tissues as well as within the thoracic and abdominal body cavities, the staking of the body, while it will release some of the gas, will not release all of it by any means—especially when you consider that, throughout much of Slavic territory, the stake had to be driven in at one blow. A second blow revived the vampire.[114] This is perhaps one of the reasons why the last-resort method of disposing of a vampire is always that of burning him.

While I had no doubt that flames would shoot from the body of a burning "vampire," I thought it best to get the opinion of an authority and asked Dr. Allen about this theory. He offered me a more striking confirmation than I could have hoped for, saying that he had a colleague who had acquired the habit of dramatizing the presence of gases in a dead body by touching them off with a match when he made his first incision. The resulting flame, according to Dr. Allen, shot between one and two feet in the air.

20. *When a vampire is killed in his grave, he is apt to scream or groan and to move suddenly, and fresh blood flows from his wounds.* It must be remembered that what is being "killed" is a bloated corpse. An attempt to drive a stake into it will force air past the glottis, which is still intact, thereby creating a very lifelike groan. Such sounds (Pensold refers to this as the "*Totenlaut*") are common even when a body is moved, let alone when the thoracic cavity is being violently compressed, as would happen in the staking of a vampire. Among medical personnel the reaction to such sounds is likely to be one of humor, as when an attendant, on hearing a body groan, said to Dr. Allen, "Don't *hurt* him!" I have also heard an account—and here we may have entered the domain of legend—of a bystander who was asked to help carry a body and, when it emitted a sound, dropped his end, saying, "If he can talk, he can walk."

It takes little imagination to conceive of how such sounds would affect the people engaged in attempting to kill a vampire. Incidentally, we have other, more pedestrian accounts in which the sounds are not interpreted as a human scream or groan at all. Wuttke, for example, cites an account in which the sound is compared to the squeal of a pig.[115] And Aribert Schroeder quotes the following account from eighteenth-century Serbia:

> The investigation of the doctors determined that the four questionable corpses, which had lain in the earth for twenty days, had remained incorrupt. Out of fear that vampires or snakes might take them over, the inhabitants of the village beheaded the corpses, drove a stake into the man's heart, whereupon they heard a loud cracking sound, and burned all the corpses.[116]

Several things about this account are particularly interesting. First of all, note that, as in many accounts of revenants, we are told that authorities have been brought in, people who might be expected to know about dead bodies. Second, note how little these authorities actually did know, as is suggested by their astonishment at finding that the bodies had not decayed, underground, in a period of twenty days. Man's final decay had long since been a literary motif, but not, it seems, a scientific study.

Finally, note the "overkill." The body is beheaded, a stake is driven into the heart, and the corpse is then burned. The account itself is very straightforward, but the rather extreme efforts to kill the revenant hint at the climate of fear in which the events took place. The hysteria over vampirism can be seen in Köhler's accounts of conflicts, in the eighteenth century, between citizens and the authorities over whether a suicide (i.e., a potential revenant) was to be buried in the churchyard—conflicts that were often resolved by military force.[117]

As for the movement of the body, clearly this occurs because the attempts to drive a stake through it causes a redistribution of the gases of decomposition—much like what happens when you push down on a balloon. I have conducted no experiments here, for all the obvious reasons.

The blood, of course, is not really fresh at all (as de Tournefort points out, by the way): it is the fact that it is *liquid* that shocks the vampire-killers. We have seen that this is a normal circumstance under certain conditions.[118] Here again one needs little imagination to conceive of the effect a bleeding corpse would have on people who already suspect that it is still alive.

21. *Garlic will protect one from a revenant.* I find myself wondering if garlic was originally a specific against the stench from the dead body, on the principle that one strong smell may be opposed with another. De Tournefort, as we have seen, describes the Greeks using frankincense to mask the odor, and de Groot, in *The Religious System of China,* makes the following remarks:

> It is a general conviction that any one who calls at a mortuary house incurs a kind of pollution, especially so if death has been untimely or caused by disease. Some condolers therefore wisely hide a few garlic roots under their garments, convinced that the strong smell will prevent the influences of death from clutching to their bodies; on leaving the house they throw the roots away in the street.[119]

Note that in China, as in Europe, the garlic is held to be useful when one is in the presence of a dead body, but in de Groot's account, it is specifically the strong smell that is held to be the active agent. This passage, by the way, clearly implies an awareness of contagion. One sees this also in accounts of how everything associated with the dead person—the utensils he ate with, the water used to wash him, the straw he lay on—must be thrown out, burned, or buried with him. As de Groot's text suggests, such "pollution" (i.e., contagion) is most to be feared when death is "untimely or caused by disease."

The "vampires" illustrate this principle well: the fear of them was simply the fear of death, brought about by agents that were known to be contagious, while the actual mechanism of contagion was not understood. (Since we do understand the mechanism, we are not afraid to "catch our death" from a victim of stroke; but our recent experience with the AIDS epidemic has had some similarities to the vampire scares of the past.)

22. *Vampires and other revenants are frequently described sitting up after death, sometimes in the grave or coffin.* Such stories are so persistent, and they occur over such a wide area,[120] that I finally began to wonder if there was something to them, although I could not think of a satisfactory explanation. The evidence remains contradictory: Dr. Allen, for example, while himself doubting that such is possible, nonetheless tells me that a colleague of his claims to have seen a movie of this very phenomenon.

The Blums quote a classic instance of such real or supposed movement of the body:

> On my mother's island a man was very ill and became unconscious. The people thought that he had died, and so they prepared the funeral. After the ceremony there was a movement in the coffin and slowly the man began to rise. Well, the people there believed he was becoming a vrikolax; in their fright they threw everything they could find at him—sticks, rocks, anything. In that way they did kill him when before he had only been in a coma.[121]

The incident may have happened this way. But if we suppose that the body can in fact "sit up like a Turk" after death, as it is frequently described doing,[122] then we would have a plausible explanation for why it is that such bodies—as in the above account—always seem to end up being dead after all.

The Greeks make distinctions between different types of revenants, and the distinctions seem always to be related to demonstrable physical characteristics of dead bodies. This can be seen most easily in the etymologies of the terms for the revenant (except for *vrykolakas*, which is clearly borrowed from the Slavic):[123]

1. τυμπανιαιος: "drumlike," because of the taut, distended skin, resulting from the bloating of the body.
2. αλυτος: "unloosed," which is to say, incorrupt. The body has not decayed.
3. σαρχωμενος: "one who has put on flesh," that is, bloated.
4. αναιχαθουμενος: "one who sits up" in his grave.
5. χαταχανας: Lawson derives this last from the Greek word for *gape*. I may be more persuaded of this etymology than Lawson was, as I can attest, by grace of the L.A. Medical Examiner's Office, that the gape of a decomposing body (brought about by the swelling) is a particularly striking and unforgettable sight. This is one of the reasons why, even now in Greece, the mouth is tied shut.[124]

In addition, he gives three terms—αναρραχο, lampasma, lampastro—that he finds unintelligible. The second two would seem to be derived from the root λαμπ-, from which our *lamp* is derived and should mean, respectively, "that which is lit up" (abstract noun) and "that which lights up" (agent form). Lawson would seem to be ignoring the obvious etymologies because they do not appear to make sense—unless, that is, one notices that such terms all seem to be related to the condition of a dead body. Then one need only look for a mechanism whereby a dead body can give off light, and W. E. D. Evans, in *The Chemistry of Death*, describes such a mechanism:

> It was observed in antiquity that dead fish and meat could appear to glow with a pale light, and the wonder and fear that this must have brought to primitive man observing the phenomenon in the darkness of night or the gloom of a cave can well be imagined. Old stories, often re-told, linger on in oral tradition telling of the glowing of exhumed human remains. ...
>
> These fearful concomitants to the exposure of entombed or buried bodies seem to have become unfashionable in recent years; perhaps modern times have made mankind too familiar with death, and by scientific pathways have come sophistication and disenchantment. At all events, the luminescence of remains is now to be explained by natural, rather than supernatural history.
>
> Luminescence of dead animal remains is most commonly due to contamination by luminous bacteria such as Photobacterium fischeri, the light emanating from the organisms and not from reactions in the decomposing tissues. The organisms swarm over the remains and give light, particularly while the temperature is in the range of 15° to 30°C.[125]

The first word, αναρραχο, would seem to be derived from ava plus ραχις ("up" plus "spine"), which becomes plausible when you consider that revenants are commonly reported sitting up after death and that Lawson has already given one derivation that suggests this habit (number 4 in the list of Greek terms above).

If this is so, then we are confronted with the following conclusion: most native Greek words for the revenant refer to demonstrable physical characteristics of a dead body. It seems most reasonable to conclude that the two concerned with sitting up do so too.

The matter is not easily resolved, but there is certainly no doubt that some movement is possible after death. Rigor mortis causes all the muscles to stiffen, and because the flexor muscles of the arms are stronger than the extensors, the arms may move slightly across the chest. Moreover, when rigor mortis ends, as it must, gravity may again cause some movement, which could account in part for the extremely common stories of bodies being found in a changed position.[126] (The bloating and bursting of the body would also change its position, and such changes presumably contribute to the idea that the body has left the grave.)[127] Cremation causes considerable movement of the corpse.[128] And movement would certainly occur—seemingly at the volition of the corpse—if one were to try to adjust the limbs of the body while it is in rigor mortis: they would spring back to their original position.

Finally, though, I must acknowledge that I have not found sufficiently clear evidence here to persuade me that I have located the source of this tradition. It may be that the phenomena are brought about by funerary or burial practices that I am not taking into account.

23. *Vampirism and class.* It is only in fiction that a vampire is likely to be from the upper classes—Count Dracula, for example. Actually, rich and important people tend to be buried properly, and their families have sufficient influence to prevent them from being dug up again. Consequently, the classic vampire—in folklore, at least—far from being the urbane count that the movies have introduced us to, tends to be a peasant with a drinking problem.[129]

ν

It has been remarked that vampire stories occur only in areas where the dead are buried, not where they are cremated,[130] and the reasons for this will now be obvious. It will also be clear why it is that such stories are by no means an isolated phenomenon but occur worldwide. They tend to correlate with the practice of exhumation, as in Greece, Bulgaria, and Serbo-Croatia, and the local variations are based on such things as whether the blood at the lips, combined with the bloating, is taken to be evidence of blood-sucking. Since the phenomena being observed are quite diverse, one would also expect to encounter in folklore creatures that are seemingly quite different from the revenant but are related by their origin: carrion-eating ghouls, for example, like those of India,[131] which serve to account for the process of decomposition, except that here the body in the grave is viewed as the victim rather than the monster. It should be an easy matter, in fact, to predict reflexes of the phenomena of decomposition; we might look for creatures that swell up, change color, drip blood, refuse to die, burst (as do trolls, for example), and give off a noisome stench.

It should also be profitable to consider the possibility that certain changes in funerary customs—the cremations of the Urnfield Culture, for example—came about not because of changes in religious beliefs, but because there was an "epidemic of vampirism." Such epidemics would tend to occur when people were forced to look closely at the decomposition of corpses, as in times of plague. Because of this, a reconsideration of the history of funerary practices would seem to be in order, approaching the question from the point of view that it is in fact very difficult to dispose of a body in such a way as to keep it disposed of, and that our funerary practices probably reflect ever-renewed attempts to deal with this problem.

And finally, after having gone to such lengths to argue that the lore of the vampire arose out of misconceptions concerning the nature of decomposition, I must concede that there are well-attested accounts of actual dead bodies being involved in the drinking of human blood. It is not as people believed, however, for by a peculiarly gruesome and chilling irony, the blood of the supposed vampire was regarded as a specific against vampirism and was baked in bread,[132] painted on the potential victim,[133] or even drunk.[134] Blood was actually consumed, in other words, but by the "victims," and it was the blood of the supposed vampire.

The vampires themselves, it would appear, were and are dead.

Notes

I would like to thank Professor Felix Oinas for his valuable comments on two versions of the manuscript of this article. The refereeing process was most helpful.

1. Jean-Jacques Rousseau, *Lettre à l'Archevêque de Paris*, quoted in Voyslav M. Yovanovitch, *"La Guzla" de Prosper Mérimée* (Paris, 1911),

316. All translations are my own unless otherwise indicated.
2. From the *Mercure galant*, 1693–4, quoted in Stefan Hock, *Die Vampyrsagen und ihre Verwertung in der deutschen Litteratur* (Berlin, 1900), 33–34.
3. Johannes Flückinger's account quoted in Georg Conrad Horst, *Zauberbibliothek*, (Mainz, 1821), vol. 1, 256.
4. Ibid., 257–258.
5. Basil Copper, *The Vampire in Legend, Fact, and Art* (Secaucus, N.J.: Citadel Press, 1974), 44.
6. See, for example, G. Willoughby-Meade, *Chinese Ghouls and Goblins* (New York, 1928), 224.
7. L. Strackerjan, *Aberglaube und Sagen aus dem Herzogthum Oldenburg* (Oldenburg, 1867), vol. 1, 154. See also Christo Vakarelski, *Bulgarische Volkskunde* (Berlin: Walter de Gruyter and Co., 1968), 30.
8. W. R. S. Ralston, *The Songs of the Russian People* (London, 1872), 409. See also J. C. Lawson, *Modern Greek Folklore and Ancient Greek Religion* (Cambridge, England, 1910), 408; Vakarelski, *Bulgarische Volkskunde*, 30.
9. Adolf Wuttke, *Der deutsche Volksaberglaube der Gegenwart* (Hamburg, 1860), 222.
10. Ibid.
11. Rossell Hope Robbins, *The Encyclopedia of Witchcraft and Demonology* (New York: Crown Publishers, 1959), p. 523. See also, Friedrich Krauss, *Slavische Volksforschungen* (Leipzig, 1908), p. 125; Lauri Honko "Finnish Mythology," in *Wörterbuch der Mythologie* (Stuttgart, 1973), vol. 2, 352.
Vampirism can also come about by a variety of other means, as when an animal jumps over the corpse. Space does not permit a complete accounting here, but I discuss these in detail in *Vampires, Burial, and Death: Folklore and Reality* (New Haven: Yale University Press, 1988).
12. Raymond McNally and Radu Florescu, *In Search of Dracula* (New York: Galahad Books, 1972), 148. See also Elwood B. Trigg, *Gypsy Demons and Divinities: The Magic and Religion of the Gypsies* (Secaucus, N.J.: Citadel Press, 1973), 155; W. Mannhardt, "Über Vampyrismus," *Zeitschrift fur deutsche Mythologie und Sittenkunde* 4 (1859): 259–282; R. P. Vukanovic, "The Vampire," *Journal of the Gypsy Lore Society* 37 (1958): 30; Krauss, *Slavische Volksforschungen*, p. 130; Vakarelski, *Bulgarische Volkskunde*, p. 239. Vukanovic's article was published in installments; I shall cite it by the year.
13. Trigg, *Gypsy Demons*, p. 157. See also D. Demetracopoulou Lee, "Greek Accounts of the Vrykolakas," *Journal of American Folklore* 55 (1942): 131; Joseph Klapper, *Schlesische Volkskunde auf kulturgeschichtlicher Grundlage* (Breslau, 1925), 213; Fr. von Hellwald, *Die Welt der Slawen* (Berlin, 1890), p. 369; Mannhardt, "Über Vampyrismus," 271; Vukanovic, "The Vampire" (1958), 22, 25; Hock, *Die Vampyrsagen*, 29.
14. Hock, *Die Vampyrsagen*, p. 3. See also Ernst Bargheer, *Eingeweide, Lebens- und Seelenkräfte des Leibesinneren im deutschen Glauben und Brauch* (Leipzig, 1931), 82; Mannhardt, "Über Vampyrismus," 264.
15. Montague Summers, *The Vampire, His Kith and Kin* (New York: University Books, 1960), 161. See also Bernhardt Schmidt, *Das Volksleben der Neugriechen und das hellenische Alterthum* (Leipzig, 1871), vol. 1, 164; Juljan Jaworskij, "Südrussische Vampyre," *Zeitschrift des Vereins für Volkskunde* 8 (1898): 331; Lawson, *Modern Greek Folklore*, 387.
16. Hock, *Die Vampyrsagen*, 31–32, 43–44. See also Johann Heinrich Zedler, *Grosses vollständiges Universal-Lexikon* (Graz: Akademische Druck- und Verlagsanstalt, 1962), vol. 44, 664. This is a reprint of an edition published in 1745. See also Mannhardt, "Über Vampyrismus," 269, 274; Bargheer, *Eingeweide*, 78–79, 85.
17. Dagmar Burkhart, "Vampirglaube und Vampirsage auf dem Balkan," in *Beiträge zur Südosteuropa-Forschung* (Munich, 1966), 219. See also Krauss, *Slavische Volksforschungen*, 125.
18. Summers, *The Vampire*, 179. See also Mannhardt, "Über Vampyrismus" 275.
19. Ibid. See also Edmund Schneeweis, *Serbokroatische Volkskunde* (Berlin: de Gruyter and Co., 1961), p. 9; Vukanovic, "The

Vampire," (1960), 47; Lawson, *Modern Greek Folklore*, p. 367.

20. Pitton de Tournefort, *Relation d'un voyage du Levant* (Paris, 1717), vol. 1, 133. See also Hanns Bächtold-Stäubli, *Handwörterbuch des deutschen Aberglaubens* (Berlin: de Gruyter, 1934–1935), vol. 6, 818; Richard Beitl, *Deutsches Volkstum der Gegenwart* (Berlin, 1933), 32; Bargheer, *Eingeweide*, 84.

21. Johann Heinrich Zopf, *Dissertatio de vampyris serviensibus* (Duisburg, 1733), 7. See also Maximilian Lambertz in *Wörterbuch der Mythologie*, 490; Schneeweis, *Serbokroatische Volkskunde*, 9.

22. Rade Uhlik, "Serbo-Bosnian Gypsy Folktales, N. 4," *Journal of the Gypsy Lore Society* 19 (1940): 49. See also Vakarelski, *Bulgarische Volkskunde*, 239; Schneeweis, *Serbokroatische Volkskunde*, 10; Lee, "Greek Accounts," 128; Vukanovic, "The Vampire" (1960), 49; Trigg, *Gypsy Demons*, 154–155.

23. Schneeweis, *Serbokroatische Volkskunde*, 9; Vukanovic, "The Vampire" (1958), 23; Schmidt, *Das Volksleben*, 168; Trigg, *Gypsy Demons*, 154; Hock, *Die Vampyrsagen,*, 27; Lawson, *Modern Greek Folklore*, 368.

24. Burkhart, "Vampirglaube," 219; McNally and Florescu, *In Search of Dracula*, 150.

25. Julius von Negelein, *Weltgeschichte des Aberglaubens*, vol. 2: *Haupttypen des Aberglaubens* (Berlin and Leipzig: de Gruyter, 1935), 124. See also Jan Machal, *Slavic Mythology* (Boston, 1918), 231; Dmitrij Zelenin, *Russische (ostslavische) Volkskunde* (Berlin and Leipzig: de Gruyter, 1927), 328; Paul Geiger, "Die Behandlung der Selbstmörder im deutschen Brauch," *Archiv für Volkskunde* 26 (1926): 158.

26. Hock, *Die Vampyrsagen*, 24, 36; Hellwald, *Die Welt der Slawen*, 368.

27. Friedrich Krauss, "Vampyre im südslawischen Volksglauben," *Globus, Illustrierte Zeitschrift fur Länder und Volkskunde* 61 (1892): 326. See also Hellwald, *Die Welt der Slawen*, 368.

28. Agnes Murgoci, "The Vampire in Roumania," *Folkore* 37 (1926): 328. Also Veselin Čajkanović, "The Killing of a Vampire," *Folklore Forum* 7, 4 (1974): 261; trans. Marilyn Sjoberg, originally published in Belgrade in 1923. See Adelbert Kuhn, *Sagen, Gebräuche und Märchen aus Westfalen* (Leipzig, 1859), 175, for early accounts of staking in Saxo Grammaticus and Burchard of Worms.

29. Trigg, *Gypsy Demons*, 152. See also G. F. Abbott, *Macedonian Folklore* (Cambridge, 1903), 219.

30. Wuttke, *Der deutsche Volksaberglaube*, 221. See also J. D. H. Temme, *Die Volkssagen von Pommern und Rügen* (Hildesheim: Georg Olms Verlag, 1976), 308; originally published in Berlin in 1840. And Paul Drechsler, *Sitte, Brauch und Volksglaube in Schlesien* (Leipzig, 1903), 317; Klapper, *Schlesische Volkskunde*, 212; Franz Tetzner, *Die Slawen in Deutschland* (Braunschweig, 1902), 462. Archaeologically, such beheading is well attested. See, for example, Ludwig Pauli, *Keltischer Volksglaube* (Munich: C. H. Beck'sche Verlagsbuchhandlung, 1975), 145–146.

31. Augustine Calmet, *The Phantom World*, ed. Henry Christmas (London, 1850), vol. 2, 38; This is a translation of his *Dissertations sur les apparitions des anges, des démons et des esprits, et sur les revenants et les vampires* (Paris, 1746). See also Hock, *Die Vampyrsagen*, 42; Bargheer, *Eigenweide*, 37; Burkhart, "Vampirglaube," 222; Lawson, *Modern Greek Folkore*, 412.

32. August Löwenstimm, *Aberglaube und Strafrecht* (Berlin, 1897), 103. See also Christopher Frayling, *The Vampyre, A Bedside Companion* (New York: Scribner, 1978), 30; Robert Pashley, *Travels in Crete* (London, 1837), vol. 2, 201; Krauss, *Slavische Volksforschungen*, 133, 135; Trigg, *Gypsy Demons*, 157; Čajkanović, "The Killing of a Vampire," 261.

33. See Aribert Schroeder's account following. See also Arthur and Albert Schott, *Walachische Maerchen* (Stuttgart and Tübingen, 1845), 297; Edm. Veckenstedt, *Wendische Sagen, Märchen und abergläubische Geschichten* (Graz, 1880), 354–355; and Harry A. Senn, *Were-Wolf and Vampire in Romania*, East European Monographs (Boulder, 1982), 67, for a summary of methods of killing the vampire.

34. Summers, *The Vampire*, 202; Schmidt, *Das Volksleben*, 167; Bächtold-Staubli,

HandWörterbuch, 819; Jaworskij, "Südrussische Vampyre," 331; Iván Balassa and Gyula Ortutay, *Ungarische Volkskunde* (Budapest: Corvina Kiadó, and Munich: C. H. Beck, 1982), 726.

35. Hock, *Die Vampyrsagen*, 28.
36. Dieter Sturm and Klaus Völker, *Von denen Vampiren oder Menschensaugern* (Carl Hanser Verlag, 1968), 524; Arthur Jellinek, "Zur Vampyrsage," *Zeitschrift des Vereins für Volkskunde* 14 (1904): 324; Bargheer, *Eigenweide*, 86; Mannhardt, "Über Vampyrismus," 260, 262, 265–265; Bächtold-Stäubli, *Handwörterbuch*, 819; Hellwald, *Die Welt der Slawen*, 367, 370; Abbott, *Macedonian Folklore*, 219–220; Beitl, *Deutsches Volkstum*, 187; Wuttke, *Der deutsche Volksaberglaube*, 222; Trigg, *Gypsy Demons*, 153; Hock, *Die Vampyrsagen*, 28; Murgoci, "The Vampire in Roumania," 341.
37. Schneeweis, *Serbokroatische Volkskunde*, 9. See also Norbert Reiter (Slavic) in *Wörterbuch der Mythologie*, 201; Vukanovic "The Vampire" (1958), 23.
38. Mannhardt, "Über Vampyrismus," 264, 268; Zedler, *Universal-Lexikon*, vol. 46, 478; Vukanovic "The Vampire" (1960), 47; Drechsler, *Sitte, Brauch*, 318; Bächtold-Stäubli, *Handwörterbuch*, 818–819; Hock, *Die Vampyrsagen*, 31–33; Trigg, *Gypsy Demons*, 157; Edward Tylor, *Primitive Culture* (London, 1871), vol. 2, 176; Joseph von Görres, *Die Christliche Mystik* (Regensburg, 1840), 282.
39. Murgoci, "The Vampire in Roumania," 334; Vakarelski, *Bulgarische Volkskunde*, 305.
40. Hellwald, *Die Welt der Slawen*, 371–372; Abbott, *Macedonian Folklore*, 219; Trigg, *Gypsy Demons*, 142, 149; Bächtold-Staubli, *Handwörterbuch*, 818.
41. Voltaire made a remark to the effect that vampires are not to be found in London or Paris (quoted in Sturm and Völker, *Von denen Vampiren* 484).
42. Tekla Dömötör, *Volkslaube und Aberglaube der Ungarn* (Corvina Kiadó, 1981), 122. Krauss points out that Medvegia, which Arnold Paole made famous, was actually in Serbia under Hungarian rule (Krauss, *Slavische Volksforschungen*, 131). See also Bargheer, *Eigenweide*, 81 and Mannhardt, "Über Vampyrismus," 273.
43. Grigore Nandris, "The Historical Dracula: The Theme of His Legend in the Western and in the Eastern Literatures of Europe," *Comparative Literature Studies* 3, 4 (1966): 369. See also Senn, *Were-Wolf*, 41ff. I am indebted to Dr. Senn for his helpful clarification (in conversation) of some details relating to the history and folklore of Romania, especially in the matter of Dracula. Incidentally, there is some question as to which of several Vlads in Romanian history was Stoker's model.
44. John Glaister and Edgar Rentoul, *Medical Jurisprudence and Toxicology* (Edinburgh and London: E. and S. Livingstone, 1966), 117. See also Albert Ponsold, *Lehrbuch der gerichtlichen Medizin* (Stuttgart: Georg Thieme Verlag, 1957), 290–296.
45. Glaister and Rentoul, *Medical Jurisprudence*, 115–116; Ponsold, *Lehrbuch*, 292–293.
46. Glaister and Rentoul, *Medical Jurisprudence*, 120.
47. Ibid.
48. Aidan and Eve Cockburn, *Mummies, Disease and Ancient Cultures* (Cambridge University Press, 1982), 1 (abridged paperback edition).
49. Glaister and Rentoul, *Medical Jurisprudence*, 124.
50. Ibid., 121.
51. Christian Fischer, "Bog Bodies of Denmark," trans. Kirstine Thomsen, in Cockburn, *Mummies*, 177. See also P. V. Glob, *The Bog People*, trans, from the Danish by Rupert Bruce-Mitford (New York: Ballantine, 1973); and Alfred Dieck, *Die europäischen Moorleichenfunde: Göttinger Schriften zur Vor-und Frühgeschichte*, ed. Herbert Jankuhn (Neumünster: Karl Wacholtz Verlag, 1965).
52. Richard and Eva Blum, *The Dangerous Hour: The Lore of Crisis and Mystery in Rural Greece* (New York: Charles Scribner's 1970), 71. Hock (*Die Vampyrsagen*, 23) also remarks that people who are not buried at all tend to become vampires. See also E. H. Meyer, *Mythologie der Germanen* (Strassburg, 1903), 94.
53. Strackerjan, *Aberglaube*, 154.

54. Glaister, and Rentoul, *Medical Jurisprudence,* 121.
55. Charles Creighton, *A History of Epidemics in Britain* (Cambridge, 1891), vol. 2, 165.
56. Creighton, *History,* vol. 2, 167.
57. Schneeweis, *Serbokroatische Volkskunde,* 90. One would expect to find a correlation between "vampirism" and the custom of exhumation. This seems to be present in the Balkans. The duration of the first burial may be from three to eighteen years, after which the body is dug up again: "If the body has still not disintegrated, then it is believed that a curse weighs on it" (Schneeweis, *Serbokroatische Volkskunde,* 103). Note that this custom implies that bodies may not disintegrate even after years in the grave, let alone days or months.

    For a discussion of the practice of exhumation in Greece, see Loring M. Danforth, *The Death Rituals of Rural Greece* (Princeton, N.J.: Princeton University Press, 1982). Danforth describes inhumations taking place after five years, in the area where he did his research. Lawson *(Modern Greek Folklore,* 372) and the Blums *(The Dangerous Hour,* 75) mention a time span of three years. See Vakarelski *(Bulgarische Volkskunde,* 309) for an account of exhumations in Bulgaria.
58. Murgoci, "The Vampire in Roumania," 327.
59. Krauss, "Vampyre," 327.
60. Glaister and Rentoul, *Medical Jurisprudence,* 111–112.
61. Hans Naumann, *Primitive Gemeinschaftskultur: Beiträge zur Volkskunde unci Mythologie* (Jena, 1921), 49. Also Vukanovic "The Vampire" (1958), 23: "... it is believed that the body which is to become a vampire turns black before burial."
62. Pauli, *Keltischer Volksglaube,* 175. See also Geiger, "Die Behandlung," 159; Reiter, *Wörterbuch,* 201; Zelenin, *Russische (ostslavische) Volkskunde,* 393; Mannhardt, "Über Vampyrismus" 260, 270; ajkanovi, "The Killing of a Vampire," 264; and Veroboj Vildomec, *Polnische Sagen,* introduction and notes by Will-Erich Peuckert (Erich Schmidt Verlag, 1979), 78.
63. See note 57: exhumation correlating with vampirism.
64. Edmund Schneeweis, *Feste und Volksbräuche der Lausitzer Wenden* (Nendeln, Liechtenstein: Kraus Reprint, 1968), 81; originally published in Leipzig, 1931. There are at least two other reasons, by the way, for blood to appear at the mouth of a corpse: a traumatic injury may cause this (as in a murder victim), as will pneumonic plague, which causes vomiting of blood. See Creighton, *History,* vol. 1, 122.
65. Ronald and Catherine Berndt, *The World of the First Australians* (Chicago: University of Chicago Press, 1965), 410. Lawson *(Modern Greek Folklore,* 405) says that, on the Greek island of Chios, "the woman who prepares the corpse for burial places on its lips a cross of wax or cotton-stuff. ..."
66. Wuttke, *Der Deutsche Volksaberglaube,* 222. See also Klapper, *Schlesische Volkskunde,* 213, and the account from the *Mercure galant* (Section I).
67. John Taylor, *African Rifles and Cartridges* (Highland Park, N.J.: Gun Room Press, 1977), facing p. 342; reprint of 1948 edition.
68. Burkhart, "Vampirglaube," 222; Trigg, *Gypsy Demons,* 156; Vukanovic, "The Vampire" (1960), 45, and (1959), 117; Otto Knoop, *Sagen unci Erzäblungen aus der Provinz Posen* (Posen, 1893), 139.
69. W. E. D. Evans, *The Chemistry of Death* (Springfield, Ill: Charles C. Thomas, 1963), 49.
70. Bächtold-Stäubli, *Handwörterbuch,* 814. This interpretation is also suggested in a curious nineteenth-century Hungarian novel that analyzes the vampire lore. I found a German translation of the novel. Ferenz Köröshazy, *Die Vampyrbraut* (Weimar, 1849), 268. (On the title page, the author's name is given in reverse order, in the Hungarian manner.) See also Karl Bartsch, *Sagen, Märchen und Gebräuche aus Meklenburg* (Vienna, 1879), 93.
71. Trigg, *Gypsy Demons,* 154.
72. Murgoci, "The Vampire in Roumania," 349; Vakarelski, *Bulgarische Volkskunde,* 239.
73. See, for example, Sturm and Völker, *Von denen Vampiren,* 511, 526, 441, 442, 444; Edward Westermarck, *Ritual and Belief in Morocco*

(London, 1926), vol. 2, 548; and Bargheer, *Eigenweide*, 79.
74. Ponsold, *Lehrbuch*, 290.
75. Jan Perkowski, *Vampires of the Slavs* (Cambridge, Mass., 1976), 109ff.
76. Glaister and Rentoul, *Medical Jurisprudence*, 52.
77. Cockburn, *Mummies*, 1.
78. Jens P. Hart Hansen, Jørgen Meldgaard, and Jørgen Nordqvist, "The Mummies of Qilakitsoq," *National Geographic* 167, 2 (February 1985): 190–207; see p. 201. See Trigg, *Gypsy Demons*, 146, for long teeth of vampire; also, Otto Knoop, "Sagen aus Kujawien," *Zeitschrift des Vereins fur Volkskunde* 16 (1906): 96.
79. J. J. Hess, *Von den Beduinen des innern Arabiens* (Zürich and Leipzig: Max Niehans Verlag, 1938), 164. Note, in this connection, the practice of throwing a rock or twig onto the place where someone was killed: Schneeweis, *Wenden*, 100–101; Geiger, "Die Behandlung," 163; Felix Liebrecht, *Zur Volkskunde* (Heilbronn, 1879), 282–283.

Edward Tripp of Yale University Press pointed out to me that, considered from this perspective, it makes sense that Anubis, the Egyptian god of tombs and embalming, would be represented with the head of a jackal. Jackals would in fact "preside" over the disposal of the dead, given the opportunity.

For an account of coffins designed to prevent bears from breaking in and eating the corpses, see Milovan Gavazzi, "The Dugout Coffin in Central Bosnia," *Man* 53, 202 (1953): 129.

For burial methods designed to protect the coffin from wolves, see Philip Tilney, "Supernatural Prophylaxes in a Bulgarian Peasant Funeral," *Journal of Popular Culture* 4, 1 (1970): 222, 223.
80. Vukanovic "The Vampire" (1960), 49; Trigg, *Gypsy Demons*, 155.
81. Burkhart, "Vampirglaube," 243.
82. Lambertz in *Wörterbuch der Mythologie*, 490.
83. Bargheer, *Eigenweide*, 84. I have in my files a newspaper account of an event of this sort: "A hand protruding from an incline near the Harbor Freeway led to the discovery of the badly decomposed body of an adult male..." (*Los Angeles Times*).
84. Meyer, *Mythologie*, 96.
85. Glaister and Rentoul, *Medical Jurisprudence*, 119–120.
86. Murgoci, "The Vampire in Roumania," 332.
87. See Burkhart, citing Schneeweis, *Serbokroatische Volkskunde*, 239, n. 141. Also, Löwenstimm, *Aberglaube*, 93–103; Friedrich Haase, *Volksglaube und Brauchtum der Ostslaven* (Hildesheim/New York: Georg Olms Verlag, 1980), 329; reprint of 1939 edition; Zelenin, *Russische (ostslavische) Volkskunde*, 329. Also, Geiger, "Die Behandlung" (Switzerland): disposal of bodies in water, 153, 155–156.
88. See, for example, Haase, *Volksglaube*, 302; E. Cabej, "Sitten und Gebräuche der Albaner," *Revue internationale des études balkaniques* (1934–35): 224; Vakarelski, *Bulgarische Volkskunde*, 303, 309; G. Lemke, *Volksthümliches in Ostpreussen* (Mohrungen, 1884), vol. 1, 56.
89. *Grettir's Saga*, trans. Denton Fox and Herman Pálsson (University of Toronto Press, 1974), 72; Vakarelski, *Bulgarische Volkskunde*, 307; Lemke, *Volksthümliches*, vol. 3, 51.
90. *Grettir's Saga*, 72, for rocks; Zelenin, *Russische (ostslavische) Volkskunde*, 327, for brush.
91. P. V. Glob gives numerous examples of this in *The Bog People*. See also Pauli, *Keltischer Volksglaube*, 174–179; Schneeweis, *Wenden*, 102; Geiger, "Die Behandlung," 158. Dieck (*Die europäischen Moorleichenfunde*, 50–127) catalogues the methods of holding down the bodies.
92. Hock, *Die Vampyrsagen*, 42; Tetzner, *Die Volkssagen*, 461.
93. Meyer, *Mythologie*, 96.
94. Reiter in *Wörterbuch der Mythologie*, 201.
95. Schneeweis, *Serbokroatische Volkskunde*, 88, 104; Krauss, *Slavische Volksforschungen*, 127–128; Vukanovic, "The Vampire" (1958), 22; Trigg, *Gypsy Demons*, 152; Burkhart, "Vampirglaube," 220.
96. Beitl, Deutsches Volkstum, 45.
97. Reiter, *Wörterbuch*, 201.

98. Jan Perkowski, "The Romanian Folkloric Vampire," *East European Quarterly* 16, 3 (September 1982): 313.
99. Arpád Csiszár, "A hazajáró lélek," *A nyiregyházi Jósa András Muzeum Évkönyve*, 8–9 (1965–66): 159–96; summary in German: 199–201; see 200.
100. Balassa and Ortutay, *Ungarische Volkskunde*, 673. See also Vakarelski, *Bulgarische Volkskunde*, 305; Schneeweis, *Serbokroatische Volkskunde*, 88; and Adolf Schullerus, *Siebenbürgisch-sächsische Volkskunde im Umriss* (Leipzig, 1926), 125.
101. Dömötör, *Volksglaube*, 251–252.
102. For death figure with scythe: Vakarelski, *Bulgarische Volkskunde*, 311; with sickle: Haase, *Volksglaube*, 301.
103. Burkhart, "Vampirglaube," 215, 229. See also Schneeweis, *Serbokroatische Volkskunde*, 11.
104. Schneeweis, *Wenden*, 85.
105. Trigg, *Gypsy Demons*, 152.
106. Stith Thompson, *Motif-Index of Folk-Literature* (Helsinki, 1932), vol. 2, 380, E442: "Ghost laid by piercing grave with stake." See also Sebestyén Karoly, "Speerhölzer und Kreuze auf dem Széklerboden," *Anzeiger der ethnographischen Abteilung des ungarischen National-Museums* (1905), vol. 2, 99; Burkhart, "Vampirglaube," 243; Ernö Kunt, *Volkskunst ungarischer Dorffriedhöfe* (Budapest: Corvina Kiadó, 1983), p. 40; translation into German by Valér Nagy.
107. Krauss, *Slavische Volksforschungen*, 127. In some areas thorns are put into the grave (see Schott, *Walachische Maerchen*, 198).
108. Strackerjan, *Aberglaube*, 154.
109. *Los Angeles Times*, Nov. 21, 1978.
110. Pauli, *Keltischer Volksglaube*, 174–179; Schneeweis, *Serbokroatische Volkskunde*, 106; Naumann, *Primitive Gemeinschaftskultur*, 105; Mannhardt, "Über Vampyrismus" 269; Karl Brunner, *Ostdeutsche Volkskunde* (Leipzig, 1925), 195; Fischer, "Bog Bodies of Denmark," 178, 182, 192.
111. Burkhart, "Vampirglaube," 223.
112. Erhard Eylmann, *Die Eingeborenen der Kolonie Südaustralien* (Berlin, 1908), 232.
113. Beitl, *Deutsches Volkstum*, 187; Schneeweis, *Serbokroatische Volkskunde*, 88; Vakarelski, *Bulgarische Volkskunde*, 303.
114. Hellwald, *Die Welt der Slawen*, 370; Schneeweis, *Serbokroatische Volkskunde*, 10; Vakarelski, *Bulgarische Volkskunde*, 303.
115. Wuttke, *Der deutsche Volksaberglaube*, 222.
116. Aribert Schroeder, *Vampirismus* (Frankfurt, 1973), 45–46. The words used here may very well refer to the sound created by the splitting open of the swollen body cavity.
117. J. A. E. Köhler, *Volksbrauch, Aberglauben, Sagen und andere alte Überlieferungen im Voigtland* (Leipzig, 1867), 257–258. See also Zelenin, *Russiche (ostslavishe) Volkskunde*, 329; Löwenstimm, *Aberglaube*, 98ff.
118. Zopf (*Dissertatio*, 11–12) cites an essay, published in 1732, in which it is remarked that it is in fact not abnormal for a corpse to bleed this way.
119. J. J. M. de Groot, *The Religious System of China* (The Hague, 1892–1910), vol. 1, 32.
120. Not just in Europe: "It is, according to the Chinese, by no means a rare thing in their country for corpses to sit up on their death-bed and strike terror and fright into the hearts of their mourning kinsfolk" (de Groot, *Religious System*, vol. 5, 750). A Chinese acquaintance from Peking also mentioned this belief to me in conversation. See also Westermarck, *Ritual and Belief*, 449.
121. Blum and Blum, *The Dangerous Hour*, 71.
122. The Turks being not only the bugbears of the Greeks but also the westernmost culture that did not necessarily use chairs. "Sitting up like a Turk," then, could mean sitting with legs straight out. Murgoci cites the expression, p. 119; also, Raymond T. McNally, *A Clutch of Vampires* (Greenwich, Conn.: New York Graphic Society, 1974), 191.
123. Lawson, *Modern Greek Folklore*, 377. The following etymologies are all Lawson's.
124. Danforth, *Death Rituals*, 52.
125. Evans, *The Chemistry of Death*, 10–11. See also R. L. Airth and G. E. Foerster, "Some Aspects of Fungal Bioluminescence," *Journal of Cellular and Comparative Physiology* 56 (1960): 173–182.
126. See, for example, Trigg, *Gypsy Demons*, 156.

127. Markus Köhbach, "Ein Fall von Vampirismus bei den Osmanen," *Balkan Studies* 20 (1979): 89.
128. Evans, *Chemistry of Death*, 84.
129. Ralston, *Songs of the Russian People*, 409; Zelenin, *Russische (ostslavische) Volkskunde*, 329–330; Haase, *Volksglaube*, 329; Löwenstimm, *Aberglaube*, 102. Such alcoholic vampires were blamed for droughts, having continued beyond death their habit of drinking everything in sight.
130. Hock, *Die Vampyrsagen*, 1; Burkhart, "Vampirglaube," 250; Wilhelm Hertz, *Der Werwolf* (Stuttgart, 1862), 126; Richard Andree, *Ethnographische Parallelen und Vergleiche* (Stuttgart, 1878), 81.
131. Trigg has an informative discussion of these: *Gypsy Demons*, 145, 178–179.
132. *Mercure galant,* quoted in Hock, *Die Vampyrsagen*, 34.
133. See "Stana" in section I. Also Arnold Paole in Sturm and Völker, *Von denen Vampiren*, 451.
134. Burkhart, "Vampirglaube," 221; Perkowski, "Romanian Folkloric Vampire," 316; Wuttke, *Der Deutsche Volksaberglaube,* 221–222; Richard Beitl, *Deutsche Volkskunde* (Berlin, 1933), 188; Mannhardt, "Über Vampyrismus" 261–262.

East European Vampires

Felix Oinas

THE VAMPIRE IS DEFINED by Jan Perkowski as "a being which derives sustenance from a victim, who is weakened by the experience. The sustenance may be physical or emotional in nature."[1] More commonly, however, the term *vampire* is used in a more restricted sense to denote a type of the dead or, actually, undead. It is a living corpse or soulless body that emerges from its grave and drinks the blood of the living. Belief in vampires is found all over the world, in India, China, Malaya, Indonesia, and elsewhere, but especially in eastern Europe—among the Slavs and their neighbors: the Greeks, Romanians, Albanians, and others.

Among the East Slavs, the vampire is well known to the Ukrainians. The Russians knew it by its name in former times (from the eleventh to the fifteenth century). The vampire tradition is well documented among the West Slavs—the Czechs, Poles, and particularly the Kashubs, who live at the mouth of the Vistula River—and among the South Slavs—Macedonians, Bulgarians, Serbs, Croats, and Slovenes. *Vampire* in Russian is *upyr*, Ukrainian *upýr'* Bulgarian *vъpir*, Czech and Slovak *upír*, Polish *upiór* (East Slavic), Kashub *wupi, lupi;* the origin of this term is uncertain. Among the South Slavs, the vampire is called by the name of the werewolf, *vukodlak* (in Serbian), *volkodlak* (Slovene), and *vъrkolak* (Bulgarian).[2] In the following essay we shall discuss the vampire primarily among the Slavs, with some references to their neighbors.

There is a host of ideas about the origin of vampires. The most common is that sorcerers, witches, werewolves, excommunicates, and those who died unnatural deaths (such as suicides and drunkards) become vampires at their deaths. People can, however, be destined from birth to become vampires. The union of a werewolf or the devil and a witch is believed to produce a vampire. Likewise, children born with a caul on their head, or with their teeth showing, or with contiguous eyebrows are expected to become vampires. There are antidotes for some of these signs, but not for all. For example, the caul has to be burned and its ashes fed to the child when it is seven years old. Some Greeks believe that children born on Christmas Day are doomed to become vampires. This is a punishment for the presumptuousness of their mothers in having conceived on the same day as the Virgin Mary. People can be made vampires even after death. This happens if a human or unclean animal (cat or dog) steps over a body or a bird flies over it. These acts are evidently connected with the idea that insufficient respect or care for the dead is shown. In order to avoid this, relatives of the deceased keep constant vigil by the corpse as long as it is at home.

Ernest Jones, in his psychoanalytical study of vampires,[3] distinguishes two basic emotions—love and hatred—as motives which are projected to the dead and urge reunion and return from the grave. Love motivates vampires to always visit relatives first, particularly their marital partners. On the other hand, an unconscious feeling of guilt causes people to fear being the targets of a vampire's hatred and revenge.

Vampires are believed to lie in their graves as undecayed corpses, leaving at midnight to go to houses and have sexual relations with or suck the blood of those sleeping, or to devour their flesh, sometimes causing the death of the victims. If the grave is opened, the presence of a vampire can be recognized by finding the body in a state of disorder, with red cheeks, tense skin, charged blood vessels, warm blood and growing hair and nails; in some cases the grave itself is bespattered with blood, doubtless from the latest victim.

A memorat recorded from a Kashub tells that "at midnight the [vampire] awakens and first eats his own dress and flesh, and then leaves the tomb and goes to visit his kinsfolk, first the near relatives and then the more distant ones, and sucks the blood from their bodies, so that they die. If all his blood-relatives have died, he rings the church bell, and, as far as the sound reaches, all who hear it must die."[4]

Vampires are occasionally considered responsible for hardships that befall households and even whole villages: bringing on a drought, causing storms, crop failures, livestock plagues, and diseases. These beliefs are identical with those connected with the "unclean dead" (those who have died unnatural deaths) and have been carried over to vampires.

Felix Oinas, "East European Vampires & Dracula," *Journal of Popular Culture*, vol. 16, no. 1, pp. 108-114. Copyright © 1982 by John Wiley & Sons, Inc. Reprinted with permission.

Vampires appear among the Slavs also as bats.[5] The bat form was added to vampirism in Europe rather late—after the return of Cortez's followers from the New World in the sixteenth century, with tales of blood-sucking bats. Only one type of sanguineous bat, Desmodontidae, exists, which is found in the former Mayan area of habitation in the South American tropics—Panama, the West Indies, and their neighborhood. This so-called vampire bat does not suck blood from its victim, but licks it. Meticulous observations have revealed that the lips of this creature are never near the initial wound, but by moving its long tongue quickly, the bat causes a pulsating ribbon of blood to flow freely into its mouth. In about twenty minutes it consumes the amount of a fair-sized wineglass. In the tropics of the New World, this curious creature had a strong effect on people's beliefs—even a blood-sucking bat god was created. When the Spaniards returned to Europe, their stories of the blood-sucking bat strengthened the superstitions already present. In about 1730 a real "vampire epidemic" broke out in Europe, especially in the Slavic countries. There was a flood of works relating cases about alleged vampires that sucked the blood of people and animals. Plague and other epidemics were attributed either to the stench of the vampires or to their attacks.

What are the ways of rendering a vampire harmless? After the diagnosis of vampirism has been made, there are numerous ways to treat the dead.[6] The simplest consist of measures calculated to afford the dead a peaceful rest, such as placing miniature poplar crosses in the coffin. One may also offer the dead a peaceful occupation by putting quantities of sand and poppy seed into the coffin. The sand and poppy seed must be counted grain by grain before the vampire can leave its coffin. The dead can be kept from leaving the grave by piling a heap of stones onto it. Sterner measures to render harmless a person judged to be a potential vampire are to pierce the body with a sharpened stake (hawthorn or aspen) by beating it into the chest or back, between the shoulder blades, or to drive a stake or nail into the head; to place thorns under the tongue to keep the vampire from sucking blood; to bind the hands of the corpse behind its back; to maim the heels and cut the tendons under the knees. In more serious cases it is desirable to strike off the head with a single stroke and to place it between the legs, or to hack the body to pieces. Some of these measures are, however, not completely foolproof; cases have been reported of an exhumed vampire who had been pierced by a stake, but had pulled the stake out. The surest method of disposing of vampires is to completely annihilate the body by burning it and scattering the ashes.

Some of these acts correspond closely to the punishments meted out, especially in the Orient, for particularly heinous murders.[7] The killing of a vampire or any other dangerous person is accomplished in such a way as to make it impossible for the soul to avenge itself.

During the vampire epidemic in Europe, and even in the United States, from the eighteenth to well into the nineteenth century, numerous cases of the mishandling of corpses believed to be vampires have become known.[8] In 1889 in Russia, the corpse of an old man who was suspected of being a vampire was dug up, and many of those present maintained that they saw a tail attached to its back. In Rhode Island, a father in 1874 exhumed the body of his own daughter and burned her heart, in the belief that she was endangering the lives of the other members of the family. In 1899, Romanian peasants in Krasova dug up no fewer than thirty corpses and tore them to pieces, expecting to stop an epidemic of diphtheria. Further instances have been reported from Hungary, Bucharest, Transylvania, and so on.

A tragic event, entitled "Immigrant's Fears of Vampires Led to Death,"[9] was reported in the *Times* of London as late as January 9, 1973. Mr. Myiciura, a Polish immigrant in Stoke on Trent, sixty-eight years of age, a retired pottery worker who had lived twenty-five years in England, was found dead in his bed. He had died from choking on a piece of garlic, which he had placed in his mouth before going to bed. The police officer explained at the inquest: "In his room was a ritual distribution of objects as antidotes to vampires. There was a bag of salt at the dead man's face, one between his legs and other containers scattered around the room. Salt was also sprinkled on his blankets. Outside his window was a washing-up-bowl containing cloves of garlic. There was garlic even in the keyhole of his lodgings."

The dead man's landlady testified: "He thought vampires were everywhere. He used salt, pepper and garlic to keep them away." And the city coroner said: "This is a strange case. This man took precautions against vampires he thought were in his neighborhood. He had a superstitious fear of vampires and choked on a clove of garlic used to ward them off." A verdict of accidental death was recorded.

Perkowski, who analyzed this case, points out that the precautions taken by Mr. Myiciura were those used in Poland to ward off vampires. "The clove in his mouth complemented by the salt near his head and between his legs effectively sealed off the portals of his body, just as the portals of his room had been sealed."[10] He might have sealed himself off either to keep the vampire from entering, or, if he was a vampire himself, then to keep his soul from leaving to wreak havoc. However, the first possibility is more plausible, considering especially the landlady's testimony.

In Yugoslavia, the vampire has merged with the werewolf (usually called *vukodlak*, and only occasionally *vampir*). The term *vukodlak* means "wolf's hair" and originally denoted "werewolf"—a man turned into a wolf. There are only traces of the *vukodlak's* werewolfism (lycanthropy) in Yugoslavia. Thus it was told, for example, that a woman changed herself into a wolf and killed forty sheep near Trebinja in about 1880. Her transformation was achieved by making a circle with a rope and—after she had disrobed—turning somersaults in it. Most often, however, the *vukodlak* appears as a vampire. As such, it comes out of the grave at night and visits people at home or in the neighborhood. He either drinks their blood or has amorous relations with his former wife, or his former girlfriends or young widows.

Since the people of Yugoslavia were very much afraid of vampires in former times, there were numerous instances of frauds and tricks played by living persons who presented themselves as vampires.[11] During periods of hunger, vampire impersonators were frequently seen at water mills and granaries. Gangs of young people clothed as vampires vandalized the villages. More frequent were cases where men used a vampire cloak for love trysts with young women. There were even accounts of women who had children by "vampires." These women were visited by other men, in the guise of their "vampire" husbands, and the frightened villagers did not dare to interfere. Joakim Vujic in his travelogue of Serbia relates that in a village near Baja a vampire appeared around midnight, creating a great din and wearing a white shroud, to visit a young widow whose husband had recently died. The frightened people ran out of the house, except for the beautiful widow, who remained in her bed. The vampire stayed with her for an hour, after which he left with much clanking and rattling. This affair continued for three months, until a bold lad with his comrades managed to capture the vampire despite his most desperate resistance. He turned out to be a neighbor of the widow. An investigation revealed that the widow, together with the "vampire," had killed her husband so as to carry on their illicit love affair. Both were sentenced to death.

The tendency to confuse vampires with werewolves is noticeable also in Russia, as indicated by a curious piece of information pertaining to vampires: "More frequently encountered was the belief in Russia that while a dead vampire destroyed people, a live one, on the contrary, defended them. According to this belief, each village had its own vampire, as if it were a guard, protecting the inhabitants from his dead comrades. But if he lost his strength and perished in the fight, he himself became an evil and dangerous destroyer."[12]

This information about the "live vampires" as the protectors of villages can hardly be correct, since it defies the basic notions about vampires. This latter role is, however, fitting for werewolves. Among various peoples, werewolves (like shamans) appear as protectors against various hostile powers. According to Serbian beliefs, certain demonic beings (related to werewolves), appearing in the shape of beasts, are benevolent to people and fight against evil spirits. A seventeenth-century report from Latvia relates that werewolves work on the side of God against sorcerers, who are on the Devil's team.[13] If the sorcerers take fertility away into hell, the werewolves bring it back. There are competitions between Latvian and Russian werewolves; if the Latvian werewolves win, the Latvian people will then have a good crop. Considering these data, we come to the conclusion that the live vampire reported in Russia cannot be a vampire but must be a werewolf functioning as the protector of the villagers against evil spirits. The Slavic werewolves are believed to become vampires after death. This is what happened to the so-called good vampire in the report: it becomes an evil and dangerous destroyer. A mix-up between vampires and werewolves in Russia is understandable, in light of the blurring of the notion of the vampire during recent centuries.

Among the Russians, especially in the north, numerous vampiristic traits have been transferred to heretics. The beliefs in heretics show them to be a conglomerate of sectarians, witches, *rusalkas*, and vampires (known by the names *eretik, eretnik, eretitsa, eretnitsa, erestun*). Various episodes among heretics betray their vampiristic essence.[14]

A. Zvonkov reports from Elatomsk District (east-central Russia) the following:

> I was told that a peasant's daughter died; the peasant invited his godfather to his house, treated him with food and drink, and asked him to dig the grave. Being drunk, the godfather, who had taken a spade along, strolled directly to the cemetery. He found a fallen-in grave, descended into it and began to dig. The spade hit a coffin, and, all of a sudden, through a rotten branch he saw an *eretitsa*'s eye. The peasant jumped out quickly and ran home without looking back. When he arrived, he climbed onto the stove, but the *eretitsa* was lying there and was looking at him with the same evil eye. The man ran to the yard and then to the manger, but the accursed *eretitsa* had anticipated him: she was lying in the manger, shaking with demonic laughter. From that time on the godfather began to wither and wither. They held services to Zosima and Savvatii, besprinkled him with holy water, but whatever they did, nothing helped, and the godfather died.

In this description, special attention should be given to the detail concerning the *eretitsa*'s eye. In Russia and Germany there is a belief that the open eyes of a corpse can draw someone into the grave; for this reason, the eyes of the deceased are closed at the time of death. The Kashubs believe that when a vampire (*vieszcy*) dies, his left eye remains open. Zvonkov's story is an indication that the Russians, like the Kashubs, were familiar with the tradition about the vampire's open eye. According to the Gypsies of Yugoslavia, some parts of the human body, such as the eye, can become vampires. The godfather is constantly followed by the *eretitsa*'s eye in the story recorded by Zvonkov. Here the eye seems to function as a full-fledged vampire that draws out the godfather's life substance and causes him to wither away.

In northern Russia, heretics appear after their deaths as evil, bloodthirsty vampires. A report given by Rybnikov from Olonets illustrates this:

> Evil sorcerers don't give peace to the Christians even after their deaths and become *erestuny;* they seize the moment when a neighbor is near his end and, as soon as the soul has left the body, they enter the deceased. After that, unpleasant things happen to the family. There are *erestuny* who 'transform themselves,' i.e., acquire another person's face and endeavor to sneak into their own or into another family. Such an *erestun* lives, it seems, as is fitting for a good peasant, but soon people in the family or in the village begin to disappear one after the other; the *erestun* eats them up. In order to

destroy the transformed sorcerer, it is necessary to take the whip used for a heavily loaded horse and give him a thorough thrashing. Then he will fall down and give up his ghost. In order to prevent him from coming to life in the grave, it is necessary to drive an aspen stake into his back between the shoulders.

There is another piece of information about heretics from northern Russia that is similar to this one. Efimenko reports that in the Shenkursk district of Karelia the same person who in his lifetime is called *koldun* (sorcerer) is called *eretik* after his death if he roams around at night in villages, captures people, and eats them. If people "get tired of him," they gather at the grave of the one who was known as a sorcerer during his lifetime, take him out of the grave, and burn him in a bonfire or pierce his back with an aspen stick; the stick prevents any further emergence from the grave.

The *eretik* as vampire appears in Russian literature as well. In M. D. Chulkov's *The Mocker, or Slavic Tales (Peresmeshnik, ili slavenskie skazki)* a rich peasant, a practitioner of black magic, picks a fight immediately after his death with a dog next to his coffin. The priest at first refuses to bury him or to read the burial service "over such a heretic *(eretik),* who has the devil within him." After he is finally buried, the corpse does not stay in the grave at night, but strolls about the village, catches people by the back of their heads, throws them out the window, and drags them by their beards along the street. People leave the village. They dare to come back only after a hunter has killed the corpse with a hatchet.

Zelenin suggests that "the idea of the bloodthirsty vampire has penetrated from Western Europe to the Ukraine and Belorussia; to the Great Russians it is unknown."[15] Zelenin's position is hardly tenable. There are clear indications that the beliefs in vampires have deep roots among the Slavs and obviously go back to the Proto-Slavic period. These beliefs are also well documented among the early Russians. The term *vampire* (*upyr'*) appears as the name of a Novgorodian prince (Upir Likhyi) as early as 1047 and resurfaces in 1495 as a peasant name. This term has also been recorded in western Russia as both a personal and a place name. The previous existence in Russia of a vampire cult is illustrated by the fight clerics waged in encyclicals against sacrifices made to them.

It is true that the term *upyr'* has been almost unknown in Russia during the last centuries. But the absence of this term does not preclude the presence of the notion of the vampire. As our examples given above show, beliefs pertaining to the vampire were transferred to the heretics. In the heretics' garb, the vampire has continued to live vigorously in the Russian north.

In Estonia, beliefs in vampires are rather undeveloped. The term for vampire in Estonia is *vampiir* (vampire), *vere-imeja* (blood-sucker), or *veripard* (blood-beard). There are numerous stories about revenants who visit people in the night and press down upon them. However, the vampire as a bloodsucking and killing revenant is little known by the people, and the idea may have been taken from their neighbors.[16]

In Hungary the vampire per se is almost unknown in folk religion. However, there are some figures that closely resemble the vampire. The *ludverc* or *luderc* is a burning shaft or star which flies through the air and enters the house through the chimney. A malevolent revenant, it takes on the appearance of the dead marriage partner of the victim and sleeps with her or him, making the person pale and drained. It is exorcised by magic. The belief in *ludverc* is known particularly in Transylvania and is probably a borrowing from Romania.[17] The belief in the living dead, too, is well known to Hungarian peasants all over the country. Though this creature scares people by its appearance, it does not suck blood, and should not be classed with the vampire.

There is also information about the presence of full-fledged vampires from Hungary. The close examination of the names of those accused in vampirism in court proceedings shows (as Linda Dégh informs me) that they were not Hungarians, but members of some minorities, especially Slavs. Since Hungary before 1918 included vast tracts with non-Hungarian population, the stories about vampires obviously came from those areas. The Hungarians, on the whole, seem to have been reluctant to assimilate these beliefs. It is of course possible that the belief in vampires may have found acceptance among the Hungarians in some restricted localities. It cannot be ascertained with certainty whether the much publicized vampire story in 1912 involves a Hungarian or a person of a national minority. According to this story a farmer in Hungary who suffered from ghostly visitations went to the cemetery one night, stuffed three pieces of garlic and three stones into his mouth, and fixed a corpse to the ground by thrusting a stake through it.[18]

Notes

1. Jan L. Perkowski, *Vampires of the Slavs* (Cambridge, Mass.: Slavica, 1976), 136. Perkowski's work has been used extensively for this article.
2. Kazimierz Moszynski, quoted by Perkowski, *Vampires of the Slavs*, 184–186.
3. Ernest Jones, *On the Nightmare* (New York: Grove Press, 1959), 99ff.
4. Perkowski, *Vampires of the Slavs*, 191.
5. Raymond L. Ditmars and Arthur M. Greenhall, quoted by Perkowski, ibid., 272ff.
6. Aleksandr N. Afanas'ev, quoted by Perkowski, ibid., 171–176; Moszynski, quoted by Perkowski, ibid, 182–184.
7. Jones, *On the Nightmare*, 116.
8. Ibid., 121–124.
9. Perkowski, *Vampires of the Slavs*, 156ff.
10. Ibid, 159.
11. Tihomir R. Djordjevic, *Veštica i vila. Vampir i druga bića* (Belgrade: Naućna knjiga, 1953), p. 185.
12. S. A. Tokarev, *Religioznye verovaniya vostochnoslavyanskikh narodov* (Moscow and Leningrad: Akademiya nauk, 1957), 41–42.
13. For details see Felix J. Oinas, "Introduction to Werewolf," in *The Golden Steed: Seven Baltic Plays*, ed. Alfreds Straumanis (Prospect Heights, Ill.: Waveland Press, 1979), 226–227.
14. See Felix J. Oinas, "Heretics as Vampires and Demons in Russia," *Slavic and East European Journal* 22 (1978): 433–438.
15. Dmitrii Zelenin, *Russische (ostslavische) Volkskunde* (Berlin and Leipzig: Walter de Gruyter, 1927), 373.
16. Oskar Loorits, *Grundzüge des estnischen Volksglaubens*, 1 (Lund: Kungl. Gustav Adolfs Akademi, 1949), 100, 563.
17. Linda Dégh, *Folktales of Hungary* (Chicago: University of Chicago Press, 1965), 349, and personal communications.
18. Jones, *On the Nightmare*, 124.

In Defense of Vampires

John V. A. Fine, Jr.

To start a discussion of vampires in Serbia during the first reign of Prince Miloš Obrenović (1815–39) it makes sense to describe how the Serbs of the time saw them. This can best be done by quoting the description of vampires presented by a contemporary Serb, who among his varied talents was a fine ethnographer, Vuk Karadžić:[1]

> A man into whom (according to popular tales) forty days after death a devilish spirit enters and enlivens (making him vampirized) is called a vukodlak. Then the vukodlak comes out at night from his grave and strangles people in their houses and drinks their blood. An honest man cannot vampirize, unless some bird or other living creature flies or jumps across his dead body. Thus everywhere people guard their dead [pre-burial] to see that nothing jumps over them. Vukodlaks most often appear in the winter (particularly between Christmas and Spasovdan [a moveable feast, forty days after Easter]). When a large number of people begin to die in a village, then people begin to blame a vukodlak from the grave (and in some places begin to say that he was seen at night with his shroud over his shoulders) and begin to guess who it might be. Then they take a black stallion without any spots or marks to the graveyard and lead it among the graves where it is suspected there are vukodlaks, for they say that such a stallion does not dare to step over a vukodlak. When they find the grave of someone they believe or guess to be a vukodlak, then they collect all the peasants and, taking with them a white thorn (or hawthorn) stake (because he fears only a white thorn stake ...), dig up the grave; and if they find in it a man who has not disintegrated, then they pierce it with that stake and throw it on a fire to be burned. They say that when they find such a vukodlak in a grave, he is fat, swollen and red with human blood ("red as a vampire"). A vukodlak sometimes returns to his wife (especially if she is young and pretty) and sleeps with her, and they say a child born of such a union has no bones. And in times of hunger vampires often gather near mills and around granaries. They say that all of them go with their shrouds over their shoulders. A vampire can also pass through the smallest hole, that is why it does not help to lock a door against them any more than it does against a witch.

Other collections of folk beliefs show variations. Evil people may turn into vampires as a result of their evil lives. Usually vampirization occurs forty days after death, but in certain places the transformation occurs immediately. In some places a child of a vampire and a human woman appears normal; however, he has special talents, one of which often is the ability to be a *vampirdžije,* or vampire-finder.

Now having seen how the Serbs viewed vampires, let us turn to the sources and see the creatures in action and the responses they elicited.

On March 8, 1820, various *kmetovi* (local elders) and other merchants of Ub wrote Prince Miloš that over the last few days people had begun to die off like flies owing to a vampire; as a result people were gathering three to one house, not daring to go out at night owing to fear. So they begged the *vladika* (bishop), who had come to collect Church taxes [*mirija*], to allow them to dig up the graveyard, but he had not allowed them to do this. So they went to [the local governor, Miloš' brother] Lord Jevrem, but he without the *vladika*'s approval was not able to give them permission. So now they begged Prince Miloš either to allow them to dig up the graveyard or to move, because they could no longer endure it.[2]

On March 10 Miloš replied to the *obština* of Ub that they might open the graves, which they suspected had vampires, to seek confirmation

---

John V. A. Fine, Jr., "In Defense of Vampires," *East European Quarterly*, vol. 21, pp. 15–23. Copyright © 1987 by John V. A. Fine, Jr. Reprinted with permission.

of their suspicions [he uses the negative term *superstition* here], but they were forbidden to inflict any injury on the corpses; rather they were to summon the parish priest or the *vladika* to then read over them the prayers for the dead according to the [Church] law.³

This halfway permission was sufficient for the peasants to follow their own bent, as is seen from a letter of April 7, 1820, that Jevrem wrote to his brother Miloš. Jevrem reports that he summoned the people of Ub and inquired how things were going with the vampire that had appeared among them; he learned that they had acted on their own without any cleric present. Instead they had called an elder from Panjuha who had taught them how to deal with vampires. Under his guidance they had excavated the suspect graves, piercing one body with a stake and chopping off its head, which was then placed at its feet; and now the graves stood open. In one case dogs had dragged out one woman's corpse, eating it.⁴

This was not Miloš' only vampire concern of that time. For on April 5, 1820, he expelled from Požarevac a *vampirdžije* (a vampire-finder) who had been familiar with vampires in Smederevo.⁵ And on April 20 he released from jail a certain *vampirdžije* named Ilija from village Duaka with a warning that if in the future he dug up any more vampires in any village he would be sentenced to a separation from his family and would remain in jail for good.⁶ The prince's actions against vampire-finders show that, as he had done in Ub, in regard to them, he tried to follow Church law and use prayers rather than mutilation techniques.

After this promising beginning, if we exclude a case reported by Joakim Vujić that did not involve Miloš, which we shall present below, nothing more is heard about vampires until the 1830s, when we find several other cases. It probably would be safe to assume that they remained active, being dealt with on a local level, through the rest of the 1820s and into the 1830s.

In any case on August 15, 1836, Jovan Obrenović informed his brother Miloš that the peasants of village Svojdrug, without the knowledge of the authorities, that July, had got together and declared Miloš Raković from their village, who had died on the last Little Spasovdan [a moveable feast, falling on the first Thursday after Spasovdan], a vampire; they had dug him up, verified their beliefs in some way, and had reburied him. A short time later they informed their priest, Zaharija, about it, and he, like the rest, superstitious, went with them to Miloš' grave, where for a second time they dug him up. The priest poured holy water on him and they buried him again. Three days later the villagers again gathered and together with the village elder [*kmet*] Aćim Milošević, went to Miloš' grave and for a third time dug it up; they shot the corpse through, cut off his head, and again buried him.⁷

On March 28, 1838, Timok Bishop Dositej Novaković wrote the *prota* [first priest] of Negotin that he had sent the *protojerej* of his diocese, Paun Radosavljević, and the priest of the village of Radujevac, Joan Matejić, to the monastery of St. Roman for a time—a common penalty for ecclesiastical misdemeanors—because they had allowed the villagers of Radujevac to dig up a corpse they believed to be a vampire.⁸ The first of April he wrote again to the *prota* of Negotin saying that he had learned that some *protojerej* in Negotin [surely the *protojerej* accused in the first letter] through the local priest had authorized the local villagers to dig up the grave of a man they had declared a vampire and to pour holy oil on him. With this permission the villagers, led by their priests, openly dug up a corpse which had died a short time before. After the priests said their prayers over the dead man, they went home, and then the villagers cut up the dead body and poured barley and boiled wine into its intestines so it would no longer vampirize and then reburied it.⁹ The bishop called on the prince to take strict action against priests participating in such affairs in order to eliminate such superstitions.

On June 1, 1839, the Timok consistory under the same bishop wrote the court of the district of Poreč about the villagers of Šarbanovac. They had become upset over nine (whose names are given) who had become vampires, and who, by the testimony of their relatives, had strangled several men, women, and children (who are named) and six little children and a certain number of animals. They had turned to their priest, who had forbidden them to do anything. Not convinced, the villagers waited until the priest was called out of town. Then to investigate the vampirism the peasants dug up the nine dead bodies. The leader of this venture was Novak Mikov, who had made an agreement with the villagers to carry out the work for ten *groša,* market rates. This Novak Mikov, according to information from the villagers, being paid ten *groša,* dug up eight vampires, extracted their hearts, cooked them [the hearts] in boiled wine, thrust them back in their places, and reburied the bodies. The ninth was Jona, spouse of Vinulov. But when they dug her up, they realized she had not suffocated people and children like the other eight vampires, and thus they reburied her whole. The consistory carried out an investigation, interviewing a variety of villagers, and then, having determined the facts of the case, passed it on to the secular district court.[10] On the eighth of July 1839 [the published text says 1838, surely a typo] the *okružni sud* (district court) of Zaječar found Novak and Radovan Petrov—one of four villagers who had taken a leading role in helping Novak—guilty of digging up the dead vampires of Šarbanovac and sentenced them to seven days in jail and thirty strokes of a cane.[11]

An extremely interesting case occurred shortly after Miloš' abdication. On March 9, 1844, the district court of Požarevac charged and on the 15th found guilty Spasoje Petrinog and Dema Jovanović from the village Manastirica, who in the company of Dema's wife, Kalina, and Stana Mijailova from superstition had dug up Spasoje's wife and damaged her body. They believed that the deceased had become a vampire, for some sheep had disappeared. The court found that they had done the action, condemned it as a violation of Christian law, and decided that Spasoje as the husband of the dead lady should receive forty strokes of the cane, Dema twenty-five, and the other two twenty-five strokes of the *kamidžija* (a whip), with the sentence to be carried out at the graveyard where the woman was buried.[12]

On June 6, 1844, the Požarevac district court also sentenced some men from Krepoljin who, holding it was a vampire, had dug up the body of one old lady, piercing it with knives and pistol shots. The leaders of the God-hated affair, Matije Ljubenović and Stojan Dunić, were to receive forty strokes and their three companions (Petar Nikolić, Todor Mijajlović, and Janko Djordjević) twenty-five.[13]

On September 22, 1844, the Požarevac district court sentenced Milić Stojadinović from the village of Šapina to five days in jail and twenty-five strokes for digging his deceased wife up from her grave, where she had lain two years, placing the part of her shroud that had covered her head over her feet, pouring wine over her, and reburying her. He had so acted because he believed she was making it impossible for him to remarry. We are not told how she prevented him from doing this.[14]

One final event of interest, occurring during Miloš' reign, but in territory to the south of his principality and still under the Turks, near Monastery Dečani, is described by Joakim Vujić. The conversation between himself and two monks, which he presents in dialogue form, occurred in 1826:[15]

> During my visit to this monastery [Monastery Klisura] there was staying one old monk, named Gerasim, who was from the monastery of Dečani, but who had just been in Bosnia to seek alms. ... And thus Father Visarion, abbot and host, gave us both dinner. And after we had dined, the following conversation occurred among the three of us.
>
> *Gerasim:* Dear brothers, can you imagine what happened two months ago in a village near Novi Pazar?
> *I:* And what happened, holy father? Come tell us.
> *Gerasim:* It happened that they dug up a vampire.
> *I:* And what did they do with him?
> *Gerasim:* What did they do? Why they ran him through with a hawthorn stake.

I: If that is what they did, it would have served them better to have gone to the tavern to drink raki, and to have left the dead body to sleep in peace.

Gerasim: And why leave the corpse in peace?

I: Because in this world there are no vampires.

Gerasim: There you are, just like our students nowadays. They don't believe in anything.

Visarion: Sir, I beg you not to speak in that way. How can you say there are no vampires in this world?

I: Because it is an impossible being. And I can't allow such a remark to pass with a clear conscience. But I beg you, Father Visarion, tell me, have you ever with your own eyes seen one?

Visarion: It is true that I have never seen one, but it is what people say.

Gerasim: But I have seen one with my own eyes; what do you say to that?

I: Then I beg you, Father Gerasim, tell me what this vampire that you saw with your own eyes looked like.

Gerasim: What it looked like! When they dug it up, it was not decomposed, its eyes were staring and its teeth were showing and clenched.

I: And what did this, your vampire, do?

Gerasim: And what did it do! At night he went about the village, scaring and strangling people; why he went into his own house and even slept with his wife.

I: Ha ha ha! He was a crude vampire, shame on him! To even have a woman on his mind. And what did his wife do, did she chase him out?

Gerasim: Of course not; she didn't dare, because he would have strangled her.

I: Tell me more, what else happened with your vampire?

Gerasim: What happened! When they dug him up, then Priest Stavro took a hawthorn stake, forced it between his teeth, and then took a piece of holy wood and put it between his teeth and along the holy wood poured into his mouth three drops of holy water and …

I: Now stop! I beg you, Father Gerasim, why didn't this vampire leap up and grab Priest Stavros by his beard?

Gerasim: You're again talking nonsense! How could he grab him by his beard, when during the day he is dead and has no strength; it is only at night that he gets power from the Unclean One, and comes to life, and then he goes about the village causing all sorts of chaos and misfortune.

I: Hmmm, so this vampire is dead in the day, but alive at night. I still just can't believe it. But tell me, what happened with your vampire in the end?

Gerasim: What happened! Why, after that, the elder Petko took that same hawthorn stake and stabbed him through the breast, and blood issued from his mouth and that was the end of him. Then they again buried him in the ground, and after that he never again left his grave, nor scared nor strangled people in the village. …

I, having listened to these words of the Monk Gerasim about the vampire, began to say to myself: God All-blessed! How can this people live in such error, ignorance, and superstition; and if a clergyman believes and talks such superstition, what will the common people think and say? And then casting my glance upward, said: All powerful God, give our lord Miloš a long and successful life that he may during his reign establish schools with talented teachers who can wipe out error and enlighten our people. And then I turned to the monk and in this way spoke to him.

I: Holy father, I from my side beg and advise you for God's sake not to believe that there are such monsters in this world as vampires, which could bring upon other men such injuries and misfortune, but the whole thing is only one simple and stupid superstition which does not serve any good purpose. And, tell me, Father Gerasim, what would you say if I said that even though you dug up your alleged vampire and found him not decomposed with staring eyes and clenched teeth, that still does not prove he was a vampire. And why not? That is because in some places is found earth which is salt-sulphur (salitrosumporita), that is it is such that when you put a dead body, in which there is still considerable blood to be found, in such ground, then the blood will coagulate and the body will swell and the earth will not allow the body to decompose, but will keep it as firm as if it were magnetic iron. And such a dead body may for 77 or more years remain undecomposed in such ground. And if we want to decompose such a body we do not need a hawthorn stake nor a priest with holy wood and water, for there is no need to torture the corpse, but one need only dig it up, take it out of the ground into the air and let it lie there for only half an hour in the air and then put it back in the grave and cover it. Then after three days dig up the corpse again and you will see that it is already half disintegrated.

And now I will tell you briefly from where vampires and such superstitions originate: From nowhere else but the imagination and craftiness of men, as I will show by narrating the following case to you. Just listen to me.

In Hungary not far from my town of Baja, where I was born, there is still today a certain village in which there once appeared a vampire, as you would say. It frightened people and rode on them as it would a donkey, but it was mostly seen around the house of one young, pretty widow, whose husband two days before [its first appearance] had died and been buried; so always at night at 12 o'clock, with its white shroud, threaded with bells, and white cap and socks, it appeared, and when it arrived the whole household would panic, and everyone from fear would flee every which way, leaving only the pretty young widow in her bed. This alleged vampire would spend an hour or so in the house with the young person, after which, with loud cries, bangs, and the ringing of bells, it would leave. This went on for three months. During this time one sharp young man decided to follow the vampire, and if possible even to capture it. So he took with him two of his trusted friends, and they hid in the kitchen behind the door, each having in his hand a stout rope. The householder and his wife knew they were there, but the pretty young widow did not know a thing about it. When all was ready and it was approaching midnight, here came our pretty vampire with his white shroud, cap, and socks, according to his custom with bangs, noise, and bells ringing. All the household flew out of the house without their caps, and then he nicely approached the young daughter-in-law and lay down beside her. At that moment the sharp young hero in the kitchen crashed into the room and seized the handsome vampire by the arms. At this the vampire began to clang, moan, and to scratch. But it did not help him, because he was well held. Meanwhile the two comrades came running in with their stout ropes to help the first tie up the handsome vampire, and then to drag him to the village hall. And there were five neighbors from her house. The next day they also took her to the courthouse, where she was put through a tough interrogation, and in the end they found, even proved, that she with her vampire had poisoned her husband whom she did not love; she had wanted to carry on a disgusting illicit love affair with the vampire and he also wanted to do it with her. But they were not able to do so with so many people living in the house, and no other place existed for them to go to. Afterwards both of them were taken to the county seat of Bač, where there took place a second intensive interrogation, and when it was clearly proved and both of them admitted their guilt, then the court announced its decision, namely that the vampire be hanged and the pretty vampirica have her head cut off below the gallows, and the sentence was carried out.

And that is your vampire, and under the name of vampires people not only carry out lustful doings, but also steal, burn houses, and commit other crimes. And as for bodies that do not decompose, and such are found naturally, there are also those that are embalmed.

[And Vujić then proceeded to explain embalming to the two monks, who had never heard of the process.]

Vujić's rational-scientific outlook should not be taken to represent a section of opinion in Serbia at the time. Vujić was a Serb from the Austro-Hungarian Empire, then on a grand tour of Serbia's churches and monasteries. He was soon, however, to settle in Serbia as director of the new theater Miloš was trying to establish in Kragujevac. The theater, which under Vujić's direction lasted only a few years, chiefly presented works of Vujić. Whether or not that explains its short life, I am in no position to judge. Vujić very well may have already been angling for such a post during his 1826 journey, which would explain the extreme flattery of Miloš—one example of which is seen in the cited passage—which runs through his whole book.

The documents cited in my text show that vampire beliefs were widespread in Serbia at this time. They were not limited to the ignorant peasantry but were also widespread among the clergy. Among Serbs the main issue was not whether or not there were vampires—for Miloš himself in not denying their existence may well not have been sure of this—but how was one to deal with them; should one use traditional village methods or should one take a more spiritual approach and call on the clergy to eliminate them through prayers? It would take many decades and the establishment of schools throughout Serbia—a task begun with vigor by Miloš—to embue people with Vujić's skeptical rejection. In fact, even today in modern Yugoslavia such beliefs have not been entirely eradicated.

What function did vampire beliefs serve? As an ancient belief passed on from generation to generation, vampires, of course, were simply a part of this world, as children learned without question from their elders. However, they did explain certain sudden and unusual events, and as blame was thrown on the dead they produced a far more harmless scapegoat than was seen when blame was thrown on the living, as also occurred in Serbia, when such ills were blamed on witches.

Notes

1. Vuk Karadžič, "Život i običaj naroda Srpskog," reprinted in V. Karadžič, *Prvi i Drugi Srpski Ustanaka* (Novi Sad and Belgrade, 1969), 330–331. The best general study of vampires in what was formerly Yugoslavia is T. Djordjević, "Vampir i druga bića u našem narodnom verovanju i predanju," published in the Serbian Academy of Sciences series, *Srpski Etnografski Zbornik*, knj. 66, second series, "Život i običaji narodni," knj. 30 (Belgrade, 1953), 149–219.

2. T. Djordjević, "Običaji narodna Srpskoga," knj. 2, published in *Srpski Etnografski Zbornik* (henceforth *SEZ*), 14 (1909): 431–432.
3. Djordjević, *SEZ*, 14 (1909): 432. This document is also contained in V. and N. Petrović, *Gradja za istoriju Kraljevine Srbije—vreme prve vlade Kneza Miloša Obrenovića,* vol. 1 (Belgrade, 1882), 393. Their text says "priest *and* vladika" (italics mine) instead of Djordjević's reading of "or." The latter's reading seems more reasonable to me.
4. Djordjević, *SEZ*, 14 (1909): 432–433.
5. Ibid., 432.
6. Ibid., 433.
7. Ibid., 433.
8. T. Djordjević, "Nekoliko arhivskih podataka o našim narodnim običijima," *Glasnik Etnografskog Museja u Beogradu*, 13 (1938): 5.
9. Ibid., 5.
10. T. Djordjević, "Gradja za Srpske narodne običaje iz vremena prve vlade Kneza Miloša," *SEZ*, 19 (1914): 464.
11. Ibid., 465.
12. S. Maksimović, *Sudjenja u Požarevačkom Magistratu, (1827–1844),* ed. V. Živković (Požarevac, 1973), 216.
13. Ibid., 216–217.
14. Ibid., 219–220.
15. Joakim Vujić, *Putešestvije po Srbije* [1826], 2 (Belgrade, 1902), 2–11..

South Slavic Countermeasures Against Vampires

Friedrich S. Krauss

About the method and manner of fully destroying a vampire, scholars have given unclear views, even though there is certainly no reason for such differences of opinion. The vampire is a dead person who comes to life during the nighttime. So one destroys him just as one would annihilate any living being, namely by killing it, in this case usually either by driving a stake through its body or by burning the corpse. The disembodied spirit is freed or takes flight and is thus no longer able to cause harm to anyone.

If a widow confesses that her deceased husband has visited her as a vampire or other signs indicate that such an event has occurred—for example, nightly noises in the house, pots and pans flying about, a sudden death in the village, or even direct encounters with the vampire at a crossroads at night—then the most respected and senior men of the village will convene. The purpose of this assembly is to obtain permission from the living relatives of the vampire to dig up the grave to exhume the deceased, this to determine whether the suspect corpse has indeed become a vampire. The Muslims say that the body of such a vampire, even though it may have been lying in its grave for a long period of time, does not decompose. Only its eyes are big as those of oxen and are bloodshot as well. In such a case, one builds a fire in the grave, sharpens a hawthorn stake, and with it impales the body. Informants state that during the impalement, the vampire's body frequently writhes and twists, and that a large amount of blood spurts out of its body. While one group of people tends to the body of the vampire, the others present anxiously watch for the appearance of a moth (or butterfly) flying away from the grave. If one does fly out of the grave, everyone runs after it in order to capture it. If it is caught, it is thrown onto a bonfire so that it will die. Only then is the vampire completely destroyed. If the butterfly escapes, however, then, alas, woe to the village, because the vampire wreaks a frightful vengeance, which does not end until finally a period of seven years runs out.

In the upper Krajina, the Muslims and Christians believe that a vampire cannot be killed by any means other than by driving a hawthorn stake *(glogovi kolac)* through its body. Some informants have stated in my presence that one may also impale a vampire with a knife which has never yet cut bread. The Herzegovinians of the Orthodox Confession pierce the vampire through the dried hide of a young bull, because they believe (like the Serbians in the Morava and the Bulgarians in Rumelia) that anyone who is bespattered with the blood of the vampire will himself turn into a vampire, and that thereupon he must soon die. The Herzegovinian Orthodox do not burn the vampire. Nor do the Catholics of Slavonia. In the Drina region of upper Bosnia at the Serbian border, the Orthodox priest accompanies the farmers to the cemetery. They proceed to scrape open the grave of the deceased, stuff it full with a wagonload of straw, drive a hawthorn stake through both the straw and the corpse, and set fire to the straw. The fire continues to be fed until the body of the vampire has completely turned to ashes. Only then do they believe that any farther return of the vampire has been prevented.

Farmer Lato Petrovic in Zabrgje reports:

> About 150 years ago in the village of Cengic in the Zvornik district, there lived the wife of an Orthodox priest. After the death of this priest's wife *(popadija)*, a raft of other deaths occurred in the village. At that time, all the members of the household of my mother's grandfather, Farmer Pero, died except for three young boys. So Pero decided to stand watch at night. In the kitchen of his own house, he lighted a large fire and waited. Suddenly, around midnight, the *popadija* appeared in the house. Pero, however, jumped up, seized a burning hawthorn branch from the fire, began to beat the *popadija* with it, and chased her out of the house. Still, she remained in front of the house and she shouted, "Come on out here, old man Pero, and beat me just a little and I will perish immediately." Pero answered, "I will not go outside and I will not let you into the house." Whereupon

Friedrich S. Krauss, "South Slavic Countermeasures Against Vampires," *The Vampire: A Casebook*, ed. Alan Dundes; trans. Johanna Jacobsen and Alan Dundes, pp. 67–71. Copyright © 1998 by the Regents of the University of Wisconsin System. Reprinted with permission by The University of Wisconsin Press.

she retorted, "Just you wait, old man Pero, no son of yours will survive with whom you could plot." At the crack of dawn, Pero, along with the village magistrate and a farmer, went to the priest and informed him that the *popadija* had been resurrected and that she was snatching away people. The priest said, "It isn't true!" But Pero went to the courthouse in Zvornik and reported that the *popadija* had turned into a vampire and that just last night in the kitchen of his house, he had covered her shroud with soot when he struck her. The court granted him permission to dig up the grave. Together with the most respected men of the village, he exhumed the grave. There they found the *popadija* swollen up like a tub and they took a sharpened hawthorn stake, planted it on the *popadija's* stomach, and with a hammer drove it into her body. Then they built a huge fire and burned her to ashes and coals. But, sure enough, as they began to fill in the grave again, a snake crawled out of it. But Pero killed the snake on the spot. From that time on, they had peace and quiet in the village, and the sudden spate of deaths ceased.

Manda Superina in Pleternika told my mother: In the village of Mihaljevci, north of Pozega, a man fell off a wagon. His head got caught under the wheels and was crushed. And so he died. Eight days after the funeral, he returned, and began to sleep with his neighbor's wife. And sure enough, she became pregnant with his child. Thereupon, she informed the priest and told other women what had happened to her. One of the women advised her that she should take hemp and spin a large skein of thread, and that when the dead man next came to her, she should tie the thread to his big toe. Then she could discover where he came from. She was also told to make ready a large hawthorn stake. In the daytime, when the priest and the village folk opened the grave, they found the dead man lying on his stomach. They drove the hawthorn stake into his head and a large flame burst out of it. The skull exploded with a sound as loud as that of a cannon. The priest then at once gave the dead man his final benediction, and the dead man never returned again. The woman, however, gave birth to a child. The child died soon thereafter, but the woman is still alive. The narrator is a Catholic woman, and oddly enough, she had appealed to the Catholic priest of Velika. As a rule, Catholic priests do not play any role in the vampire hunts of Slavonia. In Dalmatia, where the Franciscan monk is very popular and believed, the people are more likely in such situations to turn to the priest for help. The monk is more sympathetic to the requests of the parish in which he is a priest.

Should a *kozlak* die, the old women in the village and also the remaining family members of the deceased take precautions with different measures against the anticipated imminent return of the *kozlak*. In some areas, it is the custom not to sweep out the room where death occurred for several days afterward. This, however, seldom seems to work. In spite of all this, the *vukodlak* or *kozlak* comes in at a certain hour of the night to disturb the tranquillity of the household and to torment the sleeping. The *kozlak* especially likes to rattle dishes, and he takes great pleasure, if there is a wagon around, in pulling it all around farmsteads. In such a crisis, the farmer will turn to his priest, that is, to the Franciscan who deals with written amulets. The priest must say prayers, and over and above that he must betake himself to the cemetery straight to the grave where the *kozlak* rests. He then has to summon him, await his appearance, and then run him through with a thorn. This thorn has to have grown in the high mountains in a place from which point the thornbush could not have seen the sea. Only in this case, or so it is believed, will the procedure work, and the *kozlak* will leave the people in peace.

It is no accident that it is the thorn that is used for impalement. The thorn is a natural—one could even say the original—human stabbing weapon. And it is easy to understand that its age-old utilization in ritual activities—in which category, in a limited sense, we can also consider vampire-slaying—has continued up to the present day. The thorn appears in the religious ceremonies of many peoples. Yet it seems to me that Liebrecht[1] is mistaken when he seeks to demonstrate that, just because the old Germans used the thorn in cremation, this leads to the following conclusion: "This explains finally, then, as a side observation, why in the Serbian legends the body of the vampire was impaled with a stake made out of hawthorn or a thornbush. It was a symbolic cremation." As evidence, Liebrecht cites the Bohemian "Lying Chronicler" Hajck (from the year 1337). A vampire would not stop attacking the people "even when a stake had been driven through his body; only after his body was burned did he desist." For us there is no doubt that the Czechs at that time burned the corpse as a more powerful means of total annihilation in order to be fully certain of the desired result. Where do we find here even the shadow of symbolism? And where is the basis for a symbolic explanation of the custom?

In conclusion, we must consider one more belief, one which was a vital factor in the development of the custom of the blood feud. The soul of a murdered man, according to folk belief, could find no rest until revenge had been taken on the murderer. For this reason, the nearest blood-relative of the murder victim was obliged to seek blood revenge as a sacred duty. This is what is referred to in the old folk belief and legal proverb: Ko se ne osveti; taj se ne posveti (He who is not revenged, that person shall not find everlasting peace). However, blood feud is also based on principles of property law that cannot be explored here.

---

1. Ed. note: This refers to the important mid-nineteenth-century folklorist Felix Liebrecht (1812–90). For the citation referred to by Krauss, see Liebrecht, *Zur Volkskunde: Alte und neue Aufsätze* (Heilbronn: Verlag von Gebr. Henninger, 1879), 65.

Vampurella

Darwin and Count Dracula

Charles S. Blinderman

A STUDENT OF MINE some years ago confessed, blushfully, that though she didn't believe in vampires, she kept a clove of garlic on her bedroom windowsill, just in case. From at least the 4th Century B.C., garlic has been used as protection against the powers of darkness, specifically, back in the time of Theophrastus, to prevent Hecate, mother of witches, from doing mischief. Throughout both occidental and oriental medical and magical history, garlic has been used also to ward off or cure jaundice, tumors, dropsy, sunstroke, leprosy, smallpox, plague, whooping-cough, intestinal worms, and hysteria. Thus, Professor van Helsing's recommendation to the English targets of Count Dracula's attention that they surround themselves with garlic has a long history. Other aspects of the novel—and therefore of vampire fiction in general, of plays, movies, and television shows, of the rich progeny Bram Stoker generated—also have their roots in the matrix of myth. Count Dracula himself is part Vlad Tpesh, part Elizabeth Bathory, part lamia, part werewolf, and part bat—and part Darwinian Superman.

Each of these first five ingredients deserves modest explication. Dracula as Darwinian Superman is the theme of this article. Vlad Tpesh, the historical figure from whom Stoker constructed his Count, was King of Wallachia (territory encompassing Transylvania and itself encompassed by Romania) sporadically during the fifteenth century. He is noteworthy for nailing people's hats to their heads, ripping unborn children from wombs, burning the poor, and, especially—his forte—impaling thousands of his countrymen on stakes. One historiographical approach asserts that he did these things to scare the Turks and thus keep Wallachia together as a nation. It's more likely he did them because he liked doing them. This aspect of Vlad IV (nicknamed "Dracula," which means son of "Dracul," which means "dragon," since his father, Vlad III, was also a terror) enters into the Count, who is a warrior fond of spilling blood. Countess Bathory, an early seventeenth-century Romanian noblewoman, was equally fond of spilling blood—on herself. She deprived at least six hundred girls of their blood, and therefore of their lives, under the illusion that bathing in blood would keep her attractive. Jack the Ripper probably makes a similar contribution to the recipe.

And of course, there's the bat. But before we turn to that animal as an ingredient of the Count, there are two others in the menagerie worth mentioning. The first (chronologically) is the Greek lamia; a ghostly serpentine presence oozing from corpses and travelling from her natal graveyard to divest passersby of their vitality, the lamia in medieval times was translated into the succubus and in the Romantic period into the heroine of a poem by John Keats. The Count's affinity with the werewolf is signalled by his being able to transform himself into a wolf and by his hairy palms, a suggestion that he's an onanist, to which diversion this paper will return. As for the bat, which on a word-association test might be the first response elicited by "vampire," that must have been a late contribution to the vampire legend, itself traced back by Montague Summers three thousand years. The vampire bat, in European history, can be traced back only to the sixteenth century since it is indigenous to America only. The conquistadors returned to Europe with tales of El Dorado, and of the one-ounce creepy true vampire bat, occasionally a parasite of human beings. The bat became fused with a much larger cousin of the order Chiroptera, the false vampire bat (a mouse-eater), and then became absorbed into post Renaissance vampire literature.

A very early work which alludes to the vampire is Dr. Henry More's *An Antidote Against Atheism* (1653), wherein the spectre is characterized mostly by his breath, cold and "of so intolerable stinking and malignant a scent, as is beyond all imagination and expression." There are few mentions of the vampire in English literature until the Romantic Period when—in addition to Keats' "Lamia"—John Stagg's "The Vampyre" and Lord Byron's "The Giauor" both enriched the legend, the poems adorned with images of "jaws cadaverous," "clotted carnage," "ghastly haunts," "gnashing tooth," "haggard lip," and "sullen grave." Polidori's "The Vampyre" is a short story, the vampire hero of which is a take-off on Lord Byron and the moral

Charles S. Blinderman, "Vampurella: Darwin and Count Dracula," *The Massachusetts Review*, vol. 21, no. 2, pp. 411–428. Copyright © 1980 by Massachusetts Review. Reprinted with permission.

of which is that, contrary to Romantic optimism, there is evil in this world. At least four other fictional pieces prior to Bram Stoker's novel which conducted the vampire legend through fiction, two English—Rymer and Prest's *Varney the Vampire* and Sheridan LeFanu's *Carmilla*—and two French, de Maupassant's "La Horla" and, a century before that, de Sade's *Justine*.

The last is of particular relevance to this paper because of its philosophical dimensions. *Justine* is a fun-house of antic behavior—pederasty, fellation, coprophagia, scatophilia, necrophilia, blasphemy, anal intercourse, flagellation, and murder. The Count spends some of his time bleeding his wife but more of it discoursing on what such blood-letting signifies. It signifies, first of all, a view of Nature. Nature permits anything, even virtue, though she prefers crime; and the strong are impelled by their human nature to exercise power over the weak: "The only happiness of the strong lies in the exercise of their strength, that is to say, in the most absolute oppression." "The theory of loving one's neighbor is a myth which we owe to Christianity and not to Nature." Christianity may emphasize moral sensations, but human experience reveals that moral sensations are fallacious—only physical sensations are real. Sadism signifies the proper view of women, who make better victims than men do because they are more angelic, lovely, noble, and majestic, thus more suitable for sadistic violation. The Count addresses this point in language which the later Count Dracula could well have employed:

> The happy or unhappy state of the victim of our revel is totally immaterial to the satisfaction of our senses, and the state of her heart or mind is a matter of complete indifference. Women are but the instruments of pleasure whose sole function is to provide targets.

Both Counts find their "supreme ecstasy" dependent upon a tableau of death. De Sade's vision grew more comprehensive: from the violation of a few girls in *Justine*, he developed fantasies, in *Juliette*, about a corrupt financier, Saint-Fond, who, bored with poisoning drinking fountains, designed a plan to corner farm produce and thus starve half the population of France.

To proceed from de Sade to *Dracula* through Darwinism is a journey undertaken with some caution. All three are expressions of the oldest profession in the world—dualism. To some of its followers, and to most of its opponents, Darwinism seemed to take sides in the conflict between spirit and flesh, professing Lucretian or worse (such as de Sadean) materialism. *Dracula* is less ambivalent in its professing the supremacy of the spirit over the flesh, though in that novel the flesh makes a courageous stand and almost achieves victory. Darwinism was a lightning-rod for the Victorian period's grappling with dualism. One can even discover such concern in pre-Darwinian works, such as Tennyson's *In Memoriam* and Browning's "Cleon," but it was with the coming of the *Origin of Species* that the fight really began, and it is mostly through Thomas Henry Huxley's exposition of Darwinian materialism that we can discover the parallels to, and perhaps even the influences upon, the message of *Dracula*. There are a few places in the novel where something explicit is said about nineteenth-century science—to van Helsing, the very method of scientific work is a fraud. Operating within an age that is "sceptical and selfish" science attempts to explain everything, and "if it explain not," van Helsing goes on in his weird idiom, "then it says there is nothing to explain" (p. 170).[1] Claiming that "there are things which you cannot understand; and yet which are; that some people see things that others cannot" (p. 172), he goes on at stultifying length, like a voice out of the whirlwind, but petulant, to lecture at us with an itemized list of those things which science cannot explain but in which we are to have faith: hypnotism, the longevity of Methusalah and of turtles, the immortality of the parrot, the resurrection of the Indian fakir, "the altogether of comparative

---

1 Leonard Wolf, ed., *The Annotated, Dracula* (N.Y.; 1975). For similar language from a clergyman unsure of his commitment to the new science, see Charles Kingsley, *Water-Babies* (London: 1863), p. 161.

anatomy," and a giant aged oil-drinking Spanish spider. Although allegedly a scientist himself, van Helsing proposes that superstition is a force more powerful than scientific rationality, a proposition he finds validated by the appearance of Count Dracula in the midst of the "scientific, sceptical, matter-of-fact nineteenth century" (p. 212).

These comments by van Helsing, however superficial and ridiculous, give us a clue to the more profound implications developed by the novel's strategies. There are several such implications, all of them connecting *Dracula* to Darwinian materialism: 1) the "assimilation" (the concept is critical in both *Dracula* and the antecedent Huxley essay "On the Physical Basis of Life") of one being by another; 2) the contest of spirit versus flesh—Darwinian materialism tending towards the reduction of all phenomena to matter, Dracula as count agreeing with that while *Dracula* as novel resists it; 3) the extraction from philosophical materialism of carnal satisfaction, the condition aspired to by apes, vampires, and perverted gentlemen; 4) the question of immortality, a condition denied by materialism, given a new meaning by the undead vampires, and believed in by the Christian opponents of Darwinism and by the van Helsing congregation; and 5) the Social Darwinian superman, who turns out to be a parasitic leech, both literally and metaphorically.

The Protoplasmic Machine

The scenes in *Dracula* which most readily illustrate the dependence human and "undead" creatures have on other living things are not those which most readily come to mind—the assaults of Count Dracula upon Lucy and Mina, the vamps gloating over Jonathan Harker in Castle Dracula, Lucy, as the "bootiful lady," devouring children in a park. More significant than these in illustrating the transmutation of flesh into flesh is the lunatic Renfield's zoophagous appetite, which includes flies, spiders, and birds, and anticipates rats and cats. Renfield, who manages to be at the same time one of the more realistic as well as the more fantastic of the cast of characters, is a transmogrified political economist. To achieve economy, he eats the animals that have eaten the animals—thus the consumption of a cat would carry with it the life-force of several birds each of which has eaten scores of spiders each of which has eaten hundreds of flies. Implicit in the vampire act is the cannibalistic assimilation of human organs into human (or humanoid) flesh. Renfield's physician, Dr. Seward, warily notes that "it was life, strong life, and gave life to him ... what he desires is to absorb as many lives as he can" (pp. 71, 74). Renfield's own comment offers an interpretation rather than a summary, and concludes with a scriptural reference that will be examined in its proper place later:

> I used to fancy that life was a positive and perpetual entity, and that by consuming a multitude of live things, no matter how low in the scale of creation, one might indefinitely prolong life. At times I held the belief so strongly that I actually tried to take human life. The doctor here will bear me out that on one occasion I tried to kill him for the purpose of strengthening my own vital powers by the assimilation with my own body of his life through the medium of blood—relying, of course, upon the Scriptural phrase, "For the blood is the life" (p. 209).

Materialism emphasizes kinship—between the inanimate and the animate, between flora and fauna, between non-human and human animals—reducing all phenomena to matter in motion. In the materialistic conception of things, there is no spirit, no dualistic alternative to matter, and that conception is also deterministic. Issues of ethical value are at stake: conscience, freedom of the will, immortality, and the integrity of human relationship, which is tenuous enough on a cash nexus, but even more vulnerable on a protoplasmic nexus. Darwinian reduction of human actions, including the act of thinking, to physiological actions is the product especially of T. H. Huxley's speculations, and to a lesser extent of the speculations indulged in by others of the first and second generations of Darwinists, John Tyndall, G. J. Allman, and E. Ray Lankester.

The Darwinian prefiguration of Renfield's explanation of what he was about was developed by Huxley in several works, particularly in "On the Physical Basis of Life," an essay that was enormously popular and that maintained its influence for decades. Huxley was, more than anyone else, responsible for the constant expansion of the parameters of Darwinism, from its initial statement of the theory of natural selection through its associations with the theory of human evolution, with materialism, agnosticism, the Higher Criticism, and social, political, and ethical positions. Huxley always went on to something more radical than Darwin had in mind; the monistic reduction of human activity, including cerebration, to chemical turbulence was one of those extensions.

In a work earlier than "On the Physical Basis of Life"—in "The Phenomena of Organic Nature"—he had informed a working-class audience that they were organized molecules. This met with an agreeable reception. He tried that theme out again, in greater detail, in the 1868 lecture "On the Physical Basis of Life." He alerted his Edinburgh audience to the interesting fact that the physical basis of life is protoplasm, a definable combination of oxygen, hydrogen, nitrogen, and carbon which is manifest in all living things from a flower to a fly, from a whale to a man. All human action, he claimed, is

> the result of the molecular forces of the protoplasm which displays it, and if so, it must be true, in the same sense and to the same extent, that the thoughts to which I am now giving utterance, and your thoughts regarding them, are the expression of molecular changes in that matter of life which is the source of other vital phenomena (p. 163).[2]

---

2 Thomas Henry Huxley, "On the Physical Basis of Life," *Collected Essays* (London: 1893), I.

Huxley noted in the course of the lecture that the lecture itself would exhaust a certain quantity of his protoplasm, and that he would have to eat something, say mutton, to bring him back to completion again.

> A singular inward laboratory, which I possess, will dissolve a certain portion of the modified protoplasm; the solution so formed will pass into my veins; and the subtle influences to which it will then be subjected will convert the dead protoplasm into living protoplasm, and transubstantiate sheep into man (p. 147).

Except for the possibility of provoking dyspepsia, it doesn't matter what's eaten—wheat and lobster will do as well as sheep—since we enjoy a "catholicity of assimilation" in the conversion process. Huxley emphasized the kinship of all life, all living things being reducible to universal protoplasm which, created by plants and consumed by animals, is plastic enough to be variously incarnated. All of this illustrates the grand Coleridgean motto of Huxley's philosophical and aesthetic systems—unity in diversity—and that means that lower creatures will with equal facility subsist on higher creatures.

> I might sup upon lobster, and the matter of life of the crustacean would undergo the same wonderful metamorphosis into humanity. And were I to return to my own place at sea, and undergo shipwreck, the crustacean might, and probably would, return the compliment and demonstrate our common nature by turning my protoplasm into living lobster (p. 148).

The controlling image is that of a factory, the account of which has its profit and loss columns: we take in fuel and convert it to the expenditure of energy.

"On the Physical Basis of Life" was a remarkably successful address. Darwin and others of Huxley's circle were surprised that he hadn't been stoned. One contemporary letter observed that the audience had been intensely interested. The discourse was published in *The Fortnightly Review* and sent that periodical into seven reprintings. In his *Recollections,* John Morley, the review's editor, searched for a suitable analog to the excitement generated by the essay and found it only in the reception given Swift's "Conduct of the Allies" a century earlier.

Contributing to the fame of the protoplasmic theory was the *Bathybius haeckelii* incident. After examining a specimen of material gathered from the depths of the Atlantic Ocean, Huxley concluded that he had observed in the gelatinous substance fundamental protoplasm, ur-schleim animated, and he endowed it with the dignity of a taxonomic name that recognized E. H. Haeckel's work on protozoa: *Bathybius haeckelii.* It was a satisfaction for Huxley (and more so for Haeckel) to find this primordial ooze, since it could be taken to constitute the link between inert matter and physical life. Later analysis showed that *Bathybius haeckelii* was not protoplasm, but calcium sulfate precipitated out of a mixture of alcohol and marine mud. A group of similar imaginary creatures was also given taxonomic existence, among them Protamoeba, Protomonas—and Vampurella.

Representing "the protoplasmic theory as a victory for the mechanistic over the vitalistic conception of life," Huxley had both the prestige and the rhetorical ability—so claims one modern student of *Bathybius haeckelii*—to make protoplasm "quite literally a household word."[3] Initial reviews of the essay were generally hostile, critics attacking the notion of protoplasmic consanquinity (as James Hutchinson Sterling did), the defense of idealism (which defense seemed at best equivocal), and the caveat that materialism had nothing to do with ethics (but to Richard Holt Hutton and many other critics, Huxley had clearly advanced immorality).

---

[3] G. L. Geison, "The Protoplasmic Theory of Life and the Vitalist-Mechanist Debate," *Isis* 60 (1969), p. 279. On Vampurella, see N. A. Rupke, "*Bathybius haeckelii* and the Psychology of Scientific Discovery," *Studies in the History and Philosophy of Science* #7 (1976), p. 61. For another study of *Bathybius haeckelii*: Philip F. Rehbock, "Huxley, Haeckel and the Oceanographers," *Isis* 66 (1975), pp. 504–533.

After the initial burst of hostile criticism there appeared several defenses, for example Dr. James Ross's 1874 *On Protoplasm.* In an address ("Protoplasm and the Commonality of Life") to the British Association for the Advancement of Science, Professor G. J. Allman, observing in passing that protoplasm had become "a subject in whose study there has during the last few years prevailed an unwonted amount of activity," rendered a description of amoebic activity that is appropriate for vampire activity:

> A stream of protoplasm instantly runs away from the body of the Amoeba towards the destined prey, envelops it in its current, and then flows back with it to the central protoplasm, where it sinks deeper and deeper into the soft yielding mass, and becomes dissolved, digested, and assimilated in order that it may increase the size and restore the energy of its captor.

Controversy about protoplasm found its way into comical works also, for example in an 1875 Aberdeen satire the long title of which expresses both theme and tone: *Protoplasm, Powheads, and Porwiggles; and the Evolution of the Horse from the Rhinoceros; illustrating Professor Huxley's Scientific Mode of Getting up the Creation and Up*setting *Moses*, and in *The Mikado*: "I am," asserts Pooh-Bah in Act I,

> in point of fact, a particularly haughty and exclusive person, of pre-Adamite ancestral descent. You will understand this when I tell you that I can trace my ancestry back to a protoplasmal primordial globule.

Less gentle was Samuel Butler's quip from *Luck or Cunning:* "Great is Protoplasm. There is no life but protoplasm, and Huxley is its prophet."

Like the proposition that all life is kin through sharing protoplasm is the notion that the organization of the protoplasm itself is coercive, a determinant of our behavior. Huxley advanced this deterministic theory in a book, *Lessons in Elementary Physiology,* and in several addresses that were reprinted as essays. Throughout he developed a mechanical model for the human body, a model that seemed to deny free will as well as spirit. And again we find that this aspect of his popularization of Darwinian materialism caused a stir. A writer in the *Irish Church Society's Journal* for January, 1875, said that Huxley's "On the Hypothesis that Animals Are Automata" had been "universally read"; Disraeli noted with some disdain that in London society young men casually pratted about automatism; and a lecture by Professor Watts *(On the Hypothesis that Animals Are Automata)*, delivered at the Presbyterian College, London, struck the crucial note:

> Young men of Great Britain and Ireland! Will you identify yourselves with a science falsely so-called, which would identify you with brutes, and, repressing the noblest aspirations of your nature, would turn our world into a Sodom, and lay upon your brightest hopes the blight of an eternal night?

Dr. Joseph Parker, minister of City Temple, Holborn Viaduct, attacked Huxley's automatism hypothesis in the 1875 *Job's Comforters: Scientific Sympathy*; and W. H. Mallock attacked it in *The New Republic*, which describes Mr. Storks (Huxley) as "great on the physical basis of life and the imaginative basis of God" (p. 25). Dr. Jenkinson (Benjamin Jowett) reads a manuscript which discovers the problem of the day as the reconciliation of the natural with the spiritual, and then he comments on automatism:

> Witness the discussions now engaging so much public attention on the subject of animal automatism, and the marvellous results which experiments on living subjects have of late days revealed to us; a frog with half a brain having destroyed more theology than all the doctors of the Church with their whole brains can ever build up again (p. 97).

Later on, Mr. Saunders (representing mostly the Positivist Frederic Harrison) says, his voice "tremulous with excitement": "I know that in their last analysis a pig and a martyr, a prayer and a beefsteak, are just the same—atoms and atomic movement." St. George Mivart, George Romanes, Leslie Stephens, and James McCosh also contributed to the popularization of Darwinian materialism; McCosh, in his 1884 *Agnosticism of Hume and Huxley* drove to the ethical implications:

> Will the seducer be more likely to be kept from gratifying his lust when the highest philosophy teaches him that the soul of his victim is a mere collection of nerves?

In short, Huxley's exposition of physiological reductionism achieved a degree of polemical fame, throughout the 'seventies and 'eighties and even into the 'nineties. That undifferentiated protoplasm was named Vampurella, that Professor Allman's description of amoebic ingestion is appropriate to vampire courtship, and that Pooh-Bah hails his protoplasmal ancestor are points that may be only of incidental interest. What is important is that the issue was kept before the public for a long time—205,000 copies of Huxley's *Lessons in Elementary Physiology* alone were sold between 1866 and 1915. Anyone aware of what was moving in the intellectual currents of the age, as Stoker was, could not well help knowing of Darwinian materialism, the concept itself and, more to the point, of the fundamental objection that that concept might encourage vice, which translates mostly into carnal connection conducted in a new Sodom.

The Onanistic Ape

In Victorian culture, both popular and pious, the ape emerges as the embodiment of an ambulatory protoplasmic machine, characterized primarily by hairiness and horniness. Cynocephalus, the ape as virile male, is in one rendition or another a character in the legends of many cultures, Greek, Persian, Portuguese, as well as Victorian, which knew considerably more about apes than did the ancient world, but which still often preferred myth to reality.

> The hideous monster rummaged through the drawers and eventually laid hold of a razor which he flourished and chattered in evident delight. He sprang suddenly forward and attacked Mdlle. Proche, the poor lady struggling to free herself from her assailant. The gorilla inflicted severe wounds on the throat and neck of his victim who had by this time fainted from loss of blood.

The Illustrated Police News is lush with reports on sea monsters, homicidal rats, sharks, devilfish, jealous wives, and hideous apes such as the simian assailant of "A Fearful Adventure at Famber." The passage quoted from that story is accompanied by a cartoon depicting a scene of general mayhem—a painting fallen off a wall and slashed, one fainted woman, one shrieking woman, and one gorilla, who has the bloodstained razor in one hand, a woman's neck in another, a smile on his face, and the linen of an overturned table like a figleaf over his loins. The myth of the male ape as hyper-virile, jumping about the pampas chasing naked girls as in *Candide* or raping them, as in "A Fearful Adventure at Famber," continues today in the enlarged version of King Kong.

Stuart P. Sherman, in an analysis of Theodore Dreiser's debt to Darwinism, noted that in the Darwinian scheme, "the male of the species is characterized by cupidity, pugnacity, and a simian inclination for the other sex." Horrors provoked by the ape fructified not only such popular pieces as "A Fearful Adventure at Famber," but also the theological attacks on Darwin and Huxley. The hint insinuated by Darwin in the *Origin*—"Much light will be thrown on man and his history"—was enough to provoke attack after attack on the theory of natural selection by those who leapt to the warranted conclusion that somewhere on the ancestral tree drawn by Darwinism there crouched an ape. The least pleasing prospect about that ape was his sexuality. To Bishop Samuel Wilberforce, Huxley's opponent at a spring, 1860, meeting of the British Association for the Advancement of Science, the notion of "the brute origin of man" was inconsistent with man's supremacy over the earth, power of speech, gift of reason, free will and responsibility, historic fall and future redemption. The "unflinching materialism" of Darwinism, said Adam Sedgwick, came straight from "the bottom of the well." In a review of Huxley's *Man's Place in Nature* (1863), the *Athenaeum* found Huxley's aim "to degrade man" by parading before us "gibbering, grovelling apes" as our grandparents.

Sedgwick's figure, "the bottom of the well," is a hidden allusion to the boogy-man of Victorian culture, sex. Dracula is like the mythologized ape in being a creature of prodigious sexual appetite, arid the vampire has the talent of exciting in the purest of victims uncontrollable libidinous energies. The introduction to this fundamental motif of the novel occurs in the scene of Jonathan Harker's temptation in Castle Dracula. Jonathan, in "an agony of delightful anticipation," awaits the ministrations of the vamps:

> All three had brilliant white teeth, that shone like pearls against the ruby of their voluptuous lips. There was something about them that made me uneasy, some longing and at the same time some deadly fear. I felt in my heart a wicked, burning desire that they would kiss me with those red lips. … The fair girl went on her knees, and bent over me, fairly gloating. There was a deliberate voluptuousness which was both thrilling and repulsive, and as she arched her neck she actually licked her lips like an animal, till I could see in the moonlight the moisture shining on the scarlet lips and on the red tongue as it lapped the white sharp teeth (pp. 39, 41).

Such wanton display of a vagina dentata encourages Jonathan to close his eyes "in a languorous ecstasy." Mina is similarly charmed by the carnivorous love-making of Count Dracula, who is intent on transubstantiating her into him, and in giving her something of himself as well. When he turns to her veins "to refresh his thirst," she confesses, "I was bewildered, and, strangely enough, I did not want to hinder him" (p. 255). The sexual gratification to which the Count devotes his life is sometimes rendered subtly, and sometimes obviously, as he goes about the land seeking heterosexual alliances (*Dracula* is diligently heterosexual, unlike *Carmilla*). The Count not only ingests the blood of the young women he preys upon, but endows them with his blood, which might be guise for his semen—at least, according to Steven Marcus' calculation, the two fluids were sometimes considered convertible, forty ounces of blood replenishing the loss of one ounce of semen. That convertibility may lurk behind the memorable scene concluding Chapter 21, wherein the Count, after scratching wounds in his own chest, forces the delicate, pure, pious—and not altogether unwilling—Mina to sup:

> When the blood (she reports) began to spurt out, he took my hands in one of his, holding them tight, and with the other seized my neck and pressed my mouth to the wound, so that I must either suffocate or swallow some of the— (p. 255).

In estimating his victims to be "like sheep in a butcher's" (p. 271), Dracula looks upon English women much as Madam Audray looked upon her prostitutes:

> She does not keep her meat too long on the hooks. ... You may have your meat dressed to your own liking, and there is no need of cutting twice from one joint; and if it suits your taste, you may kill your own lamb or mutton, for her flock is in prime condition and always ready for sticking.[4]

A critic of the founding of the British Association for the Advancement of Science was concerned that opening science up to the public might provide for young ladies information and sights (such as elephants flirting on Sundays) calculated to bring a blush to their cheeks. Monkeys and apes—at least when caged—seem to have nothing to do except fiddle with their mates or themselves. Dr. Lawson Tait addressed himself to the simian neglect of the work ethic:

> ... luxurious living and idleness are productive of lust in monkeys as well as men. I fancy that it is rather the result of luxury living, their freedom from the strain of earning an honest livelihood that disables monkeys—and men—from training themselves in moral restraint.

This is coded language for masturbation. The symptomology of Count Dracula suggests that he experiences similar proclivities and from a similar cause. He is not as clumsy as another figure whose connection to the mythologized ape is close—Mr. Hyde, described by Stevenson as "something troglodytic," "pure evil," who scampers about the laboratory "like a monkey," retaliates with "ape-like spite," and kills with "ape-like fury." But the Count is like Mr. Hyde, and like prototypical Cynocephalus in having monstrous and depraved appetites. He is hairy-palmed (another code-phrase), fang-toothed, unemployed, and, like Dr. Acton's onanist, sallow in complexion, cold, emaciated, irritable, alienated ("he creeps about alone") and studious.[5]

"Sexuality and Fictional Convention in Dracula," Victorian Newsletter, 42 (Fall, 1972), pp. 20–22 and Phyllis A. Roth, "Suddenly Sexual Women in Bram Stoker's Dracula," Literature and Psychology, XXVII: 3 (1977), pp. 113–121. On the virile ape, see Desmond Morris, Men and Apes (N.Y.: 1966). The article "Murderous Attack by a Gorilla" is reproduced in Leonard de Vries, ed., 'Orrible Murder: Victorian Crime and Passion (N.Y.: 1971).

5 Quoted in Peter T. Cominos, "Innocent Femina Sensualis in Unconscious Conflict," in Martha Vicinus, ed., *Suffer and Be Still: Women in the*

---

4 Quoted in Ronald Pearshall, The Worm in the Bud (N.Y.: 1969), p. 259. See also Carrol Fry,

Dracula lacks so much it seems unfair to single out one quality; but if something were to be singled out as a significant omission in his character it would be the soul. Everyone knows that the vampire has no reflection in a mirror because like the ape he has no soul (while the ape has none, the onanist imperils the one he has). Bishop Wilberforce and many others were keenly aware of the Darwinian picture of the human being—a protoplasmic machine born to die, and that's all, or perhaps, as in Thomas Hardy's "Transformation," to yield his chemicals to the nutrition of a tree. When Dr. Seward teases Renfield about what an elephant's soul would taste like, Renfield replies:

> "I don't want an elephant's soul, or any soul at all!" For a few moments he sat despondently. Suddenly he jumped to his feet, with his eyes blazing and all the signs of intense cerebral excitement. "To hell with you and your souls!" he shouted. "Why do you plague me about souls?" (pp. 239–240)

Throughout the Darwinian controversies, beginning with the earliest reviews of the *Origin,* and going on right through the 'nineties, with Huxley's address on "Evolution and Ethics," and of course continuing today, a critical point of argument has revolved around the question of whether we do or do not have a soul. In two papers delivered to the Metaphysical Society during the years of the popularization of the physico-chemical basis of the human being, Huxley advanced the contention that the notion of soul is an unproven hypothesis. One of these papers is entitled "Has a Frog a Soul?" (November 8, 1870), and here Huxley again correlates vital activity with protoplasmic configuration. In his summary to the second paper, "The Views of Hume, Kant, and Whately upon the Logical Basis of the Doctrine of the Immortality of the Soul" (November 17, 1869), he notes that Hume maintained (as Huxley himself maintained):

> In the absence of proof to the contrary, the absolute dependence of the mental faculties upon the bodily organization is presumptive evidence that the former do not outlast the latter.

Then he briefly alludes to Kant's imperative that "the immortality of the soul is an hypothesis of immense moral value," and concludes:

> I follow Hume, Kant, and Whately in defending the thesis that—THE IMMORTALITY OF THE SOUL CANNOT BE DEDUCED BY SCIENTIFIC METHODS OF REASONING FROM THE FACTS OF PHYSICAL OR PSYCHICAL NATURE.

Those who find consolation in Christian credenda would agree with Kant's imperative, and would further agree with the proposition that if the tie were to be broken between immortal rewards and punishments on the one hand and mundane morality on the other, the cyrenaic rampage would be upon us, a rampage orchestrated, among others, by vampires.

The Parasitic Superman

Eight years before the publication of *Dracula* there appeared an essay, as unknown as the novel is famous, which as a definition of retrogressive metamorphosis provides a link between Darwinism and *Dracula.* Written by E. Ray Lankester, *Degeneration: A Chapter in Darwinism* is a study of evolutionary processes leading to the development of parasitic forms. Such forms are characterized by the enlargement or refinement of certain organs, and the complementary degeneration of other organs, the elaborated new structures being directed

---

Victorian Age (Bloomington: 1972), p. 162. Dracula does not manifest all the symptoms of the onanist as those symptoms are listed in Acton's *The Functions and Disorders of the Reproductive Organs*: he is not insane, careless in dress or unclean in person, he does not suffer from a stunted, weak frame, sluggish feeble intellect, loss of memory or of self-reliance, incoherence, apathy, inability to concentrate, curvature of the spine, or acne.

towards successful parasitism. Retrogressive metamorphosis occurs when the organism "becomes adapted to less varied and less complex conditions of life" than its ancestral form enjoyed. Lankester devotes most of his essay to the discussion of parasitic animals such as barnacles and ascidians; but he speaks of the process occurring also with higher animals and with civilizations:

> Any new set of conditions occurring to an animal which render its food and safety very easily attained, seems to lead, as a rule, to Degeneration; just as an active, healthy man sometimes degenerates when he suddenly becomes possessed of a fortune; or as Rome degenerated when possessed of the riches of the ancient world (pp. 18–19).

In the general argument about whether or not evolution is necessarily progressive, Lankester takes sides with Huxley (whose *Scientific Memoirs* he co-edited) and, therefore, against Lamarck and Herbert Spencer:

> Possibly we are all drifting, tending to the condition of intellectual Barnacles or Ascidians. It is possible for us—just as the Ascidian throws away its tail and its eye, and sinks into a quiescent state of inferiority—to reject the good gift of reason with which every child is born, and to degenerate into a contented life of material enjoyment accompanied by ignorance and superstition (p. 32).

In significant respects, Dracula is such a degenerate, offering to his followers the power of pleasure, eternal carnal fun, here and now—not as in Christian eschatology, spiritual integration later and somewhere unmapped. In the kingdom of heaven which the Count endeavors to establish there are no disembodied souls strumming on harps, but rather fleshly beings whose business is pleasure (and, as unhappily for them as for Paolo and Francesca, whose pleasure is business, so compulsive is the hunger). To Professor van Helsing, Count Dracula, in his providing a life of material enjoyment for his congregation, was on his way to becoming "the father or furtherer of a new order of beings, whose road must lead through Death, not Life" (p. 158). Jonathan and Mina may have been "strangely enough" bewildered by finding that they didn't want to hinder the vampires courting them; but there is really not much of a puzzle about the attraction of the carnal life. It is attractive enough even to subvert the proper Victorian maiden. Lucy—despite a couple of mysteries in her background—is such a maiden. But after Dracula's proselytism, she changes: "The sweetness was turned to adamantine, heartless cruelty, and the purity to voluptuous wantonness" (p. 189). The charismatic Dracula, leech though he is, develops potential into reality. It is the recognition of the strength of appetite and of Dracula's ability to satisfy it that motivates van Helsing to direct his search-and-destroy operation. The new order of beings that van Helsing fears, the degenerate life that Lankester warns is an option in evolution, constitutes the moral danger of materialism.

The idea of the superman emergent from Social Darwinism owes little to Darwin, and less to Huxley, but a good deal to Herbert Spencer whose construct, "the survival of the fittest," could be taken to justify, and was taken to justify, unbridled competition among tradesmen and among nations. "Brave peoples alone have an existence, an evolution or a future; the weak and cowardly perish, and perish justly." This remark could have been made by Spencer or by Count Dracula in his conversation with Jonathan Harker in Transylvania. It was made by Heinrich von Treitschke, whose *The Mystique of War* carries Social Darwinism to a militaristic extreme. The metaphor of the capitalist or the militarist consuming those weaker than themselves takes on the value of literalism in the confines of Stoker's novel. Dracula, looking upon his victims as sheep, is remorseful that blood is no longer being spilled as abundantly as it used to be in the exuberance of Wallachian wars. He longs for a return to carnage, and does his best to advance the blood lust, as his model Vlad IV did his best.

Renfield refers to Dracula as the Master and "He," Renfield playing the role of John the Baptist to Dracula as messiah. Dracula effects communion with his congregation through the sharing of blood, for instead of wine being blood, blood is transubstantiated into wine, Mina emerging from this ritual as Dracula's "bountiful wine-press"; and he offers eternal life. To these soteriological functions, he adds that of the warrior. As the great beast slouching towards London, Dracula personifies the apocalyptic future that frightens van Helsing. Van Helsing is aware that the Count's trafficking with women could lead to the propagation of a family related through blood in a genetic as well as ceremonial sense. The Lamarckian sentiment in this awareness reflects Francis Galton's thesis, in *Hereditary Genius* (1869) and "Gregariousness in Cattle and Men," that talent and genius and an "inclination" toward moral traits are hereditary—and that the leader of men is often their exploiter. Galton's view supports his cousin's:

> There is apparently much truth (wrote Darwin in the *Descent*) in the belief that the wonderful progress of the United States, as well as the character of the people, are the results of natural selection; for the more energetic, restless, and courageous men from all parts of Europe have emigrated during the last ten or twelve generations to that great country, and have there succeeded best.

The prospect of improving the species—America the model, as Rockefeller, Ford, Carnegie, Sumner, and many other American exponents of Social Darwinism saw it—is what van Helsing explicitly acknowledges in the course of the blood-transfusions, communion among the anti-Dracula forces also being achieved through the giving and taking of blood. Addressing himself to Quincey Morris' giving blood to Lucy, van Helsing comments: "If America can go on breeding men like that, she will be a power in the world indeed" (p. 158). Thus, *Dracula* presents a contest between two evolutionary options: the ameliorative, progressive, Christian congregation, or the Social Darwinian superman in the form of the ultimate parasitic degenerate, Count Dracula.

Dracula is not a faultless work of art—the dialect is often ludicrous, van Helsing's almost always; the plot is marred by many absurdities, such as Jonathan Harker's miraculous escape, convalescence, and return; the blood-transfusions are not to be recommended as clinical models. But the story does dramatize a very scary, and also tantalizing possibility: the over-coming of human compassion, of the human species itself, by a degenerate messiah. Van Helsing sees the opposition between vampirism and Christianity the way the critics of Darwinism saw that construct as opposing Christianity. One of these critics, W. Wilford Hall, wrote (*The Problem of Human Life,* 1880), in language that van Helsing might have used could he have spoken English:

> From this time on, it is either an unconditional surrender to the materialistic and atheistic evolution of Huxley and Haeckel, or it is the triumph of religion and of the unadulterated word of God.

Dracula fantasizes on what could happen were materialism to be as successful in shaping the moral basis of the human community as it has been successful in elucidating the physical basis of life.

The Taboo Upon the Dead

Sigmund Freud

The Taboo upon the Dead

WE KNOW THAT THE dead are powerful rulers; but we may perhaps be surprised when we learn that they are treated as enemies.

The taboo upon the dead is—if I may revert to the simile of infection—especially virulent among most primitive peoples. It is manifested, in the first instance, in the consequences that follow contact with the dead and in the treatment of mourners.

Among the Maoris anyone who had handled a corpse or taken any part in its burial was in the highest degree unclean and was almost cut off from intercourse with his fellow-men, or, as we might put it, was boycotted. He could not enter any house, or come into contact with any person or thing without infecting them. He might not even touch food with his hands, which, owing to their uncleanness, had become quite useless. 'Food would be set for him on the ground, and he would then sit or kneel down, and, with his hands carefully held behind his back, would gnaw at it as best he could. In some cases he would be fed by another person, who with outstretched arm contrived to do it without touching the tabooed man; but the feeder was himself subjected to many severe restrictions, little less onerous than those which were imposed upon the other. In almost every populous village there lived a degraded wretch, the lowest of the low, who earned a sorry pittance by thus waiting upon the defiled.' He alone was allowed 'to associate at arm's length with one who had paid the last offices ... to the dead. And when, the dismal term of his seclusion being over, the mourner was about to mix with his fellows once more, all the dishes he had used in his seclusion were diligently smashed, and all the garments he had worn were carefully thrown away. [Frazer, 1911*b*, 138 f.]

The taboo observances after bodily contact with the dead are the same over the whole of Polynesia, Melanesia and a part of Africa. Their most regular feature is the prohibition against those who have had such contact touching food themselves, and the consequent necessity for their being fed by other people. It is a remarkable fact that in Polynesia (though the report may perhaps refer only to Hawaii) priestly kings were subject to the same restriction while performing their sacred functions.[1] The case of the taboo upon the dead in Tonga offers a specially clear instance of the way in which the degree of prohibition varies according to the taboo power of the person upon whom the taboo is imposed. Thus anyone who touches a dead chief is unclean for ten months; but if he himself is a chief he is only tabooed for three, four, or five months according to the rank of the dead man; but if the dead man were the 'great divine chief', even the greatest chief would be tabooed for ten months. These savages believe firmly that anyone who violates the taboo ordinances is bound to fall ill and die; indeed they believe it so firmly that, in the opinion of an observer, 'no native ever made an experiment to prove the contrary'.[2]

Essentially, the same prohibitions (though from our point of view they are more interesting) apply to those who have been in contact with the dead only in a metaphorical sense: the dead person's mourning relations, widowers and widows. The observances that we have so far mentioned may seem merely to give characteristic expression to the virulence of the taboo and its contagious power. But those which now follow give us a hint at the reasons for the taboo—both the ostensible ones and what we must regard as the deep-lying ones.

'Among the Shuswap of British Columbia widows and widowers in mourning are secluded and forbidden to touch their own head or body; the cups and cooking vessels which they use may be used by no one else. ... No hunter would come near such mourners, for their presence is unlucky. If their shadow were to fall on anyone, he would be taken ill at once. They employ thorn-bushes for bed and pillow ... and thorn-bushes are also laid all around their beds.'[3] This last measure is designed to keep the dead person's ghost at a distance. The same purpose is shown still more clearly in the usage reported from another North American tribe which provides that, after her husband's death, 'a widow would wear a breech-cloth made of dry bunch-grass for several days to prevent her husband's ghost having intercourse with her.'[4] This suggests that contact 'in a metaphorical

---

Sigmund Freud, "The Taboo upon the Dead," *Totem and Taboo*, trans. James Strachey, pp. 51–63. Copyright © 1950 by Taylor & Francis Group LLC. Reprinted with permission.

sense' is after all understood as being bodily contact, for the dead man's ghost does not leave his relations and does not cease to 'hover' round them during the time of mourning.

'Among the Agutainos, who inhabit Palawan, one of the Philippine Islands, a widow may not leave her hut for seven or eight days after the death; and even then she may only go out at an hour when she is not likely to meet anybody, for whoever looks upon her dies a sudden death. To prevent this fatal catastrophe, the widow knocks with a wooden peg on the trees as she goes along, thus warning people of her dangerous proximity; and the very trees on which she knocks soon die.'[5] The nature of the danger feared from a widow such as this is made plain by another example. 'In the Mekeo district of British New Guinea a widower loses all his civil rights and becomes a social outcast, an object of fear and horror, shunned by all. He may not cultivate a garden, nor show himself in public, nor walk on the roads and paths. Like a wild beast he must skulk in the long grass and the bushes; and if he sees or hears anyone coming, especially a woman, he must hide behind a tree or a thicket.'[6] This last hint makes it easy to trace the origin of the dangerous character of widowers or widows to the danger of temptation. A man who has lost his wife must resist a desire to find a substitute for her; a widow must fight against the same wish and is moreover liable, being without a lord and master, to arouse the desires of other men. Substitutive satisfactions of such a kind run counter to the sense of mourning and they would inevitably kindle the ghost's wrath.[7]

One of the most puzzling, but at the same time instructive, usages in connection with mourning is the prohibition against uttering the name of the dead person. This custom is extremely widespread, it is expressed in a variety of ways and has had important consequences. It is found not only among the Australians and Polynesians (who usually show, us taboo observances in the best state of preservation), but also among 'peoples so widely separated from each other as the Samoyeds of Siberia and the Todas of southern India; the Mongols of Tartary and the Tuaregs of the Sahara; the Ainos of Japan and the Akamba and Nandi of central Africa; the Tinguianes of the Philippines and the inhabitants of the Nicobar Islands, of Borneo, of Madagascar, and of Tasmania.' (Frazer, 1911b, 353.) In some of these eases the prohibition and its consequences last only during the period of mourning, in others they are permanent; but it seems invariably to diminish in strictness with the passage of time.

The avoidance of the name of a dead person is as a rule enforced with extreme severity. Thus in some South American tribes it is regarded as a deadly insult to the survivors to mention the name of a dead relative in their presence, and the punishment for it is not less than that laid down for murder. (Ibid., 352.) It is not easy at first to see why the mention of the name should be regarded with such horror; but the dangers involved have given rise to a whole number of methods of evasion which are interesting and important in various ways. Thus the Masai in East Africa resort to the device of changing the dead man's name immediately after his death; he may then be mentioned freely under his new name while all the restrictions remain attached to the old one/This seems to presuppose that the dead man's ghost does not know and will not get to know his new name. [Ibid., 354.] The Adelaide and Encounter Bay tribes of South Australia are so consistently careful that after a death everyone bearing the same name as the dead man's, or a very similar one, changes it for another. [Ibid., 355.] In some instances, as for instance among certain tribes in Victoria and in North-West America, this is carried a step further, and after a death all the dead person's relations change their names, irrespective of any similarity in their sound. [Ibid., 357.] Indeed, among the Guaycurus in Paraguay, when a death had taken place, the chief used to change the name of every member of the tribe; and 'from that moment everybody remembered his new name just as if he had borne it all his life'.[8]

Moreover, if the name of the dead man happens to be the same as that of an animal or common object, some tribes think it necessary to give these animals or objects new names, so that the use of the former names shall not recall the dead man to memory. This usage leads to a perpetual change of vocabulary, which causes much difficulty to the missionaries, especially when such changes are permanent. In the seven years which the missionary Dobrizhoffer spent among the Abipones of Paraguay, 'the native word for jaguar was changed thrice, and the words for crocodile, thorn, and the slaughter of cattle underwent similar though less varied vicissitudes'.[9] The dread of uttering a dead person's name extends, indeed, to an avoidance of the mention of anything in which the dead man played a part; and an important consequence of this process of suppression is that these people possess no tradition and no historical memory, so that any research into their early history is faced by the greatest difficulties., [Ibid., 362 f.] A number of these primitive races, however, adopted compensatory usages which revive the names of dead persons after a long period of mourning by giving them to children, who are thus regarded as reincarnations of the dead. [Ibid., 364 f.]

This taboo upon names will seem less puzzling if we bear in mind the fact that savages regard a name as an essential part of a man's personality and as an important possession: they treat words in every sense as things. As I have pointed out elsewhere [Freud, 1905, Chap. IV], our own children do the same. They are never ready to accept a similarity between two words as having no meaning; they consistently assume that if two things are called by similar-sounding names this must imply the existence of some deep-lying point of agreement between them. Even a civilized adult may be able to infer from certain peculiarities in his own behaviour that his not so far removed as he may have thought from attributing importance to proper names, and that his own name has become to a very remarkable extent bound up with his personality. So, too, psycho-analytic practices comes upon frequent confirmations of this in the evidence it finds of the importance of names in unconscious mental activities.[10]

As was only to be expected, obsessional neurotics behave exactly like savages in relation to names. Like other neurotics, they show a high degree of 'complex sensitiveness'[11] in regard to uttering or hearing particular words and names; and their attitude towards their own names imposes numerous, and often serious, inhibitions upon them. One of these taboo patients of my acquaintance had adopted a rule against writing her own name, for fear that it might fall into the hands of someone who would then be in possession of a portion of her personality. She was obliged to fight with convulsive loyalty against the temptations to which her imagination subjected her, and so forbade herself to surrender any part of her person'. This included in the first place her name, and later extended to her handwriting, till finally she gave up writing altogether. We shall no longer feel surprised, therefore, at savages regarding the name of a dead person as a portion of his personality and making it subject to the relevant taboo. So, too, uttering the name of a dead person is clearly a derivative of having contact with him. We may therefore turn to the wider problem of why such contact is submitted to so strict a taboo.

The most obvious explanation would point to horror roused by dead bodies and by the changes which quickly become visible in them. Some part must also be played in the matter by mourning for the dead person, since it must be a motive force in everything relating to him. But horror at the corpse clearly does not account for all the details of the taboo observances, and mourning cannot explain why the uttering of the dead man's name is an insult to his survivors. Mourning, on the contrary, tends to be preoccupied with the dead man, to dwell upon his memory and to preserve it as long as possible. Something other than mourning must be held responsible for the peculiarities of the taboo usages, something which has very different purposes in view. It is precisely the taboo upon names that gives us the clue to this unknown motive; and if the usages alone did not tell us, we should learn it from what the mourning savages say to us themselves.

For they make no disguise of the fact that they are *afraid* of the presence or of the return of the dead person's ghost; and they perform a great number of ceremonies to keep him at a distance or drive him off.[12] They feel that to utter his name is equivalent to invoking him and will quickly be followed by his presence.[13] And accordingly they do everything they can to avoid any such evocation. They disguise themselves so that the ghost shall not recognize them,[14] or they change his name or their own; they are furious with reckless strangers who by uttering the ghost's name incite him against the survivors. It is impossible to escape the conclusion that, in the words of Wundt (1906, 49), they are victims to a fear of 'the dead man's soul which has become a demon'. Here, then, we seem to have found a confirmation of Wundt's view, which, as we have already seen (p. 24), considers that the essence of taboo is a fear of demons;

This theory is based on a supposition so extraordinary that it seems at first sight incredible: the supposition, namely, that a dearly loved relative at the moment of his death changes into a demon, from whom his survivors can expect nothing but hostility and against whose evil desires they must protect themselves by every possible means. Nevertheless, almost all the authorities are at one in attributing these views to primitive peoples. Westermarck, who, in my opinion, takes far too little notice of taboo in his book on The Origin and Development of the Moral Ideas, actually writes in his chapter on 'Regard for the Dead': 'Generally speaking, my collection of facts has led me to the conclusion that the dead are more commonly regarded as enemies than friends, and that Professor Jevons and Mr. Grant Allen are mistaken in their assertion that, according to early beliefs, the malevolence of the dead is for the most part directed against strangers only, whereas they exercise a fatherly care over the lives and fortunes of their descendants and fellow clansmen.'[15]

In an interesting volume, Rudolf Kleinpaul (1898) has used the remnants among civilized races of the ancient belief in spirits to throw light on the relation between the living and the dead. He, too, reaches the final conclusion that the dead, filled with a lust for murder, sought to drag the living in their train. The dead slew; and the skeleton which we use to-day to picture the dead stands for the fact that they themselves were slayers. The living did not feel safe from the attacks of the dead till there was a sheet of water between them. That is why men liked to bury the dead on islands or on the farther side of rivers; and that, in turn, is the origin of such phrases as 'Here and in the Beyond'. Later, the malignity of the dead diminished and was restricted to special categories which had a particular right to feel resentment—such as murdered men, for instance, who in the form of evil spirits went in pursuit of their murderers, or brides, who had died with their desires unsatisfied. But originally, says Kleinpaul, *all* of the dead were vampires, all of them had a grudge against the living and sought to injure them and rob them of their lives. It was from corpses, that the concept of evil spirits first arose.

The hypothesis that after their death those most beloved were transformed into demons clearly raises further questions. What was it that induced primitive men to attribute such a change of feeling to those who had been dear to them? Why did they make them into demons? Westermarck (1906-8, 2, 534 f.) is of the opinion that these questions can be answered easily. 'Death is commonly regarded as the gravest of all misfortunes; hence the dead are believed to be exceedingly dissatisfied with their fate. According to primitive ideas a person only dies if he is killed—by magic if not by force—and such a death naturally tends to make the soul revengeful and ill-tempered. It is envious of the living and is longing for the company of its old friends; no wonder, then, that it sends them diseases to cause their death. ...But the notion that the disembodied soul is on the whole a malicious being ... is also, no doubt, intimately connected with the instinctive fear of the dead, which is in its turn the outcome of the fear of death.'

The study of psycho-neurotic disorders suggests a more comprehensive explanation, which at the same time covers that put forward by Westermarck.

When a wife has lost her husband or a daughter her mother, it not infrequently happens that the survivor is overwhelmed by tormenting doubts (to which we give the name of 'obsessive self-reproaches') as to whether she may not herself have been responsible for the death of this cherished being through some act of carelessness or neglect. No amount of recollection of the care she lavished on the sufferer, no amount of objective disproof of the accusation, serves to bring the torment to an end. It may be regarded as a pathological form of mourning, and with the passage of time it gradually dies away. The psychoanalytic investigation of such cases has revealed the secret motives of the disorder. We find that in a certain sense these obsessive self-reproaches are justified, and that this is why they are proof against contradictions and protests. It is not that the mourner was really responsible for the death or was really guilty of neglect, as the self-reproaches declare to be the case. None the less there was something in her—a wish that was unconscious to herself—which would not have been dissatisfied by the occurrence of death and which might actually have brought it about if it had had the power. And after death *has* occurred, it is against this unconscious wish that the reproaches are a reaction. In almost every case where there is an intense emotional attachment to a particular person we find that behind the tender love there is a concealed hostility in the unconscious. This is the classical example, the prototype, of the ambivalence of human emotions. This ambivalence is present to a greater or less amount in the innate disposition of everyone; normally, there is not so much of it as to produce the obsessive self-reproaches we are considering. Where, however, it is copiously present in the disposition, it will manifest itself precisely in the subject's relation to those of whom he is most fond, in the place, in fact, where one would least expect to find it. It must be supposed that the presence of a particularly large amount of this original emotional ambivalence is characteristic of the disposition of obsessional neurotics—whom I have so often brought up for comparison in this discussion upon taboo.

We have now discovered a motive which can explain the idea that the souls of those who have just died are transformed into demons and the necessity felt by survivors to protect themselves by taboos against their hostility. Let us suppose that the emotional life of primitive peoples is characterized by an amount of ambivalence as great as that which we are led by the findings of psycho-analysis to attribute to obsessional patients. It then becomes easy to understand how after a painful bereavement savages should be obliged to produce a reaction against the hostility latent in their unconscious similar to that expressed as obsessive self-reproach in the case of neurotics. But this hostility, distressingly felt in the unconscious as satisfaction over the death, is differently dealt with among primitive peoples. The defence against it takes the form of displacing it on to the object of the hostility, on to the dead themselves. This defensive procedure, which is a common one both in normal and in pathological mental life, is known as a '*projection*'. The survivor thus denies that he has ever harboured any hostile feelings against the dead loved one; the soul of the dead harbours them instead and seeks to put them into action during the whole period of mourning. In spite of the successful defence which the survivor achieves by means of projection, his emotional reaction shows the characteristics of punishment and remorse, for he is the subject of fears and submits to renunciations and restrictions, though these are in part disguised as measures of protection against the hostile demon. Once again, therefore, we find that the taboo has grown upon the basis of an ambivalent emotional attitude. The taboo upon the dead arises, like the others, from the contrast between conscious pain and unconscious satisfaction over the death that has occurred. Since such is the origin of the ghost's resentment, it follows naturally that the survivors who have the most to fear will be those who were formerly its nearest and dearest.

In this respect taboo observances, like neurotic symptoms, have a double sense. On the one hand, in their restrictive character, they are expressions of mourning; but on the other hand they clearly betray—what they seek to conceal—hostility against the dead disguised as self-defence. We have already learned that certain taboos arise out of fear of temptation. The fact that a dead man is helpless is bound to act as an encouragement to the survivor to give free rein to his hostile passions, and that temptation must be countered by a prohibition.

Westermarck is right in insisting that savages draw no distinction between violent and natural death. In the view of unconscious thinking, a man who has died a natural death is a murdered man: evil wishes have killed him.[16] Anyone who investigates the origin and significance of dreams of the death of loved relatives (of parents or brothers or sisters) will be able to convince himself that dreamers, children and savages are at one in their attitude towards the dead—an attitude based upon emotional ambivalence.[17]

At the beginning of this essay [p. 24] disagreement was expressed with Wundt's opinion that the essence of taboo was a fear of demons. Yet we have now assented to an explanation that derives the taboo upon the dead from a fear of the soul of the dead person transformed into a demon. The apparent contradiction can easily be resolved. It is true that we have accepted the presence of demons, but not as something ultimate and psychologically unanalysable. We have succeeded, as it were, in getting behind the demons, for we have explained them as projections of hostile feelings harboured by the survivors against the dead.

Both of the two sets of feelings (the affectionate and the hostile), which, as we have good reason to believe, exist towards the dead person, seek to take effect at the time of the bereavement, as mourning and as satisfaction. There is bound to be a conflict between these two contrary feelings; and, since one of the two, the hostility, is wholly or for the greater part unconscious, the outcome of the conflict cannot be to subtract, as it were, the feeling with the lesser intensity from that with the greater and to establish the remainder in consciousness—as occurs, for instance, when one forgives a slight that one has received from someone of whom one is fond. The process is dealt with instead by the special psychical mechanism known in psycho-analysis, as I have said, by the name of 'projection.' The hostility, of which the survivors know nothing and moreover wish to know nothing, ejected from internal perception into the external world, and thus detached from them and pushed on to someone else. It is no longer true that they are rejoicing to be rid of the dead man; on the contrary, they are mourning for him; but, strange to say, *he* has turned into a wicked demon ready to gloat over their misfortunes and eager to kill them. It then becomes necessary for them, the survivors, to defend themselves against this evil enemy; they are relieved of pressure from within, but have only exchanged it for oppression from without.

It cannot be disputed that this process of projection, which turns a dead man into a malignant enemy, is able to find support in any real acts of hostility on his part that may be recollected and felt as a grudge against him: his severity, his love of power, his unfairness, or whatever else may form the background of even the tenderest of human relationships. But it cannot be such a simple matter as that. This factor alone cannot explain the creation of demons by projection. The faults of the dead no doubt provide a part of the explanation of the survivors' hostility; but they would not operate in this way unless the survivors had first developed hostility on their own account. The moment of death, moreover, would certainly seem to be a most inappropriate occasion for recalling any justifiable grounds of complaint that might exist. It is impossible to escape the fact that the true determining factor is invariably *unconscious* hostility. A hostile current of feeling such as this against a person's nearest and dearest relatives may remain latent during their lifetime, that is, its existence may not be betrayed to consciousness either directly or through some substitute. But when they die this is no longer possible and the conflict becomes acute. The mourning which derives from an intensification of the affectionate feelings becomes on the one hand more impatient of the latent hostility and, on the other hand, will not allow it to give rise to any sense of satisfaction. Accordingly, there follow the repression of the unconscious hostility by the method of projection and the construction of the ceremonial which gives expression to the fear of being punished by the demons. When in course of time the mourning runs its course, the conflict grows less acute, so that the taboo upon the dead is able to diminish in severity or sink into oblivion.

Notes

1. Frazer (loc. cit.) [quoting Ellis (1832-6, 4, 388)].
2. Frazer (1911b, 140), quoting Mariner (1818 [1, 141]).

3. [Frazier (1911b, 142), quoting Boas (1890, 643 f.).]
4. [Frazier (1911b, 143), quoting Teit (1900, 332 f.).]
5. [Frazier (1911b, 144), quoting Blumentritt (1891, 182).]
6. [Frazer (1911b, 144), quoting Guis (1902, 208 f.).]
7. The patient whose 'impossibilities' I compared with taboos earlier in this paper (see page 28) told me that whenever she met anyone dressed in mourning in the street she was filled with indignation: such people she thought, should be forbidden to go out.
8. Frazer (1911b, 357), quoting an old Spanish observer [Lozano (1733, 70)].
9. Frazer (1911b, 360), quoting Dobrizhoffer [1784, 2, 301].
10. Cf. Stekel [1911] and Abraham [1912].
11. [Komplexempfindlichkeit—a term used by Jung in connection with his word association experiments.]
12. Frazer (1911b 353) mentions the Tuaregs of the Sahara as an example of this explanation being given by the savages themselves.
13. Subject, perhaps, to the condition that some of his bodily remains are still in existence. (Ibid., 372.)
14. In the Nicobar Islands. (Ibid., 358.)
15. Westermarck (1906-8, 2, 532 ff.). In his footnotes and in the section of the text which follows, the author gives copious confirmatory evidence, often of a highly characteristic sort. For instance: 'Among the Maoris the nearest and most beloved relatives were supposed to have their natures changed by death, and to become malignant, even towards those they formerly loved. [Quoting Taylor (1870, 18).] ... Australian natives believed that a deceased person is malevolent for a long time after death, and the more nearly related the more he is feared. [Quoting Fraser (1892, 80).] ... According to ideas prevalent among the Central Eskimo, the dead are at first malevolent spirits who frequently roam around the villages, causing sickness and mischief and killing men by their touch; but subsequently they are supposed to attain rest and are 110 longer feared. [Quoting Boas (1888, 591).]'
16. Cf. the next essay in this volume.
17. [Cf. Freud: *The Interpretation of Dreams* (1900), English translation, 1932, 242 ff.]

Part III, Chapter X
THE WORKING DAY

SECTION 1—THE LIMITS OF THE WORKING DAY

WE STARTED WITH THE supposition that labour-power is bought and sold at its value. Its value, like that of all other commodities, is determined by the working time necessary to its production. If the production of the average daily means of subsistence of the labourer takes up 6 hours, he must work, on the average, 6 hours every day, to produce his daily labour-power, or to reproduce the value received as the result of its sale. The necessary part of his working day amounts to 6 hours, and is, therefore, *cæteris paribus,* a given quantity. But with this, the extent of the working day itself is not yet given.

Let us assume that the line A B represents the length of the necessary working time, say 6 hours. If the labour be prolonged 1, 3, or 6 hours beyond A B, we have 3 other lines:

Working day I.
A———B—C.
Working day II.
A———B——C.
Working day III.
A———B———C.

representing 3 different working days of 7, 9, and 12 hours. The extension B C of the line A B represents the length of the surplus labour. As the working day is A B + B C or A C, it varies with the variable quantity B C. Since A B is constant, the ratio of B C to A B can always be calculated. In working day I, it is 1/6, in working day II, 3/6, in working day III, 6/6 of A B. Since, further the ratio (surplus working time)/(necessary working time) determines the rate of the surplus-value, the latter is given by the ratio of B C to A B. It amounts in the 3 different working days respectively to 16 2/3, 50 and 100 per cent. On the other hand, the rate of surplus-value alone would not give us the extent of the working day. If this rate *e.g.,* were 100 per cent, the working day might be of 8, 10, 12, or more hours. It would indicate that the 2 constituent parts of the working day, necessary-labour and surplus-labour time, were equal in extent, but not how long each of these two constituent parts was.

The working day is thus not a constant, but a variable quantity. One of its parts, certainly, is determined by the working time required for the reproduction of the labour-power of the labourer himself. But its total amount varies with the duration of the surplus-labour. The working day is, therefore, determinable, but is, *per se,* indeterminate.[1]

Although the working day is not a fixed, but a fluent quantity, it can, on the other hand, only vary within certain limits. The minimum limit is, however, not determinable; of course, if we make the extension line B C or the surplus-labour=0, we have a minimum limit, *i.e.,* the part of the day which the labourer must necessarily work for his own maintenance. On the basis of capitalist production, however, this necessary labour can form a part only of the working day; the working day itself can never be reduced to this minimum. On the other hand, the working day has a maximum limit. It cannot be prolonged beyond a certain point. This maximum limit is conditioned by two things. First, by the physical bounds of labour-power. Within the 24 hours of the natural day a man can expend only a definite quantity of his vital force. A horse, in like manner, can only work from day to day, 8 hours. During part of the day this force must rest, sleep; during another part the man has to satisfy other physical needs, to feed, wash, and clothe himself. Besides these purely physical limitations, the extension of the working day encounters moral ones. The labourer needs time for satisfying his intellectual and social wants, the extent and number of which are conditioned by the general state of social advancement. The variation of the working day fluctuates, therefore, within physical and social bounds. But both these limiting conditions are of a very elastic nature, and allow the greatest latitude. So we find working days of 8, 10, 12, 14, 16, 18 hours, *i.e.,* of the most different lengths.

---

1 "A day's labour is vague, it may be long or short." ("An Essay on Trade and Commerce, containing observations on taxes," 8c. London, 1770, p. 78.)

Karl Marx, from *Capital.* Copyright in the Public Domain.

The capitalist has bought the labour-power at its day-rate. To him its use-value belongs during one working day. He has thus acquired the right to make the labour work for him during one day. But what is a working day?[2]

At all events, less than a natural day. By how much? The capitalist has his own views of this *ultima Thule*, the necessary limit of the working day. As capitalist, he is only capital personified. His soul is the soul of capital. But capital has one single life impulse, the tendency to create value and surplus-value, to make its constant factor, the means of production, absorb the greatest possible amount of surplus-labour.[3]

Capital is dead labour, that vampire-like, only lives by sucking living labour, and lives the more, the more labour it sucks. The time during which the labourer works, is the time during which the capitalist consumes the labour-power he has purchased of him.[4]

If the labourer consumes his disposable time for himself, he robs the capitalist.[5]

The capitalist then takes his stand on the law of the exchange of commodities. He, like all other buyers, seeks to get the greatest possible benefit out of the use-value of his commodity. Suddenly the voice of the labourer, which had been stifled in the storm and stress of the process of production, rises.

The commodity that I have sold to you differs from the crowd of other commodities, in that its use creates value, and a value greater than its own. That is why you bought it. That which on your side appears a spontaneous expansion of capital, is on mine extra expenditure of labour-power. You and I know on the market only one law, that of the exchange of commodities. And the consumption of the commodity belongs not to the seller who parts with it, but to the buyer, who acquires it. To you, therefore, belongs the use of my daily labour-power. But by means of the price that you pay for it each day, I must be able to reproduce it daily, and to sell it again. Apart from natural exhaustion through age, &c., I must be able on the morrow to work with the same normal amount of force, health and freshness as to-day. You preach to me constantly the gospel of "saving" and "abstinence." Good! I will, like a sensible saving owner, husband my sole wealth, labour-power, and abstain from all foolish waste of it. I will each day spend, set in motion, put into action only as much of it as is compatible with its normal duration, and healthy development. By an unlimited extension of the working day, you may in one day use up a quantity of labour-power greater than I can restore in three. What you gain in labour I lose in substance. The use of my labour-power and the spoliation of it are quite different things. If the average time that (doing a reasonable amount of work) an average labourer can live, is 30 years, the value of my labour-power, which you pay me from day to day is $1/365 \times 30$ or $1/10950$ of its total value. But if you consume it in ten years, you pay me daily $1/10950$ instead of $1/3650$ of its total value, *i.e.,* only $1/3$ of its daily value, and you rob me, therefore, every day of $2/3$ of the value of my commodity. You pay me for one day's labour-power, whilst you use that of 3 days. That is against our contract and the law of exchanges. I demand, therefore, a working day of normal length, and I demand it without any appeal to your heart, for in money matters sentiment is out of place. You may be a model citizen, perhaps a member of the Society for the Prevention of Cruelty to Animals, and in

---

2 This question is far more important than the celebrated question of Sir Robert Peel to the Birmingham Chamber of Commerce: What is a pound? A question that could only have been proposed, because Peel was as much in the dark as to the nature of money as the "little shilling men" of Birmingham.

3 It is the aim of the capitalist to obtain with his expended capital the greatest possible quantity of labour (d'obetnir du capital dépensé la plus forte somme de travail possible). J. G. Courcelle-Seneuil. Traité théorique et pratique des entreprises industrielles. 2nd ed. Paris, 1857, p. 63.

4 "An hour's labour lost in a day is a prodigious injury to a commercial State. ... There is a very great consumption of luxuries among the labouring poor of this kingdom: particularly among the manufacturing populace, by which they also consume their time, the most fatal of consumptions." An Essay on Trade and Commerce, 8c., p. 47 and 153.

5 "Si le manouvrier libre prend un instant de repos, l'économic sordide qui le suit des yeux avec inquiétude prétend qu'il la vole." N. Linguet. "Théorie des loix civiles," 8c. London, 1767, t. II., p. 466.

the odour of sanctity to boot; but the thing that you represent face to face with me has no heart in its breast. That which seems to throb there is my own heart-beating. I demand the normal working day because I, like every other seller, demand the value of my commodity.[6]

We see then, that, apart from extremely elastic bounds, the nature of the exchange of commodities itself imposes no limit to the working day, no limit to surplus-labour. The capitalist maintains his rights as a purchaser when he tries to make the working day as long as possible, and to make, whenever possible, two working days out of one. On the other hand, the peculiar nature of the commodity sold implies a limit to its consumption by the purchaser, and the labourer maintains his right as seller when he wishes to reduce the working day to one of definite normal duration. There is here, therefore, an antinomy, right against right, both equally bearing the seal of the law of exchanges. Between equal rights force decides. Hence is it that in the history of capitalist production, the determination of what is a working day, presents itself as the result of a struggle, a struggle between collective capital, *i.e.,* the class of capitalists, and collective labour, *i.e.,* the working class.

---

6 During the great strike of the London builders, 1860–61, for the reduction of the working day to 9 hours, their Committee published a manifesto that contained, to some extent, the plea of our workers. The manifesto alludes, not without irony, to the fact that the greatest profit-monger amongst the building masters, a certain Sir M. Peto, was in the odour of sanctity. (This same Peto, after 1867, came to an end à la Strousberg.)

Introducing the Dracula of Fiction, History, and Folklore

Raymond T. McNally and Radu Florescu

"Welcome to my house! Enter freely and of your own will!" He made no motion of stepping to meet me, but stood like a statue, as though his gesture of welcome had fixed him into stone. The instant, however, that I had stepped over the threshold, he moved impulsively forward, and holding out his hand grasped mine with a strength which made me wince, an effect which was not lessened by the fact that it seemed as cold as ice—more like the hand of a dead than a living man.

So THE VAMPIRE DRACULA first appears in Bram Stoker's novel. Published in 1897, *Dracula* is as popular now as when it was written. Millions not only have read it but have seen it at the cinema. Among the famous filmed versions are F. W. Murnau's *Nosferatu*, starring Max Schreck in 1922, Tod Browning's *Dracula* with Bela Lugosi in 1931, Terence Fisher's *Horror of Dracula* featuring Christopher Lee in 1958, John Badham's *Dracula* with Frank Langella in 1979, and Francis Ford Coppola's *Bram Stoker's Dracula* with Gary Oldman as the most recent cinematic count in 1992.

As for the book before you, the original idea is owed to one of the coauthors. But let Raymond McNally speak for himself: "More than thirty-five years ago, as a fan of Dracula horror films, I began to wonder whether there might be some historical basis for their vampire hero. I reread Stoker's *Dracula* and noted that not only this novel but almost all of the Dracula films are set in Transylvania. At first, like many Americans, I assumed that this was some mythical place, in the same imaginary region, perhaps, as Ruritania. I found out, however, that Transylvania is a province, a historical region of western Romania bounded by the Carpathian Mountains, that had been independent for almost a thousand years but under Hungarian and Turkish influence. In Stoker's novel there are some fairly detailed descriptions of the towns of Klausenburgh (called Cluj in Romanian) and Bistritz (Bistrita in Romanian) and the Borgo Pass (Birgau) in the Carpathian Mountains. When I located the Borgo Pass marked clearly on a modern Romanian map, I had an intuition that if all that geographical data were genuine, why not Dracula himself? Most people had never asked this question, being generally thrown off by the vampire story line. Since vampires do not exist, Dracula—so goes the popular wisdom—must have been the product of a wild and wonderful imagination.

"Eventually I read an authentic late fifteenth-century Slavic manuscript in an archive in St. Petersburg which described the deeds of a Romanian prince named Dracula. After researching the little that was available about the historical Dracula in several languages, I consulted with my Boston College colleague, Professor Radu Florescu, who was in Romania at the time. With his encouragement and enthusiasm I took up the study of the Romanian language and in 1969 received an American government-sponsored fellowship to travel to the very homeland of Dracula to see what more I could discover about this mysterious man and his legend. There, underlying the local traditions, was an authentic human being fully as horrifying as the vampire of fiction and film—a fifteenth-century prince who had been the subject of many horror stories even during his own lifetime; a ruler whose cruelties were committed on such a massive scale that his evil reputation in the Western world reached beyond the grave to the firesides where generations of grandmothers warned little children: 'Be good or Dracula will get you!'

"Unlike myself, an American of Irish and Austrian ancestry who knew the fictional Dracula principally through late-night movies, my colleague Radu Florescu is a native Romanian who knew of a historical Dracula through the research of earlier Romanian scholars. But his ties with this history go deeper than that. As a boy he spent many hours on the banks of the Arges River, which bounded his family's country estate deep in the Wallachian plain, not too far distant from Castle Dracula. In addition, the Florescus can trace their line back to an aristocratic family of Dracula's time with marriage connections to Dracula's family."

It was autumn of 1969 when we tracked down Castle Dracula. The castle was by then

Raymond T. McNally and Radu Florescu, from *In Search of Dracula: The History of Dracula and Vampires*, pp. 1–6. Copyright © 1994 by Houghton Mifflin Harcourt Publishing Company. Reprinted with permission.

Woodcut frontispiece of *Dracole Waida*, Nuremberg, c. 1488, a manuscript that begins "In the year of our Lord 1456 Dracula did many dreadful and curious things."

abandoned, in ruins, and known to the peasants as the castle of Vlad Tepes, or Vlad the Impaler, a ruler notorious for mass impalement of his enemies. Vlad Tepes was in fact called Dracula in the fifteenth century, and we found that he even signed his name that way on documents, but this fact was not even known by the peasants of the castle region.

Using dozens of ancient chronicles, maps, and nineteenth- and twentieth-century philological and historical works, and drawing on folklore, we pieced together a dual history—an account not only of the real fifteenth-century Dracula, Vlad Tepes, who was born and raised in Transylvania and ruled in southern Romania, but also of the vampire who exists in the legends of these same regions. In addition, we studied how Bram Stoker, during the late nineteenth century, united these two traditions to create the most horrifying and famous vampire in fiction: Count Dracula.

What was known of this dual history before our research? In 1896 a Romanian scholar, Ioan Bogdan, noted that there existed various fifteenth-century German pamphlets which described the Romanian Prince Vlad Tepes as "Dracole." The Romanian historian Karadja published the texts, but neither made the connection between these references and Stoker, nor did Bogdan, as a philologist, concern himself extensively with the history and folklore. A few pertinent discoveries were later made by others. For instance, in 1922, the late eminent historian Constantin Giurescu discovered the foundation stone of the Church of Tirgsor, which indicated that Vlad Tepes as its founder and patron was a pious ruler. And in the 1930s, amateur archaeologist Dinu Rosetti and genealogist George Florescu opened the grave of Vlad Tepes at Snagov as part of a general excavation at the site. It was not until the 1960s that the scholar Grigore Nandris began to unravel the story. He studied the philological relationship between the names Dracole and Vlad Tepes and noted that for some unknown reason Bram Stoker had associated these names in his vampire story. The German Slavicist Julius Striedter compared Slavic manuscripts and German pamphlets about Dracula. The Soviet Slavicist Isaac Lurie analyzed Slavic documents in Russian archives. But it was Nandris's philological studies which prepared the groundwork for our investigation, and Harry Ludlam's biography of author Bram Stoker, curiously titled *The Biography of "Dracula": Bram Stoker* (1962), also proved invaluable.

What follows is a complex story involving seven separate research expeditions which resulted in four books: *In Search of Dracula* (1972), *Dracula: A Biography of Vlad the Impaler* (1973), *The Essential Dracula* (1979), and *Dracula, Prince of Many Faces* (1989). Some of the search resulted in the discovery of authentic Dracula documents and sites in the present territory of Romania, Bulgaria, Hungary, Turkey, the former Yugoslavia, Germany, the United Kingdom, Ireland, Italy, Switzerland, France, and even the United States. Study of both the mythical and the historical aspects of the story encountered difficulties. Countries previously dominated by Marxist ideology discouraged research on vampire beliefs as the authorities wished to portray peasants as "modern" and not superstitious.

Regarding Dracula, the historical personage, the official Communist Party historians

In 1976 Nicolae Ceausescu's Romania issued this portrait of a rather benign-looking Vlad on a commemorative postage stamp. Ceausescu and Communist Party historians endorsed a revisionist version of the Dracula story, portraying him as a national hero and rationalizing his cruelties.

portrayed him as a national hero and played down or rationalized his cruelties. None exhibited that hero-worshipping attitude more than the late dictator Nicolae Ceausescu who, according to some authorities, shared many character traits with Dracula. Revolutionaries often caricatured him as a vampire with fangs. One incredible example of this admiration was the manner in which the five-hundred-year anniversary of Dracula's death was celebrated in 1976. Throughout Romania eulogies and panegyrics were ordered by Communist Party members; monographs, novels, works of art, a film—even a commemorative stamp was issued—to praise the Impaler. A short footnote—which to this day has not been fully elucidated—adds to the mystery of the Ceausescu-Dracula relationship. On December 22, 1989, the late dictator and his wife, surrounded by an irate crowd shouting for their death, finally realized that his reign was over. Ceausescu ordered his helicopter pilot to fly from the rooftop of the headquarters of the beleaguered Central Committee of the Communist Party in Bucharest to the palace he had built at Snagov, a short distance from where, according to tradition, Dracula lay buried. Even more mysterious were the motivations of the late dictator to try to move the capital city from Bucharest to Tirgoviste, Dracula's capital in the fifteenth century. In the last stage of the Ceausescu drama, Ceausescu ordered his pilot to leave Snagov, and then to land the helicopter on the highway leading to Tirgoviste. After highjacking two cars (one ran out of gas), Ceausescu ordered the driver toward Tirgoviste, evidently seeking solace and support in Dracula's former capital. Finally, he was arrested by the army on the outskirts of the town and confined to barracks. Following a parody of a military trial, he and his wife were shot by soldiers not very far from Dracula's palace.

Was the real Dracula a vampire? Did the peasants of his time consider him associated with the forces of evil? What connection is there between the real prince and the vampire-count created by Bram Stoker? How did the name Dracula originate? What do Romanian peasants today believe about Vlad Tepes and vampires? And have we been dealing simply with history or are there mysteries here beyond the reach of historical research?

The Archbishop's Vampires

Francesco Paolo De Ceglia

The Archbishop's Vampires Giuseppe Davanzati's *Dissertation* and the Reaction of "Scientific" Italian Catholicism to the "Moravian Events"

Francesco Paolo de Ceglia[1]

Marcantonio:
La sacc'io na canzoncella
Che li muorte fa mori.

Asdrubale:
Per berlicco, e per berlocco,
Morto spurio, morto sciocco,
Le mie carni, ch'or mi tocco,
Non mangiarti a gran ribocco,
Ma va pasciti di stocco,
E funereo baccala.[2]

News from Moravia

"Finding myself one evening some years ago in Rome in private conversation with the late Cardinal Schrattenbach, Bishop of Olomouc [Olmütz], he told me, with much discretion, that he had received in the post, from his consistory in Olomouc, a detailed report in which those ministers informed him that the disease or bloodbath of vampires was spreading greatly throughout the province of Moravia, his diocese …"[3]

---

[1] I would like to thank Sara Donahue for her help in preparing the English version of this text; Robert Halleux, Irina Podgorny. Gianna Pomata, Alberto Postigliola, Fernando Vidal and the anonymous referees for their precious suggestions.
[2] Giuseppe Palomba. *I vampiri* (Naples: 1812), 8–9. This is an *opera buffa* inspired by Davanzati's *Dissertation*. The Neapolitan verses, actually impossible to translate, would sound more or less as follows in English: Marc.: " I know a little song/ That kills the dead." Asdr.: " Don't shilly-shally/ Fake dead, imprudent dead/ My flesh, which I touch now/ Don't eat in large quantities/ But swallow my sword/ Funereal dried salted cod."
[3] Giuseppe Davanzati, *Dissertazione sopra i vampiri* [1774; 1789], ed. Giacomo Annibaldis (Nardo,

The *DISSERTAZIONE SOPRA i vampiri* by Giuseppe Davanzati opens with these words. The author was the Archbishop of Trani, who took a stand, on the periphery of the Kingdom of Naples, both against ancient devotional practices, that were by that time judged to be superstitious,[4] and against the multiplication of the holy days of obligation, which, by distancing the poor peasants from the fields, at times caused them to go hungry.[5] Published posthumously in 1774, by his grand-nephew Domenico Forges Davanzati, and then in a second edition in 1789, the tract was written "when, upon the renewal of vampire sightings in Germany in 1739, to satisfy the curiosity of a few friends he decided to write a *Dissertation* on this phenomenon. Although the author had no desire to print anything, nevertheless his work was soon distributed in manuscript form, not only in Italy, but also on the other side of the mountains."[6] The booklet was fairly successful. If it is true, as Davanzati's grand-nephew maintains, that "Burman told a subject of our kingdom that he

---

1998), henceforward referred to as *Dissertation*, 19.
[4] Davanzati fought the tradition of a phallic procession, which took place during the carnival in 18th century Trani. Luciano Carcereci, "Il Carnevalce a Trani nel XVIII sccolo," *Lares*, 65 (1999), 275–282.
[5] Franco Venturi, *Settecento riformatore: Da Muratori a Beccaria* (Torino: 1969), 143–147, 383–385; Jean-Michel Salmann, "Davanzati, Giuseppe Antonio," in *Dizionario biografico degli italiani*, 33 (Rome: 1987), 109–112; Vincenzo Ferrone, *I profeti dell'Illuminismo: Le metamorfosi della ragione nel tardo Settecento italiano* (Rome-Bari: 1989), 29–34; Pietro Sisto, "La *Dissertazione sopra i vampiri* di Giuseppe Davanzati: Tra regolata devozione e magia nalurale," in *I fantasmi della ragione: l.etteratura scientifica in Puglia Ira Illuminismo e Restaurazione* (Fasano: 2002), 7–42. During the feasts of precept, which, for instance, in December amounted to half a month, peasants were not allowed to work.
[6] Domenico Forges Davanzati, "Vita di Giuseppe Davanzati arcivescovo di Trani," in *Dissertation*. 139. We do not know why the book was not published earlier. According to some authors, the *Dissertation* contained a too open criticism to Schrattenbach and Northern prelates, nevertheless it is important to point out that, during his life, Davanzati did not publish any of his writings: *Lettera sopra la riforma delle feste; Dissertazione sopra i vampiri; Dissertazione sulle comete; Dissertazione sulta tarantula in Puglia.*

Francesco Paolo De Ceglia, "Bishop's Vampires," *Archives Internationales D'Hostoire Des Sciences*, vol. 61, no. 166–167, pp. 487–510. Copyright © 2011 by Brepols Publishers. Reprinted with permission.

had never read anything better on this topic", the manuscript must have had quite a rapid (although not widespread) circulation in order to have reached Holland before March 31, 1741, the date of the death of the Dutch classical scholar Pieter Burman (the Elder).[7]

The history of vampirism, which is too complex to be examined even in its most general characteristics in this article, certainly did not begin with the events in the Moravian diocese of Olomouc on which Davanzati, in truth, did not enter into details. Fortunately, we can reconstruct the facts from the words of Gerhard van Swieten, personal physician of the Austrian Empress Maria Theresa:[8]

> "In the year 1723 they burned the body of a man thirteen days after his death, and in the sentence alleged that the reason was that his grandmother had not lived in good repute in the community. In 1724 they burned the corpse of a man eighteenth days after death, because he was a relative of the person mentioned previously. It was enough to be related to a supposed vampire, and the trial became good and final. Thus, they burned the body of a man two days after his death for this very reason, without other testimony, that the corpse retained a good complexion after death, and joints were still flexible.... On April 23, 1723 [*sic*, in truth 1731] the Concistory of Olmouc caused nine corpses to be burned, amongst them seven of little children, since it was believed they had been infected by a vampire buried before them in the same cemetery."[9]

The "Moravian diocese" had therefore repeatedly been subject to surges of fear linked to the "return of the dead." Moreover, it had been the site of the publication of the book responsible for lighting the fuse of the debate in Western Europe in the 1700s. Indeed in 1704, before Schrattenbach's appointment, the Catholic jurist Carl Ferdinand von Schertz had published *Magia posthuma*, in which he expressed perplexity, particularly regarding its legality, about the practice of exhuming cadavers suspected of vampirism and burning them so as to destroy not only their mortal remains, often found unspoiled, but also the evil

---

7 Franco Venturi, cit., 384. Nevertheless, none of the authors who addressed this issue prior to the publication of the *Dissertation* mentions Davanzati's name.

8 The "classic" era of vampirism lasted approximately 60 years, from the case of Jure Grando (1672) to the events in Medvegja (1731–32). Hypotheses on the origins of the belief can be classified in five macro-classes: 1) universal or prehistoric genesis; 2) shamanistic; 3) oriental; 4) ancient or medieval European; 5) modern or of the Enlightenment. There is a vast quantity of literature available on the topic. For a brief overview, see Augustus Montague Summers, *The Vampire: His Kith and Kin* (London: 1928) and *The Vampire in Europe* (London: 1929); Tony Faivre, *Les vampires: Essai historique, critique et litteraire* (Paris: 1962); Paul Barber, *Vampires, Burial, and Death: Folklore and Reality* (New Haven-London: 1988); Klaus Hamberger, *Mortuus non mordet: Dokumente zum Vampirismus, 1689–1791* (Wien: 1992); *Les vampires*. Colloque de Cérisy (Paris: 1993); J. Gordon Melton, *The Vampire Hook: The Encyclopaedia of the Undead* (Detroit: 1994); Massimo Introvigne, *La stirpe di Dracula: Indagine sul vampirismo dall'antichita ai nostri giorni* (Milan: 1997); Claude Lecouteux, *Histoire des vampires: Autopsie d'un mythe* (Paris: 2009); Erik Butler, *Metamorphoses of the Vampire in Literature and Film: Cultural Transformations in Europe. 1732–1933* (Rochester, NY: 2010).

9 Gerhard van Swieten, *Considerazione intorno alla pretesa magia postuma*, Italian transl. by Giuseppe Valeriano Vannetti [1787], ed. Piero Violante (Palermo: 1988), 15–16. This report, originally written in French in 1755, was immediately translated into both German and Italian. Following its publication, Maria Theresa is said to have hurriedly issued a decree on vampires on March 1, 1755 and another on superstition and magic on August 6, 1756. The decrees were published in Constantin Franz von Kauz, *De cultibus magicis ...* (Vienna: 1767), 371–376. For more information on the topic, see Gabor Klaniczay, "Decline of Witches and Rise of Vampires in 18th Century Habsburg Monarchy," *Ethnologia Europaea*, 17 (1987), 165–180. The Prussian Society of Sciences also addressed the issue. On March 11, 1732 it published *Gutachten ... von denen Vampyren oder Blutaussagern*. The text can now be read in Klaus Hamberger, cit., 111–114.

influence that they wielded on the area in which they were buried.[10] Schertz, who frequently referred to manuals of Jesuit scholarship, such as *Loca infesta* by Peter Thyraeus and, above all, *Disquisitionum magicarum libri sex* by Martin Del Rio (which had substituted the inveterate *Malleus maleficarum* of the Dominican tradition in resolving demonological controversies),[11] expressed philosophical and theological uncertainties too. At times he superimposed, as was frequently done by others thereafter, what he was trying to explain onto the more well-known phenomenon of incubuses and succubuses, who, like vampires, tormented the wretched by "squeezing their chests and throats almost to the point of suffocating them."[12]

Almost thirty years had passed since the publication of *Magia posthuma*, during which time an assortment of interpretive hypotheses had accumulated, although none of them had shed much light on the matter.[13] The phenomenon had not died down, on the contrary, it had assumed almost epidemic proportions, causing the authorities to be concerned about issues of public health and law and order.[14] In the two capitals, Vienna and Rome, one political and the other religious, fast action was needed, since it was a widespread belief that, as van Swieten said, "vampirism ... is as contagious as scabies; because it is believed that a vampire cadaver will quickly infect all other bodies buried in the same cemetery."[15] Davanzati described how vampires presented themselves at the homes of family and friends, speaking, eating and spending time with them. It was not clear how, but it was believed that they sucked their relatives' blood—"upir" in some Slavonic languages means indeed "blood sucker"[16]—causing them to die and then become vampires themselves, in this way "spreading this misfortune among the populace a bit like the plague; sepulchres and cemeteries were full of vampires, while the aforementioned provinces had lost almost all of their inhabitants, some were dead, some had run away."[17]

Considering the embarrassed silence of the Church of Rome on the topic,[18] the only solution available to the local populace was to appeal to the civil authorities:

> "The public officials of these [courts], after having gathered precise information and holding a trial, issued a final sentence against the aforementioned vampire, in which it was solemnly and with all legal formalities decreed that the public executioner should go to the site where the vampire was buried, open the sepulchre and, with a sabre or wide sword, in the presence of the entire population, cut off the vampire's head, then with a spear open its chest and with the same spear pierce its heart from one side to the other, ripping it out, and, finally, close the tomb."[19]

What interpretation of the facts did the *Dissertation* propose? Some years later, the

---

10 In 1693 the Sorbonne had already expressed the opinion that the practice was illicit. Dom Augustin Calmet, *Traite stir les apparitions des esprits, et sur les vampires, ou les revenans de Hongrie, de Moravie, etc.* [1746], 2 (Paris: 1751), henceforth referred to as *Traite*, 307–315.

11 Peter Thyraeus, *Loca infesta ...* (Köln: 1598); Martin Del Rio, *Disquisitionum magicarum libri sex* (Louvain: 1599–1600).

12 Carl Ferdinand von Schertz, *Magia posthuma ...* (Olomouc: n.d.), A3 verso. The date is missing from the frontispiece, and sources usually date the book to 1706. Nonetheless, the imprimatur date in the back of the volume is 1704.

13 A highly useful bibliography of works on vampirism between 1679 and 1807 can be found Tony Faivre's *Du vampire villageois aux discours des clercs,* in *Les vampires,* cit., 61–74.

14 A list of the most famous eases and the various positions on the issue can be found in "Vampyren oder Blutsauger," in *Grosses vollständige Universal-Lexicon aller Wissenschaften und Künste,* ed. Johann Heinrich Zedler, 46 (Halle-Leipzig: 1745), 474–482.

---

15 Gerhard van Swieten, cit.,12.
16 Katharina M. Wilson, "The History of the Word Vampire," *Journal of the History of Ideas,* 46 (1985), 577–583.
17 *Dissertation*, 19.
18 *Traite*, 32.
19 *Dissertation*, 20.

French Benedictine Dom Augustin Calmet, speaking of the argumentation strategies used by Jean-Baptiste de Boyer, an opponent of the Catholic Church and the author of the *Lettres juives* (a text which was also well-known to Davanzati), would identify two ways to annihilate or at least to tame the belief in vampires: either tracing them back to natural phenomena or negating the truthfulness of the stories about them. In his opinion, the latter would be preferable.[20] Although Calmet did not know it, the Archbishop of Trani had followed this same two-pronged approach.

Against the Devil

Davanzati was a man of that Catholic *Aufklärung* which, shaking off the visionary excesses of Baroque mysticism, was responsible for the classics of the Italian "anti-superstitious" school of thought.[21] Concentrating, above all, on the theme of witches and celestial apparitions, these publications were circumscribing the space that, until that time, had been conceded, above all, to the action of the Devil, but in part to God as well, in this way drastically reducing the group of phenomena that tradition had considered preter- and supernatural.[22] The imperative was to explain the phenomena through the laws of nature, without unnecessarily involving the Devil, as had, instead, been done until just a few decades prior.[23] Actually Prospero Lambertini's *De servorum Dei beatificatione el sanctorum canonizatione*, on the beatification of the servants of God and on canonization of the blessed, was only the culmination and the synthesis of a process which had already begun in the 1670s–80s, when, for example, Cardinals Lorenzo Brancati and Giovanni Bona had begun to work on creating a rational foundation to the *discretio spirituum*, that is the science of distinguishing good spirits from evil ones or, in other terms, the signs of holiness from those of diabolical possession or simple folly.[24] After 1710, with the anti-Spanish turn of sentiment, first pro-French then pro-Austrian, witchcraft and possession, especially in a group, such as in the case of the "possessed" Ursuline nuns in Loudun, seemed to be subjects so outdated that the Holy Office condemned an entire series of manuals for exorcists.[25]

Davanzati, not afraid to include in his writings a long and uninhibited paean to Galileo (who was still officially a reprobate in the eyes of the Catholic Church),[26] claimed to believe in the invariability of the laws of nature, which convinced him that all that took place in his day and age could not be so different from what had happened in the past. Therefore, should vampires truly exist, they could not be anything particularly new. This led him to reinterpret their image in better known terms, comparing them to ghosts or even, reducing their dramatic force, to the more familiar *monaci* and *monacelle*, domestic elves common to the nocturnal

---

20 *Traite*, 46. The reference is to Jean-Baptiste de Boyer, Marquis d'Argens, *Lettres juives* … [1736] (La Haye: 1738), § 137. The letter is not included in the first edition.
21 Mario Rosa, "L'Aufklärung cattolica," in *Settecento religioso: Politico delta ragione e religione del cuore* (Venice: 1999), 149–184.
22 Luciano Parinetto, *Magia e ragione: Una polemica sulle streghe in Italia intorno al 1750* (Florence: 1974); Nadia Minerva, *II diavolo. Eclissi e metamorfosi nel secolo dei Lumi: Da Asmodeo a Belzebu* (Ravenna: 1990); Fernando Vidal, "Extraordinary Bodies and the Physicotheological Imagination," in *The Faces of Nature in Enlightenment Europe*, eds. Gianna Pomata and Lorraine Daston (Berlin: 2003), 61–96.
23 David Gentilcore, *Heaters and Healing in Early Modern Italy* (Manchester: 1998): 156–188.
24 Lorenzo Brancati, *Commentaria … in tertium librum sententiarum … tomus secundus … de virtuibus in genere …* (Rome: 1668); Giovanni Bona, *De discretione spirituum …* (Rome: 1672). For information on the *discretio spirituum* see Anne Jacobson Schutte, *Aspiring Saints: Pretense of Holiness, Inquisition and Gender in the Republic of Venice 1618–1750* (Baltimore-London: 2001).
25 Elena Brambilla, *Corpi invasi e viaggi dell'anima: Santita, possessione, esorcismo dalla teologia barocca alla medicina illuministica* (Rome: 2010), 123–186.
26 *Dissertation*, 49. In 1757, Benedict XIV is said to have had the books that sustained the movement of the Earth removed from the *Index librorum prohibltorum*, except for *De revolutionists* and *Dialogo sopra i due massimi sistemi del mondo*, which remained until 1835.

mythology of Southern Italy.[27] In truth, the identification of vampires with ghosts was bold from a theological point of view: the Moravian undead, as *revenans en corps*, namely creatures with a body, had a nature quite different from the merely spiritual one which the tradition accorded to ghosts, so much so that some believed they were the result of a sort of resurrection. Therefore, Davanzati accepted this identification, but only for heuristic ends. Once it was demonstrated that it was impossible for ghosts to carry out evil acts, it was then possible to derive the nonexistence of vampires, by definition bearers of misfortune and death.

This was not simply a refreshing gust of rationalism. Since the period of the Council of Trent, discussions on ghosts had assumed a strategic political importance. For the papists, ghosts were souls from Purgatory, the third realm of the afterlife, which for the Protestants—and, with some fluctuations, for the members of the Orthodox Church—was merely a Catholic invention. The Holy Roman Church's argument, which at times slid into true *petitio principii*, was in short the following: the existence of ghosts proves the existence of Purgatory and Purgatory gives credit to Catholicism over other faiths which do not accept it.[28] Therefore, the involvement of ghosts, although only temporary, was not a coincidence, but rather a method for reaffirming the "Catholic way" of dealing with the issue. Moreover, through ghosts, who were souls temporarily freed by God but still under his jurisdiction, Catholics indirectly undermined the Devil's capacity for intervention.[29]

For Protestants, spirits, if not the fruit of an overly lively imagination, could only come from Heaven or Hell and, therefore, only be either angels or demons. This rendered moot the distinction, which was instead fundamental in Rome, between *stricto sensu* ghosts (souls from Purgatory) and apparitions (Christ, the Madonna and the saints, angels and demons).[30] Vampires certainly could not be angelic visions, and, so, had to be the result of action by the Devil, who, in this way, was strengthened and endowed with an uncommon ability to influence reality. Davanzati could not allow this ...

For example, the physician Johann Wilhelm Nöbling, who had written his doctoral dissertation under the guidance of Johann Christoph Stock, and, after him, the Pietist theologian Egidius Günther Hellmund, had interpreted vampires as incubuses and succubuses, whose existence Davanzati rejected.[31] The physician hiding behind the acronym W.S.G.E. had attributed the phenomenon to a demonic operation carried out with the aid of wizards and witches, who, according to the *Dissertation*, "should be laughed at and mocked."[32] Finally, the Pietist theologian and historian Johann Heinrich Zopf had spoken of God unleashing an unfathomable decree of punishment on the inhabitants of the villages involved.[33] The Archbishop of Trani,

---

27 *Dissertation*, 25–31. The monacello (or munaciello) was a mischievous spirit, not necessarily wicked, whose presence was even interpreted as a good omen at times. Matilde Serao. *Leggende napoletane* [1881] (Naples: 2004), 119.
28 Ronald C. Finucane, *Appearances of the Dead: A Cultural History of Ghosts* (Buffalo: 1984); Fernando Vidal, "Ghosts, the Economy of Religion, and the Laws of Princes. Dom Calmet's *Treatise on the Apparitions of Spirits*," in *Gespenster und Politik. 16. bis 21. Jahrhundert*, eds. Claire Gantet and Fabrice d'Almeida (Munich: 2007), 103–126.
29 Gabrieila Zarri, "Purgatorio particolare e ritorno dei morti tra Riforma e Controriforma: L'area italiana," *Quaderni storici* 17 (1982), 466–497.

30 However, it has been demonstrated that Protestant and Catholic demonology cannot always be completely distinguished. Stuart Clark, "Protestant Demonology: Sin, Superstition, and Society (c.1520–c. 1630)," in *Early Modern European Witchcraft: Centres and Peripheries*, eds. Bengt Ankarloo and Gustav Henningsen (Oxford: 1990), 179–215.
31 Johann Christoph Stock, *Dissertatio physica de cadaveribus sanguisugis ...* (Jena: 1732); Egidius Günther Hellmund, *Judicium necrophagiae ....* in *Unerkannte Gerichte Gottes* (Idstein: 1737); cfr. *Dissertation*, 82. Instead, Prospero Lambertini accepted the existence of incubuses and succubuses. *Creder tutto. creder nulla: Il "Notae de miraculis"...* ed. Emidio Alessandrini (Assisi: 1995), C1V-CV, 5 (74-75); *De servorum Dei beatificatione et beatorum canonizatione* [1734–1738], 4 (Prato: 1841), from this point on *De beatificatione*. Pars prima, § III, 24–38.
32 W.S.G.E., *Curieuse und sehr wunderbare Relation ...* (n.c.: 1732); cfr. *Dissertation*, 74.
33 Johann Heinrich Zopf, *Dissertatio de vampiris Serviensibus* (Duisburg: 1733); *Dissertatio*

when faced with arguments of this type, could have bowed down before the inscrutability of the divine plan and admitted the supernatural nature of this phenomenon. Instead he responded with a rhetorical doubt fraught with Enlightenment snobbishness:

> "If I were to permit myself to investigate the holy mysteries of divine Providence, I would say: why do these apparitions and tricks of the Devil only take place today in poor Moravia and northern Hungary, and not elsewhere in Spain, France and our Italy?[34]

Perhaps the belief in the excessive power of the Devil, especially in the marginal lands of the Catholic community, was the fault of a few priests who took advantage of this fear. Davanzati railed against the "preachers in the pulpits," who offended God by overestimating the Devil. After all, the Archbishop was not afraid of self-criticism. Even in his *Lettera sopra la riforma delle feste*, a letter on the reform of holy days, he did not refrain from putting forth proposals (for instance, a reduction in the feasts of precept), which, if approved, would have lessened his power and that of his colleagues.[35] Similarly, during the same time period, Benedict XIV rebuked the Archbishop of the Greek rite in Lviv, who gave too much credit to the vampire phenomenon:

> "Perhaps it is the great freedom in Poland that gives you the right to stroll about after death. Here, I admit, the dead are as peaceful as they are silent … It is up to you, as the Archbishop, to eradicate these superstitions. You will discover, if you go to the source, that perhaps there are priests who corroborate them to compel the people, who are naturally credulous, to pay them for exorcisms and masses."[36]

The only way to defeat the Devil (and the Protestants with him) was to erode his powers. As a consequence, Davanzati, emphasizing what had been already said in a long theological tradition which had tried to circumscribe the prince of evil's powers within the limits of nature,[37] sustained with force a list of what the Devil was *not* allowed to do: 1) raising the dead; 2) transgressing natural laws; 3) changing people into beasts; 4) changing a "species" into another, for instance iron into gold or water into wine; 5) making "therapeutic miracles," such as restoring sight to one born blind or reattaching an amputated leg; 6) being everywhere, but only in a circumscribed and specific place; 7) knowing the future; 8) making people ill and acting on the forces of nature (winds, currents etc.); 9) appearing under the form of incubuses and succubuses, which did not exist.[38]

Apparitions caused by the Devil, if they had been admitted, could have been "gratuitous," that is, creations which only served to harm or tease mankind. That "poor" fallen angel was nevertheless so weak and incapable of doing anything without the permission of God! His apparitions were therefore not acknowledged by Davanzati, except in a few cases. On the other hand, ghosts left Purgatory and visited their families in order to communicate a warning or make a request for a mass. Their action was meant to be a tool for converting or uplifting the living. Was it rightful for a theologian

---

physico-theologica de eo quod iustum est circa cruentationem cadaverum (Duisburg : 1737).
34 *Dissertation*, 61. Even Voltaire, in the entry "Vampires" in his *Dictionnaire philosophique* (Paris: 1764) adopted the peripheral nature of the events as a proof of their scarce credibility.
35 *Dissertation*, 88. Also see Giseppe Davanzati, *Lettera sopra la riforma delle feste* [1742] (Naples: 1774). For a comparison with Ludovico Antonio Muratori's statements see Pietro Sisto, cit., 10–21.

36 Louis Antoine Caraccioli, *La vie du Pape Benoit XIV* (Paris: 1783), 192–193.
37 For instance, even the anything but moderate Henrich Kramer (and Jacob Sprenger), *Malleus maleficarum* (Strasbourg: 1487); F.ngl. transl. *The Malleus Maleficarum*, ed. by Montague Summers (London: 1928), Pars secunda, Quaestio I, Caput IX, 126.
38 *Dissertation*, 73–85.

to identify them with the never seen before *revenans en corps*? The answer was negative: vampires had completely different (evil) aims, so they simply could not be ghosts. Here Davanzati both abundantly and freely quoted Augustine, the cautious founder of the Christian doctrine of the spirits, who had judged dealings between the living and the dead to be impossible except through the mediation of God, therefore of the Church, which proposed itself as guarantor of this relationship.[39]

The strategy followed by Davanzati, much drier, more debonair and, above all, less gullible than Calmet, was, in brief, the following: 1) first of all, he "rationally"—that is, without making recourse to the authority of the conciliar decrees—minimised the Devil's actual ability to influence nature and people, being nonetheless careful not to slip into the Pyrrhonism of Pierre Bayle or the radical Cartesianism of Balthasar Bekker. 2) The operation succeeded in temporarily identifying the vampire-ghosts as souls from Purgatory. Someone had already noticed that the belief in vampires prospered mostly in areas where the existence of the third realm of the afterlife was denied.[40] Moreover, like souls from Purgatory, vampires could be interpreted as an intermediate state between saved and damned souls.[41] It was nonetheless inexpedient to go on with this identification, dangerous from a theological point of view. 3) At this point, it was only necessary to prove that these apparitions had no goals of spiritual elevation to set aside their supernatural origin. 4) Once all this was done, the last obstacle to overcome was the naturalistic interpretation of the phenomenon:

> "Anyone with a little common sense, so to speak, can clearly realise that the Devil plays no role in a story like that of these vampires; it is all a human creation, or at most a sort of tiresome illness, such as the plague, or some other epidemic disease."[42]

Is a Corpse Still Alive?

Having contained, and perhaps even negated, any possible intervention by the Devil, whose power is "very rare and limited,"[43] Davanzati scrutinised with some interest the belief that the body, even after the passing of the soul, could maintain an intimate vitality. With death, according to Cartesian philosophy, the life of a *man* would end, but not necessarily that of the *body* itself.[44] Many texts contained evidence that proved this, or that at least, though with some strain, seemed to lend credence to this interpretation. Most of them were cited by Davanzati, starting with *De miraculis mortuorum* by the Lutheran physician Christian Friedrich Garmann, member of the Leopoldina Academy of Sciences. This huge volume, based on an vast collection of sources, mostly scholarly, and with a solid philosophical structure, asserted itself as the uncontested scientific guide

---

39 *Dissertation*, 51–54; For information about Augustine as founder of the doctrine of the spirits, see Jean-Claude Schmitt, *Les revenants: Les vivants et les morts dans la societe medievale* (Paris: 1994), 31–40. Latin quotations supposed to be from *The City of God* are abundant in the *Dissertation*, nevertheless I was not able to locate them in the work by Augustine
40 Leo Allatios, with the same type of strained logic, had already found an analogy between the Greek *tympanaioi* and souls from Purgatory. Leo Allatios, *De utriusque ecclesiae occidentalis atque orientalis perpetua in dogmate de Purgatorio consensione* (Rome: 1655), 41–42. In Protestant circles there emerged a debate on the economic advantages, for example of the masses for dead souls, that the doctrine of Purgatory had for the Church of Rome. Ludwig Lavater, *De spectris, lemuribus et magnis atque insolitis fragoribus ...* [1570] (Leyden: 1659), 111–124.
41 Massimo Introvigne, "Antoine Faivre: Father of Contemporary Vampire Studies," *Esoterisme, Gnoses et Imaginaire Symholique: Melanges offerts a Antoine Faivre*, eds. by Richard Caron, Joscelyn Godwin, Wouter J. Hancegraaff and Jean-Louis Veillard-Baron (Leuven: 2001), 595–610.
42 *Dissertation*, 67.
43 *Dissertation*, 88.
44 In the medical field, Theodor Craanen, in his *Tractatus physico-medicus de homine* (Leyden: 1689), developed the "schism" between soul and life opened by Descartes in *Les passions de l'ame*.

in the "naturalistic" section of the *Dissertation*.[45] White sweats, eyes that opened after having been closed, blood losses, changes in appearance, unpleasant odours, will-o'-the-wisps, the incorruptibility of the cadaver or its movements inside and outside the grave: these were all presented as phenomena *also* attributable to natural causes, which Davanzati, however, in most cases limited himself to hypothesising on, or even, without supplying too many details, to postulating, perhaps because he was not particularly expert in the field of (post-mortem) physiology.

Apart from the role played by Cartesian philosophy, the belief, which existed at the same time on both folkloric and learned levels, that there was a sort of "physiological continuity" between life and death was ancient and widespread. It could even be defined as typical of the cultural *koine* shared by people living in the lands of Central and Eastern Europe.[46] As the Spanish Benedictine Benito Jerónimo Feijoo deliberated, "the inhabitants of those provinces describe these resurrections as factual and real and do not consider them to be miraculous. They do not imagine that [the resurrections] are the work of God, as a supernatural Creator, but the result of natural causes."[47] On the other hand, Garmann was only the epigone of a long tradition, which counted amongst its most illustrious representatives the Protestant jurist Heinrich Kornmann, whose handbook, a very uncritical compilation of *miracula*, was referred to by everyone in the debate on vampirism.[48]

However, even in so-called Latin Europe, "continuist" thought had gained some credence, particularly in the context of the natural philosophy of the Italian Renaissance. Girolamo Cardano and Tommaso Campanella had, for example, interpreted the growth of cadavers' fingernails in these terms.[49] Nevertheless, the Tridentine policy had been severe with them and reaffirmed with Tertullian that "if death does not arrive wholly as a single event, it is not death. If some element of the soul remains, it is life: death mixes with life no more than the night with the day."[50] The resolve with which the Catholic Church imposed the personal soul of divine origin as man's one and only life principle prevented the body from having any independent vitality.[51] The limited dissemination on the Italian peninsula of Paracelsianism and Helmontianism (the latter was more

---

45 The reference edition is the posthumous one, in three books of over 1,200 pages, excluding the indexes: Christian Friedrich Garmann, *De miraculis mortuorum* (Dresden and Leipzig: 1709). The work, at the time quite popular, but almost unknown today, is a monumental encyclopaedia of post mortem phenomena. There is a German translation of the shorter 1670 edition, just over 100 pages, edited by Silvio Benetello and Bernd Herrmann (Gottingen: 2003).
46 Aristotelis, *De invent.*, IV, 469b; XV, 475a; XXIII, 479a; Lynn Thorndike, *A History of Magic and Experimental Science*, 7 (New York: 1958), 238–39; 278–280; Claudio Milanesi, *Morte apparente e morte intermedia: Medicina e mentalita net dibattito sull'incertezza dei segni della morte (1740–1789)* (Rome: 1989): 67–92; Katharine Park, "The Life of the Corpse: Division and Dissection in Late Medieval Europe," *Journal of the History of Medicine and Allied Sciences*, 50 (1995), 111–132.
47 Benito Jeronimo Feijoo y Montenegro, *Cartas eruditas y curiosas ... 4* [1753] (Madrid: 1770), Carta 20, § 30, 245.
48 The 1670 edition of Garmann's *De miraculis mortuorum* was added to the *Index* with a decree dated December 6, 1678. Kornmann had also written a *De miraculis mortuorum* (Frankfurt: 1610), which, however, was never formally condemned by the Church of Rome, unlike his *Sybilla Trig-Andriana seu de virginitate ...* (Frankfurt: 1610), included in the *Index* with a decree dated March 16, 1620.
49 Girolamo Cardano, *In librum Hippocratis de alimento commentaria ...* (Rome: 1574), 6, § 54, 552; Tommaso Campanella, *De sensu rerum et magia* (Frankfurt: 1620), 4, § 9, 297–298; § 14, 325.
50 The classic reference to Tertullian is from *De anima*, 51b. Cardano's writings (not medical texts, to tell the truth) were forbidden by the Tridentine *Index* of 1564; Campanella's with a decree dated April 21, 1632.
51 The differences between Catholics and Protestants regarding the body's possibility to have independent vitality also emerged a few centuries later in the context of the 18th–19th century controversy over apparent death. G Rüve, *Scheinlod. Zur kulturellen Bedeutung der Schwelle zwischen Leben und Tod um 1800* (Bielefeld: 2008), 168–210; Francesco P. de Ceglia, "Sepolti vivi! Discussioni ottocentesche sulla morte apparente," *S-nodi pubblici e privati nella storia contemporanea*, 6 (2010), 15–42.

suspect than has commonly been believed)[52] did the rest, limiting the Italians' "thanatological" interests above all to the practice of embalming.[53] Therefore if a body showed a postmortem vitality, this had to be ascribed to a transcendent cause.[54]

Certainly, outside Italy (and the Catholic world) not everyone interpreted postmortem phenomena in natural terms[55] Moreover, the 18th century vampire entertains a clear evolutionary link, on the one hand, with the *Nachzehrer*, the dead which chews on its own shroud in the tomb causing misfortune in local communities[56], on the other, with the *vrykolakas* and, above all, with the less-known *tympaniaios*, that is the deceased who remains incorrupt as a result of having been excommunicated. The latter two were often combined into a single figure, which had caused a great stir in Western Europe through the writings of Leo Allatios and Joseph Pitton de Tournefor.[57] Nevertheless, in the previous century, also as a result of the spread of Paracelsianism, Helmontianism and a renewed magicism of vague Cartesian ancestry, there had been in Central and Eastern Europe an increase in interpretations based on sympathies, astral emanations, spirits, *archei* and general vital principles. The pervasiveness in these same areas on all levels of a fierce demonological culture had not been an obstacle. On the contrary, thanks to this background, post-mortem phenomena had been noted, accepted and investigated: it had only been their interpretation that had needed to be partially changed. Demonology—anything but a thing of the past, mind you—[58] had in other terms supplied knowledge and sensibility toward that type of phenomena; as a result of it, there would soon be "scientific" studies of *miracula mortuorum*.[59]

The Evangelical scholar Michael Ranft was renowned among those who proposed a natural-magic interpretation.[60] He was the

---

52 Robert Halleux, "Le proces d'inquisition du chimiste Jean Baptiste Van Helmont (1578–1644): Les enjeux et les arguments," *Comptes-rendus des seances de l'Academie des Inscriptions et Belles-Lettres*, 2 (2004), 1059–1086.
53 Silvia Marinozzi and Gino Fornaciari, *Le mummie e l'arte medica nell'evo moderno* (Rome: 2005), 23–74.
54 Per Binde, *Bodies of Vital Matter: Notions of Life Force and Transcendence in Traditional Southern Italy* (Goteborg: 1999), 114–143.
55 A famous example of a demonological interpretation of post mortem phenomena is found in Philipp Rohr's *Dissertatio historico-philosophica de masticatione mortuorum* (Leipzig: 1679).
56 Thomas Schürmann, *Nachzehrerglauben in Mitteleuropa* (Marburg: 1990); *Elle mangeait son linceul: Fantomes, revenants. vampires et esprits frappeurs.* ed. Claude Lecouteux (Paris: 2006), 183–199. Calmet labelled chewing by cadavers a "childish imagination." *Traite*, 215.
57 Leo Allatios, *De Graecorum hodie quorundam opinationibus* (Koln: 1645), §§ XIV–XVIII, 149–158; Joseph Pitton de Tournefort, *A Voyage into the Levant* [1717], English transl., 3 vols. (London: 1741) 1, 103–107; *Traite*, 122–139 ; Karen Hartnup, "*On the Beliefs of the Greeks": Leo Allatios and Popular Orthodoxy* (Leiden-Boston: 2004), 173–236. Davanzati had met Tournefort personally. Domenico Forges Davanzati, cit., 144. On the relations between vampires and werewolves see Carla Corradi Musi, *Vampiri europei e vampiri dell'aria sciamanica (*Soveria Mannelli: 1995), 63–165.
58 Christoph Friedrich Demelius, *Philosophischer Versuch …* (n.c.: 1732); Johann Conrad Dippel, "Der Todten Essen und Trinken," in *Geistliche Fama*, 8 (1732), 22 and fol.; Gottlob Heinrich Vogt, *Kurtzes Bedenken von denen Actenmassigen Relationen wegen derer Vampiren …* (Leipzig: 1732), 2 pts.
59 Stuart Clark, *Thinking with Demons: the Idea of Witchcraft in Early Modern Europe* (Oxford: 1997). The theologisation of medicine, which asserted itself above all in Italy at the end of the 16th century, made it possible for many physicians—like Scipione Mercurio, Giovan Battista Codronchi, Paolo Zacchia and Pietro Piperno—not infrequently to attribute the origin of disease to the Devil. However, I have found no evidence that either they or theologians and/or exorcists—from Girolamo Menghi to Candido Brugnoli—concerned themselves with questions related to the Devil having an effect on dead bodies.
60 In some eases a sort of *reductio ad naturam* was created, capable of medicalising the calamity that had struck the local peoples. Peter Mario Kreuter, *Vom "üblen Geist" zum "Vampier": Die Darstellung des Vampirs in den Berichten osterreichischer Militarazte zwischen 1725 und 1756*, in *Poetische Widerganger*, eds. Julia Bertschik and Christa Agnes Tuczay (Tubingen: 2005), 113–129; Daniel Arlaud, *Vampire, Aufklarung und Staat: Eine militarmedizinische Mission in Ungarn, 1755–1756*, in *Gespenster und Politik*, cit., 127–141.

author of the Latin dissertation *De masticatione mortuorum in tumulis*, printed in 1725, and then in a second edition in 1728. Expanded and exasperated in its interpretive choice, it was re-edited in German in 1734, after the events in Medvegja, with a title that significantly associated the chewing dead and vampires.[61] Matter, for Ranft, although he did not disdain some Cartesian influences, was intimately active, not mere extension. It was endowed with vegetative life and a sort of consciousness, strong enough to exert an influence from a distance. The cause of vampiric phenomena lay, consequently, in the imagination (understood not as a simple psychological faculty, but rather as an operative force, capable, even after death, of generating illness from a distance, through the transmission of spiritual images), the vegetative soul and the astral body: in natural causes, therefore, which, in his opinion, would not be recognised by the Catholics.[62] Indeed, in Ranft's opinion, they, unlike the Protestants, would never understand the naturalness of many of the phenomena, and would be forced to either reject them or judge them to be miraculous.[63]

The idea that cadavers were capable of taking some kind of action in their tombs that influenced the living, as already mentioned, had been a shared belief in this part of the world for centuries.[64] The "Latin" Europeans, nonetheless, began to be fully aware of this approach to the dead body only at the end of the 17th century. At this time the circulation, even on the international level, of publications belonging to what could be defined as proto-scientific and cultural journalism, brought the issue to public attention in periodicals such as *[Nouveau] Mercure galant* (1672–1724, and later *Mercure de France*), *Mercure historique et politique* (1686–1782) and *Glaneur historique* (1731–1733). An important role was played, above all, by *Commercium litterarium* (1731–1745) of Nuremberg, which featured 18 articles on the subject from March to September 1732, some of which would be cited by Benedict XIV himself.[65] The political situation also had an effect: the peace treaty of Passarowitz (1718) assigned parts of Serbia and Wallachia to Austria, which changed how ancient beliefs, now communicated to the capital city and the rest of Europe, were rationalised.

The Archbishop of Trani did not disdain the natural interpretation, which he constantly entertained in the *Dissertation*, even giving, in a few circumstances, the impression of leaning toward the hypothesis that vampirism was nothing more than an epidemic disease.[66] Suddenly, how-

---

61 Michael Ranft, *Dissertatio historico-critica de masticatione mortuorum in tumulis* (Leipzig: 1725, 1728); French transl. *De la mastication des morts dans leurs tombeaux*, ed. Danielle Sonnier (Grenoble: 1995); German augmented transl. *Tractat von dem Kauen und Schmatzen der Todten in Grabern, worin die wahre Beschaffenheit derer Hungarischen Vampyrs und Blut-Sauger gezeigt ...* (Leipzig: 1734). The events in the Serbian village of Medvegja concern the case of Arnold Paole and people who died from his "contagion." Surgeons were summoned from Belgrade: they inspected some buried bodies and found "unmistakable signs of vampirism." Word of their findings reached the Emperor, who ordered an inquiry. The new report, *Visum et repertum*, which confirmed the surgeons' first impressions, was sent to Vienna in 1732 and widely circulated throughout Europe.
62 Calmet was severe with the possibility to admit the astral body, because it was incompatible with the Catholic doctrine of the soul. *Traite*, 299–300.
63 For information on the political situation, see Mario Rosa, "Le chiese cristiane a meta secolo," in *Settecento religioso*, cit., 111–127. The entry in Zedler's *Lexicon* highlights the difference between the "Occidental" and "Oriental" points of view. "Vampyren oder Blutsauger," cit.

64 Philippe Aries, *The Hour of Our Death* [1977], English transl. by H. Weaver (New York: 1991), 357.
65 *De beatificatione*, Pars prima, § XXI, 241–242.
66 Many had already undertaken a medicalisation of the phenomenon. For Gottlob Heinrich Vogt a sort of poison caused vampirism. Gottlob Heinrich Vogt, cit. Again in Leipzig, which was the capital of the Central European debate, Johann Christoph Meinig, writing under the pseudonym Putoneus, and Johann Christoph Fritsch, who published his paper anonymously, blamed the bovine plague for everything. Eating infected meat was the cause of fevers and hallucinations, in his opinion. Meinig and Fritsch's hypotheses were then touched on and completed by Johann Christoph Harenberg (a disciple of Christian Wolff), who invited to carry out "scientific" autopsies on the bodies of presumed vampires. Putoneus, *Besondere Nachricht, von denen Vampyren* (Leipzig: 1732); Anon., *Muthmassliche Gedanken*

ever, he changed course, saying that "although the aforementioned system is approved by the experience of witnesses who are trustworthy, of doctrine and great authority; despite all of this, not being very sure, I have deliberated, if not on whether to disapprove of it as erroneous, at least not to embrace it as true ... "[67] The reader, guided with care through a reasoning based on the search for natural causes, was, in this way, suddenly invited, without an explicit reason, to abandon the path he had begun and to choose a new road, defined as being more simple. Why?

Problems of Incorruptibility

The epistemic status of the dead body may have played more than a minor role. During the controversy, Ranft introduced some irony:

> "They [the Catholics] set the non-putrefaction of the bodies among the miracles for confirming the authority of their orthodoxy and their religion. Do they not think that the bodies of saints remain immune from corruption? That is why they have acknowledged a number of saints so great that, if they wanted to celebrate them all, a millennium would barely be sufficient."[68]

The dispute was ancient and the Protestant mockery little more than a *topos*. However, the problem, observed the scholar and anti-Catholic controversialist Otto Graf zum Stein, was now renewed by the very discovery of these new unspoiled bodies.[69] The lack of putrefaction of the vampires' bodies could have been a parody set up by the Devil to mock the Roman beliefs regarding the incorruptibility of saints, added the already Johann Heinrich Zopf.[70] Because the Catholics, noted another anonymous polemicist, were even driven to canonise John of Nepomuk because they found his tongue intact, and then, did they not want to admit that the Devil could also act on cadavers, rendering them incorruptible?[71] In other terms, many asked, what difference was there between the body of a saint, a vampire or any other individual preserved naturally? The vampire question was, in this way, used to support anti-Catholic views, just as, for instance, the success of exorcism had been used to support the anti-Protestant point of view.[72]

Davanzati was working in a period in which the Roman Church was redefining its ambivalent relationship with uncorrupted bodies. To shed light on this phase, it may be useful to compare the canonisation manual used at the time of the "Moravian events," that is the *Novissimus de sanctorum canonizatione tractatus* by the Bishop Carlo Felice de Matta, from 1678, and the one which immediately followed, written at the time of a reconsideration of ancient certainties, *De servorum Dei beatiftcatione et sanctorum canonizatione* by Prospero Lambertini, from 1734–38. The chapter "De incorruptione" in the first handbook, gave credence to the most improbable tales, often taken from the compilation by Kornmann and vaguely rationalised in the light of the "Quaestio 34" of the *Elysius ... campus* by the Portuguese physician Gaspar de Los Reyes Franco. Certainly, there was approval and support for the possibility that a body could be

---

von denen Vampyren ... (Leipzig: 1732); Johann Christoph Harenberg, *Vernunftige und Christliche Gedanken über die Vampire ...* (Wolfenbüttel: 1733). Only in 1756 did Georg Tallar, in a medical report presented to the Austrian court of inquiry, point out how the soldiers who had arrived to guard the area, despite eating the same food as the locals and being exposed to the same environmental conditions, had not experienced vampirism. This report was not published until 1784. Georg Tallar, *Visum repertum anatomico-chirirgicum* (Vienna-Leipzig: 1784).
67 *Dissertation*, 94.
68 Ranft, cit., 72.

69 Otto Graf zum Stein, Unterredungen von dem Reiche der Geister (Leipzig: 1730).
70 Johann Heinrich Zopf, *Dissertatio de vampiris Serviensibus* (Duisburg: 1733); *Dissertatio physico-theologica de eo quod lustum est circa cruentationem cadaverum* (Duisburg: 1737).
71 W.S.G.E., cit., 22, 24, 30–31.
72 Daniel P. Walker. *Unclean Spirits: Possession and Exorcism in France and England in the Late Sixteenth and Early Seventeenth Centuries* (Philadelphia: 1981).

preserved by natural causes within conditions of magic and influxionism, typical of certain later Renaissance philosophies. These causes could be: environmental conditions, including the influence of the stars; the texture of the cadaver, at times too dry; a lightning bolt, which renders that which it strikes incorruptible; the "ratio dierum," because cadavers of people born on January 27 and 30, as well as February 13, do not decompose; the presence of a bronze nail driven into the flesh; the use of preserving spices and ointments, etc.[73]

It is worth paying attention to three aspects: 1) first of all, in continuity with what an eclectic tradition, medico-legal as well, affirmed, a certain importance was conceded to the role played by the Devil in the preservation of some cadavers; 2) despite a few premises to the contrary, the incorruption of the body, "above all, if soft and flexible," was still considered an important "indicium santitatis"; and 3) finally, even though not formally admitted, the possibility of autonomous activity on the part of the cadaver was at least considered, "moreover, Liévin Lemmens ... believes that the dead have a vegetative force [*vim vegetantem*] which makes hair, teeth and fingernails grow ... ,nevertheless, Gaspar de Los Reyes Franco ... demonstrates that it comes from the outflow [*effluxu*] of its own substance ... and Paolo Zacchia agrees with him."[74] To sum up: a) a holy body is soft and flexible; b) nevertheless, it is important to pay attention to the Devil's nasty jokes; c) as well as to the intimate vitality of the cadaver (whatever its origin may be). All three of these positions were scaled down by the new "regulated devotion" of the 18th century.[75]

The partial *reductio* of the Devil's role has already been discussed. Regarding the supernatural dimension of the incorruptibility of the holy body, the Roman Church had already been taking a cautious, although anything but renunciative, stand for some time. In 1678, the year of the publication of De Matta's manual, the Sacred Congregation of Rites had already established that the medical commission should not only evaluate the evidence adopted by the postulators, but also scrutinise the evidence provided by the *promotor fidei*.[76] This had conferred more importance to the voice of science, so that Caterina Vigri, better known as Saint Catherine of Bologna, had been canonised for two therapeutic miracles and not thanks to the striking incorruption of her body (which she was known for in most of Europe), that had instead been considered to be the result of natural desiccation.[77]

Lambertini, who conceded very little to actions by the Devil, abandoned, despite his "skeptical-saint-making," the "phenomenological" criteria of softness and flexibility.[78] Therefore, he anchored the semeiotics of incorruptibility to the ascertainment of heroic virtues, to which he attributed an importance that was previously unheard of.[79] As early as the Middle Ages, when

---

73 Carlo Felice de Matta, *Novissimus de sanctorum canonizatione tractatus* (Rome: 1678), Pars tertia, § XIV, 187–191. These were explicitly refused by Lambertini. *De beatificatione,* Pars prima, § XXX, 340.

74 Carlo Felice de Matta, cit., Pars tertia, § XIII, 193. The references are respectively: Lievin Lemmens, *De miraculis occultis naturae* (Antwerp: 1559), 2, § VI; Gaspar de Los Reyes Franco, *Elysius ... campus* (Brussels: 1661), Quaestio 33, § IX; Paolo Zacchia, *Quaestiones medico-legales* (Rome: 1621–51), 4, I, Quaestio 10, § XXXVII.

75 Mario Rosa, "Mistica visionaria e *regolata devozione*", in *Settecento religioso,* cit., 47–73.

76 Francesco Antonelli, *De inquisitione medico-legali super miraculis ...* (Rome: 1962), 75.

77 Gianna Pomata, "Malpighi and the Holy Body: Medical Experts and Miracolous Evidence in Seventeenth-century Italy," *Renaissance Studies,* 21 (2007), 568–586. Pomata clearly points out how the subject of medical investigation was the determination of the "mollities" of the body. Regardless of the official pronouncements of the Church, the incorruption of Catherine's body was considered miraculous by most everyone, to the point that the Protestants pointed to this belief as evidence of the Catholics' credulity. W.S.G.E., cit., 24.

78 *De beatificatione,* Pars prima, § XXXI, 355; § XXX, 340

79 For information on the heroic virtues, conceived of in part in answer to the Lutheran doctrine of justification by faith alone, see Alfred de Bonhome, "Heroicite des vertus," in *Dictionnaire de Spiritualite,*

miracles played a central and almost exclusive role in the canonisation process, Rome had begun to assume a prudent stance,[80] which, by the mid-17th century, in conjunction with the publication of the Augustinian monk Fortunato Scacchi's celebrated volume, had invested the criteria for ascertainment of virtues and the definition of that which could be considered "heroic."[81] With Lambertini, who opened the "De cadaverum incorruptione" section of his *vade mecum* with a reference to Scacchi, the critical attitude toward preter- and supernatural phenomena finally matured: miracles were no longer considered proof of heroic virtues, but a consequence thereof.

A Pope who even corresponded with Voltaire had to have been aware that times had changed. Relics that became smaller or lighter to allow them to be moved, the bodies of saints which blinded, crippled or even killed anyone who came near them without due respect or which had an ominous influence on the area in which they were buried until an object that had been taken from them was returned ... at this time these things were out of style: even Calmet had sensed this.[82] Therapeutic miracles were now defined as such on the basis of seven precise characteristics of extraordinariness and unexplainableness, which recognised in the event something that was phenomenologically different from ordinary recovery of health, be it spontaneous or induced. Clearly it was medical science which played a primary role in ascertaining this "otherness."[83]

Rebus sic stantibus, which was the role of theology? Aside from Canon Law, Lambertini tried to carve around the holy body a space relatively free from the influence of scientists, whose assertions were more debatable than they would have had lay people believe. Indeed, "incorruptibility occurs as an act of God by the infusion of a *natural* quality, thanks to which the cadavers are protected and immune from receiving extraneous qualities, as a result of which ... they are wont to rot." The limit of research carried out by means of the autopsy was that it was impossible to rule out that " since the cause was of the *natural* kind, the miracle of incorruptibility is no longer miraculous."[84] After the Church's ascertainment of the heroic virtues, it was science that, by classifying some healings as non-natural, de facto led them to be considered as miraculous. Juridically speaking, the alleged non-putrefaction underwent the same process, but, to quote Blaise Pascal, "the heart has reasons which reason knows nothing of." Incorruption, although judged by science (and law) to be natural, could nevertheless be considered as miraculous.[85] Theologically speaking, at least. Clearly, Lambertini had in his mind the already mentioned case of Saint Catherine of Bologna: her incorruption was purely natural for the physicians, therefore, on the basis of

---

ascetique et mystique, 7 (Paris: 1968), 337–343; Romeo De Maio, "L'ideale eroico nei processi di canonizzazione della Controriforma," *Ricerche di storia sociale e religiosa,* (July–December 1972), 139–160. For information on Lambertini's role in the evolution of the process of canonisation, see Fernando Vidal, "Miracles, Science, and Testimony in Post-Tridentine Saint-Making," *Science in Context,* 20 (2007), 481–508. Lambertini begins the chapter "De cadaverum incorruptione" with a remark on heroic virtues. *De beatificatione,* Pars prima, § XXX, 336.

80 Andre Vauchez, *La saintete en Occident aux derniers siecles du Moyen Age: d'apres les proces de canonisation et les documents hagiographiques* (Rome: 1988), 510–520.

81 Fortunato Scacchi, *De cultu et veneratione servorum Dei* (Rome: 1639), 117–275.

82 Carlo Dogheria, *Santi e vampiri: Le avventure del cadavere* (Viterbo: 2006). For Calmet's opinion, see *Traite,* VII–VIII.

83 It is necessary: 1) for the disease to be serious, incurable or difficult to treat; 2) that the patient not be in a stage from which it is possible to recover spontaneously; 3) that no treatment has been attempted or, if attempted, that the fact that it has not taken effect is ascertained; 4) that healing be sudden and instantaneous; 5) that it be perfect, not flawed or partial; 6) that it has not been preceded by excretions or attacks; 7) that the disease healed never return. *De beatificatione,* Pars prima, § VIII, 88–106.

84 *De beatificatione,* Pars prima, § XXX, 351 (italics mine).

85 Relations between physicians and judges in Italian courts were often strained. Alessandro Pastore, *Il medico in tribunal: La perizia medico nella procedura penale d'antico regime (secoli XVI–XVIII)* (Bellinzona: 1998).

the rules approved in 1678, for the Sacred Congregation of Rites; nonetheless it was (unofficially) miraculous for the community of the Catholic faithful and ... the Protestants.[86] Belief was not, in other terms, a matter of science.[87]

What were the consequences for the probative strength of incorruption? The preservation of the holy body, which had traditionally been *the* miracle and, somehow, which would never completely let go of that honour,[88] became *a* miracle and moreover *sui generis*, "even more so because the bodies of saints that have decayed are much more numerous than those which have remained incorrupt."[89] Whilst a scientific truth was valid, at least theoretically, *erga omnes*, a theological one could be effective only *inter partes*. The individuation of the body's incorruption, whenever acquired by making use of a reasoning shared only inside the community of the faithful, had therefore to be translated into a supernumerary miracle, which was accepted as an object of veneration,[90] even though it lacked the effects for the canonization process.[91] In this way, the intimately theological nature of the investigation into the verification of miracles was recovered. The difference between an unspoiled body of a saint and a naturally preserved cadaver was not, as a consequence, phenomenological, but semiotic.[92] In other words, aside from the formal requirements of the canonization process, incorruption was miraculous when the theologians, not the physicians, verified it as such.

Davanzati, in keeping with this line of thinking, limited the boundaries of the area for research to the natural causes of the phenomenon:

> "And although it would not be difficult for me to believe that said circumstance could be a purely natural thing in some cadavers, I demand it be a supernatural and miraculous thing in those servants of God whose moral virtues in heroic status have been proved as such by the Holy Mother Church and by the Sacred Roman Rota."[93]

---

86 *De beatificatione,* Pars prima, § XXX. 337–338; then 347–350 *passim.*

87 Lambertini showed an analogous ambivalent attitude towards the case of Filippo Neri, beatified in 1615 and canonized in 1622, so before the reform. While meditating, Neri had once fell a ball of fire go through the month into his breast; years later, during his autopsy, physicians had found his pulmonary artery and heart abnormally enlarged. Lambertini reflected on the saint's aneurisms and explained that his heart had been enlarged "ex morbo naturali." Nonetheless, he concluded that it was necessary to admit a supernatural agent too: "who will not recognize the finger of God acting on the nature?" *De beatificatione,* Pars prima, § XIX, 209–224; Nancy G. Siraisi, "Signs and Evidence: Autopsy and Sanctity in the Late Sixteenth-Century Italy," in *Medicine and the Italian Universities: 1250–1600,* ed. by Nancy G. Siraisi (Leiden: 2001), 356–380; Fernando Vidal, *Miracles. Science, and Testimony,* cit.

88 Peter Brown, *The Cult of the Saints: Its Rise and Function in Latin Christianity* (Chicago: 1981): 86–126; John S. Strong, "Relics," in *The Encyclopaedia of Religion,* ed. Mircea Eliade, 12 (London: 1982), 275–282; Luigi Canetti, *Frammenti di eternita: Corpi e reliquie tra antichita e Medioevo* (Rome: 2002). To understand the ties that part of the Catholic culture still has with the body of saints, just consider how mass media in Italy have treated the discovery of the partially uncorrupted. in other words corrupted, body of Saint Pio of Pietrelcina (2008).

89 *De beatificatione,* Pars prima, § XXX, 342.

90 See, for example, a volume such as the one by Joan Carroll Cruz, *The Incorruptibles: A Study of the Incorruption of the Bodies of Various Catholic Saints and Beati* (Charlotte: 1977). Published with the ecclesiastical "nihil obstat" and "imprimatur," it reviews 102 cases of incorruptibility, some of which have never been "procedurally" recognised by the Roman Church.

91 *De beatificatione,* Pars prima, § XXX, 348. In effect, the incorruptibility of the body was of increasingly lesser importance in eases of sanctification starting in the second half of the 18th century. Jacalyn Duffin, *Medical Miracles: Doctors, Saints, and Healing in the Modern World* (Oxford: 2009), 100–102.

92 Davanzati did not attribute much importance to secondary differences, such as odour, swollen abdomen, etc. For example, the semiotic (not phenomenological) difference between monsters and exotic species is examined in the first chapter of Lorraine Daston and Katharine Park, *Wonders and the Order of Nature, 1150–1750* (New York: 1998).

93 *Dissertation,* 126. Davanzati concretely promoted the veneration of relics in his own diocese. On this topic, see the document preserved in the Trani

Not only: the premise according to which the body was meant to conserve its own vitality even after death presented theological implications that were difficult to control. Setting aside the positions of the ancient philosophers, such as Pythagoras, Empedocles and Aristippus, who explained the post-mortem phenomena by speaking of a semi-material soul or a *medium quid* between soul and body, Davanzati considered the hypotheses of a few modern thinkers, including Paracelsus, Johann Sophron Kozack, Gerard Feltmann, Jan Marek Marci and Fortunio Liceti, many of whom he drew upon from Garmann's book. It was only an extrinsic and academic reference, by the author of the *Dissertation*, as a hurried conclusion clearly revealed:

> "This opinion disavows itself in many aspects. Firstly, because these two souls do not exist in man, since the sensitive soul, according to the common opinion of modem thinkers, should also be immortal and spiritual: which would lead to the admission of two spiritual souls in a man. That goes against all reason and, in particular, is contrary to what the Holy Mother Church sacrosanctly thinks. Secondly, cui bono is understood and what is the purpose of this sensitive and vegetative soul? All of man's actions are duly saved with only the spiritual and rational soul, which regulates all of the lower type of senses through the manner and order in which it influences the body."[94]

To sum up, the *de miraculis mortuorum* tradition was to be taken with a grain of salt, because, when it did not attribute too great a role to the Devil and did not cast doubts on the supernaturalness of the preservation of the holy body, it tended to multiply the number of souls or vital principles. Lambertini himself, in fighting that belief, referred back to the authority of the Jesuit Théophile Raynaud (who, in turn, based his observations on the *postpraxis medica* studies by Antonio Santorelli, physician of the University of Naples),[95] who believed "nonetheless, it is not possible to accept the reasoning adopted by Plato to explain the permanence of the integrity of bodies, that is to say the indissolubility of the soul—as Tertullian says above—which is said to persist in the body of the dead. In fact, it is preposterous that the soul should remain in a dead body."[96] Therefore, from a philosophical and theological point of view, Tertullian's *De anima* got the better of Plato's *Republic*.[97] The soul remained one and indivisible. The Latin post-Tridentine tradition won out, on the one hand, over the Italian philosophy of the late Renaissance, on the other hand, over the Greek as well as the Central and Eastern European culture. Lambertini, faithful to the late Zacchia—the personal physician of the popes Innocent X and Alexander VII, legal advisor to the Rota Romana and head of the health system in the Papal States[98]—ascribed the movement of the cadaver to animal spirits stuck in its fibres, while the growth of fingernails, hair and teeth, as the ambivalent Liceti had guessed, to the depression or emptying of skin, flesh and gums. What had once seemed to be a phenomenon related to the residual activity of the organism, was nothing but the expression of its shrivelling up.[99] The paragraph on vampires

---

Diocesan Archives, *Archivio Capitolare di Trani, Mss C3795. 1726, c. scritta n. I.*
94 *Dissertation*, 45.

95 Antonio Santorelli, *Postpraxis medica ...* (Naples: 1629), 58–63.
96 Theophile Raynaud, *De incorruptione cadaverum ...* (1645), in *Philologica ...* (Leyden: 1665), 28.
97 In actual fact, at the heart of the dispute on vampires, even the Protestants cast a suspicious eye upon the multiplication of souls. Johann Christoph Stock, cit., 9–13; Franz Anton Ferdinand Stebler, "Sub vampyri, aut sanguisugae larva ... " in *Acta physico-medica Academiae Caesareae Lepoldino-Carolinae naturae curiosorum*, 4 (1737), 89–112, above all 97–100.
98 On his influential (and controversial) figure see the precious *Paolo Zacchia: Alle origini della medicina legale (1584–1659)*, eds. By Alessandro Pastore and Giovanni Rossi (Milan: 2008).
99 *De beatificatione,* Pars prima, § XXXI, 356. The reference is to Paolo Zacchia, cit., 4, I, Quaestio 10,

was only included in the second edition of *De servorum Dei heatificatione et sanctorum canonizatione*, published in 1749, when the author had already ascended to the papal throne with the name Benedict XIV. In the end, the phenomenon would be defined as the fruit of "imagination, terror and fear."[100]

The Problems of a "Corrupt and Depraved" Imagination

Even Davanzati—who seemed to have a more or less Cartesian vision of the anatomy of the brain, which, in his opinion, was made of "fan-shaped" membranes—considered vampire apparitions to be purely the "effect of imagination."[101] Many scholars, influenced by the assonances in their pronouncements as well as by the attestation of the grand-nephew-biographer, have attributed excessive weight to the prelate's familiarity with Prospero Lambertini and Ludovico Antonio Muratori.[102] Nevertheless, the relationships could not have been particularly close.[103] The Archbishop of Trani was not the *longa manus* of Benedict XIV; nor is it certain that the *Dissertation* was the reason why the pontiff included the paragraph on vampires in the second edition of *De servorum Dei beatificatione et sanctorum canonizatione*, since the only articles he quoted were those that had appeared in *Commercium litterarium*, which Davanzati does not mention and perhaps never read. Therefore, the harmony between the Archbishop of Trani and the Pope must be understood in a wider sense as being coherent with a cultural project that was being carried forward by the Italian Catholic culture (more than by the Church *stricto sensu*). The relationship with Muratori should be interpreted in the same way. In 1745 he did not speak specifically about vampirism in *Della forza della fantasia umana*, that is on the power of human fantasy, but tried to find first-hand information on the subject through private correspondence, apparently with little luck.[104]

In other Catholic countries like France, for example, there was stronger evidence of the contrast between those who, like Calmet,

---

§§ XXXI-XXXII; Fortunio Liceti, *De quaesitis per epistolas ...* (Bologna: 1640), 2, LX.

100 *De beatificatione*, Pars prima, § XXXI, 323–324. Actually, there is another, less famous, part of the text in which vampires are mentioned. It is the chapter "De sanguine a cadavere manantibus," when it is deemed that blood can remain fluid as a result of pent-up heat in the body. *De beatificatione*, Pars prima, § XXXI, 358. The scientific reference is Georg Bernhard Bilfinger, *Elementa physices ...* (Leipzig: 1742), 258–272.

101 *Dissertation*, 105–115.

102 The battle against some superstitious practices created problems for Davanzati with the traditionalist Pope Benedict XIII. Instead his relationship with Clement XII, Benedict's successor, was one of mutual esteem. Clement nominated him for an important diplomatic mission. Finally, to demonstrate the great regard that Benedict XIV had for him, the Archbishop's grand-nephew Giuseppe Forges Davanzati related two short missives from the pontiff. The first, dated 12 January 1743, thanks Davanzati for the copy of the *Dissertation* received as a gift. The second, dated 2 August 1746, communicates the Archbishop's promotion to Patriarch of Alexandria. His grand-nephew also claimed that "in Italy [Davanzati] met the aged Redi, Muratori and Maffei, in Geneva Mr. Clercq, in Paris Tournefort, in Rotterdam the aged Bayle, in Vienna Mr. Leibniz." Domenico Forges Davanzati, cit., respectively, 141, 142, 144.

103 The documents preserved in the Vatican Secret Archives make no hints at privileged relations with the Pope. In *Archivio Concistoriale, Acta Camerarii 27*, for example, mention is made of financial petitions advanced by Davanzati, who had to scheme quite a bit to obtain (partially) what he wanted. Even the information that can be drawn from letters sent to Rome, in *Segreteria di Stato, Vescovi. 135, 144, 145, 146, 150, 255, 265*, adds little of use to this study. The documents preserved in the Trani Diocesan Archives contain administrative information. Instead, the absence of Davanzati from Muratori's imposing group of correspondents is indicative. *Carteggio muratoriano: corrispondenti e bibliografia*, eds. Federica Missere Fontana and Roberta Turricchia (Modena: 2008). Incidentally, even his relationship with Leibniz after his stay in Vienna was reduced to the exchange of three letters in all.

104 Giuseppe Trenti, "Curiosita del mondo dell'occulto nel carteggio muratoriano," in *Atti e memorie: Deputazione di storia patria per le antiche Provincie modenesi*, 6 (1984), 149–153.

appeared to be confused by these events,[105] and those who, whether they were religious or Pyrrhonistic, from the author of the entry "Vampire, Wampire, Oupire & Upire" in the *Dictionnaire de Trévoux* to Lenglet du Fresnoy or Voltaire himself, distanced themselves or even ridiculed such credulity.[106] On the contrary, in Italy, almost everyone took more or less the same position. In 1749 Girolamo Tartarotti published the *Congresso notturno delle Lammie*, or nocturnal gathering of witches, in which vampirism was considered to be "a pure dream, born of apprehension and fear."[107] Two years later, Costantino Grimaldi medicalised it in his *Dissertazione* on the three types of magic, attributing the cause to "the foods eaten by the inhabitants of the North." Embracing a "dietary etiopathogenesis" borrowed from Friedrich Hoffmann, he explained that vampires had appeared "in places where beer with too much hop is drunk, and where hard foods like peas, fava beans, heavy bread and pork are eaten." These foods easily generated nightmares, even more so "under a heavy and cold sky." Thus, it was not by chance that one heard nothing of such phenomena in places where people ate better and drank wine instead of beer, like in Italy and France.[108]

The prince of evil was the deceiver *par excellence*. He made people believe in his power through illusions able to affect their imagination: "It is no wonder that the Devil can deceive the outer human senses, since ... he can illude the inner sense, by bringing to actual perception ideas that are stored in the imagination."[109] Even Socrates had been deceived by his daemon, which was anything but the Devil.[110] An abundant literature on the Devil's tricks already existed, but times had changed: 18th century authors were slowly shifting their attention to the purely natural causes affecting the imagination above all of women and simple-minded people. Imagination, to which Lambertini dedicated much more space in his treatise on canonisation than his predecessors ever had,[111] became that slippery slope down which the sphere of the preter- and supernatural descended toward the natural: in the light of theological (Thomas Aquinas) and scientific (Thomas Feyens) authorities, many of the phenomena once attributed to God or the angels (good or bad) were now understood to be *figmenta* of a *phantasia* which were, nonetheless, only able to affect the body of the imagining subject or, at most, in the case of a pregnant woman, the body of the unborn child. Although it was exalted in its intra-corporeal potential, the imagination was in other words negated all possible extracorporeal action.[112]

Instead, Davanzati, despite his past battles against superstitious practices, felt the full weight of certain widespread beliefs at every

---

105 It is important to point out that Calmet's attitude towards vampires was more complex than generally believed. Fernando Vidal, "Ghosts, the Economy of Religion, and the Laws of Princes." cit.

106 "Vampire, Wampire, Oupire & Upire," in *Dictionnaire de Trevoux* (Paris: 1771. 6th ed.), vol. 8, 285. The caustic works by the libertine and Pyrrhonist Nicolas Lenglet Du Fresnoy are the *Traite historique el dogmatique* (Avignon: 1751) and the *Recueil de dissertations ...* (n.c.: 1751). Reference has already been made to Voltaire. In the German-speaking area, as has been shown, the debate was even more varied. On the topic, Tony Faivre, *Du vampire villageois aux discours des cleres*, cit.

107 Girolamo Tartarotti, *Congresso notturno delle Lammie* (Rovereto: 1749), 140.

108 Costantino Grimaldi, *Dissertazione in cui si investiga ... magia diabolica ... magie artificiale e naturale* (Rome: 1751), 68.

109 Henrich Kramer (and Jacob Sprenger), cit., Pars prima, Quaestio IX, 59.

110 Giovan Franccsco Pico della Mirandola, *Strix, sive de hidificatione daemonum* (Bologna: 1523); French transl. *La sorciere: Dialogue en trois livres sur la tromperie des demons*, ed. by Alfredo Perifano (Turhout: 2007), 111–112.

111 de Matta dedicated only a few remarks to imagination in the chapter "de occultis naturae viribus." Carlo Felice de Matta, cit., Pars tertia, § XIX, 267–273.

112 To be precise, Lambertini supported Thomas Aquinas *(Summa theologica,* III, Quaest. 3, Art. 3, ad 3) in thinking that imagination only influenced the bodily processes strictly related to it, like the passions of the soul or the movement of spirits, and certainly not corporal organisation such as the shape of a hand or a foot. Fernando Vidal, *Miracles, Science, and Testimony*, cit.

social and cultural level in the Kingdom of Naples in general and in Apulia in particular, one of "the most remote and unknown parts of Italy."[113] Not to admit the force of spells or that which, starting from the years in which the *Dissertation* was published, was called "jettatura," would mean to close his eyes to the evidence.[114] Datur actio in distans: this was his persuasion, although admittedly reluctant, and formulated in terms of generic fluids and interacting spirits. Therefore, it was necessary to warn parents and nursemaids not to allow certain dirty and deformed old women to come too close to their children, because their bleary and watery eyes transmitted "some poisonous and evil airs and spirits into the pores of the little children." Only "relics of the saints and holy things" were effective against them.[115]

Based on such conditions, imagination became (or returned to being) for Davanzati a real operative force, able to act outside of the confines of the body of the imaginer:

> "If imagination with the vehemence of its spirits has the power to operate physically as well inside the subject as outside of it, this means it can produce real and physical effects in its own body and in those of others, ... why could it not have the force to cause in us a simple ephemeral and purely imaginary operation, such as the simple representation of one image in the place of another?"[116]

Vampires were the result of a collective suggestion, in which, however, the imagination of one person "effectively" acted on that of another, triggering a "spiritual epidemic." This thesis, clearly, could not but have wider consequences. An imagination able to produce "real" effects could place the concept of the miracle itself in doubt. The dilemma was: couldn't otherwise inexplicable apparitions and healing have been the result of an imagination acting in an extracorporeal manner? This was basically what Pietro Pomponazzi had sustained, in that if people believed that the bones of a dog were those of a saint, those bones would perform miracles in the same way as the bones of a saint.[117] The question was thorny and it was to be the subject of the debate between miraculists and anti-miraculists in the centuries that followed.[118]

Going too far with one's imagination was dangerous. Not too far from Trani was the town of Copertino [Cupertino], where Giuseppe was born and raised. He was beatified in 1753, by Lambertini himself, then canonised in 1767 by Clement XIII. A mystic, he was the subject of much discussion because he actually took flight during his moments of ecstasy. It is quite likely that Davanzati referred to him when he tells that:

> "There is, among others, a certain anonymous philosopher not of low doctrine, who openly asserts that it is possible for a man overwrought by a strong imagination to be able to lift his whole body naturally into the air ... To tell the truth this seems paradoxical, yet it is held to be true by a certain physician from this area, a learned and honest man."[119]

---

113 George Berkeley, Letter to John Percival, 18 June 1717, in *Correspondence*, ed. Benjamin Rand (Cambridge: 1914), 166. Nonetheless, Trani was a patrician city, the seat of an important and active court.
114 Francesco P. de Ceglia, "*It's not true, but I believe it*: Discussions on Jettatura between the End of the 18th and Beginning of the 19th Century," *Journal of the History of Ideas*, 72 (2011), 75–97.
115 *Dissertation*, 81.
116 *Dissertation*, 107.
117 Pietro Pomponazzi, *De naturalium effectuum admirandorum causis sive de incantationibus liber* (Basel: 1556), 249–250. Added to the Parma *Index* in 1580, then to the Roman *Index* in 1596.
118 Kenneth L. Woodward, *Making Saints: How the Catholic Church Determines Who Becomes a Saint, Who Doesn't, and Why* (New York: 1990); Pierre Delooz, *Les miracles: Un défi pour la science?* (Brussels: 1997).
119 *Dissertation*, 97; Catrien Santig, "Tirami su: Pope Benedict XIV and the Beatification of the Flying Saint Giuseppe da Copertino," in *Medicine and Religion in Enlightenment Europe*, eds. Ole Peter Grell and Andrew Cunningham (Aldershot: 2007), 79–99.

In short, the excessive power of the imagination annihilated the supernatural. Davanzati was not hiding. On the contrary, he was sure of his answer, but he had gone too far beyond the boundaries of the area of imagination established by Lambertini, not to trip up in argumentative paradoxes. The author of *De servorum Dei beatificatione el sanctorum canonizatione* had, in fact, had to cede ground regarding the probationary strength of the theological (rather than scientific and juridical) ascertainment of the holy body's incorruptibility, which became valid as to say only *inter partes*. However, negating the *actio in distans*, he had guaranteed a "scientific" definition to the other (therapeutic) miracles, which remained valid, at least theoretically, *erga omnes*.

In the *Dissertation*, Davanzati, for whom there was no scientifically ascertainable difference in the incorruptibility of a holy body as compared with a cadaver preserved by natural causes, transferred this logic to the interpretation and ascertainment of all other miracles. Or better, he did not make the same courageous epistemological leap as Lambertini, the promoter of the new skeptical-saint-making. He remained faithful to the practice of subordination of medicine to theology that was particularly widespread in the Kingdom of Naples, culturally closer to Spain.[120] Therefore, he appealed to the heroic virtues, which could gestaltically reorganise the phenomena, otherwise interpretable as natural:

"From this it can be deduced that fear of the adversary is pointless, so, by attributing so many almost miraculous operations to the imagination, damage is done to the virtue of real miracles and the canonisation of saints. The miracles of the latter will always be real miracles, each time, as previously said, when they happen concurrently with heroic virtues. When this is not the case, these same supposed miracles will always be considered the natural effects of fantasy."[121]

While for Hume, during this same period, a miracle was "a transgression of a law of nature by a particular volition of the Deity, or by the interposition of some invisible agent,"[122] for Davanzati it tautologically remained what theologically was decreed to be a miracle. The recognition of the efficient cause—natural vs. preter- and supernatural—depended on the individuation of the final cause: aetiology was subordinate to teleology (and theology). Vampires, in conclusion, were for him figments of the imagination, not because they were otherwise inexplicable from a scientific point of view, so much as because the miracle of their existence made no sense theologically. Nonetheless, had the foundations *de fide* of the reasoning been disowned, as was possible for the Protestants, the whole logical construction would have collapsed.

---

120 Romeo De Maio, *Societa e vita religiosa a Napoli neu eta moderna, 1656–1799* (Naples: 1971); Jean-Michel Sallmann, *Naples et ses saints a l'age baroque: 1540–1750* (Paris: 1994); Giulio Sodano, *Modelli e selezione del santo moderno: Periferia napoletana e centro romano* (Milan: 2002).

121 *Dissertation*, 114.
122 David Hume, *An Enquiry Concerning Human Understanding* (London: 1748), X, i, 90n.

Absent Presences in Liminal Places

Murnau's *Nosferatu* and the Otherworld of Stoker's *Dracula*

Saviour Catania

"Life is nothings"[1]
—Bram Stoker

ALTHOUGH THE CREDITS OF F.W. Murnau's *Nosferatu*[2] acknowledge Bram Stoker's *Dracula* as the fictional source of Henrik Galeen's screenplay,[3] most critics tend to dismiss any thematic connection between novel and film. To Lane Roth, for instance, *Nosferatu*, far from being "an individual filmmaker's vision of a literary work," is essentially "an expression of the German *Zeitgeist*" of the Weimar Republic and, particularly, of the "mysticism and fantasy" that the expressionist *Schauerfilm* had inherited from traditional German Romanticism (312–13). David Walker concurs, adding that *Nosferatu*'s "teutonic flavor" actually undermines it as an "adaptation that best captures the spirit [of *Dracula*]" (48). Such exclusively "Germanic" interpretations should not go unquestioned, however, for Murnau takes more than just a few plot elements from *Dracula*. I intend to examine this issue, thereby redressing the balance in favor of Stoker's influence by suggesting that *Dracula* offered Murnau a complex reworking of major Gothic motifs extracted from Germanic literature and culture. Arguably, then, what seems to have inspired Murnau to rework *Dracula* on film was an awareness that Stoker had appropriated much of Murnau's own aesthetic affinities with the German Romantic spirit in his novel. In order to demonstrate how Murnau distills the *Stimmung* or existential mood of German Romanticism through Stoker's influence, I shall focus on two intermeshed aspects of what critics label *Nosferatu*'s fantastic Germanness: absent presence and liminal landscape.

As Angela Dalle Vacche rightly remarks, Murnau "slim[s] his protagonist down to an evanescent, flickering fragment of the German nocturnal imagination ..." (182). Lloyd Michaels echoes her insight by observing that what distinguishes the Murnau and Herzog *Nosferatu*s from other non-German film versions of *Dracula* is that their vampire-counts, "[un]like their English-speaking counterparts ... manage to signify elusiveness, rather than presence, lack rather than excess ..." (68). The implication is that there is something innately Germanic about the motif of absent presence on which Murnau pivots his *Nosferatu*, and which he culturally bequeaths to Werner Herzog's 1979 remake. Conversely, it could be argued that Murnau inherited this bizarre theme from, say, Friedrich de la Motte Fouqué, whose novel *The Magic Ring* epitomizes the German Romantic obsession with the shadowy self fragmenting into a more insubstantial parallel realm. Such a preoccupation with the ghostly double of a dislocated or dissolving personality is clearly an earlier manifestation of *Helldunkel*, which Lotte H. Eisner defines as "a sort of twilight of the German soul" (8). In terms of *Nosferatu* as adaptation, however, this is only half the point. For absent presence is a reiterated theme in *Dracula*. That Nosferatu terrifies the *Empusa*'s sailor by his diaphanous appearance owes, in fact, much less to such Hoffmann *doppelgänger* tales as "The Story of the Lost Reflection" than to Stoker's description of the *Demeter* mate's ordeal with Dracula's physical vacuity: "On the watch last night I saw It, like a man, tall and thin, and ghastly pale. It was in the bows, and looking out. I crept behind It, and gave It my knife, but the knife went through It, empty as the air" (113). Such testimony confirms that Dracula's disappearing act before Olgaren's eyes is neither a product of madness on this sailor's part nor a trick of the dark, but rather Dracula's uncanny ability to be, and not to be, simultaneously. Evidently, then, what haunts the *Empusa*'s hold—an entity through whose insubstantiality stacked coffins are clearly visible—originates from what lurks on the *Demeter*'s bow: the spectre of "no one" (112). The disclosure that Dracula's realm is darkly ethereal is further proof that he is the literary prototype of Murnau's translucent count. "I love the shade and the shadow" (32), Dracula tells Harker, whose initial encounter with him as the dark driver establishes the latter's physicality as one of immaterial materiality: "When he [Dracula] stood between me and the flame he didn't obstruct it, for I could see its ghostly flicker all the same" (18).

Gwenyth Hood implicitly draws attention to this incorporeal materiality in her comparison of

Saviour Catania, "Absent Presences in Liminal Places: Murnau's Nosferatu and the Otherworld of Stoker's Dracula," *Literature/Film Quarterly*, vol. 32, no. 3, pp. 229–236. Copyright © 2004 by Literature/Film Quarterly. Reprinted with permission.

J. R. R. Tolkien's Sauron with Stoker's vampire: "Unlike Dracula, he [Sauron] has completely lost his body ..." (223). As retribution for having defied the ban of the Valar prohibiting the invasion of the Undying Lands, Sauron's fair physique dissolves into what Tolkien calls "a dark wind" (III, 317). Dracula is really no such evil discarnate. Still, Dracula's is the body of no body, and thus what he most closely anticipates in Tolkien's world is what Patricia Meyer Spacks calls the "physical nothingness" (86) of the Nazgûls or Ringwraiths. What the Black Riders, and indeed both Sauron and Nosferatu, inherit from Dracula then is his unholy hollowness. Hence Dracula's shadowlessness. Dracula, in Van Helsing's words, "throws no shadow [and] make[s] in the mirror no reflect" (289), further indicating that it is again in Stoker that Murnau finds his thematic justification for that startling shadow that renders Nosferatu so untypical of the Victorian Gothic vampire. The crucial point here is that it is partially because of the shadow he casts that Nosferatu comes to embody the disembodiment of his shadowless counterpart. Nosferatu *as* shadow is, in fact, one of Murnau's ingenious ways of incarnating in visual images Stoker's verbal descriptions of what is visible but incorporeal. This is true especially of Nosferatu's preying scenes, where Hutter (Harker) and his wife have to contend with the swelling insubstantiality of a silhouette. While recognizing that Murnau clearly displays in such scenes "the taste for shadows" (133) that Eisner finds prevalent in "most film-makers of Germanic origin" (133), one cannot really endorse Roth's interpretation of Nosferatu's shadow as just an expressionistic manifestation of the Romantic literary *doppelgänger* motif, whose source Roth traces to the "traditional Germanic preoccupation with *Dualismus*" (5). Judith Mayne delves deeper into such "dualislic categories of thought" in both in Murnau and Stoker: "Central to both *Dracula* and *Nosferatu* ... is a dangerous territory where opposing terms are not so easily distinguishable" (27). For Murnau's is essentially not a vision of polarities. Nor for that matter is Stoker's. Indeed, *Nosferatu* comes closest to *Dracula* in its appropriation of the central Stokerean notion that light is darkness. This motif is a vital variant of the "absent presence" theme in both novel and film.

Consider, for instance, those two scenes depicting the *Empusa* captain's deserted cabin where Murnau's focal point is literally the most minimal of visual details—what Eisner accurately describes as "the reflection of the sustained, monotonous swinging of a suspended lamp" (105). What should be added, however, is

that the lamplight subtly evokes by its sudden abrupt shifting the vampire's jerky movement, thereby hinting at Nosferatu's ethereal presence in the cabin. *Nosferatu* powerfully exemplifies Murnau's "cinema of thin air" (15), as Gilberto Perez insightfully labels it, through such haunting moments as this one when the ethereal darkness that heralds Nosferatu's rattish entry into Ellen's (Mina's) bedroom suddenly becomes a wild oscillation of light. Gregory A. Waller seems therefore off the mark when he writes that "in *Nosferatu,* opening a door or window is an action ... that creates the possibility for ... letting in the sunlight and letting in infection and darkness" (182). For Murnau conceives light in tenebrous terms, and dawn becomes no less deadly than twilight—as the vampire's sunlit death dramatically demonstrates. Murnau could have hardly conceived a more elementally fitting demise for his vampire of dark light than this change from Dracula's death by impalement of the heart to Nosferatu's dissolution by the sun.

Murnau's denouement may be superior to Stoker's but this in no way minimizes, however, what the German film owes to *Dracula*. For the concept of the "dark light" vampire is Stoker's. It would be best, in fact, to emphasize that the three vampiresses at Castle Dracula are, significantly, spectres of dark light when first they gleam on Harker's sight. Indeed, what alarms Harker terribly is that their "phantom shapes become ... gradually materialised from the moonbeams" (60): and much to his amazement, they again "fade into the rays of the moonlight" (53) after their visitation. Rather than simply deleting Stoker's vampiresses, then, Murnau rightly appropriates for *Nosferatu* their "moonlight" properties as a means of recreating Van Helsing's vision of the vampiric count "com[ing]" on moonlight rays as elemental dust" (290). Such Stokerean images are also evidently the source of Nosferatu's weird and allegorized surrogate: the polyp that Professor Bulwer, the film's noncrusading Van Helsing, presents as evidence of a preying force that is paradoxically a visible invisibility, "transparent ... almost incorporeal ... almost a phantom"(252). If *Nosferatu* is viewed in terms of André Bazin's imprint concept of the cinematic image as a kind of death-mask moulding through light manipulation (12), one might say that what Murnau imprints on screen is Dracula's insubstantial substantiality. Nosferatu is almost the quintessence of Dracula's evanescence: an ethereal manifestation of that "unmirrorable image" (74) that David Glover rightly labels "physiognomy's true vanishing point" (74). Hence Murnau's reliance in the latter half of his film on high-angled long shots that establish quite disturbingly the viewpoint of something unseen hovering over the Bremen streets. As Perez says of Nosferatu's sightlessness: "His presence is felt in the air" (19), much like Dracula's is in Whitby, where old Mr. Swales draws Mina's attention to it in words of eerie poetry: "Maybe it's in that wind out of the sea that's bringin' with it loss and wreck, and sore distress, and sad hearts. Look! look! ... there's something in that wind and in that hoast beyont that sounds, and looks, and tastes, and smells like death. It's in the air" (99). Just like Dracula in Whitby, Nosferatu in Bremen is essentially a flitting liminality.

What Nosferatu crucially shares with Dracula is this threshold kind of existence: they are borderers or liminal figures helplessly hedged between the seen and the unseen. Significantly, while edging into Ellen's sight, Nosferatu manifests invisibly in terms of a symbology of infinity, which finds embodiment in the illimitable seascape Ellen scans from the beach cemetery where she stands. Dalle Vacche roots this culturally in the influence on Murnau of David Caspar Friedrich's "elegiac or sublime" (171) marine painting, and specifically of *The Monk by the Sea* (1809–1810). That Murnau shares Friedrich's aesthetic preoccupation with "mak[ing] visible the invisible" (168), as Dalle Vacche rightly puts it, can hardly be denied. It is, however, highly debatable as to what extent this shared concern is simply the result, as Dalle Vacche suggests, of Carl Neuman, Murnau's art mentor at Heidelberg, having convinced his pupil that he should concern himself "with what makes German art German" (165). Notwithstanding the likelihood of such Wölflinian nationalistic aesthetic tendencies (164–65), Murnau's beach scene ultimately owes its inspiration to Stoker—and not to Friedrich. What is truly at stake here is that Murnau's Ellen only seemingly shares Friedrich's monk's marine edge—for the awe of the "hollow space" (17), to quote Perez's phrase, that she confronts at this existential border, recalls not Friedrich's monk but Mina Harker. Mina is not only another *Rückenfigur,* but also one whose scrying of the seascape from an equally liminal location, the churchyard cliff at Whitby, powerfully portends in terms of Burkean limitlessness the *horror vacui* of her German equivalent. As Mina notes in her journal: "The horizon is lost in a grey mist. All is vastness; the clouds are piled up like giant rocks, and there is a 'brool' over the sea that sounds like some presage of doom" (98). As in Murnau's beach scene, the terror of the Stokerean Undead is all the more invisibly grand because it is not visually affirmed. It is evident that it is to Stoker's seascape of unrelieved greyness, and not to Friedrich's darker sea redeemed by intimations of immortality through seagulls on the wing, that Murnau owes the sublimity of the vampire's vacuity.

It is rather strange then that Dalle Vacche should pivot her Murnau/Friedrich beach parallel on the following quotation from Joseph Leo Koerner: "Friedrich empties his canvas in order to imagine, through an invocation of the void, an infinite, unrepresentable God" (16). What Koerner's trenchant comment recalls to mind, rather, is Friedrich's Wordsworthian pantheistic statement: "The divine is everywhere, even in a grain of sand; there I represented it in the reeds" (16).[4] The Wordsworthian echo is unmistakable, for Friedrich's vision of ubiquitous divinity is not dissimilar to what "Tintern Abbey" extols—the "spirit roll[ing] through all things" (ll. 100, 102; 262).[5] Significantly, what Friedrich's *Rückenfigur* evokes in this respect is what Koerner calls Wordsworth's "halted traveller" (183) since both are figures in an epiphanic landscape where what remains visually out of reach is a nevertheless immanent divinity. As Charles Sala states, what we have in Friedrich is "landscape as spiritual hierograph" (78). But what Friedrich says about his painting *Swans in the Rushes* (c. 1819–1820), and particularly about the divine essence of his reeds, is in no way applicable to the reedy dunes of Murnau's beach. Admittedly, Murnau's seascape, like Friedrich's in *The Monk by the Sea,* is a meditation on spatial vacuity; but what Murnau's void leaves unrepresented is not a divine transcendence but its inverted presence or what may be termed an anti-divine state. Murnau's Nosferatu incarnates in this respect S. L. Varnado's concept of his Stokerean progenitor as the embodiment of Rudolf Otto's "negative numinous" (Varnado 101–102).[6] Hence Murnau's tottering crosses, which suggest that the "contamination" (8) Robin Wood rightly detects in Murnau's beach scene, with its promise of sea-borne pestilential coffins, is essentially a malaise of the spirit. Murnau inverts the traditional association of the sea with what Wood calls "purity, or purification" (8), rooting the point of liminality in a beach cemetery.

To conclude, however, as Rona Unrau does, that what therefore concerns Murnau is not Stoker's "fear of becoming Un-Dead"(236) but "fear of human extinction [or] mortality" (236–37)—a feature she finds "typically German" (237)—is to simplify both film and novel. What is central in both Murnau and Stoker is not fear of the Undead, of being in an absent present state, but the ambivalent attraction/repulsion that such a state elicits in mortals. Significantly, though Harker shares none of his filmic counterpart's interest in the vampire's coffined body, but simply his revulsion, Hutter's advancing/retreating movements in the "crypt coffin" sequence are as explicitly at cross purposes as Lucy's repeatedly clutching and dropping the antivampiric garlic in Stoker's novel. Wood rightly intuits that, no less than *Nosferatu, Dracula* is "about the human fear of death" (16),[7] for it is fundamentally such a fear that determines the attraction/repulsion complex in both Murnau and Stoker. The vampire attracts and repulses simultaneously by offering immortality to nonliving entities. Hence the absent presence and its mesmerizing/terrifying influence on Ellen. But Ellen's sea vigil is set on a Stokerean beach of graves, since Death is equally the *genius loci* of Whitby. More thematically apposite in this context is the visual parallel Dalle Vacche draws in terms of "spectral quality" (164) between the image of Nosferatu crossing a Bremen canal in a boat "which glides across the water by itself" (164) and Arnold Böcklin's barge scene in the painting *The Isle of the Dead* (1880). For Murnau's Ellen, as has been stated, is sublimely perched on the edge of a seat of death that the unseen Nosferatu navigates like the Stygian ferryman. But once again, Murnau's vision of Nosferatu's ship as a self-steered Charon skiff recalls Stoker rather than Böcklin—for Dracula's "strange ship" (100), riding the gales beyond Mina's gaze, is, unlike Böcklin's barge of death, supernaturally steered like the ghostly galleon in Coleridge's *Rime of the Ancient Mariner*. As Devendra P. Varma observes: "In its voyage from Varna to Whitby the *Material Ship* turns into a *Phantom Ship*" (211). There is, however, no supernatural navigation in Böcklin's 1880 painting, which Dalle Vacche reproduces in her text, nor for that matter, in any other version of *The Isle of the Dead*.

Every element, then, in both the canal and beach scenes points to Stoker's *Dracula* as the major source of Murnau's uncanny vision. The very name of Stoker's ship, *Demeter*, reinforces, for instance, Evans Lansing Smith's reading of Murnau's vessel as "the mother of Death" (243), since "Demeter is the name of the mother of Persephone whose yearly abduction into Hades" (243) leaves an absent presence in its wake. Even the way old Swales describes Dracula's ship when he glimpses it—"steered mighty strangely ... changes about with every puff of wind" (100) prefigures visually Murnau's wildly shifting patch of light in the captain's cabin. As James Craig Holte asserts: "No other adaptation of *Dracula* has captured the terror of the discovery of evil aboard an isolated vessel as effectively as *Nosferatu*" (32). Here, as elsewhere, what really haunts Murnau is Stoker's *nada*. Indeed, rather than pondering on divine imponderables as Friedrich does in the alleged self-portrait of the sea monk, Murnau's Ellen surveys the abysmal absence of the self—for when Friedrich's spiritual horizon disappears, what then appears is the horizon of soullessness. Ellen is then not fundamentally different to her Stokerean equivalent whose experience at Whitby cliff similarly reveals the nothingness beneath her feet. True, Stoker refrains from tossing Mina over the edge, but it is still to Stoker, and not to Friedrich, that Murnau owes his inspiration for Ellen's plunge into perdition. *Nosferatu* recreates *Dracula* in the sense that it propels Stoker's text onto what both the Victorian novelist and Weimar filmmaker anticipate: the Heideggerian/Sartrean vision of the nothingness of being.

Murnau's unsettling journey into the darkest of existential liminal territories is essentially a voyage into the Stokerean nothing; and this is further evidenced by Hutter's phantasmal coach ride that Dalle Vacche associates exclusively with German Romantic expressionist painting: "Hutter's cross[ing] into the land of phantoms ... provides a possible reference to Alfred Kubin's fantastic pictures of coaches travelling through the forest ..." (170). Admittedly, what Thomas Elsaesser notes about Albin Grau, that he was "a friend of novelist-painter Alfred Kubin" (13), seems to validate such intriguing attempts to trace the negative or reversed phantom carriage sequence to the coach drawings of Kubin. For it was Grau who designed the film's costumes and décor for Murnau. Quite understandably, then, Michel Bouvier and J. L. Leutrat go further than Dalle Vacche and actually suggest that Murnau's source could be Kubin's *The Road to Zwickledt* (323).[8] It should be noted, however, that though Murnau's negative image transforms Galeen's "fairy-tale forest" (*Murnau* 242) into a *Märchenwald* of spectral paleness, it still retains the carriage's blackness, thereby differentiating the latter from Kubin's *Zwickledt* moonlit equivalent. Ironically, it is Murnau's carriage sequence with its reversal of what Bert Cardullo calls "the usual positions of light and shadow on objects" (29) that creates the "chaos of light and shadow"(18) in which, as Eisner says, Kubin usually excels. What Murnau charts through the progress of the black calèche is a geography of unearthliness. For the coach's startling unbleached appearance in a completely bleached landscape hints at a realm that transcends the eerie forest of Kubin to evoke the liminal portal of Stoker. What the carriage's saccadic or fast-motion rhythm suggests, in fact, is the chilling line which, as Diane Milburn rightly notes,

Stoker "slightly misquote[s]" (45) from Burger's ballad "Lenore": "For the dead travel fast" (15). Significantly, Murnau's carriage plunges into the descent of no return by accelerating to the spirit speed of its Stokerean counterpart at the Borgo Pass—that equally bizarre border of paradoxes where a Zeno-like trajectory of "straight road[s]" (16) takes Harker's calèche "over and over the same ground again" (16).

Again, despite the intriguing parallels David B. Dickens draws between Lenore's "midnight ride" (136)[9] and Harker's, with their shared preternatural celerity that makes "time race ... past [while] also seem[ing] interminable" (136), the nightmarish spatiality of Bürger's road ballad, like that of Goethe's "The Erl King" that it prefigures, lacks the antithetical Stokerean motif of journeying in linear circles. So does Goethe's *Faust*—for though its Mephistopheles does mention the damnation of "endless circles" (34),[10] as Dickens quoting Leonard Wolf re-emphasizes (16 n.58), such circular movement differs radically from Harker's whose fate is to circulate by travelling straight. Such is the Stokerean road to nowhere—what Clive Leatherdale calls a "dream-like unreality" (169)—that leads Harker to the invisible approach to Castle Dracula. Murnau similarly shows a path where there is none by subjecting Hutter to a journey conceived as "unmappable in [its] contours" (93)[11]—a journey in negative images whose inverted chiaroscuro properties hint at phantomland unseen, or what Perez filmically calls "the space off screen" (16). The right realm, one would say, for an absent present wraith: the realm of the "out of frame" (16), to use again Perez's phrase. In Derridean terms, *Nosferatu* excels because it recreates Stoker's verbal text (where, as Glover states, what matters is "matter out of place" [71]) in an out-of-filmic text, beyond the frame: the *hors-champ* is virtually its (un)seen world. The source of this extraordinary achievement remains Stoker's less experimental novel, however, with its alluring twilit liminality blurring worldly and otherworldly slates of being. Consider, as a final example, how Murnau transforms the Dracula/Lucy tryst at Whitby, with its full moon highlighting their odd whiteness, into the odder unreality of a white night scene: Hutter's carriage ride through the white forest of phantom night. Intensely uncompromising in its stunning metamorphosis of Stoker's vision, *Nosferatu* remains, as Mayne says, "almost resolutely in ... twilight" (28). Still *Dracula's* "setting sun" (443) ending is not devoid of twilight associations. If, as Eisner states, "[t]he German soul instinctively prefers twilight to daylight" (51), so does Stoker who, like Murnau, distills his art through a Gothic *grisaille*.

Saviour Catania
University of Malta

Notes

1. See Bram Stoker, *The Essential Dracula*, edited and annotated by Leonard Wolf (New York: Plume. 1993) 287. Subsequent references to this edition are given after quotations in the text.
2. All references to Murnau's *Nosferatu* are to the Redemption videocassette copy of the film.
3. Gertrud Mander's translation of Galeen's script for *Nosferatu* is included in Eisner's *Murnau* 227–72.
4. Cited in Koerner 16.
5. See Wordsworth's poem in De Selincourt 262.
6. For an insightful analysis of Dracula as a Victorian specimen of the "negative numinous," see Varnado 101–02.
7. See also Wheeler's comments on Philippe Aries's analysis of the Victorian dread of physical extinction, 32–33.
8. See illustration in Bouvier and Leutrat 323.
9. See also Ruther's comments on German and English "vampiric 'cross-fertilization,'" 55.
10. See Dickens's article in Miller 31–40.
11. See Shepard 93.

Works Cited

Bazin. André. *What is Cinema? Vol. 1.* Trans. Hugh Gray. Berkeley: U. of California P., 1967.

Bouvier, Michel, and J. I. Leutrat. *Nosferatu*. Paris: Gallimard, 1981.

Cardullo, Bert. "Expressionism and *Nosferatu*." *San Jose Studies* 11 (1985): 25–33.

Dalle Vacche, Angela. *Cinema and Painting: How Art is Used in Film*. London: Athlone, 1996.

Derrida, Jacques. *Of Grammatology*. Trans. Gayatri Chakravorty Spivak. Baltimore: Johns Hopkins UP, 1976.

Dickens, David B. "Bürger's Ballad 'Lenore': En Route to *Dracula*." *Visions of the Fantastic*. Ed. Allienne R. Becker. Westport: Greenwood, 1996. 131–38.

—. "The German Matrix of Stoker's *Dracula*." *Dracula: The Shade and the Shadow*. Ed. Elizabeth Miller. Essex: Desert Island, 1998. 31–40.

Eisner, Lotte H. *The Haunted Screen: Expressionism in the German Cinema and the Influence of Max Reinhardt*. London: Seeker and Warburg, 1973.

—. *Murnau*. London: Seeker and Warburg, 1973.

Elsaesser, Thomas. "Six Degrees of *Nosferatu*." *Sight and Sound* n.s. 11 (2001): 12–15.

Glover, David. *Vampires, Mummies and Liberals: Bram Stoker and the Politics of Popular Fiction*. Durham: Duke UP, 1996.

Holte, James Craig. *Dracula in the Dark: The Dracula Film Adaptations*. Westport: Greenwood, 1997.

Hood, Gwnyeth. "Sauron and Dracula." *Dracula: The Vampire and the Critics*, Ed. Margaret L. Carter. Ann Arbor: UMI Research P, 1988. 215–30.

Koerner, Joseph Leo. *Caspar David Friedrich and the Subject of Landscape*. New Haven: Yale UP, 1990.

Leatherdale, Clive. *Dracula: The Novel and the Legend*. Wellingborough: Aquarian, 1985.

Mayne, Judith. "Dracula in the Twilight: Murnau's *Nosferatu* (1922)." *German Film and Literature: Adaptations and Transformations*. Ed. Eric Rentschler. London: Methuen, 1986. 25–39.

Michaels, Lloyd. *The Phantom of the Cinema: Character in Modern Films*. New York: State U of New York P, 1998.

Milburn, Diane. "For the Dead Travel Fast": *Dracula* in Anglo-German Context." *Dracula: The Shade and the Shadow*. Ed. Elizabeth Miller. Essex: Desert Island, 1998. 41–53.

Murnau, F. W., dir. *Nosferatu*. Perf. Max Schreck and Greta Schroeder. 1922. Videocassette. Redemption (RETN 012).

Perez, Gilberto. "*Nosferatu*." *Ravitan* 13 (1993): 1–33.

Roth, Lane. "Dracula meets the *Zeitgeist*: *Nosferatu* (1922) as Film Adaptation." *Literature/Film Quarterly* 7 (1979): 309–13.

—. "Nosferatu: Shadow of Evil." *Gore Creatures* 24 (1975): 4–6.

Ruther, Clemens. "Bloodsuckers with Teutonic Tongues: The German-Speaking World and the Origins of *Dracula*." *Dracula: The Shade and the Shadow*. Ed. Elizabeth Miller. Essex: Desert Island, 1998. 54–67.

Sala, Charles. *Caspar David Friedrich and Romantic Painting*. Trans. Jean-Marie Clarke and Robin Ayres. Paris: Terrail, 1994.

Shepard, Jim. "Nosferatu." *Triquarterly* 87 (1993): 88–117.

Smith, Evans Lansing. "Framing the Underworld: Threshold Imagery in Murnau, Cocteau and Bergman." *Literature/Film Quarterly* 24 (1996): 241–54.

Spacks, Patricia Meyer. "Power and Meaning in *The Lord of the Rings*." *Tolkien and the Critics: Essays on J. R. R. Tolkien's The Lord of the Rings*. Ed. Neil D. Isaacs and Rose A. Zimbardo. Notre Dame: U of Notre Dame P, 1968. 81–99.

Stoker, Bram. *The Essential Dracula*. Ed. Leonard Wolf. New York: Plume, 1993.

Unrau, Rona. "Eine Symphonie des Grauens or the Terror of Music: Murnau's *Nosferatu*." *Literature/Film Quarterly* 24 (1996): 234–40.

Varma, Devendra P. "Dracula's Voyage: From Pontus to Hellespontus." *Dracula: The Vampire and the Critics*. Ed. Margaret L. Carter. Ann Arbor: UMI Research P, 1988. 207–13.

Varnado, S. L. *Haunted Presence: The Numinous in Gothic Fiction.* Tuscaloosa: U of Alabama P, 1987.

Walker, David. *"Nosferatu:* The Unauthorized Undead." *Video Watchdog* 19 (1993): 48–61.

Waller, Gregory A. *The Living and the Undead: From Stoker's Dracula to Romero's Dawn of the Dead.* Urbana: U of Illinois P, 1986.

Wheeler, Michael. *Death and the Future Life in Victorian Literature and Theology.* Cambridge: Cambridge UP, 1990.

Wood, Robin. "Murnau's Midnight and *Sunrise."* *Film Comment* 12 (1976): 4–19.

—. "Burying the Undead: The Use and Obsolescence of Count Dracula." *Mosaic* 16 (1983): 175–87.

Wordsworth, William. "Tintern Abbey." *The Poetical Works of William Wordsworth.* Ed. E. De Selincourt. Oxford: Clarendon, 1952. 259–63.

Dracula Horror Stories of the Fifteenth Century

Raymond T. McNally and Radu Florescu

MORE FASCINATING THAN THE official archives, which concentrate on political and diplomatic history, is *la petite histoire*—the more intimate story—which in the case of Dracula is found in contemporary German pamphlets. In modern parlance, these pamphlets not only created bad press for Dracula, but also became bestsellers in the extensive medieval Germanic world from Brasov to Strasbourg. The Saxons' desire for vengeance was realized, at least after Dracula's death, by defaming his character for centuries to come. Although this is controversial, the experiences of and stories told by Transylvanian Saxon refugees may well lie at the basis of all the accounts of Dracula's misdeeds.

To date, many accounts concerning Dracula have been found, in places as diverse as the Strasbourg public archives, the Benedictine monastery of St. Gall (now known as the Stiff Library) in Switzerland, and the Benedictine monastery of Lambach near Salzburg. Most are printed, some illustrated with crude woodcuts, and four are in manuscript form. Such pamphlets were the principal medium for transmitting stories and images to the general public in the fifteenth century.

Most of the stories concerning Dracula are tales of horror with some sort of moral for the reader. Though distortion is unquestionable, their amazing accuracy of historical, geographical, and topographical detail leads scholars to accept much in them as fact. The German stories about Dracula can be considered bona fide, historical sources; they constitute a credible account of Dracula's life and times, particularly when they coincide with the formal diplomatic dispatches.

Those responsible for starting the legend were hardly gothic authors but German Catholic monks from Transylvania, refugees who fled the country because of Dracula's brutal attempt to destroy the Catholic institutions and confiscate their wealth. Like all fugitives, they had a story to tell, and, as so often happens in these instances, the story exaggerated their plight.

The oldest surviving manuscript was once housed in the library at the monastery of Lambach, near Salzburg; the original has been lost, but a copy was made by a German scholar, W. Wattenbach, in 1896 (one year before the publication of Stoker's *Dracula*). Other manuscripts are now located at the British Museum and the public library in Colmar, France, as well as in the Stiff Library in St. Gall, Switzerland.

The separate segments of the St. Gall narrative, all very similar in style and composition, initially strike the reader as very brief summaries of horror stories, undoubtedly among the first of their kind. They seem to be designed for an unsophisticated audience. Dracula is portrayed as a demented psychopath, a sadist, a gruesome murderer, a masochist, "one of the worst tyrants of history, far worse than the most depraved emperors of Rome such as Caligula and Nero." Among the crimes attributed to this Dracula are impalement, boiling alive, burning, decapitation, and dismemberment.

Recent research has enabled us to reconstruct the route followed by the author of that manuscript—Brother Jacob of the Benedectine order—and describe the circumstances of his first encounter with Dracula. Brother Jacob, together with two companions, Brothers Hans and Michael, were chased out of their abbey, called Gorrion (present-day Gorjni grad in Slovenia), for refusal to abide by the new rules adopted by the order. Forced into exile, the monks crossed the Danube and fled north to Wallachia, where they found asylum in a fifteenth-century Franciscan monastery still extant in Tirgoviste, not very far from Dracula's palace. A chance encounter with Dracula took place outside the princely palace. Dracula, always suspicious of visiting ecclesiastics (particularly Catholics), invited the monks to his throne room. He first ironically addressed Brother Michael, wishing to ascertain whether God had a place reserved for him in paradise notwithstanding the many victims he had sent to death. "In a way,' added the prince, "could one in the eyes of God be considered a saint, if one has shortened the heavy burdens of so many unfortunate people on this earth?" What concerned Dracula most was the expiation of his sins after death, a concern implicit in his attention to good works as a means of atonement: construction of and gifts to monasteries, services for the dead. Obviously intimidated by the awesome Impaler, Brother Michael attempted to assuage Dracula's

Raymond T. McNally and Radu Florescu, from *In Search of Dracula: The History of Dracula and Vampires*, pp. 78–92. Copyright © 1994 by Houghton Mifflin Harcourt Publishing Company. Reprinted with permission.

From the pamphlet publisher by ambrosius Huber in 1499 at Nuremberg. The text above the impalement scene states: Here begins a very cruel frightening story about a wild bloodthirsty man, Dracula the voevod. How he impaled people and roasted them and with their heads boiled them in a kettle, and how he skinned people and hacked them into pieces like a head of cabbage. He also roasted the children of mothers and they had to eat their children themselves. And many other horrible things are written in this tract and also in which land he ruled.

fears of hellfire. "Sire, you can obtain salvation," replied the monk, "for God in His mercy has saved many people." Thus, with hypocritical words Brother Michael succeeded in saving his own neck. But Dracula needed additional reassurance from the other monks. He therefore summoned Hans the Porter, asking him more bluntly this time, "Sire monk, tell me truly, what will be my fate after death?" The latter, who had the courage of his convictions, was forthright in his answer and reprimanded the prince for his crimes: "Great pain and suffering and pitiful tears will never end for you, since you, demented tyrant, have spilled and spread so much innocent blood. It is even conceivable that the devil himself would not want you. But if he should, you will be confined to hell for eternity." Then, with a pause, Brother Hans added: "I know that I will be put to death by impalement without judgment for the honesty of my words devoid of flattery, but before doing so, give me the privilege of ending my sermon." Annoyed yet fearful, Dracula allowed the friar to proceed: "Speak as you will. I will not cut you off." Then followed what surely must have been one of the most damning soliloquies that Dracula ever allowed anyone to utter in his presence: "You are a wicked, shrewd, merciless killer; an oppressor, always eager for more crime; a spiller of blood; a tyrant; and a torturer of poor people! What are the crimes that justify the killing of pregnant women … ? What have their little children done … whose lives you have snuffed out? You have impaled those who never did any harm to you. Now you bathe in the blood of the innocent babes who do not even know the meaning of evil! You wicked, sly, implacable killer! How dare you accuse those whose delicate and pure blood you have mercilessly spilled! I am amazed at your murderous hatred! What impels you to seek revenge upon them? Give me an immediate answer to these charges!" These extraordinary words both amazed and enraged Dracula. He contained his anger, however, and replied calmly, reasserting his own Machiavellian political philosophy, "I will reply willingly and make my answer known to you now. When a farmer wishes to clear the land he must not only cut the weeds that have grown but also the roots that lie deep underneath the soil. For should he omit cutting the roots, after one year he has to start anew, in order that the obnoxious plant does not grow again. In the same manner, the babes in arm who are here will someday grow up into powerful enemies, should I allow them to reach manhood. Should I do otherwise, the young heirs will easily avenge their fathers on this earth."

Hans knew his fate was sealed but insisted on having the last word: "You mad tyrant, do you really think you will be able to live eternally? Because of the blood you have spilled on this earth, all will rise before God and His kingdom demanding vengeance. You foolish madman and senseless, unhearing tyrant, your whole being belongs to hell!" Dracula became mad with anger. The monk had pricked him where it hurt most, in his conscience and in his belief that because he was appointed prince by God, who, in His mercy, would have pity on his soul. He seized the monk with his own hands and killed him on the spot. Forsaking the usual procedure, he forced the monk to lie down on the floor and repeatedly stabbed him in the head. Writhing in pain on the bloodstained floor, Hans died quickly. Dracula had him hanged by his feet from a cord. He then hoisted the unfortunate wretch on a high stake in front of the Franciscan monastery. For good measure he impaled his donkey as well.

One can well imagine the effect of this gruesome sight on the remaining monks. Terrified, they quickly abandoned the monastery. Brother Michael, whose cowardice had saved his life, and Brother Jacob, his surviving companion, crossed into Transylvania, then sought refuge in various Benedictine houses in lower Austria and at St. Gall in Switzerland. There they related their unsavory adventures to other monks, the tales obviously colored by the anguish of a close escape. It was in this manner that the first Dracula horror story was born at the end of 1462.

Brother Jacob settled at Melk, a large abbey on the Danube. This abbey, the inspiration for Umberto Eco's detective thriller *The Name of the Rose*, still occupies its commanding position on a hill dominating the river and is one of the most palatial Benedictine houses in Europe. It was at Melk that Brother Jacob met other Benedictine refugees from Transylvania. Dracula's horrors undoubtedly became a highlight of conversation among the Romanian and German monks attached to this grandiose monastery, and some of these stories were inserted into the annals of the abbey. It was also at Melk that Brother Jacob met the court poet of the emperor Frederick III, Michel Beheim, who lived at Wiener Neustadt, just a few miles from the abbey. By that time Beheim's skill at writing history in verse was well established. Among his many historical poems was a history of the Varna crusade, highlighting the role of Dracula's brother Mircea. Information of Brother Jacob's misadventures at Dracula's court whetted Beheim's appetite for yet another poem on the extraordinary Dracula family. The courtier sought out the monk in the summer of 1463. The poem was likely completed in that year.

This poem represents by far the most extensive contemporary account of Dracula's life story. Over a thousand lines, the original manuscript is housed in the library of the University of Heidelberg, where most of Beheim's other original manuscripts are kept. He entitled the poem *Story of a Bloodthirsty Madman Called Dracula of Wallachia* and read it to the Holy Roman Emperor Frederick III during the late winter of 1463. This story of Dracula's cruelties was evidently to the emperor's taste, for it was read on several occasions from 1463 to 1465 when he was entertaining important guests.

The progressive popularization of the Dracula story, however, was due to the coincidence of the invention of the printing press in the second half of the fifteenth century and the production of cheap rag paper. The first Dracula news sheet destined for the public at large was printed in 1463 in either Vienna or Wiener Neustadt. Later, money-hungry printers saw commercial possibilities in such sensational stories and continued printing them for profit. This confirms the fact that the horror genre conformed to the tastes of the fifteenth-century reading public as much as it does today. We suspect that Dracula narratives became bestsellers in the late fifteenth century, some of the first pamphlets with a nonreligious theme. One example of the many unsavory but catchy titles is: *The Frightening and Truly Extraordinary Story of a Wicked Blood-thirsty Tyrant Called Prince Dracula*.

No fewer than thirteen different fifteenth- and sixteenth-century Dracula stories have been discovered thus far in the various German states within the former empire. Printed in Nuremberg, Lübeck, Bamberg, Augsburg, Strasbourg, Hamburg, etc., many of them exist in several editions.

The following excerpt from the title page of a German pamphlet is a lurid preview of what lay in store for the reader:

> The shocking story of a MONSTER and BERSERKER called Dracula who committed such unchristian deeds as killing men by placing them on stakes, hacking them to pieces like cabbage, boiling mothers and children alive and compelling men to acts of cannibalism.

Woodcut portrait of Dracula from Ioan Bogdan's 1896 publication *Vlad Tepes*, where its source is identified as fifteenth- or sixteenth-century German pamphlet that was in Budapest.

By way of further enticement, the anonymous pamphleteers promised many other shocking revelations, plus mention of the country over which Dracula ruled. For dramatic purposes, the frontispiece of several pamphlets included a woodcut depicting the tyrant Dracula dining happily amid a forest of his impaled victims. Others simply showed Dracula's face, but with distorted features. One printed in 1494 has a woodcut portraying a bleeding, suffering Christ.

The deeds attributed to Dracula in the German narratives are so appalling that the activities of Stoker's bloodsucking character seem tame by comparison. The following excerpt is an example of "Dracula's unspeakable tortures unequaled by even the most blood-thirsty tyrants of history such as Herod, Nero and Diocletian."

> Once he had a great pot made with two handles and over it a staging device with planks and through it he had holes made, so that a man would fall through the planks head first. Then he had a great fire built underneath the

heads and had water poured into the pot and boiled men in this way.

The woodcuts graphically demonstrate that there were many methods of impalement: the stake penetrating the navel, the rectum, or piercing the heart—as vampires might say it—causing instant death. The "berserker" was not deterred by age, sex, nationality, or religion. Pamphlets mention the killing of native Romanians, Hungarians, Germans, Turks, and Jews; Gypsies, it seems, incurred Dracula's wrath on frequent occasions. Catholics, Orthodox Christians, Moslems, and heretics also perished. Mothers and even sucklings were executed; sometimes children's heads were impaled on their mother's breasts. There was, it seems, a stake in constant readiness at Dracula's palace.

The German writers relate that aside from impaling his victims, Dracula decapitated them; cut off noses, ears, sexual organs, limbs; hacked them to pieces; and burned, boiled, roasted, skinned, nailed, and buried them alive. In one verse Beheim described Dracula as dipping his bread in the blood of his victims, which technically makes him a living vampire—a reference that may have induced Stoker to make use of this term. According to the German sources he also compelled others to eat human flesh. His cruel refinements included smearing salt on the soles of a prisoner's feet and allowing animals to lick it off. If a relative or friend of an impaled victim dared remove the body from the stake, he was apt to hang from the bough of a nearby tree. Dracula terrorized the citizenry, leaving cadavers at various strategic places until beasts or the elements or both had reduced them to bones and dust.

How credible are these stories? Were they based on concrete historical fact, were they the product of sadistic propagandists seeking to awe or amuse, or were they written by monks simply to offer diversion from the daily fare of religious literature? Or, as some critics of these anecdotes have suggested, were they in fact contrived on orders of the Hungarian court to destroy Dracula's reputation and justify the harsh treatment subsequently meted out to him in prison? It would then follow that a common model inspired all the fifteenth-century Dracula narratives, whether German or not.

The Hungarian court had strong reasons for discrediting Dracula and having him safely removed from power. Aside from other factors, his strong autocratic rule threatened Hungarian hegemony in Transylvania. However, even granting that a common German anti-Dracula model may have inspired the accounts of the official Hungarian court chronicler, Antonio Bonfinius, one finds it hard to account for the similarity of the many other Dracula narratives written in a variety of languages and circulating over widely scattered geographic and political regions. For instance, the Russian Dracula manuscript closely coincides with the German stories. Yet to assume that all of these were mere translations of an original German source is to credit the fifteenth century with twentieth-century efficiency of transmission. In addition, the Russian and other narratives are sufficiently different in their explanation of the crimes to account for a single source.

One major argument against the theory of a common horror story prototype is provided by the oral ballads and traditions that contain anecdotes similar to those mentioned elsewhere, yet explain away the Impaler's crimes by providing rational motives. The Romanian peasants could understand neither German nor Slavonic, nor read or write even their own language. The Romanian Dracula narratives were stories composed in his lifetime, simply transmitted orally from one generation to another, very much in the manner of the Viking sagas. Not until the twentieth century were they formally committed to print, and it is safe to assume that a few Romanian anecdotes still go unrecorded.

One can pursue the argument against a single source by pointing out that identical stories about Dracula appeared in the reports of official chroniclers, diplomats, and travelers; in the folklore of neighboring states; and in a great number of languages: Italian, French, Latin, Czech, Polish, Serbian, and Turkish, obviously written by independent observers or commentators or sung by peasants.

To the determined skeptic, a sound yardstick of credibility is provided by the reports of diplomats stationed in the nearby capitals of Buda and Constantinople. Diplomats reporting to their home governments are usually wary of embellished facts, and their dispatches have to be terse and to the point. Here is a quote from the papal legate at Buda, Nicholas of Modrussa, reporting to Pope Pius II in 1464, referring to a specific massacre in which Dracula killed 40,000 men and women of all ages and nationalities:

> He killed some by breaking them under the wheels of carts; others stripped of their clothes were skinned alive up to their entrails; others placed upon stakes, or roasted on red-hot coals placed under them; others punctured with stakes piercing their heads, their breasts, their buttocks and the middle of their entrails, with the stake emerging from their mouths; in order that no form of cruelty be missing he stuck stakes in both the mother's breasts and thrust their babies unto them. Finally he killed others in various ferocious ways, torturing them with many kinds of instruments such as the atrocious cruelties of the most frightful tyrant could devise.

A contemporary papal nuncio, Gabriele Rangone, bishop of Erlau, reported in 1475 that by that date Dracula had personally authorized the murders of 100,000 people. This figure, if true, is equivalent to at least one-fifth of the total population of Dracula's principality, though the number obviously includes Turks, Germans, and other enemies.

In fairness to the narratives of the German monks, one should note that by mentioning precise locations in Transylvania and elsewhere, dates, historical figures, cities, districts and townships, and specific fortresses and churches, a measure of credibility is added to their accounts. In addition, they provide a fairly accurate geopolitical and topographical description of Transylvania. With pinpoint accuracy one German pamphlet, published in Nuremberg in 1499, refers to individual sections of Brasov, or Kronstadt (Kranstatt in Low German dialect cited below).

> And he led away all those whom he had captured outside the city called Kranstatt near the chapel of St. Jacob. And at that time Dracula ... had the entire suburb burned. Also ... all those whom he had taken captive, men and women, young and old, children, he had impaled on the hill by the chapel and all around the hill, and under them he proceeded to eat at table and enjoyed himself in that way.

This particular horror occurred outside the fortifications of Brasov in April 1459, undoubtedly one of Dracula's most dramatized atrocities. Dracula's famous meal among the impaled cadavers was immortalized in two woodcuts, one printed at Nuremberg in 1499, the other at Strasbourg in 1500. The mention of smaller townships, individual villages, monasteries, and fortresses further strengthens the historicity of the accounts. Although identification is at times difficult since most German names in use during the fifteenth century have been replaced by Romanian ones, and some ancient townships have now disappeared, it has been possible with the help of sixteenth-century maps to retrace Dracula's path of destruction through Transylvania.

Among the sources to which the historian can turn to verify the authenticity of the German accounts is the rich primary documentation in the archives of Brasov and Sibiu, fortified cities that figure prominently in all the German accounts. The Sibiu archive includes, among other items, one missive by Dracula himself, bearing the awesome signature DRAKULYA, a nickname that he adopted to demonstrate that he considered himself son of the crusading Dragon.

As the criminal investigator seeking the truth about a suspect looks for a motive, so the historian testing the veracity of these German stories looks for Dracula's motivation to commit his horrible deeds. Undoubtedly there was the occasional irrational streak in his character, but we have found all along that such moments were often accompanied by a keen awareness of the problem he was attempting to resolve. Some of his motives mentioned in the various German horror stories are best summarized below.

Revenge. The killing of Dracula's father and brother, Dracul and Mircea, related in the first episode of the St. Gall manuscript, are authentic historical facts. The assassinations both took place in 1447. Dracula's investigation into Mircea's murder prompted his enslavement of the nobles and citizens of Tirgoviste, which led to the construction of Castle Dracula.

The execution in 1456 of Vladislav II, Dracula's predecessor, can also be credited to revenge, since Vladislav was in part responsible for the assassination of Dracula's father.

Inter-family feuds. The struggle between the two rival factions of the Wallachian princely family, the Draculas and the Danestis, was a struggle for survival; it helps account for many of Dracula's massive raids. For example, it was because of the defection and betrayal of his half brother, Vlad the Monk, that Dracula destroyed cities and villages in his own enclave.

Protection of Transylvanian commerce. Most of Dracula's vindictiveness against the German Saxon population of Transylvania was due to an ill-defined but rising patriotism, directed in this instance against the commercial monopoly exercised by the German Transylvanian Saxons in all Romanian provinces. For instance, the incident mentioned by Beheim of Dracula's arrest of German youths traveling in Wallachia illustrates this intense belief in the national sovereignty of his state. In 1459 after secretly recalling his own Wallachian merchants from Transylvania, Dracula apprehended four hundred German-speaking Transylvanian trainees who had come to Wallachia in order to learn the Romanian language. He had them assembled in a room and burned alive. Dracula undoubtedly saw these apprentices less as trainees than as spies sent by the Saxon merchants of Brasov and Sibiu to learn about native methods of production.

Establishment of personal authority. As previously related, when Dracula first came to rule in 1456 Wallachia was beset by internal anarchy, *boyar* intrigue, rival factions, and Hungarian political pressure. The mass *boyar* impalement is vividly described in Beheim's poem and recounted in other sources. (The killings resulted from the lighthearted answers of the *boyar* council to Dracula's question: "How many reigns have you my loyal subjects personally experienced in your lifetime?") Thus Wallachia was immediately and horribly instructed that the princely title, and all that it implied, was not to be taken lightly. Moreover, the property of the victims was distributed to Dracula adherents, who formed a new nobility with a vested interest in the survival of the regime.

Affirmation of national sovereignty. Some of Dracula's motives to commit atrocities against the Turks were surely personal in nature, the result of the suffering he experienced during his imprisonment in Egrigoz when he was a boy. But he was impelled by national concerns, as well.

Dracula's defiance of the Turks included the famous scene in the throne room of Tirgoviste, when Turkish representatives failed to remove their turbans. This story, concluding with Dracula's moralizing about the impropriety of imposing Turkish customs upon another nation, clearly indicates his intention of affirming full national sovereignty over limited sovereignty.

Another indication of the veracity of the German stories is what they omit. For example, Beheim's poem includes an invaluable, detailed description of Dracula's last days of freedom in the fall of 1462, when he appealed to the Hungarian king for help and protection following his flight to Castle Dracula. It does *not* include an account of Dracula's subsequent imprisonment in Hungary; an understandable omission since German Transylvanian witnesses could hardly have been present in Buda.

In addition to anecdotes which can easily be placed in a geographical or historical context are a number which cannot be connected to any specific place or date, but which are nevertheless mentioned in the various German texts and form an integral part of the story.

The authenticity of such anecdotes can be substantiated because they occur in all three variants, German, Slavonic, and Romanian, and, for reasons explained, they could not have derived from a common literary model. In terms of content, moral and political philosophy, and even specific methods of punishment, they coincide fairly closely with those anecdotes that do have historical validity. They reveal characteristics of Dracula which correspond with traits expounded in the other anecdotes. They describe events and policies which can be verified.

One story tells of a famous fountain in a deserted square in Tirgoviste where travelers habitually would rest and refresh themselves. Dracula ordered a golden cup to be permanently stationed here for all to use. Never did that cup disappear throughout his reign. He was, after all, a "law and order" ruler.

A second anecdote tells of a foreign merchant who spent the night at an inn and, being aware of the reputation of Dracula's country for honesty, left his treasure-laden cart in the street. Next morning, to his amazement, he found that one hundred sixty gold ducats were missing. He immediately sought an audience with the prince. Dracula simply replied, "Tonight you will find your gold." To the citizens of Tirgoviste he gave the ultimatum: "Either you find the thief or I will destroy your town." Certain of success in advance, Dracula commanded that one hundred sixty substitute ducats plus one extra one be placed in the cart during the night. Duly the thief and the original ducats were found. Having proved the honesty of his capital, Dracula desired to test the ethics of the foreigner. Fortunately, he was honest and admitted to the additional ducat. While impaling the thief, Dracula told the merchant that such would undoubtedly have been his fate had he proved dishonest.

Both of these stories are in keeping with contemporary references to Dracula's attempt to set a strict code of ethics in his land — a most difficult thing to implement in a society known for its Byzantine cynicism and absence of moral standards, but not an impossible one, since Dracula enforced public morality by means of severe punishment. Narratives about burning the poor and the sick are more difficult to rationalize. Perhaps because of the exigencies of war Dracula could ill afford to feed useless mouths. Regarding the poor, Dracula may have imagined he was sending them to Paradise where they would suffer less, in accordance with Scripture. In the case of the sick, one might argue it was a form of mercy killing or perhaps an attempt to rid the country of the plague or other disease.

Throughout the various sagas one also notes a sadistic sexuality: the ritual and manner of impalement, a husband's forced cannibalism of his wife's breasts, and similar horrors. Here, again, Dracula employs morbid measures to impose puritanical morality. The extent of Dracula's indignation against an unfaithful woman almost surpasses belief. Dracula ordered her sexual organs to be cut out. She was then skinned alive and displayed in public, her skin hanging separately from a pole in the middle of the marketplace. The same punishment was applied to maidens who did not keep their virginity, and to unchaste widows. In other instances, Dracula was known to have nipples cut from women's breasts, or a red-hot iron stake shoved through the vagina until the instrument emerged from the mouth.

What explanation might successfully reconcile Dracula's apparent attraction to women with the savagery of his sexual crimes? One obvious conjecture suggested by the phallic use of the stake is some sort of sexual inadequacy, most likely partial impotence.

There are other, general considerations which must be kept in mind when evaluating Dracula's criminality. One is the proverbial concern of viewing a man's actions according to the standards of his time. Dracula's age was that of the spider king, Louis XI; Ludovico Sforza the Moor; the Borgia pope, Alexander VI; his son Cesare; and Sigismondo Malatesta. One could go on and on enumerating their brutal contemporaries. The point is that the Renaissance, for all its humanism, was marked by extraordinary inhumanity.

Impalement, though never before or since practiced on so wide a scale, was not Dracula's invention. It was known in Asia and practiced by the Turks. One recorded instance in the West is attributed to John Tiptoft, Earl of Worcester, during the War of the Roses, and he had learned it from the Turks.

Dracula's cruel traits were not unique in his family, either. We know little about his father, except that he was a crusader of the Order of the Dragon. Dracula's eldest legitimate son is remembered as Mihnea the Bad. Also, Dracula spent more years in prison than he did on the throne; his first imprisonment, by the Turks, began when he was no more than fifteen. But most of his experiences seemed to reinforce one fact: life was insecure—and cheap. His father was assassinated; a brother was buried alive; other relatives were killed or tortured; his first wife killed herself; subjects conspired against him; his cousin, a sworn friend, betrayed him; Hungarians, Germans, and Turks pursued him. When reviewing Dracula's life in light of his imprisonment and the chaos of his early years, it becomes all too clear that horror begets horror.

Dark Shamans

Kanaimà and the Poetics of Violent Death

Neil L. Whitehead

Introduction

THE TERM *KANAIMÀ* REFERS both to a mode of ritual mutilation and killing and to its practitioners. The term also can allude to a more diffuse idea of active spiritual malignancy, in existence from the beginning of time, that consumes the assassins. This book is about those killers and the reasons they give for their actions. It is also about their victims.

Kanaimà as an ethnographic issue is complex to research because it is a discourse that operates at a number of levels, referring simultaneously to the dynamics of the spirit world, physical aggression by individuals, the tensions and jealousies between villagers and family members, and the suspicions of distant enemies and outsiders. This means that any ethnography of kanaimà necessarily involves a broad appreciation of cultural life and social organization, not least because one of kanaimà's key characteristics is that it is regional, not just local, in its practice. It is therefore part of the cultural repertoire of a number of Amerindian groups, and is known of and suffered by their closest neighbors as well. As a result, one is simultaneously dealing with convincing case histories, wild rumors, considered attributions of blame, false accusations, ungrounded gossip, and justified suspicion.

This pervasive and profound discourse of kanaimà is a central ethnographic fact of the lives of the people of the Guyana Highlands. Both dramatizing the human condition and indicating its futility, kanaimà is a daily subject of conversation and closely influences the decisions that people make with its vision of a cosmos filled with predatory gods and spirits whose violent hungers are sated by humans. Decisions to go to the farm, to make a journey with someone else or not, to carry a gun or not, to pass by the spirit abode of a famed killer, or to walk by a longer route are thus woven into the texture of everyday life, influencing its practical aspects as much as the ideational. For those that participate in this discourse there is also the distant but steady drum beat of the killings that are the discursive proof of the malign nature of the cosmos and the enmity of others.

For these reasons the following study examines the discourse of kanaimà as well as the histories of the killings. This is not just for the good theoretical reason that acts and ideas cannot properly be treated as separate realms, but also because our notions of causality and facticity are challenged by the nature of kanaimà. Such has been the case in the study of magical and spiritual phenomena worldwide, particularly where the possibility of dark shamanism, "witchcraft," and assault sorcery is under discussion. While this is not a unique problem, however, this book is not about the philosophy of causation or the conceptual conflicts between "science" and "magic" but about the way in which such issues are woven into the fabric of everyday life; that is, this book looks at the poetics of kanaimà and the violent, mutilating death it envisages. This poetic is neither a system of empirical observation nor a fanciful embellishment of the inexplicable—it is both. The term *poetic*, in this sense, suggests that the meaning of violent death cannot be entirely understood by reference to biological origins, sociological functions, or material and ecological necessities but must also be appreciated as a fundamental and complex cultural expression. Such cultural expression itself, if it is to be understood, must necessarily involve competence in the manipulation of signs and symbols. Any particular act of manipulation—that is, any given cultural performance—is therefore akin to the poetical in that it involves discursive forms of allusion and implication that are highly specialized, albeit rarely textual. In short, I am not concerned with the formal properties of signs, symbols, and rituals—semiotics—but how those signs are used performatively through time—poetics.

I have been researching kanaimà among the Patamuna since 1992. Because the Patamuna and Makushi frequently intermarry, some of my information is derived from Makushi informants; however, as kanaimà is fundamentally a supra-ethnic phenomenon and is practiced by Amerindian groups throughout the Guyana Highlands, this regional perspective actually helps delineate the nature of kanaimà. Numbering around 5,000, the Patamuna are distributed in villages whose populations range

Neil L. Whitehead, from *Dark Shamans: Kanaimà and the Poetics of Violent Death*, pp. 1–9, 11–40. Copyright © 2002 by Duke University Press. Reprinted with permission.

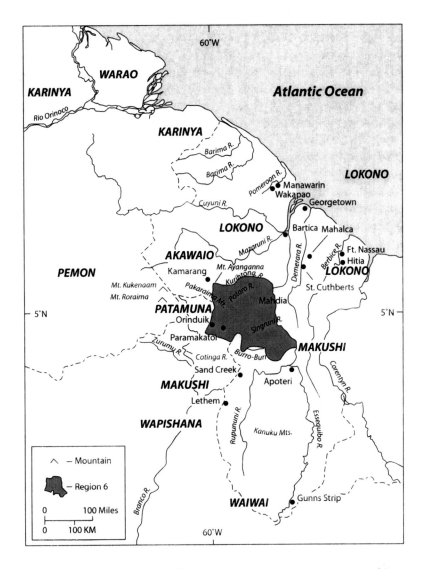

Map I. Map of the Guyana Highlands and Surrounding Region.

from 50 to nearly 1,000 people, the latter being the case for Paramakatoi, where I was largely based. However, many individual family *benab* (houses) or settlements of several benabs are strung out like beads along the main trails through the forest. Despite their tiny populations, these lone settlements may also have a deep historical resonance (e.g., Wandàpatoi). Such relatively isolated settlements once provided the context for kanaimà activity, but periodic warfare might sometimes have led to the formation of larger villages. Such aggregations would have split up eventually as the threat of raiding faded and people reverted to the "ideal" household context of forest seclusion. Today, even in a large settlement like Paramakatoi, the houses stand apart, placed on low hills surrounding the small savanna rather than being clustered in an overtly organized relationship to one another. However, particularly in Paramakatoi and a few other central settlements like Kato and Kopinan, during the recent period of rapid change following the arrival of the missionaries and the spread of the government's presence, larger villages have aggregated around landing strips, schools, medical posts, police stations, and stores. In addition, mining, logging, and the cross-border trade with Brazil have all served as dynamic influences in the social-structural changes. The Guyana Highlands comprise the upper reaches of the Essequibo River and its tributaries to the north (Mazaruni, Cuyuni, and Potaro) and are bounded by the Ireng River, the border with Brazil, to the south. At the heart of this region are the Pakaraima mountains, so named for the *pakara* (basket) shape of the *tepui* (granitic uplifts) that characterize the region. At the center of this mountain range and forming the point where the borders of Brazil, Venezuela, and Guyana meet is Roraima mountain, rising to an elevation of nearly 9,000 feet. Mount Kowa, which overlooks Paramakatoi, rises to about 3,000 feet, and there are numerous smaller elevations, "bumps," that are in the 1,000- to 2,000-foot range. Patamuna *asanda* (paths) use such bumps to cross from one valley to the next. Communication between villages involves walking these asanda, and most major settlements are about a day's walk apart, with smaller clusters of houses sometimes occurring in between.

Regions of Patamuna settlement are usually in the heavily forested valleys, such as the Yawong to the north of the Ireng, which to its south gives way to vast savannas of low scrub and grasses. The Patamuna and Makushi see themselves as primarily oriented to one or other of these ecotones and as a result the Patamuna are known to the Makushi as a people preferring the cool wetness of the forest to the hot, dry savannas. Both the Patamuna and Makushi are Cariban speakers, and their languages are somewhat related, although the Patamuna are linguistically closer to the Akawaio to their north. The general lifestyle of the Patamuna is well known from the many descriptions of tropical forest manioc farmers that already exist, although no particular ethnographic study of the Patamuna has been made so far. As will be evident from chapter 1, this work is not intended to be a general ethnography of the Patamuna but rather an ethnographic and historical study of kanaimà, in the context of the contemporary Patamuna. Socially the Patamuna also broadly conform to other, better-known Cariban groups of the region, practicing cross-cousin marriage, which is ideally combined with a uxorilocal residence. However, Patamuna society is very much in flux, and kanaimà itself plays an important role in the construction and persistence of particular forms of sociality.

Kanaimà is a form of dark shamanism, and one purpose of this work is to disaggregate our concept of "shamanism" and to show how it has obscured important differences and purposes in the range of shamanic techniques, as in the case of the Patamuna. This work identifies three distinct but related shamanic complexes: *piya*, *alleluia*, and kanaimà. Piya shamanism, most often described in general anthropological literature, refers to individuals who have the power to cure and kill but who are primarily sought after for the former purpose. At the end of the nineteenth century a new form of shamanism, influenced by contacts with missionaries, was invented in the Guyana Highlands and involved a direct relationship with *Katú/Akwa* (God). The key ritual technique of this complex is the possession of chants; these chants make use of certain non-Patamuna words or phrases, such as the term *alleluia* for which this ritual practice is named. The nature and meaning of kanaimà, a form of assault sorcery, and how it relates to these other shamanic complexes is the subject of this work.

Kanaimà involves the mutilation and lingering death of its victims and as such clearly involves criminal activity. Therefore, I have changed or obscured personal names, and occasionally places, in order to protect those who confided information to me. These informants included the families of victims, as well as avowed killers and kanaimà practitioners. These latter individuals were extremely difficult, as one might imagine, to interview. The interviews with killers in particular were both complex to arrange and expensive, though not all such interviewees were as knowledgeable as they sometimes pretended. I also interviewed practicing piya, *alleluia'san* (chant owners), and *kàyik* (eminent men) who have an excellent contextual knowledge of kanaimà. More difficult was to produce a statistical profile of kanaimà killing. My own assessment, based on the situation in Paramakatoi, was that such killings were regular but infrequent, amounting to around one per year. In any case, Guyanese law does not recognize the category of "kanaimà death,"

Map 2. Map of the Patamuna Region.

so cause of death is sometimes falsified to satisfy this bureaucratic nicety, as the interview with a government nurse indicates (see chapter 3). Such inattention from the Guyanese government and police led in part to the exceptional support I received from Patamuna in making this study. At the same time, no one would wish to inflict a campaign of "law and order" on the people of the Highlands, for such exercises are themselves apt to become indiscriminately lethal. Given this, kanaimà has become somewhat accepted and is endured as a mark of Amerindian autonomy. Since the politics of ethnographic representation in Amazonia are complex, this work was not written as promptly as it might have been, the issue of how it might be used beyond the anthropological community needing careful assessment; in other words, I wanted to avoid using anthropological representation in service of the state.

This work falls into six chapters. Chapter 1 details the chronology of my own fieldwork in the Pakaraima mountains and explains the circumstances under which I first learned of the kanaimà complex, how I was myself threatened by kanaimàs, and how I went on to interview avowed killers and their victims. The purpose of this will be to reflect on the entanglements that fieldwork involves, the ethical duties we have to our informants, and the unforeseen consequences of close ethnographic engagement. Chapter 2 gives a history of kanaimà as far back as it can be reconstructed, since sixteenth-century materials also point to the presence of the kanaimà complex. I give particular attention to the way in which kanaimà was presented by colonial, anthropological, and literary authors, especially those who claimed direct experience of kanaimà.

Chapter 3 opens with a synthetic account of kanaimà ritual practice, derived from the result of all the interviews. Patamuna testimony on the kanaimà is then presented, and such materials appear in all the subsequent chapters. Where possible I have reproduced verbatim narratives of kanaimà and the interviews with both killers and the families of their victims. All testimonies and stories were recorded on audio or video tape. If Patamuna was spoken, then the testimony was translated orally by a Patamuna and taped by myself. The resulting translation is reproduced verbatim, as are all materials originally spoken in Guyanese English, according to my transcription of the tapes. Synoptic accounts of events or persons derive from my field notes or conversations held in both English and Patamuna. I hope in this way to allow a fairly direct presentation of native voices, though clearly my acts of translation and editing necessarily obscure that aim to some extent. These materials are then discussed in terms of their thematic and empirical contents with a view to delineating the nature of kanaimà ideas and practices among the Patamuna and neighboring peoples.

Chapter 4 presents further ethnographic and historical materials relevant to shamanic warfare between kanaimà, piya, and alleluia prophets, as well as the Christian missionaries. This analysis of the war for the souls of the Patamuna is intended to draw out the historical changes in the meaning and practice of shamanic rituals and how those changes were connected to, and reciprocally influenced by, Christian evangelism and other forms of colonial intrusion. I also present an account of a particular shamanic battle between a piya and a kanaimà.

Chapter 5 then moves consideration of occult violence and its cultural meanings to a global stage. I suggest that, however unique South American kanaimà shamanism may be, it is still comparable to other resurgent forms of occult violence, assault sorcery, and even state-led campaigns of terror. The way in which the state itself co-opts occult magic is thus an important theme in the discussion, as is the way in which the advent of modernity relates to the expression of hypertraditionality in the form of kanaimà. In particular, I argue that kanaimà violence is an authentic and legitimate form of cultural expression and is mimetically linked to the violence of economic and political "development." The ethnographic materials for this chapter include accounts of alleluia, discussion of the mining frontier and its effect on the practice of kanaimà, current representational practices, and the making of a "snuff film" dealing with kanaimà.

Chapter 6 provides a comparative ethnological discussion of kanaimà and other forms of assault sorcery and also reviews current literature on warfare and violence in Amazonia, thus bringing together two bodies of theory—that of European and that of North American anthropologists—that have in large part developed independently. Examination of the kanaimà presents opportunities for both forms of analyses that makes use of the strengths of both schools of thought.

Chapter 1: The Ethnographer's Tale

As I got off the plane in Paramakatoi in 1992, I had not a thought of kanaimà in mind. The purpose of my journey was to make, in collaboration with the Walter Roth Museum of Anthropology, a preliminary survey of archaeological sites, in particular cave occupation sites, urn burials, and old villages. I hoped with that survey to begin to counter the exceptionally negative view that the region was sparsely populated and devoid of cultural time-depth, a view that had been promulgated in the archaeological literature outside of Guyana. I was accompanied by a Lokono man from the Mahaica River who was a highly experienced field archaeologist. He had been through the region a couple of years previously and had already examined the kinds of sites—old villages, burials, battle sites—that we were now interested in documenting as systematically as we could. We planned to walk out from Paramakatoi, south toward the Ireng River, then follow the north bank of the Ireng to Puwa village, turn north to Kurukabaru and then south again to Kato, where we would be able to catch a flight to Georgetown. Logistically and physically this was a difficult itinerary since we would have to carry most of what we needed over a terrain that features numerous mountains covered in dense tropical forest alternating with savannas. However, with the aid of various Patamuna who were enthusiastically behind the project, it seemed feasible to accomplish within the six to eight weeks we had planned to be away.

I want to emphasize the active participation of Patamuna individuals, both at the outset of this project and in subsequent ethnographic investigations. I do so to indicate not only their interest in my work but also the way in which my research was shaped by their priorities. While this may sound ideal, it meant that my research risked becoming partisan as it became more closely identified with the interests and ambitions of certain individuals, albeit that they were legitimate leaders of the community. This is not to suggest that there can be any "unpositioned" viewpoint; clearly any researcher is necessarily part of one kind of social network and therefore not another. However, the public authority of the individuals involved—or, later, their lack of it—became a particularly significant factor in the history of my fieldwork in the Pakaraimas between 1992 and 1997. It also fundamentally influenced my ability to gain otherwise relatively obscure, and even dangerous, knowledge.

Although this was not my first visit, Guyana had been relatively off-limits to anthropologists and most outsiders during the years of the Peoples National Congress government. Policies of self-reliance and an understandable antipathy to intellectual colonization by the United States and United Kingdom meant that foreign researchers were often judged superfluous. However, the Walter Roth Museum, under the directorship of Denis Williams, provided invaluable support for my field trips into the Pakaraimas, and without that assistance it is doubtful I could have worked in Guyana at all. I was therefore doubly pleased to not just be in Guyana but to have the opportunity to reach an interior region that was largely unknown in recent archaeology or ethnography.

Unknown to me at the moment the plane touched down, but soon apparent, the kanaimà would come to dominate that trip's research, as well as subsequent fieldwork in the region. Within thirty minutes of landing, we were visited by the Nurse for Paramakatoi, who politely listened to our plans, then launched into a startling account of what we "should really be investigating"—the kanaimà, especially because of the interest (not all of it favorable) that the earlier work of my Lokono companion had aroused.

It is hard now to reconstruct how much I knew or had heard of kanaimà before that moment, as it has come to dominate my thoughts over nearly the whole of the last decade. However, being reasonably well read in the anthropological and historical literature of northeastern South America, I had certainly heard the term. I had also at some point read Walter Roth's classic synthesis of materials on the kanaimà and so vaguely recalled kanaimà as some peculiar revenge cult that was probably in substance a colonially projected idea of native savagery. I had even referred to Brett's account of an "unappeased" kanaimà in a publication on Karinya warfare, but only as a possible example of the results of colonial suppression of warfare in the nineteenth century (Whitehead 1990b). I was therefore intrigued and surprised to find kanaimà being almost the first topic of conversation, since I had assumed that the phenomenon had simply faded away, which had seemed to be the implication of Roth's account. I could not have been more wrong.

The sequence of my own intellectual interest in kanaimà seems, as an anthropological issue and category of ethnographic description, to closely reproduce the history of anthropological debate about "cannibalism." As will become evident, nonnative ideas about kanaimà, as with cannibalism more widely, cannot be taken as simply reflecting impartial results of an encounter with some objectively present form of native savagery or exoticism. Rather, our interest in the savagery of others, in particular when it appears to take the form of cannibalism, clearly has served an ideological purpose in both politically justifying and morally enabling violent conquest and occupation of native South America (Arens 1979; Hulme 1986, 2000; Hulme and Whitehead 1992; Whitehead 1988, 1995a, 1995c). Nonetheless, ideological agendas aside, some cultural practices are undeniably challenging to interpret, in that they apparently give meaning and value to acts that we might abhor or simply deny as "real." However, this lack of "reality" often reflects our own lack of understanding, and what we actually mean is that those acts are "incomprehensible."

Kanaimà perfectly instantiates such a category, for the term invokes truly strange and troubling acts. In both the colonial literature and native oral testimony, kanaimà refers to the killing of an individual by violent mutilation of, in particular, the mouth and anus, into which are inserted various objects. The killers are then enjoined to return to the dead body of the victim in order to drink the juices of putrefaction.

> The ... victim will first become aware of an impending attack when the *Kanaimàs* approach his house by night, or on lonely forest trails [*asanda*], making a characteristic whistling noise. ... a direct physical attack might come at any point, even years thereafter, for during this period of stalking the victim is assessed as to their likely resistance and their suitability as "food."... In some attacks the victims may have minor bones broken, especially fingers, and joints dislocated, especially the shoulder, while the neck may also be manipulated to induce spinal injury and back pain. This kind of attack is generally considered to be a preliminary to actual death and mutilation; ... fatal attack will certainly follow but, informants stress, many months, or even a year or two, later. When a fatal physical attack is intended, victims are always struck from behind and physically restrained. ... A variety of procedures, intended to produce a lingering death, are then enacted. The victim has their tongue pierced with the fangs of a snake, is turned over and either an iguana or an armadillo tail is inserted into their rectum so that the anal muscles can be stripped out through repeated rubbing. Then, pressing on the victim's stomach, a section of the sphincter muscle is forced out and cut. Finally, the victim's body is rubbed down with astringent plants ... and a thin flexed twig is forced into the rectum, so that it opens the anal tract. Packets of herbs are then rammed in as deeply as possible. This is said to begin a process of auto-digestion, creating the special aroma of *Kanaimà* enchantment, rotting pineapple. ... As a result of the completion of these procedures, the victim is unable to speak or to take any sustenance by mouth. Bowel control is lost and the clinical cause of death becomes acute dehydration through diarrhoea. ... the *Kanaimàs* will try and discover the burial place of their victim and await the onset of

putrefaction in the corpse that usually occurs within three days. ... [When] the grave site is discovered, a stick is inserted through the ground directly into the cadaver, then the stick is retracted and the *maba* (honey-like) juices sucked off. ... If the corpse is indeed sufficiently "sweet," it will be partially disinterred in order to recover bone material and, ideally, a section of the anal tract. The use of previous victim's body parts is necessary to facilitate the location and killing of the next victim. (Whitehead 2001b)

One can readily appreciate, then, how issues of "representing others" are brought forcibly to mind by apparently "objectively encountering" such a ritual complex not as a textual remnant from colonial days but as the earnest testimony of living individuals. Moreover, I was to learn that the idea of kanaimà exercises a constant and intense influence over the cultural imagination of the Patamuna and their neighbors, the Akawaio and Makushi. However, my initial reactions to the Nurse were to try to fold her testimony into that more general discourse on "witchcraft" and to see her declarations as a performance of Patamuna alterity and desire to differentiate and distance themselves from others, especially white anthropologists.

However, the Nurse's—and later other's—absolute insistence on the physical reality of kanaimà, coupled with her sophisticated acknowledgment of its wider discursive properties, was unsettling; it challenged me to truly confront a kind of cultural difference that it had been easy to assume had been eroded by the long histories of colonial contact in this region, even if the Patamuna had not been in the forefront of that process. Indeed, I found that my hesitation to immediately acknowledge the reality of kanaimà put me alongside the British missionaries who had, according to the Nurse, assumed that kanaimà was just part of the "superstitious nonsense" cooked up by "primitive" peoples. The missionaries, lacking cultural competence, simply dismissed kanaimà as some kind of spirit, an example of Wittgenstein's observation that "Wherever our language leads us to believe there is a body, but no body exists, there is a spirit" (1953,1:36).

Nonetheless, if I had not then encountered something more "real" than "just talk," presumably I, too, would have remained within the standard view of the anthropological literature, that is, that whatever may have been true in the past, accusations of kanaimà exemplified the social functions of belief in witchcraft as a mechanism for community inclusion/exclusion. So they may be, but that by no means exhausts the matter—and not just because such a discourse might serve as a rich realm of cultural performance and signification, but because people actually die in ways consistent with the notion of kanaimà attack. I have never witnessed such an attack, nor have I attempted to do so, even though the lack of eyewitness accounts has rightly been adduced as an ethnographic weakness in anthropological discussions of cannibalism. Nonetheless, a moment's reflection should indicate that to witness physical violence is in itself extremely dangerous and necessarily entails complex ethical judgments as to how (and whether) such events should be described or published. Yet it is equally clear that the only difference between my position and that of the missionaries would be a willingness to take seriously what was so evidently being impressed on me—that kanaimàs are real people who do real killing of specific and identifiable individuals.

We were due to leave Paramakatoi early the day after next in order to keep to our itinerary, and though I made copious notes of that first conversation, I did not yet seriously entertain deviating from our original plan. So we walked from Paramakatoi, which is on a small savanna at the top of a mountain at the end of the Yawong River valley, down into the valley to search for our chief Patamuna collaborator, whom I call "Waiking." It was on this day that archaeology and kanaimà came together in a startling way. We learned that, at the head of the valley, there was a small cave, Kuyali'yen (Macaw Cave), in which an urnburial had recently been found. This was exactly the kind of information we had hoped to gather, and it immediately justified our decision to organize the research in a way that directly involved Patamuna. To have uncovered this site through physical survey would have been much more time-consuming and uncertain. We decided to visit the site immediately so that we could walk out of the valley, as planned, the following day.

When I first saw the "burial" I was disappointed as it was evident that the "burial" vessel was very small, not nearly large enough to contain a complete human set of remains. It was accompanied by a small *tumi* (offering bowl). It had not been my intention to collect archaeological materials; we not only wished to be alert to Patamuna sensitivities about the handling of ancestral remains, but we were also in no position to carry heavy and fragile ceramics for the remaining six weeks. However, what happened next was to become, both in my mind and that of others, a defining moment: as the Patamuna with us would not "trouble" the pot in any way, my Lokono companion moved the pot to the cave mouth where I could photograph it—and where I, too, without thinking, touched it.

This act came to define my identity to many Patamuna in many ways. Indeed, I believe I was to some degree manipulated into this "archaeological discovery," since I was not the first non-Patamuna to see it. It also transpired that the reasons for showing it to me were substantially more connected with contemporary conflicts than with the archaeological past, for the pot was in fact a ritual vessel still being used by a kanaimà, as was evident from the contents of the pot—it contained human skeletal and tissue material that appeared, and was later verified to be, very recent indeed, not at all archaeological. As yet, though, none of this was apparent.

At the time, and despite the obviously ethnographic nature of the context, we nonetheless had given an archaeological commitment to the Walter Roth Museum, which we honored by measuring and photographing the pot and, unfortunately, by removing a sample of the bone material to determine its age. I say "unfortunately" because this act, as far as can be said with certainty, may have been the immediate reason for an apparent attempt to poison me. The less-than-favorable light in which the earlier archaeological survey was held by some Patamuna thus came to have a real and definite consequence.

On our way back from the cave, my Patamuna companions suggested that this was something "kanaimà" and that we should return via the benab of an individual whom I call "Pirai." At that moment, I presumed that this was because Pirai was living the closest to the cave, but it transpired that he had a much more substantive connection with the vessel. I could not follow the initial part of the conversation with Pirai on arriving at his benab, but it was obvious that he was very excited and upset about something, and the word *kanaimà* occurred a number of times. We climbed back up the bump to Paramakatoi to find that news of the "discovery" was already in the village and that, in the opinion of those villagers who spoke to me about it, it was an excellent development and should enable the museum "to let everyone know the truth of those kanaimàs." But, whatever the intriguing ethnographic aspects, the implications of the ritual vessel seemed to be something I could better pursue on a subsequent visit and that anyway might not please the museum, on which I was reliant for future permissions to work anthropologically in the interior. All that was changed dramatically by the events that followed.

We were lodged at the boarding school for the duration of our visit, since it was still the Christmas vacation and the children had returned to their home villages. We also had use of the refectory, and while we were starting to prepare some food that evening, a Makushi woman came in and offered to cook for us. As she did so she started to talk animatedly about kanaimà, although we had not raised the topic, but neither of us spoke Makushi and her English was fragmented. I must confess that I had had quite enough of the topic for one day and was more concerned with how I was going to physically meet the challenges of six weeks of hard trekking. I knew that, among other things, eating properly was a basic rule, and I wished that she would simply serve up the rations that we had given her to prepare. The food was execrable. Although it was simply rice and a few dried shrimp, she had managed to make it taste absolutely horrible. My Lokono companion suggested that it was just the *casareep* (manioc juice) that she had used to flavor the dried shrimp and that I was being a typical "white boy" in my excessive delicacy of taste. But I had eaten casareep before and so just concluded that she was a lousy chef.

I have no proof otherwise and make no accusations, but I started feeling extremely ill within a few minutes of finishing that meal, and the symptoms got steadily and acutely worse during the next few days. I was quite unable to sleep that night because of a high temperature and incessant vomiting. I was feeling very weak by sunrise when, nevertheless, we set off back down the Yawong valley to rendezvous with Waiking. Thinking that my illness was a reaction to some form of food poisoning, I ignored my physical state as well as I could. However, in the general conversation we had while redistributing our loads at Waiking's house, the matter of my "illness" came up, as the *droghers* (carriers) were concerned about taking me into the bush while in such a condition. When I jokingly blamed the poor culinary arts of the Makushi woman, someone, I don't recall whom, remarked that to have let her cook for us was "a stupid thing to do, boy. Don't you know she lives by Pirai?" Of course we hadn't known, but with that strange luminosity that comes with feverish thought, I suddenly appreciated that what was being suggested was not poisoning *by* my food but *of* my food.

During that day my condition got worse and worse until, when we were almost at the summit of Aluatatupu on the other side of the Yawong valley, I collapsed with severe retching and stomach cramps. I had never ever lain down on the forest floor before, for the obvious reason that it is home to many voracious biting insects, but neither can I recall having felt quite so grim, even though I have had malaria, hepatitis, and pneumonia, as well as "normal" food poisoning. My companions carried me to the summit, about a half mile farther on. I was laid down and I cried by the waters of Akaikalakparu. In the crossing place of this creek is a small, submerged stone; carved on it is the face of a *totopù* (spirit guardian) who died right there, from exhaustion, as he couldn't make it down into the valley. We eyed each other balefully.

Everyone was thoroughly alarmed at the prospect of having me die, for it was acknowledged that even Patamuna could simply "fall down on the line [asanda]," that a fear of "not making it" would kill you as certainly as any accident or other misfortune. Of course, the Patamuna regularly walked this route and could easily make the next village, Taruka, from Paramakatoi. However, as the petroglyph of the to-topù's face at Akaikalakparu suggested, longer journeys were always a challenge for small parties or lone individuals, given the food shortages that could occur if the bumps weren't walked in sufficient time. It was not that people had no food, or indeed would refuse to share it if someone were desperate, but there was not necessarily enough food to buy or trade, and what there was had become extremely expensive due to the mining activities throughout the region. We had planned to reach Taruka in one day and Monkey Mountain in one or two days after that and so had only minimal rations with us. These were immediately exhausted by meals that night and the next morning. I slept for a few hours and actually felt better, if weak, the next day. My load was distributed among the others: Waiking; his brother, Yabiku; and Hashiro, my Lokono companion.

It took us all of that day to reach Taruka. On the line we had another uncanny experience when Pirai passed us in the company of two adolescent boys. What was peculiar was that he, as well as his companions, simply refused to address anyone. They emerged right behind us on the trail as we stopped by a creek to drink, and while Pirai made eye contact with us all, he responded neither to greetings nor to the insults shouted after him as he proceeded up the mountain trail. When we finally arrived at Taruka we were greeted politely and offered bowls of *cassiri* (manioc beer), but only one of my companions accepted, which I knew to be a real breach of etiquette. Taruka was a Makushi village at that time, and the conviction that the Makushi were kanaimàs was certainly part of Patamuna ethnic prejudices, but refusal of cassiri seemed to imply a very particular judgment about this village. Perhaps unsurprisingly, then, no one had food to sell us. This was a serious matter, as we had no food left and the only place to buy it would be Monkey Mountain, which we could clearly see some twenty miles away toward the Brazilian border.

We were stuck. We could not go on, or at least I couldn't, because I could hardly walk to the latrine, let alone Monkey Mountain, and my symptoms now became far worse, developing into a constant diarrhea and nausea. All that night I had to keep leaving the house we were lodged in. On one occasion I staggered some twenty yards from the house, squatted, and looked out over the savanna toward Siparuni mountain. The moon was bright, and as I tried to enjoy the beauty of the scene I saw in the distance some movement that appeared to be two distinct figures moving along the ground toward me. My first thought was that they were dogs, but as they turned to flank me they appeared instead to have the shape of anteaters because of the elongated head and tail. As I pulled up my pants, I looked away, then could not find the figures again when I looked back. Although that seemed odd, I reflected that, all other things considered, perhaps this was to be taken seriously. I would not recount this incident at all were it not for the unpleasant effect it had on everyone else, who immediately took the distant figures to have been kanaimàs and who were now convinced that the interest of the kanaimàs was centered on us. It was rather unsettling to be sick, to be a long walk from the next village, and to feel menaced by something I could not easily understand or explain away.

The next morning it had become vital that we either try to go on or go back, and we were fortunate that someone did finally sell us three eggs and some pieces of *tasso* (dried meat). We were not technically starving as yet. It was fortunate also that Waiking had been able to persuade someone to fetch a horse, Sharon, so that I could be carried down the trail to Monkey Mountain. Since everyone was now weak and tired from hunger, our progress was slow. Although I do not think we ate the whole of that day either, we did occasionally find wild cashew trees in fruit, which inhibited my diarrhea. As we finally reached Monkey Mountain early the next morning, we passed the remains of a crashed aircraft, a token of the mining frontier, once used by a Brazilian diamond trader who had been flown in to buy up stones. In Monkey Mountain we were able to purchase food, and we also met Johnny Roth, the great-grandson of Walter Roth. Having eaten at last, everyone was feeling better, including myself, and we planned to continue toward Puwa with a good store of rations. It was not to be.

I have taken some pains to depict the palette of events and ideas from which each of us constructed our pictures of what happened next, and I am not suggesting that we were necessarily all in perfect accord. I can therefore only speak to my impressions, but that certainly does not exclude suggesting the motivations present in others—that being the essence of any attempt at anthropological explanation or cultural interpretation. The pervasive nature of kanaimà as a cultural discourse and the manner in which I had entered into it—by inviting enmity as a result of "troubling" the vessel in Kuyali'yen—entailed certain consequences that were beyond my control.

I was lying in my hammock while the others had gone to the shop at Monkey Mountain, when, to my surprise, one of the youths who had been with Pirai on the line into Monkey Mountain appeared in the doorway. He said not a word at first and didn't respond to my questions. He then began to speak rapidly but deliberately in Patamuna, which I couldn't clearly follow. Waiking, Yabiku, and Hashiro saw the youth as they returned and they let out a loud shout, at which he bolted off. When I explained what had happened they suggested that he had been sent to "check you out" and that he had been threatening me. Whether or not this was the case, and I certainly don't like to think it was so, this at least suggested that we should abandon our original itinerary. It had been a key aspect of the project that it should be done with Patamuna cooperation and, although I was receiving support from some of them, it seemed that my presence was simply not welcome to others among them. Since this was actually the inference of my Patamuna companions, I also took this to mean that persisting at this point was likely to be a cause of further trouble for them.

In retrospect it is clear that tension was building with Pirai and that Hashiro and I were unwittingly increasing that tension, since we must have seemed intent on uncovering kanaimà pots as much as burials. Nonetheless, we all had the sense that we were being forced to give up something that was important and useful. Waiking and others in Paramakatoi, such as the Nurse, believed that a key aspect of future political and economic opportunities for the Patamuna was to possess a recognizable and distinct external ethnic identity. Archaeology and ethnography were seen as part of the means by which that could be achieved. In addition the Walter Roth Museum itself had been making a series of efforts to more adequately inform the Guyanese about the interior populations. The aim was to establish the antiquity of the Amerindian presence in Guyana through excavation and also to document the little-known highland peoples through broad archaeological and/or ethnographic surveys, such as the one we were conducting, as well as through longer term fieldwork.

At that moment it seemed to me that the best way to return to this survey, or another project in Paramakatoi, would be to leave now before the suspicions of kanaimà grew out of hand and something worse happened. In any case I was still very ill. I discussed the possibility of leaving with both Hashiro and Waiking, and we agreed that we should do so but that we would return and make the kanaimà itself the focus of investigation—not least because it was evident that the ritual vessel we had disturbed was very significant. To answer why that should be and to find further the physical evidence of kanaimà activity seemed feasible, if risky, given our own direct encounters with those held to be kanaimà. Moreover, to leave and then return, rather than continue on, seemed preferable at that point, not just because I was very sick but also because it would allow us to plan properly and let things calm down a bit. In addition, Waiking was adamant that it would be possible to interview piya on the matter, since there was a general feeling that the "work of the kanaimà had to be better known," and setting up those interviews would take time. The Nurse's testimony was further evidence of this appeal for openness about ritual practice, and I was intrigued to find myself already cast in the role of "ethnographer." Usually an ethnographer is expected to justify and explain that role as a precondition of extended research. So I was very impressed by the sophistication of Patamuna in exploiting the interest of outsiders for their own benefit. In fact, I came to understand that this theme had been very deeply inscribed on their historical consciousness, as the "fetching" of both alleluia and various missionaries into Paramakatoi, which I discuss later, clearly showed. In this sense it was not me as such but the need for a certain kind of external connection that made me appropriate and useful in the political aims of Patamuna.

So that was it. We used the police radio at Monkey Mountain to contact the bush-pilot Derek Leung who extracted Hashiro and myself the following morning. We had promised Waiking that we would return at a future date.

Once in Georgetown we decided to utilize the remaining weeks with a survey of archaeological sites on the Berbice River which proved to be highly productive. But with time and distance I found myself more and more intrigued by what had "really happened" in Paramakatoi, and the kanaimà remained for me a continual topic of conversation, reflection, and inquiry. I had felt a bit better when I returned to Georgetown, with only intermittent fever, vomiting, and diarrhea, but I became alarmed again when I started urinating blood after a couple of days in Berbice. I had now begun to be persuaded that whatever the cause of my sickness it was not routine, as the symptoms did not match readily with any particular cause. Hashiro then had the suggestion that I fight "fire with fire" by consulting someone on the Berbice who had knowledge of bush-medicine. This we did and I swallowed what I was given. I stopped passing blood.

It was only then that Hashiro told me something which he had not previously mentioned—his own father had been killed by kanaimàs. According to Hashiro, his father was working as a woodcutter at the time and had gone upriver to Mahaica, only stopping at St. Cuthbert's, where they lived, to collect pineapples. He returned unusually late, around 6:30 P.M., saying he couldn't remember why or what had happened. His wife began to worry about him, but he bathed as usual. He then started feeling very sick and from then on his condition deteriorated rapidly. Despite seeking medical help in Georgetown the very next day and being given a clean bill of health and a release form, he died suddenly on the third day. As he was being prepared for burial the family noticed finger marks and bruising on his arms and back. For the family this was evidence of the *yawáho* (kanaimà) but they insisted that this was actually a case of an attack gone wrong, in that the man who claimed the killing had mistakenly identified Hashiro's father as the intended victim. According to Hashiro, they also pointed to the fact that the killing was "not done that way," implying that the attackers had actually realized their misidentification and had therefore stopped short of enacting the full kanaimà ritual. However, Hashiro further surprised me by making an explicit connection between his own earlier work in the Paramakatoi region, the possibility that his father's death might have been intended for himself, and the menacing circumstances we had just encountered. In short, Hashiro felt that I was becoming involved in an active contest between the kanaimàs and those who would "expose" them.

I was not able to return to Paramakatoi until 1995 as I had accepted a post in the United States, at the University of Wisconsin. The demands of migrating from England to a new country with a wife and two small children, none of whom had visited the United States before, had meant I could not visit South America in 1993. Prior to this, on my return from Paramakatoi in 1992, my father had been diagnosed with inoperable colorectal cancer, on top of which my maternal uncle died just before Christmas of that year. I will say that this deeply affected me, as the loss of a father in particular would affect anyone, but that it also affected my view of the events in Guyana. In that time of stress it was hard not to recall that Hashiro's father had been "mistakenly" killed for his son and to not let form the idea that the anal wounding of the typical kanaimà victim was somehow being recalled and reduplicated, first in the rectal pain I had suffered as a consequence of being continually sick, and then in the fatal rot that was eating away my father's insides. He did not go quietly into that long night, and my family situation meant that it fell to me to nurse him in his last weeks of life in the spring of 1994. Again, then, I was unable to return to Paramakatoi, although I had kept the connection with Waiking active with the help of the museum and Hashiro.

In 1995, however, I was able to plan my return to Paramakatoi for the summer months. By that time, having had many reasons to contemplate the cultural forms of death and dying, I was also resentful and angry toward those who, it seemed, had tried to poison me—for on my return to Guyana I found that this was the story being told. This story was heard not just in Paramakatoi, where anthropologist Duncan Kilgour had recorded it in 1994, but it also had spread right across the highland region to Lethem and eventually even as far as Dominica in the Caribbean. My return to Paramakatoi was thus considered highly significant, both because it signaled a refusal to be intimidated by the possibility of kanaimà and because I could be of definite use as an ethnographic recorder. In fact, it was my work on historical themes that proved the most important, as the textual recording of oral history was, for the Patamuna in Paramakatoi, the principal benefit of my presence. The investigation of kanaimà was certainly a secondary consideration for some Patamuna and was therefore always going to be the more provocative and divisive subject of research. However, there was also strong support for bringing kanaimà "into the open," to publish accounts of their practices, to "collect" their ritual equipment, and to interview avowed kanaimàs directly so that their "reality" could finally be established in the minds of outsiders and so that their violent criminality, as it was then pictured, might somehow be curbed.

During 1995 I collected both oral histories about the Patamuna generally and about

Paramakatoi in particular (Whitehead 1996c). I was also able to interview piya on the subject of kanaimà and, eventually, a powerful kanaimà himself. The centerpiece of the oral historical materials was undoubtedly the testimony on warfare, alleluia, and the arrival of the missionaries; such testimony was given in rather a formal way. I was not encouraged to ask questions as such, but rather to be as faithful a recorder as possible. Testimony was always given in Patamuna, tape-recorded, then translated and transcribed into English by myself and an English-speaking Patamuna. The Patamuna also insisted on the adoption of particular spellings for Patamuna words, since they felt that misspelling was a particularly damaging form of misrepresentation by outsiders, given their overall commitment to resisting language loss.

As a result of achieving the aims of addressing Patamuna wishes for a record of key events in the history of both Paramakatoi and the initial occupation of the Yawong Valley by the Patamuna ancestors, I then received full support for researching the issue of kanaimà. The key interviews with piya and kanaimà occurred during my 1995 research trip. Without the assistance of Waiking, the initial interviews could not have been easily achieved, but once I had identified the key kanaimà, I then made independent approaches. These interviews were hard to broker, but the lure of money and the sense that, whether or not they granted interviews, I was going to say or do something which might affect them did encourage some kanaimàs to speak with me. This in turn built a momentum such that more senior kanaimàs, their ritual tutors, finally also agreed to speak directly with me. I avoided Pirai, however, because of a suspicion that he was behind the problems I had experienced in 1992. The younger kanaimàs were often braggarts and sometimes really quite ignorant of ritual matters, but they did allow me to form a picture of possible motivations for becoming involved in kanaimà practices. The older kanaimàs were much more intimidating, less given to freely explaining their motives or procedures, and physically wasted in appearance. Interviews with piya were also complex to arrange and conduct but were not tinged with the same air of menace. The most forthcoming of the older kanaimàs, whom I call "Emewari," probably supplied the bulk of the information I had from these sources, and other interviews were really confirmations (or not) of what he said. The other key interview was with a piya who is known widely across the region, and it was he who made a shamanic attack on a kanaimà while I was present, though I think not at my behest.

The interview with Emewari was of course invaluable, not just for the detailed information he gave but also because the conviction that kanaimà lacked "reality" had arisen in part from the absence of anyone avowing to be a killer. I should note that Emewari asked for, and got, a considerable sum of money for information on the kanaimà. Although I was initially suspicious of the fact that such knowledge would be "for sale" at all, I found that for the kanaimà, as for the piya, material rewards serve as tokens of spiritual eminence and power. I would also add that, as with all the other avowed killers I have encountered, Emewari had a marked tendency to boast about what he could achieve. Since most avowed killers admit to no specific killing and allusions to killing are often given metaphorically—as when it is said "we tied a cow" to mean "trussed up a victim"—it is perhaps unsurprising, then, that Emewari was extremely difficult to interpret, speaking of certain events through allusions to individuals I could not identify and using words that were not of Patamuna origin. Although I had linguistic assistance from a Patamuna, who I cannot name for obvious reasons, the results of this much-anticipated encounter were still frustratingly incomplete—one always thinks of the best questions only with hindsight. However, what I did understand was illuminating, even if still somewhat inconclusive, which I'll discuss in chapter 3.

As mentioned, I was able to supplement this interview by seeking out alleged kanaimàs in more distant villages, and even in Georgetown, the capital of Guyana. None of these individuals would admit to any specific incidence of violence, but most were grimly keen to "educate" me in generalities. For this, I had to play my role as one who was morbidly fascinated with kanaimà and with "manly" violence more generally, and who was quite ready to recount my own "experiences" of inflicting pain and violence in return for theirs. The catalog of violence in and by Western cultures from which I could draw such "experiences" is sufficiently replete and shocking to have made kanaimà appear quite tame at times. In particular, I remember that tales of Nazi atrocities and the refinements of modern "antipersonnel" armaments, such as the Claymore mine, particularly captured the imagination of one of these individuals.

The reasons that these interviews were possible at all were, I believe, closely connected to the political positioning that was going on in Paramakatoi in 1995 with regard to promised, or at least rumored, development schemes. I think the Patamuna felt that, if it were to be the subject of an ethnography, kanaimà would no longer be merely a "cultural problem" for the Patamuna but could be repositioned as a political and law enforcement "problem" for the government. As various interest groups vied for the scarce resources of the Guyanese state, the issue of kanaimà, it was supposed, would politically dramatize the situation of the Patamuna and therefore encourage attention to their overall situation.

Operating on a subtler level were the more local conflicts that led some individuals to see my "research" as a way of getting back at those boasting of their kanaimà connections or knowledge. If such supposedly "secret" knowledge could be made available to all, through writing about it and publishing the results, then the "real story" of kanaimàs could be told and their influence undermined. It is certainly the case that the very vagueness, yet pervasiveness, of the presence of kanaimà allows it to assume a central place in indigenous imagination. Given this, the kind of "documentation" that outsiders are particularly good at producing serves to make exact and particular what otherwise can be elusive and uncertain. In this sense kanaimà is a joint and mutual cultural production not just by practitioners but by victims, bystanders, and outsiders, as well.

Nonetheless, community support resulted in interviews not only with avowed kanaimàs but also with many of the victims' families, as well as with piya who had experienced spirit battles with kanaimàs. The atmosphere in Paramakatoi, however, began to intensify as more people learned that we had been "troubling" kanaimà and, worst of all, had recovered some ritual paraphernalia used by a killer (see page 89 and plate III). As a result I received a very alarming note from Waiking, warning me off further inquiry into the topic and withdrawing his hitherto vital assistance and protection. This was quite understandable under the circumstances, but it left me feeling very exposed and uncertain—perhaps I had been too successful and thus was inviting attacks on those who had helped me, or even on myself?

Such thoughts were not dispelled by the various warnings I then began to receive, sometimes from individuals with whom I had never spoken, warnings to the effect that I had "gone too far," that I should not have troubled such things. It was therefore particularly unsettling to be visited, on three successive nights, by an unidentified person(s). I was lodged in Paramakatoi in a four-room concrete building next to the clinic. The windows had firmly locking shutters, and the only door was also secured by a strong lock, although there were, of course, gaps in the fit of both windows and doors. I was alone, since only other visitors would sleep there. Although I had assumed that, whatever the case in 1992, the passage of time and my apparent ability to culturally negotiate interviews with kanaimàs had rendered me irrelevant or external to the politics of ritual assassination, those illusions were ended over those three nights. Each night, I would clearly hear the approach of one person, maybe more, followed by the sound of a deliberate scratching at the doorframe and windows. I would call out but receive no reply. Then, once again, I would hear scratching that moved in a circle round the building, ending back at the doorway each time. I might have taken this as a (not very funny) prank by the young men had it not been that on each occasion I found afterward a *yamaliwok* (coral snake) somewhere in the house.

I would have been much happier to think of these incidents as coincidence and overactive imagination—and I admit that my imagination had been put into overdrive by that point. However, the very unwelcome news soon came that "Bishop," held to be the most adept kanaimà from the Kopinan River, had already left there five days before to come over and "check me." The bearer of these tidings was particularly alarmed because that meant that he must already be "in the bush outside PK [Paramakatoi]," as he had not come into the village. I was also visited by one of my most knowledgeable informants, whom I call "Acoori," as well as by the village *Tushau* (chief), who both warned me quite strongly to now desist as "bad things were happening."

With only about ten days left in my planned time in the Paramakatoi region, I decided that this was definitely the moment to go, but only after having first promised to return when the oral historical materials were in a published form. Around that time, I also began to get high fevers in the night, which I could not separate in my imagination from the alleged presence of Bishop and the unsettling events around my own house. In fact these fevers continued for about two months after my return to the United States. The doctors were unable to identify a cause as such, but while investigating all possible angles they discovered that I had incurable hepatitis C, probably contracted from contact with a large amount of infected human blood when I went to the aid of someone accidentally who had severed an artery with a cutlass while working on his *mùloka* (farm). So it felt as if the kanaimàs had gotten me anyway!

The Walter Roth Museum responded magnificently to both the historical materials and the desire of Patamuna leaders to see them published. Denis Williams suggested that I put the materials into order and that the museum would then print them up in pamphlet form for distribution as widely as possible among the Patamuna villages. The result was published in 1996, and I returned in 1997 to carry the 5,000 pamphlets up to Paramakatoi and help with their distribution.

When I returned to Paramakatoi in the summer of 1997, various Patamuna expressed a great deal of satisfaction with the outcome of my previous visit and held a parade and ceremony to hand over the "little history" that had been made. At this point I also hoped to be able to reinterview some people as, inevitably, there were many aspects to kanaimà magic and ritual that remained obscure. However, interest and support for this had waned, and those who had previously supported the research were now quite hostile to me. I found out that the reasons for this were threefold. First, a strong suspicion had developed that all along I had only been trying to initiate myself as a kanaimà. This threw me somewhat, as quite the opposite had always been the basis of our collaboration, but it was sufficient indication that I should not look to the same set of individuals for more assistance with this. Nonetheless, I very much needed to dispel this suspicion, which had been "proven" by a sequence of deaths that had occurred since my last visit, among them the wife of Pirai and the father of the family that lived next to him. I countered that the deaths of my uncle and father were equal proof that I was not the origin of the "magical death" sent against them. In addition, some argued that the white man was probably trying to steal kanaimà, just like he stole cocaine from the Amerindians, and that he would put kanaimà to use against the Amerindians, just as he had done with cocaine. On this occasion I countered that the white man had no need of kanaimà, that the whole of the Yawong valley could be made a desert if the white man called in an airstrike, so that we had no need of kanaimà. I don't know how convincing this ultimately was, but it abated talk of my "becoming kanaimà." Connected to their suspicions was also the charge that I had stirred up trouble between Paramakatoi and neighboring villages by having published, in the oral history pamphlet, Patamuna accounts of warfare that featured a well-known raid by the Kopinan on Paramakatoi. Unfortunately my protestations that I had only faithfully done what I had been asked to do could not overturn the impression that this might be another example of my "kanaimà-like" propensities for conflict.

A second reason for hostility was the emergence of a new antipathy to external researchers in general and the threat that such researchers might steal from or otherwise exploit indigenous people for their cultural knowledge. The figure of the ethnobotanist, I must say, rather than the ethnographer was the chief villain of the piece. The debate around intellectual property rights, quite rightly, had become a big issue with all the Amerindian people in Guyana, but the effect for me was to have to continually explain why the notion that I could "make millions" from my research was unfair, if not entirely inaccurate in relative terms. Clearly I was better off materially than all the Patamuna, so I could certainly pay them for assistance at a rate that reflected that relative wealth, but unfortunately not at the level that the rhetoric of the foreign nongovernmental organizations suggested.

A third reason for encountering new difficulties may have stemmed from the "magical force" of the pamphlet itself. By this I mean that the mere fact of the pamphlet, whatever its particular contents, stimulated excitement because of an association, initiated in alleluia shamanism, between texts and divine power. Alleluia thus comprises both alleuia'san and *iwepyatàsak* (prophets) and, as will later become clear, such prophetism has often been evidenced through the possession of special texts. That may also be the reason why I was told that both the pamphlet and my presence had been prophesied. Either way, that was not a recommendation for those already becoming ill-disposed to the research.

Given these obstacles, the opportunity to interview kanaimàs farther seemed unlikely, if not foolish. I therefore decided to examine the relationship between kanaimà and alleluia more closely, since it had struck me that there was perhaps a ritual and a historical connection. I also knew that alleluia had gone "underground" in Paramakatoi after the arrival of the Pilgrim Holiness missionaries but was not by any means extirpated. Unfortunately, those who had formerly assisted me were not only now reluctant to speak out about kanaimà but also showed a similar disinterest in discussing alleluia. I therefore got to know Alfred Edwin one of the still-practicing alleluia singers, and his son, Roger. From Alfred, and with the translation assistance of Roger, I recorded both alleluia songs and a whole series of mythic tales and historical accounts. In particular Alfred guided us to many of the alleluia places in the Yawong valley that had fallen into disuse. This was the happiest of times, and the materials we gathered will certainly be the subject of further publication, but the practice of alleluia also carries political implications. Neither did we ignore the subject of kanaimà ignored, and it was precisely the disinterest of my earlier collaborators that now encouraged other Patamuna to relate their experiences and even act them out.

These changing orientations of my research directly replicated some of the social and political divisions in Paramakatoi itself. No longer being exclusively involved with one extended family, I was now able to be much more involved with others, like the Edwins. They did not have a high status in Paramakatoi, and this was partly connected to their obdurate practice of alleluia. Alfred's brother, Roy, is a lay pastor in the village and therefore gave up being an alleluia singer against Alfred's wishes, evidence that even close family ties were affected by decisions to abandon, or not, the practice of alleluia. Roger wanted his father's songs to be heard again in the village and to have a film record made of the event. The idea thus evolved that I would sponsor an alleluia event that would enable Alfred to sing alleluia in Paramakatoi for the first time since the 1960s. Roger therefore spent an enormous amount of time and effort to build an "Alleluia House" as a venue for this rather subversive event, which was simultaneously a snub to those who had withdrawn their support for my researches. The resulting event was filmed, but what the film cannot adequately communicate was the background conflicts that were played out that day and night.

People began assembling at the Alleluia House the day before the singing was to begin, and I was surprised to see that people had traveled up from as far as Lethem to join in the event. This did not mean that all who had come had come to see it succeed, and my heart fell when a group from Lethem wired a boom box to a car battery and started playing Brazilian samba and passing out bottles of rum. Given the sacral nature of alleluia, such behavior would ruin the possibility of the event vindicating alleluia in Paramakatoi. The next day was to be the commencement of the alleluia singing, but the following morning the samba party was still in full swing. A showdown had to be engineered to eject the interlopers, if not quiet them. As the day wore on, more and more people from Paramakatoi arrived at Roger's place, and it became clear from the reactions of the crowd, that the "moral majority" was definitely in favor of hearing "real" alleluia, and the loutish elements were quickly quelled.

So it was that the first alleluia songs were heard in Paramakatoi for over forty years, and I can only say that it was a true privilege to have been there. Indeed, those who had abandoned me so suddenly were now insisting that I return with video equipment as soon as possible in order to record "proper" alleluia. These same individuals had boycotted Roger's event, considering it too much of a "spree" (drinking party), just as the outsiders from Lethem had wanted. Indeed, the disruption by the outsiders from Lethem may have been directly encouraged by these individuals, since a younger brother of one was prominent in the attempt to wreck the event.

This was the closing scene from that 1997 trip, and I returned to Georgetown and again received the enthusiastic support of the Walter Roth Museum for a publication containing all the materials on alleluia and kanaimà I had just gathered, which would then be distributed among Patamuna villages, as had happened with my first set of materials. But I should have known that such things cannot be easily repeated. Even as I was rushing to complete the manuscript for the museum back in the United States, Denis Williams, the director of the museum, was dying of what had become symbolically potent to me: colorectal cancer. While Williams did review and approve my manuscript before he died, which was a comfort to me, he was not always an easy person and was therefore a controversial figure in Guyanese political life. The Ministry of Culture, which took over the administration of the museum after Denis died, saw only a minimal academic product in my manuscript and so declined to publish the work, even though the galleys were already at the printer. Unlike Denis, the ministry saw no political value in the production and donation of this text to the Patamuna. The Patamuna themselves, I later learned, had come to suspect the museum of selling the earlier work at a great profit, since there was a nominal cover charge for tourists or visitors who purchased a copy at the museum itself.

On top of this I was given a final "sign" that the project, so precipitously begun in 1992, was probably at an end. Derek Leung—the bush-pilot without whom not only my fieldwork but more important the daily life of the people in Paramakatoi would have been infinitely more difficult, for want of emergency medical assistance and supplies of gasoline, tools, and the like—was killed. His plane lost instrumentation just outside Mahdia, his base of operations, and, according to air-traffic control, his last words were, in that inimitable terseness that was his hallmark, "Ooooh fuck." The logistical and political obstacles to my return seemed insurmountable, and the writing of this book is partly a symptom of that frustration.

The way in which ethnographers might become enmeshed in the beliefs and desires of those they study has been addressed before in the anthropological literature, and the book that I read in 1995 that seemed best to provide an analogy with my own situation was Paul Stoller's and Cheryl Olkes's (1987) account of their time with Songhay sorcerers in the Republic of Niger. What struck me about the account was that, in seeking to understand Songhay sorcery more closely, Stoller was sucked in as an unknowing agent of sorcery, even to the extent of possibly having been responsible for someone's death. This story is still, strangely, something of a comfort, as I remain anxious as to the reason for the shamanic assassination of a particular kanaimà, since its occasion was so conveniently timed to satisfy and so closely tied to my intense interest in such shamanic warfare, as I discuss later.

In South American ethnology in general, the topic of violent and aggressive shamanism has rarely been broached, and I made a point of canvasing colleagues as to whether or not they had had any similar experiences, or even experience of killing shamanism at all. I was surprised, and somewhat relieved, to find that this phenomenon was more common than I had thought, though it was not part of my colleagues' research projects at the time. Darell Posey, an anthropologist of the Kayapó, wrote the following to me in 1996: "I REALLY enjoyed our brief encounter in Madison. Your research is certainly interesting and, well, frightening. I have seen so much of this stuff up close and from around the edges ... and, frankly, one of the reasons I left the Kayapó was that I was learning too much about these things. The other dimensions (death-shamanism) have a physical component, but the visible is only the mask."

Terry Roopnaraine, a fellow anthropologist born in Guyana, wrote to me in June 1997, just after my departure from that country. He had returned from the Pomeroon, where he had decided to make inquiries about kanaimà, being intrigued and perhaps a little skeptical of my reports from Paramakatoi since he had himself done his doctoral research in Monkey Mountain:

> "This is pretty much everything I have on kanaimà. I believe that there is more information to be had, but frankly I got too nervous to pursue the matter. As I said on the phone, I had three successive nights of identical nightmares. For about a week, I was very edgy and quick-tempered. All in all, I had the feeling that there was something awful crawling in my head. Sometimes, for no apparent reason, all the hair on my arms would stand up. On a couple of occasions, I just started crying, apropos of nothing. So I am sorry, but I am very reluctant to continue these inquiries in the field. There are some things best left alone. I was getting genuinely worried about you in the Pakaraimas, and I am very glad you're OK."

Terry expressed well the emotional state that dealing with kanaimà generates, and certainly a daily focus on kanaimà meant I often felt I was just "getting through it." Both Darrell and Terry were also right to raise the possibility that such things might be better left alone, but, as I related, the intensity with which an investigation of kanaimà was initially supported and the genuinely affecting stories of those who had suffered from their attacks had caused me to persist. Of course, these were not the only reasons; no academic can help being seduced by the prospect of discovering what has previously been secreted or hidden, of making that original contribution to the ethnographic literature of the region, so I suppose that motive must have been in there, too, crowded out though it was at the time by the sheer vividness and immediacy of kanaimà violence. I also think that a certain anger, connected to my grief after the death of my father, was focused into my research on kanaimà and that such anger led me to persist in the face of difficult or trying circumstances.

Despite my personal rage, there has also been a wider mythopoetic dimension to my experiences, in that they at times seem to uncannily recapitulate the experiences of other outsiders who encounter kanaimà. Graham Burnett (2000, 183–89) provides a nice discussion of the reactions of various nineteenth-century travelers to the "demon landscape" of the interior of Guyana, pointing out how the discovery and desecration of native spirit places, as well as their occasional defacement, served to enable the possession of that landscape through a mapping and surveying that exorcized the genius loci. In a less literally geographical sense, ethnography also, through its explanations, undoubtedly robs cultures of some of the force of their performative expression. In this sense, knowledge itself becomes colonial (Whitehead 1995b). However, as Burnett also notes, the very "recognition of the hallucinatory power of the landscape placed the explorer at risk; it was a short step from empathy to the kind of collapse—the 'going native' (or mad)—that disqualified the explorer," and also the ethnographer, no doubt.

In the hallucinatory landscape of kanaimà, tales or allegations of whites poisoned or killed by the kanaimà are of particular interest for the way in which they reveal the nature of kanaimà as a cultural discourse. As such, kanaimà is not just directed toward other Amerindian groups, nor only toward co-villagers, but also toward the agents of eighteenth- and nineteenth-century "colonial" and twentieth-century "modernizing" development. The colonial development of the interior, principally under the Dutch, was intended to occur through trade for forest products, which included slaves. By 1750 it was already apparent that such trade had indeed had a considerable effect on the peoples of the interior, particularly in the Essequibo-Rupununi-Rio Branco corridor. In his report of that year to the Dutch West India Company, the colony's *commandeur*, Storm van's Gravesande, noted that the traders "act so badly towards the natives that several have already been murdered by the latter; others get poisoned and expose the Colony to danger of war with the savage tribes" (Harris and Villiers 1911, 260). Van's Gravesande also noted that the trade in "red slaves" from the upper Essequibo region was "fairly large" and that some of the traders "do not hesitate even to go with some tribes to make war upon others ... and selling them as slaves, and abusing Indian women. Hence it was that in the year 1747 the rovers G. Goritz and H. Bannink were murdered by the Indians [in upper Essequibo], some others poisoned, and others forced to flee" (Harris and Villiers 1911, 269).

Colonial development under the British administration of the nineteenth century was at best "absent minded" (Rivière 1995) and so largely devolved into the missionary effort that I describe later. At the forefront of evangelical progress in the highlands was the British missionary Thomas Youd. His case is examined more fully below, but the tale of his poisoning by kanaimàs has become notorious. Although there are reasons to question the accuracy of this tale, its place in the discourse of kanaimà is undeniable. Lesser known in twentieth-century literature but equivalent to the case of Youd was that of one Pastor Davis. Theodor Koch-Grüneberg described Davis as having died in a village by Roraima "from a hemorrhage, as it was described, and was buried here" and indicated that it was a killing enacted by Patamuna or Makushi kanaimàs (1979, 1:103, 109, 114; 3:186).

Either way, the notion of the susceptibility of whites to death by kanaimà is not just a particular claim about the forensic causes of death in any given instance but a wider attempt to bring whites within native categories in a way that renders them less powerful and threatening. This is how I have come to understand the "legend" of my own poisoning by kanaimàs, as well as that of other whites, about which I was carefully and deliberately informed. In particular, the case of Bengi, eventually shotgunned in the late 1960s, was related to me on a number of occasions by different persons, so as to firmly impress it on my thinking, as a relatively recent example of how avaricious whites might fall victim to shamanic attack. Bengi and his brother were known as practicing kanaimàs who went to work for a white man in a *balata*-bleeding (rubber-gathering) operation on the Siparuni. However, the white man got angry because he thought they were being lazy. They in turn demanded a payment of cigarettes, but when the confrontation ended, they were smiling. Everyone in the balata camp wondered if the white man would try to chase them out of the camp, and everyone thought that since he had a concrete house that could be closed up tight he was safe. But it is said that Bengi and his brother must have gotten into the white man's house, because they left the next morning and he was sick on waking. He died within a week. Clearly other forms of assault sorcery are not being distinguished from specifically kanaimà attack in the way these events are narrated, but the point for those who recount this incident is to suggest the susceptibility of whites to Amerindian occult forces.

The cultural contextualization of specific histories like these thus allows us to see that such multiple versions erode the authority of the idea of History itself. How can we say "what happened" if the cultural meanings of a story *(histoire)* diverge in such a way as to appropriate the key events, which are registered in all versions but in culturally specific ways? Probably only by counting all versions as relevant and legitimate historiographical expressions. As a result, whatever such kanaimà deaths may have involved, including the clear possibility that they were not examples of ritual violence, they should not be interpreted as we once thought they might be, as opportunities for the destruction of the Mythical by the Historical. This was the notion that drove the colonial occupation and exorcism of the "demon landscape" in the nineteenth century.

A more adequate response, in the light of nearly a hundred years of ethnographic engagements, must be to recognize the discursive origins of apparently empirical claims and that the proof of such claims is established by reference to the discourse from which they emerge, not by a suprahistorical procedure in factual verification. In one sense it really does not matter if I, or anyone else, was clinically poisoned—it is the claims made to that effect that are anthropologically significant for our understanding of the histories and historicities of others. As with Hugh Goodwin's death on the Orinoco in the sixteenth century, or the death of Captain Cook which has exercised the anthropological imagination more widely, the "apotheosis" of whites in the cosmologies of others, their relevance to the cultural discourses of history, reflects not their historical importance as we understand it but precisely an attempt to negate that potential. The effort, then, to disprove or prove kanaimà deaths becomes the vehicle for the colonization of the historical experience of others by bringing it within an external model of historiography. It remains important to ethnographers to know who did or didn't die and how, but our knowledge of the cultural plurality of notions of death, individuality, and agency also teaches us the limits of our own notion of history.

The purpose of this chapter has been, among other things, to illustrate the entanglements that fieldwork involves, the ethical duties we have to our informants, and the unforeseen consequences of close ethnographic engagement. My experience is not presented as an example of how those difficulties might be avoided, but rather to suggest that, even with the best of intentions, they are inevitable. At the same time, if the classic injunction of ethnographic fieldwork—to be a participant observer—is not to be taken as a mere tautology, then it must mean that our manner of "participation" should be no less an object of our theoretical and methodological reflection than the issues of "observation" that have been the focus of discussion since the early 1990s.

In the case of the kanaimà, participation has, of course, been fraught with difficulty, if not outright danger, but it has resulted, I believe, in a distinct and new view of kanaimà as a shamanic practice. Moreover, in negotiating the sometimes contradictory and shifting attitudes and statements that are made with regard to kanaimà, it becomes apparent that its "reality" as conceived of within an empiricist and rationalist tradition of thought is quite different from its "reality" for those who live kanaimà and its consequences. This is why the matter must be approached as a form of discourse whose practice is simultaneously and in varying degrees verbal, emotional, psychological, sociological, and cultural—in a word, *real*. Kanaimà, therefore, is not just a matter of "forensic" evidence, although the following chapters certainly contain such evidence, since it is certainly the more culturally satisfying to minds trained in the traditions of rational empiricism. Nonetheless, as I will attempt to show, kanaimà is much more than the poisoned and mutilated bodies it produces.

Giving up the Ghost

Nina Auerbach

From Christabel to Carmilla: Friends and Lovers

CARMILLA, SHERIDAN LE FANU'S languid and pedigreed vampire, sighs longingly toward Laura, her enthralled prey: "I wonder whether you feel as strangely drawn towards me as I do to you; I have never had a friend—shall I find one now?" For Jane Austen, an effusive vampire might be a "freind" but never that soberer, more cherished being, a "friend." Neither Laura nor Le Fanu can afford such nice distinctions: as Laura tells her own story, she lives, motherless and exiled, with her myopic father and two silly governesses in a Styrian castle. She is cut off from England and other women. When Carmilla penetrates her household—through dreams and tricks as well as bites—she presents herself as Laura's only available source of intimacy. Everything male vampires seemed to promise, Carmilla performs: she arouses, she pervades, she offers a sharing self. This female vampire is licensed to realize the erotic, interpenetrative friendship male vampires aroused and denied.

Ruthven, Varney, and the rest are blasphemous by definition, but their emotional life is as compartmentalized as that of any Victorian patriarch: women fill their biological needs, but men kindle emotional complexity. Women exist to be married or depleted or rescued. They are as consummately made as Frankenstein's creature, their condition a barometer of the vampire's power. When a woman becomes a vampire herself, she has no more agency than she did when she was human: Clara rises from her coffin as the pièce de résistance that finally ends *Varney the Vampire's* feast of blood, but she has nothing to say. Her wordless appearance is testimony to Varney's evil artistry: "And now the light ... shone on a mass of white clothing within the coffin, and in another moment that white clothing was observed to be in motion. Slowly the dead form that was there rose up, and they all saw the pale and ghastly face. A streak of blood was issuing from the mouth, and the eyes were open" (p. 837). Clara's features are no longer her own: "the" face, "the" mouth, "the" eyes are Varney's fabrications. For all the individuality it expresses, Clara's ghastly face is indistinguishable from her white clothing. Even her name is an abstraction, as is that of the snarling ingenue Clara inspired, Bram Stoker's Lucy Westenra. These girls whose names mean "light" exist only to be extinguished and relit by a vampire master.

Carmilla's is a different story. Her origins are obscure and remote; as far as Laura perceives, she sleeps, prowls, and falls in love on her own authority. If anyone directs her, it is the mother who engineers the supposed carriage accident that deposits Carmilla at the castle of Laura's father. That mother in turn may be directed by a figure only Laura's governess sees, "a hideous black woman, with a sort of coloured turban on her head, who was gazing all the time from the carriage window, nodding and grinning derisively toward the ladies, with gleaming eyes and large white eyeballs, and her teeth set as if in fury" (p. 83).

We never learn who the black woman is, where she comes from, or her degree of power over the action. Carmilla is not the product of a single maker's potency, but the spirit of an elusive female community who may be her makers or merely her confederates, and whose power only women perceive; from the beginning, Laura's father is strangely blind to the women's plot. The "hideous black woman" may be the devil herself in the form of a voodoo priestess; her exotic associations, racial and spiritual, hint at a geographic range of female magic beyond Byron's male-ruled Orient or *Varney*'s Nordic lore. Remembering back through the centuries, Carmilla tells Laura of the "cruel love—strange love" that turned her into a vampire (p. 101). Though she leaves her lover's gender unspecified, the word *strange,* the Swinburnian euphemism for homosexual love, suggests that Carmilla's original maker was female. But like many women—and unlike Varney and the egomaniacal Dracula—Carmilla's maker leaves no signature. As Laura tells her story. Camilla's hunger is her own, not the projection of some megalomaniacal creator.

Carmilla has all the agency of our male vampires with none of their erotic ambivalence. Like Ruthven and the rest, she compartmentalizes her emotions, but in a subtler manner only

Nina Auerbach, from *Our Vampires, Ourselves*, pp. 38–60. Copyright © 1995 by University of Chicago Press. Reprinted with permission.

an expert can explicate. Thus. Le Fanu brings in one Baron Vordenburg at the end to explain vampirism's "curious lore":

> The vampire is prone to be fascinated with an engrossing vehemence resembling the passion of love, by particular persons. In pursuit of these it will exercise inexhaustible patience and stratagem, for access to a particular object may be obstructed in a hundred ways. It will never desist until it has satiated its passion, and drained the very life of its coveted victim. But it will, in these cases, husband and protract its murderous enjoyment with the refinement of an epicure, and heighten it by the gradual approaches of an artful courtship. In these cases it seems to yearn for something like sympathy and consent. In ordinary ones it goes direct to its object, overpowers with violence, and strangles and exhausts often at a single feast. (P. 136)

Leaving aside the Baron's condescending, cataloging tone, which aims, unlike Laura's narrative, to make typical Carmilla's idiosyncratic emotional ebbs and flows, the Baron locates scientifically for the first time in literature the division we have seen in male vampires between feeding and friendship. Ruthven fed on women while draining his male friend by the intangible tie of an oath. Carmilla feeds only on women with a hunger inseparable from erotic sympathy, distinguishing among her prey only on the sterling British basis of class. She preys on peasant girls but falls in love with Laura, a protected lady like herself whose relative in fact she is: Laura's dead mother was a Karnstein, part of the "bad family" that produced Carmilla. The Baron, like later Victorian sexologists, glibly turns Carmilla's passion into pathology, but he neglects to tell us that unlike many humans, Carmilla loves only those she understands.

Carmilla is one of the few self-accepting homosexuals in Victorian or any literature. One might assume that her vampirism immunizes her from human erotic norms, but most members of her species were more squeamish: no male vampire of her century confronts the desire within his friendship. Despite Mario Praz's portentous division between heroic male and decadent female vampires, the two are interdependent: the women perform for the men. Among vampires, as in more reputable species, homosexuality itself is figured as female.

In the self-conscious 1890s, females would dominate vampire iconography, but their horrible hunger is not Carmilla's: fin-de-siècle literary vampires like Dracula's three sister-brides, theatrical vampires from Mrs. Pat Campbell to Theda Bara, or pictorial vampires like Edvard Munch's *Vampire*—whose face virtually disappears as she chews on her man—are horrible because heterosexual, dreadful because they feast on men. The poem Rudyard Kipling wrote to accompany Philip Burne-Jones's powerful painting of Mrs. Pat Campbell as a vampire excoriates her sins against gender rather than God:

> The Fool was stripped to his foolish hide (Even as you and I!)
> Which she might have seen when she threw him aside—
> (But it isn't on record the lady tried)
> So some of him lived but the most of him died—(Even as you and I!)
>
> *And it isn't the shame and it isn't the blame*
> *That stings like a white-hot brand—*
> *It's coming to know that she never knew why*
> *(Seeing, at last, she could never know why)*
> *And never could understand!*

To Kipling's male readers in 1897, an enraged, cohesive "us," female vampires are an alien gender to whom men's wrenching adoration is incomprehensible. In 1872, Carmilla is the known. Her story is less an account of predation than it is of the recognition that underlies all vampire literature before the close of the nineteenth century. This erotic recognition is not a tender alternative to the coldness of male vampires, but a performance, featuring female characters, of the homoerotic identification men, even vampires, dare not act on.

Varney plays with the affinity between vampires and humans, but an incidental aphorism denies (with characteristic hedging) the sort of intense sharing Carmilla exemplifies: "Two people don't dream of the same thing at the same time; I don't of course deny the possibility of such a thing, but it is too remarkable a coincidence to believe all at once" (Varney, p. 796). But Carmilla and Laura do dream the same dream at the same time. As a child, Laura dreams of a caressing young lady entering her bed and biting her breast. When Carmilla comes to the castle years later, they recognize each other's faces from their common childhood dream. Though Carmilla characterizes her feelings by the Swinburnian code word *strange*, her enchantment is her familiarity.

Carmilla has no use for the moon that had been central to the animation of male vampires; she drinks life only through Laura. The moon is at its brightest just *before* Carmilla appears, and it is analyzed to florid death by Laura's "metaphysical" governess, who declares "that when the moon shone with a light so intense it was well known that it indicated a special spiritual activity. The effect of the full moon in such a state of brilliancy was manifold. It acted on dreams, it acted on lunacy, it acted on nervous people; it had marvelous physical influences connected with life. ... The moon, this night ... is full of odylic and magnetic influence" (pp. 78–79).

Parodying Boucicault's ornate stage effects and the pseudo-poetry of *Varney the Vampire*, Le Fanu introduces a moon brimming with signification that resuscitates no one. *Varney's* poetic commentary about the moon is an invariable prelude to a lunar resurrection, but Carmilla upstages the moon. Under her dominion, it shrinks to the decorative prop it remains in horror stories, no longer energizing Carmilla, but courteously illuminating her. "How beautiful [Carmilla] looked in the moonlight!" Laura exclaims conventionally (p. 98); at the end, vampire-killing men use moonlight to track Carmilla with no fear that the moon will resurrect her. Carmilla's hunger to absorb another life is the end of the Lunarian vampire. Turning from the sky toward the living, Carmilla lets nothing distract her from the interpenetration that is the essence of the nineteenth-century vampire's hunger.

Carmilla and Laura not only share dreams or visions; they share a life even before Carmilla murmurs, "I live in your warm life and you shall die—die, sweetly die—into mine ... you and I are one for ever" (pp. 89-90). Both have lost their mothers and their countries; each suffuses the image of the other's absent mother. In their common dream, each perceives the other as a "beautiful young lady," not another child. Like Laura's dead mother, Carmilla is a Karnstein, a vibrant remnant of an apparently extinct family. When Laura's mother breaks protectively into a vampire reverie, her message is so ambiguous that Laura misconstrues it, turning herself into Carmilla and her own mother into her friend's. Hearing a sweet and terrible warning, "Your mother warns you to beware of the assassin," seeing Carmilla bathed in blood at the foot of her bed, Laura fuses self, killer, and mother: "I wakened with a shriek, possessed with the one idea that Carmilla was being murdered" (p. 106). In the flow of female dreams, murderer and murdered, mother and lover, are one; women in *Carmilla* merge into a union the men who watch them never see.

Le Fanu's unconventional imagery brings vampirism home. There are no mediating rituals like Byron's numerology, Polidori's oath, or Varney's lunar resurrections, nor, compared to *Dracula*, does Le Fanu dwell on blood; water is the vampire's medium. "Certain vague and strange sensations visited me in my sleep. The prevailing one was of that pleasant, peculiar cold thrill which we feel in bathing, when we move against the current of a river" (p. 105). Considering the elaborate, arcane rituals in which most vampires indulge, Laura's homely sensation of swimming is neither vague nor strange. Her feelings are as familiar as Carmilla is herself, modulating into caresses and orgiastic shudders: "My heart beat faster, my breathing rose and fell rapidly and full drawn; a sobbing, that rose into a sense of strangulation, supervened, and turned into a dreadful convulsion, in which my senses left me, and I became unconscious" (p. 106).

For Le Fanu, the strangeness of vampirism is its kinship to the commonplace. Its identification with cold water rather than hot blood or spectral moonbeams releases it from both perversity and enchantment; as the lives of Carmilla and Laura flow into each other, with the voice of one spectral mother summoning both girls, so the occult flows into intimate physical sensations. Le Fanu's ghosts have been defined by their chillingly modern absurdity, but his vampire invokes rather the horror inherent in the Victorian dream of domestic coziness, the restoration of lost intimacy and comfort.

In her association with bathing rather than moonbeams or blood, her play with the life of the body rather than the abstractions of magic, Carmilla is no ghost. Waking suddenly, Laura sees at her bed a collage of Carmillas, all of them solid:

> I saw something moving round the foot of the bed, which at first I could not accurately distinguish. But I soon saw that it was a sooty black animal that resembled a monstrous cat. It appeared to me about four or five feet long, for it measured fully the length of the hearth-rug as it passed over it; and it continued to-ing and fro-ing with the lithe sinister restlessness of a beast in a cage.... I felt it spring lightly on the bed. The two broad eyes approached my face, and suddenly I felt a stinging pain as if two large needles darted, an inch or two apart, deep into my breast. I waked with a scream ... and I saw a female figure standing at the foot of the bed, a little at the right side. It was in a dark loose dress, and its hair was drawn and covered its shoulders. A block of stone could not have been more still. There was not the slightest stir of respiration. As I stared at it, the figure appeared to have changed its place, and was now nearer the door; then, close to it, the door opened, and it passed out. (P. 102)

The miracle of this description, in its own time as now, is its breathtaking freedom from convention. There are no fangs, no slavering, no red eyes, no mesmerism, and no dematerialization, only a larger-than-average cat and a door that opens. The opening door is the key to this vampire: she is all body, though a mutating one, with no vampire trap to enforce transparency. Male vampires took their authority from the ghost of Hamlet's father, but Carmilla's is as cozy as a cat, though one eerily elongated.

Later on, one of the storytelling father figures who enter at the end will negate Laura's perceptions by turning Carmilla back into a phantom, equipped with the old disembodying vampire trap: "How did she pass out from her room, leaving the door locked on the inside? How did she escape from the house without unbarring door or window?" (p. 125). In her immateriality, the General's Carmilla is a monstrous mystery, while Laura's is as solid as the domestic settings. Laura's Carmilla may be strange, but her face and the sensations she arouses are indelibly familiar, and her body is as material as a door.

Laura's story is unique in its freedom from the rituals and conventions that are the usual substance of vampire tales, but its strange familiarity is an incisive comment on the vampires of its time. Carmilla differs from Ruthven, Varney, and the rest in intensity rather than kind: as a woman, the vampiric friend releases a boundless capacity for intimacy. The Byronic vampire was a traveling companion; Camilla comes home to share not only the domestic present, but lost mothers and dreams, weaving herself so tightly into Laura's perceptions that without a cumbersome parade of male authorities to stop her narrative, her story would never end.

Carmilla initially seems devoid of authorities; Carmilla is so emotionally direct, so indifferent to occultism, that learned translators seem superfluous. Dr. Hesselius, Le Fanu's guide to the supernatural in other tales, comes on only indirectly, in a brief prologue authenticating the "conscientious particularity" of Laura's narrative; he plays no rescuing role. Like many Victorian fathers, Laura's is a venerated fool, impervious to the plot that brings a vampire to his castle, laughing ever more affably as his daughter drifts closer to death. But just as Laura's life is melting into Carmilla's, the story is forced on track by the entrance of the General, whose daughter was Carmilla's previous victim. The General is as competent a father as Laura's is idiotic. His narrative is a variant of Laura's, though its plotting mother seems to take orders, not from a voodoo priestess, but from "a gentleman, dressed in black" with a deathly pallor. The General's tale thus restores male authority on both a diabolical and a domestic plane.

More experts follow the General: a woodman expert in Karnstein revenants, a grotesque old baron who is a trove of vampire lore, a priest, and two medical men who authenticate Carmilla's decapitation, which a "report of the Imperial Commission" verifies. Laura's point of view shrivels under this invasion of experts and official language, as does the vitality of Le Fanu's story. Ruthven and Varney were credible monsters as well as seductive friends, but Carmilla has no monstrous life. Diagnosed as a horror, she dies as a presence; compared to the writhings and bloody foamings of Bram Stoker's staked Lucy, Carmilla's ritual decapitation is an abstract anticlimax to the vividness of her seduction. The Carmilla experts dispatch it as characterless as the blob the General sees attacking his daughter: "I saw a large black object, very ill-defined, crawl, as it seemed to me, over the foot of the bed, and swiftly spread itself up to the poor girl's throat, where it swelled, in a moment, into a great, palpitating mass" (p. 130).

In contrast to the General's ill-defined object, Laura's Carmilla—sharer, cat, mother, and lover—is a vividly defined subject. It is that sharing, individualized vampire—the loved and known companion, not the "great, palpitating mass"—whom nineteenth-century readers believed in and feared. In her suggestive concluding sentence, Laura restores that friend to some sort of life: "It was long before the terror of recent events subsided; and to this hour the image of Carmilla returns to memory with ambiguous alterations—sometimes the playful, languid, beautiful girl; sometimes the writhing fiend I saw in the ruined church; and often from a reverie I have started, fancying I heard the light step of Carmilla at the drawing-room door" (p. 137).

Unlike conventional vampirized ingenues—*Varney's* Flora or *Dracula's* Mina—Laura has no congregation of embracing men to welcome her back from the dead; she returns only to the father-ruled solitude of her pre-Carmilla existence. Her final sentence is not merely elegiac: as effectively as the moonlight under which dead male vampires quivered, Laura's memories restore Carmilla's physical life. The "light step" is as material as ever, while the final "door" reminds us that Carmilla is no phantom, but flesh, who, like us, must open doors to pass into rooms. Her oath, "I live in your warm life and you shall die—die, sweetly die—into mine … you and I are one for ever," is more warmly inescapable than Ruthven's was: Carmilla does live in Laura's life at the end. Her resurrection raises a lurking question about Laura's own condition: if a "strange love" transformed Carmilla into a vampire, hasn't her own love the power to transform Laura, making their lives literally one? The cryptic announcement in the Prologue that Laura "died" after writing her story (p. 72) does not preclude her being also alive—on the verge, like Carmilla, of opening the door.

Ruthven's oath was formal, ritual, orchestrating his ceremonial burial; Carmilla's is a private, apparently spontaneous outburst, ensuring her continuing life. Nonetheless, in a genre that simultaneously expressed and inhibited its century's dream of homoerotic friendship, Carmilla speaks for the warier vampires who came before her. Her vampirism, like theirs, is an interchange, a sharing, an identification, that breaks down the boundaries of familial roles and the sanctioned hierarchy of marriage.

Carmilla's oath was so binding and seductive that it had no immediate progeny: for generations after Le Fanu, erotic friendship with vampires became unthinkable. Its major source, Coleridge's haunting fragment *Christabel* (1816), has a strange, scarcely cited half-life among vampire works. *Christabel* is a fantastic seduction poem whose serpent-woman Geraldine, like Carmilla, invades the castle and the identity of the motherless Christabel; like Laura's, Christabel's danger is intensified by her father's fatuous misconstructions. *Christabel*, whose main action is the interchange of identity between the two women, was one unacknowledged model for the Byronic vampire, though Byron's persona is too self-absorbed to acknowledge any play among women.

Nonetheless, *Christabel* fed Ruthven. Shortly before the famous ghost-story contest, Byron recited part of it at the Villa Diodati to terrifying effect: Geraldine's exposed bosom sent Percy Shelley shrieking out of the room, possessed by a vision of a woman "who had eyes instead of nipples." The bosoms in Coleridge's poem may or may not have eyes, but they are potent tokens of forbidden friendship. They scared a new generation of Romantics toward their own tales of terror, but no bosoms invade those manuscripts; in *Frankenstein* as well as Byron and Polidori's vampire tales, friends, villains, lovers, and sufferers all are men. Byron admitted no affinity between Coleridge's vampire and his own: his journal claims that he recited Coleridge's "verses ... of the *witch's* breast" (Macdonald, pp. 92–93; my italics), relegating Geraldine to a different order of monstrosity than that of his own inscrutable Darvell.

Yet by her century's definition Geraldine is unquestionably a vampire: she is, like Darvell, a best friend who offers dangerous sympathy. Neither Byron nor Polidori nor their many adapters acknowledged Geraldine as a model of friendship. Until Le Fanu restored and translated into prose its erotic female plot, *Christabel* was both too strange and too disturbingly familiar to be acknowledged as the origin of the nineteenth-century vampire legend.

Aside from providing the outline of a plot *Carmilla* rationalizes and develops, *Christabel*, like *Carmilla,* strips its story of occult trappings that distract from the erotic interchange of identities between vampire and prey. Intimacy arouses these vampires, not blood or the moon. Like Carmilla, Geraldine outshines the moon that rules Ruthven and Varney. As Christabel hurries to the wood at midnight, ostensibly to pray but actually to encounter Geraldine, the moon recedes: "The moon is behind, and at the full; / And yet she looks both small and dull" (*Coleridge,* I, ll. 18–19). Geraldine, on the other hand, radiates her own light. Christabel encounters a "damsel bright, / Dressed in a silken robe of white, / That shadowy in the moonlight shone" (I, ll. 58–60): the robe the moon casts into shadow nevertheless mysteriously shines. So does Geraldine's body, revealing even her veins: "Her blue-veined feet unsandaled were, / And wildly glittered here and there / The gems entangled in her hair" (I, ll. 63–65).

Geraldine eludes the decorporealizing vampire trap. Male vampires are slighter than doors, walls, and moons; female vampires are solid. The moon resurrects males, but shrinks before females. Moreover, while the power of Varney and Alan Raby takes the form of continual deaths and resurrections, Geraldine's, like Carmilla's, lies in her unquenchable life; neither woman has to die to prove she is always alive. The vitality of female vampires is an extreme embodiment of the vampire legend in the nineteenth century: these glittering companions have a corporeality men evade.

Like Carmilla, Geraldine is eerily inseparable from the spirit of her victim's mother, whom she both displaces and becomes. When she first sees Geraldine, Christabel cries, "Mary mother, save me now!"; once under Geraldine's spell, she prays ineffectually to Christ. Having brought Geraldine to her bedroom, she gives her "a wine of virtuous powers" her mother has made, adding plaintively, "O mother dear! that thou wert here!" and receiving the cryptic response, "'I would,' said Geraldine, 'she were!'" Christabel or Geraldine or the two together summon that mother's spirit, leading Geraldine to attempt an exorcism: "Off, wandering mother! Peak and pine! ... Though thou her guardian spirit be, / Off, woman, off! 'tis given to me" (I, ll. 190–213). Having apparently expelled Christabel's mother, Geraldine exposes her own bosom, the climactic if undefined sight that transfixes Christabel and terrified Shelley. Her seduction ends in a lullaby, restoring the mother she claimed to have banished:

And lo! the worker of these harms,
That holds the maiden in her arms,
Seems to slumber still and mild
As a mother with her child.

No doubt, she [Christabel] hath a vision sweet.
What if her guardian spirit 'twere,
What if she knew her mother near?
(I, ll. 296–99; 326–28)

Like Carmilla, Geraldine is simultaneously the lost mother's antagonist and her embodiment. The ambiguous exorcism in *Christabel* is the genesis of the cry in *Carmilla*—a cry that simultaneously denounces Carmilla and protects her—"Your mother warns you to beware of the assassin." These female vampires become the mothers they dispel, restoring the life they consume. In both works, moreover, when the supposedly dead mother returns, she is as subversive an outsider as the tender vampire. She does not heal the family, but dissipates its boundaries by supplanting the inept father who was its sole authority.

In *Christabel*'s cryptic second half, which takes place under the father's impercipient eye, Christabel is so imbued with Geraldine that, like Le Fanu's Laura at the end of her narrative, she can only turn into her. Laura, prosaic to the last, hears a familiar step at the door; the more baroque Christabel hisses like the serpent who is Geraldine's essence while her father caresses the lovely intruder. Vampire and victim are so entwined that, like *Carmilla*, the story has no logical end, for no character can be saved or damned. Le Fanu's experts plod in and chop Carmilla out of the narrative; Coleridge simply stops his poem. In nineteenth-century iconography, male vampires are allies of death who end their narratives by killing or dying, but females are so implicated in life's sources that their stories overwhelm closure.

Christabel and *Carmilla* isolate vampirism as an extract of alien femaleness. The itinerant Byronic vampire has the world as his stage; Geraldine and Carmilla flourish in the obscure privacy of women's bedrooms and dreams. But not all female vampires in the nineteenth century offer overpowering empathy; Keats's *Lamia* (1820) features, like *Christabel*, a vampiric serpent woman, but the sinuously heterosexual Lamia does not mingle her identity with that of her bemused prey. She is an artist of the occult whose powers demand spectators, not sharers. Since her magic is stronger than her body, the philosopher Apollonius, Keats's male expert, easily deciphers her art and destroys her.

Christabel has no expert to decipher Geraldine, whose art is her being. Her power lies in a bosom that controls the poem, even though it may not exist at all, for its revelation enforces concealment: "Behold! her bosom and half her side— / A sight to dream of, not to tell" (I, ll. 252–53). "Behold!" is exactly what we cannot do, just as Christabel, confronted with the bosom, cannot speak: "In the touch of this bosom there worketh a spell, / Which is lord of thy utterance, Christabel!" (ll. 267–68). The bosom—or charismatic nonbosom—feeds dreams but blocks narrative. It may be large; it may drip milk; it may have shriveled into nonexistence (in part II, Christabel remembers it as "old" and "cold"); it may, like the vision that sent Shelley shrieking out of the room, be able to see you. Whatever it looks like, it is inseparable from Geraldine's body; it is neither magic to be shared nor an illusion to be dissipated, but a proclamation of femaleness.

Men acquire, through occult rigmarole, the vampirism women embody. Male vampires declare their condition by their deathly aura; Geraldine's inheres in the life of her body. Its entanglement with the source of life and with the identity of its prey may well have sent Shelley shrieking. Byron evaded Geraldine's spell by translating her bosom into the formal, purely verbal oath that binds vampire to mortal; Keats evaded it by abstracting it into a spell legible to experts. Throughout the century, male writers of vampirism followed their example: their vampires offer a friendship mystified into occult abstractions. Only among women, those specialists in romantic friendship, is vampirism embodied in a physical, psychic union the experts of the next century would label "homosexual." The touch of Geraldine's bosom crystallizes the spell male vampires cast but refuse to perform.

Compared to the polished formulations and logical structure of later vampire works, Coleridge's unfinished poem is so elliptical and eccentric that its influence was easy to ignore. The ghost of Hamlet's father is a suitably stately progenitor of Darvell, Ruthven, Alan Raby, and Varney, all of whom by implication disown the touchable Geraldine. Even when Le Fanu succumbed to *Christabel* by recasting it in prose, he evaded Geraldine's bosom. Initially, that bosom is the site not of the vampire's power, but of the victim's wound: Laura's childhood dream of Carmilla concludes with "a sensation as if two needles ran into my breast very deep at the same moment" (p. 74), and as an adult she describes "a stinging pain as if two large needles darted, an inch or two apart, deep into my breast" (p. 102). Carmilla remembers her own transformation similarly: "'I was all but assassinated in my bed, wounded *here*,' she touched her breast, 'and never was the same since'" (p. 101).

But under the eyes of her father and a male doctor, Laura's wound creeps chastely upward until it rests on the neutral neck to which Stoker would confine vampires:

> "You mentioned a sensation, like that of two needles piercing the skin, somewhere about your neck, on the night when you experienced your first horrible dream. ...Can you indicate with your finger about the point at which you think this occurred?"
>
> "Very little below my throat—*here*," I answered.
>
> I wore a morning dress, which covered the place I pointed to.
>
> "Now you can satisfy yourself," said the doctor. "You won't mind your papa's lowering your dress a very little. It is necessary, to detect a symptom of the complaint under which you have been suffering."
>
> I acquiesced. It was only an inch or two below the edge of my collar. (P. 111)

Considering her desperate circumstances, Laura is oddly insistent about her wound's ascent from bosom to neck. So was the vampire literature *Christabel* inspired. A century of alluring vampire friends evade erotic sites, the shared reality of bodies, on behalf of an abstract bond and a purely surgical violence. In 1897, *Dracula* provided a lexicon of vampirism for the twentieth century. Predators were identifiable by their fangs, victims by two little holes in their neck. After *Dracula*, contact between vampire and victim is as external to the body as possible. Moving from the erotic to the clinical, from affinity to penetration, vampire iconography abandons bosoms, fastening with scientific precision on higher, cleaner wounds.

Carmilla's Progress

Carmilla is the climax and the end of a dream of an intimacy so compelling only vampires could embody it. She survives through the twentieth century, but she shrinks to conform to our own century's embarrassed decorum. The loss of her obsessed generosity is an index of an intensifying cultural repression evident in her passage from a Victorian novel about romantic friendship through a slew of sexy twentieth-century films.

Twentieth-century adaptations abandon Geraldine's bosom. In most of these, voyeurism supplants friendship: most structure the women's story around the responses of a male watcher, explicit or implied. *Carmilla*'s men might be experts but they were incompetent watchers: Laura's father was blind to women's plots, and even the General saw the vivid Carmilla only as a blob. In twentieth-century film adaptations, by contrast, female vampires spring to life only under men's eyes. In Andrea Weiss's categorical but depressingly accurate diagnosis, "What has survived of *Carmilla* from Victorian literature and worked its way into twentieth-century cinema is its muted expression of lesbians, no longer sympathetically portrayed but now reworked into a male pornographic fantasy." The physical and psychic sharing available only to women, according to nineteenth-century ideologies of gender, is scarcely possible in our own, more squeamish *Carmilla*s.

Carl Dreyer's stately *Vampyr* (1932) is the first canonical vampire film not based on *Dracula;* it claims to be, instead, a loose adaptation of *Carmilla*. Despite its source, *Vampyr* scrupulously avoids not only erotic intimacy, but all contact between its characters, whether they are human or preterhuman; its key images involve a solitude so solemnly intense that it is scarcely a vampire film at all. Dreyer's fastidious distance from his source guarantees his artistry for many critics: according to Pauline Kael, "most vampire movies are so silly that this film by Carl Dreyer—a great vampire film—hardly belongs to the genre." To achieve art status for his film, a director must drain away his vampires.

Dreyer's protagonist is neither Carmilla (here a blind old crone less visible than her diabolical male henchmen) nor Laura, whose character is split into two sisters: the stricken Léone, who spends most of the movie in bed, sobbing and shuddering over her own damnation, and the beleaguered Gisèle, whom the hero rescues at the end. The center of the film is the man who sees them. The opening title affirms the primacy of a male watcher: "This story is about the strange adventures of young Alan Gray. His studies of devil worship and vampire terror of earlier centuries have made him a dreamer, for whom the boundary between the real and the unreal has become dim." Like the dreamer/director Carl Dreyer, this poetic spectator retains full control over the mysterious world he observes.

The story is indeed "about" Alan Gray's oblique experience of vampirism. We watch him watching the interplay between satanic shadows and human characters; intently reading experts' accounts (as have less exalted vampire-watchers from Boucicault's melodramas through Hammer films and the inhabitants of Stephen King's *Salem's Lot*); dreaming of his own burial alive, which he observes from his coffin in horror; sailing into mist with Gisèle once the crone has been staked. Vampirism here is Alan Gray's experience, his dream, or his creation. The viewer is barred from participating in it; we watch only Alan watching.

Vampirism is purged of sharing or interchange. The crone and Léone are scarcely together. When they are, the physical contrast between the massive blind woman and the frail girl is so controlling that vampirism comes to resemble self-hypnosis rather than affinity. In one dreamlike sequence, Léone wanders into the garden, where Alan and the spectators find her sprawled on a rock with the crone leaning over her. The scene freezes into a tableau that realizes Fuseli's famous painting, *The Nightmare*; its stylization deflects attention from active physical interchange toward a poetic spectator who appreciates cinematic painting.

Other scenes among women are similarly purged of affinity. Large close-ups of Léone or Gisèle with sorrowing or stern older women—the old servant, the austere nursing nun—force the women's visual incompatibility on the viewer: old and young, imposing and frail, dark and blond, seem to inhabit different physical universes. These insistent contrasts replace the amorphous maternal spirit of *Carmilla*, who both protects against and embodies the vampire. When Léone, half-transformed, bares her teeth, Gisèle shrinks away into the nun's arms, expressing no empathy with her beloved sister. Later, we hear from behind a closed door a woman's seductive plea, "Come with me! We will be one soul, one body! Death is waiting," but we see neither speaker nor hearer. *Vampyr* is that rarity in the vampire canon, a work that forecloses intimacy.

Its two most famous sequences have little to do with vampires: in both, men experience the claustrophobic solitude of burial alive. In a vision, Alan Gray observes his own funeral, watching the grave close over him through a glass window in his coffin; at the end, the sinister doctor Marc is trapped in a flour mill, flailing helplessly as a blizzard of whiteness covers him. These splendid sequences throw the focus away from vampirism, women, or any emotional interchange; the men who helplessly, silently, watch themselves sink recapitulate the director's lonely terror at his own submergence in images. The one canonical masterpiece *Carmilla* inspired announces implicitly that female vampires are incompatible with art's mastery.

Roger Vadim's art movie *Et mourir de plaisir* (1960; released in America in 1961 under the appropriately painterly title *Blood and Roses*) is less stark than *Vampyr*, but its visual dynamic is the same: a blond and a dark woman, here more striking in their visual contrast than in their acting ability, parade erotically before the ambivalent eyes of a male watcher—Mel Ferrar, a Karnstein descendant both of them love. Carmilla, the apparent vampire, is in reality only a *reincarnation* of the eighteenth-century vampire Millarca, who in her life murdered all the mortal women male Karnsteins wanted to marry—represented here by the dark Georgia, to whom Mel Ferrar is engaged. Erotic affinity is chastely sublimated in a heterosexual romantic triangle. In the same soothing spirit, the vampire is less a character than a personification of the haunting stately past she commemorates in her chanted refrain: "My name is Millarca. I lived in the past. I live now."

Le Fanu's intensity fades into remote and decorative effects. Like *Vampyr*, *Blood and Roses* is made to be watched, not shared. Its sleepy actors are there to display the director's gorgeous red-and-white imagery: spreading bloodstains emphasize the bosoms under pristine white dresses; in a floral conceit that replaces contact with mortals, swollen roses wither under a vampire's touch. When Carmilla vampirizes Georgia at last, her visit swells into a dream sequence so ornate that it obliterates any potential affinity between the women. As in *Vampyr*, visual spectacle displaces the erotic plot. We are spectators of somnolent women who (at least in the bowdlerized American version) scarcely notice each other as they drift about erotically for our delectation.

The Vampire Lovers (1970, dir. Roy Ward Baker), one of the later, softer products of England's prolific Hammer Studios, learns its technique from Dreyer and Vadim, but this *Carmilla* variation is giddily hostile to high art. Like all Hammer films, it exudes a cheerful semi-pornographic opulence bold in its time; but as in *Vampyr* and *Blood and Roses*, the predations of the vampire are dependent on the obsessions of a watching male, here a famous vampire-killer who comes on at the beginning and the end to control the action, framing the women's story in narrative voice-over. Primarily, though, that watcher is the drooling adolescent in the audience. Baker multiplies Le Fanu's two women into five sexy vampires, victims, and intermediates: the nameless Karnstein decapitated by a strapping Baron in the opening sequence, Carmilla, Laura (whom Carmilla quickly kills), Emma (the Laura figure), and Emma's German tutor, sinister because intellectual, who becomes, without being bitten, Carmilla's slavish acolyte. For the body of the movie, these women parade around in various combinations, displaying to caressing close-ups blown-up breasts celestially echoed by a swollen moon. Not only does this breast fetishism "reduce lesbian desire to an infantile, pre-Oedipal phase of development" (Weiss, *Vampires and Violets,* p. 96); it muffles the vampire's mouth, the dominant weapon in Hammer's *Dracula* series, not only submerging her in maternal fleshiness, but silencing her. In both art and commercial film, Le Fanu's characters forfeit their story to become cinematic spectacles.

One would expect feminist chic to radicalize female vampires, and in one sense it has: they have become success symbols. In the iconoclastic *Daughters of Darkness* (1971, dir. Harry Kümel), where Delphine Seyrig's suave vampire does overcome the perverse sadism of the supposedly normal husband, this cool creature is a victor, but scarcely a friend: though Seyrig and the battered wife kill the husband and go off together, Seyrig's Countess Bathory is an imperious aristocrat like Dracula, not a sharer like Carmilla.

Miriam Blaylock in *The Hunger* (1983, dir. Tony Scott), the affluent Carmilla of the 1980s, has roots in the self-obsessed, almost airless cinematic art of the 1930s and the teasing spectacles of the 1960s and '70s. Neither Scott's film nor the Whitley Strieber novel on which it is based acknowledges Le Fanu directly. Strieber does allude to Keats's Lamia, who, like Miriam, specializes less in dreams and desire than in gorgeous decor, but Lamia enchants only men, while Miriam's seduction of Sarah, the scientist trying to study her, is at the center of *The Hunger*. Unlike the sleepwalkers in earlier movies, Miriam and Sarah almost manage to be friends; unlike most women in vampire movies, they do talk to each other; but in both film and novel, their creators' conventions come between them.

Whitley Strieber's novel is an exactingly intelligent myth of "another species, living right here all along. An identical twin" of humanity, but a twin glowingly superior, self-regenerating, attuned to the laws of history through surviving the repeated rise and decline of empires. Strieber's Miriam is a dominant, superior consciousness who has survived centuries of arrogant imperial persecution. Tony Scott's film fractures Strieber's vivid imagination of higher organisms. Scott's Miriam is far from timeless. She epitomizes the glamour of the 1980s, subordinating history to seductive objects: jewelry, furniture, lavish houses in glamorous cities, leather clothes. Responding to the success stories of her consuming decade, Miriam lives through her things. She kills, not with her teeth, but with her jewelry, an ankh that hides a knife. She preserves her desiccated former lovers, who age eternally once their vampirism wears off, as carefully as she does her paintings. These things, along with the music and the cityscapes over which she presides, make us envy Miriam's accoutrements instead of her immortality. Vampires in *The Hunger* are not their powers, but their assets.

The movie reduces Miriam not only by subordinating her to her props, but by appropriating the staccato visual techniques of MTV. The characters, like the look of the film, are fractured. Miriam loses not only the memories that, in Strieber's novel, take her back to the beginning of Western civilization, but her controlling consciousness. Originally a figure of lonely integrity throughout the waste of empires, Scott's Miriam becomes an icon of glamorous discontinuity.

Dreyers and Vadim's vampire women shrank to stylized figments of a male artist's dream, Baker's into interchangeable stuffed breasts. Scott too turns his characters into parts of themselves. Mouths predominate, often crosscut with the giant grimace of a laboratory monkey, but Scott also cuts between disjointed eyes, hands, nipples, teeth, throats, blood, and (in the love scene between Miriam and Sarah) legs and breasts, fetishizing fragments until the audience scarcely knows what eye or hand belongs to which man or woman, or (in the love and murder scenes) who is doing what to whom. Although Catherine Deneuve's soft blond Miriam and Susan Sarandon's dark edgy Sarah are contrasting visual types whose rhythms evoke different centuries, Scott's slashing camera makes them effectively indistinguishable in key scenes. Postmodern cinema aligns itself with 1930s high art and 1960s soft porn, creating a collusion between director and viewer that dwarfs personality and overpowers the chief gift of Victorian vampires: their friendship.

Moreover, while Le Fanu's Laura became Carmilla by remembering her at the end, Sarandon's Sarah becomes Miriam by dismembering her: after flexing her new vampirism by butchering her male lover, Sarah defies and displaces Miriam. In *Blood and Roses* and *Daughters of Darkness,* the seemingly dead vampire lived on in her female victim at the end, but Susan Sarandon is more conqueror than possession. *The Hunger* ends with an opaque shot of Sarah and a female lover looking down over another city; her distinctive style, her rhythm, her decor, all have turned into Miriam's. The vampirism that meant sharing in the 1870s adapts to the competitive business ethos that reigned over America in the 1980s. There is room for only one at the top.

Strieber's provocative novel features an omnipotent Miriam who continues to reign at the end, but in the novel too, the triumph of vampirism is the failure of sharing. *Carmilla*-like promises abound, only to be denied as wicked illusions: "[Sarah's] mother kept coming to mind. She had not felt this sense of intimate female friendship since she was a child" (p. 183). "Then she smiled and Sarah wanted to laugh with delight at the radiance of it. Her whole being seemed to rise to higher and higher levels as Miriam continued to look into her eyes. It was as if she could feel Miriam's feelings inside of herself, and those feelings were pure and loving and good" (p. 241).

The intimacy, the sharing, the maternal suffusion, were the essence, in the nineteenth century, of the vampire's allure. Le Fanu's Laura never stopped feeling Carmilla's feelings inside her, nor did she bother to question whether those feelings were good. Strieber, however, sunders the friendship with jarringly abrupt moralism. Once Sarah has killed her male lover, she suddenly sees Miriam in a higher heterosexual light: "You love only yourself! You're worse than a monster. Much worse! … You can't love me or anybody else. You're incapable of it!" (p. 295). Strieber hammers the diagnosis home by forcing even the victorious Miriam to acknowledge Sarah's sexual and spiritual superiority: "Miriam now realized that the gift she could confer was not above one such as Sarah, but beneath her" (p. 306). The vampire's uncharacteristic humility at the end disavows her earlier, exalted disrespect for human love: "Sarah had despaired of ever really being loved. She wanted Tom, enjoyed him sexually, but the old hollowness asserted itself, the reality once again emerging. Miriam could work in the forest of Sarah's emotions. She knew well her role in this age: the bringer of truth" (p. 141). But Miriam's cynical truth is never allowed to prevail: once Tom is dead, love conquers all. Strieber's sophisticated account of science, aesthetics, the tenacity of intelligence, and the fall of empires ends by capitulating to an emotional normalcy to which the Victorian Le Fanu was supremely indifferent. The journey into unknown countries is forbidden.

The real twentieth-century talisman against vampires is not garlic or a crucifix, but Sarah's diagnostic cry: "You can't love me or anybody else. You're incapable of it!" Dracula, the father of our vampires, was vulnerable to the same accusation from a former lover: "You yourself never loved; you never love!" The twentieth-century vampires Dracula spawned mean many things, but they have lost the love they brought to those they knew.

In the nineteenth century, vampires were vampires *because* they loved. They offered an intimacy, a homoerotic sharing, that threatened the hierarchical distance of sanctioned relationships. Generally contorted and vicarious, that love expressed itself most fully through men's imaginations of women, those licensed vehicles of intimacy. *The Hunger* grafts twentieth-century denials—formal and moral—to an essentially nineteenth-century vision of union. The vampires our own century creates are empire builders who repudiate the "intimacy, or friendship" of their sentimental predecessors.

Hungary and Czecho-Slovakia

Montague Summers

HUNGARY, IT MAY NOT untruly be said, shares with Greece and Slovakia the reputation of being that particular region of the world which is most terribly infested by the Vampire and where he is seen at his ugliest and worst. Nor is this common reputation undeserved. It was owing to a number of extraordinary and terrible occurrences towards the end of the seventeenth century, which visitations persisted into the earlier years of the eighteenth century, that general attention was drawn to the problem of the Vampire, that theologians and students of the occult began to collect data of these happenings which made sufficient noise to be reported in such journals as the *Mercure galant* and the *Glaneur Hollandois*. There followed, such was the universal interest aroused by these events, very many monographs and academic dissertations to which attention has already been drawn. It will suffice here to remind ourselves of just a few of these, such works for example as Philip Rohr's *De masticatione mortuorum*, Leipzig, 1679; the *Magia posthuma* of Charles Ferdinand de Schertz, which was published at Olmutz in 1706, and which directly dealt with a case of vampirism that had come under the author's notice. This will be treated in detail a little later. We also have early in the eighteenth century the *De masticatione mortuorum in tumulis liber* of Michael Ranftius, Leipzig, 1728; a *Dissertatio de cadaueribus sanguisugis* by John Christian Stock, Jena, 1732; *Relation von den Vampyren oder Menschensaugern*, Leipzig, 1732; *Relation von denen in Servien sich erzeigenden Blutsaugern*, 1732; *Besondere Nachricht von denen vampyren oder sogennanten Blut-Saugern*, 1732; *Uisus et repertus über die sogenannten Vampyren*, Nuremburg, 1732; *Dissertatio de hominibus post mortem sanguisugis, vulgo dictis Uampyrea*, Leipzig, 1732, of John Christopher Rohlius and John Hertelius; *Dissertatio de Vampyris Seruiensibus* of John Henry Zopfius and Francis van Dalen, 1733; a second work of Michael Ranftius printed at Leipzig, 1734, *Tractatus von dem Kauen und Schmatzen der Todten in Gräbern, worin die wahre Beschassenheit der Hungarischen Vampyrs oder Blut-Sauger gezeiget,. auch alle von dieser Materie bisher edirten Schriften recensiret werden;* nor must we forget the important *Von Vampyren* of John Christian Harenberg, issued in 1739. This list of rare treatises, many of which were published at Leipzig, might be almost indefinitely prolonged, but a sufficient number of names has been given to show the extraordinary attention that was being excited by the problem of vampirism, an attention evoked by actual happenings. In fact one student many years later wrote an article, which seems to have escaped general notice, to which he gave the name *Le Diable à Leipzig*.

In his famous work *An Antidote against Atheism: or, An Appeal to the Natural Faculties of the Mind of Man, whether there be not a God*, 1653 (second edition with Appendix, 1655), the great Cambridge Platonist Henry More relates the following, which are probably the first histories to be recorded concerning Vampires by an English author since the Chroniclers of the twelfth century.

A certain Shoemaker in one of the chief Towns of *Silesia,* in the year 1591, *Septemb.* 20, on a Friday betimes in the morning, in the further part of his house, where there was adjoining a little Garden, cut his own Throat with his Shoemaker's knife. The Family, to cover the foulness of the fact, and that no disgrace might come upon his Widow, gave out, that he died of an Apoplexy, declined all visits of friends and neighbours, in the meantime got him washed, and laid Linens so handsomely about him, that even they that saw him afterwards, as the Parson, and some others, had not the least Suspicion but that he did die of that disease; and so he had honest Burial, with a funeral Sermon, and other circumstances becoming one of his rank and reputation. Six weeks had not past, but so strong a rumour broke out, that he died not of any disease, but had laid violent hands upon himself, that the Magistracy of the place could not but bring all those that had seen the corps, to a strict examination. They shuffled off the matter as well as they could at first, with many fair Apologies, in behalf of the deceased, to remove all suspicion of so heinous an act: but it being pressed more home to their Conscience, at last they confessed, he died a violent death, but desired their favour and clemency to his widow

Montague Summers, from *The Vampire in Europe*. Copyright in the Public Domain.

and children, who were in no fault; adding also, that it was uncertain but that he might be slain by some external mishap, or, if by himself, in some irresistible fit of phrency or madness.

Hereupon the Councel deliberate what is to be done, Which the Widow hearing, and fearing they might be determining something that would be harsh, and to the discredit of her Husband, and herself, being also animated thereto by some busie bodies, makes a great complaint against those that raised these reports of her Husband, and resolved to follow the Law upon them, earnestly contending that there was no reason, upon mere rumours and idle defamations of malevolent people, that her Husband's body should be digged up, or dealt with as if he had been either *Magician*, or *Self-murtherer*. Which boldness and pertinacity of the woman, though after the confession of the fact, did in some measure work upon the Council, and put them to a stand.

But while these things are in agitation, to the astonishment of the Inhabitants of the place, there appears a *Spectrum* in the exact shape and habit of the deceased, and that not only in the night, but at mid-day. Those that were asleep it terrified with horrible visions; those that were waking it would strike, pull, or press, lying heavy upon them like an *Ephialtes*: so that there were perpetual complaints every morning of their last night's rest through the whole Town. But the more freaks this *Spectrum* play'd, the more diligent were the friends of the deceased to suppress the rumours of them, or at least to hinder the effects of those rumours; and therefore made their addresses to the President, complaining how unjust a thing it was, that so much credit should be given to idle reports and blind suspicions, and therefore beseech'd him that he would hinder the Council from digging up the corps of the deceased, and from all ignominious usage of him: adding also, that they intended to appeal to the Emperour's Court, that their Wisdoms might rather decide the Controversy, than that the cause should be determined from the light conjectures of malicious men.

But while by this means the business was still protracted, there were such stirs and tumults all over the Town, that they are hardly to be described. For no sooner did the Sun hide his head, but this *Spectrum* would be sure to appear, so that every body was fain to look about him, and stand upon his guard, which was a sore trouble to those whom the Labours of the Day made more sensible of the want of rest in the night. For this terrible *Apparrition* would sometimes stand by their bed-sides, sometimes cast itself upon the midst of their beds, would lie close to them, would miserably suffocate them, and would so strike them and pinch them, that not only blue marks, but plain impressions of his fingers would be upon sundry parts of their bodies in the morning. Nay, such was the violence and impetuousness of this Ghost, that when men forsook their beds, and kept their dining-rooms, with Candles lighted, and many of them in company together, the better to secure themselves from fear and disturbance; yet he would then appear to them, and have a bout with some of them, notwithstanding all this provision against it. In brief, he was so troublesome, that the people were ready to forsake their houses, and seek other dwellings, and the Magistrates so awakend at the perpetual complaints of them, that at last they resolved, the President agreeing thereto, to dig up the Body.

He had lain in the ground near eight months, *viz.* from *Sept.* 22, 1591, to *April* 18, 1592. When he was digged up, which was in the presence of the Magistracy of the Town, his body was found entire, not at all putrid, no ill smell about him, saving the mustiness of the Grave-cloaths, his joints limber and flexible, as in those that are alive, his skin only flaccid, but a more fresh grown in the room of it, the wound of his throat gaping, but no gear nor corruption in it; there was also observed a Magical mark in the great toe of his right foot, *viz.* an Excrescency in the form of a Rose. His body was kept out of the earth from *April* 18, to the *24th,* at what time many both of the same town and others came daily to view him. These unquiet stirs did not cease for all this, which they after attempted to appease, by burying the corpse under the Gallows, but in vain; for they were as much as ever, if not more, he now not sparing his own Family: insomuch that his Widow at last went her self to the Magistrate, and told them, that she should be no longer against it, if they thought fit to fall upon some course of more strict proceedings touching her Husband.

Wherefore the seventh of *May* he was again digged up, and it was observable, that he was grown more sensibly fleshy since his last interment. To be short, they cut off the Head, Arms, and Legs of the Corps, and opening his Back, took out his Heart, which was as fresh and intire as in a Calf new kill'd. These, together with his Body, they put on a pile of wood, and burnt them to Ashes, which they carefully sweeping together, and putting into a Sack (that none might get them for wicked uses) poured them into the River, after which the *Spectrum* was never seen more.

As it also happen'd in his Maid that dy'd after him, who appeared within eight days after her death, to her fellow servant, and lay so heavy upon her, that she brought upon her a great swelling of the eyes. She so grievously handled a Child in the cradle, that if the Nurse had not come to his help, he had been quite spoil'd; but she crossing her self, and calling upon the Name of *Jesus*, the Spectre vanished. The next night she appeared in the shape of an *Hen,* which, when one of the Maids of the house took to be so indeed, and followed her, the Hen grew into an immense bigness, and presently caught the Maid by the throat, and made it swell, so that she could neither eat nor drink of a good while after.

She continued these stirs for a whole month, slapping some so smartly, that the stroke were heard of them that stood by, pulling the bed also from under others, and appearing sometime in one shape, sometimes in another, as of a Woman, of a Dog, of a Cat, and of a Goat. But at last her body being digged up, and burnt, the Apparition was never seen more.

These things being done at *Breslaw* in *Silesia,* where this *Weinrichius* then lived, which makes the Narration more considerable. This concealing the name of the parties, I conceive, was in way of civility to his deceased Towns-man, his Towns-mans's Widow and their Family.

The other Story he sets down he is not the first Pen-man of, (though the things were done in his time, and, as I conceive, some while after what was above related, as a passage in the Narration seems to intimate) but he transcrib'd it from one that not only dwelt in the place, but was often infested with the noisom occursions of that troublesome *Ghost*, that did so much mischief to the place where he dwelt. The Relation is somewhat large, I shall bring it into as narrow compass as I can.

Johannes Cuntius, a Citizen of *Pentsch* in *Silesia,* near sixty years of age, and one of the *Aldermen* of the Town, very fair in his carriage, and unblameable, to men's thinking, in the whole course of his life, having been sent for to the *Mayor's* house (as being a very understanding man, and dexterous at the dispatch of businesses) to end some controversies concerning certain Waggoners, and a Merchant of *Pannonia* having made an end of those affairs, is invited by the *Mayor* to Supper: he gets leave first to go home to order some businesses, leaving this sentence behind him, *It's good to he merry while we may, for mischiefs grow up fast enough daily.*

This *Cuntius* kept five lusty Geldings in his Stable, one whereof he commanded to be brought out, and his shoe being loose, had him ty'd to the next post: his Master with a Servant busied themselves to take up his leg to look on his hoof, the Horse being mad and mettlesome, struck them both down; but *Cuntius* received the greatest share of the blow: one that stood next by help'd them both up again. *Cuntius* no sooner was up and came to him self, but cry'd out, *Wo is me, how do I burn, and am all on a fire!* which he often repeated. But the parts he complain'd of most, the Women being put out of the room, when they were searched, no appearance of any stroke or hurt was found upon them. To be short, he fell downright sick, and grievously afflicted in Mind, loudly complaining, that his Sins were such, that they were utterly unpardonable, and that the least part of them were bigger than all the Sins of the World besides; but would have no Divine come to him, nor did particularly confess them to any. Several rumours indeed there were that once he had sold one of his Sons, but when, and to whom, it was uncertain; and that he had made a Contract with the Devil, and the like. But it was observed, and known for certain, that he had grown beyond all expectation rich, and that four days before this mischance, he being witness to a Child, said, that that was the last he should be ever witness to.

The night he dy'd, his eldest Son watched with him. He gave up the Ghost about the third hour of the night, at what time a black Cat, opening the Casement with her nails, (for it was shut) ran to his bed, and did so violently scratch his face and the bolster, as if she endeavoured by force to remove him out of the place where he lay. But the Cat afterwards suddenly was gone, and she was no sooner gone, but he breathed his last. A fair Tale was made to the Pastor of the Parish, and the Magistracy of the Town allowing it, he was buried on the right side of the Altar, his Friends paying well for it. No sooner *Cuntius* was dead, but a great Tempest arose, which raged most at his very Funeral, there being such impetuous Storms of Wind with Snow, that it made men's bodies quake, and their teeth chatter in their heads. But so soon as he was interred, of a sudden all was calm.

He had not been dead a day or two, but several rumours were spread in the town of a *Spiritus incubus,* or *Ephialtes,* in the shape of *Cuntius,* that would have forced a Woman. This happen'd before he was buried. After his burial, the same *Spectre* awaken'd one that was sleeping in his dining room, saying, *I can scarce withhold my self from beating thee to death.* The voice was the voice of *Cuntius*. The watchmen of the Town also affirmed, that they heard every night great stirs in *Cuntius* his House, the fallings and throwings of things about, and that they did see the gates stand wide open betimes in the mornings, though they were never so diligently shut o'er night; that his Horses were very unquiet in the Stable, as if they kick'd, and bit one another; besides unusual barkings and howlings of the Dogs all over the Town. But these were but preludious suspicions to further evidence, which I will run over as briefly as I may.

A Maid-servant of one of the Citizens of *Pentsch* (while these Tragedies and Stirs were so frequent in the Town) heard, together with some others lying in their beds, the noise and tramplings of one riding about the House, who at last ran against the Walls with that violence, that the whole House shaked again, as if it would fall, and the windows were all fill'd with flashings of light. The Master of the house being informed of it, went out of doors in the morning to see what the matter was; and he beheld in the Snow the impressions of strange feet, such as were like neither Horses, nor Cows, nor Hogs, nor any Creature that he knew.

Another time, about eleven of the clock in the night, *Cuntius* appears to one of his Friends that was a witness to a Child of his, speaks unto him, and bids him be of good courage, for he came only to communicate unto him a matter of great importance. *I have left behind me,* said he, *my youngest Son* James, *to whom you are God-father. Now there is at my eldest Son* Steven's, *a Citizen of* Jegerdorf, *a certain Chest, wherein I have put four hundred and fifteen Florens: This I tell you, that your God-son may not be defrauded of any of them, and it is your duty to look after it; which if you neglect, wo be to you.* Having said this, the *Spectre* departed, and went up into the upper rooms of the House, where he walked so stoutly that all rattled again, and the roof swagged with his heavy stampings. This *Cuntius* his Friend told to the Parson of the Parish a day or two after for a certain truth.

But there are also several other notorious passages of this *Cuntius*. As his often speaking to the Maid that lay with her Mistress, his Widow, to give him place, for it was his right; and if she would not give it him, he would writh her neck behind her.

His galloping up and down like a wanton horse in the Court of his House. He being divers times seen to ride, not only in the streets, but along the vallies of the fields, and on the Mountains, with so strong a trot, that he made the very ground flash with fire under him.

His bruising of the body of a Child of a certain Smiths, and making his very bones so soft, that you might wrap the corps on heaps like a glove.

His miserably tugging all night with a *Jew* that had taken up his Inn in the Town, and tossing him up and down in the lodging where he lay.

His dreadful accosting of a Waggoner, an old acquaintance of his, while he was busie in the stable, vomiting out fire against him to terrify him, and biting of him so cruelly by the foot, that he made him lame.

What follows, as I above intimated, concerns the Relator himself, who was the Parson of the Parish, whom his Fury so squeez'd and press'd when he was asleep, that wakening he found himself utterly spent, and his strength quite gone, but could not imagine the reason. But while he lay musing with himself what the matter might be, this *Spectre* returns again to him, and holding him all over so fast, that he could not wag a finger, rowled him in his bed backwards and forwards a good many times together. The same happen'd also to his Wife another time, whom *Cuntius*, coming thro' the casement in the shape of a little Dwarf, and running to her bed-side, so wrung and pulled as if he would have torn her throat out, had not her two Daughters come in to help her.

He pressed the lips together of one of this *Theologer's* Sons so, that they could scarce get them asunder.

His House was so generally disturbed with this unruly Ghost, that the Servants were fain to keep together anights in one room, lying upon straw, and watching the approaches of this troublesome Fiend. But a Maid of the House, being more courageous than the rest, would needs one night go to bed, and forsake her company. Whereupon *Cuntius* finding her alone, presently assaults her, pulls away the bedding, and would have carried her away with him; but she hardly escaping fled to the rest of the Family, where she espied him standing by the candle, and straightway after vanishing.

Another time he came into her Master's Chamber, making a noise like a Hog that eats grain, smacking and grunting very sonorously. They could not chase him away, by speaking to him; but ever as they lighted a Candle, he would vanish.

On another Time about Evening, when this *Theologer* was sitting with his Wife and Children about him, exercising himself in Musick, according to his usual manner, a most grievous stink arose suddenly, which by degrees spread itself to every corner of the room. Here upon he commends himself and his family to God by Prayer. The smell nevertheless encreased, and became above all measure pestilently noisom, insomuch that he was forced to go up to his chamber. He and his Wife had not been in bed a quarter of an hour, but they find the same stink in the bed-chamber; of which, while they are complaining one to another, out steps the Spectre from the Wall, and creeping to his bed-side, breathes upon him an exceeding cold breath, of so intolerable stinking and malignant a scent, as is beyond all imagination and expression. Here upon the *Theologer*, good soul, grew very ill, and was fain to keep his bed, his face, belly, and guts swelling as if he had been poysoned; whence he was also troubled with a difficulty of breathing, and with a putrid inflammation of his eyes, so that he could not well use them of a long time after.

But taking leave of the sick Divine, if we should go back, and recount what we have omitted, it would exceed the number of what we have already recounted. As for example, The trembling and sweating of *Cuntius* his Gelding, from which he was not free night nor day: The burning blue of the Candles at the approaches of *Cuntius* his Ghost: His drinking up the milk in the milk-bowls, his flinging dung into them, or turning the milk into blood: His pulling up posts deep set in the ground, and so heavy, that two lusty Porters could not deal with them: his discoursing with several men he met concerning the affairs of the Waggoners: His strangling of old men: His holding fast the Cradles of Children, or taking them out of them: His frequent endeavouring to force women: His defiling the Water in the Font, and fouling the Cloth on the Altar on that side that did hang towards his grave with dirty bloody spots: His catching up Dogs in the streets, and knocking their brains against the ground: His sucking dry the Cows, and tying their tails like the tail of an Horse: His devouring of Poultry, and his flinging of Goats bound into the Racks: His tying of an Horse to an empty oat-tub in the Stable, to clatter up and down with it, and the hinder foot of another to his own head-stall: His looking out of the Window of a low Tower, and then suddenly changing himself into the form of a long staff: His chiding of a Matron for suffering her servant to wash dishes on a Thursday, at what time he laid his hand upon her, and she said, it felt more cold than ice: His pelting one of the Women that washed his corps, so forcibly, that the print of the Clods he flung, were to be seen upon the wall: His attempting to ravish another, who excusing herself and saying, *My Cuntius, thou seest how old, wrinkled, and deformed I am, and how unfit for those kind of sports,* he suddenly set up a loud laughter, and vanished.

But we must insist upon these things; only we will add one passage more that is not a little remarkable. His gravestone was turned of one side, shelving, and there were several holes in the earth, about the bigness of mouse-holes, that went down to his very Coffin, which, however they were filled up with earth over night, yet they would be sure to be laid open the next morning.

It would be a tedious business to recite these things at large, and prosecute the Story in all its particular Circumstances. To conclude therefore, their calamity was such, from the frequent occursions of this restless fury, that there was none but either pitied them, or despis'd them; none would lodge in their Town, Trading was decayed, and the Citizens impoverished by the continual stirs and tumults of this unquiet Ghost.

And though the *Atheist* may perhaps laugh at them, as men undone by their own Melancholy and vain imaginations, or by the waggery of some ill neighbours; yet if he seriously consider what has been already related, there are many passages that are by no means to be resolved into any such Principles; but what I shall now declare, will make it altogether unlikely that any of them are.

To be short therefore, finding no rest, nor being able to excogitate any better remedy, they dig up *Cuntius* his body with several others buried both before and after him. But those both after and before were so putrify'd and rotten, their Sculls broken, and the Sutures of them gaping, that they were not to be known by their shape at all, having become in a manner but a rude mass of earth and dirt; but it was quite otherwise in *Cuntius*: His Skin was tender and florid, his Joynts not at all stiff, but limber and moveable, and a staff being put into his hand, he grasped it with His fingers very fast; his Eyes also of themselves would be one time open, and another time shut; they opened a vein in his Leg, and the blood sprang out as fresh as in the living; his Nose was entire and full, not sharp, as in those that are ghastly sick, or quite dead: and yet *Cuntius* his body had lien in the grave from *Feb.* 8 to *July* 20 which is almost half a year.

It was easily discernible where the fault lay. However, nothing was done rashly, but Judges were constituted, Sentence was pronounced upon *Cuntius* his Carcase, which (being animated thereto from success in the like case, some few years before in this very Province of *Silesia*, I suppose he means at *Breslaw*, where the Shoemakers body was burnt) they adjudged to the fire.

Wherefore there were Masons provided to make a hole in the wall near the Altar to get his body through, which being pulled at with a rope, it was so exceeding heavy, that the rope brake, and they could scarce stir him. But when they had pull'd him through, and gotten him on a Cart without, which *Cuntius* his Horse that had struck him (which was a lusty-bodied Jade) was to draw; yet it put him to it so, that he was ready to fall down ever and anon, and was quite out of breath with striving to draw so intolerable a load, who not withstanding could run away with two men in the same Cart presently after, their weight was so inconsiderable to his strength.

His body, when it was brought to the fire, proved as unwilling to be burnt, as before to be drawn; so that the Executioner was fain with hooks to pull him out, and cut him into pieces to make him burn. Which, while he did, the blood was found so pure and spiritous, that it spurted into his face as he cut him; but at last, not without the expence of two hundred and fifteen great billets, all was turned into ashes. Which they carefully sweeping up together, as in the foregoing Story, and casting them into the River, the *Spectre* never more appeared.

I must confess, I am so slow witted myself that I cannot so much as imagine, what the *Atheist* will excogitate for a subterfuge or hiding place, from so plain and evident Convictions.

In his *Historia naturalis curiosa regni Poloniae* published at Sandomir in 1721 Gabriel Rzazcynsci, a learned Jesuit, writes: "De cruentationibus cadauerum in specie agens, mira profert de mortuis in tumulis adhuc uoracibus et uicinis uiuentes in spectorum modum trucidantibus a Polonis speciali nomine *Upiers* et *Upierryea* appellatis. De quibus quae producit authentica documenta ulteriorem fortasse disquisitionem merentur."

The following document was guaranteed by Monsieur de Vassimont, a councillor of the Confederation of Bar in Podolia, who had been sent as an envoy to Moravia by his Royal Highness Leopold I, Duke of Lorraine, in order to conduct certain businesses on behalf of his brother, Prince Charles Joseph of Lorraine, Bishop of Olmutz and Osnabruck and later Archbishop of Tréves (1698–1715). Monsieur de Vassimont was generally informed that in those districts it was no unusual thing to see men who had been dead for some long time suddenly appear in the midst of a general assembly, and that not infrequently they entered a room and took their place at table with friends or acquaintance, that they never uttered a word, but that some sign either with the head or the hand was given to one of those present and that this person almost certainly died not very many days later. These extraordinary phenomena were vouched for by many very respectable individuals, and amongst others by an aged rector who declared that he had actually witnessed more than one instance of this.

The bishops and the priests of that province officially consulted Rome with regard to such extraordinary occurrences; but it appears they received no reply, because no doubt, all this was regarded as purely imaginary and as having no existence beyond the fancy of the common folk. They determined then to exhume the bodies of those who returned in this way and to cremate them, or at any rate entirely to destroy them in some other manner. And thus, at length, they were freed from the importunity of these phantoms who nowadays are far less frequently to be seen in this country than in former times. The rector, a learned and most honoured man, solemnly declared that what he related was entirely true.

It was, indeed, the report of these apparitions which gave Charles Ferdinand de Schertz the occasion to write his book *Magia posthuma*, which, as has been mentioned above, appeared at Olmutz in 1706, and which was dedicated to Prince Charles of Lorraine, Bishop of Olmutz and Osnabruck. Schertz relates that in a certain village a woman who had recently died without receiving the last Sacraments was buried in the usual way in the cemetery. Four days after her decease the inhabitants of the village heard an extraordinary noise and a terrible storm arose, when they saw a ghost which appeared to some people in the form of a dog, to others in the shape of a gaunt and hideous man, and who was seen not only by one individual but by many, and who caused persons the greatest alarm and torment by assaulting them fiercely, by seizing their throats so that they were almost suffocated, by exhausting the strength from their whole frame so that they were reduced to the last degree of feebleness and everyone noted how pale, attenuated and ill they appeared.

The ghost even attacked animals, and cows were found half dead just as if they had been severely beaten. These poor beasts by their mournful lowing showed what pains they were suffering. Horses were observed overcome with fatigue, sweating and trembling, over-heated, breathless, covered with foam, as if they had just been roughly driven at full gallop along some long and difficult road. These troubles persisted for many months.

Schertz, who was an eminent lawyer, argues the facts from a legal point of view. He examines the circumstances with perfect impartiality, and he weighs the evidence in the nicest manner according to precedent and routine. Granting that these troubles, these noises, these disturbances actually emanate from the person who is suspected of being their cause he inquires whether her body should be burned, as is the usual procedure in the case of the bodies of other apparitions who return from the grave and inflict injuries upon the living. He cites several examples of similar happenings and particularly describes the evil consequences which ensued. There was for instance a herdsman belonging to the village of Blau near the town of Kodon in Bohemia who after his death appeared to several persons in the district, and he used to call these unfortunate wretches loudly by name. Whether it was from fright, or whether it was because this Vampire exhausted their vitality, those whom he had thus summoned expired, it was remarked, within the course of a few days, invariably less than a week. The peasants of Blau exhumed the body, and drove a large stake right through the heart so that it was pinned to the ground. In spite of this precaution that very night the body appeared again and in so awful a guise that he frightened several persons to death, whilst he attacked and actually suffocated a yet greater number. He jeered horribly at those who had thought to have put an end to this plague, and mockingly thanked them for having given him a fine stick to drive away the dogs. When morning had come the place was in a panic, and the village authorities caused the body once again to be disinterred. It was then handed over to the common executioner who threw it into a tumbril and conveyed it beyond the village to a waste piece of ground where it was burned. The corpse, bloated and swollen, yelled like a madman kicking and tearing as though it had been alive, and when they pierced it with sharpened piles of white thorn it howled horribly, writhing and champing its blub red lips with the long white teeth whilst streams of warm red blood spurted out in all directions. At last it was thrown on a blazing pyre, and when execution had been duly performed, and the body reduced to ashes, the apparitions and molestations at last ceased.

Schertz says that exactly the same procedure has been followed in a great many other districts, and that to his knowledge many villages had been annoyed in this way. In each case when they have exhumed the body the Vampire was discovered as if it were alive, with a fresh complexion. Several other writers of authority are quoted and these fully bear out what he relates concerning these spectres, who, he remarks, particularly infest the mountainous districts of Silesia and Moravia, particularly the Carpathian ranges. Not only do they appear at night but they are often seen during the day, and, what is very extraordinary, objects which have belonged to the dead persons are moved from one place to another and are conveyed from room to room without anybody who visibly touches them. According to Schertz, the only remedy is to disinter the body, cut off the head, and burn the corpse to ashes. But this, says he, must not be done without due authority, and such proceedings are to be carried out in a formal and official manner. An inquiry must be held; witnesses are to be called and examined; the evidence is not to be too readily accepted; when the bodies in question have been exhumed they must be examined by medical men and theologians who may determine whether it is actually these persons who are molesting the living, and who may note the marks which undoubtedly evince vampirism. Should these conditions appear, then the bodies shall be officially handed over to the common executioner who will be instructed to burn them. It is said that cases are known when apparitions appear for some three or four days after the body has been burned. Should such an instance be authentic, and there is no reason to suppose otherwise, it must follow that this is not a Vampire but a ghost, and the spectre can neither draw upon nor nourish itself with the vitality of the living, although, indeed, it is quite true that ghosts themselves can be actually harmful and there are many cases upon record where spectres who are particularly malignant have actually attacked living persons and endeavoured to strangle them. So it must not be supposed that the evil powers of an apparition are only confined to frightening and alarm. It is particularly related that the clothes of a person who is a Vampire will often be moved from one place where they were hanging to another, as for example even though a suit of clothes may be locked up in a wardrobe, it has been found that these are mysteriously laid out upon a bed as if ready set for the person to change his attire. Schertz mentions that not many months before he wrote, there occurred at Olmutz certain disturbances that were very widely talked of and discussed. A house was troubled by an apparition which moved the furniture and pelted persons with stones and other missiles. But it would seem that here we have to deal with a poltergeist, a species of haunting very prevalent at the present day, and indeed, often investigated because it is so common. There are reported a very large number of examples of this especial haunting. One of the latest instances of these disturbances which took place at a house in Eland Road, Lavender Hill, London, S.W. 11, during January of last year (1928) caused a tremendous sensation.

The following incidents which happened about the year 1720 are placed beyond all manner of doubt both on account of the number and the position of the witnesses as also on account of the weight of the evidence which is sensible, circumstantial and complete. A soldier, who was billeted at the house of a farmer residing at Haidam, a village on the frontiers of Hungary, when one day he was at table with his host, the master of the house and the family, saw a stranger enter and take his place at the board among them. There seemed nothing extraordinary in this circumstance, but the goodman exhibited symptoms of unusual terror, as indeed did the rest of the company. Although he did not know what to think of it the soldier refrained from any comment, although it was impossible that he should not have remarked their confusion and fear. On the next morning the farmer was discovered dead in his bed, and then the reason for their perturbation could no longer be kept secret. They informed the soldier that the mysterious stranger was the farmer's old father, who had been dead and buried for more than ten years, and who had thus come and taken his place by the side of his son to forewarn him of his death, which indeed the terrible visitant had actually caused.

As might have been expected, the soldier recounted this extraordinary incident to his friends and companions and so it came to the ears of several officers by whom it was carried to the general. A consultation was held, and it was resolved that the Count de Cadreras, commander of a corps of the Alandetti Infantry, should institute a full inquiry into so extraordinary circumstances. Accordingly this gentleman with several other officers, an army surgeon and a notary, paid an official visit to Haidam. Here they took the sworn depositions of all the people belonging to the house, and these without exception gave it on oath that the mysterious stranger was the father of the late master of the house, and that all the soldier had said and reported was the exact truth. These statements were unanimously corroborated by all the persons who lived in that district. In consequence of this the officers decided that the body must be exhumed, and although ten years had passed it was found lying like a man who had just died, or even rather, like one who was in a heavy slumber, since when a vein was pierced the warm blood flowed freely as if that of a living person. The Count de Cadreras gave orders that the head should be completely severed, and then the corpse was once more laid in his grave. During their inquiry they also received information of many others who returned from the tomb, and among the rest of a man who had died more than thirty years before, who had come back no less than three times to his house at the hour of the evening's meal; and that on each occasion he had suddenly sprung upon an individual whose neck he bit fiercely, sucking the blood, and then vanishing with indescribable celerity. The first time he thus attacked his own brother, the second time one of his sons, and the third time one of the servants of the farm, so that all three expired instantly upon the spot. When this had been attested upon oath the Commissioner ordered that this man also should be disinterred, and he was found exactly like the first, just as a person who was still alive, the blood gushing out slab and red when an incision was made in the flesh. Orders were given that a great twopenny nail should be driven through the temples, and that afterwards the body should be laid again in the grave.

A third, who had been buried more than sixteen years, and who had caused the death of two of his sons by sucking their blood, was considered especially dangerous and forthwith cremated. The Commissioner made his report to the highest army tribunal, and they were so struck by the narration that they required him personally to deliver it to the Emperor Charles VI, who was so concerned at these extraordinary facts that he ordered a number of eminent lawyers, officers of the highest rank, the most skilled surgeons and physicians, and his most learned theologians to visit the district and conduct a most searching inquiry into the causes of these unusual and terrible occurences. The papers dealing with the case are still extant and the whole story was related in 1730 by the Count de Cadreras himself to a responsible official of the University of Fribourg who took down the details from the Count's own lips. It is hard to see how more reliable evidence is to be obtained of any happening or event.

The following history is given by several authorities and is also related in the *Lettres Juives,* by the Marquis d'Argens, a well-known book the first edition of which was translated into English and published London, 1729 as *The Jewish Spy,* "being a philosophical, historical, and critical correspondence by letters which lately pass'd between certain Jews in Turkey, Italy, France, etc." In this work which through the supposed medium of a foreigner, whose views are unbiased by the ideas and associations to which the mind of a native is habituated, are presented remarks on the manners and customs of a nation, interspersed with accounts of any extraordinary happenings that may recently have attracted particular notice. Although the medium is imaginary it must not by any manner of means be supposed that these letters had not a very serious import and intention. This method was perhaps the safest and most popular way in which one might criticize existing institutions and correct prevalent abuses, and the various histories which the author presents are related as facts deserving grave attention and communicated to his readers because they contain something extraordinary which demands scientific investigation and the consideration of a philosopher. When the question of vampirism was so largely occupying the attention of the learned it was natural that in such a work as the *Lettres Juives* some history of this kind, well authenticated and officially sanctioned, should find a place. The following was attested by two officers of the tribunal of Belgrade and by an officer in command of the imperial army at Gradiska, all three of whom investigated the affair in the year 1725. At the beginning of September, 1728, in a village named Kisolova, which is about nine or ten miles from Gradiska, there died a farmer by name Peter Plogojowitz who still appeared hale and hearty being only sixty-two years of age. Three days after his death, at midnight, he appeared to enter his house and asked his son for food. When this was set before him it seemed as if he partook of it and then left the room. On the next day the son who had been exceedingly alarmed told his friends and neighbours what had happened. That night the father did not appear, but on the following night he was again seen and he again asked for food. This time the son refused it upon which the apparition regarded him with a threatening look and on the next day he was found to have suddenly expired. Within a very few hours five or six other persons fell ill in the village. Their symptoms were complete exhaustion and a faintness as though from excessive loss of blood. They complained that they had been visited by a fearful dream in which the dead Plogojowitz seemed to glide into the room, catch them by the throat biting hard and suck the blood out of the wound. In this way he killed nine persons in less than a week. In spite of all that the local apothecary could do the sick men expired within a few days. The chief magistrate of the district learning what had taken place from the parish priest at once committed the facts to writing and sent them to Gradiska where there happened to be staying the Commander of the Imperial forces. Taking with him two officers of great experience and ordering the common executioner to attend, he visited the village of Kisilova which was thus tormented. They opened the graves of all who had died since the first week in September, and when they came to that of the farmer they found him as though he were in a trance, gently breathing, his eyes wide open and glaring horribly, his complexion ruddy, the flesh plump and full. His hair and nails had grown, and when the scarfskin came off there appeared a new and healthy cuticle. His mouth was all slobbered and stained with fresh blood. Thence they at once concluded it was he who must be the Vampire thus molesting the district, and it was necessary at once to put a stop to his ravages in case he should infect the whole village. The executioner armed with a heavy mallet drove a sharp stake through his heart, during which the grave was deluged with the blood that gushed from the wound, his nose, ears, and every orifice of the body. A big pyre of logs and brushwood having been built, the body was placed thereon. It was dry weather and the wood when kindled soon burned brightly, the flames being fanned by a gentle breeze. In a very short time the body was reduced to ashes. No marks of vampirism being found upon the other bodies they were reburied with due precautions, garlic and whitethorn being placed in the coffins, and thenceforth the village was freed from any molestation.

One of the best-attested, most detailed, and most famous histories of vampirism is concerned with the village of Meduegna near Belgrade, just at the time when the two dioceses of Belgrade and Smederevo were united by Benedict XIII, and Vincent Bagradin became the first holder of the double title. As will be later seen the document which gives full particulars of the following history was signed on 7 January, 1732, by three army surgeons and formally countersigned by a lieutenant-colonel and a sub-lieutenant. Of its authenticity and absolute fidelity no doubt at all can be entertained.

In the spring of 1727 there returned from service in the Levant to his native village Meduegna, a young man named Arnold Paole, who although he had seen military service but a few years had, according to his own accounts, met with many and varied adventures in that part of the world, a career which afforded him opportunity to save enough to purchase a good cottage and an acre or two of land in his native place, whence he was determined not to stir for the remainder of his days. It appeared a little remarkable to some that a man in the early prime of life, far from ill-looking, one who must have seen the rough as well as the smooth and companied with many a good fellow, should settle down so early in a quiet and out-of-the-way village. Yet his scrupulous honesty in all business transactions, his disciplined habits of work, his steady conduct, soon showed that the adventures with which he must have met in his travels had not, as is only too often the case with young soldiers, affected his probity and self-control. Nevertheless some noticed a certain uneasiness, a certain strangeness in his manner, which gave them food for suspicions, although they could not exactly tell whither these suspicions tended. It seemed as though he almost systematically avoided meeting Nina, the daughter of a rich farmer whose land ran along his own. And yet, as the gossips of the village said, what more equal match could there be? He was young; he had a decent property which in time would greatly improve; he had health, he was obviously of industrious habits, and he himself had been heard to declare that he had formed no connexions and had no ties in other lands.

As time passed on Arnold could not always avoid the society of his neighbours, and no surprise was felt when it was announced that he had been formally betrothed to Nina. And yet, as she often told her friends, the maiden felt that there was a shadow between them. At last she resolved to tackle him on the subject and she boldly asked what trouble so continually oppressed him. After a while he consented to tell her, and having informed her that he was always haunted by the fear of an early death he related a strange adventure which had befallen him at Kostartsa near Granitsa whilst he was on active service. He said that in those parts of Greece the dead returned to torment the living. By some evil chance they had been stationed in a terribly haunted spot, and he had experienced the first visitation. Immediately he sought the unhallowed grave and executed summary vengeance upon the Vampire. He had then, in spite of the persuasion of his superiors, sent in his resignation from the army, and had literally fled to his native village. It was true that so far he experienced no ill effects, and he trusted that he might have been able to counteract the evil. It so happened that during the harvest-home Arnold fell from the top of a loaded hay-waggon and was picked up insensible from the ground. They carried him to bed but he had evidently received some serious injury for after lingering a short time he died. In a few days his body was laid to rest, as they thought, in the village churchyard. About a month later, however, reports began to be circulated that Arnold after night-fall had been seen wandering about the village, and several persons, whose names are entered upon the official report, complained that they were haunted by him, and that after he had appeared to them they felt in a state of extraordinary debility. But a short time went by when several of these persons died, and something like a panic began to spread through the neighbourhood. As the dark winter nights approached no man dared to venture outside his doors when once dusk had fallen, yet it was whispered that the spectre was able easily to penetrate closed windows and walls, that no locks or bars could keep him out if he wished to enter. Throughout the whole winter the wretched village seems to have lived in a state of frantic terror and dismay. The evil, as we may well imagine, was aggravated by the cold hungry nights of a snow-tossed December and January. At length some ten weeks, or rather more, after his funeral it was resolved that the body of Arnold must be disinterred with a view of ascertaining whether he was indeed a vampire. The party consisted of two officers, military representatives from Belgrade, two army surgeons, *Unterfeldscherern*, a drummer boy who carried their cases of instruments, the authorities of the village, the old sexton and his assistants. Dr. Mayo thus reconstructs the scene. "It was early on a grey morning that the commission visited the quiet cemetery of Meduegna, which, surrounded with a wall of unhewn stone, lies sheltered by the mountains that, rising in undulating green slopes, irregularly planted with fruit trees, ends in an abrupt craggy ridge, feathered with underwood. The graves were, for the most part, neatly kept, with borders of box, or something like it, and flowers between; and at the head of most a small wooden cross, painted black, bearing the name of the tenant. Here and there a stone had been raised. One of considerable heighth, a single narrow slab, ornamented with grotesque Gothic carvings, dominated over the rest. Near this lay the grave of Arnold Paole, towards which the party moved. The work of throwing out the earth was begun by the bent crooked old sexton, who lived in the Leichenhaus beyond the great crucifix. He seemed unconcerned enough;" but, as might well be supposed the young drummer boy was gazing intently, fascinated by horror and suspense. Before very long the coffin was rather roughly dragged out of the ground, and the grave-digger's assistant soon knocked off the lid. It was seen that the corpse had moved to one side, the jaws gaped wide open and the blub lips were moist with new blood which had trickled in a thin stream from a corner of the mouth. All unafraid the old sexton caught the body and twisted it straight. "So," he cried, "You have not wiped your mouth since last night's work." Even the officers accustomed to the horrors of the battlefield and the surgeons accustomed to the horrors of the dissecting room shuddered at so hideous a spectacle. It is recorded that the drummer boy swooned upon the spot. Nerving themselves to their awful work they inspected the remains more closely, and it was soon apparent that there lay before them the thing they dreaded—the vampire. He looked indeed, as if he had not been dead a day. On handling the corpse the scarfskin came off, and below there were new skin and new nails. Accordingly they scattered garlic over the remains and drove a stake through the body, which it is said gave a piercing shriek as the warm blood spouted out in a great crimson jet.

When this dreadful operation had been performed they proceeded to exhume the bodies of four others who had died in consequence of Arnold's attacks. The records give no details of the state in which these were found. They simply say that whitethorn stakes were driven through them and that they were all five burned. The ashes of all were replaced in consecrated ground.

It might have been thought that these measures would have put an end to vampirism in the village, but such unhappily was not the case, which shows that the original vampire at Kostartsa must have been of an exceptionally malignant nature. About half-a-dozen years after the body of Arnold Paole had been cremated the infection seems to have broken out afresh and several persons died apparently through loss of blood, their bodies being in a terribly anæmic and attenuated condition. This time the officials did not hesitate immediately to cope with the danger, and they determined to make a complete examination of all the graves in the cemetery to which any suspicion attached. Accordingly several surgeons of eminence were summoned from Belgrade and a very thorough investigation took place which yielded the most extraordinary results. The medical reports from which the following cases of vampirism are quoted were officially signed on 7 January, 1732, at Meduegna by three distinguished army surgeons, Johannes Flickinger, Isaac Siedel, Johann Friedrich Baumgartner, and formally countersigned by the lieutenant-colonel and a sub-lieutenant then in residence at Belgrade.

The most remarkable examples were the following:

A woman by name Stana, twenty years of age, who had died three months before, after an illness which only lasted three days and which followed directly after her confinement. Upon her death bed she confessed that she had anointed herself with the blood of a vampire to liberate herself from his persecutions. Nevertheless, she, as well as her baby, had died. The body of the child, owing to a hasty and careless interment, had been half scraped up and devoured by wolves. The body of the woman, Stana, was untouched by decomposition. When it was opened the chest was found to be full of fresh blood, the viscera had all the appearance of soundest health. The skin and nails of both hands and feet were loose and came off, but underneath was a clean new skin and nails.

A woman of the name of Miliza, who had died after an illness lasting three months. The body had been buried nearly one hundred days before. In the chest was liquid blood, and the bowels were sound and entirely healthy. The corpse was declared by a heyduk who recognized it to look better and to be far plumper than during life. The body of a child eight years old, that had likewise been buried ninety days. It was in the Vampire condition.

The son of a heyduk named Milloc, a lad some sixteen years old. The body had been buried ninety days; it was rosy and flabber, wholly in the Vampire condition.

One Joachim, a boy of seventeen, who was likewise the son of a heyduk. He had died after a short illness of three days, and had lain buried for eight weeks and four days. His complexion was fresh, and the body unmistakably in the Vampire condition.

A woman, named Ruscha. She had died after a sickness lasting ten days. She was buried six weeks before. New blood and warm was found in her chest and in fundo uentriculi.

A young girl ten years of age, who had died two months before. Her body was in the Vampire condition, and when pierced with a stake a great quantity of hot blood poured forth and swilled the grave.

The wife of a villager named Hadnuck, who had been buried seven weeks before; and that of her babe, eight weeks old, who had lain interred only twenty-one days. It was remarked that these corpses although buried in the same ground and hard by the others were far gone in decomposition.

A serving-man, Rhade, who was twenty-three years old. He had ailed for some three months before his death, and the body which had been buried for five weeks was much tainted with corruption.

A woman and a child who had been buried five weeks, and whose bodies were entire, showing every trace of vampirism.

A heyduk named Stanko, a much-respected and important character in the village. He had died six weeks previously at the age of sixty. In the chest and abdomen there was found to be a quantity of rich new blood, and the whole body was in the Vampire condition.

Millock, a heyduk, twenty-five years old. The body which bore every trace of vampirism had been in the earth six weeks.

Stanjoika, the wife of a heyduk, twenty years old. She died after a brief illness of three days and had been buried more than a fortnight before. Her face was full and florid; the limbs supple and without any cadaverous coldness. There was a quantity of new blood in her chest and *in ventriculo cordis*. The viscera were sound and healthy. The skin appeared fresh and comely as in life.

It should be observed that this list by no means exhausts the cases of vampirism which were then collected, and particular details, moreover, have been most fully recorded in each instance, but to amplify the catalogue would involve much reiteration that might prove wearisome without adding anything material to the tale of a demonstration already conclusively established.

Erasmus Franciscus in his commentary upon Baron Valvasor's *Die Ehre des Herzogthums Krain*, Ljubljana, 1689, gives an interesting account of a Vampire in Carniola. There lived in the district of Kranj, and not far from the city of that name, a certain peasant, a landowner, who was called Grando. During his life he had always been held a quiet industrious man of good repute, but after his death the neighbourhood was much plagued by the attacks of a vampire and there could be no doubt that this was Grando. Accordingly the ecclesiastical authorities gave directions that he should be disinterred. When they opened his grave, after he had been buried for many months, the body was found as though he slept. Not only was his complexion fresh and ruddy, but the features gently quivered as if the dead man smiled. He even parted his lips as if he would inhale fresh air. He opened his eyes wide, and those engaged began to recite litanies and prayers, whilst a priest holding aloft the Crucifix adjured the Vampire in these words: "Raise thine eyes and look upon Jesus Christ who hath redeemed us from the pains of hell by His most Holy Passion and His precious Death upon the Rood," whereupon an expression of extraordinary sadness came over the dead man's face and tears began to flow fast down his cheeks. Finally after a solemn commendation of his soul they struck his head from the body which moved just as if it had been alive.

It will not be impertinent to quote here a very interesting passage which occurs in *The Travels of three* English *Gentlemen*, written about 1734, and published in the *Harleian Miscellany*, vol. iv, 1745. The travellers have arrived at Laubach.

"We must not omit Observing here, that our Landlord seemed to pay some Regard to what Baron *Valvasor* has related of the *Vampyres*, said to infest some Parts of this Country. These *Vampyres* are supposed to be the Bodies of deceased Persons, animated by evil Spirits, which come out of the Graves, in the Night-time, suck the Blood of many of the Living, and thereby destroy them. Such a Notion will, probably, be looked upon as fabulous and exploded, by many People in *England;* however, it is not only countenanced by Baron *Valvasor,* and many *Carnioleze* Noblemen, Gentlemen, &c. as we were informed, but likewise actually embraced by some Writers of good Authority. M. *Jo. Henr. Zopfius,* Director of the *Gymnasium* of *Essen,* a Person of great Erudition, has published a Dissertation upon them, which is extremely learned and curious, from whence we shall beg Leave to transcribe the following Paragraph: "The *Vampyres*, which come out of the Graves in the Nighttime, rush upon People sleeping in their Beds, suck out all their Blood, and destroy them. They attack Men, Women, and Children, sparing neither Age nor Sex. The People attacked by them complain of Suffocation, and a great Interception of Spirits; after which, they soon expire. Some of them, being asked, at the Point of Death, what is the Matter with them, say they suffer in the Manner just related from People lately dead, or rather the Spectres of those People; upon which, their Bodies, from the Description given of them, by the sick Person, being dug out of the Graves, appear in all Parts, as the Nostrils, Cheeks, Breast, Mouth, &c. turgid and full of Blood. Their Countenances are fresh and ruddy; and their Nails, as well as Hair, very much grown. And, though they have been much longer dead than many other Bodies, which are perfectly putrified, not the least Mark of Corruption is visible upon them. Those who are destroyed by them, after their Death, become *Vampyres*; so that, to prevent so spreading an Evil, it is found requisite to drive a Stake through the dead Body, from whence, on this Occasion, the Blood flows as if the Person was alive. Sometimes the Body is dug out of the Grave, and burnt to Ashes; upon which, all Disturbances cease. The *Hungarians* call these Spectres *Pamgri*, and the *Servians Vampyres*; but the Etymon, or Reason of these Names, is not known." Vid. *Dissert. de* Vampyres Serviensibus *quam Suprem. Numin. Auspic. Præsid.* M. Joan. Henr. Zopfio *Gymnas.* Assind. *Direct. publice defend.* &c. Christ. Frid. Van Dalen Emmericens, &c. P. 6, 7. Duisburgi *ad* Rhenum, Typis Johannis Sas, Academiæ Typographi, Anno MDCCXXXIII.

These Spectres are reported to have infested several Districts of *Servia*, and the Bannat of *Temeswaer,* in the Year 1725, and for seven or eight Years afterwards, particularly those of *Mevadia,* or *Meadia,* and *Parakin,* near the *Morava.* In 1732, we had a Relation of some of their Feats in the Neighbourhood of Cassovia; and the publick Prints took Notice of the Tragedies, they acted in the Bannat of *Temeswaer,* in the Year 1738. Father *Gabriel Rzaczynski,* in his Natural History of the Kingdom of *Poland,* and the great Duchy of *Lithuania,* published at *Sendomir,* in 1721, affirms, that in *Russia, Poland,* and the great Dutchy of *Lithuania,* dead Bodies, actuated by infernal Spirits, sometimes enter People's Houses in the Night, fall upon Men, Women, and Children, and attempt to suffocate them; and that of such Diabolical Facts his Countrymen have several very authentic Relations. The *Poles* call a Man's Body thus informed *Upier,* and that of a woman *Upierzyca,* i.e. *a winged* or *feathered Creature;* which Name seems to be deduced from the surprising Lightness and Activity of these incarnate Demons. If we remember right, an Account of them also, from *Poland,* is to be met with, in some of the News-Papers for 1693, perfectly agreeing with those of the *Servian Vampyres* given us by M. *Zopfius.* In Fine, the Notion of such pestiferous Beings has prevailed from time immemorial over a great Part of *Hungary, Servia, Carniolo, Poland,* &c. as is evinced by several Authors in Conjunction with the aforesaid M. *Zopfius.* To which we shall beg Leave to add, that the antient *Greeks* also seem to have been firmly persuaded, that dead Bodies were sometimes acted by evil Spirits, as appears from a Fragment of *Phlegon.* Neither is this Opinion, however it may be ridiculed by many People, altogether without Foundation; since the Supreme Being *may* make wicked Spirits his Instruments of Punishment here, as well as Plagues, Wars, Famines, &c. and, that he *actually has* done so, is sufficiently apparent from Scripture, to omit what has been said on this Head by some of the most eminent profane Authors.

Before we take Leave of the City of *Laubach,* it will be proper to observe, that, though the Bulk of the People there speak the *Carniolian,* or *Sclavanian,* Tongue, and have some Customs peculiar to themselves, they agree in most Points with the other *Germans.* All the People of Fashion and Distinction speak *German* fluently and purely—*Laubach* was taken by *Ottocar,* King of *Bohemia,* in 1269; and attacked ineffectually by the *Turks* in 1472, and 1484. *Albert,* Archduke of *Austria,* likewise failed in his Attempt upon it, in 1441. The Streets are not very broad, nor the Houses grand; though, every Thing considered, it may be esteemed a fine City. Here we lay, for the first Time, betwixt two Feather-beds; which threw the Writer of this Account into so violent a Sweat, that he had scarce any Rest all Night, and found himself extremely faint the next Morning. Many of the *Germans,* however, like this Sort of Lodging; though it is very disagreeable, for the most Part, to Gentlemen of other Nations."

About the years 1730–32 occurred the case of Stephen Hubner of Treautenau, who after his death returned and not only attacked individuals but also killed cattle. From the official report it would seem that this vampire strangled them. This case was very shortly taken in hand and by order of the supreme court of the district the body was disinterred. Although actually five months had passed since the time of burial it was found with all the marks of vampirism. Being taken to the public gallows it was there decapitated by the common executioner. The remains were burned to ashes and scattered to the wind. For precautions sake the bodies of those near Hubner were exhumed and reverently cremated, and then once again interred in their original resting place.

Although these histories belong for the most part to the eighteenth century the belief in vampires among Slavonic peoples is yet as strong as ever. The Serbians still paint crosses with tar on the doors of their houses and barns to keep out the vampires, just as in the old days among the Highlanders of Scotland it was believed that tar daubed on a door kept off witches. In many districts of Bosnia, when the women of a village go to pay a visit to a neighbour's house where a death has recently occurred they put a sprig of hawthorn (*Weissdorn*) behind their head-cloth, and just after they have left the house they throw it away in the road. If the dead has turned into a vampire he will be so busily engaged in picking up the hawthorn that it will not be possible for him to track them to their own homes.

In various parts of Germany, especially in certain districts of West Prussia the Vampire tradition long prevailed, and even now instances of vampirism are occasionally, if rarely, found in the remoter thorps and burghs. No new features or extraordinary happenings are recorded, and it is but seldom that cases excited any very general attention. Among the most remarkable were those of a citizen of Egwanschiftz who in 1617 was attacked and long tormented by a vampire who at last slew the victim whereupon the bodies both of the vampire and the luckless prey were cremated in two several pyres at a deserted spot some distance from human habitation. Two hundred years later, in 1820, a rich landowner whose possession of extensive properties in the vicinity of Danzig made him a very prominent figure throughout the district was sorely beset by a vampire, and only delivered from these attacks by the prayers and mortifications of certain holy Cistercian monks who had been ejected from their house by the abominable decrees of the Prussian government of 28 April, 1810.

In his chronicle under the year 1343 Sebastian Moelers relates that during a terrible visitation of the Black Death cases of vampirism were numerous in the Tyrol, and the Benedictine abbey of Marienberg was much infested, one at least of the monks, Dom Steino von Netten, being commonly reputed to have been slain by a vampire. In 1348 the plague swept off every inmate of this famous cloister except Abbot Wyho, a priest, one lay brother, and Goswin who later became the eminent chronicler.

At Danzig in 1855 there was a fearful outbreak of cholera, and it was bruited throughout the whole province that the dead returned as Vampires to fetch the living. It is said that the fears of the people terribly increased the mortality.

From time immemorial in many parts of Europe the peasants at a season of especial distress, particularly when the cattle have been attacked by some wasting disease, are wont to resort to a ceremonial kindling of bonfires, the general name for which is need-fire. The exact signification of this name is a little doubtful. Grimm would derive it from *need* "necessity"(German, noth), so that the term need-fire signifies a "forced fire." This is also the interpretation given by Lindenbrog. (Eum ergo ignem *nodfeur* et *nodfyr*, quasi necessarium. ignem uocant.) On the other hand C. L. Rochholz connects the word need with a verb *nieten* "to churn," in which case need-fire would mean a "churned fire." The superstition of kindling need-fires comes down through the ages from Pagan times, and it was one of those heathen practices the continuance of which was again and again forbidden. Whilst King Pepin was ruling the Franks a synod which had been convened under S. Boniface in 750 prohibited the kindling "illos sacrilegos ignes, quos *niedfyr* uocant" as heathenish and profane. Nevertheless the tradition persisted and with other Pagan practices the knowledge of it was handed down by the covens and colleges of witches. In the year 1598 when a fatal epidemic was raging at Neustadt, near Marburg, a sorcerer by name John Kohler actually persuaded the burgomaster and leading citizens to assay this magic operation. All fires upon the hearths and elsewhere having been extinguished sparks were produced by friction and from these a pyre was kindled between the gates of the town and all the cattle driven through the smoke and flames. Throughout the town all fires were relit by means of brands which had been taken from the public bonfire. It is not surprising to learn that this piece of witchcraft had no good effect; the pest raged as before; and the only result appears to have been that grave suspicion attached itself to Kohler who in December 1605 was burned having been found guilty of midnight conjurations and necromancy.

Nevertheless in many parts of Germany until the middle of the nineteenth century, in Lower Saxony, in the Hartz Mountains, in Brunswick, in Silesia and Bohemia, the practice still prevailed. In 1682 it was forbidden by Gustavus Adolphus, Duke of Mecklenburg, but his law had no effect. The need-fire is said still to survive in the remoter parts of Switzerland, of Norway and Sweden; and, although the fact is hardly recognized, in

Yorkshire and in Northumberland on the occasion of rinderpest the practice of lighting needfires continued well within living memory, and, it has been said, is not altogether unknown in the remoter districts even to-day.

There are many ways of preparing the needfire, but it is essential that it should not be struck with flint and steel, nor, of course, must a match be used. The first sparks are to be made by prolonged friction, and it is usual to have ready tow, a piece of linen or some other inflammable substance which will immediately burst into a flame whence the brush wood or straw can be set ablaze. Unless every light in the village shall have been previously put out the fire will probably fail of its effect. Formerly in many parts it was kindled annually as a preventive, but in more recent times it was only resorted to in the case of an actual murrain.

However, in Russia (at least until lately), in Poland, in Serbia and among the Slavonic peoples generally, an epidemic among the cattle is generally ascribed to a vampire who is draining them of their vitality. Accordingly the reason for the need-fire takes a slightly different aspect. It is kindled with a very definite reason, to wit that the flames may keep off the vampire who cannot pass through them. One of the chief days, in Poland at any rate, upon which it was usual to kindle these fires, was the feast of S. Roch who during his lifetime devoted himself both to persons and animals stricken by the plague, as is related in an old sequence which is found in the fifteenth century missels of Sarum, Utrecht, Autun, Toulouse and other cities.

> At post mortem sui patris
> Et decessum suae matris,
> Peregre diuertitur;
> Et ad domos infirmorum
> Peste dira perpessorum
> Festine ingreditur
> Jesum Christum Deum clamat,
> Signo crucis cunctos sanat
> Sua prouidentia.
> Ad quem uenit uir beatus,
> Prorsus fuit hic sanatus
> Diuina potentia.
>   Ciuitates Italiæ,
>   Romæ, Longobardiæ,
> Sanat suis precibus.
> Hospitali Placentiæ
> Percussus pestis silice,
> Abiectus e mœnibus;
>   Languens dum in silua sitit
> Fontem Deus sibi mittit
> Præostensa nebula.
> Paruus canis panes portat
> A Gothardo, et reportat;
> Cane uiro regula.
>   Sic uir sanctus confortatur
> Dum Gothardo consolatur
> In ualle miseriæ;
> Et per angelum sanatur
> Qui a Deo mittebatur,
> Raphael in nomine.

In 1414 during the council of Constance when the plague broke out in that city the fathers of the council ordered public prayers and processions in honour of S. Roch, and immediately the pestilence ceased. Accordingly with S. Sebastian and S. Adrian he is generally invoked against the plague, and in Poland he is regarded as the saint who will protect against the ravages of vampires since they spread their infection as a poisonous pestilence.

That well-known occult investigator and authority the late Dr. Franz Hartmann has given us particulars of some cases of vampirism which actually came under his own observation. The following which were related in *Borderland,* vol. III 1895, occurred in the neighbourhood of Vienna but a short time before they were published.

A young lady at G—had an admirer who asked her in marriage, but as he was a drunkard she refused and married another. Thereupon the lover shot himself, and soon after that event a vampire, assuming his form, visited her frequently. She could not see him but felt his presence in a way that could leave no room for doubt. The medical faculty did not know what to make of the case, they called it "hysterics," and tried in vain every remedy in the pharmacopœia, until she had at last the spirit exorcised by a man of strong faith. In this case there is an elemental making use of, and being aided by, the elementary of the suicide.

A very similar example, which has already been quoted at length (p. 115), was related by the Hon. Ralph Shirley in the *Occult Review*.

Dr. Hartmann also gives the following typical instances of vampirism, and these may serve for many thus avoiding superfluous repetition. A miller at D— had a healthy servant-boy, who soon after entering his service began to fail. He acquired a ravenous appetite, but nevertheless grew daily more feeble and emaciated. Being interrogated, he at last confessed that a thing which he could not see, but which he could plainly feel, came to him every night about twelve o'clock and settled upon his chest, drawing all the life out of him, so that he became paralised for the time being, and neither could move nor cry out. Thereupon the miller agreed to share the bed with the boy, and made him promise that he should give a certain sign when the vampire arrived. This was done, and when the signal was made the miller putting out his hands grasped an invisible but very tangible substance that rested upon the boy's chest. He described it as apparently elliptical in shape, and to the touch feeling like gelatine, properties which suggest an ectoplasmic formation. The thing writhed and fiercely struggled to escape, but he gripped it firmly and threw it on the fire. After that the boy recovered, and there was an end of these visits. "Those who like myself," remarks Dr. Hartmann, "have, on innumerable occasions removed 'astral tumours,' and thereby cured the physical tumours will find the above neither 'incredible' nor 'unexplainable.' Moreover, the above accounts do not refer to events of the past but to persons still living in this country."

"A woman in this vicinity has a ghost, or as she calls it, a 'dual' with whom she lives on the most intimate terms as wife and husband. She converses with him and he makes her do the most irrational things. He has many whims, and she being a woman of means, gratifies them. If her dual wants to go and see Italy 'through her eyes,' she has to go to Italy and let him enjoy the sights. She does not care for balls and theatres; but her dual wants to attend them, and so she has to go. She gives lessons to her dual and 'educates' him in the things of this world and commits no end of follies. At the same time her dual draws all the strength from her, and she has to vampirize every one she comes in contact with to make up for the loss."

Mrs. Volet Tweedale in her *Ghosts I have Seen* gives a very curious account of a certain Prince Valori who was everywhere attended by a familiar or "satyr," invisible to many people, but often seen in his company by those who had psychic faculties. The familiar became attached to him on an occasion when he had had the incredible folly to attend a Sabbat in the Vosges. A Russian clairvoyante who knew all the circumstances informed Mrs. Tweedale that a certain ancestor of her own, the Bohemian noble de Laski, famous as having befriended Dr. Dee and Kelly, entertained a familiar called Buisson. As among the covens of witches two centuries since the familiars who wait upon modern adepts of black magic have various names, Minette, Verdelet, etc., Mrs. Tweedale tells us that "General Elliot, who commanded the forces in Scotland" and "was a very well-known society man about twenty-five years ago" had a familiar, Wononi, and used actually to speak aloud with him in the middle of a dinner-party. "To look at he was the very last man that one would associate with matters occult."

The erotic familiar is by no means unknown to-day. As in former times he is often required to assume the likeness of some person whom the witch lusts to enjoy. There is an allusion to this practice in Middleton's drama *The Witch*, where when the young gallant visits the witch's abode Hecati cries on seeing him:

'Tis Almachildes—fresh blood stirs
in me—
The man that I have lusted to enjoy:
I've had him thrice in incubus
already.

It will readily be remembered that in *La-Bas*—and Huysmans here is not writing fiction—Madame Chantelouve says to Durtal: "Enfin, tenez, je vous possède quand et comment il me plaît, de même qui j'ai longtemps possédé Byron, Baudclaire, Gérard de Nerval, ceux qui j'aime …

—Vous dites?

—Je dis qui je n'ai qu' à les désirer, qu' à vous désirer vous, maintenant, avant de m'endormir…

—Et ?

—Et vous seriez inférieur à ma chimère, au Durtal que j'adore et dont les caresses rendent mes nuits folles.

—Il la regarda, stupéfié. Elle avait ses yeux dolents et troubles; elle semblait même ne plus le voir et parler dans le vide. Il hésita, apercut en un éclair de pensées, ces scènes de l'incubat dont Gévingey parlait …"

Sinistrari in his famous treatise *De Daemonialitate* gives several instances which actually came under his own notice of incubi who attach themselves with vampirish pertinacity to certain individuals and who are only expelled and dismissed with great difficulty. He also relates the case of a woman who confessed to long and indecent intercourse with an erotic incubus who appeared to her under the form of a comely youth and exhausted her vitality.

Under the heading "A Modern Case of Vampirism" Dr. Hartmann relates the following, by which we see that the strong wish to injure another can be sufficiently concentrated to form a psychic tie between the person who is bitterly antagonistic and his enemy so that there can actually take place the absorption of vitality from the one to the other. "In the night of 31 December, 1888, Mr. and Mrs. Rose (the names in this story are pseudonyms, but the facts are true) went to bed as poor people and on the morning of 1 January, 1889, they woke up finding themselves rich. An uncle to whom they owed their poverty because he kept them from coming into the legal possession of their rightful property, had died during the night. There are some occurences of an occult character, connected with this event, which will be interesting to those who wish to find practical proofs and demonstrations in their investigations of the 'night side of nature.'

"Mr. Rose is a young, but very clever, professional man in this city, who being at the beginning of his career has, therefore, only an exceedingly limited number of clients. His young wife is one of the most amiable ladies whom it has been my good fortune to meet; a spiritually minded woman and more of a poetess than an economist. She had been brought up under the most affluent circumstances, her father being very rich, and she was the only and therefore the pet child in her luxurious home. It would be too complicated a task to tell how it happened that the property which she inherited fell first into the hands of her uncle, a spiteful and avaricious man. Sufficient to say that this man, whom we will call Helleborus, had by his intrigues and law-suits managed to keep Mrs. Rose's property in his hands; giving her and her husband no support whatever. More than once they were forced to borrow money from their friends, in order to keep themselves from starvation.

"As 'Uncle Helleborus' was in the last stage of consumption, their only hope was that his death would soon put an end to his law-suits, and bring them into possession of what rightfully belonged to them.

"Uncle Helleborus, however, did not seem inclined to die. Year after year he kept on coughing and expectorating; but with all this he out-lived many who predicted his death. After making to Mr. and Mrs. Rose a proposal of a settlement, which would have left him in possession of nearly all the property and given to them only a pittance, he went to Meran, last autumn, to avoid the cold climate of Vienna.

"In their embarrassing circumstances, they were much inclined to accept the settlement; but they concluded to first consult about it a friend, an eminent lawyer; and this gentleman (whom we will call Mr. Tulip, as everybody in Vienna knows his real name) advised them to the contrary. This enraged Helleborus against Tulip; and starting into a blind rage, he swore that if he found an opportunity of killing Tulip, he would surely do so.

"Mr. Tulip was an extraordinary strong, well-built and healthy man; but at the beginning of December last, soon after Mr. Helleborus's departure for Meran, he suddenly failed in health. The doctors could not locate the disease, and he grew rapidly thinner and weaker, complaining of nothing but extreme lassitude, and feeling like a person who was daily bled. Finally, on 20 December, last, all Vienna was surprised to hear that Mr. Tulip had died. Post-mortem examination showing all the organs in a perfectly normal condition, the doctors found nothing better to register but death from *marasmus* (emaciation), as the cause of this extraordinary event. Strange to say, during the last days of the disease (if it can be so called), when his mind became flighty, he often imagined that a stranger was troubling him, and the description which he gave of that invisible personage fitted Mr. Helleborus with perfect accuracy.

"During Mr. Tulip's sickness, news came from Meran that Mr. Helleborus was rapidly gaining strength and recovering from his illness in a most miraculous manner; but there were some people who expressed grave doubts as to whether this seeming recovery would be lasting. On the day of Mr. Tulip's funeral, Mr.—, a prominent member of the Theosophical Society, now in Austria, remarked to Mrs. Rose: 'You will see that now that Mr. Tulip is dead, his Vampire will die too.'

"On 1 January, 1889, Mr. Rose dreamed that he saw Uncle Helleborus looking perfectly healthy. He expressed his surprise about it, when a voice, as if coming from a long distance said: 'Uncle Helleborus is dead.' The voice sounded a second time, and this once far more powerfully, repeating the same sentence: and this time Mr. Rose awoke with the sound of that voice still ringing in his ears, and communicated to his wife the happy news that 'Uncle Helleborus was dead.' Two hours afterwards a telegram came from Meran, announcing the demise of Uncle Helleborus, which had occurred on that very night, and calling upon Mr. Rose to come and attend to the funeral. It was found that Mr. Helleborus had begun to grow rapidly worse from the day when Mr. Tulip died.

"The only rational explanation of such cases I have found in Paracelsus."

In *The Occult Review* for September, 1909, under the title "An Authenticated Vampire Story" was given the following history which was contributed by Dr. Hartmann.

On 10 June. 1909, there appeared in a prominent Vienna paper *(The Neues Wiener Journal)* a notice saying that the castle of B—had been burned by the populace, because there was a great mortality among the peasant children, and it was generally believed that this was due to the invasion of a Vampire, supposed to be the last Count B—, who died and acquired that reputation. The castle was situated in a wild and desolate part of the Carpathian Mountains, and was formerly a fortification against the Turks. It was not inhabited, owing to its being believed to be in the possession of ghosts: only a wing of it was used as a dwelling for the caretaker and his wife.

Now it so happened that, when I read the above notice, I was sitting in a coffee-house at Vienna in company with an old friend of mine who is an experienced occultist and editor of a well-known journal, and who had spent several months in the neighbourhood of the castle. From him I obtained the following account, and it appears that the Vampire in question was probably not the old Count, but his beautiful daughter, the Countess Elga, whose photograph, taken from the original painting, I obtained. My friend said: "Two years ago I was living at Hermannstadt, and being engaged in engineering a road through the hills, I often came within the vicinity of the old castle, where I made the acquaintance of the old castellan, or caretaker, and his wife, who occupied a part of the wing of the house, almost separate from the main body of the building. They were a quiet old couple and rather reticent in giving information or expressing an opinion in regard to the strange noises which were often heard at night in the deserted halls, or of the apparitions which the Wallachian peasants claimed to have seen when they loitered in the surroundings after dark. All I could gather was that the old Count was a widower and had a beautiful daughter, who was one day killed by a fall from her horse, and that soon after the old man died in some mysterious manner, and the bodies were buried in a solitary graveyard belonging to a neighbouring village. Not long after their death an unusual mortality was noticed among the inhabitants of the village; several children and even some grown people died without any apparent illness; they merely wasted away; and thus a rumour was started that the old Count had become a Vampire after his death. There is no doubt that he was not a saint, as he was addicted to drinking, and some shocking tales were in circulation about his conduct and that of his daughter; but whether there was any truth in them, I am not in a position to say.

"Afterwards the property came into the possession of —, a distant relative of the family, who is a young man and officer in a cavalry regiment at Vienna. It appears that the heir enjoyed his life at the capital and did not trouble himself much about the old castle in the wilderness; he did not even come to look at it, but gave his directions by letter to the janitor, telling him merely to keep things in order and to attend to repairs, if any were necessary. Thus the castellan was actually master of the house, and offered its hospitality to me and my friends.

"One evening I and my two assistants, Dr. E—, a young lawyer, and Mr. W—, a literary man, went to inspect the premises. First we went to the stables. There were no horses as they had been sold; but what attracted our special attention was an old, queer-fashioned coach with gilded ornaments and bearing the emblems of the family. We then inspected the rooms, passing through some halls and gloomy corridors, such as may be found in any old castle. There was nothing remarkable about the furniture; but in one of the halls there hung in a frame an oil-painting, a portrait, representing a lady with a large hat and wearing a fur coat. We were all involuntarily startled on beholding this picture—not so much on account of the beauty of the lady, but on account of the uncanny expression of her eyes; and Dr. E—, after looking at the picture for a short time, suddenly exclaimed: 'How strange. The picture closes its eyes and opens them again, and now it begins to smile.'

"Now Dr. E— is a very sensitive person, and has more than once had some experience in spiritism, and we made up our minds to form a circle for the purpose of investigating this phenomenon. Accordingly, on the same evening we sat around a table in an adjoining room, forming a magnetic chain with our hands. Soon the table began to move and the name *Elga* was spelled. We asked who this Elga was, and the answer was rapped out: 'The lady whose picture you have seen.'

"'Is the lady living?' asked Mr. W—. This question was not answered; but instead it was rapped out: 'If W— desires it, I will appear to him bodily to-night at two o'clock.' W— consented, and now the table seemed to be endowed with life and manifested a great affection for W—; it rose on two legs and pressed against his breast, as if it intended to embrace him.

"We inquired of the castellan whom the picture represented; but to our surprise he did not know. He said that it was the copy of a picture painted by the celebrated painter Hans Markart of Vienna, and had been brought by the old Count because its demoniacal look pleased him so much.

"We left the castle, and W— retired to his room at an inn a half-hour's journey distant from that place. He was of a somewhat sceptical turn of mind, being neither a firm believer in ghosts and apparitions nor ready to deny their possibility. He was not afraid, but anxious to see what would come of his agreement, and for the purpose of keeping himself awake he sat down and began to write an article for a journal.

"Towards two o'clock he heard steps on the stairs and the door of the hall opened; there was the rustling of a silk dress and the sound of the feet of a lady walking to and fro in the corridor.

"It may be imagined that he was somewhat startled; but taking courage, he said to himself: 'If this is Elga let her come in.' Then the door of the room opened and Elga entered. She was most elegantly dressed, and appeared still more youthful and seductive than the picture. There was a lounge on the other side of the table where W— was writing, and there she silently posted herself. She did not speak, but her looks and gestures left no doubt in regard to her desires and intentions.

"Mr. W— resisted the temptation and remained firm. It is not known whether he did so out of principle or timidity or fear. Be this as it may, he kept on writing, looking from time to time at his visitor and silently wishing that she would leave. At last, after half an hour, which seemed to him much longer the lady departed in the same manner in which she came.

"This adventure left W— no peace, and we consequently arranged several sittings at the old castle, where a variety of uncanny phenomena took place. Thus, for instance, once the servant-girl was about to light a fire in the stove, when the door of the apartment opened and Elga stood there. The girl, frightened out of her wits, rushed from the room, tumbling down the stairs in terror with the lamp in her hand, which broke, and came very near to setting her clothes on fire. Lighted lamps and candles went out when brought near the picture, and many other 'manifestations' took place which it would be tedious to describe; but the following incident ought not to be omitted.

"Mr. W— was at that time desirous of obtaining the position as co-editor of a certain journal, and a few days after the above-narrated adventure he received a letter in which a noble lady of high position offered him her patronage for that purpose. The writer requested him to come to a certain place the same evening, where he would meet a gentleman who would give him further particulars. He went, and was met by an unknown stranger, who told him that he was requested by the Countess Elga to invite Mr. W— to a carriage drive, and that she would await him at midnight at a certain crossing of two roads, not far from the village. The stranger then suddenly disappeared.

"Now it seems that Mr. W—had some misgivings about the meeting and drive, and he hired a policeman as detective to go at midnight to me appointed place, to see what would happen. The policeman went and reported next morning that he had seen nothing but the well-known, old-fashioned carriage from the castle, with two black horses, standing there as if waiting for somebody, and that as he had no occasion to interfere, he merely waited until the carriage moved on. When the castellan of the castle was asked, he swore that the carriage had not been out that night, and in fact it could not have been out, as there were no horses to draw it.

"But that is not all, for on the following day I met a friend who is a great sceptic and disbeliever in ghosts, and always used to laugh at such things. Now, however, he seemed to be very serious and said: 'Last night something very strange happened to me. At about one o'clock this morning I returned from a late visit, and as I happened to pass the graveyard of the village, I saw a carriage with gilded ornaments standing at the entrance. I wondered about this taking place at such an unusual hour, and being curious to see what would happen, I waited. Two elegantly dressed ladies issued from the carriage. One of these was very young and pretty, but threw at me a devilish and scornful look as they both passed by and entered the cemetery. There they were met by a well-dressed man, who saluted the ladies and spoke to the younger one, saying: "Why, Miss Elga! Are you returned so soon?" Such a queer feeling came over me that I abruptly left and hurried home.'

"This matter has not been explained; but certain experiments which we subsequently made with the picture of Elga brought out some curious facts.

"To look at the picture for a certain time caused me to feel a very disagreeable sensation in the region of the solar plexus. I began to dislike the portrait and proposed to destroy it. We held a sitting in the adjoining room; the table manifested a great aversion to my presence. It was rapped out that I should leave the circle, and that the picture must not be destroyed. I ordered a Bible to be brought in, and read the beginning of the first chapter of St. John, whereupon the above-mentioned Mr. E— (the medium) and another man present claimed that they saw the picture distorting its face. I turned the frame and pricked the back of the picture with my penknife in different places, and Mr. E—, as well as the other man, felt all the pricks, although they had retired to the corridor.

"I made the sign of the pentagram over the picture, and again the two gentlemen claimed that the picture was horribly distorting its face.

"Soon afterwards we were called away and left that country. Of Elga I heard nothing more."

That a belief, and a very well founded belief in vampirism, still retains in Hungary, is evident from the following account which was reported in *The Daily Telegraph*, 15 February, 1912. "A Buda-Pest telegram to the *Messaggero* reports a terrible instance of superstition. A boy of fourteen died some days ago in a small village. A farmer, in whose employment the boy had been, thought that the ghost of the latter appeared to him every night. In order to put a stop to these supposed visitations, the farmer, accompanied by some friends, went to the cemetery one night, stuffed three pieces of garlic and three stones in the mouth, and thrust a stake through the corpse, fixing it to the ground. This was to deliver themselves from the evil spirit, as the credulous farmer and his friends stated when they were arrested."

Of Montenegro in his *Voyage Historique et Politique au Montenegro* M. le Colonel L. C. Vialla de Sommières writes as follows: "In no country is the belief in ghosts, in witches, and in evil spirits stronger than in Montenegro. Apparitions, dreams, omens ceaselessly haunt their brains, but nothing equals the terror inspired by *brucolaques*, that is to say the dead bodies of those who died excommunicate, and which are huddled into the earth without any burial rites or prayer. The very ground which has covered them is for ever accursed; the spot is shunned and avoided by all, and if a thought of the place crosses a man's mind he believes that he is being pursued by avenging ghosts. In fine these men who court every danger and dare every peril think of nothing but of witches and of demons; they are for ever discoursing of the terror with which evil spirits inspire them. It would require no mean authority on demonology with a facile pen to write the long narratives of all manner of devils which they never tire of relating and the myriad adventures of this sort that they love to tell."

A little later the author gives a somewhat farcical adventure which happened to a man whom he himself had known, and who was alive as late as 1813. "A certain *Zanetto*, a droll sort of fellow, who was something given to drink, one day when he was rather more than half seas over happened to be caught in a heavy shower. Having stumbled home he threw himself on his bed fully dressed as he was, well-warmed with wine but chilled with the drenching rain. Suddenly he was seized by terrible convulsions; about eleven o'clock he fell into a state of coma, he was icy cold, he did not even breathe; at last he was surely dead ... at eight o'clock the next morning they were going to bury him. In order to carry him from his house to the Church the *cortège* had to climb a very difficult path and to descend by one which was even worse. The irregularity of the ground, for the whole way was strewn with rocks and large stones, compelled the bearers from time to time to make sudden and abrupt movements. This continual shaking up recalled *Zanetto* to life. He began to stir himself briskly and to some effect; he sat up, looked all around him and bawled out at the top of his voice: 'What the devil are you about you drunken rascals?' At these words the bearers flung down their burden and thunder-struck one and all fairly took to their heels. Those who were following the bier scattered helter skelter among the vineyards on either side uttering piercing cries as they ran; those who went before looked back and terrified at the sight they rushed pell-mell as far as the neighbouring town where they spread the utmost alarm since some were dumb with terror, whilst others told the wildest tales, but all of them were shaking with fear. Only the priests remained in the funeral train, and they were wondering what might be the cause of this disorder, when they heard these words shouted out by the awakened *Zanetto*: 'You fiends, you borachios, I will make you pay for this; you trapped me finely at home and have brought me all this way; and you will carry me back to my house again; if not in good earnest I will send the lot of you to the very place where you thought you were going to pack me off for good and all; yes, and this time I'll drink everything up; I won't leave you the value of a ha'penny.' But the priests with great gentleness and without any sort of hurry or impatience conveyed him back to his house. There they did all in their power to quiet the fellow and calm his temper, for he was raving away like a frenzied bedlamite. I have heard him tell the tale himself in merry mood."

In *The Observer,* 2 September, 1923, there was an account of an apparition which appeared in Belgrade and haunted a house, No. 61, Bosanska Street, which runs from the old "Gates of the Town," near the railway station, into the well-known thoroughfare Balkanska Street. Bricks and stones seemed to have been thrown at the house until all the windows were broken and the family barracaded the apertures with boards, tables and chairs. The furniture was shifted violently from place to place, and often thrown down to be smashed to pieces. A procession of devout persons proceeded throughout the premises, entering every room and also proceeding round the exterior of the house chanting psalms and sprinkling holy water. It was stated that the troublesome apparition was a Vampire, although its activities certainly seemed to be those of a poltergeist. It is, of course, quite possible that a Vampire who wished to annoy and molest the inhabitants of a house might resort to poltergeist tricks which albeit generally merely mischievous and vexing, can prove, as records show, dangerous in no small degree.

It is true that Professor Barrett in a discussion of the poltergeist phenomena says: "The movement of objects is usually quite unlike that due to gravitational or other attraction. They slide about, rise in the air, move in eccentric paths, sometimes in a leisurely manner, often turn round in their career, and usually descend quietly without hurting the observers ... Stones are frequently thrown, but no one is hurt." Yet during the disturbances at Lenagh, Mountfield, Co. Tyrone, in 1864–65 the inmates of the house were so pelted with bricks that they had to fly the place, and an incredulous visitor whilst boasting of his superior unbelief was so sharply assaulted by a shower of stones which pelted his back that he rubbed off without any further ceremony. A girl also was struck by a hard clod of earth and knocked into a pail of water. In a more recent case, the Battersea poltergeist of Eland Road, Lavender Hill, London, S.W.11, whose doings caused so great a sensation in January, 1928, Miss Robinson who resided in the house related how "Lumps of coal, potatoes, onions and other missiles have come hurtling through the air both day and night breaking our back windows, and threatening our welfare. ... In the room in which my brother sleeps a wardrobe collapsed with no apparent reason. ... A china bowl on a side table in my sister's room splintered to pieces and crashed on to the ground." Indeed her father's health had broken down under the strain and he had been obliged to remove elsewhere.

Although I would not without further inquiry assert that all these phenomena and similar sporadic happenings which might be collected from well nigh every county are in their origin necessarily demoniacal, yet it certainly does appear warrantable that in the majority of cases they can safely be assigned to a Satanic source. At the same time a quota may be the effluence of volitional but eccentric forces in some way directed by mysterious and seemingly invisible entities who find an outlet for their manifestation through an unconscious medium, generally a young person of either sex. In their details far too many of these curious cases nearly resemble the violent disturbances, and even the physical assaults upon the Saints, which are recorded in hagiography, and which (we know) were the work of the devil, to be deemed anything but suspect in the very highest degree. In the life of Blessed Christina of Stommeln it is told that on 21 December, 1267, when she was first visited by Peter of Dacia, a Dominican of Gotland who was in Cologne as a pupil of Blessed Albertus Magnus, the holy maiden was actually thrown to the ground several times in succession and severely wounded without it being apparent that anyone had touched her. The evil spirits were wont to plague and vex her in the most noisome ways very often drenching her with stinking ordure and fæces that burned like fire. They flung stones about the house, so that her father was seriously wounded in the head and well nigh had his arm broken owing to a blow. A jewess who visited Christina and who began to mock at the ouphs and elfin rogues, as she dubbed them was so pelted with brickbats that her body was bruised from head to foot before she could escape into the street beyond the range of the missiles.

Blessed Franco, a Carmelite, was long vexed and persecuted beyond measure by what might seem to be a series of poltergeist molestations. Objects of which he had need would be suddenly snatched away and at length found hidden in a distant part of the cloister. When he was in the kitchen the pans, dishes, bowls and plates were frequently whisked out of sight and only discovered after a painful search. But when he commanded in a loud voice: "In the Name of Jesus of Nazareth, I bid thee, foul wretch, be gone," yells of hideous laughter were heard after which all was suddenly still and for a while there were no more disturbances.

A good Jesuit of Sassari in Sardinia, Father Sebastian del Campo, would frequently be annoyed by showers of stones cast by an unseen hand. As they struck him they caused a more than ordinary pain but no bruise nor livid marks appeared after the blows.

In her chamber the stigmatized Marie de Möerl, who died in 1868, was plagued in a very similar manner. Often she would be thrown out of her bed with insane violence; at midnight in the midst of a freezing winter her blankets and coverlet would be filched away, whilst the most horrible racket aroused the whole household. The Bishop, however, enjoined exorcisms after which the diabolic persecution in this kind was stayed.

Perhaps the most famous and most rigidly documented case in more recent years is that of S. John Baptist Vianney, the Curé d'Ars. The *grappin*, as the Saint had dubbed his demoniac persecutor "would seem to be hammering nails into the floor, cleaving wood, planing boards, or sawing, like a carpenter busy at work in the inside of the house; or he would drum upon the table, the chimney-piece, the waterjug, or on whatever would make the greatest noise." In the winter of 1826 when the holy Curé was staying at the Presbytery of St. Trivier-sur-Moignans several of the priests who were also sleeping in the house somewhat disdainfully discussed these vexations to which the abbé Vianney was subjected and "agreed that all this infernal mysticism was nothing in the world but reverie, delusion, and hallucination." Some attributed the noises to squadrons of rats, for these animals no doubt kept high revels in the presbytery at Ars, since it was a forlorn and crazy building of a truly venerable antiquity. And so all went to bed to sleep their soundest. "But, behold! at midnight they are awakened by a most terrible commotion. The presbytery is turned upside down, the doors slam, the windows rattle, the walls shake, and fearful cracks seem to betoken that they are about to fall prostrate."

Among the older authorities who deal with these manifestations the following may be profitably consulted: Pierre Le Loyer, *Discours et histoires des spectres, visions, apparitions des esprits, anges, demons, et ames se monstrans visibles aux hommes*, first edition, Angers, 2 vols., 1586; Robert du Triez, *Les ruses, finesses et impostures des Esprits malins*, Cambrai, 1563; and the third book, *De Terrificationibus Nocturnisque Tumultibus* of the *De Spirituum apparitione*, Cologne, 1594, by Peter Thyraeus, S.J., sometime Professor of Theology at Mainz.

To conclude this chapter I have judged it not impertinent to give, with due cautels, a translation of the famous *Dissertatio De Masticatione Mortuorum* which was pronounced by Phillip Rohr at the University of Leipzig, 16 August, 1679, and was printed at that city in the same year. The book is exceedingly scarce, and although it is not quite so fully considered as the longer works of Zopfius and Rohlius it is one of the earliest and most typical of these treatises. There are, of course, theological errors and these not a few, but I think my notes will be a sufficient safeguard in this respect.

Philip Rohr in his day stood in fair repute for his scholarship and he was also known as an occult investigator. His work on the Kobolts who haunt mines is held in esteem. It may be remarked, however, that the subject had previously been treated by Georg Landmann, the famous metallurgist, in his *De Animantibus subterraneis*, which with other of his treatises was published at Bale, folio, 1657.

Dissertatio Historico-Philosophica De Masticatione Mortuorum, Quam Dei & Superiorum indultu, in illustri Academ. Lips. sistent Praeses M. Philippus Rohr Marckran-stadio-Misnic. & Respondens Benjamin Frizschius, Musilavia Misnicus, Alumni Electorales, ad diem XVI. Augusti Ann. M. DC. LXXIX. H. L. Q. C. Lipsiae, Typis Michaelis Vogtii.

a and *w*. Those who have written of the history of funeral rites and of the mysteries of death have not neglected to place on record that there have been found from time to time bodies who appear to have devoured the grave clothes in which they were wound, their cerements, and whilst doing so to have uttered a grunting noise like the sound of porkers chawing and rooting with their groyns. Now different writers have pronounced very different opinions upon this matter, and some learned men have ascribed this phenomenon to natural causes which are not clearly known to us; whilst others have only been able to explain it by assuming that there are certain animals which glut their hunger for human flesh by feeding upon corpses, but what animals these may be they do not tell; and others again have advanced yet other opinions. This phenomenon then seemed to us to be a fit subject which might be treated in a public and formal disputation, all the rules and regulations being duly observed, in order that we might arrive at the best explanation of this matter and to some extent at any rate elucidate it. Accordingly we determined and resolved after due study to set down the sum of our researches in the following pages, relying upon the kindly indulgence of our readers to make full allowances for the extreme obscurity of those points upon which it has not been possible to pronounce a definite opinion, and also taking our stand upon the authority of those Eminent Doctors and writers whose opinions, and often whose very words, we have quoted in resolving these hard matters. The subject would seem obviously to fall into two parts, of which the first may be reviewed historically; whilst the second demands to be closely examined from a purely philosophical point of view (alteram philosophican διασκεψιν sibi uendicat).

Bram Stoker and the Search for Castle Dracula

Raymond T. McNally and Radu Florescu

HIGH UP IN THE Transylvanian Alps we came to a halt. There, atop a black volcanic rock formation, bordering the Arges River and framed by a massive alpine snow-capped landscape, lay the twisted battlements of Castle Dracula, its remains barely distinguishable from the rock of the mountain itself, a sheer thousand-foot drop on all sides. This was hardly the grandiose, macabre mausoleum described by Bram Stoker, yet no matter how modest nor how tortured by time, it was a *historic* edifice, one challenging the historian to solve its mystery, to push back an unconquered frontier.

For our party of five, composed of two Americans and three Romanians, this was the end of a long trail. Our search for Castle Dracula had begun in a light vein at the University of Bucharest. It continued as an expedition marred by every possible frustration and by mysterious accidents.

This search began, as did so many other Dracula hunts, because of the extraordinary hold the Dracula vampire mystique still exercises upon popular imagination throughout the world. Unperturbed by the vampire myth, however, a handful of skeptics have always claimed that there was a factual basis for the Dracula story and that part of the setting indeed lay in Transylvania.

Bram Stoker, at the very beginning of his story, tells of his own painstaking efforts both to consult well-known Orientalists such as Arminius Vambery, professor at the University of Budapest and a frequent visitor to England, and to study the available literature concerning the frontier lands between the Christians and Turks. Even Stoker's mention of consulting maps of the area available at the British Museum library in London are intended to stress the historicity of the plot; he tells us they were not too reliable, but they proved to be far more accurate than he thought.

In Stoker's novel, the town of Bistrita, for instance, is accurately described and located, as are such small villages as Fundu and Veresti, places you will not find marked on any modern tourist map. The famed Borgo Pass leading from Transylvania to Moldavia, the northernmost province of Romania, really exists, and is beautifully described in Stoker's novel. The historic context, the century-old struggle between Romanians and Turks that was sparked in the fifteenth century, is authentic. The ethnic minorities of Transylvania—the Saxons, Romanians, Szekelys, and Hungarians—are known and are distinguished from each other by Stoker.

Dracula was in fact an authentic fifteenth-century Wallachian prince who was often described in the contemporary German, Byzantine, Slavonic, and Turkish documents and in popular horror stories as an awesome, cruel, and possibly demented ruler. He was known mostly for the amount of blood he indiscriminately spilled, not only the blood of the infidel Turks—which, by the standards of the time, would make him a hero—but that of Germans, Romanians, Hungarians, and other Christians. His ingenious mind devised all kinds of tortures, both physical and mental, and his favorite way of imposing death earned him the name "the Impaler."

In a rogues' gallery Dracula would assuredly compete for first prize with Cesare Borgia, Catherine de Médicis, and Jack the Ripper, owing not only to the quantity of his victims, but to the refinement of his cruelty. To his contemporaries, the story of his misdeeds was widely publicized—in certain instances by some of his intended victims. The Dracula story, in fact, was a "bestseller" throughout Europe four hundred years before Stoker wrote his version. Many of the German-originated, fifteenth-century accounts of the Dracula legend have been found in dusty archives of monasteries and libraries.

The names of Dracula and his father, Dracul, are of such importance to this story that they require a precise explanation. Both father and son had the given name Vlad. The names Dracul and Dracula and variations thereof in different languages (such as Dracole, Draculya, Dracol, Draculea, Draculios, Draculia, Tracol) are really nicknames. What's more, both nicknames had two meanings. Dracul meant "devil," as it still does in Romanian today; in addition it meant "dragon." In 1431, the Holy Roman Emperor Sigismund invested Vlad the father with the Order of the Dragon, a semimonastic, semimilitary organization dedicated to fighting the Turkish infidels. Dracul in the sense of dragon

Raymond T. McNally and Radu Florescu, from *In Search of Dracula: The History of Dracula and Vampires*, pp. 7–14. Copyright © 1994 by Houghton Mifflin Harcourt Publishing Company. Reprinted with permission.

Coins minted by Vlad Dracul showing the sign of the Dragon, and the eagle of Wallachia on the reverse side.

stems from this. It also seems probable that when the simple, superstitious peasants saw Vlad the father bearing the standard with the dragon symbol they interpreted it as a sign that he was in league with the devil.

As for the son, we now know that he had two nicknames: he was called Vlad Tepes (pronounced *tsep-pesh*), which means Vlad the Impaler, and he was also called Dracula, a diminutive meaning "son of the dragon" or "son of the devil." (A final point in this discussion of nomenclature: the association of the words "devil" and "dragon" in Romanian may be just one of the many reasons for the association of Dracula with vampirism in the eyes of his detractors.)

Other male Draculas, too, were known by evil epithets. Dracul's second son was Mihnea the Bad; another descendant was Mihnea II, the Apostate, and yet another indirect descendant was known as the Little Impaler. In an age of violence, all the Draculas lived violently, and with few exceptions died violently.

In his lifetime, Dracula had fame and notoriety throughout much of Europe, but rarely has such recognition of a public figure become so lost to posterity. Indeed, when Stoker mentioned Dracula in the late nineteenth century, few of his readers knew he was writing about a historical character. One obstacle to understanding arose from the fact that the Dracula stories circulated in diverse languages (German, Hungarian, Romanian, Slavic, Greek, Turkish) and in different worlds having little relation to each other. A chief difficulty, however, was the confusion caused by the name itself. Was it Dracula the son of the Devil, Dracula the son of the man invested with the Order of the Dragon, or simply Dracula the Impaler? Small wonder that the Byzantine scholar reading about Dracula's deeds of heroism against the Turks, the German reading of the atrocities of the Devil against his fellow Saxons, and the Romanian studying the Impaler's achievements, failed to attribute these actions to the same man. It is only of very recent date that Romanian historians themselves have pieced together some of the fragments of the formidable Dracula story.

If Stoker's Dracula story was essentially correct in points of history, if Dracula existed, why not a Castle Dracula? Since Transylvania was so minutely described by Stoker, what could be more logical than to begin the hunt in northeastern Transylvania, where the author set his plot on an isolated mountain peak, a few miles east of Bistrita on the road leading to the Borgo Pass.

Over the years, many persons had set out to find Castle Dracula in this general direction. They had traveled the way of Stoker's hero, Jonathan Harker, from Cluj to Bistrita and from Bistrita to the Borgo Pass. The travelers found countless superstitious peasants and were struck by the majestic beauty of this abandoned Carpathian frontier region separating Transylvania proper from Bukovina to the northeast and Moldavia to the east. But none had found the castle. Several expeditions ended on the same dismal note—not a trace of *any* castle.

Undeterred by past failures, we decided to undertake the venture and set forth on the Stoker trail, if for no other reason than to satisfy our curiosity. From the standpoint of scenery alone, it is easy to excuse Stoker for setting the story in the wrong part of Transylvania, thus leading the Dracula hunter some hundred miles or more astray. The anchor town of Bistrita, the departure point for any Dracula excursion, is a quaint medieval city, more German than Romanian in its character, with a mixed population of Romanians, Hungarians, and those mysterious Szekelys, whom Stoker erroneously took to be possible ancestors of Dracula. (Some historians claim just as formidable a pedigree of horror for the Szekelys, tracing them back to Attila's Huns.) From the crumbling walls of the old city, the most unsophisticated traveler can judge that at one time Bistrita must have been an impressive frontier point; from its oversized marketplace surrounded by the colorful baroque German-style homes of the well-to-do, one may safely conclude that the town was an important trading center, with goods plying north from Transylvania to Poland and Bohemia and east to Moldavia.

Beyond Bistrita, the road finally climbs to the Borgo Pass, along the Dorne depression, passing through several rustic mountain villages where life has not changed much in a thousand years. The peasants still wear their traditional garb—the fur cap or *caciula,* the embroidered shirt with motifs that vary from village to village, the sheepskin-lined vest or *cojoc* (lately sold as après-ski apparel in the elegant resorts of Europe), the roughly stitched pigskin shoes or *opinci.* These farm people are not without an artistic side. The women embroider; the men mold clay products with a technique kept secret, although the quality of the local clay certainly contributes to its success. The peasant house, made almost entirely of wood, delights one with the imaginative carvings of its *pridvor,* a kind of porch surrounding the house, and the decorative patterns of the main gate, giving the only access to the courtyard. Local folklore is rich: the *doinas,* a plaintive folksong the *strigaturi* or lyrical poetry, the *basme* or fairy tales, the ballads, and the *legende* or popular epics, all combine natural and supernatural elements. In the *doinas* there are frequent references to the wolves, which, traveling in packs at night in the midst of winter, were thought to do their worst to man and beast alike. In the *basme* the bat is often mentioned, and in Romania this creature is a messenger of bad luck. In the legends of old, one species of vampire is a supernatural being of demonic origin, fighting Fat-Frumos, the fairy prince who embodies moral power. The wolf-headed serpent is the motif used on the ancient standard of the Dacians, the ancestors of the Romanians.

Also interesting for our purposes are the historical ballads that speak of the ancient battleground among Romanians, Tartars, Turks, and Poles. These ballads commemorate countless heroes and villains, preserving by word of mouth a fascinating history—one quite as remarkable as the sagas of the Vikings.

Of late, the more wily peasants, impressed by the number of foreign tourists seeking Dracula's castle, have decided to play along with the search; and they do it well for the price of a few cigarettes and packs of chewing gum. Unwilling to disappoint the Dracula hunter, one imaginative peasant from the village of Prundul-Birgaului made numerous allusions to a castle that was *mai la munte,* a favorite Romanian expression of vagueness which means "a little farther up the mountain" (of course, when you reach one peak, as every alpinist knows, there is always another behind it). However, as historians have often found in regard to folklore, where there is smoke, there is fire. It so happened that the folklore references implying the existence of a castle near the Borgo Pass were quite correct. At Rodna, not far from the Borgo Pass, lie the remains of a small fortress. Only it was not the Castle Dracula that we were searching for, even though Dracula visited it during his lifetime, since he often traveled the solitary highway winding through the Romanian and Hungarian lands.

The historic route of the Borgo Pass was initially traveled by Romania's feudal leaders at the close of the fourteenth century, when they set forth from their haven in the Transylvanian plateau to found the principality of Moldavia. It goes through majestic country—Stoker's Mittel Land "green and brown where grass and rock mingled, ... an endless perspective of jagged rock and pointed crags."

Beyond the lower mountains, surrounding the Dorne depression, and rising to three thousand feet, lie the higher peaks, often snow-capped even during the summer. These are the mountains of Bukovina, a favorite alpinist playground which demands the skill and sometimes the equipment of the expert for tricky ascents of upwards of 6,500 feet. On the Moldavian side of the border, one reaches the watering spa of Vatra

Hunedoara, castle of John Hunyadi

Dornei. Today this town is an important tourist center, not only because of the health-restoring springs, but because it gives approach to a dozen famed monasteries in Bukovina and Moldavia proper, representing extraordinary jewels of fifteenth-century Romanian artistry. The biblical scenes and history on the exterior walls of the monasteries, dating back to Dracula's time, are painted in shades of deep blue and purple, and they have survived virtually unscathed through some five hundred rigorous winters.

Castle Bistrita, located near the Borgo Pass, may also have served as a model for the castle in Stoker's novel. It was John Hunyadi who actually completed Castle Bistrita around 1449, four years before the fall of Constantinople. The *voevod* or warlord of Transylvania, foremost Balkan crusader, governor of Severin, hereditary duke of Timisoara, count of Bistrita, in charge of the Hungarian kingdom, John Hunyadi was in fact in control of the political destinies of what was left of the east and central European lands in their last and most desperate struggle with the Turks. He died in 1456 while defending Belgrade, the last great Christian bastion on the Danube, the year that Dracula was enthroned as prince. Hunyadi was the father of Matthias Corvinus, the Hungarian king who kept Dracula imprisoned in his citadel on the Danube for twelve years, from 1462 to 1474. Relations between the Hunyadis and the Draculas were initially friendly, though never intimate.

During the years 1451 to 1456 Dracula may have stayed near Bistrita, a fortified town at that time, but few of the fortifications of Bistrita remain today. It is likely that Stoker heard the legends connecting Dracula to this region. The Saxon population of Bistrita, who disliked the Romanians and the Hungarians, doubtless heard of Dracula's atrocities against their brethren farther south in the towns of Brasov and Sibiu, where most of the horrors were committed and recorded. It is quite plausible that some Saxon refugee from southern Transylvania wrote a description of them. However, if there is a Bistrita document about Dracula, it is not known today. In any event, Bistrita Castle was attacked, ransacked, and totally destroyed by the German population of the city at the close of the fifteenth century as an apparent gesture of defiance against the Hunyadi family.

Castle Bistrita was built on a small hill in the middle of the quaint twelfth-century German township surrounded by ditches and towers built by the various guilds for protection. The castle was later given to Dracula, who controlled it in recompense for his services to the Hunyadis at a crucial time of conflict with the local German merchants. Much of what was left of the original town was destroyed by the Turks during the Austro-Turkish wars of the seventeenth century, and in addition, as Stoker noted in *Dracula,* "Fifty years ago a series of great fires took place, which made terrible havoc on five separate occasions."

Castle Bistrita seems to have been a smaller version of Hunyadi's formidable castle of Hunedoara, one hundred miles to the southwest; a most impressive structure dating back to 1260 and today completely and beautifully restored. This is the castle of the Hunyadis where Dracula was greeted as an ally and friend in 1452, but as a foe in 1462. With its imposing donjon, smaller towers, massive walls, battlements, and drawbridge, it seems custom-made for a vampire film. But neither Bistrita nor Hunedoara convey the eerie atmosphere of the real Castle Dracula. Nonetheless, in the impressive Hall of Knights, with its lovely marble columns, once hung all the portraits of the "greats" of Dracula's time, including John Hunyadi and, undoubtedly, Dracula. A hostile hand, possibly that of a revengeful German, destroyed all these portraits. Fortunately, three paintings of Dracula and a number of woodcut portraits have survived the furies of the past.

In his novel, Stoker describes Dracula as "a tall old man, cleanshaven save for a long white moustache, and clad in black from head to foot, without a single speck of colour about him anywhere." The author depicts Dracula's moustache as heavy, his teeth as sharp and white, and his skin as sallow and pallid. In the portrait of Dracula that survives in the collection at Castle Ambras, the real Dracula is as startling and arresting in appearance as the figure created in words by Stoker, or the character created some years later by Max Schreck, in Murnau's 1922 classic horror film, *Nosferatu.*

The Quick and the Undead

Visual and Political Dynamics in *Blood: The Last Vampire*

Christopher Bolton

IN THE FILMS OF Oshii Mamoru, political struggle is not only palpable—it is positively sensual. Oshii's films chart the efforts of people to make a difference or leave a trace in a politicized, mediated world where the importance of the individual is increasingly uncertain. The threat to individual agency is represented by political or technological networks that are ubiquitous but also invisible—power structures governing individual lives so completely that the structures themselves escape detection. They can script an individual's actions, rewrite memories, even substitute their own simulated reality for an individual's lived life, all without leaving a mark.

Opposing the tyranny of these structures is a longing for individual significance that is often expressed as a sensuous desire for the individual body. Time and again in Oshii's films, it is romantic and carnal desire that assert the worth of the human. We see it in *Patlabor 2* (1993), whose mecha pilots must strip off their claustrophobic mechanical suits in order to make human contact; in Oshii's script for *Jin-Roh* (2000), where factional politics are momentarily suspended by a fairy-tale love story between a terrorist and a secret policeman; and in *Ghost in the Shell* (1995), where the ambivalent narrative about networked, disembodied consciousness is countered by the shapely physique of the cyborg heroine.[1] All this produces an interesting paradox in Oshii's films: his characters are sometimes described as ghosts in the machine—the last traces of resistance haunting these political and technological networks—but, in fact, his human characters are the films' most reassuringly tangible features, while the machinery and technology of these invisible, inescapable networks are often far more ghostly and far more haunting.

A noteworthy example is *Blood: The Last Vampire*, directed by Kitakubo Hiroyuki and a team of young artists working under Oshii's tutelage.[2] *Blood* is a vampire story set on an American air force base in Japan during the Vietnam War. Released in 2000, it was one of the first anime to make heavy use of photorealistic digital effects, though at many points it preserves the stylized quality of conventional animation. While the vampires and human characters are largely two-dimensional, the planes taking off and landing in the background are rendered as more photorealistic three-dimensional forms. At one level, the planes disrupt the film's fantasy by evoking the realities of Vietnam, realities that are in many ways more frightening than any ghost story. But at the same time, the planes have a ghostly quality of their own that makes them much more complex signifiers. They represent not only the reality of politics but its unrealities as well.

These unrealities include the cracks and contradictions in the national identity that was forged for Japan after World War II. Japan became a newly pacifist nation that renounced the militarism of the thirties and forties, but it has also supported and profited from American wars in Vietnam and elsewhere. Japan's ability to formulate an independent defense policy has been hindered by fears in Japan and in the rest of Asia that Japanese pacifism is only a thin veneer and that prewar militarism could reassert itself at any time. In *Blood*, the planes visually represent the weight and solidity of present realities, as well as the illusory quality of Japanese politics and the country's suppressed but still-haunting memories of its own wartime aggression.

At the same time, the film's two-dimensional vampire heroine Saya seems at first to be a cartoonish fantasy—a camp parody of anime vixens. But Saya's sexiness and violence have a reassuring physicality that promises an escape from the intangibility and uncertainty of politics. In this sense, *Blood* is a film that could only have been made as an anime: it is the work's strange admixture of fantasy and photorealism that comments most provocatively on Japan's present historical moment. This essay begins by examining political dynamics in *Blood*'s plot and then links this to the film's physical dynamics—the way mass and motion are portrayed by the film's unique combination of two- and three-dimensional animation.

Christopher Bolton, "The Quick and the Undead: Visual and Political Dynamics," *Mechademia 2: Networks of Desire*, pp. 125–142. Copyright © 2007 by University of Minnesota Press. Reprinted with permission.

From Ghosts In The Machine To Vampires On The Subway: The Plot Of *Blood*

Blood opens on a nearly deserted Tokyo subway train as it approaches its final stop of the night. A coldly attractive young girl stares at the only other passenger in the car, an exhausted office worker. Interior and exterior shots of the train alternate with shots of the two characters and the opening credits, building tension while showcasing the 3-D animation used to render several very complex perspective shots inside and outside the moving train. Suddenly the girl leaps from her seat, races toward her fellow passenger, and cuts him down with a samurai sword.

As the girl exits the train, she is met by two American agents of an unnamed secret organization, and we learn from their conversation that her victim belonged to a vampirelike race of monsters who can take human form. The monsters are called chiropterans (after the biological order that includes bats), and the girl, Saya, has been enlisted to hunt them down. This terse dialogue between Saya and the agent named David is the only background the film provides, but it establishes that Saya is also a vampire herself. The link and the distinction between her and the chiropterans are explained only with David's cryptic comment that "she is the only remaining original."

The scene also sets up the mission that will occupy Saya for the rest of the fifty-minute film: the monsters have emerged from hibernation and infiltrated the U.S. air force base in Yokota, where they have already murdered several people. Saya poses as a student to visit the base school where the last murder took place, in hopes of ferreting out the chiropterans who are passing as humans. She locates them on Halloween night and fights three of them in a running battle, climaxing with a dramatic fight in a burning hangar and a chase across the runways.

The monsters are killed, and the incident is hushed up. In the final scene, some days later, the sole civilian witness (the school nurse) wonders what she has seen. All of the scenes up to now have been in the fading light of late afternoon or at night, but now in daylight, the monsters seem no more than a bad dream. At the same time, a suspicion or a fear that has lurked in the shadows for the whole film now comes into the light: it is clear right from the opening shot (of a rotary dial telephone) that the film is set in the near past, but aside from small details in the background of one or two scenes, for most of the film there is no indication of the year. In the closing minutes, though, we see a calendar marked 1966, and the final shot shows a B-52 bomber taking off into the clear blue sky while an English voice-over describes the bombing war in Vietnam. The end credits alternate with dim and grainy (ghostly) news footage of the war.

The ending leaves no doubt that vampirism is a metaphor for the U.S.–Japan military relationship, though the vampire in this case could be either America or Japan. The U.S. bases established in Japan after the occupation have been a staging area for U.S. wars in Korea, Vietnam, and the Middle East. In the heated debates that center on these bases, one position portrays the United States as a foreign parasite that has exploited its Japanese host in order to prosecute its own wars; another accuses Japan of being the parasite—of enjoying the shelter of the U.S. military umbrella with minimal risk and expenditure.

This dialectic of exploitation and dependence is reproduced in local communities around the base. Like Dracula's manor, large U.S. bases form the foundation of local economies. But in Okinawa, for example, well-publicized incidents of U.S. marines raping local girls have created a nationwide image of the bases as harboring monsters who raid the populace and then escape back to the safety of the castle. And the deafening jet noise from bases like Yokota has become a charged symbol of U.S. indifference to the surrounding Japanese communities. In *Blood*, the G.I. bars and brothels around Yokota are a hunting ground for the chiropterans. When the body of a murdered hostess is discovered early in the film, one character speculates that the woman's American boyfriend might be involved in her death, but the comment is all but drowned out by the noise of a passing plane.

The Vampire As Metaphor

In Western literature, the vampire is a privileged figure for otherness and a powerful metaphor for racial or cultural mixing. The vampire is familiar but also foreign; it crosses gender lines as an effeminately alluring male or a castrating female; and it breaches blood and body boundaries in a way that suggests sexual communion but also perversion and pollution. It is for these reasons that Donna Haraway makes the vampire a central metaphor as she traces constructions of race in twentieth-century biology.

> A figure that both promises and threatens racial and sexual mixing, the vampire feeds off the normalized human. ... Deeply shaped by murderous ideologies since their modern popularization in the European accounts of the late eighteenth century—especially racism, sexism and homophobia—stories of the undead also exceed and invert each of those systems of discrimination to show the violence infesting supposedly wholesome life and nature and the revivifying promise of what is supposed to be decadent and against nature.[3]

Kotani Mari argues that the vampire represents a similar kind of otherness in Japanese manga and prose fiction, but an otherness that is doubled because the vampire enters Japanese literature as a foreign genre. Kotani writes that vampires have represented the threat and appeal of a Western other since the first Japanese vampire fiction in the thirties. But she also describes recent authors like Kasai Kiyoshi who have reversed this paradigm, casting the Japanese as a race of vampires themselves. The nationalist metaphor is transformed further by Kikuchi Hideyuki's hybrid human/vampire heroes, as well as Ohara Mariko's parasitic vampires that infest and manipulate their human hosts: both authors blur or erase the lines between native and foreign, or self and other, and show us "how we should speculate on the topic of hybridity in a post-colonialist and post-creolian age."[4]

Like Haraway's vampire, the vampires in *Blood* symbolize racial or cultural difference and conflict, including the racialized violence of colonialism or imperialism. But *Blood* also shows the confusions and reversals that Kotani predicts. It is a film about familiarity and unfamiliarity: the way that one culture can regard another as monstrous, but also the blurring of boundaries between the monsters and us. The chiropterans are batlike creatures who can masquerade as humans, and Saya is clearly one of Kotani's hybrid heroines, a creature somewhere between us and them. Saya is on "our" side, but she sneers at the humans she protects and feels a kinship with the chiropterans she kills.

The ambiguity of Saya's vampire identity is matched by a cultural ambiguity: she seems simultaneously American and Japanese. *Blood* has an interracial and international cast of black, white, Japanese, and seemingly bicultural characters, and while some are drawn in a way that seems to deliberately emphasize racial stereotypes, Saya and others are ambiguous.[5] More than one character asks Saya uncertainly if she is Japanese, but she pointedly refuses to answer. She speaks both Japanese and English with seeming fluency. And she seems to be passing for a Japanese visitor at the base school, although she is unfamiliar with Japanese customs: David has to explain to her that the sailor suit she has been given to wear is a Japanese school uniform.

This schoolgirl's uniform is a distinctly sexual fetish in *Blood* (as in so many other anime), but it takes on a strangely ironic status on Saya, who has become jaded and perverted over the course of a hundred years, even as she retains the body of a little girl. Saya is sexy in the vampire's liminal, transgressive way, but her eternal youth, her threatening allure, and the rest of her vampiric sex appeal have been translated into a series of exaggerated anime archetypes: she is savior and avenger, executioner and demon lover, a sword-wielding sorceress in a middy uniform.

On the night of the base Halloween party (a backdrop that further ironizes these horror stereotypes), Saya shows up at the school infirmary just in time to save the school nurse from two chiropterans disguised as female students. (The nurse is the film's emblematic victim, and she too seems alternately American and Japanese: she possesses the apparently bicultural name Masako Caroline Asano, and many of the same ambiguous qualities as Saya [Figure 2].) Saya kills one monster and wounds the other, but her sword is broken in the struggle, and the remaining monster abducts the nurse. The creatures are immune to gunfire, and only a genuine warrior's sword is strong enough to cut them, so Saya steals a replacement sword from the window of a nearby antique store and gives chase. When she strikes the chiropteran, however, the sword turns out to be a fake modern reproduction, and it bends in half. With the tables turned, the monster traps the weaponless Saya and the nurse in a hangar, which catches fire. In the scene's feverish climax, the monster is about to devour Saya when David arrives with a genuine sword that he flings desperately toward her. Framed dramatically against the flames, Saya screams for the sword and then catches, draws, and swings the blade in one motion to cut the chiropteran in half.

This conclusion does not provide a simple answer to the question of who is the vampire and who is the victim in the U.S.–Japan relationship. Neither the heroine nor the central victim is definitively American or Japanese. Both are threatened by the chiropterans, but do these monsters represent America menacing Japan, or Japan taking its revenge on the American interloper?

The tangled symbolism stems precisely from the tangled politics of postwar Japan. The chiropterans can probably best be associated with violence, militarism, and war itself—not only U.S. cold war imperialism and interventionism but also the Japanese militarism of World War II. Like the hibernating monsters, that militarism has lain dormant or disguised since the occupation, but now it threatens to reemerge. Clothed in a military-style school uniform and armed with a samurai sword, Saya seems to represent a truer, nobler, and more disciplined warrior spirit that will actually rein in the violence. In the logic of this and other films connected to Oshii, Japan is threatened by a crisis of that true spirit, symbolized by the sword that turns out to be fake. If it does not regain its martial and cultural identity, Japan will fall into the kind of violence represented by the chiropterans—supporting U.S. imperialism by proxy or resorting to military adventurism itself. Japanese and not-Japanese, Saya represents a new Japan that rediscovers its samurai values, a strong Japan that now fights against war itself.

The contradiction of a warrior who fights war stems in part from the collision of Oshii's leftist politics with the violent military/action genre he favors. But it is also a tension that reflects the contradictions and conflicting desires of postwar Japanese national identity. After World War II, the American occupation disarmed Japan and imposed a constitution that renounced the right to wage war and maintain an army. The military pact between the two countries assumed that Japan would maintain only "defensive" forces and would be protected by American troops, in return for supporting U.S. bases and combat operations diplomatically, logistically, and monetarily. The legacy of this policy is a Japanese national identity that is arguably split: a militarily noninterventionist and constitutionally pacifist country that was also a launching pad for several American wars.

The defense pact incited protests when it was signed in the fifties and again when it was renewed in the sixties. More recently, the government's decision to deploy support troops in the Gulf and Iraq wars has fostered national debate. The paradox of Japan's position is seen in the fact that calls for a more militarily independent Japan now come from the Right and the Left—from some who think Japan should commit its own troops to combat in Iraq and elsewhere, and from others who want Japan to stand up and oppose U.S. aggression. But for many in Japan and Asia, the idea of a militarily independent Japan (especially Japanese troops abroad), represents an alarming echo of the country's wartime past. Like other Oshii films (where this political critique is sometimes even more explicit), *Blood* seems to yearn for a Japan that is militarily strong and independent but also peace loving and noninterventionist.[6]

So while Saya's character has the elements of a sexual fantasy cobbled together from fetishistic images, she is more importantly a fantasy of national agency and identity—a fantasy that is almost sexually stirring and disturbing, inevitable and naive. Her physical power and presence represent the hope for a force that can cut through the perceived inaction and paralysis of Japanese politics. By the time it achieves violent release in the burning hangar, the repressed tension between David and Saya is as much political as it is sexual: from David (that is, from the United States), she receives the sword she could not find. With it, she regains the warrior spirit Japan lost after World War II, and with this new blade she incarnates a new Japan, one on an independent equal footing with the West. With youth's innocent strength and age's sad wisdom, Saya can rescue the Japanese–U.S. partnership (maybe in the person of the nurse) from falling into the militarism and imperialism it has in the past—a threat represented by the ravening chiropterans. With her sword reforged, she will conquer war itself and guard the peace.

There is an ironic, even tongue-in-cheek quality to the film's idea that Japan's savior will take the form of a sword-wielding vampire schoolgirl in a sailor suit. What the mix of seriousness and pastiche in these overlapping sexual and national fantasies really conveys is the idea that Saya does not represent a real political solution so much as she points out the paradoxes of Japan's political identity vis-à-vis the United States and the contradictions that seem to inhere in every (im)possible solution. In fact, the film's hope is tinged with such irony that it sometimes verges on nihilism, a kind of despair we see more clearly in the edgy *Blood* manga that Tamaoki Benkyo based on the film. This work shows us Saya in the present day, now caged like an animal by the U.S. military and released only to hunt. Tamaoki is best known for his pornographic comics, and here Saya's nemesis is a sadistic lesbian vampire who leads a motorcycle gang and uses her cell phone to troll for disillusioned youth. Saya defeats her, but there is ultimately little distinction between good and evil: the villain turns out to be Saya's own alter ego and twin.[7]

The film is slightly more sanguine. In the ironic, self-referential style that characterizes so many anime, the film is shot through with a stirring but always slightly sardonic optimism. Just as Donna Haraway relies on fantastic, ironic narratives about vampires or cyborgs to make her most dangerous claims, *Blood* reflects on dangerous issues by translating them into a fantastic genre and an animated medium that allow us to deal with these painful realities from a distance. Yet at several points, *Blood*'s more realistic 3-D animation threatens to disrupt that metaphoric quality and break into the real. This is the subject taken up below.

Spaces And Planes: The Visual Dynamics Of *Blood*

This brings us to the visual differences between anime and live action, and the formal style of *Blood*. Here I would like to start with a question about the final climactic battle with the chiropterans. After Saya kills the monster inside the burning hangar, a third chiropteran appears and perches dramatically on the hangar roof, then grows wings and glides out over the runways. As Saya and David pursue it in a jeep, they realize it is heading for a plane that is taxiing toward takeoff. For some reason, they must stop it before it reaches the plane, but it is not exactly clear why. Will it attack and crash the aircraft? Or will it cling to the wing and escape beyond David and Saya's reach? If the chiropteran only wants to get away, why did it come to the base in the first place, and why aren't David and Saya content to see it go? A viewer can construct several plausible explanations, but the urgency of this final scene suggests the need for a decisive answer. The second half of this essay works toward such an answer, by considering what Saya and the planes represent on a visual level.

Thomas LaMarre has argued compellingly that the most interesting approach to anime connects its meaning with its specific visual qualities, particularly those qualities that set it apart from live-action cinema. LaMarre's essay "From Animation to Anime" takes up the case of "limited animation," anime's practice of reducing the number of illustrations that make up an animated sequence.[8] Originally a cost-cutting expedient, limited animation has given rise to a number of specific effects that have now come to be regarded as positive parts of anime's aesthetic. Among these are long close-ups in which nothing moves except the characters' mouths or eyes, a jerky energy when characters do move (caused by drawing fewer intermediate stages of a given motion), and an image-compositing technique that replaces an articulated moving figure with a single static drawing of the figure, which is then photographed as it slides in front of a static background. This last practice of "moving the drawing" instead of "drawing the movement" produces rigid figures that appear to float across the background in a layer of their own, rather than articulated figures that move in and out of the background in three dimensions.

For LaMarre, this last effect generates a kind of weightless, floating quality that creates a sense of freedom for the character and spectator alike. LaMarre supports this with a clever reading of the flying scenes in Miyazaki Hayao's *Castle in the Sky* (1986, *Tenku no shiro Rapyuta*), where these static figures in horizontal movement produce a sense of gliding weightlessly on the wind. In this way, the formal visual quality of the movement mirrors the story's theme (and that of several other Miyazaki stories), in which characters gain freedom by harnessing the wind and their own inner potential rather than by relying on a mechanical technology fueled by scarce resources. "Minimum technology" becomes both the environmentalist mandate of Miyazaki's films and the philosophy of their production. For LaMarre, this freedom enables the protagonist to escape the burden of history in a way that is suggestive for *Blood*. *Castle*'s heroine Sheeta is among the last descendants of a people who ruled floating cities equipped with apocalyptic weapons, yet Sheeta has an inner freedom that empowers her to reject this legacy and gives her the strength to destroy the last remnants of her people's dangerous technology.

Like most animation of the time, *Castle in the Sky* was produced by drawing and painting figures on transparent celluloid, layering these "cels" over background paintings, and photographing them for each frame. The limited number of layers and the difficulty of portraying movement toward or away from the camera both reinforced the flat, sliding quality of the motion, according to LaMarre. *Blood*'s innovation was to include backgrounds and objects that were modeled in three dimensions using computer graphics imagery (CGI).[9] A computer can calculate the appearance of these elements and environments from any angle and generate as many frames as needed, allowing the animators to produce sequences in which intricate shapes can rotate smoothly and the virtual camera can move through complex sets. Some software can also calculate the motion of drawn objects in ways that take into account inertia and other dynamic forces. This gives computer-rendered objects a sense of depth, mass, and momentum that hand-drawn characters do not have.

While many of the characters in *Blood* are two-dimensional caricatures, the planes in the background are rendered in three dimensions, in historically accurate detail (Figures 3–5). Harnessing a persistent bias that cinematic or photographic realism is somehow closer to unmediated experience than two-dimensional drawing, the filmmakers use this photorealism to associate the planes with a more profound reality. As they take off or return from a destination we can imagine as Vietnam, these aircraft are the film's most prominent signifier for the world of war and geopolitics outside the vampire story. But what is more interesting is the way that *Blood* juxtaposes three-dimensional computer-rendered elements with the kind of limited animation LaMarre describes. In the opening scene, when Saya races through the train car toward the disguised chiropteran, the train cars are rendered with an almost exaggerated linear perspective, while Saya remains a "moving drawing"—a static figure who flies through the car toward her target. Here Saya evokes the same sense of weightlessness and freedom as Miyazaki's Sheeta. Faster than a locomotive, she is also free of its ponderous inertia. As she strikes down postwar political threats in the person of the chiropteran, Saya may even be quick enough to dodge around the historical dilemmas *Blood* presents—in effect escaping the difficult legacy of World War II just as Sheeta escapes the burden of her family history. This fast freedom is the ultimate object of desire that Saya represents. But in the end it is probably unattainable: all around her, the ponderous shapes of other figures—the train, the planes—remind us of a weightier reality.[10]

These, then, are the links between political and visual dynamics—political movements and physical motion—in the film. At the most intuitive level, *Blood* lulls us into a fantasy world not only with its occult plot but with its flat visuals; yet, whenever a plane appears, it has a cinematic realism that calls us back to the reality of Vietnam. At a more complex level, the juxtaposition is not just between two-dimensional cartoonishness and three-dimensional realism but between visions of fast, floating freedom versus the lumbering weighty responsibilities imposed on postwar Japan. There is a further wrinkle in the fact that while the planes seem real and weighty, they also have a ghostly quality of their own, a quality of the dead returned to life. Often this is achieved with lighting and sound effects: a cargo plane that roars overhead appears only as a looming silhouette. A fighter taxiing away from the camera floats lightly into the air behind a shimmering veil of heat (Figures 4 and 5). In the climax, a huge C-130 transport or gunship lumbers into the sky, glowing eerily in the dawn light, while Saya stands in front of it, a tiny, flat silhouette. The planes also gain a ghostly quality by combining detailed three-dimensionality with a drawn quality that they never lose. They become uncanny by approaching cinematic realism and stopping short.

Resurrected Memories: Computer Graphics And The Undead

Livia Monnet explains the ghostly quality of CGI's *almost* cinematic realism in a reading of *Final Fantasy: The Spirits Within* (2001), an ostensibly photorealistic film in which everything is computer modeled and rendered. Monnet points out that despite their visual realism, the film's characters have a ghostly, uncanny, or undead quality generated by the many layers of simulation that separate them from the human. Each CGI body is "a *ghostly, invaded body*, a computer-animated trace of a real, referential movement"—for example, the movement of a human motion-capture actor whose gestures have been recorded and copied to animate a 3-D model of a human body:

> The elastic, dot-constellation figures produced by the computer from motion-capture data provided by real human actors absorbed, as it were, the latter's "lifeblood," which then became the "living material" of the digital actor's "lifelike" behavior. ... *Final Fantasy*'s virtual actors perform as undead, digital vampires or zombies.[11]

Monnet sees these formal visual qualities as intimately intertwined with the film's science fiction plot, which involves a set of monstrous phantoms that infect and devour human bodies. The phantoms are also undead—a malevolent spiritual energy left over from an extinct civilization. Monnet identifies the reason for this plot and style as an impulse *Final Fantasy* inherits from early cinema, an urge to confront and overcome death. Just as early film theory attributed an animism to motion pictures, *Final Fantasy* strives like Doctor Frankenstein to animate its figures, but ends up with uncanny characters that seem half alive.

Freud identifies the uncanny with the return of repressed ideas or beliefs—the "primitive" belief that a lifeless object can come to life, as well as sexual fears that have been repressed. Extending and critiquing Freud, Monnet notes that the heroine of *Final Fantasy* is a passive host, or "medium," in which the action plays out. Monnet thereby relates the uncanny quality of the film's CGI actors with the haunting return of this suppressed female agency.

These ideas are helpful for thinking about undead agency in *Blood*. But just as Miyazaki's

Castle in the Sky turns limited animation into a virtue, *Blood* leverages the uncanny limitations of CGI to good effect, using them to acknowledge and foreground issues of lost agency and lost or repressed memory. For a Japanese audience, this includes the perceived loss of Japan's historical or political agency after World War II, as well as the fear of reclaiming that agency and risking a return to prewar aggression. For many in and out of Japan, what has been repressed is thoughtful debate about Japan's wartime responsibilities and history. U.S. viewers may also be reminded of America's own repressed complicity in all of the above, as well as the willfully forgotten lessons of Vietnam. This is why the F-4 Phantoms and other planes are the film's true ghosts, spookier and scarier than the chiropterans: they haunt us with the return of an uncomfortable reality—not just an everyday reality we set aside when we entered the theater but political truths we have suppressed in our everyday lives. Only a Harawayan figure like Saya—the product of "desire and fear," "shaped by murderous ideologies" herself—can bring this suppressed violence to the surface and simultaneously head it off.

Planes, Trains, And The Air Mobile: *Blood's* Climax And Crisis

We can now revisit and reread the film's final chase. Why must David and Saya prevent the chiropteran from reaching the plane? The aircraft is not in danger. It is a C-130 Galaxy, a hundred feet long and forty feet tall, and as we get closer, it towers over Saya and the monster. The real worry is what powers the monster will gain if it joins with this mechanical behemoth. If the chiropterans represent an awakening Japanese militarism, the fear of renewed Japanese intervention abroad is figured as the threat that the monster will escape Japan's shores on America's back and reach out as far as Vietnam. This will repeat the grim history of 1940, when Japan's expansion into French Indochina was a prelude to the Pacific War.[12]

More broadly, and more in line with the visual argument above, the fear in this scene is that latent Japanese militarism (which has been pushed back into the realm of fantasy up to now) will somehow merge with the three-dimensional world of the plane and reassert itself. The fear that the chiropteran will reach the plane is the fear that Japan's imperialists will rise from the (un)dead, that the two-dimensional nightmare will somehow become a three-dimensional reality. This is the catastrophe Saya averts. When David pulls the speeding jeep alongside the plane, she fatally slashes the monster just short of the plane's wing. As the aircraft turns away from her and wheels into the sky, Saya remains a flattened silhouette in the foreground. She has succeeded in keeping the creature in her own two-dimensional world, but she cannot enter the real world either. In this film, the rearmed peaceful Japan she symbolizes is ultimately just a pipe dream.

For *Blood's* audience, then, the sexual and political fantasies that Saya represents both remain unattainable. Anime bodies and beings can certainly provoke sexual desire in the viewer, but without even an actor or actress to stand in for the character in our fantasies, that desire for the anime body must be tinged with a particular hopelessness. All the more so when the character is a self-conscious pastiche of fetishes like Saya. In *Blood*, the frustrated sexual desire that is a feature of so many anime becomes an analogue for unconsummated political yearnings as well. Exiled from the fantasy, the spectator remains trapped in the real world.

This sense of foreclosed possibilities on the part of the spectator is also discussed by LaMarre. He suggests that Miyazaki's use of sliding layers gives an increased freedom and agency not only to his characters but to the viewer as well. The spectator and the characters occupy adjacent layers that are in "relative motion." The world "is sensed but not quite objectifiable (in the sense of forming stable points of reference)," opening the possibility that anime might help us spectators alter or rethink the deterministic roles imposed on us by modern film and modern history.[13] For LaMarre, this space of possibility is represented by a train, a moving environment whose windows flash sequential images in a way that leaves us unsure if it is the world or we ourselves that are in motion.

Writing on very similar visual issues in anime by Miyazaki and fiction by Edogawa Ranpo, Thomas Looser sees the view from a train window in the opposite way. With its differential movement of near and far objects, Looser regards it as a triumph of three-dimensional linear perspective and a dominating imperialistic gaze.[14] So what kind of train is the subway we board with Saya in the opening scenes of *Blood*? In fact, its exaggerated linear perspective associates it with Looser's more pessimistic vision. There is even a sense in which the subway scenes and other rendered environments seem to fix the spectator's position more firmly, trapping and pinning us down in return for letting us see things that cel-based animation cannot show.

This difference between the two trains speaks to the difference between Miyazaki and Oshii. If Miyazaki makes his points by freeing the spectator, Oshii makes them by implicating us uncomfortably in the projects he criticizes. He provokes our desire for freedom but frustrates it by confining us claustrophobically inside the machine. For example, when the chiropteran stands on the roof of the burning hangar preparing to fly, the camera rotates around the building in an ostentatiously perspectival view, while the frame shakes in a way that mimics news footage taken from a helicopter. (Less than a minute later, a shot of agents in a helicopter brings the association to the surface.) In the aerial shot of the hangar, we have been transported inside the plane. In LaMarre's parlance, we have become the "viewing machine-subject" that Miyazaki so carefully avoids.[15] Now we are not only watching; we have become part of the machine's projects. Now it is we who are providing air support.

If there is optimism in *Blood* and Oshii's other work, it is less a dream of political revolution than a more modest and more visual hope that anime might allow us to see things hidden by other media, or perhaps remember scenes that we have repressed. In this way, the darkness of *Blood* does shine some light on postwar Japanese political identity, and the film hopes that this knowledge might make some small difference. As *Blood*'s spectators, we cannot share Saya's inhuman speed or agency, but Oshii seems to hope that if we can see the train coming, we just might be able to get out of the way.

Notes

This essay is based on papers delivered at two conferences: "Digital Cultures in Asia" at Academia Sinica in Taiwan, July 2005, and "Schoolgirls and Mobile Suits" at the Minneapolis College of Art and Design, October 2005. I benefited greatly from comments by the conference participants, as well as from feedback by Kotani Mari and Eliot Corley at earlier stages in the project.

1. *Kokaku kidotai: Ghost in the Shell*, dir. Oshii Mamoru (1995); translated as *Ghost in the Shell*, DVD (Manga Entertainment, 1998); *Kido keisatsu patoreibaa 2: The Movie*, dir. Oshii Mamoru (1993); translated as *Patlabor 2: The Movie*, DVD (Manga Video, 2000); *Jinro*, dir. Okiura Hiroyuki, script by Oshii Mamoru (2000); translated as *Jin-Roh: The Wolf Brigade*, DVD (Viz, 2002).
2. *Blood: The Last Vampire*, dir. Kitakubo Hiroyuki, planning assistance by Oshii Mamoru (2000); translated on DVD (Manga Entertainment, 2001). For more on Oshii's key role in the collaborative process, see the documentary "Making of *Blood: The Last Vampire*" on the American DVD. For various interpretations of the film by the various creators, see Brian Ruh, *Stray Dog of Anime: The Films of Mamoru Oshii* (New York: Palgrave, 2004), 154–64.
3. Donna Haraway, *Modest_Witness@Second_Millennium.FemaleMan©_Meets_OncoMouse™: Feminism and Technoscience* (New York: Routledge, 1977), 214–15.
4. Kotani Mari, "Techno-Gothic Japan: From Seishi Yokomizo's *The Death's-Head Stranger* to Mariko Ohara's *Ephemera the Vampire*," in *Blood Read: The Vampire as Metaphor in Contemporary Culture*, ed. Joan Gordon and

Veronica Hollinger (Philadelphia: University of Pennsylvania Press, 1997), 194.

5. At one point in the film, a woman fleeing from the chiropteran runs into a black airman drawn as a caricature, with a large flat nose, bulging white eyes, and enormous lips. In a scene calculated to startle (and perhaps disturb) the viewer, she looks into his face and screams for several seconds before realizing that he is not a monster himself. The uncomfortable joke evokes civilian and military racial tensions in the sixties and the monstrousness of the black other (or black soldier) in the racist imagination. The scene drives its point home by lynching this character a few frames later: a chiropteran lurking in a tree grabs him from above and pulls his head into the branches, then kills him as his twitching legs dangle from the tree. Once noticed, the violent symbolism of this scene threatens to overwhelm the whole film.

6. For example, see Oshii's *Patlabor 2*, released shortly after the first Gulf war. Michael Fisch and I have both considered these issues in the context of that film. Michael Fisch, "Nation, War, and Japan's Future in the Science Fiction Anime Film *Patlabor 2*," *Science Fiction Studies* 27, no. 1 (2000): 49–68; Christopher Bolton, "The Mecha's Blind Spot: *Patlabor 2* and the Phenomenology of Anime," in *Robot Ghosts and Wired Dreams: Japanese Science Fiction from Origins to Anime*, ed. Christopher Bolton, Istvan Csicsery-Ronay Jr., and Takayuki Tatsumi (Minneapolis: University of Minnesota Press, 2007).

7. Other *Blood* spin-offs include a television series set and released in 2005 and a sequence of novels, including a recently translated novel by Oshii himself (reviewed in this volume). Tamaoki Benkyo, *Blood: The Last Vampire 2000*; translated by Carl Gustav Horn as *Blood: The Last Vampire 2002* (San Francisco: Viz, 2002); Oshii Mamoru, *Blood The Last Vampire: Kemonotachi no yoru* (Tokyo: Kadokawa horaa bunko, 2002); translated by Camellia Nieh as *Blood The Last Vampire: Night of the Beasts* (Milwaukie, Ore.: DH Press, 2005); *Blood+*, TV series (2005-); available on Japanese DVD (Aniplex, 2005–).

8. Thomas LaMarre, "From Animation to Anime: Drawing Movements and Moving Drawings," *Japan Forum* 14, no. 2 (2002): 329–67.

9. *Blood*'s animators also increased the number of layers that compose in each shot using software like Photoshop. For technical details, see the "Making of" documentary on the American DVD.

10. LaMarre argues that a deliberate gap between cel and digital animation can push us to abandon these very assumptions about cinema's nearness to reality, as well as broader notions about the historical indexicality of (visual) language. This opens the possibility of thinking in new ways about history itself. While I identify Saya's two-dimensionality as representing an attractive freedom that is ultimately unrealistic, LaMarre sees a more radical and more sustainable freedom in the heroine of Rintaro's *Metropolis* (2001), a cyborg who combines two- and three-dimensional attributes in a single character. Thomas LaMarre, "The First Time as Farce: Digital Animation and the Repetition of Cinema," in *Cinema Anime: Critical Engagements with Japanese Animation*, ed. Steven T. Brown (New York: Palgrave, 2006), 161–88.

11. Livia Monnet, "Invasion of the Women Snatchers: The Problem of A-Life and the Uncanny in *Final Fantasy: The Spirits Within*," in Bolton, Csicsery-Ronay Jr., and Tatsumi, *Robot Ghosts and Wired Dreams*.

12. This fear is born out in the 2005 television series, which begins with a scene of Saya and the chiropterans slaughtering American soldiers and local villagers in Vietnam.

13. LaMarre, "From Animation to Anime," 364–65.

14. Thomas Looser, "From Edogawa to Miyazaki: Cinematic and *Anime*-ic Architectures of Early and Late Twentieth-Century Japan," *Japan Forum* 14, no. 2 (2002): 297–327.

15. LaMarre, "From Animation to Anime," 364.

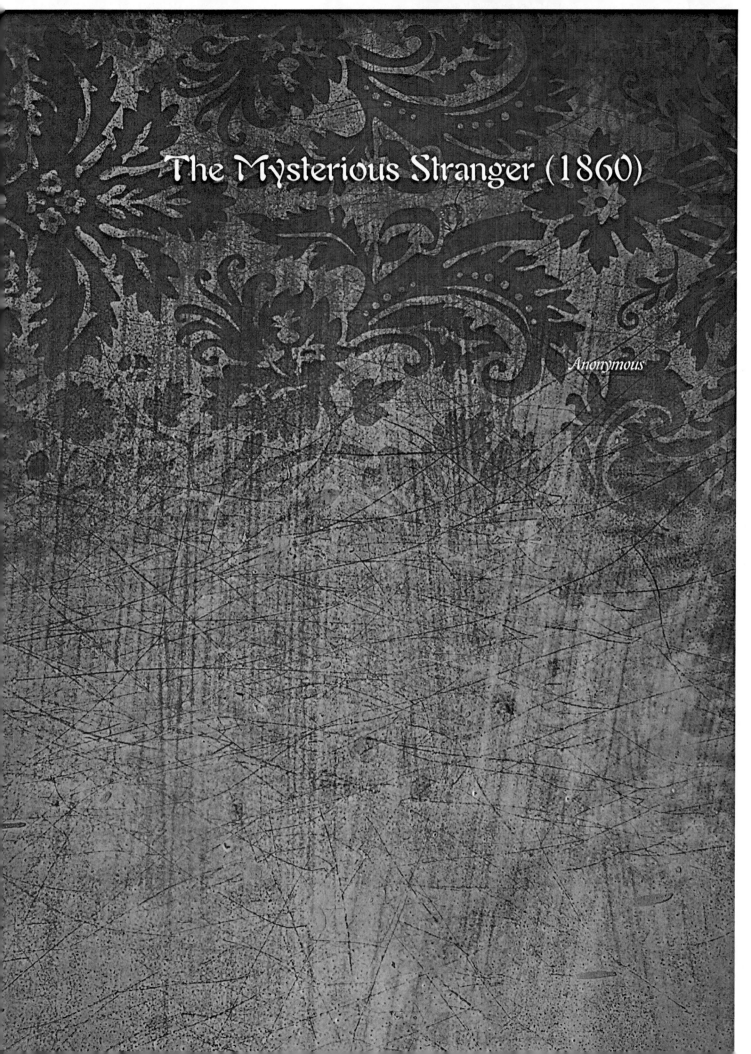

"To die, to sleep, To sleep, perchance to dream, ay, there's the rub ..."
                                    Hamlet.

BOREAS, THAT FEARFUL NORTH-WEST wind, which in the spring and autumn stirs up the lowest depths of the wild Adriatic, and is then so dangerous to vessels, was howling through the woods, and tossing the branches of the old knotty oaks in the Carpathian Mountains, when a party of five riders, who surrounded a litter drawn by a pair of mules, turned into a forest-path, which offered some protection from the April weather, and allowed the travellers in some degree to recover their breath. It was already evening, and bitterly cold; the snow fell every now and then in large flakes. A tall old gentleman, of aristocratic appearance, rode at the head of the troop. This was the Knight of Fahnenberg, in Austria. He had inherited from a childless brother a considerable property, situated in the Carpathian Mountains; and he had set out to take possession of it, accompanied by his daughter Franziska, and a niece about twenty years of age, who had been brought up with her. Next to the knight rode a fine young man of some twenty and odd years—the Baron Franz von Kronstein; he wore, like the former, the broad-brimmed hat with hanging feathers, the leather collar, the wide riding-boots—in short, the travelling-dress which was in fashion at the commencement of the seventeenth century. The features of the young man had much about them that was open and friendly, as well as some mind; but the expression was more that of dreamy and sensitive softness than of youthful daring, although no one could deny that he possessed much of youthful beauty.

As the cavalcade turned into the oak wood the young man rode up to the litter, and chatted with the ladies who were seated therein. One of these—and to her his conversation was principally addressed—was of dazzling beauty. Her hair flowed in natural curls round the fine oval of her face, out of which beamed a pair of starlike eyes, full of genius, lively fancy, and a certain degree of archness. Franziska von Fahnenberg seemed to attend but carelessly to the speeches of her admirer, who made many kind inquiries as to how she felt herself during the journey, which had been attended with many difficulties: she always answered him very shortly, almost contemptuously; and at length remarked, that if it had not been for her father's objections, she would long ago have requested the baron to take her place in their horrid cage of a litter, for, to judge by his remarks, he seemed incommoded by the weather; and she would so much rather be mounted on the spirited horse, and face wind and storm, than be mewed up there, dragged up the hills by those long-eared animals, and mope herself to death with ennui. The young lady's words, and, still more, the half-contemptuous tone in which they were uttered, appeared to make the most painful impression on the young man: he made her no reply at the moment, but the absent air with which he attended to the kindly-intended remarks of the other young lady, showed how much he was disconcerted.

"It appears, dear Franziska," said he at length in a kindly tone, "that the hardships of the road have affected you more than you will acknowledge. Generally so kind to others, you have been very often out of humour during the journey, and particularly with regard to your humble servant and cousin, who would gladly bear a double or triple share of the discomforts, if he could thereby save you from the smallest of them."

Franziska showed by her look that she was about to reply with some bitter jibe, when the voice of the knight was heard calling for his nephew, who galloped off at the sound.

"I should like to scold you well, Franziska," said her companion somewhat sharply, "for always plagueing your poor Cousin Franz in this shameful way; he who loves you so truly, and who, whatever you may say, will one day be your husband."

"My husband!" replied the other angrily. "I must either completely alter my ideas, or he his whole self, before that takes place. No, Bertha! I know that this is my father's darling wish, and I do not deny the good qualities Cousin Franz may have, or really has, since I see you are making a face; but to marry an effeminate man—never!"

Anonymous, "The Mysterious Stranger." Copyright in the Public Domain.

"Effeminate! You do him great injustice," replied her friend quickly. "Just because instead of going off to the Turkish war, where little honour was to be gained, he attended to your father's advice, and stayed at home, to bring his neglected estate into order, which he accomplished with care and prudence; and because he does not represent this howling wind as a mild zephyr—for reasons such as these you are pleased to call him effeminate."

"Say what you will, it is so,'" cried Franziska obstinately. "Bold, aspiring, even despotic, must be the man who is to gain my heart; these soft, patient, and thoughtful natures are utterly distasteful to me. Is Franz capable of deep sympathy, either in joy or sorrow? He is always the same—always quiet, soft and tiresome."

"He has a warm heart, and is not without genius," said Bertha.

"A warm heart! that may be," replied the other; "but I would rather be tyrannized over, and kept under a little by my future husband, than be loved in such a wearisome manner. You say he has genius, too. I will not exactly contradict you, since that would be impolite, but it is not easily discovered. But even allowing you are right in both statements, still the man who does not bring these qualities into action is a despicable creature. A man may do many foolish things, he may even be a little wicked now and then, provided it is in nothing dishonourable; and one can forgive him, if he is only acting on some fixed theory for some special object. There is, for instance, your own faithful admirer the Castellan of Glogau, Knight of Woislaw; he loves you most truly, and is now quite in a position to enable you to marry comfortably. The brave man has lost his right hand—reason enough for remaining seated behind the stove, or near the spinning-wheel of his Bertha; but what does he do?—He goes off to the war in Turkey; he fights for a noble thought—"

"And runs the chance of getting his other hand chopped off, and another great scar across his face," put in her friend.

"Leaves his lady-love to weep and pine a little," pursued Franziska, "but returns with fame, marries, and is all the more honoured and admired! This is done by a man of forty, a rough warrior, not bred at court, a soldier who has nothing but his cloak and sword. And Franz—rich, noble—but I will not go on. Not a word more on this detested point, if you love me, Bertha."

Franziska leaned back in the corner of the litter with a dissatisfied air, and shut her eyes as though, overcome by fatigue, she wished to sleep.

"This awful wind is so powerful, you say, that we must make a detour to avoid its full force," said the knight to an old man, dressed in a fur-cap and a cloak of rough skin, who seemed to be the guide of the party.

"Those who have never personally felt the Boreas storming over the country between Sessano and Trieste, can have no conception of the reality," replied the other. "As soon as it commences, the snow is blown in thick long columns along the ground. That is nothing to what follows. These columns become higher and higher, as the wind rises, and continue to do so until you see nothing but snow above, below, and on every side—unless, indeed, sometimes, when sand and gravel are mixed with the snow, and at length it is impossible to open your eyes at all. Your only plan for safety is to wrap your cloak around you, and lie down flat on the ground. If your home were but a few hundred yards off, you might lose your life in the attempt to reach it."

"Well, then, we owe you thanks, old Kumpan," said the knight, though it was with difficulty he made his words heard above the roaring of the storm; "we owe you thanks for taking us this round as we shall thus be enabled to reach our destination without danger."

"You may feel sure of that, noble sir," said the old man. "By midnight we shall have arrived, and that without any danger by the way, if—" Suddenly the old man stopped, he drew his horse sharply up, and remained in an attitude of attentive listening.

"It appears to me we must be in the neighborhood of some village," said Franz von Kronstein; "for between the gusts of the storm I hear a dog howling."

"It is no dog, it is no dog!" said the old man uneasily, and urged his horse to a rapid pace.

"For miles around there is no human dwelling; and except in the castle of Klatka, which indeed lies in the neighborhood, but has been deserted for more than a century, probably no one has lived here since the creation.—But there again," he continued; "well, if I wasn't sure of it from the first."

"That howling seems to bother you, old Kumpan," said the knight, listening to a long-drawn fierce sound, which appeared nearer than before, and seemed to be answered from a distance.

"That howling comes from no dogs," replied the old guide uneasily. "Those are reed-wolves; they may be on our track; and it would be as well if the gentlemen looked to their firearms."

"Reed-wolves? What do you mean?" inquired Franz in surprise.

"At the edge of this wood," said Kumpan, "there lies a lake about a mile long, whose banks are covered with reeds. In these a number of wolves have taken up their quarters, and feed on wild birds, fish and such like. They are shy in the summer-time, and a boy of twelve might scare them; but when the birds migrate, and the fish are frozen up, they prowl about at night, and then they are dangerous. They are worst, however, when the Boreas rages, for then it is just as if the fiend himself possessed them: they are so mad and fierce that man and beast become alike their victims; and a party of them have been known even to attack the ferocious bears of these mountains, and, what is more, to come off victorious." The howl was now again repeated more distinctly, and from two opposite directions. The riders in alarm felt for their pistols and the old man grasped the spear which hung at his saddle.

"We must keep close to the litter; the wolves are very near us," whispered the guide. The riders turned their horses, surrounded the litter, and the knight informed the ladies, in a few quieting words, of the cause of this movement.

"Then we *shall* have an adventure—some little variety!" cried Franziska with sparkling eyes.

"How can you talk so foolishly?" said Bertha in alarm.

"Are we not under manly protection? Is not Cousin Franz on our side?" said the other mockingly.

"See, there is a light gleaming among the twigs; and there is another," cried Bertha. "There must be people close to us."

"No, no," cried the guide quickly. "Shut up the door, ladies. Keep close together, gentlemen. It is the eyes of wolves you see sparkling there." The gentlemen looked towards the thick underwood, in which every now and then little bright spots appeared, such as in summer would have been taken for glowworms; it was just the same greenish-yellow light, but less unsteady, and there were always two flames together. The horses began to be restive, they kicked and dragged at the rein; but the mules behaved tolerably well.

"I will fire on the beasts, and teach them to keep their distance," said Franz, pointing to the spot where the lights were thickest.

"Hold, hold, Sir Baron!" cried Kumpan quickly, and seized the young man's arm. "You would bring such a host together by the report, that, encouraged by numbers, they would be sure to make the first assault. However, keep your arms in readiness, and if an old she-wolf springs out—for these always lead the attack—take good aim and kill her, for then there must be no further hesitation." By this time the horses were almost unmanageable, and terror had also infected the mules. Just as Franz was turning towards the litter to say a word to his cousin, an animal, about the size of a large hound, sprang from the thicket and seized the foremost mule.

"Fire, baron! A wolf!" shouted the guide.

The young man fired, and the wolf fell to the ground. A fearful howl rang through the wood.

"Now, forward! Forward without a moment's delay!" cried Kumpan. "We have not above five minutes' time. The beasts will tear their wounded comrade to pieces, and, if they are very hungry, partially devour her. We shall, in the meantime, gain a little start, and it is not more than an hour's ride to the end of the forest. There—do you see—there are the towers of Klatka between the trees—out there where the moon is rising, and from that point the wood becomes less dense."

The travellers endeavoured to increase their pace to the utmost, but the litter retarded their progress. Bertha was weeping with fear, and even Franziska's courage had diminished, for she sat very still. Franz endeavoured to reassure them. They had not proceeded many moments when the howling recommenced, and approached nearer and nearer.

"There they are again and fiercer and more numerous than before," cried the guide in alarm.

The lights were soon visible again, and certainly in greater numbers. The wood had already become less thick, and the snowstorm having ceased, the moonbeams discovered many a dusky form amongst the trees, keeping together like a pack of hounds and advancing nearer and nearer till they were within twenty paces, and on the very path of the travellers. From time to time a fierce howl arose from their centre which was answered by the whole pack, and was at length taken up by single voices in the distance.

The party now found themselves some few hundred yards from the ruined castle of which Kumpan had spoken. It was, or seemed by moonlight to be, of some magnitude. Near the tolerably preserved principal building lay the ruins of a church which must have once been beautiful, placed on a little hillock dotted with single oak-trees and bramble-bushes. Both castle and church were still partially roofed in, and a path led from the castle gate to an old oak-tree, where it joined at right angles the one along which the travellers were advancing.

The old guide seemed in much perplexity.

"We are in great danger, noble sir," said he. "The wolves will very soon make a general attack. There will then be only one way of escape: leaving the mules to their fate, and taking the young ladies on your horses."

"That would be all very well, if I had not thought of a better plan," replied the knight. "Here is the ruined castle; we can surely reach that, and then, blocking up the gates, we must just await the morning."

"Here? In the ruins of Klatka?—Not for all the wolves in the world!" cried the old man. "Even by daylight no one likes to approach the place, and, now, by night!—The castle, Sir Knight, has a bad name."

"On account of robbers?" asked Franz.

"No; it is haunted," replied the other.

"Stuff and nonsense!" said the baron. "Forward to the ruins; there is not a moment to be lost."

And this was indeed the case. The ferocious beasts were but a few steps behind the travellers. Every now and then they retired, and set up a ferocious howl. The party had just arrived at the old oak before mentioned and were about to turn into the path to the ruins, when the animals, as though perceiving the risk they ran of losing their prey, came so near that a lance could easily have struck them. The knight and Franz faced sharply about, spurring their horses amidst the advancing crowds, when suddenly, from the shadow of the oak stepped forth a man who in a few strides placed himself between the travellers and their pursuers. As far as one could see in the dusky light the stranger was a man of a tall and well-built frame; he wore a sword by his side and a broad-brimmed hat was on his head. If the party were astonished at his sudden appearance, they were still more so at what followed. As soon as the stranger appeared the wolves gave over their pursuit, tumbled over each other, and set up a fearful howl. The stranger now raised his hand, appeared to wave it, and the wild animals crawled back into the thickets like a pack of beaten hounds.

Without casting a glance at the travellers, who were too much overcome by astonishment to speak, the stranger went up the path which led to the castle and soon disappeared beneath the gateway.

"Heaven have mercy on us!" murmured old Kumpan in his beard, as he made the sign of the cross.

"Who was that strange man?" asked the knight with surprise, when he had watched the stranger as long as he was visible, and the party had resumed their way.

The old guide pretended not to understand, and riding up to the mules, busied himself with arranging the harness, which had become disordered in their haste: more than a quarter of an hour elapsed before he rejoined them.

"Did you know the man who met us near the ruins and who freed us from our fourfooted pursuers its such a miraculous way?" asked Franz of the guide.

"Do I know him? No, noble sir; I never saw him before," replied the guide hesitatingly.

"He looked like a soldier, and was armed," said the baron. "Is the castle, then, inhabited?"

"Not for the last hundred years," replied the other. "It was dismantled because the possessor in those days had iniquitous dealings with some Turkish-Sclavonian hordes, who had advanced as far as this; or rather"—he corrected himself hastily—"he is *said* to have had such, for he might have beam as upright and good a man as ever ate cheese fried in butter."

"And who is now the possessor of the ruins and of these woods?" inquired the knight.

"Who but yourself, noble sir?" replied Kumpan. "For more than two hours we have been on your estate, and we shall soon reach the end of the wood."

"We hear and see nothing more of the wolves," said the baron after a pause. "Even their howling has ceased. The adventure with the stranger still remains to me inexplicable, even if one were to suppose him a huntsman—"

"Yes, yes; that is most likely what he is," interrupted the guide hastily, whilst he looked uneasily round him. "The brave good man, who came so opportunely to our assistance, must have been a huntsman. Oh, there are many powerful woodsmen in this neighborhood! Heaven be praised!" he continued, taking a deep breath, "there is the end of the wood, and in a short hour we shall be safely housed."

And so it happened. Before an hour had elapsed the party passed through a well-built village, the principal spot on the estate, towards the venerable castle, the windows of which were brightly illuminated, and at the door stood the steward and other dependents, who, having received their new lord with every expression of respect, conducted the party to the splendidly furnished apartments.

Nearly four weeks passed before the travelling adventures again came on the *tapis.* The knight and Franz found such constant employment in looking over all the particulars of the large estate, and endeavouring to introduce various German improvements, that they were very little at home. At first Franziska was charmed with everything in a neighborhood so entirely new and unknown. It appeared to her so romantic, so very different from her German Father-land, that she took the greatest interest in everything, and often drew comparisons between the countries, which generally ended unfavourably for Germany. Bertha was of exactly the contrary opinion: she laughed at her cousin, and said that her liking for novelty and strange sights must indeed have come to a pass when she preferred hovels in which the smoke went out of the doors and windows instead of the chimney, walls covered with soot, and inhabitants not much cleaner, and of unmannerly habits, to the comfortable dwellings and polite people of Germany. However, Franziska persisted in her notions, and replied that everything in Austria was flat, *ennuyant,* and common; and that a wild peasant here, with his rough coat of skin, had ten times more interest for her than a quiet Austrian in his holiday suit, the mere sight of whom was enough to make one yawn.

As soon as the knight had gotten the first arrangements into some degree of order the party found themselves more together again. Franz continued to show great attention to his cousin, which, however, she received with little gratitude, for she made him the butt of all her fanciful humours, that soon returned when after a longer sojourn she had become more accustomed to her new life. Many excursions into the neighborhood were undertaken but there was little variety in the scenery, and these soon ceased to amuse.

The party were one day assembled in the old-fashioned hall, dinner had just been removed, and they were arranging in which direction they should ride. "I have it," cried Franziska suddenly, "I wonder we never thought before of going to view by day the spot where we fell in with our night-adventure with wolves and the Mysterious Stranger."

"You mean a visit to the ruins—what were they called?" said the knight.

"Castle Klatka," cried Franziska gaily. "Oh, we really must ride there! It will be so charming to go over again by daylight, and in safety, the ground where we had such a dreadful fright."

"Bring round the horses," said the knight to a servant; "and tell the steward to come to me immediately." The latter, an old man, soon after entered the room.

"We intend taking a ride to Klatka," said the knight: "we had an adventure there on our road—"

"So old Kumpan told me," interrupted the steward.

"And what do you say about it?" asked the knight.

"I really don't know what to say," replied the old man, shaking his head. "I was a youth of twenty when I first came to this castle, and now my hair is grey; half a century has elapsed during that time. Hundreds of times my duty has called me into the neighbourhood of those ruins, but never have I seen the Fiend of Klatka."

"What do you say? Whom do you call by that name?" inquired Franziska, whose love of adventure and romance was strongly awakened.

"Why, people call by that name the ghost or spirit who is supposed to haunt the ruins," replied the steward. "They say he only shows himself on moon-light nights—"

"That is quite natural," interrupted Franz smiling. "Ghosts can never bear the light of day; and if the moon did not shine, how could the ghost be seen, for it is not supposed that any one for a mere freak would visit the ruins by torch-light."

"There are some credulous people who pretend to have seen this ghost," continued the steward. "Huntsmen and woodcutters say they have met him by the large oak on the crosspath. That, noble sir, is supposed to be the spot he inclines most to haunt, for the tree was planted in remembrance of the man who fell there."

"And who was he?" asked Franziska with increasing curiosity.

"The last owner of the castle, which at that time was a sort of robbers' den, and the headquarters of all depredators in the neighbourhood," answered the old man. "They say this man was of superhuman strength, and was feared not only on account of his passionate temper, but of his treaties with the Turkish hordes. Any young woman, too, in the neighbourhood to whom he took a fancy, was carried off to his tower and never heard of more. When the measure of his iniquity was full, the whole neighbourhood rose in a mass, besieged his stronghold, and at length he was slain on the spot where the huge oak-tree now stands."

"I wonder they did not burn the whole castle, so as to erase the very memory of it," said the knight.

"It was a dependency of the church, and that saved it," replied the other. "Your great-grandfather afterwards took possession of it, for it had fine lands attached. As the Knight of Klatka was of good family, a monument was erected to him in the church, which now lies as much in ruin as the castle itself."

"Oh, let us set off at once! Nothing shall prevent my visiting so interesting a spot," said Franziska eagerly. "The imprisoned damsels who never reappeared, the storming of the tower, the death of the knight, the nightly wanderings of his spirit round the old oak, and lastly, our own adventure, all draw me thither with an indescribable curiosity."

When a servant announced that the horses were at the door, the young girls tripped laughingly down the steps which led to the coachyard. Franz, the knight, and a servant well acquainted with the country followed; and in a few minutes the party was on the road to the forest.

The sun was still high in the heavens when they saw the towers of Klatka rising above the trees. Everything in the wood was still except the cheerful twitterings of the birds as they hopped about amongst the bursting buds and leaves and announced that spring had arrived.

The party soon found themselves near the old oak at the bottom of the hill on which stood the towers, still imposing in their ruin. Ivy and bramble bushes had wound themselves over the walls, and forced their deep roots so firmly between the stones that they in a great measure held these together. On the top of the highest spot a small bush in its young fresh verdure swayed lightly in the breeze.

The gentlemen assisted their companions to alight, and leaving the horses to the care of the servant, ascended the hill to the castle. After having explored this in every nook and cranny, and spent much time in a vain search for some trace of the extraordinary stranger whom Franziska declared she was determined to discover, they proceeded to an inspection of the adjoining church. This they found to have better withstood the ravages of time and weather; the nave, indeed, was in complete dilapidation, but the chancel and altar were still under roof, as well as a sort of chapel which appeared to have been a place of honour for the families of the old knights of the castle. Few traces remained, however, of the magnificent painted glass which must once have adorned the windows, and the wind entered at pleasure through the open spaces.

The party were occupied for some time in deciphering the inscriptions on a number of tombstones, and on the walls, principally within the chancel. They were generally memorials of the ancient lords, with figures of men in armour, and women and children of all ages. A flying raven and various other devices were placed at the corners. One gravestone, which stood close to the entrance of the chancel, differed widely from the others: there was no figure sculptured on it, and the inscription, which on all besides was a mere mass of flattering eulogies, was here simple and unadorned; it contained only these words: "Ezzelin von Klatka fell like a knight at the storming of the castle"—on such a day and year,

"That must be the monument of the knight whose ghost is said to haunt these ruins," cried Franziska eagerly. "What a pity he is not represented in the same way as the others—I should so like to have known what he was like!"

"Oh, there is the family vault, with steps leading down to it, and the sun is lighting it up through a crevice," said Franz, stepping from the adjoining vestry.

The whole party followed him down the eight or nine steps which led to a tolerably airy chamber, where were placed a number of coffins of all sizes, some of them crumbling into dust. Here, again, one close to the door was distinguished from the others by the simplicity of its design, the freshness of its appearance, and the brief inscription: "Ezzelinus de Klatka, Eques."

As not the slightest effluvium was perceptible, they lingered some time in the vault; and when they reascended to the church, they had a long talk over the old possessors, of whom the knight now remembered he had heard his parents speak. The sun had disappeared, and the moon was just rising as the explorers turned to leave the ruins. Bertha had made a step into the nave, when she uttered a slight exclamation of fear and surprise. Her eyes fell on a man who wore a hat with drooping feathers, a sword at his side, and a short cloak of somewhat old-fashioned cut over his shoulders. The stranger leaned carelessly on a broken column at the entrance; he did not appear to take any notice of the party; and the moon shone full on his pale face.

The party advanced towards the stranger.

"If I am not mistaken," commenced the knight; "we have met before."

Not a word from the unknown.

"You released us in an almost miraculous manner," said Franziska, "from the power of those dreadful wolves. Am I wrong in supposing it is to you we are indebted for that great service?"

"The beasts are afraid of me," replied the stranger in a deep fierce tone, while he fastened his sunken eyes on the girl, without taking any notice of the others.

"Then you are probably a huntsman," said Franz, "and wage war against the fierce brutes."

"Who is not either the pursuer or the pursued? All persecute or are persecuted, and Fate persecutes all," replied the stranger without looking at him.

"Do you live in these ruins?" asked the knight hesitatingly.

"Yes; but not to the destruction of your game, as you may fear, Knight of Fahnenberg," said the unknown contemptuously. "Be quite assured of this; your property shall remain untouched—"

"Oh! my father did not mean that," interrupted Franziska, who appeared to take the liveliest interest in the stranger. "Unfortunate events and sad experiences have, no doubt, induced you to take up your abode in these ruins, of which my father would by no means dispossess you."

"Your father is very good, if that is what he meant," said the stranger in his former tone;

and it seemed as though his dark features were drawn into a slight smile; "but people of my sort are rather difficult to turn out."

"You must live very uncomfortably here," said Franziska, half vexed, for she thought her polite speech had deserved a better reply.

"My dwelling is not exactly uncomfortable, only somewhat small—still quite suitable for quiet people," said the unknown with a kind of sneer. "I am not, however, always quiet; I sometimes pine to quit the narrow space, and then I dash away through forest and field, over hill and dale; and the time when I must return to my little dwelling always comes too soon for me."

"As you now and then leave your dwelling," said the knight, "I would invite you to visit us, if I knew—"

"That I was in a station to admit of your doing so," interrupted the other; and the knight started slightly, for the stranger had exactly expressed the half-formed thought. "I lament," he continued coldly, "that I am not able to give you particulars on this point—some difficulties stand in the way: be assured, however, that I am a knight, and of at least as ancient a family as yourself."

"Then you must not refuse our request," cried Franziska, highly interested in the strange manners of the unknown. "You must come and visit us."

"I am no boon-companion, and on that account few have invited me of late," replied the other with his peculiar smile; "besides, I generally remain at home during the day; that is my time for rest. I belong, you must know, to that class of persons who turn day into night, and night into day, and who love everything uncommon and peculiar."

"Really? So do I! And for that reason, you must visit us," cried Franziska. "Now," she continued smiling, "I suppose you have just risen, and you are taking your morning airing. Well, since the moon is your sun, pray pay a frequent visit to our castle by the light of its rays. I think we shall agree very well, and that it will be very nice for us to be acquainted."

"You wish it?—You press the invitation?" asked the stranger earnestly and decidedly.

"To be sure, for otherwise you will not come," replied the young lady shortly.

"Well, then, come I will!" said the other, again fixing his gaze on her. "If my company does not please you at any time, you will have yourself to blame for an acquaintance with one who seldom forces himself, but is difficult to shake off."

When the unknown had concluded these words he made a slight motion with his hand, as though to take leave of them, and passing under the doorway, disappeared among the ruins. The party soon after mounted their horses and took the road home.

It was evening of the following day, and all were again seated in the hall of the castle. Bertha had that day received good news. The knight Woislaw had written from Hungary that the war with the Turks would soon be brought to a conclusion during the year, and that although he had intended returning to Silesia, hearing of the Knight of Fahnenberg having gone to take possession of his new estates, he should follow the family there, not doubting that Bertha had accompanied her friend. He hinted that he stood so high in the opinion of his duke on account of his valuable services, that in future his duties would be even more important and extensive; but before settling down to them, he should come and claim Bertha's promise to become his wife. He had been much enriched by his master, as well as by booty taken from the Turks. Having formerly lost his right hand in the duke's service, he had essayed to fight with his left; but this did not succeed very admirably, and so he had an iron one made by a very clever artist. This hand performed many of the functions of a natural one, but there had been still much wanting; now, however, his master had presented him with one of gold, an extraordinary work of art, produced by a celebrated Italian mechanic. The knight described it as something marvellous, especially as to the superhuman strength with which it enabled him to use the sword and lance. Franziska naturally rejoiced in the happiness of her friend, who had had no news of her betrothed for a long time before. She launched out every now and then, partly to plague Franz, and partly to express her own feelings, in the highest praise and admiration of the bravery and enterprise of the knight, whose adventurous qualities she lauded to the skies. Even the scar on his face and his want of a right hand were reckoned as virtues; and Franziska at last saucily declared that a rather ugly man was infinitely more attractive to her than a handsome one, for as a general rule handsome men were conceited and effeminate. Thus, she added, no one could term their acquaintance of the night before handsome, but attractive and interesting he certainly was. Franz and Bertha simultaneously denied this. His gloomy appearance, the deadly hue of his complexion, the tone of his voice, were each in turn depreciated by Bertha, while Franz found fault with the contempt and arrogance obvious in his speech. The knight stood between the two parties. He thought there was something in his bearing that spoke of good family, though much could not be said for his politeness; however, the man might have had trials enough in his life to make him misanthropical. Whilst they were conversing in this way, the door suddenly opened and the subject of their remarks himself walked in.

"Pardon me, Sir Knight," he said coldly, "that I come, if not uninvited, at least unannounced; there was no one in the ante-chamber to do me that service."

The brilliantly lighted chamber gave a full view of the stranger. He was a man of about forty, tall, and extremely thin. His features could not be termed uninteresting—there lay in them something bold and daring—but the expression was on the whole anything but benevolent. There were contempt and sarcasm in the cold grey eyes, whose glance, however, was at times so piercing that no one could endure it long. His complexion was even more peculiar than the features: it could neither be called pale nor yellow; it was a sort of grey, or, so to speak, dirty white, like that of an Indian who has been suffering long from fever; and was rendered still more remarkable by the intense blackness of his beard and short cropped hair. The dress of the unknown was knightly, but old-fashioned and neglected; there were great spots of rust on the collar and breastplate of his armour; and his dagger and the hilt of his finely worked sword were marked in some places with mildew. As the party were just going to supper, it was only natural to invite the stranger to partake of it; he complied, however, only in so far that he seated himself at the table, for he ate no morsel. The knight, with some surprise, inquired the reason.

"For a long time past I have accustomed myself never to eat at night," he replied with a strange smile. "My digestion is quite unused to solids, and indeed would scarcely confront them. I live entirely on liquids."

"Oh, then we can empty a bumper of Rhine-wine together," cried the host.

"Thanks; but I neither drink wine nor any cold beverage," replied the other; and his tone was full of mockery. It appeared as if there was some amusing association connected with the idea.

"Then I will order you a cup of hippocras"—a warm drink composed of herbs—"it shall be ready immediately," said Franziska.

"Many thanks, fair lady; not at present," replied the other. "But if I refuse the beverage you offer me now, you may be assured that as soon as I require it—perhaps very soon—I will request that, or some other of you."

Bertha and Franz thought the man had something inexpressibly repulsive in his whole manner, and they had no inclination to engage him in conversation; but the baron, thinking that perhaps politeness required him to say something, turned towards the guest, and commenced in a friendly tone: "It is now many weeks since we first became acquainted with you; we then had to thank you for a singular service—"

"And I have not yet told you my name, although you would gladly know it," interrupted the other dryly. "I am called Azzo; and as"—this he said again with his ironical smile—"with the permission of the Knight of Fahnenberg, I live at the castle of Klatka, you can in future call me Azzo von Klatka."

"I only wonder you do not feel lonely and uncomfortable amongst those old walls," began Bertha. "I cannot understand—"

"Why my business is there? Oh, about that I will willingly give you some information, since you and the young gentleman there take such a kindly interest in my person," replied the unknown in his tone of sarcasm.

Franz and Bertha both started, for he had revealed their thoughts as though he could read their souls. "You see, my lady," he continued, "there are a variety of strange whims in the world. As I have already said, I love what is peculiar and uncommon, at least what would appear so to you. It is wrong in the main to be astonished at anything, for, viewed in one light, all things are alike; even life and death, this side of the grave and the other, have more resemblance than you would imagine. You perhaps consider me rather touched a little in my mind, for taking up my abode with the bat and the owl; but if so, why not consider every hermit and recluse insane? You will tell me that those are holy men. I certainly have no pretension that way; but as they find pleasure in praying and singing psalms, so I amuse myself with hunting. Oh, away in the pale moonlight, on a horse that never tires, over hill and dale, through forest and woodland! I rush among the wolves, which fly at my approach, as you yourself perceived, as though they were puppies fearful of the lash."

"But still it must be lonely, very lonely for you," remarked Bertha.

"So it would by day; but I am then asleep," replied the stranger dryly; "at night I am merry enough."

"You hunt in an extraordinary way," remarked Franz hesitatingly.

"Yes; but, nevertheless, I have no communication with robbers, as you seem to imagine," replied Azzo coldly.

Franz again started—that very thought had just crossed his mind. "Oh, I beg your pardon; I do not know—" he stammered.

"What to make of me," interrupted the other. "You would therefore do well to believe just what I tell you, or at least to avoid making conjectures of your own, which will lead to nothing."

"I understand you: I know how to value your ideas, if no one else does," cried Franziska eagerly. "The humdrum, everyday life of the generality of men is repulsive to you; you have tasted the joys and pleasures of life, at least what are so called, and you have found them tame and hollow. How soon one tires of the things one sees all around! Life consists in change. Only in what is new, uncommon, and peculiar, do the flowers of the spirit bloom and give forth scent. Even pain may become a pleasure if it saves one from the shallow monotony of everyday life—a thing I shall hate till the hour of my death."

"Right, fair lady—quite right! Remain in this mind: this was always my opinion, and the one from which I have derived the highest reward," cried Azzo; and his fierce eyes sparkled more intensely than ever. "I am doubly pleased to have found in you a person who shares my ideas. Oh, if you were a man, you would make me a splendid companion; but even a woman may have fine experiences when once these opinions take root in her, and bring forth action!"

As Azzo spoke these words in a cold tone of politeness, he turned from the subject, and for the rest of his visit only gave the knight monosyllabic replies to his inquiries, taking leave before the table was cleared. To an invitation from the knight, backed by a still more pressing one from Franziska to repeat his visit, he replied that he would take advantage of their kindness, and come sometimes.

When the stranger had departed, many were the remarks made on his appearance and general deportment. Franz declared his most decided dislike of him. Whether it was as usual to vex her cousin, or whether Azzo had really made an impression on her, Franziska took his part vehemently. As Franz contradicted her more eagerly than usual, the young lady launched out into still stronger expressions; and there is no knowing what hard words her cousin might have received had not a servant entered the room.

The following morning Franziska lay longer than usual in bed. When her friend went to her room, fearful lest she should be ill, she found her pale and exhausted. Franziska complained she had passed a very bad night; she thought the dispute with Franz about the stranger must have excited her greatly, for she felt quite feverish and exhausted, and a strange dream, too, had worried her, which was evidently a consequence of the evening's conversation. Bertha, as usual, took the young man's part, and added that a common dispute about a man whom no one knew, and about whom anyone might form his own opinion, could not possibly have thrown her into her present state. "At least," she continued, "you can let me hear this wonderful dream."

To her surprise, Franziska for a length of time refused to do so.

"Come, tell me," inquired Bertha, "what can possibly prevent you from relating a dream—a mere dream? I might almost think it credible, if the idea were not too horrid, that poor Franz is not very far wrong when he says that the thin, corpse-like, dried-up, old-fashioned stranger has made a greater impression on you than you will allow."

"Did Franz say so?" asked Franziska. "Then you can tell him he is not mistaken. Yes, the thin, corpse-like, dried-up, whimsical stranger is far more interesting to me than the rosy-cheeked, well-dressed, polite, and prosy cousin."

"Strange," cried Bertha. "I cannot at all comprehend the almost magic influence which this man, so repulsive, exercises over you."

"Perhaps the very reason I take his part, may be that you are all so prejudiced against him," remarked Franziska pettishly. "Yes, it must be so; for that his appearance should please my eyes is what no one in his senses could imagine. But," she continued, smiling and holding out her hand to Bertha, "is it not laughable that I should get out of temper even with you about this stranger?—I can more easily understand it with Franz—and that this unknown should spoil my morning, as he has already spoiled my evening and my night's rest?"

"By that dream, you mean?" said Bertha, easily appeased, as she put her arm round her cousin's neck and kissed her. "Now, do tell it to me. You know how I delight in hearing anything of the kind."

"Well, I will, as a sort of compensation for my peevishness towards you," said the other, clasping her friend's hands. "Now, listen! I had walked up and down my room for a long time; I was excited—out of spirits—I do not know exactly what. It was almost midnight ere I lay down, but I could not sleep. I tossed about, and at length it was only from sheer exhaustion that I dropped off. But what a sleep it was! An inward fear ran through me perpetually. I saw a number of pictures before me, as I used to do in childish sicknesses. I do not know whether I was asleep or half awake. Then I dreamed, but as clearly as if I had been wide awake, that a sort of mist filled the room, and out of it stepped the knight Azzo. He gazed at me for a time, and then letting himself slowly down on one knee, imprinted a kiss on my throat. Long did his lips rest there; and I felt a slight pain, which always increased, until I could bear it no more. With all my strength I tried to force the vision from me, but succeeded only after a long struggle. No doubt I uttered a scream, for that awoke me from my trance. When I came a little to my senses I felt a sort of superstitious fear creeping over me—how great you may imagine when I tell you that, with my eyes open and awake, it appeared to me as if Azzo's figure were still by my bed, and then disappearing gradually into the mist, vanished at the door!"

"You must have dreamed very heavily, my poor friend," began Bertha, but suddenly paused. She gazed with surprise at Franziska's throat. "Why, what is that?" she cried. "Just look: how extraordinary—a red streak on your throat!"

Franziska raised herself, and went to a little glass that stood in the window. She really saw a small red line about an inch long on her neck, which began to smart when she touched it with her finger.

"I must have hurt myself by some means in my sleep," she said after a pause; "and that in some measure will account for my dream."

The friends continued chatting for some time about this singular coincidence—the dream and the stranger; and at length it was all turned into a joke by Bertha.

Several weeks passed. The knight had found the estate and affairs in greater disorder than he at first imagined; and instead of remaining three or four weeks, as was originally intended, their departure was deferred to an indefinite period. This postponement was likewise in some measure occasioned by Franziska's continued indisposition. She who had formerly bloomed like a rose in its young fresh beauty was becoming daily thinner, more sickly and exhausted, and at the same time so pale, that in the space of a month not a tinge of red was perceptible on the once glowing cheek. The knight's anxiety about her was extreme, and the best advice was procured which the age and country afforded; but all to no purpose. Franziska complained from time to time that the horrible dream with which her illness commenced was repeated, and that always on the day following she felt an increased and indescribable weakness. Bertha naturally set this down to the effects of fever, but the ravages of that fever on the usually clear reason of her friend filled her with alarm.

The knight Azzo repeated his visits every now and then. He always came in the evening, and when the moon shone brightly. His manner was always the same. He spoke in monosyllables, and was coldly polite to the knight; to Franz and Bertha, particularly to the former, contemptuous and haughty; but to Franziska, friendliness itself. Often when, after a short visit, he again left the house, his peculiarities became the subject of conversation. Besides his odd way of speaking, in which Bertha said there lay a deep hatred, a cold detestation of all mankind with the exception of Franziska, two other singularities were observable. During none of his visits, which often took place at supper-time, had he been prevailed upon to eat or drink anything, and that without giving any good reason for his abstinence. A remarkable alteration, too, had taken place in his appearance: he seemed an entirely different creature. The skin, before so shrivelled and stretched, seemed smooth and soft, while a slight tinge of red appeared in his cheeks, which began to look round and plump. Bertha, who could not at all conceal her ill-will towards him, said often, that much as she hated his face before, when it was more like a death's-head than a human being's, it was now more than ever repulsive; she always felt a shudder run through her veins whenever his sharp piercing eyes rested on her. Perhaps it was owing to Franziska's partiality, or to the knight Azzo's own contemptuous way of replying to Franz, or to his haughty way of treating him in general, that made the young man dislike him more and more. It was quite observable that whenever Franz made a remark to his cousin in the presence of Azzo, the latter would immediately throw some ill-natured light on it or distort it to a totally different meaning. This increased from day to day, and at last Franz declared to Bertha that he would stand such conduct no longer, and that it was only out of consideration for Franziska that he had not already called him to account.

At this time the party at the castle was increased by the arrival of Bertha's long-expected guest. He came just as they were sitting down to supper one evening, and all jumped up to greet their old friend. The knight Woislaw was a true model of the soldier, hardened and strengthened by war with men and elements. His face would not have been termed ugly, if a Turkish sabre had not left a mark running from the right eye to the left cheek, and standing out bright red from the sunburned skin. The frame of the Castellan of Glogau might almost be termed colossal. Few would have been able to carry his armour, and still fewer move with his lightness and ease under its weight. He did not think little of this same armour, for it had been a present from the palatine of Hungary on his leaving the camp. The blue wrought-steel was ornamented all over with patterns in gold; and he had put it on to do honour to his bride-elect, together with the wonderful gold hand, the gift of the duke.

Woislaw was questioned by the knight and Franz on all the concerns of the campaign; and he entered into the most minute particulars relating to the battles, which, with regard to plunder, had been more successful than ever. He spoke much of the strength of the Turks in a hand-to-hand fight, and remarked that he owed the duke many thanks for his splendid gift, for in consequence of its strength many of the enemy regarded him as something superhuman. The sickliness and deathlike paleness of Franziska was too perceptible not to be immediately noticed by Woislaw; accustomed to see her so fresh and cheerful, he hastened to inquire into the cause of the change. Bertha related all that had happened, and Woislaw listened with the greatest interest. This increased to the utmost at the account of the often-repeated dream, and Franziska had to give him the most minute particulars of it; it appeared as though he had met with a similar case before, or at least had heard of one. When the young lady added that it was very remarkable that the wound on her throat, which she had at first felt had never healed, and still pained her, the knight Woislaw looked at Bertha as much as to say that this last fact had greatly strengthened his idea as to the cause of Franziska's illness.

It was only natural that the discourse should next turn to the knight Azzo, about whom everyone began to talk eagerly. Woislaw inquired as minutely as he had done with regard to Franziska's illness about what concerned this stranger, from the first evening of their acquaintance down to his last visit, without, however, giving any opinion on the subject. The party were still in earnest conversation, when the door opened, and Azzo entered. Woislaw's eyes remained fixed on him, as he, without taking any particular notice of the new arrival, walked up to the table, and seating himself, directed most of the conversation to Franziska and her father, and now and then made some sarcastic remark when Franz began to speak. The Turkish war again came on the *tapis,* and though Azzo only put in an occasional remark, Woislaw had much to say on the subject. Thus they had advanced late into the night, and Franz said smiling to Woislaw: "I should not wonder if day had surprised us, whilst listening to your entertaining adventures."

"I admire the young gentleman's taste," said Azzo, with an ironical curl of the lip. "Stories of storm and shipwreck are, indeed, best heard on *terra firma,* and those of battle and death at a hospitable table or in the chimney-corner. One has then the comfortable feeling of keeping a whole skin, and being in no danger, not even of taking cold." With the last words, he gave a hoarse laugh, and turning his back on Franz, rose, bowed to the rest of the company, and left the room. The knight, who always accompanied Azzo to the door, now expressed himself fatigued, and bade his friends good night.

"That Azzo's impertinence is unbearable," cried Bertha when he was gone. "He becomes daily more rough, unpolite, and presuming. If only on account of Franziska's dream, though of course he cannot help that, I detest him. Now, tonight, not one civil word has he spoken to anyone but Franziska, except, perhaps, some casual remark to my uncle."

"I cannot deny that you are right, Bertha," said her cousin. "One may forgive much to a man whom fate had probably made somewhat misanthropical; but he should not overstep the bounds of common politeness. But where on earth is Franz?" added Franziska, as she looked uneasily round. The young him had quietly left the room whilst Bertha was speaking.

"He cannot have followed the knight Azzo to challenge him?" cried Bertha in alarm.

"It were better he entered a lion's den to pull his mane!" said Woislaw vehemently. "I must follow him instantly," he added, as he rushed from the room.

He hastened over the threshold, out of the castle, and through the court before he came up to them. Here a narrow bridge with a slight balustrade passed over the moat by which the castle was surrounded. It appeared that Franz had only just addressed Azzo in a few hot words, for as Woislaw, unperceived by either, advanced under the shadow of the wall, Azzo said gloomily: "Leave me, foolish boy—leave me; for by that sun"—and he pointed to the full moon above them—"you will see those rays no more if you linger another moment on my path."

"And I tell you, wretch, that you either give me satisfaction for your repeated insolence, or you die," cried Franz, drawing his sword.

Azzo stretched forth his hand, and grasping the sword in the middle, it snapped like a broken reed. "I warn you for the last time," he said in a voice of thunder as he threw the pieces into the moat. "Now, away—away, boy, from my path, or, by those below us, you are lost!"

"You or I! you or I!" cried Franz madly as he made a rush at the sword of his antagonist and strove to draw if from his side. Azzo replied not; only a bitter laugh half escaped from his lips; then seizing Franz by the chest, he lifted him up like an infant, and was in the act of throwing him over the bridge when Woislaw stepped to his side. With a grasp of his wonderful hand, into the springs of which he threw all his strength, he seized Azzo's arm, pulled it down, and obliged him to drop his victim. Azzo seemed in the highest degree astonished. Without concerning himself further about Franz, he gazed in amazement on Woislaw.

"Who art thou who darest to rob me of my prey?" he asked hesitatingly. "Is it possible? Can you be—"

"Ask not, thou bloody one! Go, seek thy nourishment! Soon comes thy hour!" replied Woislaw in a calm but firm tone.

"Ha, now I know!" cried Azzo eagerly. "Welcome, blood-brother! I give up to you this worm, and for your sake will not crush him. Farewell; our paths will soon meet again."

"Soon, very soon; farewell!" cried Woislaw, drawing Franz towards him. Azzo rushed away and disappeared.

Franz had remained for some moments in a state of stupefaction, but suddenly started as from a dream. "I am dishonoured, dishonoured forever!" he cried, as he pressed his clenched hands to his forehead.

"Calm yourself; you could not have conquered," said Woislaw.

"But I will conquer, or perish!" cried Franz incensed. "I will seek this adventurer in his den, and he or I must fall."

"You could not hurt him," said Woislaw. "You would infallibly be the victim."

"Then show me a way to bring the wretch to judgment," cried Franz, seizing Woislaw's hands, while tears of anger sprang to his eyes. "Disgraced as I am, I cannot live."

"You shall be revenged, and that within twenty-four hours, I hope; but only on two conditions—"

"I agree to them! I will do anything—" began the young man eagerly.

"The first is, that you do nothing, but leave everything in my hands," interrupted Woislaw. "The second, that you will assist me in persuading Franziska to do what I shall represent to her as absolutely necessary. That young lady's life is in more danger from Azzo than your own."

"How? What?" cried Franz fiercely. "Franziska's life in danger! And from that man? Tell me. Woislaw, who is this fiend?"

"Not a word will I tell either the young lady or you, until the danger is passed," said Woislaw firmly. "The smallest indiscretion would ruin everything. No one can act here but Franziska herself, and if she refuses to do so she is irretrievably lost."

"Speak, and I will help you. I will do all you wish, but I must know—"

"Nothing, absolutely nothing," replied Woislaw. "I must have both you and Franziska yield to me unconditionally. Come now, come to her. You are to be mute on what has passed, and use every effort to induce her to accede to my proposal."

Woislaw spoke firmly, and it was impossible for Franz to make any further objection; in a few moments they both entered the hall, where they found the young girls still anxiously awaiting them.

"Oh, I have been so frightened," said Franziska, even paler than usual, as she held out her hand to Franz. "I trust all has ended peaceably."

"Everything is arranged; a couple of words were sufficient to settle the whole affair," said Woislaw cheerfully. "But Master Franz was less concerned in it than yourself, fair lady."

"I! How do you mean?" said Franziska in surprise.

"I allude to your illness," replied the other.

"And you spoke of that to Azzo? Does he, then, know a remedy which he could not tell me himself?" she inquired, smiling painfully.

"The knight Azzo must take part in your cure; but speak to you about it he cannot, unless the remedy is to lose all its efficacy," replied Woislaw quietly.

"So it is some secret elixir, as the learned doctors who have so long attended me say, and through whose means I only grow worse," said Franziska mournfully.

"It is certainly a secret, but is as certainly a cure," replied Woislaw.

"So said all, but none has succeeded," said the young lady peevishly.

"You might at least try it," began Bertha.

"Because your friend proposes it," said the other smiling. "I have no doubt that you, with nothing ailing you, would take all manner of drugs to please your knight; but with me the inducement is wanting, and therefore also the faith."

"I did not speak of any medicine," said Woislaw.

"Oh! a magical remedy! I am to be cured—what was it the quack who was here the other day called it?—'by sympathy.' Yes, that was it."

"I do not object to your calling it so, if you like," said Woislaw smiling; "but you must know, dear lady, that the measures I shall propose must be attended to literally, and according to the strictest directions."

"And you trust this to me?" asked Franziska.

"Certainly," said Woislaw hesitating; "but—"

"Well, why do you not proceed? Can you think that I shall fail in courage?" she asked.

"Courage is certainly necessary for the success of my plan," said Woislaw gravely; "and it is because I give you credit for a large share of that virtue, I venture to propose it at all, although for the real harmlessness of the remedy I will answer with my life, provided you follow my directions exactly."

"Well, tell me the plan, and then I can decide," said the young lady.

"I can only tell you that when we commence our operations," replied Woislaw.

"Do you think I am a child to be sent here, there, and everywhere, without a reason?" asked Franziska, with something of her old pettishness.

"You did me great injustice, dear lady, if you thought for a moment I would propose anything disagreeable to you, unless demanded by the sternest necessity," said Woislaw; "and yet I can only repeat my former words."

"Then I will not do it," cried Franziska. "I have already tried so much—and all ineffectually."

"I give you my honour as a knight, that your cure is certain, but you must pledge yourself solemnly and unconditionally to do implicitly what I shall direct," said Woislaw earnestly.

"Oh, I implore you to consent, Franziska. Our friend would not propose anything unnecessary," said Bertha, taking both her cousin's hands.

"And let me join my entreaties to Bertha's," said Franz.

"How strange you all are!" exclaimed Franziska, shaking her head; "You make such a secret of that which I must know if I am to accomplish it, and then you declare so positively that I shall recover, when my own feelings tell me it is quite hopeless."

"I repeat, that I will answer for the result," said Woislaw, "on the condition I mentioned before, and that you have courage to carry out what you commence."

"Ha! now I understand; this, after all, is the only thing which appears doubtful to you," cried Franziska. "Well, to show you that our sex are neither wanting in the will nor in the power to accomplish deeds of daring, I give my consent."

With the last words, she offered Woislaw her hand.

"Our compact is thus sealed," she pursued smiling. "Now say, Sir Knight, how am I to commence this mysterious cure?"

"It commenced when you gave your consent," said Woislaw gravely. "Now, I have only to request that you will ask no more questions, but hold yourself in readiness to take a ride with me tomorrow an hour before sunset. I also request that you will not mention to your father a word of what has passed."

"Strange!" said Franziska.

"You have made the compact; you are not wanting in resolution; and I will answer for everything else," said Woislaw encouragingly.

"Well, so let it be. I will follow your directions," said the lady, although she still looked incredulous.

"On our return you shall know everything; before that, it is quite impossible," said Woislaw in conclusion. "Now go, dear lady, and take some rest; you will need strength for tomorrow."

It was on the morning of the following day; the sun had not risen above an hour, and the dew still lay like a veil of pearls on the grass or dripped from the petals of the flowers swaying in the early breeze, when the knight Woislaw hastened over the fields towards the forest, and turned into a gloomy path, which by the direction one could perceive led towards the towers of Klatka. When he arrived at the old oak-tree we have before had occasion to mention, he sought carefully along the road for traces of human footsteps, but only a deer had passed that way. Seemingly satisfied with his search, he proceeded on his way, though not before he had half drawn his dagger from its sheath, as though to assure himself that it was ready for service in time of need.

Slowly he ascended the path; it was evident he carried something beneath his cloak. Arrived in the court, he left the ruins of the castle to the left, and entered the old chapel. In the chancel he looked eagerly and earnestly around. A deathlike stillness reigned in the deserted sanctuary, only broken by the whispering of the wind in an old thorn-tree which grew outside. Woislaw had looked round him ere he perceived the door leading down to the vault; he hurried towards it and descended. The sun's position enabled its rays to penetrate the crevices, and made the subterranean chamber so light that one could read easily the inscriptions at the head and feet of the coffins. The knight first laid on the ground the packet he had hitherto carried under his cloak, and then going from coffin to coffin, at last remained stationary before the oldest of them. He read the inscription carefully, drew his dagger thoughtfully from its case, and endeavoured to raise the lid with its point. This was no difficult matter, for the rusty iron nails kept but a slight hold of the rotten wood. On looking in, only a heap of ashes, some remnants of dress, and a skull were the contents. He quickly closed it again, and went on to the next, passing over those of a woman and two children. Here things had much the same appearance, except that the corpse held together till the lid was raised, and then fell into dust, a few linen rags and bones being alone perceptible. In the third, fourth, and nearly the next half-dozen, the bodies were in better preservation: in some, they looked a sort of yellow-brown mummy; whilst in others a skinless skull covered with hair grinned from the coverings of velvet, silk, or mildewed embroideries; all, however, were touched with the loathsome marks of decay. Only one more coffin now remained to be inspected; Woislaw approached it, and read the inscription. It was the same that had before attracted the Knight of Fahnenberg: Ezzelin von Klatka, the last possessor of the tower, was described as lying therein. Woislaw found it more difficult to raise the lid here; and it was only by the exertion of much strength that he at length succeeded in extracting the nails. He did all, however, as quietly as if afraid of rousing some sleeper within; he then raised the cover, and cast a glance on the corpse. An involuntary "Ha!" burst from his lips as he stepped back a pace. If he had less expected the sight that met his eyes, he would have been far more overcome. In the coffin lay Azzo as he lived and breathed, and as Woislaw had seen him at the supper-table only the evening before. His appearance, dress, and all were the same; besides, he had more the semblance of sleep than of death—no trace of decay was visible—there was even a rosy tint on his cheeks. Only the circumstance that the breast did not heave distinguished him from one who slept. For a few moments Woislaw did not move; he could only stare into the coffin. With a hastiness in his movements not usual with him, he suddenly seized the lid, which had fallen from his hands, and laying it on the coffin, knocked the nails into their places. As soon as he had completed this work, he fetched the packet he had left at the entrance, and laying it on the top of the coffin, hastily ascended the steps, and quitted the church and the ruins.

The day passed. Before evening, Franziska requested her father to allow her to take a ride with Woislaw, under pretense of showing him the country. He, only too happy to think this a sign of amendment in his daughter, readily gave his consent; so followed by a single servant, they mounted and left the castle. Woislaw was unusually silent and serious. When Franziska began to rally him about his gravity and the approaching sympathetic cure, he replied that what was before her was no laughing matter; and that although the result would be certainly a cure, still it would leave an impression on her whole future life. In such discourse they reached the wood, and at length the oak, where they left their horses. Woislaw gave Franziska his arm, and they ascended the hill slowly and silently. They had just reached one of the half-dilapidated outworks where they could catch a glimpse of the open country, when Woislaw, speaking more to himself than to his companion, said: "In a quarter of an hour, the sun will set, and in another hour the moon will have risen; then all must be accomplished. It will soon be time to commence the work."

"Then, I should think it was time to entrust me with some idea of what it is," said Franziska, looking at him.

"Well, my lady," he replied, turning towards her, and his voice was very solemn, "I entreat you, Franziska von Fahnenberg, for your own good, and as you love the father who clings to you with his whole soul, that you will weigh well my words, and that you will not interrupt me with questions which I cannot answer until the work is completed. Your life is in the greatest danger from the illness under which you are laboring; indeed, you are irrecoverably lost if you do not fully carry out what I shall now impart to you. Now, promise me to do implicitly as I shall tell you; I pledge you my knightly word it is nothing against Heaven, or the honour of your house; and, besides, it is the sole means for saving you." With these words, he held out his right hand to his companion, while he raised the other to heaven in confirmation of his oath.

"I promise you," said Franziska, visibly moved by Woislaw's solemn tone, as she laid her little white and wasted hand in his.

"Then, come; it is time," was his reply, as he led her towards the church. The last rays of the sun were just pouring through the broken windows. They entered the chancel, the best preserved part of the whole building; here there were still some old kneeling-stools, placed before the high altar, although nothing remained of that but the stonework and a few steps; the pictures and decorations had all vanished.

"Say an *Ave;* you will have need of it," said Woislaw, as he himself fell on his knees.

Franziska knelt beside him, and repeated a short prayer. After a few moments, both rose.

"The moment has arrived! The sun sinks, and before the moon rises, all must be over," said Woislaw quickly.

"What am I to do?" asked Franziska cheerfully.

"You see there that open vault!" replied the knight Woislaw, pointing to the door and flight of steps; "You must descend. You must go alone; I may not accompany you. When you have reached the vault you will find, close to the entrance, a coffin, on which is placed a small packet. Open this packet, and you will find three long iron nails and a hammer. Then pause for a moment; but when I begin to repeat the *Credo* in a loud voice, knock with all your might, first one nail, then a second, and then a third, into the lid of the coffin, right up to their heads."

Franziska stood thunderstruck; her whole body trembled, and she could not utter a word. Woislaw perceived it.

"Take courage, dear lady!" said he. "Think that you are in the hands of Heaven, and that, without the will of your Creator, not a hair can fall from your head. Besides, I repeat, there is no danger."

"Well, then, I will do it," cried Franziska, in some measure regaining courage.

"Whatever you may hear, whatever takes place inside the coffin," continued Woislaw, "must have no effect upon you. Drive the nails well in, without flinching: your work must be finished before my prayer comes to an end."

Franziska shuddered, but again recovered herself. "I will do it; Heaven will send me strength," she murmured softly.

"There is one thing more," said Woislaw hesitatingly; "perhaps it is the hardest of all I have proposed, but without it your cure will not be complete. When you have done as I have told you, a sort of"—he hesitated—"a sort of liquid will flow from the coffin; in this dip your finger, and besmear the scratch on your throat."

"Horrible!" cried Franziska. "This liquid is blood. A human being lies in the coffin."

"An *unearthly* one lies therein! That blood is your own, but it flows in other veins," said Woislaw gloomily. "Ask no more; the sand is running out."

Franziska summoned up all her powers of mind and body, went towards the step which led to the vault, and Woislaw sank on his knees before the altar in quiet prayer. When the lady had descended, she found herself before the coffin on which lay the packet before mentioned. A sort of twilight reigned in the vault, and everything around was so still and peaceful, that she felt more calm, and going up to the coffin opened the packet. She had hardly seen that a hammer and three long nails were its contents when suddenly Woislaw's voice rang through the church, and broke the stillness of the aisles.

Franziska started, but recognized the appointed prayer. She seized one of the nails, and with one stroke of the hammer drove it at least an inch into the cover. All was still; nothing was heard but the echo of the stroke. Taking heart, the maiden grasped the hammer with both hands, and struck the nail twice with all her might, right up to the head into the wood. At this moment commenced a rustling noise; it seemed as though something in the interior began to move and to struggle. Franziska drew back in alarm. She was already on the point of throwing away the hammer and flying up the steps, when Woislaw raised his voice so powerfully, and so entreatingly, that in a sort of excitement, such as would induce one to rush into a lion's den, she returned to the coffin, determined to bring things to a conclusion. Hardly knowing what she did, she placed a second nail in the centre of the lid, and after some strokes this was likewise buried to its head. The struggle now increased fearfully, as if some living creature were striving to burst the coffin. This was so shaken by it, that it cracked and split on all sides. Half distracted, Franziska seized the third nail; she thought no more of her ailments, she only knew herself to be in terrible danger, of what kind she could not guess: in an agony that threatened to rob her of her senses and in the midst of the turning and cracking of the coffin, in which low groans were now heard, she struck the third nail in equally tight. At this moment, she began to lose consciousness. She wished to hasten away, but staggered; and mechanically grasping at something to save herself by, seized the corner of the coffin, and sank fainting beside it on the ground.

A quarter of an hour might have elapsed when she again opened her eyes. She looked around her. Above was the starry sky, and the moon, which shed her cold light on the ruins and on the tops of the old oak-trees. Franziska was lying outside the church walls, Woislaw on his knees beside her, holding her hand in his.

"Heaven be praised that you live!" he cried, with a sigh of relief. "I was beginning to doubt whether the remedy had not been too severe, and yet it was the only thing to save you."

Franziska recovered her full consciousness very gradually. The past seemed to her like a dreadful dream. Only a few moments before, that fearful scene; and now this quiet all around her. She hardly dared at first to raise her eyes, and shuddered when she found herself only a few paces removed from the spot where she had undergone such terrible agony. She listened half unconsciously, now to the pacifying words Woislaw addressed to her, now to the whistling of the servant, who stood by the horses, and who, to while away his time, was imitating the evening-song of a belated cowherd.

"Let us go," whispered Franziska, as she strove to raise herself. "But what is this? My shoulder is wet, my throat, my hand—"

"It is probably the evening dew on the grass," said Woislaw gently.

"No; it is blood!" she cried, springing up with horror in her tone. "See, my hand is full of blood!"

"Oh, you are mistaken—surely mistaken," said Woislaw, stammering. "Or perhaps the wound on your neck may have opened! Pray, feel whether this is the case." He seized her hand and directed it to the spot.

"I do not perceive anything; I feel no pain," she said at length, somewhat angrily.

"Then, perhaps, when you fainted you may have struck a corner of the coffin, or have torn yourself with the point of one of the nails," suggested Woislaw.

"Oh, of what do you remind me!" cried Franziska shuddering. "Let us away—away! I entreat you, come! I will not remain a moment longer near this dreadful, dreadful place."

They descended the path much quicker than they came. Woislaw placed his companion on her horse, and they were soon on their way home.

When they approached the castle, Franziska began to inundate her protector with questions about the preceding adventure; but he declared that her present state of excitement must make him defer all explanations till the morning, when her curiosity should be satisfied. On their arrival, he conducted her at once to her room, and told the knight his daughter was too much fatigued with her ride to appear at the supper-table. On the following morning, Franziska rose earlier than she had done for a long time. She assured her friend it was the first time since her illness commenced that she had been really refreshed by her sleep, and, what was still more remarkable, she had not been troubled by her old terrible dream. Her improved looks were not only remarked by Bertha, but by Franz and the knight; and with Woislaw's permission, she related the adventures of the previous evening. No sooner had she concluded, than Woislaw was completely stormed with questions about such a strange occurrence.

"Have you," said the latter, turning towards his host, "ever heard of Vampires?"

"Often," replied he; "but I have never believed in them."

"Nor did I," said Woislaw; "but I have been assured of their existence by experience."

"Oh, tell us what occurred," cried Bertha eagerly, as a light seemed to dawn on her.

"It was during my first campaign in Hungary," began Woislaw, "when I was rendered helpless for some time by this sword-cut of a janizary across my face, and another on my shoulder. I had been taken into the house of a respectable family in a small town. It consisted of the father and mother, and a daughter about twenty years of age. They obtained their living by selling the very good wine of the country, and the taproom was always full of visitors. Although the family were well-to-do in the world, there seemed to brood over them a continual melancholy, caused by the constant illness of the only daughter, a very pretty and excellent girl. She had always bloomed like a rose, but for some months she had been getting so thin and wasted, and that without any satisfactory reason: they tried every means to restore her, but in vain. As the army had encamped quite in the neighbourhood, of course a number of people of all countries assembled in the tavern. Amongst these there was one man who came every evening, when the moon shone, who struck everybody by the peculiarity of his manners and appearance; he looked dried up and deathlike, and hardly spoke at all; but what he did say was bitter and sarcastic. Most attention was excited towards him by the circumstance, that although he always ordered a cup of the best wine, and now and then raised it to his lips, the cup was always as full after his departure as at first."

"This all agrees wonderfully with the appearance of Azzo," said Bertha, deeply interested.

"The daughter of the house," continued Woislaw, "became daily worse, despite the aid not only of Christian doctors, but of many amongst the heathen prisoners, who were consulted in the hope that they might have some magical remedy to propose. It was singular that the girl always complained of a dream, in which the unknown guest worried and plagued her."

"Just the same as your dream, Franziska," cried Bertha.

"One evening," resumed Woislaw, "an old Sclavonian—who had made many voyages to Turkey and Greece, and had even seen the New World—and I were sitting over our wine, when the stranger entered, and sat down at the table. The bottle passed quickly between my friend and me, whilst we talked of all manner of things, of our adventures, and of passages in our lives, both horrible and amusing. We went on chatting thus for about an hour, and drank a tolerable quantity of wine. The unknown had remained perfectly silent the whole time, only smiling contemptuously every now and then. He now paid his money, and was going away. All this had quietly worried me—perhaps the wine had gotten a little into my head—so I said to the stranger: 'Hold, you stony stranger; you have hitherto done nothing but listen, and have not even emptied your cup. Now you shall take your turn in telling us something amusing, and if you do not drink up your wine, it shall produce a quarrel between us.' 'Yes,' said the Sclavonian, 'you must remain; you shall chat and drink, too'; and he grasped—for although no longer young, he was big and very strong—the stranger by the shoulder, to pull him down to his seat again: the latter, however, although as thin as a skeleton, with one movement of his hand flung the Sclavonian to the middle of the room, and half stunned him for a moment. I now approached to hold the stranger back. I caught him by the arm; and although the springs of my iron hand were less powerful than those I have at present, I must have gripped him rather hard in my anger, for after looking grimly at me for a moment, he bent towards me and whispered in my ear: 'Let me go: from the grip of your fist, I see you are my brother, therefore do not hinder me from seeking my bloody nourishment. I am hungry!' Surprised by such words, I let him loose, and almost before I was aware of it, he had left the room. As soon as I had in some degree recovered from my astonishment, I told the Sclavonian what I had heard. He started, evidently alarmed. I asked him to tell me the cause of his fears, and pressed him for an explanation of those extraordinary words. On our way to his lodging, he complied with my request. 'The stranger,' said he, 'is a Vampire!'"

"How?" cried the knight, Franziska, and Bertha simultaneously, in a voice of horror. "So this Azzo was—"

"Nothing less. He also was a Vampire!" replied Woislaw. "But at all events *his* hellish thirst is quenched for ever; he will never return. But I have not finished. As in my country Vampires had never been heard of, I questioned the Sclavonian minutely. He said that in Hungary, Croatia, Dalmatia, and Bosnia, these hellish guests were not uncommon. They were deceased persons, who had either once served as nourishment to Vampires, or who had died in deadly sin, or under excommunication; and that whenever the moon shone, they rose from their graves, and sucked the blood of the living."

"Horrible!" cried Franziska. "If you had told me all this beforehand, I should never have accomplished the work."

"So I thought; and yet it must be executed by the sufferers themselves, while someone else performs the devotions," replied Woislaw. "The Sclavonian," he continued after a short pause, "added many other facts with regard to these unearthly visitants. He said that whilst their victim wasted, they themselves improved in appearance, and that a Vampire possessed enormous strength—"

"Now I can understand the change your false hand produced on Azzo," interrupted Franz.

"Yes, that was it," replied Woislaw. "Azzo, as well as the other Vampire, mistook its great power for that of a natural one, and concluded I was one of his own species. You may now imagine, dear lady," he continued, turning to Franziska, "how alarmed I was at your appearance when I arrived: all you and Bertha told me increased my anxiety; and when I saw Azzo, I could doubt no longer that he was a Vampire. As I learned from your account that a grave with the name Ezzelin von Klatka lay in the neighbourhood, I had no doubt that you might be saved if I could only induce you to assist me. It did not appear to me advisable to impart the whole facts of the case, for your bodily powers were so impaired, that an idea of the horrors before you might have quite unfitted you for the exertion; for this reason, I arranged everything in the manner in which it has taken place."

"You did wisely," replied Franziska shuddering. "I can never be grateful enough to you. Had I known what was required of me, I never could have undertaken the deed."

"That was what I feared," said Woislaw; "but fortune has favored us all through."

"And what became of the unfortunate girl in Hungary?" inquired Bertha.

"I know not," replied Woislaw. "That very evening there was an alarm of Turks, and we were ordered off. I never heard anything more of her."

The conversation upon these strange occurrences continued for some time longer. The knight determined to have the vault at Klatka walled up for ever. This took place on the following day; the knight alleging as a reason that he did not wish the dead to be disturbed by irreverent hands.

Franziska recovered gradually. Her health had been so severely shaken, that it was long ere her strength was so much restored as to allow of her being considered out of danger. The young lady's character underwent a great change in the interval. Its former strength was, perhaps, in some degree diminished, but in place of that, she had acquired a benevolent softness, which brought out all her best qualities. Franz continued his attentions to his cousin; but, perhaps owing to a hint from Bertha, he was less assiduous in his exhibition of them. His inclinations did not lead him to the battle, the camp, or the attainment of honours; his great aim was to increase the good condition and happiness of his tenants; and to this he contributed the whole energy of his mind. Franziska could not withstand the unobtrusive signs of the young man's continued attachment; and it was not long ere the credit she was obliged to yield to his noble efforts for the welfare of his fellow-creatures, changed into a liking, which went on increasing, until at length it assumed the character of love. As Woislaw insisted on making Bertha his wife before he returned to Silesia, it was arranged that the marriage should take place at their present abode. How joyful was the surprise of the Knight of Fahnenberg, when his daughter and Franz likewise entreated his blessing, and expressed their desire of being united on the same day! That day soon came round, and it saw the bright looks of two happy couples.

Good Lady Ducayne (1896)

Mary Elizabeth Braddon

Like most Victorian authors, Braddon did not hesitate to produce melodramatic and thrilling "sensation" stories when they were in demand, and "Good Lady Ducayne," first published in *The Strand Magazine* for February 1896, is one of her best.

I

BELLA ROLLESTON HAD MADE up her mind that her only chance of earning her bread and helping her mother to an occasional crust was by going out into the great unknown world as companion to a lady. She was willing to go to any lady rich enough to pay her a salary and so eccentric as to wish for a hired companion. Five shillings told off reluctantly from one of those sovereigns which were so rare with the mother and daughter, and which melted away so quickly, five solid shillings, had been handed to a smartly-dressed lady in an office in Harbeck Street, London, W., in the hope that this very Superior Person would find a situation and a salary for Miss Rolleston. The Superior Person glanced at the two half-crowns as they lay on the table where Bella's hand had placed them, to make sure they were neither of them florins, before she wrote a description of Bella's qualifications and requirements in a formidable-looking ledger.

"Age?" she asked, curtly.

"Eighteen, last July."

"Any accomplishments?"

"No; I am not at all accomplished. If I were I should want to be a governess—a companion seems the lowest stage."

"We have some highly accomplished ladies on our books as companions, or chaperon companions."

"Oh, I know!" babbled Bella, loquacious in her youthful candor. "But that is quite a different thing. Mother hasn't been able to afford a piano since I was twelve years old, so I'm afraid I've forgotten how to play. And I have had to help mother with her needlework, so there hasn't been much time to study."

"Please don't waste time upon explaining what you can't do, but kindly tell me anything you can do," said the Superior Person, crushingly, with her pen poised between delicate fingers waiting to write. "Can you read aloud for two or three hours at a stretch? Are you active and handy, an early riser, a good walker, sweet tempered, and obliging?"

"I can say yes to all those questions except about the sweetness. I think I have a pretty good temper, and I should be anxious to oblige anybody who paid for my services. I should want them to feel that I was really earning my salary."

"The kind of ladies who come to me would not care for a talkative companion," said the Person, severely, having finished writing in her book. "My connection lies chiefly among the aristocracy, and in that class considerable deference is expected."

"Oh, of course," said Bella; "but it's quite different when I'm talking to you. I want to tell you all about myself once and forever."

"I am glad it is to be only once!" said the Person, with the edges of her lips.

The Person was of uncertain age, tightly laced in a black silk gown. She had a powdery complexion and a handsome clump of somebody else's hair on the top of her head. It may be that Bella's girlish freshness and vivacity had an irritating effect upon nerves weakened by an eight-hour day in that overheated second floor in. Harbeck Street. To Bella the official apartment, with its Brussels carpet, velvet curtains and velvet chairs, and French clock, ticking loud on the marble chimney-piece, suggested the luxury of a palace, as compared with another second floor in Walworth where Mrs. Rolleston and her daughter had managed to exist for the last six years.

"Do you think you have anything on your books that would suit me?" faltered Bella, after a pause.

"Oh, dear, no; I have nothing in view at present," answered the Person, who had swept Bella's half-crowns into a drawer, absentmindedly, with the tips of her fingers. "You see, you are so very unformed—so much too young to be companion to a lady of position. It is a pity

Mary Elizabeth Braddon, "Good Lady Ducayne." Copyright in the Public Domain.

you have not enough education for a nursery governess; that would be more in your line."

"And do you think it will be very long before you can get me a situation?" asked Bella, doubtfully.

"I really cannot say. Have you any particular reason for being so impatient—not a love affair, I hope?"

"A love affair!" cried Bella, with flaming cheeks. "What utter nonsense. I want a situation because mother is poor, and I hate being a burden to her. I want a salary that I can share with her."

"There won't be much margin for sharing in the salary you are likely to get at your age—and with your—very—uniformed manners," said the Person, who found Bella's peony cheeks, bright eyes, and unbridled vivacity more and more oppressive.

"Perhaps if you'd be kind enough to give me back the fee I could take it to an agency where the connection isn't quite so aristocratic," said Bella, who—as she told her mother in her recital of the interview—was determined not to be sat upon.

"You will find no agency that can do more for you than mine," replied the Person, whose harpy fingers never relinquished coin. "You will have to wait for your opportunity. Yours is an exceptional case: but I will bear you in mind, and if anything suitable offers I will write to you. I cannot say more than that."

The half-contemptuous bend of the stately head, weighted with borrowed hair, indicated the end of the interview. Bella went back to Walworth—tramped sturdily every inch of the way in the September afternoon—and "took off" the Superior Person for the amusement of her mother and the landlady, who lingered in the shabby little sitting-room after bringing in the tea-tray, to applaud Miss Rolleston's "taking off."

"Dear dear, what a mimic she is!" said the landlady. "You ought to have let her go on the stage, mum. She might have made her fortune as an actress."

II

Bella waited and hoped, and listened for the postman's knocks which brought such store of letters for the parlors and the first floor, and so few for that humble second floor, where mother and daughter sat sewing with hand and with wheel and treadle, for the greater part of the day. Mrs. Rolleston was a lady by birth and education; but it had been her bad fortune to marry a scoundrel; for the last half-dozen years she had been that worst of widows, a wife whose husband had deserted her. Happily, she was courageous, industrious, and a clever needle-woman; and she had been able just to earn a living for herself and her only child, by making mantles and cloaks for a West-end house. It was not a luxurious living. Cheap lodgings in a shabby street off the Walworth Road, scanty dinners, homely food, well-worn raiment, had been the portion of mother and daughter; but they loved each other so dearly, and Nature had made them both so light-hearted, that they had contrived somehow to be happy.

But now this idea of going out into the world as companion to some fine lady had rooted itself into Bella's mind, and although she idolized her mother, and although the parting of mother and daughter must needs tear two loving hearts into shreds, the girl longed for enterprise and change and excitement, as the pages of old longed to be knights, and to start for the Holy Land to break a lance with the infidel.

She grew tired of racing downstairs every time the postman knocked, only to be told "nothing for you, miss," by the smudgy-faced drudge who picked up the letters from the passage floor. "Nothing for you, miss," grinned the lodging-house drudge, till at last Bella took heart of grace and walked up to Harbeck Street, and asked the Superior Person how it was that no situation had been found for her.

"You are too young," said the Person, "and you want a salary."

"Of course I do," answered Bella; "don't other people want salaries?"

"Young ladies of your age generally want a comfortable home."

"I don't," snapped Bella: "I want to help mother."

"You can call again this day week," said the Person; "or, if I hear of anything in the meantime, I will write to you."

No letter came from the Person, and in exactly a week Bella put on her neatest hat, the one that had been seldomest caught in the rain, and trudged off to Harbeck Street.

It was a dull October afternoon, and there was a greyness in the air which might turn to fog before night. The Walworth Road shops gleamed brightly through that grey atmosphere, and though to a young lady reared in Mayfair or Belgravia such shop-windows would have been unworthy of a glance, they were a snare and temptation for Bella. There were so many things that she longed for, and would never be able to buy.

Harbeck Street is apt to be empty at this dead season of the year, a long, long street, an endless perspective of eminently respectable houses. The Person's office was at the further end, and Bella looked down that long, grey vista almost despairingly, more tired than usual with the trudge from Walworth. As she looked, a carriage passed her, an old-fashioned, yellow chariot, on cee springs, drawn by a pair of high grey horses, with the stateliest of coachmen driving them, and a tall footman sitting by his side.

"It looks like the fairy godmother's coach," thought Bella. "I shouldn't wonder if it began by being a pumpkin."

It was a surprise when she reached the Person's door to find the yellow chariot standing before it, and the tall footman waiting near the doorstep. She was almost afraid to go in and meet the owner of that splendid carriage. She had caught only a glimpse of its occupant as the chariot rolled by, a plumed bonnet, a patch of ermine.

The Person's smart page ushered her upstairs and knocked at the official door. "Miss Rolleston," he announced, apologetically, while Bella waited outside.

"Show her in," said the Person, quickly; and then Bella heard her murmuring something in a low voice to her client.

Bella went in fresh, blooming, a living image of youth and hope, and before she looked at the Person her gaze was riveted by the owner of the chariot.

Never had she seen anyone as old as the old lady sitting by the Person's fire: a little old figure, wrapped from chin to feet in an ermine mantle; a withered, old face under a plumed bonnet—a face so wasted by age that it seemed only a pair of eyes and a peaked chin. The nose was peaked, too, but between the sharply pointed chin and the great, shining eyes, the small, aquiline nose was hardly visible.

"This is Miss Rolleston, Lady Ducayne."

Claw-like fingers, flashing with jewels, lifted a double eyeglass to Lady Ducayne's shining black eyes, and through the glasses Bella saw those unnaturally bright eyes magnified to a gigantic size, and glaring at her awfully.

"Miss Torpinter has told me all about you," said the old voice that belonged to the eyes. "Have you good health? Are you strong and active, able to eat well, sleep well, walk well, able to enjoy all that there is good in life?"

"I have never known what it is to be ill, or idle," answered Bella.

"Then I think you will do for me."

"Of course, in the event of references being perfectly satisfactory," put in the Person.

"I don't want references. The young woman looks frank and innocent. I'll take her on trust."

"So like you, dear Lady Ducayne," murmured Miss Torpinter.

"I want a strong young woman whose health will give me no trouble."

"You have been so unfortunate in that respect," cooed the Person, whose voice and manner were subdued to a melting sweetness by the old woman's presence.

"Yes, I've been rather unlucky," grunted Lady Ducayne.

"But I am sure Miss Rolleston will not disappoint you, though certainly after your unpleasant experience with Miss Tomson, who looked the picture of health—and Miss Blandy, who said she had never seen a doctor since she was vaccinated—"

"Lies, no doubt," muttered Lady Ducayne, and then turning to Bella, she asked, curtly,

"You don't mind spending the winter in Italy, I suppose?"

In Italy! The very word was magical. Bella's fair young face flushed crimson.

"It has been the dream of my life to see Italy," she gasped.

From Walworth to Italy! How far, how impossible such a journey had seemed to that romantic dreamer.

"Well, your dream will be realized. Get yourself ready to leave Charing Cross by the train deluxe this day week at eleven. Be sure you are at the station a quarter before the hour. My people will look after you and your luggage."

Lady Ducayne rose from her chair, assisted by her crutch-stick, and Miss Torpinter escorted her to the door.

"And with regard to salary?" questioned the Person on the way.

"Salary, oh, the same as usual—and if the young woman wants a quarter's pay in advance you can write to me for a check," Lady Ducayne answered, carelessly.

Miss Torpinter went all the way downstairs with her client, and waited to see her seated in the yellow chariot. When she came upstairs again she was slightly out of breath, and she had resumed that superior manner which Bella had found so crushing.

"You may think yourself uncommonly lucky, Miss Rolleston," she said. "I have dozens of young ladies on my books whom I might have recommended for this situation—but I remembered having told you to call this afternoon—and I thought I would give you a chance. Old Lady Ducayne is one of the best people on my books. She gives her companion a hundred a year, and pays all travelling expenses. You will live in the lap of luxury."

"A hundred a year! How too lovely! Shall I have to dress very grandly? Does Lady Ducayne keep much company?"

"At her age! No, she lives in seclusion—in her own apartments—her French maid, her footman, her medical attendant, her courier."

"Why did those other companions leave her?" asked Bella.

"Their health broke down!"

"Poor things, and so they had to leave?"

"Yes, they had to leave. I suppose you would like a quarter's salary in advance?"

"Oh, yes, please. I shall have things to buy."

"Very well, I will write for Lady Ducayne's check, and I will send you the balance—after deducting my commission for the year."

"To be sure, I had forgotten the commission."

"You don't suppose I keep this office for pleasure."

"Of course not," murmured Bella, remembering the five shillings entrance fee; but nobody could expect a hundred a year and a winter in Italy for five shillings.

III

From Miss Rolleston, at Cap Ferrino, to Mrs. Rolleston, in Beresford Street, Walworth, London:

"How I wish you could see this place, dearest; the blue sky, the olive woods, the orange and lemon orchards between the cliffs and the sea—sheltering in the hollow of the great hills—and with summer waves dancing up to the narrow ridge of pebbles and weeds which is the Italian idea of a beach! Oh, how I wish you could see it all, mother dear, and bask in this sunshine, that makes it so difficult to believe the date at the head of this paper. November! The air is like an English June—the sun is so hot that I can't walk a few yards without an umbrella. And to think of you at Walworth while I am here! I could cry at the thought that perhaps you will never see this lovely coast, this wonderful sea, these summer flowers that bloom in winter. There is a hedge of pink geraniums under my window, mother—a thick, rank hedge, as if the flowers grew wild—and there are Dijon roses climbing over arches and palisades all along the terrace—a rose garden full of bloom in November! Just picture it all! You could never imagine the

luxury of this hotel. It is nearly new, and has been built and decorated regardless of expense. Our rooms are upholstered in pale blue satin, which shows up Lady Ducayne's parchment complexion; but as she sits all day in a corner of the balcony basking in the sun, except when she is in her carriage, and all the evening in her armchair close to the fire, and never sees anyone but her own people, her complexion matters very little.

"She has the handsomest suite of rooms in the hotel. My bedroom is inside hers, the sweetest room—all blue satin and white lace—white enamelled furniture, looking-glasses on every wall, till I know my pert little profile as I never knew it before. The room was really meant for Lady Ducayne's dressing-room, but she ordered one of the blue satin couches to be arranged as a bed for me—the prettiest little bed, which I can wheel near the window on sunny mornings, as it is on castors and easily moved about. I feel as if Lady Ducayne were a funny old grandmother, who had suddenly appeared in my life, very, very rich, and very, very kind.

"She is not at all exacting. I read aloud to her a good deal, and she dozes and nods while I read. Sometimes I hear her moaning in her sleep—as if she had troublesome dreams. When she is tired of my reading she orders Francine, her maid, to read a French novel to her, and I hear her chuckle and groan now and then, as if she were more interested in those books than in Dickens or Scott. My French is not good enough to follow Francine, who reads very quickly. I have a great deal of liberty, for Lady Ducayne often tells me to run away and amuse myself; I roam about the hills for hours. Everything is so lovely. I lose myself in olive woods, always climbing up and up towards the pine woods above—and above the pines there are the snow mountains that just show their white peaks above the dark hills. Oh, you poor dear, how can I ever make you understand what this place is like—you, whose poor, tired eyes have only the opposite side of Beresford Street? Sometimes I go no farther than the terrace in front of the hotel, which is a favorite lounging-place with everybody. The gardens lie below, and the tennis courts where I sometimes play with a very nice girl, the only person in the hotel with whom I have made friends. She is a year older than I, and has come to Cap Ferrino with her brother, a doctor—or a medical student, who is going to be a doctor. He passed his M.B. exam at Edinburgh just before they left home, Lotta told me. He came to Italy entirely on his sister's account. She had a troublesome chest attack last summer and was ordered to winter abroad. They are orphans, quite alone in the world, and so fond of each other. It is very nice for me to have such a friend as Lotta. She is so thoroughly respectable. I can't help using that word, for some of the girls in this hotel go on in a way that I know you would shudder at. Lotta was brought up by an aunt, deep down in the country, and knows hardly anything about life. Her brother won't allow her to read a novel, French or English, that he has not read and approved.

"'He treats me like a child,' she told me, 'but I don't mind, for it's nice to know somebody loves me, and cares about what I do, and even about my thoughts.'

"Perhaps this is what makes some girls so eager to marry—the want of someone strong and brave and honest and true to care for them and order them about. I want no one, mother darling, for I have you, and you are all the world to me. No husband could ever come between us two. If I ever were to marry he would have only the *second place in my heart. But I don't suppose I ever shall marry, or even know what it is like to have an offer of marriage. No young man can afford to marry a penniless girl nowadays. Life is too expensive.*

"*Mr. Stafford, Lotta's brother, is very clever, and very kind. He thinks it is rather hard for me to live with such an old woman as Lady Ducayne, but then he does not know how poor we are—you and I—and what a wonderful life this seems to me in this lovely place. I feel a selfish wretch for enjoying all my luxuries, while you, who want them so much more than I, have none of them—hardly know what they are like—do you, dearest?—for my scamp of a father began to go to the dogs soon after you were married, and since then life has been all trouble and care and struggle for you.*"

This letter was written when Bella had been less than a month at Cap Ferrino, before the novelty had worn off the landscape, and before the pleasure of luxurious surroundings had begun to cloy. She wrote to her mother every week, such long letters as girls who have lived in closest companionship with a mother alone can write; letters that are like a diary of heart and mind. She wrote gaily always; but when the new year began Mrs. Rolleston thought she detected a note of melancholy under all those lively details about the place and the people.

"My poor girl is getting homesick," she thought. "Her heart is in Beresford Street."

It might be that she missed her new friend and companion, Lotta Stafford, who had gone with her brother for a little tour to Genoa and Spezia, and as far as Pisa. They were to return before February; but in the meantime Bella might naturally feel very solitary among all those strangers, whose manners and doings she described so well.

The mother's instinct had been true. Bella was not so happy as she had been in that first flush of wonder and delight which followed the change from Walworth to the Riviera. Somehow, she knew not how, lassitude had crept upon her. She no longer loved to climb the hills, no longer flourished her orange stick in sheer gladness of heart as her light feet skipped over the rough ground and the coarse grass on the mountain side. The odor of rosemary and thyme, the fresh breath of the sea, no longer filled her with rapture. She thought of Beresford Street and her mother's face with a sick longing. They were so far—so far away! And the she thought of Lady Ducayne, sitting by the heaped-up olive logs in the overheated salon—thought of that wizened-nutcracker profile, and those gleaming eyes, with an invincible horror.

Visitors at the hotel had told her that the air of Cap Ferrino was relaxing—better suited to age than to youth, to sickness than to health. No doubt it was so. She was not so well as she had been at Walworth; but she told herself that she was suffering only from the pain of separation from the dear companion of her girlhood, the mother who had been nurse, sister, friend, flatterer, all things in this world to her. She had shed many tears over that parting, had spent many a melancholy hour on the marble terrace with yearning eyes looking westward, and with her heart's desire a thousand miles away.

She was sitting in her favorite spot, an angle at the eastern end of the terrace, a quiet little nook sheltered by orange trees, when she heard a couple of Riviera habitués talking in the garden below. They were sitting on a bench against the terrace wall.

She had no idea of listening to their talk, till the sound of Lady Ducayne's name attracted her, and then she listened without any thought of wrong-doing. They were talking no secrets—just casually discussing a hotel acquaintance.

They were two elderly people whom Bella only knew by sight. An English clergyman who had wintered abroad for half his lifetime; a stout, comfortable, well-to-do spinster, whose chronic bronchitis obliged her to migrate annually.

"I have met her about Italy for the last ten years," said the lady; "but have never found out her real age."

"I put her down at a hundred—not a year less," replied the parson. "Her reminiscences all go back to the Regency. She was evidently then in her zenith; and I have heard her say things that showed she was in Parisian society when the First Empire was at its best—before Josephine was divorced."

"She doesn't talk much now."

"No; there's not much life left in her. She is wise in keeping herself secluded. I only wonder that wicked old quack, her Italian doctor, didn't finish her off years ago."

"I should think it must be the other way, and that he keeps her alive."

"My dear Miss Manders, do you think foreign quackery ever kept anybody alive?"

"Well, there she is—and she never goes anywhere without him. He certainly has an unpleasant countenance."

"Unpleasant," echoed the parson, "I don't believe the foul fiend himself can beat him in ugliness. I pity that poor young woman who has to live between old Lady Ducayne and Dr. Parravicini."

"But the old lady is very good to her companions."

"No doubt. She is very free with her cash; the servants call her good Lady Ducayne. She is a withered old female Croesus, and knows she'll never be able to get through her money, and doesn't relish the idea of other people enjoying it when she's in her coffin. People who live to be as old as she is become slavishly attached to life. I daresay she's generous to those poor girls—but she can't make them happy. They die in her service."

"Don't say they, Mr. Carton; I know that one poor girl died at Mentone last spring."

"Yes, and another poor girl died in Rome three years ago. I was there at the time. Good Lady Ducayne left her there in an English family. The girl had every comfort. The old woman was very liberal to her—but she died. I tell you, Miss Manders, it is not good for any young woman to live with two such horrors as Lady Ducayne and Parravicini."

They talked of other things—but Bella hardly heard them. She sat motionless, and a cold wind seemed to come down upon her from the mountains and to creep up to her from the sea, till she shivered as she sat there in the sunshine, in the shelter of the orange trees in the midst of all that beauty and brightness.

Yes, they were uncanny, certainly, the pair of them—she so like an aristocratic witch in her withered old age; he of no particular age, with a face that was more like a waxen mask than any human countenance Bella had ever seen. What did it matter? Old age is venerable, and worthy of all reverence; and Lady Ducayne had been very kind to her. Dr. Parravicini was a harmless, inoffensive student, who seldom looked up from the book he was reading. He had his private sitting-room, where he made experiments in chemistry and natural science—perhaps in alchemy. What could it matter to Bella? He had always been polite to her, in his far-off way. She could not be more happily placed than she was—in his palatial hotel, with this rich old lady.

No doubt she missed the young English girl who had been so friendly, and it might be that she missed the girl's brother, for Mr. Stafford had talked to her a good deal—had interested himself in the books she was reading, and her manner of amusing herself when she was not on duty.

"You must come to our little salon when you are 'off,' as the hospital nurses call it, and we can have some music. No doubt you play and sing?" Upon which Bella had to own with a blush of shame that she had forgotten how to play the piano ages ago.

"Mother and I used to sing duets sometimes between the lights, without accompaniment," she said, and the tears came into her eyes as she thought of the humble room, the half-hour's respite from work, the sewing machine standing where a piano ought to have been, and her mother's plaintive voice, so sweet, so true, so dear.

Sometimes she found herself wondering whether she would ever see that beloved mother again. Strange forebodings came into her mind. She was angry with herself for giving way to melancholy thoughts.

One day she questioned Lady Ducayne's French maid about those two companions who had died within three years.

"They were poor, feeble creatures," Francine told her. "They looked fresh and bright enough when they came to Miladi; but they ate too much, and they were lazy. They died of luxury and idleness. Miladi was too kind to them. They had nothing to do; and so they took to fancying things; fancying the air didn't suit them, that they couldn't sleep."

"I sleep well enough, but I have had a strange dream several times since I have been in Italy."

"Ah, you had better not begin to think about dreams, or you will be like those other girls. They were dreamers—and they dreamt themselves into the cemetery."

The dream troubled her a little, not because it was a ghastly or frightening dream, but on account of sensations which she had never felt before in sleep—a whirring of wheels that went round in her brain, a great noise like a whirlwind, but rhythmical like the ticking of a gigantic clock: and then in the midst of this uproar as of winds and waves she seemed to sink into a gulf of unconsciousness, out of sleep into far deeper sleep—total extinction. And then, after that black interval, there had come the sound of voices, and then again the whirr of wheels, louder and louder—and again the black—and then she awoke, feeling languid and oppressed.

She told Dr. Parravicini of her dream one day, on the only occasion when she wanted his professional advice. She had suffered rather severely from the mosquitoes before Christmas—and had been almost frightened at finding a wound upon her arm which she could only attribute to the venomous sting of one of these torturers. Parravicini put on his glasses, and scrutinized the angry mark on the round, white arm, as Bella stood before him and Lady Ducayne with her sleeve rolled up above her elbow.

"Yes, that's rather more than a joke," he said; "he has caught you on the top of a vein. What a vampire! But there's no harm done, signorina, nothing that a little dressing of mine won't heal. You must always show me any bite of this nature. It might be dangerous if neglected. These creatures feed on poison and disseminate it."

"And to think that such tiny creatures can bite like this," said Bella; "my arm looks as if it had been cut by a knife."

"If I were to show you a mosquito's sting under my microscope you wouldn't be surprised at that," replied Parravicini.

Bella had to put up with the mosquito bites, even when they came on the top of a vein, and produced that ugly wound. The wound recurred now and then at longish intervals, and Bella found Dr, Parravicini's dressing a speedy cure. If he were the quack his enemies called him, he had at least a light hand and a delicate touch in performing this small operation.

Bella Rolleston to Mrs. Rolleston—April 14th:

"*Ever Dearest,*

Behold the check for my second quarter's salary—five and twenty pounds. There is no one to pinch off a whole tenner for a year's commission as there was last time, so it is all for you, mother, dear. I have plenty of pocket-money in hand from the cash I brought away with me, when you insisted on my keeping more than I wanted. It isn't possible to spend money here—except on occasional tips to servants, or sous to beggars and children—unless one had lots to spend, for everything one would like to buy—tortoise-shell, coral, lace—is so ridiculously dear that only a millionaire ought to look at it. Italy is a dream of beauty: but for shopping, give me Newington Causeway.

"*You ask me so earnestly if I am quite well that I fear my letters must have been very dull lately. Yes, dear, I am well—but I am not quite so strong as I was when I used to trudge to the West-end to buy half a pound of tea— just for a constitutional walk—or to Dulwich to look at the pictures. Italy is relaxing; and I feel what the people here call 'slack.' But I fancy I can see your dear face looking worried as you read this. Indeed, and indeed, I am not ill. I am only a little tired of this lovely scene—as I suppose one might get tired of looking at one of Turner's pictures if it hung on a wall that was always opposite one. I think of you every hour in every day—think of you and our homely little room—our dear little shabby parlor, with the armchairs from the wreck of your old home, and Dick singing in his cage over the sewing machine. Dear, shrill, maddening Dick, who, we flattered ourselves, was so passionately fond of us. Do tell me in your next letter that he is well.*

"My friend Lotta and her brother never came back after all. They went from Pisa to Rome. Happy mortals! And they are to be on the Italian lakes in May; which lake was not decided when Lotta last wrote to me. She has been a charming correspondent, and has confided all her little flirtations to me. We are all to go to Bellaggio next week—by Genoa and Milan. Isn't that lovely? Lady Ducayne travels by the easiest stages—except when she is bottled up in the train deluxe. We shall stop two days at Genoa and one at Milan. What a bore I shall be to you with my talk about Italy when I come home.

"Love and love—and ever more love from your adoring, Bella."

IV

Herbert Stafford and his sister had often talked of the pretty English girl with her fresh complexion, which made such a pleasant touch of rosy color among all those sallow faces at the Grand Hotel. The young doctor thought of her with a compassionate tenderness—her utter loneliness in that great hotel where there were so many people, her bondage to that old, old woman, where everybody else was free to think of nothing but enjoying life. It was a hard fate; and the poor child was evidently devoted to her mother, and felt the pain of separation—"only two of them, and very poor, and all the world to each other," he thought.

Lotta told him one morning that they were to meet again at Bellaggio. "The old thing and her court are to be there before we are," she said. "I shall be charmed to have Bella again. She is so bright and gay—in spite of an occasional touch of homesickness. I never took to a girl on a short acquaintance as I did to her."

"I like her best when she is homesick," said Herbert; "for then I am sure she has a heart."

"What have you to do with hearts, except for dissection? Don't forget that Bella is an absolute pauper. She told me in confidence that her mother makes mantles for a West-end shop. You can hardly have a lower depth than that."

"I shouldn't think any less of her if her mother made matchboxes."

"Not in the abstract—of course not. Matchboxes are honest labor. But you couldn't marry a girl whose mother makes mantles."

"We haven't come to the consideration of that question yet," answered Herbert, who liked to provoke his sister.

In two years' hospital practice he had seen too much of the grim realities of life to retain any prejudices about rank. Cancer, phthisis, gangrene, leave a man with little respect for the humanity. The kernel is always the same—fearfully and wonderfully made—a subject for pity and terror.

Mr. Stafford and his sister arrived at Bellaggio in a fair May evening. The sun was going down as the steamer approached the pier; and all that glory of purple bloom which curtains every wall at this season of the year flushed and deepened in the glowing light. A group of ladies were standing or the pier watching the arrivals, and among them Herbert saw a pale face that startled him out of his wonted composure.

"There she is," murmured Lotta, at his elbow, "but how dreadfully changed. She looks a wreck."

They were shaking hands with her a few minutes later, and a flush had lighted up her poor pinched face in the pleasure of meeting.

"I thought you might come this evening," she said. "We have been here a week."

She did not add that she had been there every evening to watch the boat in, and a good many times during the day. The Grand Bretagne was close by, and it had been easy for her to creep to the pier when the boat bell rang. She felt a joy in meeting these people again; a sense of being with friends; a confidence which Lady Ducayne's goodness had never inspired in her.

"Oh, you poor darling, how awfully ill you must have been," exclaimed Lotta, as the two girls embraced.

Bella tried to answer, but her voice was choked with tears.

"What has been the matter, dear? That horrid influenza, I suppose?"

"No, no, I have not been ill—I have only felt a little weaker than I used to be. I don't think the air of Cap Ferrino quite agreed with me."

"It must have disagreed with you abominably. I never saw such a change in anyone. Do let Herbert doctor you. He is fully qualified, you know. He prescribed for ever so many influenza patients at the Londres. They were glad to get advice from an English doctor in a friendly way."

"I am sure he must be very clever!" faltered Bella, "but there is really nothing the matter. I am not ill, and if I were ill, Lady Ducayne's physician—"

"That dreadful man with the yellow face? I would as soon one of the Borgias prescribed for me. I hope you haven't been taking any of his medicines."

"No, dear, I have taken nothing. I have never complained of being ill."

This was said while they were all three walking to the hotel. The Staffords' rooms had been secured in advance, pretty ground-floor rooms, opening into the garden. Lady Ducayne's statelier apartments were on the floor above.

"I believe these rooms are just under ours," said Bella.

"Then it will be all the easier for you to run down to us," replied Lotta, which was not really the case, as the grand staircase was in the center of the hotel.

"Oh, I shall find it easy enough," said Bella. "I'm afraid you'll have too much of my society. Lady Ducayne sleeps away half the day in this warm weather, so I have a good deal of idle time; and I get awfully moped thinking of mother and home."

Her voice broke upon the last word. She could not have thought of that poor lodging which went by the name of home more tenderly had it been the most beautiful that art and wealth ever created. She moped and pined in this lovely garden, with the sunlit lake and the romantic hills spreading out their beauty before her. She was homesick and she had dreams; or, rather, an occasional recurrence of that one bad dream with all its strange sensations—it was more like a hallucination than dreaming—the whirring of wheels, the sinking into an abyss, the struggling back to consciousness. She had the dream shortly before she left Cap Ferrino, but not since she had come to Bellaggio, and she began to hope the air in this lake district suited her better, and that those strange sensations would never return.

Mr. Stafford wrote a prescription and had it made up at the chemist's near the hotel. It was a powerful tonic, and after two bottles, and a row or two on the lake, and some rambling over the hills and in the meadows where the spring flowers made earth seem paradise, Bella's spirits and looks improved as if by magic.

"It is a wonderful tonic," she said, but perhaps in her heart of hearts she knew that the doctor's kind voice, and the friendly hand that helped her in and out of the boat, and the lake, had something to do with her cure.

"I hope you don't forget that her mother makes mantles," Lotta said warningly.

"Or matchboxes; it is just the same thing, so far as I am concerned."

"You mean that in no circumstances could you think of marrying her?"

"I mean that if ever I love a woman well enough to think of marrying her, riches or rank will count for nothing with me. But I fear—I fear your poor friend may not live to be any man's wife."

"Do you think her so very ill?"

He sighed, and left the question unanswered.

One day, while they were gathering wild hyacinths in an upland meadow, Bella told Mr. Stafford about her bad dream.

"It is curious only because it is hardly like a dream," she said. "I daresay you could find some commonsense reason for it. The position of my head on my pillow, or the atmosphere, or something."

And then she described her sensations; how in the midst of sleep there came a sudden sense of suffocation; and then those whirring wheels, so loud, so terrible; and then a blank, and then a coming back to waking consciousness.

"Have you ever had chloroform given you—by a dentist, for instance?"

"Never—Dr. Parravicini asked me that question one day."

"Lately?"

"No, long ago, when we were in the train deluxe."

"Has Dr. Parravicini prescribed for you since you began to feel weak and ill?"

"Oh, he has given me a tonic from time to time, but I hate medicine, and took very little of the stuff. And then I am not ill, only weaker than I used to be. I was ridiculously strong and well when I lived at Walworth, and used to take long walks every day. Mother made me take those tramps to Dulwich or Norwood, for fear I should suffer from too much sewing machine; sometimes—but very seldom—she went with me. She was generally toiling at home while I was enjoying fresh air and exercise. And she was very careful about our food—that, however plain it was, it should be always nourishing and ample. I owe it to her care that I grew up such a great, strong creature."

"You don't look great or strong now, you poor dear," said Lotta.

"I'm afraid Italy doesn't agree with me."

"Perhaps it is not Italy, but being cooped up with Lady Ducayne that has made you ill."

"But I am never cooped up. Lady Ducayne is absurdly kind, and lets me roam about or sit in the balcony all day if I like. I have read more novels since I have been with her than in all the rest of my life."

"Then she is very different from the average old lady, who is usually a slave driver," said Stafford. "I wonder why she carries a companion about with her if she has so little need of society."

"Oh, I am only part of her state. She is inordinately rich—and the salary she gives me doesn't count. Apropos of Dr. Parravicini, I know he is a clever doctor, for he cures my horrid mosquito bites."

"A little ammonia would do that, in the early stage of the mischief. But there are no mosquitoes to trouble you now."

"Oh, yes, there are; I had a bite just before we left Cap Ferrino." She pushed up her loose lawn sleeve, and exhibited a scar, which he scrutinized intently, with a surprised and puzzled look.

"This is no mosquito bite," he said.

"Oh yes it is—unless there are snakes or adders at Cap Ferrino."

"It is not a bite at all. You are trifling with me. Miss Rolleston—you have allowed that wretched Italian quack to bleed you. They killed the greatest man in modern Europe that way, remember. However foolish of you."

"I was never bled in my life, Mr. Stafford."

"Nonsense! Let me look at your other arm. Are there any more mosquito bites?"

"Yes; Dr. Parravicini says I have a bad skin for healing, and that the poison acts more virulently with me than with most people."

Stafford examined both her arms in the broad sunlight, scars new and old.

"You have been very badly bitten, Miss Rolleston," he said, "and if ever I find the mosquito I shall make him smart. But, now tell me, my dear girl, on your word of honor, tell me as you would tell a friend who is sincerely anxious for your health and happiness—as you would tell your mother if she were here to question you—have you no knowledge of any cause for these scars except mosquito bites—no suspicion even?"

"No, indeed! No, upon my honor! I have never seen a mosquito biting my arm. One never does see the horrid little fiends. But I have heard them trumpeting under the curtains and I know that I have often had one of the pestilent wretches buzzing about me."

Later in the day Bella and her friends were sitting at tea in the garden, while Lady Ducayne took her afternoon drive with her doctor.

"How long do you mean to stop with Lady Ducayne, Miss Rolleston?" Herbert Stafford asked, after a thoughtful silence, breaking suddenly upon the trivial talk of the two girls.

"As long as she will go on paying me twenty-five pounds a quarter."

"Even if you feel your health breaking down in her service?"

"It is not the service that has injured my health You can see that I have really nothing to do—to read aloud for an hour or so once or twice a week; to write a letter once in a while to a London tradesman. I shall never have such an easy time with anybody. And nobody else would give me a hundred a year."

"Then you mean to go on till you break down; to die at your post?"

"Like the other two companions? No! If ever I feel seriously ill—really ill—I shall put myself in a train and go back to Walworth without stopping."

"What about the other two companions?"

"They both died. It was very unlucky for Lady Ducayne. That's why she engaged me; she chose me because I was ruddy and robust. She must feel rather disgusted at my having grown white and weak. By-the-bye, when I told her about the good your tonic had done me, she said she would like to see you and have a little talk with you about her own case."

"And I should like to see Lady Ducayne. When did she say this?"

"The day before yesterday."

"Will you ask her if she will see me this evening?"

"With pleasure! I wonder what you will think of her? She looks rather terrible to a stranger; but Dr. Parravicini says she was once a famous beauty."

It was nearly ten o'clock when Mr. Stafford was summoned by message from Lady Ducayne, whose courier came to conduct him to her ladyship's salon. Bella was reading aloud when the visitor was admitted; and he noticed the languor in the low, sweet tones, the evident effort.

"Shut up the book," said the querulous old voice. "You are beginning to drawl like Miss Blandy."

Stafford saw a small, bent figure crouching over the piled up olive logs; a shrunken old figure in a gorgeous garment of black and crimson brocade, a skinny throat emerging from a mass of old Venetian lace, clasped with diamonds that flashed like fireflies as the trembling old head turned towards him.

The eyes that looked at him out of the face were almost as bright as the diamonds—the only living feature in that narrow parchment mask. He had seen terrible faces in the hospital—faces on which disease had set dreadful marks—but he had never seen a face that impressed him so painfully as this withered countenance, with its indescribable horror of death outlived, a face that should have been hidden under a coffin-lid years and years ago.

The Italian physician was standing on the other side of the fireplace, smoking a cigarette, and looking down at the little old woman brooding over the hearth as if he were proud of her.

"Good evening, Mr. Stafford; you can go to your room, Bella, and write your everlasting letter to your mother at Walworth," said Lady Ducayne. "I believe she writes a page about every wild flower she discovers in the woods and meadows. I don't know what else she can find to write about," she added, as Bella quietly withdrew to the pretty little bedroom opening out of Lady Ducayne's spacious apartment. Here, as at Cap Ferrino, she slept in a room adjoining the old lady's.

"You are a medical man, I understand, Mr. Stafford."

"I am a qualified practitioner, but I have not begun to practice."

"You have begun upon my companion, she tells me."

"I have prescribed for her, certainly, and I am happy to find my prescription has done her good; but I look upon that improvement as temporary. Her case will require more drastic treatment."

"Never mind her case. There is nothing the matter with the girl—absolutely nothing—except girlish nonsense; too much liberty and not enough work."

"I understand that two of your ladyship's previous companions died of the same disease," said Stafford, looking first at Lady Ducayne, who gave her tremulous old head an impatient jerk, and thee at Parravicini, whose yellow complexion had paled a little under Stafford's scrutiny.

"Don't bother me about my companions, sir," said Lady Ducayne. "I sent for you to consult you about myself—not about a parcel of anemic girls. You are young, and medicine is a progressive science, the newspapers tell me. Where have you studied?"

"In Edinburgh—and in Paris."

"Two good schools. And know all the new-fangled theories, the modern discoveries—that remind one of the medieval witchcraft, of Albertus Magnus, and George Ripley; you have studied hypnotism—electricity?"

"And the transfusion of blood," said Stafford, very slowly, looking at Parravicini.

"Have you made any discovery that teaches you to prolong human life—any elixir—any mode of treatment? I want my life prolonged, young man. That man there has been my physician for thirty years. He does all he can to keep me alive—after his lights. He studies all the new theories of all the scientists—but he is old; he gets older every day—his brain-power is going—he is bigoted—prejudiced—can't receive new ideas—can't grapple with new systems. He will let me die if I am not on my guard against him."

"You are of an unbelievable ingratitude, Ecclenza," said Parravicini.

"Oh, you needn't complain. I have paid you thousands to keep me alive. Every year of my life has swollen your hoards; you know there is nothing to come to you when I am gone. My whole fortune is left to endow a home for indigent women of quality who have reached their ninetieth year. Come, Mr. Stafford, I am a rich woman. Give me a few years more in the sunshine, a few years more above ground, and I will give you the price of a fashionable London practice—I will set you up at the West-end."

"How old are you, Lady Ducayne?"

"I was born the day Louis XVI was guillotined."

"Then I think you have had your share of the sunshine and the pleasures of the earth, and that you should spend your few remaining days in repenting your sins and trying to make atonement for the young lives that have been sacrificed to your love of life."

"What do you mean by that, sir?"

"Oh, Lady Ducayne, need I put your wickedness and your physician's still greater wickedness in plain words? The poor girl who is now in your employment has been reduced from robust health to a condition of absolute danger by Dr. Parravicini's experimental surgery; and I have no doubt those other two young women who broke down to your service were treated by him in the same manner. I could take upon myself to demonstrate—by most convincing evidence, to a jury of medical men—that Dr. Parravicini has been bleeding Miss Rolleston after putting her under chloroform, at intervals, ever since she has been in your service. The deterioration in the girl's health speaks for itself; the lancet marks upon the girl's arms are unmistakable; and her description of a series of sensations, which she calls a dream, points unmistakably to the administration of chloroform while she was sleeping. A practice so nefarious, so murderous, must, if exposed, result in a sentence only less severe than the punishment of murder."

"I laugh," said Parravicini, with an airy motion of his skinny fingers; "I laugh at once at your theories and at your threats. I, Parravicini Leopold, have no fear that the law can question anything I have done."

"Take the girl away, and let me hear no more of her," cried Lady Ducayne, in the thin, old voice, which so poorly matched the energy and fire of the wicked old brain that guided its utterances. "Let her go back to her mother—I want no more girls to die in my service. There are girls enough and to spare in the world, God knows."

"If you ever engage another companion—or take another English girl into your service, Lady Ducayne, I will make all England ring with the story of your wickedness."

"I want no more girls. I don't believe in his experiments. They have been full of danger for me as well as for the girl—an air bubble, and I should be gone. Ill have no more of his dangerous quackery. I'll find some new man—a better man than you, sir, a discoverer like Pasteur, or

Virchow, a genius—to keep me alive. Take your girl away, young man. Marry her if you like. I'll write a check for a thousand pounds, and let her go and live on beef and beer, and get strong and plump again. I'll have no more such experiments. Do you hear, Parravicini?" she screamed, vindictively, the yellow, wrinkled face distorted with fury, the eyes glaring at him.

The Staffords carried Bella Rolleston off to Varese next day, she very loath to leave Lady Ducayne, whose liberal salary afforded such help for the dear mother. Herbert Stafford insisted, however, treating Bella as coolly as if he had been the family physician, and she had been given over wholly to his care.

"Do you suppose your mother would let you stop here to die?" he asked. "If Mrs. Rolleston knew how ill you are, she would come post haste to fetch you."

"I shall never be well again till I get back to Walworth," answered Bella, who was low-spirited and inclined to tears this morning, a reaction after her good spirits of yesterday.

"We'll try a week or two at Varese first," said Stafford. "When you can walk halfway up Monte Generoso without palpitation of the heart, you shall go back to Walworth."

"Poor mother, how glad she will be to see me, and how sorry that I've lost such a good place."

This conversation took place on the boat when they were leaving Bellaggio. Lotta had gone to her friend's room at seven o'clock that morning, long before Lady Ducayne's withered eyelids had opened to the daylight, before even Francine, the French maid, was astir, and had helped to pack a Gladstone bag with essentials, and hustled Bella downstairs and out of doors before she could make any strenuous resistance.

"It's all right," Lotta assured her. "Herbert had a good talk with Lady Ducayne last night, and it was settled for you to leave this morning. She doesn't like invalids, you see."

"No," sighed Bella, "she doesn't like invalids. It was very unlucky that I should break down, just like Miss Tomson and Miss Blandy."

"At any rate, you are not dead, like them," answered Lotta, "and my brother says you are not going to die."

It seemed rather a dreadful thing to be dismissed in that offhand way, without a word of farewell from her employer.

"I wonder what Miss Torpinter will say when I go to her for another situation," Bella speculated, ruefully, while she and her friends were breakfasting on board the steamer.

"Perhaps you may never want another situation," said Stafford.

"You mean that I may never be well enough to be useful to anybody?"

"No, I don't mean anything of the kind."

It was after dinner at Varese, when Bella had been induced to take a whole glass of Chianti, and quite sparkled after that unaccustomed stimulant, that Mr. Stafford produced a letter from his pocket.

"I forgot to give you Lady Ducayne's letter of adieu!" he said.

"What, did she write to me? I am so glad—I hated to leave her in such a cool way; for after all she was very kind to me, and if I didn't like her it was only because she was too dreadfully old."

She tore open the envelope. The letter was short and to the point:—

"Goodbye, child. Go and marry your doctor. I enclose a farewell gift for your trousseau.
—Adeline Ducayne

"A hundred pounds, a whole year's salary—no—why, it's for a—A check for a thousand!" cried Bella. "What a generous old soul! She really is the dearest old thing."

"She just missed being very dear to you, Bella," said Stafford.

He had dropped into the use of her Christian name while they were on board the boat. It seemed natural now that she was to be in his charge till they all three went back to England.

"I shall take upon myself the privileges of an elder brother till we land at Dover," he said; "after that—well, it must be as you please."

The question of their future relations must have been satisfactorily settled before they crossed the Channel, for Bella's next letter to her mother communicated three startling facts.

First, that the inclosed check for £1,000 was to be invested in debenture stock in Mrs. Rolleston's name, and was to be her very own income and principal, for the rest of her life.

Next, that Bella was going home to Walworth immediately.

And last, that she was going to be married to Mr. Herbert Stafford in the following autumn.

"And I am sure you will adore him, mother, as much as I do," wrote Bella.

"It is all good Lady Ducayne's doing. I never could have married if I had not secured that little nest-egg for you. Herbert says we shall be able to add to it as the years go by, and that wherever we live there shall be always a room in our house for you. The word 'mother-in-law' has no terrors for him."

Clarimonde

Théophile Gautier

BROTHER, YOU ASK ME if I have ever loved. Yes. My story is a strange and terrible one; and though I am sixty-six years of age, I scarcely dare even now to disturb the ashes of that memory. To you I can refuse nothing; but I should not relate such a tale to any less experienced mind. So strange were the circumstances of my story, that I can scarcely believe myself to have ever actually been a party to them. For more than three years I remained the victim of a most singular and diabolical illusion. Poor country priest though I was, I led every night in a dream—would to God it had been all a dream!—a most worldly life, a damning life, a life of Sardanapalus. One single look too freely cast upon a woman well-nigh caused me to lose my soul; but finally by the grace of God and the assistance of my patron saint, I succeeded in casting out the evil spirit that possessed me. My daily life was long interwoven with a nocturnal life of a totally different character. By day I was a priest of the Lord, occupied with prayer and sacred things; by night, from the instant that I closed my eyes I became a young nobleman, a fine connoisseur in women, dogs, and horses; gambling, drinking, and blaspheming; and when I awoke at early daybreak, it seemed to me, on the other hand, that I had been sleeping, and had only dreamed that I was a priest. Of this somnambulistic life there now remains to me only the recollection of certain scenes and words which I cannot banish from my memory; but although I never actually left the walls of my presbytery, one would think to hear me speak that I were a man who, weary of all worldly pleasures, had become a religious, seeking to end a tempestuous life in the service of God, rather than a humble seminarist who has grown old in this obscure curacy, situated in the depths of the woods and even isolated from the life of the century.

Yes, I have loved as none in the world ever loved—with an insensate and furious passion—so violent that I am astonished it did not cause my heart to burst asunder. Ah, what nights—what nights!

From my earliest childhood I had felt a vocation to the priesthood, so that all my studies were directed with that idea in view. Up to the age of twenty-four my life had been only a prolonged novitiate. Having completed my course of theology I successively received all the minor orders, and my superiors judged me worthy, despite my youth, to pass the last awful degree. My ordination was fixed for Easter week.

I had never gone into the world. My world was confined by the walls of the college and the seminary. I knew in a vague sort of a way that there was something called Woman, but I never permitted my thoughts to dwell on such a subject, and I lived in a state of perfect innocence. Twice a year only I saw my infirm and aged mother, and in those visits were comprised my sole relations with the outer world.

I regretted nothing; I felt not the least hesitation at taking the last irrevocable step; I was filled with joy and impatience. Never did a betrothed lover count the slow hours with more feverish ardour; I slept only to dream that I was saying mass; I believed there could be nothing in the world more delightful than to be a priest; I would have refused to be a king or a poet in preference. My ambition could conceive of no loftier aim.

I tell you this in order to show you that what happened to me could not have happened in the natural order of things, and to enable you to understand that I was the victim of an inexplicable fascination.

At last the great day came. I walked to the church with a step so light that I fancied myself sustained in air, or that I had wings upon my shoulders. I believed myself an angel, and wondered at the sombre and thoughtful faces of my companions, for there were several of us. I had passed all the night in prayer, and was in a condition well-nigh bordering on ecstasy. The bishop, a venerable old man, seemed to me God the Father leaning over His Eternity, and I beheld Heaven through the vault of the temple.

You well know the details of that ceremony—the benediction, the communion under both forms, the anointing of the palms of the hands with the Oil of Catechumens, and then the holy sacrifice offered in concert with the bishop.

Ah, truly spake Job when he declared that the imprudent man is one who hath not made a covenant with his eyes! I accidentally lifted

Théophile Gautier, "Clarimonde," trans. Lafcadio Hearn. Copyright in the Public Domain.

my head, which until then I had kept down, and beheld before me, so close that it seemed that I could have touched her—although she was actually a considerable distance from me and on the further side of the sanctuary railing—a young woman of extraordinary beauty, and attired with royal magnificence. It seemed as though scales had suddenly fallen from my eyes. I felt like a blind man who unexpectedly recovers his sight. The bishop, so radiantly glorious but an instant before, suddenly vanished away, the tapers paled upon their golden candlesticks like stars in the dawn, and a vast darkness seemed to fill the whole church. The charming creature appeared in bright relief against the background of that darkness, like some angelic revelation. She seemed herself radiant, and radiating light rather than receiving it.

I lowered my eyelids, firmly resolved not to again open them, that I might not be influenced by external objects, for distraction had gradually taken possession of me until I hardly knew what I was doing.

In another minute, nevertheless, I reopened my eyes, for through my eyelashes I still beheld her, all sparkling with prismatic colours, and surrounded with such a penumbra as one beholds in gazing at the sun.

Oh, how beautiful she was! The greatest painters, who followed ideal beauty into heaven itself, and thence brought back to earth the true portrait of the Madonna, never in their delineations even approached that wildly beautiful reality which I saw before me. Neither the verses of the poet nor the palette of the artist could convey any conception of her. She was rather tall, with a form and bearing of a goddess. Her hair, of a soft blonde hue, was parted in the midst and flowed back over her temples in two rivers of rippling gold; she seemed a diademed queen. Her forehead, bluish-white in its transparency, extended its calm breadth above the arches of her eyebrows, which by a strange singularity were almost black, and admirably relieved the effect of sea-green eyes of unsustainable vivacity and brilliancy. What eyes! With a single flash they could have decided a man's destiny. They had a life, a limpidity, an ardour, a humid light which I have never seen in human eyes; they shot forth rays like arrows, which I could distinctly *see* enter my heart. I know not if the fire which illumined them came from heaven or from hell, but assuredly it came from one or the other. That woman was either an angel or a demon, perhaps both. Assuredly she never sprang from the flank of Eve, our common mother. Teeth of the most lustrous pearl gleamed in her ruddy smile, and at every inflection of her lips little dimples appeared in the satiny rose of her adorable cheeks. There was a delicacy and pride in the regal outline of her nostrils bespeaking noble blood. Agate gleams played over the smooth lustrous skin of her half-bare shoulders, and strings of great blonde pearls—almost equal to her neck in beauty of colour—descended upon her bosom. From time to time she elevated her head with the undulating grace of a startled serpent or peacock, thereby imparting a quivering motion to the high lace ruff which surrounded it like a silver trellis-work.

She wore a robe of orange-red velvet, and from her wide ermine-lined sleeves there peeped forth patrician hands of infinite delicacy, and so ideally transparent that, like the fingers of Aurora, they permitted the light to shine through them.

All these details I can recollect at this moment as plainly as though they were of yesterday, for notwithstanding I was greatly troubled at the time, nothing escaped me; the faintest touch of shading, the little dark speck at the point of the chin, the imperceptible down at the corners of the lips, the velvety floss upon the brow, the quivering shadows of the eyelashes upon the cheeks—I could notice everything with astonishing lucidity of perception.

And gazing I felt opening within me gates that had until then remained closed; vents long obstructed became all clear, permitting glimpses of unfamiliar perspectives within; life suddenly made itself visible to me under a totally novel aspect. I felt as though I had just been born into a new world and a new order of things. A frightful anguish commenced to torture my heart as with red-hot pincers. Every successive minute seemed to me at once but a second and yet a century. Meanwhile the ceremony was proceeding, and I shortly found myself transported far from that world of which my newly born desires were furiously besieging the entrance.

Nevertheless I answered 'Yes' when I wished to say 'No,' though all within me protested against the violence done to my soul by my tongue. Some occult power seemed to force the words from my throat against my will. Thus it is, perhaps, that so many young girls walk to the altar firmly resolved to refuse in a startling manner the husband imposed upon them, and that yet not one ever fulfils her intention. Thus it is, doubtless, that so many poor novices take the veil, though they have resolved to tear it into shreds at the moment when called upon to utter the vows. One dares not thus cause so great a scandal to all present, nor deceive the expectation of so many people. All those eyes, all those wills seem to weigh down upon you like a cope of lead, and, moreover, measures have been so well taken, everything has been so thoroughly arranged beforehand and after a fashion so evidently irrevocable, that the will yields to the weight of circumstances and utterly breaks down.

As the ceremony proceeded the features of the fair unknown changed their expression. Her look had at first been one of caressing tenderness; it changed to an air of disdain and of mortification, as though at not having been able to make itself understood.

With an effort of will sufficient to have uprooted a mountain, I strove to cry out that I would not be a priest, but I could not speak; my tongue seemed nailed to my palate, and I found it impossible to express my will by the least syllable of negation. Though fully awake, I felt like one under the influence of a nightmare, who vainly strives to shriek out the one word upon which life depends.

She seemed conscious of the martyrdom I was undergoing, and, as though to encourage me, she gave me a look replete with divinest promise. Her eyes were a poem; their every glance was a song.

She said to me:

'If thou wilt be mine, I shall make thee happier than God Himself in His paradise. The angels themselves will be jealous of thee. Tear off that funeral shroud in which thou art about to wrap thyself. I am Beauty, I am Youth, I am Life. Come to me! Together we shall be Love. Can Jehovah offer thee aught in exchange? Our lives will flow on like a dream, in one eternal kiss.

'Fling forth the wine of that chalice, and thou art free. I will conduct thee to the Unknown Isles. Thou shalt sleep in my bosom upon a bed of massy gold under a silver pavilion, for I love thee and would take thee away from thy God, before whom so many noble hearts pour forth floods of love which never reach even the steps of His throne!'

These words seemed to float to my ears in a rhythm of infinite sweetness, for her look was actually sonorous, and the utterances of her eyes were reechoed in the depths of my heart as though living lips had breathed them into my life. I felt myself willing to renounce God, and yet my tongue mechanically fulfilled all the formalities of the ceremony. The fair one gave me another look, so beseeching, so despairing that keen blades seemed to pierce my heart, and I felt my bosom transfixed by more swords than those of Our Lady of Sorrows.

All was consummated; I had become a priest.

Never was deeper anguish painted on human face than upon hers. The maiden who beholds her affianced lover suddenly fall dead at her side, the mother bending over the empty cradle of her child, Eve seated at the threshold of the gate of Paradise, the miser who finds a stone substituted for his stolen treasure, the poet who accidentally permits the only manuscript of his finest work to fall into the fire, could not wear a look so despairing, so inconsolable. All the blood had abandoned her charming face, leaving it whiter than marble; her beautiful arms hung lifelessly on either side of her body as though their muscles had suddenly relaxed, and she sought the support of a pillar, for her yielding limbs almost betrayed her. As for myself, I staggered toward the door of the church, livid as death, my forehead bathed with a sweat bloodier than that of Calvary; I felt as though I were being strangled; the vault seemed to have flattened down upon my shoulders, and it seemed to me that my head alone sustained the whole weight of the dome.

As I was about to cross the threshold a hand suddenly caught mine—a woman's hand! I had never till then touched the hand of any woman. It was cold as a serpent's skin, and yet its impress remained upon my wrist, burnt there as though branded by a glowing iron. It was she. 'Unhappy man! Unhappy man! What hast thou done?' she exclaimed in a low voice, and immediately disappeared in the crowd.

The aged bishop passed by. He cast a severe and scrutinising look upon me. My face presented the wildest aspect imaginable: I blushed and turned pale alternately; dazzling lights flashed before my eyes. A companion took pity on me. He seized my arm and led me out. I could not possibly have found my way back to the seminary unassisted. At the corner of a street, while the young priest's attention was momentarily turned in another direction, a negro page, fantastically garbed, approached me, and without pausing on his way slipped into my hand a little pocket-book with gold-embroidered corners, at the same time giving me a sign to hide it. I concealed it in my sleeve, and there kept it until I found myself alone in my cell. Then I opened the clasp. There were only two leaves within, bearing the words, 'Clarimonde. At the Concini Palace.' So little acquainted was I at that time with the things of this world that I had never heard of Clarimonde, celebrated as she was, and I had no idea as to where the Concini Palace was situated. I hazarded a thousand conjectures, each more extravagant than the last; but, in truth, I cared little whether she were a great lady or a courtesan, so that I could but see her once more.

My love, although the growth of a single hour, had taken imperishable root. I did not even dream of attempting to tear it up, so fully was I convinced such a thing would be impossible. That woman had completely taken possession of me. One look from her had sufficed to change my very nature. She had breathed her will into my life, and I no longer lived in myself, but in her and for her. I gave myself up to a thousand extravagancies. I kissed the place upon my hand which she had touched, and I repeated her name over and over again for hours in succession. I only needed to close my eyes in order to see her distinctly as though she were actually present; and I reiterated to myself the words she had uttered in my ear at the church porch: 'Unhappy man! Unhappy man! What hast thou done?' I comprehended at last the full horror of my situation, and the funereal and awful restraints of the state into which I had just entered became clearly revealed to me. To be a priest!—that is, to be chaste, to never love, to observe no distinction of sex or age, to turn from the sight of all beauty, to put out one's own eyes, to hide for ever crouching in the chill shadows of some church or cloister, to visit none but the dying, to watch by unknown corpses, and ever bear about with one the black soutane as a garb of mourning for oneself, so that your very dress might serve as a pall for your coffin.

And I felt life rising within me like a subterranean lake, expanding and overflowing; my blood leaped fiercely through my arteries; my long-restrained youth suddenly burst into active being, like the aloe which blooms but once in a hundred years, and then bursts into blossom with a clap of thunder.

What could I do in order to see Clarimonde once more? I had no pretext to offer for desiring to leave the seminary, not knowing any person in the city. I would not even be able to remain there but a short time, and was only waiting my assignment to the curacy which I must thereafter occupy. I tried to remove the bars of the window; but it was at a fearful height from the ground, and I found that as I had no ladder it would be useless to think of escaping thus. And, furthermore, I could descend thence only by night in any event, and afterward how should I be able to find my way through the inextricable labyrinth of streets? All these difficulties, which to many would have appeared altogether insignificant, were gigantic to me, a poor seminarist who had fallen in love only the day before for the first time, without experience, without money, without attire.

'Ah!' cried I to myself in my blindness, 'were I not a priest I could have seen her every day; I might have been her lover, her spouse. Instead of being wrapped in this dismal shroud of mine I would have had garments of silk and velvet, golden chains, a sword, and fair plumes like other handsome young cavaliers. My hair, instead of being dishonoured by the tonsure, would flow down upon my neck in waving curls; I would have a fine waxed moustache; I would be a gallant.' But one hour passed before an altar, a few hastily articulated words, had for ever cut me off from the number of the living, and I had myself sealed down the stone of my own tomb; I had with my own hand bolted the gate of my prison! I went to the window. The sky was beautifully blue; the trees had donned their spring robes; nature seemed to be making parade of an ironical joy. The *Place* was filled with people, some going, others coming; young beaux and young beauties were sauntering in couples toward the groves and gardens; merry youths passed by, cheerily trolling refrains of drinking-songs—it was all a picture of vivacity, life, animation, gaiety, which formed a bitter contrast with my mourning and my solitude. On the steps of the gate sat a young mother playing with her child. She kissed its little rosy mouth still impearled with drops of milk, and performed, in order to amuse it, a thousand divine little puerilities such as only mothers know how to invent. The father standing at a little distance smiled gently upon the charming group, and with folded arms seemed to hug his joy to his heart. I could not endure that spectacle. I closed the window with violence, and flung myself on my bed, my heart filled with frightful hate and jealousy, and gnawed my fingers and my bedcovers like a tiger that has passed ten days without food.

I know not how long I remained in this condition, but at last, while writhing on the bed in a fit of spasmodic fury, I suddenly perceived the Abbé Sérapion, who was standing erect in the centre of the room, watching me attentively. Filled with shame of myself, I let my head fall upon my breast and covered my face with my hands.

'Romuald, my friend, something very extraordinary is transpiring within you,' observed Sérapion, after a few moments' silence; 'your conduct is altogether inexplicable. You—always so quiet, so pious, so gentle—you to rage in your cell like a wild beast! Take heed, brother—do not listen to the suggestions of the devil. The Evil Spirit, furious that you have consecrated yourself for ever to the Lord, is prowling around you like a ravening wolf and making a last effort to obtain possession of you. Instead of allowing yourself to be conquered, my dear Romuald, make to yourself a cuirass of prayers, a buckler of mortifications, and combat the enemy like a valiant man; you will then assuredly overcome him. Virtue must be proved by temptation, and gold comes forth purer from the hands of the assayer. Fear not. Never allow yourself to become discouraged. The most watchful and steadfast souls are at moments liable to such temptation. Pray, fast, meditate, and the Evil Spirit will depart from you.'

The words of the Abbé Sérapion restored me to myself, and I became a little more calm. 'I came,' he continued, 'to tell you that you have been appointed to the curacy of C—. The priest who had charge of it has just died, and Monseigneur the Bishop has ordered me to have you installed there at once. Be ready, therefore, to start to-morrow.' I responded with an inclination of the head, and the Abbé retired. I opened my missal and commenced reading some prayers, but the letters became confused and blurred under my eyes, the thread of the ideas entangled itself hopelessly in my brain, and the volume at last fell from my hands without my being aware of it.

To leave to-morrow without having been able to see her again, to add yet another barrier to the many already interposed between us, to lose for ever all hope of being able to meet her, except, indeed, through a miracle! Even to write to her, alas! would be impossible, for by whom could I dispatch my letter? With my sacred character of priest, to whom could I dare unbosom myself, in whom could I confide? I became a prey to the bitterest anxiety.

Then suddenly recurred to me the words of the Abbé Sérapion regarding the artifices of the devil; and the strange character of the adventure, the supernatural beauty of Clarimonde, the phosphoric light of her eyes, the burning imprint of her hand, the agony into which she had thrown me, the sudden change wrought within me when all my piety vanished in a single instant—these and other things clearly testified to the work of the Evil One, and perhaps that satiny hand was but the glove which concealed his claws. Filled with terror at these fancies, I again picked up the missal which had slipped from my knees and fallen upon the floor, and once more gave myself up to prayer.

Next morning Sérapion came to take me away. Two mules freighted with our miserable valises awaited us at the gate. He mounted one, and I the other as well as I knew how.

As we passed along the streets of the city, I gazed attentively at all the windows and balconies in the hope of seeing Clarimonde, but it was yet early in the morning, and the city had hardly opened its eyes. Mine sought to penetrate the blinds and window-curtains of all the palaces before which we were passing. Sérapion doubtless attributed this curiosity to my admiration of the architecture, for he slackened the pace of his animal in order to give me time to look around me. At last we passed the city gates and commenced to mount the hill beyond. When we arrived at its summit I turned to take a last look at the place where Clarimonde dwelt. The shadow of a great cloud hung over all the city; the contrasting colours of its blue and red roofs were lost in the uniform half-tint, through which here and there floated upward, like white flakes of foam, the smoke of freshly kindled fires. By a singular optical effect one edifice, which surpassed in height all the neighbouring buildings that were still dimly veiled by the vapours, towered up, fair and lustrous with the gilding of a solitary beam of sunlight—although actually more than a league away it seemed quite near. The smallest details of its architecture were plainly distinguishable—the turrets, the platforms, the window-casements, and even the swallow-tailed weather-vanes.

'What is that palace I see over there, all lighted up by the sun?' I asked Sérapion. He shaded his eyes with his hand, and having looked in the direction indicated, replied: 'It is the ancient palace which the Prince Concini has given to the courtesan Clarimonde. Awful things are done there!'

At that instant, I know not yet whether it was a reality or an illusion, I fancied I saw gliding along the terrace a shapely white figure, which gleamed for a moment in passing and as quickly vanished. It was Clarimonde.

Oh, did she know that at that very hour, all feverish and restless—from the height of the rugged road which separated me from her, and which, alas! I could never more descend—I was directing my eyes upon the palace where she dwelt, and which a mocking beam of sunlight seemed to bring nigh to me, as though inviting me to enter therein as its lord? Undoubtedly she must have known it, for her soul was too sympathetically united with mine not to have felt its least emotional thrill, and that subtle sympathy it must have been which prompted her to climb—although clad only in her nightdress—to the summit of the terrace, amid the icy dews of the morning.

The shadow gained the palace, and the scene became to the eye only a motionless ocean of roofs and gables, amid which one mountainous undulation was distinctly visible. Sérapion urged his mule forward, my own at once followed at the same gait, and a sharp angle in the road at last hid the city of S— for ever from my eyes, as I was destined never to return thither. At the close of a weary three-days' journey through dismal country fields, we caught sight of the cock upon the steeple of the church which I was to take charge of, peeping above the trees, and after having followed some winding roads fringed with thatched cottages and little gardens, we found ourselves in front of the façade, which certainly possessed few features of magnificence. A porch ornamented with some mouldings, and two or three pillars rudely hewn from sandstone; a tiled roof with counterforts of the same sandstone as the pillars—that was all. To the left lay the cemetery, overgrown with high weeds, and having a great iron cross rising up in its centre; to the right stood the presbytery under the shadow of the church. It was a house of the most extreme simplicity and frigid cleanliness. We entered the enclosure. A few chickens were picking up some oats scattered upon the ground; accustomed, seemingly, to the black habit of ecclesiastics, they showed no fear of our presence and scarcely troubled themselves to get out of our way. A hoarse, wheezy barking fell upon our ears, and we saw an aged dog running toward us.

It was my predecessor's dog. He had dull bleared eyes, grizzled hair, and every mark of the greatest age to which a dog can possibly attain. I patted him gently, and he proceeded at once to march along beside me with an air of satisfaction unspeakable. A very old woman, who had been the housekeeper of the former curé, also came to meet us, and after having invited me into a little back parlour, asked whether I intended to retain her. I replied that I would take care of her, and the dog, and the chickens, and all the furniture her master had bequeathed her at his death. At this she became fairly transported with joy, and the Abbé Sérapion at once paid her the price which she asked for her little property.

As soon as my installation was over, the Abbé Sérapion returned to the seminary. I was, therefore, left alone, with no one but myself to look to for aid or counsel. The thought of Clarimonde again began to haunt me, and in spite of all my endeavours to banish it, I always found it present in my meditations. One evening, while promenading in my little garden along the walks bordered with box-plants, I fancied that I saw through the elm-trees the figure of a woman, who followed my every movement, and that I beheld two sea-green eyes gleaming through the foliage; but it was only an illusion, and on going round to the other side of the garden, I could find nothing except a footprint on the sanded walk-a footprint so small that it seemed to have been made by the foot of a child. The garden was enclosed by very high walls. I searched every nook and corner of it, but could discover no one there. I have never succeeded in fully accounting for this circumstance, which, after all, was nothing compared with the strange things which happened to me afterward.

For a whole year I lived thus, filling all the duties of my calling with the most scrupulous exactitude, praying and fasting, exhorting and lending ghostly aid to the sick, and bestowing alms even to the extent of frequently depriving myself of the very necessaries of life. But I felt a great aridness within me, and the sources of grace seemed closed against me. I never found that happiness which should spring from the fulfilment of a holy mission; my thoughts were far away, and the words of Clarimonde were ever upon my lips like an involuntary refrain. Oh, brother, meditate well on this! Through having but once lifted my eyes to look upon a woman, through one fault apparently so venial, I have for years remained a victim to the most miserable agonies, and the happiness of my life has been destroyed for ever.

I will not longer dwell upon those defeats, or on those inward victories invariably followed by yet more terrible falls, but will at once proceed to the facts of my story. One night my door-bell was long and violently rung. The aged housekeeper arose and opened to the stranger, and the figure of a man, whose complexion was deeply bronzed, and who was richly clad in a foreign costume, with a poniard at his girdle, appeared under the rays of Barbara's lantern. Her first impulse was one of terror, but the stranger reassured her, and stated that he desired to see me at once on matters relating to my holy calling. Barbara invited him upstairs, where I was on the point of retiring. The stranger told me that his mistress, a very noble lady, was lying at the point of death, and desired to see a priest. I replied that I was prepared to follow him, took with me the sacred articles necessary for extreme unction, and descended in all haste. Two horses black as the night itself stood without the gate, pawing the ground with impatience, and veiling their chests with long streams of smoky vapour exhaled from their nostrils. He held the stirrup and aided me to mount upon one; then, merely laying his hand upon the pommel of the saddle, he vaulted on the other, pressed the animal's sides with his knees, and loosened rein. The horse bounded forward with the velocity of an arrow. Mine, of which the stranger held the bridle, also started off at a swift gallop, keeping up with his companion. We devoured the road. The ground flowed backward beneath us in a long streaked line of pale gray, and the black silhouettes of the trees seemed fleeing by us on either side like an army in rout. We passed through a forest so profoundly gloomy that I felt my flesh creep in the chill darkness with superstitious fear. The showers of bright sparks which flew from the stony road under the ironshod feet of our horses remained glowing in our wake like a fiery trail; and had any one at that hour of the night beheld us both—my guide and myself—he must have taken us for two spectres riding upon nightmares. Witch-fires ever and anon flitted across the road before us, and the night-birds shrieked fearsomely in the depth of the woods beyond, where we beheld at intervals glow the phosphorescent eyes of wild cats. The manes of the horses became more and more dishevelled, the sweat streamed over their flanks, and their breath came through their nostrils hard and fast. But when he found them slacking pace, the guide reanimated them by uttering a strange, gutteral, unearthly cry, and the gallop recommenced with fury. At last the whirlwind race ceased; a huge black mass pierced through with many bright points of light suddenly rose before us, the hoofs of our horses echoed louder upon a strong wooden drawbridge, and we rode under a great vaulted archway which darkly yawned between two enormous towers. Some great excitement evidently reigned in the castle. Servants with torches were crossing the courtyard in every direction, and above lights were ascending and descending from landing to landing. I obtained a confused glimpse of vast masses of architecture—columns, arcades, flights of steps, stairways—a royal voluptuousness and elfin magnificence of construction worthy of fairyland. A negro page—the same who had before brought me the tablet from Clarimonde, and whom I instantly recognised—approached to aid me in dismounting, and the major-domo, attired in black velvet with a gold chain about his neck, advanced to meet me, supporting himself upon an ivory cane. Large tears were falling from his eyes and streaming over his cheeks and white beard. 'Too late!' he cried, sorrowfully shaking his venerable head. 'Too late, sir priest! But if you have not been able to save the soul, come at least to watch by the poor body.'

He took my arm and conducted me to the death-chamber. I wept not less bitterly than he, for I had learned that the dead one was none other than that Clarimonde whom I had so deeply and so wildly loved. A *prie-dieu* stood at the foot of the bed; a bluish flame flickering in a bronze pattern filled all the room with a wan, deceptive light, here and there bringing out in the darkness at intervals some projection of furniture or cornice. In a chiselled urn upon the table there was a faded white rose, whose leaves—excepting one that still held—had all fallen, like odorous tears, to the foot of the vase. A broken black mask, a fan, and disguises of every variety, which were lying on the armchairs, bore witness that death had entered suddenly and unannounced into that sumptuous dwelling. Without daring to cast my eyes upon the bed, I knelt down and commenced to repeat the Psalms for the Dead, with exceeding fervour, thanking God that He had placed the tomb between me and the memory of this woman, so that I might thereafter be able to utter her name in my prayers as a name for ever sanctified by death. But my fervour gradually weakened, and I fell insensibly into a reverie. That chamber bore no semblance to a chamber of death. In lieu of the fetid and cadaverous odours which I had been accustomed to breathe during such funereal vigils, a languorous vapour of Oriental perfume—I know not what amorous odour of woman—softly floated through the tepid air. That pale light seemed rather a twilight gloom contrived for voluptuous pleasure, than a substitute for the yellow-flickering watch-tapers which shine by the side of corpses. I thought upon the strange destiny which enabled me to meet Clarimonde again at the very moment when she was lost to me for ever, and a sigh of regretful anguish escaped from my breast. Then it seemed to me that some one behind me had also sighed, and I turned round to look. It was only an echo. But in that moment my eyes fell upon the bed of death which they had till then avoided. The red damask curtains, decorated with large flowers worked in embroidery and looped up with gold bullion, permitted me to behold the fair dead, lying at full length, with hands joined upon her bosom. She was covered with a linen wrapping of dazzling whiteness, which formed a strong contrast with the gloomy purple of the hangings, and was of so fine a texture that it concealed nothing of her body's charming form, and allowed the eye to follow those beautiful outlines—undulating like the neck of a swan—which even death had not robbed of their supple grace. She seemed an alabaster statue executed by some skilful sculptor to place upon the tomb of a queen, or rather, perhaps, like a slumbering maiden over whom the silent snow had woven a spotless veil.

I could no longer maintain my constrained attitude of prayer. The air of the alcove intoxicated me, that febrile perfume of half-faded roses penetrated my very brain, and I commenced to pace restlessly up and down the chamber, pausing at each turn before the bier to contemplate the graceful corpse lying beneath the transparency of its shroud. Wild fancies came thronging to my brain. I thought to myself that she might not, perhaps, be really dead; that she might only have feigned death for the purpose of bringing me to her castle, and then declaring her love. At one time I even thought I saw her foot move under the whiteness of the coverings, and slightly disarrange the long straight folds of the winding-sheet.

And then I asked myself: 'Is this indeed Clarimonde? What proof have I that it is she? Might not that black page have passed into the service of some other lady? Surely, I must be going mad to torture and afflict myself thus!' But my heart answered with a fierce throbbing: 'It is she; it is she indeed!' I approached the bed again, and fixed my eyes with redoubled attention upon the object of my incertitude. Ah, must I confess it? That exquisite perfection of bodily form, although purified and made sacred by the shadow of death, affected me more voluptuously than it should have done; and that repose so closely resembled slumber that one might well have mistaken it for such. I forgot that I had come there to perform a funeral ceremony; I fancied myself a young bridegroom entering the chamber of the bride, who all modestly hides her fair face, and through coyness seeks to keep herself wholly veiled. Heartbroken with grief, yet wild with hope, shuddering at once with fear and pleasure, I bent over her and grasped the corner of the sheet. I lifted it back, holding my breath all the while through fear of waking her. My arteries throbbed with such violence that I felt them hiss through my temples, and the sweat poured from my forehead in streams, as though I had lifted a mighty slab of marble.

There, indeed, lay Clarimonde, even as I had seen her at the church on the day of my ordination. She was not less charming than then. With her, death seemed but a last coquetry. The pallor of her cheeks, the less brilliant carnation of her lips, her long eyelashes lowered and relieving their dark fringe against that white skin, lent her an unspeakably seductive aspect of melancholy chastity and mental suffering; her long loose hair, still intertwined with some little blue flowers, made a shining pillow for her head, and veiled the nudity of her shoulders with its thick ringlets; her beautiful hands, purer, more diaphanous, than the Host, were crossed on her bosom in an attitude of pious rest and silent prayer, which served to counteract all that might have proven otherwise too alluring—even after death—in the exquisite roundness and ivory polish of her bare arms from which the pearl bracelets had not yet been removed. I remained long in mute contemplation, and the more I gazed, the less could I persuade myself that life had really abandoned that beautiful body for ever. I do not know whether it was an illusion or a reflection of the lamplight, but it seemed to me that the blood was again commencing to circulate under that lifeless pallor, although she remained all motionless. I laid my hand lightly on her arm; it was cold, but not colder than her hand on the day when it touched mine at the portals of the church. I resumed my position, bending my face above her, and bathing her cheek with the warm dew of my tears. Ah, what bitter feelings of despair and helplessness, what agonies unutterable did I endure in that long watch! Vainly did I wish that I could have gathered all my life into one mass that I might give it all to her, and breathe into her chill remains the flame which devoured me. The night advanced, and feeling the moment of eternal separation approach, I could not deny myself the last sad sweet pleasure of imprinting a kiss upon the dead lips of her who had been my only love. ... Oh, miracle! A faint breath mingled itself with my breath, and the mouth of Clarimonde responded to the passionate pressure of mine. Her eyes unclosed, and lighted up with something of their former brilliancy; she uttered a long sigh, and uncrossing her arms, passed them around my neck with a look of ineffable delight. 'Ah, it is thou, Romuald!' she murmured in a voice languishingly sweet as the last vibrations of a harp. 'What ailed thee, dearest? I waited so long for thee that I am dead; but we are now betrothed: I can see thee and visit thee. Adieu, Romuald, adieu! I love thee. That is all I wished to tell thee, and I give thee back the life which thy kiss for a moment recalled. We shall soon meet again.'

Her head fell back, but her arms yet encircled me, as though to retain me still. A furious whirlwind suddenly burst in the window, and entered the chamber. The last remaining leaf of the white rose for a moment palpitated at the extremity of the stalk like a butterfly's wing, then it detached itself and flew forth through the open casement, bearing with it the soul of Clarimonde. The lamp was extinguished, and I fell insensible upon the bosom of the beautiful dead.

When I came to myself again I was lying on the bed in my little room at the presbytery, and the old dog of the former curé was licking my hand, which had been hanging down outside of the covers. Barbara, all trembling with age and anxiety, was busying herself about the room, opening and shutting drawers, and emptying powders into glasses. On seeing me open my eyes, the old woman uttered a cry of joy, the dog yelped and wagged his tail, but I was still so weak that I could not speak a single word or make the slightest motion. Afterward I learned that I had lain thus for three days, giving no evidence of life beyond the faintest respiration. Those three days do not reckon in my life, nor could I ever imagine whither my spirit had departed during those three days; I have no recollection of aught relating to them. Barbara told me that the same coppery-complexioned man who came to seek me on the night of my departure from the presbytery had brought me back the next morning in a close litter, and departed immediately afterward. When I became able to collect my scattered thoughts, I reviewed within my mind all the circumstances of that fateful night. At first I thought I had been the victim of some magical illusion, but ere long the recollection of other circumstances, real and palpable in themselves, came to forbid that supposition. I could not believe that I had been dreaming, since Barbara as well as myself had seen the strange man with his two black horses, and described with exactness every detail of his figure and apparel. Nevertheless it appeared that none knew of any castle in the neighbourhood answering to the description of that in which I had again found Clarimonde.

One morning I found the Abbé Sérapion in my room. Barbara had advised him that I was ill, and he had come with all speed to see me. Although this haste on his part testified to an affectionate interest in me, yet his visit did not cause me the pleasure which it should have done. The Abbé Sérapion had something penetrating and inquisitorial in his gaze which made me feel very ill at ease. His presence filled me with embarrassment and a sense of guilt. At the first glance he divined my interior trouble, and I hated him for his clairvoyance.

While he inquired after my health in hypocritically honeyed accents, he constantly kept his two great yellow lion-eyes fixed upon me, and plunged his look into my soul like a sounding-lead. Then he asked me how I directed my parish, if I was happy in it, how I passed the leisure hours allowed me in the intervals of pastoral duty, whether I had become acquainted with many of the inhabitants of the place, what was my favourite reading, and a thousand other such questions. I answered these inquiries as briefly as possible, and he, without ever waiting for my answers, passed rapidly from one subject of query to another. That conversation had evidently no connection with what he actually wished to say. At last, without any premonition, but as though repeating a piece of news which he had recalled on the instant, and feared might otherwise be forgotten subsequently, he suddenly said, in a clear vibrant voice, which rang in my ears like the trumpets of the Last Judgment:

"The great courtesan Clarimonde died a few days ago, at the close of an orgie which lasted eight days and eight nights. It was something infernally splendid. The abominations of the banquets of Belshazzar and Cleopatra were re-enacted there. Good God, what age are we living in? The guests were served by swarthy slaves who spoke an unknown tongue, and who seemed to me to be veritable demons. The livery of the very least among them would have served for the gala-dress of an emperor. There have always been very strange stories told of this Clarimonde, and all her lovers came to a violent or miserable end. They used to say that she was a ghoul, a female vampire; but I believe she was none other than Beelzebub himself.'

He ceased to speak, and commenced to regard me more attentively than ever, as though to observe the effect of his words on me. I could not refrain from starting when I heard him utter the name of Clarimonde, and this news of her death, in addition to the pain it caused me by reason of its coincidence with the nocturnal scenes I had witnessed, filled me with an agony and terror which my face betrayed, despite my utmost endeavours to appear composed. Sérapion fixed an anxious and severe look upon me, and then observed: 'My son, I must warn you that you are standing with foot raised upon the brink of an abyss; take heed lest you fall therein. Satan's claws are long, and tombs are not always true to their trust. The tombstone of Clarimonde should be sealed down with a triple seal, for, if report be true, it is not the first time she has died. May God watch over you, Romuald!'

And with these words the Abbé walked slowly to the door. I did not see him again at that time, for he left for S— almost immediately.

I became completely restored to health and resumed my accustomed duties. The memory of Clarimonde and the words of the old Abbé were constantly in my mind; nevertheless no extraordinary event had occurred to verify the funereal predictions of Sérapion, and I had commenced to believe that his fears and my own terrors were over-exaggerated, when one night I had a strange dream. I had hardly fallen asleep when I heard my bed-curtains drawn apart, as their rings slided back upon the curtain rod with a sharp sound. I rose up quickly upon my elbow, and beheld the shadow of a woman standing erect before me. I recognised Clarimonde immediately. She bore in her hand a little lamp, shaped like those which are placed in tombs, and its light lent her fingers a rosy transparency, which extended itself by lessening degrees even to the opaque and milky whiteness of her bare arm. Her only garment was the linen winding-sheet which had shrouded her when lying upon the bed of death. She sought to gather its folds over her bosom as though ashamed of being so scantily clad, but her little hand was not equal to the task. She was so white that the colour of the drapery blended with that of her flesh under the pallid rays of the lamp. Enveloped with this subtle tissue which betrayed all the contour of her body, she seemed rather the marble statue of some fair antique bather than a woman endowed with life. But dead or living, statue or woman, shadow or body, her beauty was still the same, only that the green light of her eyes was less brilliant, and her mouth, once so warmly crimson, was only tinted with a faint tender rosiness, like that of her cheeks. The little blue flowers which I had noticed entwined in her hair were withered and dry, and had lost nearly all their leaves, but this did not prevent her from being charming—so charming that, notwithstanding the strange character of the adventure, and the unexplainable manner in which she had entered my room, I felt not even for a moment the least fear.

She placed the lamp on the table and seated herself at the foot of my bed; then bending toward me, she said, in that voice at once silvery clear and yet velvety in its sweet softness, such as I never heard from any lips save hers:

'I have kept thee long in waiting, dear Romuald, and it must have seemed to thee that I had forgotten thee. But I come from afar off, very far off, and from a land whence no other has ever yet returned. There is neither sun nor moon in that land whence I come: all is but space and shadow; there is neither road nor pathway: no earth for the foot, no air for the wing; and nevertheless behold me here, for Love is stronger than Death and must conquer him in the end. Oh what sad faces and fearful things I have seen on my way hither! What difficulty my soul, returned to earth through the power of will alone, has had in finding its body and reinstating itself therein! What terrible efforts I had to make ere I could lift the ponderous slab with which they had covered me! See, the palms of my poor hands are all bruised! Kiss them, sweet love, that they may be healed!' She laid the cold palms of her hands upon my mouth, one after the other. I kissed them, indeed, many times, and she the while watched me with a smile of ineffable affection.

I confess to my shame that I had entirely forgotten the advice of the Abbé Sérapion and the sacred office wherewith I had been invested. I had fallen without resistance, and at the first assault. I had not even made the least effort to repel the tempter. The fresh coolness of Clarimonde's skin penetrated my own, and I felt voluptuous tremors pass over my whole body. Poor child! in spite of all I saw afterward, I can hardly yet believe she was a demon; at least she had no appearance of being such, and never did Satan so skillfully conceal his claws and horns. She had drawn her feet up beneath her, and squatted down on the edge of the couch in an attitude full of negligent coquetry. From time to time she passed her little hand through my hair and twisted it into curls, as though trying how a new style of wearing it would become my face. I abandoned myself to her hands with the most guilty pleasure, while she accompanied her gentle play with the prettiest prattle. The most remarkable fact was that I felt no astonishment whatever at so extraordinary an adventure, and as in dreams one finds no difficulty in accepting the most fantastic events as simple facts, so all these circumstances seemed to me perfectly natural in themselves.

'I loved thee long ere I saw thee, dear Romuald, and sought thee everywhere. Thou wast my dream, and I first saw thee in the church at the fatal moment. I said at once, "It is he!" I gave thee a look into which I threw all the love I ever had, all the love I now have, all the love I shall ever have for thee—a look that would have damned a cardinal or brought a king to his knees at my feet in view of all his court. Thou remainedst unmoved, preferring thy God to me!

'Ah, how jealous I am of that God whom thou didst love and still lovest more than me!

'Woe is me, unhappy one that I am! I can never have thy heart all to myself, I whom thou didst recall to life with a kiss—dead Clarimonde, who for thy sake bursts asunder the gates of the tomb, and comes to consecrate to thee a life which she has resumed only to make thee happy!'

All her words were accompanied with the most impassioned caresses, which bewildered my sense and my reason to such an extent, that I did not fear to utter a frightful blasphemy for the sake of consoling her, and to declare that I loved her as much as God.

Her eyes rekindled and shone like chrysoprases. 'In truth?—in very truth?—as much as God!' she cried, flinging her beautiful arms around me. 'Since it is so, thou wilt come with me; thou wilt follow me whithersoever I desire. Thou wilt cast away thy ugly black habit. Thou shalt be the proudest and most envied of cavaliers; thou shalt be my lover! To be the acknowledged lover of Clarimonde, who has refused even a Pope! That will be something to feel proud of. Ah, the fair, unspeakably happy existence, the beautiful golden life we shall live together! And when shall we depart, my fair sir?'

'To-morrow! To-morrow!' I cried in my delirium.

'To-morrow, then, so let it be!' she answered. 'In the meanwhile I shall have opportunity to change my toilet, for this is a little too light and in nowise suited for a voyage. I must also forthwith notify all my friends who believe me dead, and mourn for me as deeply as they are capable of doing. The money, the dresses, the carriages—all will be ready. I shall call for thee at this same hour. Adieu, dear heart!' And she lightly touched my forehead with her lips. The lamp went out, the curtains closed again, and all became dark; a leaden, dreamless sleep fell on me and held me unconscious until the morning following.

I awoke later than usual, and the recollection of this singular adventure troubled me during the whole day. I finally persuaded myself that it was a mere vapour of my heated imagination. Nevertheless its sensations had been so vivid that it was difficult to persuade myself that they were not real, and it was not without some presentiment of what was going to happen that I got into bed at last, after having prayed God to drive far from me all thoughts of evil, and to protect the chastity of my slumber.

I soon fell into a deep sleep, and my dream was continued. The curtains again parted, and I beheld Clarimonde, not as on the former occasion, pale in her pale winding-sheet, with the violets of death upon her cheeks, but gay, sprightly, jaunty, in a superb travelling-dress of green velvet, trimmed with gold lace, and looped up on either side to allow a glimpse of satin petticoat. Her blond hair escaped in thick ringlets from beneath a broad black felt hat, decorated with white feathers whimsically twisted into various shapes. In one hand she held a little riding-whip terminated by a golden whistle. She tapped me lightly with it, and exclaimed: 'Well, my fine sleeper, is this the way you make your preparations? I thought I would find you up and dressed. Arise quickly, we have no time to lose.'

I leaped out of bed at once.

'Come, dress yourself, and let us go,' she continued, pointing to a little package she had brought with her. 'The horses are becoming impatient of delay and champing their bits at the door. We ought to have been by this time at least ten leagues distant from here.'

I dressed myself hurriedly, and she handed me the articles of apparel herself one by one, bursting into laughter from time to time at my awkwardness, as she explained to me the use of a garment when I had made a mistake. She hurriedly arranged my hair, and this done, held up before me a little pocket-mirror of Venetian crystal, rimmed with silver filigree-work, and playfully asked: 'How dost find thyself now? Wilt engage me for thy valet de chambre?'

I was no longer the same person, and I could not even recognise myself. I resembled my former self no more than a finished statue resembles a block of stone. My old face seemed but a coarse daub of the one reflected in the mirror. I was handsome, and my vanity was sensibly tickled by the metamorphosis.

That elegant apparel, that richly embroidered vest had made of me a totally different personage, and I marvelled at the power of transformation owned by a few yards of cloth cut after a certain pattern. The spirit of my costume penetrated my very skin and within ten minutes more I had become something of a coxcomb.

In order to feel more at ease in my new attire, I took several turns up and down the room. Clarimonde watched me with an air of maternal pleasure, and appeared well satisfied with her work. 'Come, enough of this child's play! Let us start, Romuald, dear. We have far to go, and we may not get there in time.' She took my hand and led me forth. All the doors opened before her at a touch, and we passed by the dog without awaking him.

At the gate we found Margheritone waiting, the same swarthy groom who had once before been my escort. He held the bridles of three horses, all black like those which bore us to the castle—one for me, one for him, one for Clarimonde. Those horses must have been Spanish genets born of mares fecundated by a zephyr, for they were fleet as the wind itself, and the moon, which had just risen at our departure to light us on the way, rolled over the sky like a wheel detached from her own chariot. We beheld her on the right leaping from tree to tree, and putting herself out of breath in the effort to keep up with us. Soon we came upon a level plain where, hard by a clump of trees, a carriage with four vigorous horses awaited us. We entered it, and the postillions urged their animals into a mad gallop. I had one arm around Clarimonde's waist, and one of her hands clasped in mine; her head leaned upon my shoulder, and I felt her bosom, half bare, lightly pressing against my arm. I had never known such intense happiness. In that hour I had forgotten everything, and I no more remembered having ever been a priest than I remembered what I had been doing in my mother's womb, so great was the fascination which the evil spirit exerted upon me. From that night my nature seemed in some sort to have become halved, and there were two men within me, neither of whom knew the other. At one moment I believed myself a priest who dreamed nightly that he was a gentleman, at another that I was a gentleman who dreamed he was a priest. I could no longer distinguish the dream from the reality, nor could I discover where the reality began or where ended the dream. The exquisite young lord and libertine railed at the priest, the priest loathed the dissolute habits of the young lord. Two spirals entangled and confounded the one with the other, yet never touching, would afford a fair representation of this bicephalic life which I lived. Despite the strange character of my condition, I do not believe that I ever inclined, even for a moment, to madness. I always retained with extreme vividness all the perceptions of my two lives. Only there was one absurd fact which I could not explain to myself—namely, that the consciousness of the same individuality existed in two men so opposite in character. It was an anomaly for which I could not account—whether I believed myself to be the curé of the little village of C—, or *Il Signor Romualdo,* the titled lover of Clarimonde.

Be that as it may, I lived, at least I believed that I lived, in Venice. I have never been able to discover rightly how much of illusion and how much of reality there was in this fantastic adventure. We dwelt in a great palace on the Canaleio, filled with frescoes and statues, and containing two Titians in the noblest style of the great master, which were hung in Clarimonde's chamber. It was a palace well worthy of a king. We had each our gondola, our *barcarolli* in family livery, our music hall, and our special poet. Clarimonde always lived upon a magnificent scale; there was something of Cleopatra in her nature. As for me, I had the retinue of a prince's son, and I was regarded with as much reverential respect as though I had been of the family of one of the twelve Apostles or the four Evangelists of the Most Serene Republic. I would not have turned aside to allow even the Doge to pass, and I do not believe that since Satan fell from heaven, any creature was ever prouder or more insolent than I. I went to the Ridotto, and played with a luck which seemed absolutely infernal. I received the best of all society—the sons of ruined families, women of the theatre, shrewd knaves, parasites, hectoring swashbucklers. But notwithstanding the dissipation of such a life, I always remained faithful to Clarimonde. I loved her wildly. She would have excited satiety itself, and chained inconstancy. To have Clarimonde was to have twenty mistresses; ay, to possess all women: so mobile, so varied of aspect, so fresh in new charms was she all in herself—a very chameleon of a woman, in sooth. She made you commit with her the infidelity you would have committed with another, by donning to perfection the character, the attraction, the style of beauty of the woman who appeared to please you. She returned my love a hundred-fold, and it was in vain that the young patricians and even the Ancients of the Council of Ten made her the most magnificent proposals. A Foscari even went so far as to offer to espouse her. She rejected all his overtures. Of gold she had enough. She wished no longer for anything but love—a love youthful, pure, evoked by herself, and which should be a first and last passion. I would have been perfectly happy but for a cursed nightmare which recurred every night, and in which I believed myself to be a poor village curé, practising mortification and penance for my excesses during the day. Reassured by my constant association with her, I never thought further of the strange manner in which I had become acquainted with Clarimonde. But the words of the Abbé Sérapion concerning her recurred often to my memory, and never ceased to cause me uneasiness.

For some time the health of Clarimonde had not been so good as usual; her complexion grew paler day by day. The physicians who were summoned could not comprehend the nature of her malady and knew not how to treat it. They all prescribed some insignificant remedies, and never called a second time. Her paleness, nevertheless, visibly increased, and she became colder and colder, until she seemed almost as white and dead as upon that memorable night in the unknown castle. I grieved with anguish unspeakable to behold her thus slowly perishing; and she, touched by my agony, smiled upon me sweetly and sadly with the fateful smile of those who feel that they must die.

One morning I was seated at her bedside, and breakfasting from a little table placed close at hand, so that I might not be obliged to leave her for a single instant. In the act of cutting some fruit I accidentally inflicted rather a deep gash on my finger. The blood immediately gushed forth in a little purple jet, and a few drops spurted upon Clarimonde. Her eyes flashed, her face suddenly assumed an expression of savage and ferocious joy such as I had never before observed in her. She leaped out of her bed with animal agility—the agility, as it were, of an ape or a cat—and sprang upon my wound, which she commenced to suck with an air of unutterable pleasure. She swallowed the blood in little mouthfuls, slowly and carefully, like a connoisseur tasting a wine from Xeres or Syracuse. Gradually her eyelids half closed, and the pupils of her green eyes became oblong instead of round. From time to time she paused in order to kiss my hand, then she would recommence to press her lips to the lips of the wound in order to coax forth a few more ruddy drops. When she found that the blood would no longer come, she arose with eyes liquid and brilliant, rosier than a May dawn; her face full and fresh, her hand warm and moist—in fine, more beautiful than ever, and in the most perfect health.

'I shall not die! I shall not die!' she cried, clinging to my neck, half mad with joy. 'I can love thee yet for a long time. My life is thine, and all that is of me comes from thee. A few drops of thy rich and noble blood, more precious and more potent than all the elixirs of the earth, have given me back life.'

This scene long haunted my memory, and inspired me with strange doubts in regard to Clarimonde; and the same evening, when slumber had transported me to my presbytery, I beheld the Abbé Sérapion, graver and more anxious of aspect than ever. He gazed attentively at me, and sorrowfully exclaimed: 'Not content with losing your soul, you now desire also to lose your body. Wretched young man, into how terrible a plight have you fallen!' The tone in which he uttered these words powerfully affected me, but in spite of its vividness even that impression was soon dissipated, and a thousand other cares erased it from my mind. At last one evening, while looking into a mirror whose traitorous position she had not taken into account, I saw Clarimonde in the act of emptying a powder into the cup of spiced wine which she had long been in the habit of preparing after our repasts. I took the cup, feigned to carry it to my lips, and then placed it on the nearest article of furniture as though intending to finish it at my leisure. Taking advantage of a moment when the fair one's back was turned, I threw the contents under the table, after which I retired to my chamber and went to bed, fully resolved not to sleep, but to watch and discover what should come of all this mystery. I did not have to wait long, Clarimonde entered in her nightdress, and having removed her apparel, crept into bed and lay down beside me. When she felt assured that I was asleep, she bared my arm, and drawing a gold pin from her hair, commenced to murmur in a low voice:

'One drop, only one drop! One ruby at the end of my needle. … Since thou lovest me yet, I must not die! … Ah, poor love! His beautiful blood, so brightly purple, I must drink it. Sleep, my only treasure! Sleep, my god, my child! I will do thee no harm; I will only take of thy life what I must to keep my own from being for ever extinguished. But that I love thee so much, I could well resolve to have other lovers whose veins I could drain; but since I have known thee all other men have become hateful to me.…Ah, the beautiful arm! How round it is! How white it is! How shall I ever dare to prick this pretty blue vein!' And while thus murmuring to herself she wept, and I felt her tears raining on my arm as she clasped it with her hands. At last she took the resolve, slightly punctured me with her pin, and commenced to suck up the blood which oozed from the place. Although she swallowed only a few drops, the fear of weakening me soon seized her, and she carefully tied a little band around my arm, afterward rubbing the wound with an unguent which immediately cicatrised it. Further doubts were impossible. The Abbé Sérapion was right. Notwithstanding this positive knowledge, however, I could not cease to love Clarimonde, and I would gladly of my own accord have given her all the blood she required to sustain her factitious life. Moreover, I felt but little fear of her. The woman seemed to plead with me for the vampire, and what I had already heard and seen sufficed to reassure me completely. In those days I had plenteous veins, which would not have been so easily exhausted as at present; and I would not have thought of bargaining for my blood, drop by drop. I would rather have opened myself the veins of my arm and said to her: 'Drink, and may my love infiltrate itself throughout thy body together with my blood!' I carefully avoided ever making the least reference to the narcotic drink she had prepared for me, or to the incident of the pin, and we lived in the most perfect harmony.

Yet my priestly scruples commenced to torment me more than ever, and I was at a loss to imagine what new penance I could invent in order to mortify and subdue my flesh. Although these visions were involuntary, and though I did not actually participate in anything relating to them, I could not dare to touch the body of Christ with hands so impure and a mind defiled by such debauches whether real or imaginary. In the effort to avoid falling under the influence of these wearisome hallucinations, I strove to prevent myself from being overcome by sleep. I held my eyelids open with my fingers, and stood for hours together leaning upright against the wall, fighting sleep with all my might; but the dust of drowsiness invariably gathered upon my eyes at last, and finding all resistance useless, I would have to let my arms fall in the extremity of despairing weariness, and the current of slumber would again bear me away to the perfidious shores. Sérapion addressed me with the most vehement exhortations, severely reproaching me for my softness and want of fervour. Finally, one day when I was more wretched than usual, he said to me: 'There is but one way by which you can obtain relief from this continual torment, and though it is an extreme measure it must be made use of; violent diseases require violent remedies. I know where Clarimonde is buried. It is necessary that we shall disinter her remains, and that you shall behold in how pitiable a state the object of your love is. Then you will no longer be tempted to lose your soul for the sake of an unclean corpse devoured by worms, and ready to crumble into dust. That will assuredly restore you to yourself.' For my part, I was so tired of this double life that I at once consented, desiring to ascertain beyond a doubt whether a priest or a gentleman had been the victim of delusion. I had become fully resolved either to kill one of the two men within me for the benefit of the other, or else to kill both, for so terrible an existence could not last long and be endured. The Abbé Sérapion provided himself with a mattock, a lever, and a lantern, and at midnight we wended our way to the cemetery of —, the location and place of which were perfectly familiar to him. After having directed the rays of the dark lantern upon the inscriptions of several tombs, we came at last upon a great slab, half concealed by huge weeds and devoured by mosses and parasitic plants, whereupon we deciphered the opening lines of the epitaph:

Here lies Clarimonde Who was famed in her life-time As the fairest of women.*

*Ici gît Clarimonde Qui fut de son vivant La plus belle du monde.

The broken beauty of the lines is unavoidably lost in the translation.

'It is here without a doubt,' muttered Sérapion, and placing his lantern on the ground, he forced the point of the lever under the edge of the stone and commenced to raise it. The stone yielded, and he proceeded to work with the mattock. Darker and more silent than the night itself, I stood by and watched him do it, while he, bending over his dismal toil, streamed with sweat, panted, and his hard-coming breath seemed to have the harsh tone of a death rattle. It was a weird scene, and had any persons from without beheld us, they would assuredly have taken us rather for profane wretches and shroud-stealers than for priests of God. There was something grim and fierce in Sérapion's zeal which lent him the air of a demon rather than of an apostle or an angel, and his great aquiline face, with all its stern features, brought out in strong relief by the lantern-light, had something fearsome in it which enhanced the unpleasant fancy. I felt an icy sweat come out upon my forehead in huge beads, and my hair stood up with a hideous fear. Within the depths of my own heart I felt that the act of the austere Sérapion was an abominable sacrilege; and I could have prayed that a triangle of fire would issue from the entrails of the dark clouds, heavily rolling above us, to reduce him to cinders. The owls which had been nestling in the cypress-trees, startled by the gleam of the lantern, flew against it from time to time, striking their dusty wings against its panes, and uttering plaintive cries of lamentation; wild foxes yelped in the far darkness, and a thousand sinister noises detached themselves from the silence. At last Sérapion's mattock struck the coffin itself, making its planks re-echo with a deep sonorous sound, with that terrible sound nothingness utters when stricken. He wrenched apart and tore up the lid, and I beheld Clarimonde, pallid as a figure of marble, with hands joined; her white winding-sheet made but one fold from her head to her feet. A little crimson drop sparkled like a speck of dew at one corner of her colourless mouth. Sérapion, at this spectacle, burst into fury: 'Ah, thou art here, demon! Impure courtesan! Drinker of blood and gold!' And he flung holy water upon the corpse and the coffin, over which he traced the sign of the cross with his sprinkler. Poor Clarimonde had no sooner been touched by the blessed spray than her beautiful body crumbled into dust, and became only a shapeless and frightful mass of cinders and half-calcined bones.

'Behold your mistress, my Lord Romuald!' cried the inexorable priest, as he pointed to these sad remains. 'Will you be easily tempted after this to promenade on the Lido or at Fusina with your beauty?' I covered my face with my hands, a vast ruin had taken place within me. I returned to my presbytery, and the noble Lord Romuald, the lover of Clarimonde, separated himself from the poor priest with whom he had kept such strange company so long. But once only, the following night, I saw Clarimonde. She said to me, as she had said the first time at the portals of the church: 'Unhappy man! Unhappy man! What hast thou done? Wherefore have hearkened to that imbecile priest? Wert thou not happy? And what harm had I ever done thee that thou shouldst violate my poor tomb, and lay bare the miseries of my nothingness? All communication between our souls and our bodies is henceforth for ever broken. Adieu! Thou wilt yet regret me!' She vanished in air as smoke, and I never saw her more.

Alas! she spoke truly indeed. I have regretted her more than once, and I regret her still. My soul's peace has been very dearly bought. The love of God was not too much to replace such a love as hers. And this, brother, is the story of my youth. Never gaze upon a woman, and walk abroad only with eyes ever fixed upon the ground; for however chaste and watchful one may be, the error of a single moment is enough to make one lose eternity.

The Family of a Vourdalak

Alexis Tolstoy

GATHERED IN VIENNA IN the year 1815 was the cream of Europe's intellectuals, the elite of the international diplomatic set and all the towering social figures of the day. The congress was coming to an end. Royalist émigrés were preparing to return to their restored châteaux, and Russian fighters to their forsaken homes, while a number of discontented Poles were scheming to bring to Cracow their dreams of liberty and freedom, dubiously promised them by Prince Metternich, Prince Gartenberg and Count Nesselrode.

The scene resembled the aftermath of an animated social ball. For, in those late hours, after the fanfare and revelry had subsided, there remained a small core of people who, still possessing a taste for amusement and the delightful company of the Austrian ladies, were delaying their departures. This congenial circle, of which I was a member, gathered twice weekly in the manor of the Dowager Princess Schwartzenberg, several miles from the city on the outskirts of the tiny village, Gitzing. The aristocratic bearing of the mistress of the manor, her gracious amiability and her astute intellect held for her guests a magnetic attraction. On these blissful occasions, the mornings were devoted to promenades, and the afternoons to lunching in the manor or its environs. Evenings we spent luxuriating by the hearth, chatting—but never about politics, which was strictly forbidden. We surely had had our fill of that. Sometimes we related tales, either the superstitions and legends of our mother countries or our own experiences.

One evening, after a round of story-telling which left everyone in that strained condition relieved only by the enveloping semidarkness, the Marquis d'Urfé, an elderly émigré who was loved for his youthful gaiety and penetrating wit, interrupted the ensuing silence.

"Your tales, gentlemen, are unusual of course, but each, it seems to me, lacks the critical ingredient of personal involvement. I don't know whether any of you has ever actually witnessed the supernatural phenomenon of which you speak or if you can back it up with your word of honor."

Since not one of us could comply, the old man continued, decorously straightening his jabot.

"As for myself, gentlemen, I know of only one case similar to yours, but so strange, horrible and, what is most essential, authentic is it that even the most incredulous man will be left horror-stricken. I unfortunately was both witness and actor, and though I rarely like to recall the experience, I will do so if our charming ladies will only grant me their permission."

General consent followed immediately. A few apprehensive faces glanced toward the moonlit squares on the parquet marble of the hall where we were assembled. Slowly our small circle drew closer together, silently awaiting the tale. The marquis took out his gold snuffbox, drew a pinch, languourously inhaled and thus began.

"First of all, mesdames, I wish to ask your forgiveness if during my story I allude to my affairs of the heart more often than is agreeable for a man my age. But, as you will see, they are essential for the clarity of my story. And since it is excusable in old age to forget oneself, I hope none of you will mind if I imagine myself a young man again. It was in 1769 that I fell hopelessly in love with the exquisite Duchesse de Gramont. This passion, which at the time I considered deep indeed, left me no peace either day or night, and the duchess, like most beautiful women, prolonged my anguish. In a moment of extreme agitation, I requested and received a diplomatic mission to the Gospodar of Moldavia, where negotiations were being held with Versailles on matters of great importance to France. Before my departure, I visited the duchess. She greeted me less mockingly than ever before; in fact, with genuine concern.

"'D'Urfé, you are acting like a madman. But I know you, and I know you will never change your mind. And so, I beg you for only one thing. Please accept this small cross as a token of my friendship. Wear it until you return. It's a family relic which we value highly.'

"With gallantry perhaps misplaced at that moment, I kissed not the family relic but the delicate hand and fastened the cross around my neck. I have never removed it since.

Alexis Tolstoy, "The Family of a Vourdalak," *Vampires: Stories of the Supernatural*, trans. Fedor Nikanov, pp. 92–107, 109–125. Copyright © 1969 by The Estate of Fedor Nikanov.

"I shan't tire you, mesdames, with the details of my trip, with my observations about the Hungarians and Serbs—those poor but brave and honest people who, in spite of Turkish enslavement, had forsaken neither their dignity nor their former independence. It's enough to tell you that having learned Polish during my extended stay in Warsaw, I also managed to acquire some Serbian. Thus, I was able to make myself understood when I finally came upon a particular village, the name of which does not matter. Upon arriving at my quarters, I found my hosts in a state of profound confusion. This seemed especially strange since it was Sunday, the day Serbs abandon themselves to such amusements as dancing, sharpshooting, wrestling and the like. Ascribing their mood to some recent misfortune, I was about to depart when an imposing young man approached and took my hand.

"'Enter. Enter, foreigner,' he urged. 'Don't be upset by our sadness. You will understand when I explain its origin.'

"He told me that his elderly father, Gorcha, a restless and wild-tempered man, arose one morning and took a long Turkish rifle from the wall.

"'Childen,' said he to his two sons, George and Peter, 'I'm going up in the mountains to join the brave ones who are chasing the scoundrel, Ali Beg.'

"Such was called the Turkish bandit who continued to harass the neighborhood.

"'Wait ten days for me, and if by then I do not return, have a priest say a funeral Mass, for it will mean that I have been killed. But,' added old Gorcha sternly, 'if, and may God save you, I should return after those ten days, then, for your own sakes, do not permit me to enter the house. I order you to pierce me with a stake made of ash, regardless of what I will say or do. Because then I will no longer be myself, but rather a cursed vourdalak come to suck your blood.'

"I must digress, mesdames, to explain that the vourdalaks, or vampires, are, according to local opinion in Slavic nations, dead bodies that rise from graves in order to suck blood from the living. Although their habits are similar to vampires of other countries, vourdalaks prefer to suck the blood of close relatives and friends, who die and become vampires also. In Estonia and Herzegovina entire villages may be composed of vourdalaks. Indeed, the Abbot Augustine Colliné, in his curious book on ghosts, indicates terrible examples of this phenomenon. Moreover, commissioners appointed by German emperors to investigate cases of vampirism have printed evidence of vourdalaks, who, being pierced through the heart with ash stakes, were buried in the village squares. Testimony offered by those officials who had been present at the piercings assure us that they heard the corpses moaning as the stakes struck their hearts. I might add that all such testimony was delivered under oath and backed by signatures and authoritative seals.

"Keeping this in mind, it should be easy, mesdames, for you to comprehend the effect of Gorcha's words upon his sons. Both threw themselves at his feet, pleading that he let them go to the mountains in his place. Gorcha didn't even reply. He simply turned his back on them and set forth, whistling an old ballad.

"The day I arrived in this village was the day appointed by Gorcha for his return, so it was not difficult for me to appreciate his family's alarm. Also, this was a fine family. George, the elder of the two sons, married and with two children, seemed to be the serious and firm one. His brother, Peter, a handsome eighteen-year-old youth, had a gentle manner. He was obviously a favorite of his younger sister, Zdenka, a true Slavic beauty. I was immediately struck by her resemblance to the Duchesse de Gramont, particularly with respect to one characteristic, a delicate line on her forehead. To this day, I have never seen it on anyone other than those two. This faint line, which did not seem appealing at first, became irresistible once you had noticed it a few times.

"Perhaps I was too impressionable then, or maybe this characteristic resemblance combined with Zdenka's charming naïveté was, in fact, irresistible. Having spoken to her briefly, I felt an affection that was destined to become even more tender.

"I remember we were all sitting at the table that was set with farmer's cheese and a jug of milk. Zdenka was weaving; her sister-in-law was preparing supper for the children who were playing in the sand at her feet. Peter was lightheartedly whistling as he cleaned his *jitagan,* a long Turkish dagger. George, who was leaning his elbows on the table with his chin in his hands, could not take his eyes off the main road. He sat there brooding.

"I, also confused by the melancholy atmosphere, stared at the evening clouds and at the monastery rising above the pines of a nearby forest. This monastery, as I later discovered, had been famous at one time for its miraculous icon of the Holy Virgin which, according to legend, was brought by the angels and hung on the branches of an oak tree. During the preceding century, the invading Turks had slaughtered the monks and destroyed this cloister. Now there remained only the walls and a shrine where a mysterious hermit served Mass. He also guided travelers through the ruins and sheltered pilgrims who, journeying from shrine to shrine, preferred to stop at Our Lady under the Oak. Of course, I learned all of this later, since that evening my thoughts were hardly on the archeology of Serbia. As often happens when one gives free rein to thought, I became engrossed with memories of earlier days, with the enchanting period of my childhood and with friends whom I had left for this remote and uncivilized country. And I was dreaming about the Duchesse de Gramont, and—but what is the use of hiding my sinful thoughts?—I mused, mesdames, about several other contemporaries of your grandmothers', whose beauty, in spite of my will, reminded me, each in turn, of the charming duchess. Thus obsessed, I was soon oblivious to my hosts and their anxiety.

"Suddenly, George broke the silence to ask his wife about the exact time the old man had left.

"'At eight o'clock,' she replied. 'I remember hearing the monastery bell strike then.'

"'Well, now it must be no later than half past seven,' he said, becoming pensive and gazing again at the long road leading into the forest.

"I failed to mention, mesdames, that when the Serbs suspect someone of vampirism, they avoid referring to him directly. Otherwise they would call him forth from his grave. Consequently, George alluded to his father as the 'old man.'

"Several minutes of silence lasted until one of the boys pulled Zdenka by the apron, asking, 'Auntie, when is Grandfather coming home?'

"George responded to this question with a violent slap. The child began to cry, whereupon his younger brother asked, surprised and frightened, 'Why do you forbid us, Father, to speak of Grandfather?' Another slap silenced him instantly. Then both began to howl as the rest of the family made a sign of the cross. At that very moment, the monastery clock struck the first chime of eight and a human figure emerged from the forest.

"'It's he, thank God!' exclaimed Zdenka, Peter and their sister-in-law all at once.

"'God protect us!' George cried. 'And how are we to tell if the ten days appointed by him have passed or not?'

"Everyone gazed at him in horror. Meanwhile, the human figure was approaching closer, closer, closer. A tall old man with a gray mustache and a pale and stern face dragged himself with the aid of a stick. The closer he drew, the gloomier George became. Finally, the newcomer stopped and circled his family with a look that seemed oblivious, so glazed and distant were his eyes.

"'Well,' he said in a timbreless voice, 'why does no one meet me? What does this silence mean? Don't you see I'm wounded?'

"Then we all noticed that the old man's left side was drenched with blood.

"'Hold your father up,' I motioned to George. 'And you, Zdenka, give him something to strengthen him; otherwise, he will collapse.'

"'Father,' said George approaching Gorcha, 'show me your wound. I know about wounds and I'll bandage it for you.' But as soon as the son attempted to take off his coat, the old man pushed him away viciously, clasping his side with both hands.

"'Let go, clumsy one. You are hurting me.'

"'That means you're wounded in the heart!' George exclaimed, his face blanching. 'Take off your coat! Take it off, do you hear! It's crucial, do you hear me!'

"The old man rose to his full height. 'Watch out!' he warned, in that same flat voice. 'If you touch me, I shall curse you.'

"Peter placed himself between George and his father. 'Let him be. You must see he's suffering.'

"'Don't go against his will,' his wife advised. 'You know he'll never tolerate such a thing.'

"At that moment we saw the herd heading toward the house in a cloud of dust. It was not certain whether the dog escorting them did not recognize her old master or if something else influenced her, for as soon as she spied Gorcha, she halted. Her fur bristled. She growled, shivering in her tracks as if she were seeing something extraordinary.

"'What's the matter with the dog?' the old man asked, his frown deepening. 'Have I become a stranger to my own family? Did the ten days in the mountain change me so much that my own dog does not recognize me?'

"'Do you hear?' George nudged his wife.

"'What, George?'

"'He said himself that ten days have passed.'

"'Oh, no! And did he not come at the appointed hour?'

"'Yes, yes. It's clear what has to be done.'

"'The accursed dog is still howling. Shoot her!' Gorcha commanded. 'Do you hear me?'

"George didn't move. But Peter, with tears in his eyes, arose, lifted his father's rifle and shot the dog which whimpered, rolling in the dust. 'This one was my favorite,' he said huskily. 'I don't know why my father had to have her killed.'

"'Because that's all she was worth,' Gorcha snapped. 'But it has grown cool. I want to be under the roof.'

"While all this took place, Zdenka prepared a drink of vodka with pears, honey and raisins for the old man, which he pushed away with disgust. He displayed the same loathing for the lamb and rice that George placed before him. Then he went to sit in a corner, muttering unintelligibly.

"The pine logs were flaming in the fireplace, their flicker illuminating the old man's gaunt and pallid face. Were it not for the fire's glow, he could have been taken for a dead man. Zdenka sat down beside him.

"'Father, you do not eat or rest. But do tell us about your adventures in the mountain.'

"By saying this, the girl knew she was striking the most sensitive cord in the old man's heart. He loved to recount his battles and exploits against the Turks. A faint smile crossed his livid lips, though his eyes remained unexpressive. He responded by stroking his daughter's lovely blond hair.

"'Zdenka,' he said, 'I will tell you what I saw in the mountain, but not now, not today. I am tired after all. I can tell you one thing. Ali Beg is dead. He perished by your father's stroke. If anyone doubts it, here is the proof!' He pulled open the bag which was slung across his shoulder, removing a bloody head, not much less cadaverous than his own. We all turned away with a shudder. Gorcha, handing it to Peter, said, 'Hang it over the door of our house so that all those who pass may know that Ali Beg is dead, that the roads are free of villains—unless one counts the Yanychars of the Sultan!'

"Peter obeyed, though with obvious aversion. 'Now everything's clear to me,' he reflected. 'The poor dog was growling because she smelled dead flesh.'

"'Yes, she smelled dead flesh ...' George mumbled, after having returned unobtrusively with something in his hand which he rested in a nearby corner. It looked like a sharply pointed pole.

"'George,' whispered his wife, 'you don't mean you intend to ...'

"'Brother,' murmured Zdenka, 'what do you have in mind? No, no, no. You're not going to do this! It's inconceivable!'

"'Let me be,' warned George. 'I know what I'm doing and it won't be anything rash.'

"Meanwhile, night had fallen and the family wandered off to sleep in that part of the house which was separated from my own room by a thin partition. I must confess that everything I had observed affected me strangely. I snuffed out the candle. The moon shone through my window, casting bluish reflections on the floor—similar to those, mesdames, you see before your very own eyes. I felt sleepy, but, needless to say, I could not fall asleep. Attributing it to the moonlight, I searched for something to drape across the window. But I couldn't find anything. I was startled by voices coming from the other side of the partition and strained to hear what they were saying.

"'Lie down, wife,' George said soothingly. 'You, Peter, and you, Zdenka, don't worry about anything. I'll stand watch.'

"'No, George,' answered his wife. 'It's I who should not be sleeping. You worked all last night; you're exhausted. Besides, I have to attend our elder son who's been ill since yesterday. Don't worry. Lie down. I'll watch for you.'

"'Brother,' Zdenka said in her caressing voice, 'it seems that nobody has to watch for anything. See how peacefully Father sleeps.'

"'Not my wife, nor you, nor anyone seems to have much sense,' George replied in a voice that left no room for contradiction. 'Now I've told you to go to sleep. I'll be the guard!'

"Complete silence followed. Soon, my eyelids grew heavy, and I too fell asleep. The slow creaking of my door awakened me. The old man, Gorcha was entering. I could feel his presence through the pitch darkness. He seemed to be observing me through his vacant eyes. He lifted one foot after another, stealthily, until he was by my side. Consumed with terror, I nevertheless managed to remain still. The old man bent over me, his livid face so close to mine that I could feel his corpselike breath. Then, exerting superhuman effort, I discovered myself sitting up in bed, perspiring profusely. No one was in the room. But through the window I detected Gorcha, his face pressed against the pane, his uncanny eyes riveted upon me. I didn't have the strength to cry out, only enough composure to remain in bed and pretend I saw nothing. The old man was evidently reassuring himself that I was asleep, for, having stared at me thus, he slowly moved away from the window. George was snoring so loudly that the walls rattled. Then I heard Gorcha's voice in the next room. The sick child coughed.

"'You're not asleep, my little boy?' Gorcha asked.

"'No, Grandfather, and I'd like very much to talk to you.'

"'Ah, you want to talk with me. And what will it be about?'

"'I'd like you to tell me how you fought the Turks because I also want to fight them.'

"'I thought you would, my dear child. Tomorrow, I will give you the small dagger I've been saving.'

"'Oh, Grandfather, please give it to me now.'

"'Well, my little one, why didn't you talk with me earlier today?'

"'Because … because Father wouldn't let me.'

"'Your father is very cautious. But you want the dagger very much …'

"'Yes, I want it *very* much. Only not here because Father might wake up.'

"'Where, then?'

"'Well, let's go outside quietly, Grandfather, so no one can hear us.'

"Gorcha seemed to laugh as the boy got out of bed. I didn't believe in vampires. But my nerves had been so shattered by my nightmare that I got up and slammed my fist against the partition lest I reproach myself later. No one woke, though my blow sounded loud enough to waken the seven sleepers in the Arabian fairy tale. Determined to save the child, I hurled myself against the door, but it was locked from the outside. To intensify my frustration, the old man was already passing the window with the child in his arms.

"'Get up! Get up!' I screamed with all my might, shaking the partition vehemently. Only then did George awaken.

"'Hurry,' I cried. 'He's carrying your child away.' With one swift kick, George broke down the door and darted toward the forest. With some trouble I wakened Peter, then his sister-in-law and Zdenka. Huddled in front of the house, we saw George a few minutes later returning with the boy in his arms. The child had already fainted when George stumbled upon him on the main highway. We revived him, though he appeared no sicker than before. To our anxious interrogation, he explained that Grandfather had done him no harm, that they had strolled together, quietly chatting; that once they were in the fresh air, he had fainted, though he couldn't remember how or why.

"Gorcha was nowhere to be found, so the remainder of the night was spent in hushed consultation.

"The next morning I learned that ice was floating in the river, preventing anyone from crossing to the mainland for several days. Even if it were possible for me to leave, however, I could not have done so. The more I saw Zdenka, the more I craved her. And, mesdames, I am not, mind you, one of those who believe in sudden, uncontrollable passion, the kind exalted in novels. Yet I do believe that love can sometimes develop more quickly than is usual. In Zdenka's remarkable beauty I encountered the Duchesse de Gramont, the duchess transformed by pastoral garb and melodious foreign speech. The characteristic line both had on their foreheads was the *coup de grâce*. Yet perhaps it really was the incredible situation in which I had become an actor that ignited my intense passion.

"During that day I overheard Zdenka speaking with her younger brother. 'What do you think about Father, Peter?' she asked. 'I can't believe you suspect him.'

"'I dare not suspect him, especially since the boy assured us that Father didn't harm him. As for his sudden disappearance, well, you know he has done this before and never explained his activities and departures.'

"'I know,' Zdenka agreed. 'But you know that George is—'

"'Yes, I know. I know. It's useless talking to him. I'm afraid we'll have to hide the stake. He won't be able to get another one. There are no ash trees on this side of the mountain.'

"'Yes, let's hide it. But don't tell the children, for they'll surely tell George.'

"'We must be cautious,' Peter urged, and they separated.

"Night came, and still not a trace of the old man, Gorcha. Like the previous night, I was in bed, distracted by the moonbeams that illuminated my room. Sleep was beginning to distort my thoughts when I instinctively felt the presence of the old man. Opening my eyes, I saw his deathlike face pressed against the pane. This time I tried to get up, but my limbs were paralyzed. I heard the old man go around the house and knock on George's window. The child tossed and moaned in his sleep. For a while, silence prevailed. Then there was a knock at the child's window. He moaned again and woke up.

"'Is that you, Grandfather?'

"'It's me,' he answered solemnly. 'I brought you the little dagger.'

"'I don't dare come out. Father has forbidden it.'

"'But you don't have to. Just open the window and kiss me.'

"As the window was being opened, I summoned all my nerve, jumped off the bed and began knocking on the partition. George was immediately up. I heard him cursing and his wife screaming. A minute later the entire household clustered around the fainted child. As before, Gorcha had vanished. We revived the child, though he was weak and could barely breathe. The poor little thing didn't understand why he had fainted. His mother and Zdenka ascribed it to the child's fear of being caught in a forbidden conversation with his grandfather. I said nothing. When the boy grew quiet, everyone but George went to sleep. At dawn, I heard him awaken his wife. They were whispering. Zdenka joined them. The women were crying.

"The child died. I shall not elaborate on the family's despair, except to mention that, peculiarly enough, nobody attributed his death to Gorcha. At least not publicly.

"George remained reticent, his gloomy expression menacing. For two days the old man did not reappear. The third night, on the day of the little one's burial, I sensed that somebody was roaming through the house murmuring the name of the child who was still alive. It even seemed to me, momentarily, that Gorcha glanced into my window. I couldn't be sure, since the moon was obscured by clouds. Nevertheless, I reported this to George. He questioned the child, who acknowledged that he had heard his grandfather calling him and had seen him at the window outside his room. George commanded his son to awaken him the next time the old man appeared.

"These events curiously intensified my tenderness for Zdenka. I existed in constant agitation. During the day it was impossible to speak with her alone. At night, I was tormented by the prospect of my imminent departure.

"Zdenka's room was separated from mine by a hall which led on one side to the street, on the other to the yard. On my way for a walk before sleeping, I passed through the hall and noticed her door slightly ajar.

In spite of myself, I stood behind it, listening. The familiar rustle of her dress made my heart pound. She was singing a song about a Serbian knight saying farewell to his girl.

"Oh, my young poplar," the old king said, "I am off to the wars and you will forget me. The trees that grow at the foot of the mountain are slender and easily bent, but your young body is even more slender and even more easily bent. Bittersweet berries are red. They are effortlessly blown by the wind. But your lips are redder than the berries. And I am like the old oak without leaves; my beard whiter than the Danube's foam. You will forget me, little heart, and I will perish from longing, for the enemy will not dare to kill the old king." Then the beautiful girl answered. "I swear to remain faithful to you, never to forget you. If I break my oath, then return after death to suck my heart's blood." To which the old king replied, "Amen." He went off to war and the beautiful girl forgot him.

"Here Zdenka stopped as if afraid to finish the song. I could no longer contain myself. Her soft eloquence was an echo of the Duchesse de Gramont. Disregarding the consequences, I flung open the door. My intrusion made her blush, for she had just removed her outer garment and was wearing only a gold-embroidered red silk blouse and a richly colored petticoat. The outline of her supple limbs was visible, her abundant blond hair unbraided. In this state of half-undress, she looked more ravishing than ever.

"'Zdenka, my life, please do not fear me,' I implored. 'Everybody is asleep. Only the crickets in the grass and the dragonfly in the air can hear what I'm going to tell you.'

"'Go away, go away, my dearest. If my brother sees us, I'm lost.'

"'Zdenka, I will not leave until you promise to love me as the lovely maiden in your song promised to love the king. Zdenka, I soon will have to depart. Who knows whether we shall ever see each other again. I love you more than my own soul, more than my salvation. My life and my blood are yours. Won't you give me but an hour?'

"'Too much can happen in an hour,' Zdenka said softly, leaving her hand in mine. 'You don't know my brother. I have a premonition that he will see us.'

"'Don't worry, Zdenka, my darling Zdenka. Your brother is exhausted by these sleepless nights. He is lulled by the wind rustling through the trees. His slumber is deep. Our night is long, and I beg you for only one hour, whereas the farewell may last forever.'

"'No, no. Not forever!'

"'Perhaps, Zdenka. Yet I see only you, hear only you. I am no longer master over my own fate. It's as if I were compelled by a superior power. Forgive me!' and like a madman I pressed her to my heart.

"'You're not a friend to me, no, no, no,' she gasped, breaking away from my arms and hiding in a corner.

"I don't recall what I replied to her at that moment, for my sudden boldness alarmed me, though not because I was inhibited in the past, but because, in spite of my passion, I deeply respected Zdenka's purity. Thus, my gallant manner, so successful with the beautiful maidens of the time, shamed me. I realized that the young girl, in all her simplicity, had not fathomed the intent of my artful words, though, mesdames, judging from your smiles, I can see it is readily apparent to you. I stood before her bewildered, when unexpectedly she pointed toward the window, shivering. There was Gorcha peering at us. A heavy arm grabbed my shoulder. I turned around. It was George.

"'What are you doing here?' he scowled.

"Embarrassed by this turn of events, I directed his attention toward his father, who was still standing at the window but who vanished once George saw him.

"'I heard the old man and came to warn your sister,' I explained. George stared as if to penetrate my innermost thoughts. Taking my arm, he walked me to my room and left without a word.

"The next day the family was gathered in front of the house at a table set with dairy foods.

"'Where is the boy?' asked George.

"'In the yard,' his wife answered. 'He's playing his favorite game, imagining that he's fighting against the Turks.'

"No sooner had she said this than to our great surprise we detected the hulking form of old Gorcha lumbering toward us from the forest, in a manner reminiscent of his initial arrival.

"'You are most welcome, Father,' said his daughter-in-law in a low tone.

"'We are happy to see you, Father,' chorused Zdenka and Peter.

"'Father,' George said, 'we were expecting you. Will you say grace?'

"The old man turned away, frowning.

"'Say grace this very minute, urged George, 'and make the sign of the cross. Or, I swear by St. George …'

"Zdenka and her sister-in-law begged the old man to say grace.

"'No,' insisted Gorcha. 'He doesn't dare give me orders. If he tries to force me, I will curse him.'

"George darted into the house, returning in a fury. 'Where is the stake?' he cried. 'Where did you put the stake?'

"Zdenka and Peter glanced at each other furtively.

"'You corpse!' George shouted at his father. 'What have you done with my elder son? Give me my son, you dead man!'

"Speaking this way, he turned more and more pale as rage burned in his eyes. The old man stood motionless, an evil sneer on his lips.

"'Where in heaven's name is the stake? Where is that stake?' George continued. 'Let misery befall those who have hidden it, all the misery possible in one lifetime.'

"Then the most terrible thing occurred. Riding toward us on an enormous stake was the younger son, his blood-curdling laughter resounding in our ears. As he neared us, he screeched the Serbian battle cry.

"George flushed, grabbing the stake away from the child. The youngster threw himself on his father, who let forth a howl, and then darted away in the direction of the forest with a speed that seemed supernatural. George chased him across the field and also faded out of sight. The sun had already set when George, pale as death, his hair on end, came back. As he sat by the fire, his teeth seemed to be chattering. Nobody dared question him. As bedtime approached, he regained his self-control and, calling me to his side, spoke in a casual manner.

"'My dear guest, I just saw that the river is cleared of ice. Nothing detains you any longer. No need to say good-bye to my family,' he added, glancing at Zdenka. 'She wishes you well and hopes you remember us kindly. At dawn, you will find your horse saddled and a guide to direct you out of the village. Farewell, and forgive your hosts for the difficult times you spent with them.'

"George seemed almost friendly as he accompanied me to my room and shook my hand for the last time. Then he shuddered and his teeth chattered as if from the cold.

"Once alone, I thought of the despair I had suffered over former love affairs, the tenderness, jealousy and rage. Yet never until that moment, not even during encounters with the Duchesse de Gramont, had I experienced such despondence. I changed into my traveling clothes before the sun had risen, hoping to see Zdenka before my departure. But George was already awaiting me in the hall.

"I spurred my horse on, promising myself that I would stop at the village when returning from Yassa. Although this was a long time off, the prospect relieved my sadness. I was already contemplating a pleasurable return, and my imagination was working out the sweet details, when my horse bolted, almost hurling me from the saddle. She stopped, stretched out her forelegs and snorted as if in danger. I looked about in every direction until I noticed a wolf about a hundred steps ahead of us, digging in the ground. Seeing us, it raced away. I rode over and found a freshly dug hole, with a stake sticking out a few inches above the ground. Yet I couldn't be sure of this, since I rode by swiftly."

At this point, the marquis stopped talking and took a pinch of snuff.

"Is that all?" the ladies asked.

"Oh, no, not at all," assured d'Urfé. "It's very painful for me to recall what I am about to relate. Gladly would I forfeit worldly pleasures to free my mind forever of these memories.

"It took me about half a year to conclude my affairs in Yassa, much longer than anticipated. How can I tell you what I experienced through that stretch of time? It's the sad truth that stable emotions do not exist in this world. The success of my negotiations regarding the revolting politics which have recently caused so much trouble brought me strong praise from Versailles. But my tormenting memories of Zdenka were intensified. Even the ladies, particularly the wife of the Seigneur of Moldavia—a beauty who spoke our language to perfection and who singled me out from all the other young foreigners in Yassa—could not relieve my pain. Yet, reared according to French gallantry and ruled by the Gallic blood in my veins, I, of course, could not refuse this lady's flattering approaches. Moreover, considering that I was the French representative at the court of her husband, I regarded it my singular duty to satisfy the desires of the seigneur's noble wife. As you can see, mesdames, I always put the interests of my country above all else …

"Upon my return home, I journeyed by the same road I had taken to Yassa. By then I had forgotten Zdenka and her family and was reminded of them while riding through a field where I heard a bell ring eight times. Its ring was familiar. My guide informed me that it came from a nearby shrine, the Monastery of Our Lady under the Oak. With this, I headed for the guest house which was swarming with pilgrims. A monk assured me I could find lodging practically anywhere, that, due to "damned Gorcha," there were many empty houses.

"'Do you mean,' I gasped, 'that the old man is still alive?'

"'No. Apparently, he is lying quietly in the earth with a stake through his heart. He sucked the blood of his grandson, the younger child of George. One night, the little boy knocked at the house begging to be admitted, crying that he was cold. His foolish mother, though she herself had buried him that very day, was unable to summon the courage to send her son back to his grave. No sooner had she let him in than he threw himself upon her, sucking her life's blood. After she was buried, she in turn came for the blood of her husband and her brother-in-law. They all shared the same fate.'

"'And Zdenka? What happened to her?' I asked, trembling.

"'Well, as for her, the poor thing went mad from sorrow. It's really better we don't speak of her.'

"The monk's comments were puzzling, but I had no heart to pursue them further.

"'Still,' he continued, 'vampirism is contagious. Many families in the village suffer from it. If you accept my advice, you'll remain in the monastery for the night. Out there, whether the vourdalaks get you or not, you'll undergo such terror that your hair will turn snow white before I ring for early Mass. Of course, I'm only a poor monk, yet the generosity of the travelers enables me to care for their needs. I can offer you such excellent farmer's cheese and currants that your mouth will water at the sight of them. There are a few bottles of Tokay wine which are as fine as those served at the table of His Holiness.'

"I seemed to be speaking with an innkeeper rather than a monk, and his purpose in relating these horror stories appeared bent upon coercing me into imitating the generosity of the other travelers who provided the holy man with the means of gratifying their needs. Aside from this, the word 'terror' never fails to affect me like a trumpet affects a war horse. How ashamed I would have been had I not proceeded instantly to investigate the rumors!

"My shivering guide begged permission, which I granted, to remain at the monastery. I thus arrived alone at the deserted village. No lights were on; no songs sung. Through the eerie silence, I passed those familiar houses until I reached George's. Whether I was influenced by a romantic whim or simply by youthful boldness, I resolved to spend the night, though no one answered my knock at the gates. Pushing,

I managed to get them open. I tied my saddled horse to the shed and crept up to the house. Not a single door was locked, yet the house seemed abandoned. Zdenka's room appeared to have been forsaken that very day. Several dresses lay across the bed. A few pieces of jewelry, gifts from me, were scattered on the bureau. A small enamel cross, which I had purchased in Budapest, sparkled in the moonlight.

"My heart pounded at a dreadful speed. Regardless of my waning love, I sighed, wrapped myself in my cape, stretched out on the bed and slept. I can't recall the precise details, but I do remember envisioning Zdenka as a charming, ingenuous, devoted creature shamed by my fickleness. How, I agonized, could I have forgotten the sweet maiden who had loved me so very much? The vision of her became intertwined with my memories of the Duchesse de Gramont, and, in those two silhouettes, I saw one and the same person. Kneeling at Zdenka's feet, I prayed for her forgiveness. My entire being, my very soul, became infused with both sadness and happiness. Thus, I continued to dream until gently wakened by wheat stalks waving in the wind. I heard the distant chirping of birds, the rushing of a waterfall and the brushing of leaves, when it seemed that all those sounds could actually have emanated from the rustling of a lady's dress. With this notion, I opened my eyes and beheld Zdenka by my bedside. So bright was the moon that I could distinguish every feature, each more enchanting than I remembered. She was dressed in the garb she had worn on the eve of our farewell: her silk peasant blouse embroidered in gold and dirndl skirt gathered tightly around her slim waist.

"'Zdenka,' I cried, rising quickly from the bed. 'Is it you?'

"'Yes, it is me,' she responded in a small, pathetic voice. 'Yes, it is your forgotten Zdenka. Why didn't you return sooner? Now everything is ended and you must leave at once. A moment's delay and you are lost. Farewell, my friend. Farewell forever.'

"'Zdenka. Zdenka, you have been through so much sorrow. Please speak with me at least. It will relieve your anxiety.'

"'My friend, do not believe all you hear about us. But do go. Go quickly, or else you will die without reprieve.'

"'But Zdenka, what is there to fear? Is it possible you will not grant me an hour?' She shuddered and for a second seemed almost imperceptibly transformed.

"'All right. An hour—just one. Is it not the same request you made the night you overheard me singing about the old king? So be it again. I'll permit you this hour ... But no, no,' she screamed, as if coming to her senses. 'Go. Run. Run far away. I'm telling you to hurry while you still have the chance.'

"A wild frenzy distorted her features. I couldn't understand what forced her to speak this way. I only knew how lovely she was and decided to remain in spite of her wishes. Finally, complying with my request, she sat beside me and confessed that she had loved me at first sight. As she spoke, the change in her became gradually more and more distinct. Her eyes glinted boldly. Her movements challenged me provocatively. Indeed, she was emerging as someone quite unmaidenly, even wicked, completely different from the reserved young virgin of my memories.

"Is it possible, I asked myself, that Zdenka was never the chaste girl she appeared to be six months ago? Is it possible that being afraid of her brother, she had assumed a convenient disguise? Had I been tricked by a modest façade? But then, I countered, why did she urge me to leave? Was this simply a coy move? I imagined for the moment that I saw the former Zdenka ... But no, she was still transfigured ... If Zdenka is not the Diana I thought she was, could she not be compared to another goddess at least as charming? Anyway, I prefer the fate of Adonis to that of Acteon.[1] If this classical reference seems out of place, mesdames, please remember that I am relating events of 1769. At that time, mythology was à la mode, and I made the pretense of being

---

[1] Adonis, after being slain by a wild boar, spent four months out of every year with Persephone, four with Aphrodite, and four wherever he chose; Acteon was transformed into a stag after he saw the goddess of chastity bathing.-Ed.

avant-garde. Since then, times have changed, for the revolution has eclipsed both paganism and Christianity. The new religion, reason, is erected in their place. I never favored this cult, reason, especially in the company of women. As my story was transpiring, I was particularly unwilling to worship this deity. Quite naturally, I abandoned myself to Zdenka, responding pleasurably to her irresistible advances. Some time passed in sweet forgetfulness. Zdenka amused me by trying on one piece of jewelry after another, until it occurred to me to place the enamel cross around her swanlike neck. Anticipating my intention, Zdenka withdrew with a shudder.

"'Enough of this foolishness, my love,' she smiled, regaining her composure. 'Let us leave all these trinkets and discuss you and your intentions.'

"In spite of my feelings, Zdenka's odd behavior forced me to study her more closely. Unlike the past, she did not have on the holy medals and relics which Serbians commonly wear from childhood to death. I questioned her about this.

"'I lost them,' she answered, impatient to change the subject.

"A sense of foreboding came over me. I decided to leave, but Zdenka stood in my way.

"'What's the meaning of this?' she scowled. 'You begged me for an hour of my time, and now you're leaving so abruptly.'

"'Zdenka, you were right in convincing me to leave. I just heard a noise. I'm afraid we will be discovered together,' I said, attempting to conciliate her.

"'Don't worry, my friend. Everyone around us is asleep. Only the cricket in the grass and the dragonfly in the air can hear what we say.'

"'No, no, Zdenka, this won't do. I must go.'

"'Please wait,' she implored. 'I love you more than my own soul, more than my salvation. You once told me that your life and blood were mine.'

"'But your brother! I have the feeling he is about to arrive.'

"'Be still, my heart. My brother is asleep, too, lulled by the wind that is rustling in the trees. His sleep is deep and the night is long. I am requesting but a moment longer.'

"As she said this, Zdenka looked so beautiful that the anxiety that had gripped me vanished with my desire to remain by her side. A strange mixture of fright and rapture filled me. Slowly, as my will weakened, Zdenka became increasingly tender. I resolved to give in to her while I maintained my guard. But alas! I was only half sensible, as usual. Noticing my reserve, she offered me a few drafts of wine to warm myself, saying that she had purchased it from the good monk. My compliance elicited a smile, and the wine surely produced its intended effect. After the second glass, my reservations over the little cross and holy medals were completely erased from my consciousness. Zdenka, in her informal attire, her blond hair unbraided, her bracelets gleaming in the moonlight, was hopelessly enticing. I could not restrain myself and impulsively embraced her.

"Then, mesdames, then one of those inexplicable signs appeared. I have never been able to explain it to myself. In fact, at that time I was inclined not to believe in it at all. Nevertheless, when I pressed Zdenka's body to my own, one of the points of the cross, which the Duchesse de Gramont had given me, stuck into my chest. That momentary pain served as a bolt from heaven. Glancing at Zdenka, I saw that her features, though beautiful, were imprinted with death, that her eyes were glazed and that her smile was convulsed with the agony of a condemned prisoner. Simultaneously, I sensed in the room a putrid odor like some half-opened tomb. The loathsome truth stunned me. Only too late did I recall the monk's warning. What a desperate situation I was in! Everything depended upon boldness and cunning. Not wanting her to notice my doubt, I turned away. My gaze passed for a second across the window where Gorcha was leaning on a bloody stake, peering at me with the eyes of a hyena. In the other window stood George, looking exactly like his father. They were both following my movements closely. Undoubtedly they would descend upon me at my slightest effort to escape. So I pretended not to have seen them but continued, with all my will, to caress Zdenka as if nothing unusual were happening. My mind raced through plans of escape. The wailing of women and children floated in from the yard, piercing the silence like the howling of wild cats.

"It is time to escape, I said to myself, and the sooner the better. Turning to Zdenka, I spoke loudly enough for her ghastly relatives to hear. 'I am tired, my dearest, and must lie down for a while. Yet, first, my horse should be fed. I beg you not to leave. Wait for me,' I said, kissing her cold mouth. Outside, my horse was covered with foam, trying vainly to gallop out of the shed. Her neighing made me wary lest she give me away. But the vourdalaks who overheard my conversation with Zdenka did not move. Certain that the gates were ajar, I jumped onto the saddle and spurred my horse on. Having passed swiftly through the gates, I barely noticed the crowd gathered round the house, gaping through the windows. My sudden departure must have startled them. Yet for those first few moments I only concentrated on the rhythmic clatter of my horse's hoofs as they resounded in the unearthly silence.

"On the verge of congratulating myself on a safe escape, I was interrupted by a noise that resembled a hurricane. Voices moaned, howled and argued with one another. Silence. Then a resounding beat as if a corps of infantrymen were in hot pursuit, I spurred on until my horse spurted blood and my veins almost burst from the fire within. A voice was calling me.

"'Wait, wait, my dear. I love you more than my soul, more than my salvation. Wait, wait. Your blood is mine.'

"A cold breath touched my ears as Zdenka leaped upon my horse from behind.

"'My Heart, my soul,' she whispered to me. 'I see only you. I want only you. I have no power over myself. I obey a superior force. Forgive me, my dear one, forgive me.' Placing her arms around me, she bit my neck and tried to throw me from my horse.

"A terrible struggle ensued between us. Mustering all my energy, I managed to grab Zdenka with one arm around her waist, the other hand on her braids. Lifting myself in the stirrups, I hurled her to the ground. My strength drained, I became delirious. Gruesome images menaced me. First George, then Peter, was running along the road's edge trying to veer me off course. Neither one succeeded. I was rejoicing over this victory when, turning back, I saw old man Gorcha leaning on his stake, making incredible leaps with it as the Tyroleans do when they jump over crevices. But even he remained behind. His daughter-in-law, who was dragging the two children, threw one of them to him. He caught it on a sharp point, then, operating the stake like a slingshot, hurled the child at me. I avoided the blow, but the child, like a fierce bulldog, set his teeth in the neck of my horse. With some effort, I tore him away. Gorcha discharged the other one at me, but he was crushed under my horse's hoofs. I don't know what happened next. When I regained consciousness, it was already daylight, and I was sprawled at the edge of the road, my horse dying nearby.

"And so, mesdames, ended the love affair which, it would seem, should have numbed all my subsequent desires to search for others among your grandmothers. Those who still survive will testify that I did become far more sensible.

"The events I have related to you this evening are strange indeed. To this very day I shiver at the thought that I had fallen into the power of my enemies. I might have become a vampire in turn. But Providence did not permit this, and I, mesdames, am not thirsty for your blood. And, though an old man, I am prepared to defend you till the last drop of blood courses from my veins."

Dracula's Guest (1897)

Bram Stoker

When we started for our drive the sun was shining brightly on Munich and the air was full of the joyousness of early summer. Just as we were about to depart, Herr Delbrück (the *maître d'hôtel* of the Quatre Saisons, where I was staying) came down, bareheaded, to the carriage and, after wishing me a pleasant drive, said to the coachman, still holding his hand on the, handle of the carriage door: "Remember you are back by nightfall. The sky looks bright but there is a shiver in the north wind that says there may be a sudden storm. But I am sure you will not be late." Here he smiled and added, "for you know what night it is."

Johann answered with an emphatic, *"Ja, mein Herr,"* and, touching his hat, drove off quickly. When we had cleared the town, I said, after signalling to him to stop: "Tell me, Johann, what is tonight?"

He crossed himself as he answered laconically: "Walpurgisnacht." Then he took out his watch, a great, old-fashioned German silver thing as big as a turnip, and looked at it, with his eyebrows gathered together and a little impatient shrug of his shoulders. I realized that this was his way of respectfully protesting against the unnecessary delay and sank back in the carriage, merely motioning him to proceed. He started off rapidly, as if to make up for lost time. Every now and then the horses seemed to throw up their heads and sniffed the air suspiciously. On such occasions I often looked round in alarm. The road was pretty bleak, for we were traversing a sort of high, wind-swept plateau. As we drove, I saw a road that looked but little used and which seemed to dip through a little, winding valley. It looked so inviting that, even at the risk of offending him, I called Johann to stop—and when he had pulled up I told him I would like to drive down that road. He made all sorts of excuses and frequently crossed himself as he spoke. This somewhat piqued my curiosity so I asked him various questions. He answered fencingly and repeatedly looked at his watch in protest. Finally I said: "Well, Johann, I want to go down this road. I shall not ask you to come unless you like; but tell me why you do not like to go, that is all I ask." For answer he seemed to throw himself off the box, so quickly did he reach the ground. Then he stretched out his hands appealingly to me and implored me not to go. There was just enough of English mixed with the German for me to understand the drift of his talk. He seemed always just about to tell me something—the very idea of which evidently frightened him, but each time he pulled himself up, saying, as he crossed himself: "Walpurgisnacht!"

I tried to argue with him, but it was difficult to argue with a man when I did not know his language. The advantage certainly rested with him, for although he began to speak in English, of a very crude and broken kind, he always got excited and broke into his native tongue—and every time he did so he looked at his watch. Then the horses became restless and sniffed the air. At this he grew very pale and, looking around in a frightened way, he suddenly jumped forward, took them by the bridles and led them on some twenty feet. I followed and asked why he had done this. For answer he crossed himself, pointed to the spot we had left and drew his carriage in the direction of the other road, indicating a cross, and said, first in German, then in English: "Buried him—him what killed themselves."

I remembered the old custom of burying suicides at cross-roads: "Ah! I see, a suicide. How interesting!" But for the life of me I could not make out why the horses were frightened.

Whilst we were talking we heard a sort of sound between a yelp and a bark. It was far away, but the horses got very restless and it took Johann all his time to quiet them. He was pale and said, "It sounds like a wolf—but yet there are no wolves here now."

"No?" I said, questioning him; "isn't it long since the wolves were so near the city?"

"Long, long," he answered, "in the spring and summer, but with the snow the wolves have been here not so long."

Whilst he was petting the horses and trying to quiet them, dark clouds drifted rapidly across the sky. The sunshine passed away and a breath of cold wind seemed to drift past us. It was only a breath, however, and more in the nature of a warning than a fact, for the sun came out brightly again. Johann looked under his lifted hand

Bram Stoker, "Dracula's Guest." Copyright in the Public Domain.

at the horizon and said: "The storm of snow, he comes before long time." Then he looked at his watch again and, straightway, holding his reins firmly—for the horses were still pawing the ground restlessly and shaking their heads—he climbed to his box as though the time had come for proceeding on our journey.

I felt a little obstinate and did not at once get into the carriage.

"Tell me," I said, "about this place where the road leads," and I pointed down.

Again he crossed himself and mumbled a prayer before he answered, "It is unholy."

"What is unholy?" I enquired.

"The village."

"Then there is a village?"

"No, no. No one lives there hundreds of years."

My curiosity was piqued. "But you said there was a village."

"There was."

"Where is it now?"

Whereupon he burst out into a long story in German and English, so mixed up that I could not quite understand exactly what he said, but roughly I gathered that long ago, hundreds of years, men had died there and been buried in their graves; and sounds were heard under the day and when the graves were opened, men and women were found rosy with life, and their mouths red with blood. And so, in haste to save their lives (aye, and their souls!—and here he crossed himself) those who were left fled away to other places, where the living lived and the dead were dead and not—not something. He was evidently afraid to speak the last words. As he proceeded with his narration he grew more and more excited. It seemed as if his imagination had got hold of him and he ended in a perfect paroxysm of fear—white-faced, perspiring, trembling and looking round him, as if expecting that some dreadful presence would manifest itself there in the bright sunshine on the open plain. Finally, in an agony of desperation, he cried: "Walpurgisnacht!" and pointed to the carriage for me to get in. All my English blood rose at this and, standing back, I said: "You are afraid, Johann—you are afraid. Go home, I shall return alone; the walk will do me good." The carriage door was open. I took from the seat my oak walking-stick—which I always carry on my holiday excursions—and closed the door, pointing back to Munich, and said, "Go home, Johann—Walpurgisnacht doesn't concern Englishmen."

The horses were now more restive than ever and Johann was trying to hold them in, while excitedly imploring me not to do anything so foolish. I pitied the poor fellow, he was deeply in earnest, but all the same I could not help laughing. His English was quite gone now. In his anxiety he had forgotten that his only means of making me understand was to talk my language, so he jabbered away in his native German. It began to be a little tedious. After giving the direction, "Home!" I turned to go down the cross-road into the valley.

With a despairing gesture, Johann turned his houses towards Munich. I leaned on my stick and looked after him. He went slowly along the road for a while: then there came over the crest of the hill a man tall and thin. I could see se much in the distance. When he drew near the horses, they began to jump and kick about, then to scream with terror. Johann could not hold them in; they bolted down the road, running away madly. I watched them out of sight, then looked for the stranger, but I found that he, too, was gone.

With a light heart I turned down the side road through the deepening valley to which Johann had objected. There was not the slightest reason, that I could see, for his objection, and I daresay I tramped for a couple of hours without thinking of time or distance, and certainly without seeing a person or a house. So far as the place was concerned it was desolation itself. But I did not notice this particularly till, on turning a bend in the road, I came upon a scattered fringe of wood; then I recognized that I had been impressed unconsciously by the desolation of the region through which I had passed.

I sat down to rest myself and began to look around. It struck me that it was considerably colder than it had been at the commencement of my walk—a sort of sighing sound seemed to be around me, with, now and then, high overhead, a sort of muffled roar. Looking upwards I noticed that great thick clouds were drifting rapidly across the sky from north to south at a great height. There were signs of coming storm in some lofty stratum of the air. I was a little chilly and, thinking that it was the sitting still after the exercise of walking, I resumed my journey.

The ground I passed over was now much more picturesque. There were no striking objects that the eye might single out, but in all there was a charm of beauty. I took little heed of time and it was only when the deepening twilight forced itself upon me that I began to think of how I should find my way home. The brightness of the day had gone. The air was cold and the drifting of clouds high overhead was more marked. They were accompanied by a sort of far-away rushing sound, through which seemed to come at intervals that mysterious cry which the driver had said came from a wolf. For a while I hesitated. I had said I would see the deserted village, so on I went and presently came on a wide stretch of open country, shut in by hills all around. Their sides were covered with trees which spread down to the plain, dotting, in clumps, the gentler slopes and hollows which showed here and there. I followed with my eye the winding of the road and saw that it curved close to one of the densest of these clumps and was lost behind it.

As I looked there came a cold shiver in the air and the snow began to fall. I thought of the miles and miles of bleak country I had passed and then hurried on to seek the shelter of the wood in front. Darker and darker grew the sky and faster and heavier fell the snow, till the earth before and around me was a glistening white carpet, the farther edge of which was lost in misty vagueness. The road was here but crude and when on the level its boundaries were not so marked, as when it passed through the cuttings; and in a little while I found that I must have strayed from it, for I missed underfoot the hard surface and my feet sank deeper in the grass and moss. Then the wind grew strong and blew with ever increasing force, till I was fain to run before it. The air became icy cold and in spite of my exercise I began to suffer. The snow was now falling so thickly and whirling around me in such rapid eddies that I could hardly keep my eyes open. Every now and then the heavens were torn asunder by vivid lightning, and in the flashes I could see ahead of me a great mass of trees, chiefly yew and cypress, all heavily coated with snow.

I was soon amongst the shelter of the trees, and there, in comparative silence, I could hear the rush of the wind high overhead Presently the blackness of the storm had become merged in the darkness of the night. By and by the storm seemed to be passing away: it now only came in fierce puffs or blasts. At such moments the weird sound of the wolf appeared to be echoed by many similar sounds around me.

Now and again, through the black mass of drifting cloud, came a straggling ray of moonlight, which lit up the expanse and showed me that I was at the edge of a dense mass of cypress and yew trees. As the snow had ceased to fall, I walked out from the shelter and began to investigate more closely. It appeared to me that, amongst so many old foundations as I had passed, there might be still standing a house in which, though in ruins, I could find some sort of shelter for a while. As I skirted the edge of the copse I found that a low wall encircled it, and following this I presently found an opening. Here the cypresses formed an alley leading up to a square mass of some kind of building. Just as I caught sight of this, however, the drifting clouds obscured the moon and I passed up the path in darkness. The wind must have grown colder, for I felt myself shiver as I walked; but there was hope of shelter and I groped my way blindly on.

I stopped, for there was a sudden stillness. The storm had passed and, perhaps in sympathy with nature's silence, my heart seemed to cease to beat. But this was only momentarily, for suddenly the moonlight broke through the clouds, showing me that I was in a graveyard and that the square object before me was a great massive tomb of marble, as white as the snow that lay on and all around it. With the moonlight there came a fierce sigh of the storm, which appeared to resume its course with a long, low howl, as of many dogs or wolves. I was awed and shocked and felt the cold perceptibly grow upon me till it seemed to grip me by the heart Then, while the flood of moonlight still fell on the marble tomb, the storm gave further evidence of renewing, as though it was returning on its track. Impelled by some sort of fascination I approached the sepulchre to see what it was and why such a thing stood alone in such a place. I walked around it and read, over the Doric door, in German:

COUNTESS DOLINGEN OF GRATZ
IN STYRIA
SOUGHT AND FOUND DEATH
1801

On the top of the tomb, seemingly driven through the solid marble — for the structure was composed of a few vast blocks of stone — was a great iron spike or stake. On going to the back I saw, graven in great Russian letters:

THE DEAD TRAVEL FAST.

There was something so weird and uncanny about the whole thing that it gave me a turn and made me feel quite faint. I began to wish, for the first time, that I had taken Johann's advice. Here a thought struck me, which came under almost mysterious circumstances and with a terrible shock. This was Walpurgis Night!

Walpurgis Night, when, according to the belief of millions of people, the devil was abroad — when the graves were opened and the dead came forth and walked. When evil things of earth and air and water held revel. This very place the driver had specially shunned. This was the depopulated village of centuries ago. This was where the suicide lay; and this was the place where I was alone — unmanned, shivering with cold in a shroud of snow with a wild storm gathering again upon me! It took all my philosophy, all the religion I had been taught, all my courage, not to collapse in a paroxysm of fright.

And now a perfect tornado burst upon me. The ground shook as though thousands of horses thundered across it, and this time the storm bore on its icy wings, not snow, but great hailstones which drove with such violence that they might have come from the thongs of Balearic slingers — hailstones that beat down leaf and branch and made the shelter of the cypresses of no more avail than though their stems were standing corn. At the first I had rushed to the nearest tree, but I was soon fain to leave it and seek the only spot that seemed to afford refuge, the deep Doric doorway of the marble tomb. There, crouching against the massive bronze door, I gained a certain amount of protection from the beating of the hailstones, for now they only drove against me as they ricocheted from the ground and the side of the marble.

As I leaned against the door it moved slightly and opened inwards. The shelter of even a tomb was welcome in that pitiless tempest and I was about to enter it when there came a flash of forked lightning that lit up the whole expanse of the heavens. In the instant, as I am a living man, I saw, as my eyes were turned into the darkness of the tomb, a beautiful woman with rounded cheeks and red lips, seemingly sleeping on a bier. As the thunder broke overhead I was grasped as by the hand of a giant and hurled out into the storm. The whole thing was so sudden that, before I could realize the shock, moral as well as physical, I found the hailstones beating me down. At the same time I had a strange, dominating feeling that I was not alone. I looked towards the tomb. Just then there came another blinding flash, which seemed to strike the iron stake that surmounted the tomb and to pour through to the earth, blasting and crumbling the marble, as in a burst of flame. The dead woman rose for a moment of agony, while she was lapped in the flame, and her bitter scream of pain was drowned in the thundercrash. The last thing I heard was this mingling of dreadful sound, as again I was seized in the giant-grasp and dragged away, while the hailstones beat on me, and the air around seemed reverberant with the howling of wolves. The last sight that I remembered was a vague, white, moving mass, as if all the graves around me had sent out the phantoms of their sheeted-dead, and that they were closing in on me through the white cloudiness of the driving hail.

Gradually there came a sort of vague beginning of consciousness, then a, sense of weariness that was dreadful. For a time I remembered nothing, but slowly my senses returned. My feet seemed positively racked with pain, yet I could not move them. They seemed to be numbed.

There was an icy feeling at the back of my neck and all down my spine, and my ears, like my feet, were dead, yet in torment; but there was in my breast a sense of warmth which was, by comparison, delicious. It was as a nightmare—a physical nightmare, if one may use such an expression—for some heavy weight on my chest made it difficult for me to breathe.

This period of semi-lethargy seemed to remain a long time, and as it faded away I must have slept or swooned. Then came a sort of loathing, like the first stage of sea-sickness, and a wild desire to be free from something—I knew not what. A vast stillness enveloped me, as though all the world were asleep or dead—only broken by the low panting as of some animal close to me. I felt a warm rasping at my throat, then came a consciousness of the awful truth, which chilled me to the heart and sent the blood surging up through my brain. Some great animal was lying on me and now licking my throat. I feared to stir, for some instinct of prudence bade me lie still, but the brute seemed to realize that there was now some change in me, for it raised its head. Through my eyelashes I saw above me the two great flaming eyes of a gigantic wolf. Its sharp white teeth gleamed in the gaping red mouth and I could feel its hot breath fierce and acrid upon me.

For another spell of time I remembered no more. Then I became conscious of a low growl, followed by a yelp, renewed again and again. Then, seemingly very far away, I heard a "Holloa! holloa!" as of many voices calling in unison. Cautiously I raised my head and looked in the direction whence the sound came, but the cemetery blocked my view. The wolf still continued to yelp in a strange way and a red glare began to move round the grove of cypresses, as though following the sound. As the voices drew closer, the wolf yelped faster and louder. I feared to make either sound or motion. Nearer came the red glow, over the white pall which stretched into the darkness around me. Then all at once from beyond the trees there came at a trot a troop of horsemen bearing torches. The wolf rose from my breast and made for the cemetery. I saw one of the horsemen (soldiers, by their caps and their long military cloaks) raise his carbine and take aim. A companion knocked up his arm, and I heard the ball whizz over my head. He had evidently taken my body for that of the wolf. Another sighted the animal as it slunk away and a shot followed. Then, at a gallop, the troop rode forward—some towards me, others following the wolf as it disappeared amongst the snow-clad cypresses.

As they drew nearer I tried to move, but was powerless, although I could see and hear all that went on around me. Two or three of the soldiers jumped from their hones and knelt beside me. One of them raised my head and placed his hand over my heart.

"Good news, comrades!" he cried. "His heart still beats!"

Then some brandy was poured down my throat; it put vigour into me and I was able to open my eyes fully and look around. Lights and shadows were moving among the trees and I heard men call to one another. They drew together, uttering frightened exclamations, and the lights flashed as the others came pouring out of the cemetery pell-mell, like him possessed. When the farther ones came close to us, those who were around me asked them eagerly: "Well, have you found him?"

The reply rang out hurriedly: "No! no! Come away quick—quick! This is no place to stay, and on this of all nights!"

"What was it?" was the question, asked in all manner of keys. The answer came variously and all indefinitely as though the men were moved by some common impulse to speak, yet were restrained by some common fear from giving their thoughts.

"It—it—indeed!" gibbered one, whose wits had plainly given out for the moment.

"A wolf—and yet not a wolf!" another put in shudderingly.

"No use trying for him without the sacred bullet," a third remarked in a more ordinary manner.

"Serve us right for coming out on this night! Truly we have earned our thousand marks!" were the ejaculations of a fourth.

"There was blood on the broken marble," another said after a pause—"the lightning never brought that there. And for him—is he safe?

Look at his throat! See, comrades, the wolf has been lying on him and keeping his blood warm."

The officer looked at my throat and replied: "He is all right, the skin is not pierced. What does it all mean? We should never have found him but for the yelping of the wolf."

"What became of it?" asked the man who was holding up my head and who seemed the least panic stricken of the party, for his hands were steady and without tremor. On his sleeve was the chevron of a petty officer.

"It went to its home," answered the man, whose long face was pallid and who actually shook with terror as he glanced around him fearfully. "There are graves enough there in which it may lie. Come, comrades—come quickly! Let us leave this cursed spot."

The officer raised me to a sitting posture, as he uttered a word of command, then several men placed me upon a horse. He sprang to the saddle behind me, took me in his arms, gave the word to advance and, turning our faces away from the cypresses, we rode away in swift, military order.

As yet my tongue refused its office and I was perforce silent. I must have fallen asleep, for the next thing I remembered was finding myself standing up, supported by a soldier on each side of me. It was almost broad daylight and to the north a red streak of sunlight was reflected, like a path of blood, over the waste of snow. The officer was telling the men to say nothing of what they had seen, except that they found an English stranger, guarded by a large dog.

"Dog! that was no dog," cut in the man who had exhibited such fear. "I think I know a wolf when I see one."

The young officer answered calmly: "I said a dog."

"Dog!" reiterated the other ironically. It was evident that his courage was rising with the sun and, pointing to me, he said, "Look at his throat. Is that the work of a dog, master?"

Instinctively I raised my hand to my throat, and as I touched it I cried out in pain. The men crowded round to look, some stooping down from their saddles, and again there came the calm voice of the young officer: "A dog, as I said. If aught else were said we should only be laughed at."

I was then mounted behind a trooper and we rode on into the suburbs of Munich. Here we came across a stray carriage, into which I was lifted, and it was driven off to the Quatre Saisons—the young officer accompanying me, whilst a trooper followed with his horse and the others rode off to their barracks.

When we arrived, Heir Delbrück rushed so quickly down the steps to meet me that it was apparent he had been watching within. Taking me by both hands he solicitously led me in. The officer saluted me and was turning to withdraw when I recognized his purpose, and insisted that he should come to my rooms. Over a glass of wine I warmly thanked him and his brave comrades for saving me. He replied simply that he was more than glad and that Herr Delbrück had at the first taken steps to make all the searching party pleased; at which ambiguous utterance the *maître d'hôtel* smiled, while the officer pleaded duty and withdrew.

"But Herr Delbrück," I enquired, "how and why was it that the soldiers searched for me?"

He shrugged his shoulders, as if in deprecation of his own deed, as he replied: "I was so fortunate as to obtain leave from the commander of the regiment in which I served, to ask for volunteers."

"But how did you know I was lost?" I asked.

"The driver came hither with the remains of his carriage, which had been upset when the horses ran away."

"But surely you would not send a search-party of soldiers merely on this account?"

"Oh, no!" he answered, "but even before the coachman arrived I had this telegram from the Boyar whose guest you are," and he took from his pocket a telegram which he handed to me, and I read:

Bistritz
Be careful of my guest—his safety is most precious to me. Should aught happen to him, or if he be missed, spare nothing to find him and ensure his safety. He is English and therefore adventurous. There are often dangers from snow and wolves and night. Lose not a moment if you suspect harm

to him. I answer your zeal with my fortune—*Dracula*.

As I held the telegram in my hand the room seemed to whirl around me, and if the attentive *maître d'hôtel* had not caught me I think I should have fallen. There was something so strange in all this, something so weird and impossible to imagine, that there grew on me a sense of my being in some way the sport of opposite forces—the mere vague idea of which seemed in a way to paralyze me. I was certainly under some form of mysterious protection. From a distant country had come, in the very nick of time, a message that took me out of the danger of the snow-sleep and the jaws of the wolf.

Varney the Vampyre, or, the Feast of Blood (excerpt) (1845)

James Malcolm Rymer

Chapter 1

THE SOLEMN TONES OF an old cathedral clock have announced midnight—a strange death-like stillness pervades all nature. Like the ominous calm which precedes some more than usually terrific outbreak of the elements, they seem to have paused even in their ordinary fluctuations, to gather a terrific strength for the great effort. A faint peal of thunder now comes from far off. Like a signal gun for the battle of the winds to begin, it appeared to awaken them from their lethargy, and one awful, warring hurricane swept over a whole city, producing more devastation in the four or five minutes it lasted, than would a half century of ordinary phenomena.

Oh, how the storm raged! Hail—rain—wind. It was, in very truth, an awful night.

There is an antique chamber in an ancient house. Curious and quaint carvings adorn the walls, and the large chimney-piece is a curiosity of itself. The ceiling is low, and a large bay window, from roof to floor, looks to the west. The window is latticed, and tiled with curiously painted glass and rich stained pieces, which send in a strange, yet beautiful light, when sun or moon shines into the apartment. There is but one portrait in that room, although the walls seem panelled for the express purpose of containing a series of pictures. That portrait is of a young man, with a pale face, a stately brow, and a strange expression about the eyes, which no one cared to look on twice.

There is a stately bed in that chamber, of carved walnut-wood is it made, rich in design and elaborate in execution; one of those works of art which owe their existence to the Elizabethan era. It is hung with heavy silken and damask furnishing; nodding feathers are at its corners—covered with dust are they, and they lend a funereal aspect to the room. The floor is of polished oak.

God! how the hail dashes on the old bay window! Like an occasional discharge of mimic musketry, it comes clashing, beating, and cracking upon the small panes; but they resist it—their small size saves them; the wind, the hail, the rain, expend their fury in vain.

The bed in that old chamber is occupied. A creature formed in all fashions of loveliness lies in a half sleep upon that ancient couch—a girl young and beautiful as a spring morning. Her long hair has escaped from its confinement and streams over the blackened coverings of the bedstead; she has been restless in her sleep, for the clothing of the bed is in much confusion. One arm is over her head, the other hangs nearly off the side of the bed near to which she lies. A neck and bosom that would have formed a study for the rarest sculptor that ever Providence gave genius to, were half disclosed. She moaned slightly in her sleep, and once or twice the lips moved as if in prayer—at least one might judge so, for the name of Him who suffered for all came once faintly from them.

She has endured much fatigue, and the storm does not awaken her; but it can disturb the slumbers it does not possess the power to destroy entirely. The turmoil of the elements wakes the senses, although it cannot entirely break the repose they have lapsed into.

Oh, what a world of witchery was in that mouth, slightly parted, and exhibiting within the pearly teeth that glistened even in the faint light that came from that bay window. How sweetly the long silken eyelashes lay upon the cheek. Now she moves, and one shoulder is entirely visible—whiter, fairer than the spotless clothing of the bed in which she lies, is the smooth skin of that fair creature, just budding into womanhood, and in that transition state which presents to us all the charms of the girl—almost of the child, with the more matured beauty and gentleness of advancing years.

Was that lightning? Yes—an awful, vivid, terrifying flash—then a roaring peal of thunder, as if a thousand mountains were rolling one over the other in the blue vault of Heaven! Who sleeps now in that ancient city? Not one living soul. The dread trumpet of eternity could not more effectually have awakened any one.

The hail continues. He wind continues. The uproar of the elements seems at its height. Now she awakens—that beautiful girl on the antique bed; she opens those eyes of celestial blue, and a

James Malcolm Rymer, "Varney the Vampyre, or, the Feast of Blood." Copyright in the Public Domain.

faint cry of alarm bursts from her lips. At least it is a cry which, amid the noise and turmoil without, sounds but faint and weak. She sits upon the bed and presses her hands upon her eyes. Heavens! what a wild torrent of wind, and rain, and hail! The thunder likewise seems intent upon awakening sufficient echoes to last until the next flash of forked lightning should again produce the wild concussion of the air. She murmurs a prayer—a prayer for those she loves best; the names of those dear to her gentle heart come from her lips; she weeps and prays; she thinks then of what devastation the storm must surely produce, and to the great God of Heaven she prays for all living things. Another flash—a wild, blue, bewildering flash of lightning streams across that bay window, for an instant bringing out every colour in it with terrible distinctness. A shriek bursts from the lips of the young girl, and then, with eyes fixed upon that window, which, in another moment, is all darkness, and with such an expression of terror upon her face as it had never before known, she trembled, and the perspiration of intense fear stood upon her brow.

"What—what was it?" she gasped; "real, or a delusion? Oh, God, what was it? A figure tall and gaunt, endeavouring from the outside to unclasp the window. I saw it. That flash of lightning revealed it to me. It stood the whole length of the window."

There was a lull of the wind. The hail was not falling so thickly—moreover, it now fell, what there was of it, straight, and yet a strange clattering sound came upon the glass of that long window. It could not be a delusion—she is awake, and she hears it. What can produce it? Another flash of lightning—another shriek—there could be now no delusion.

A tall figure is standing on the ledge immediately outside the long window. It is its fingernails upon the glass that produces the sound so like the hail, now that the hail has ceased. Intense fear paralysed the limbs of that beautiful girl. That one shriek is all she can utter—with hands clasped, a face of marble, a heart beating so wildly in her bosom, that each moment it seems as if it would break its confines, eyes distended and fixed upon the window, she waits, froze with horror. The pattering and clattering of the nails continue. No word is spoken, and now she fancies she can trace the darker form of that figure against the window, and she can see the long arms moving to and fro, feeling for some mode of entrance. What strange light is that which now gradually creeps up into the air? red and terrible—brighter and brighter it grows. The lightning has set fire to a mill, and the reflection of the rapidly consuming building falls upon that long window. There can be no mistake. The figure is there, still feeling for an entrance, and clattering against the glass with its long nails, that appear as if the growth many years had been untouched. She tries to scream again but a choking sensation comes over her, and she cannot. It is too dreadful—she tries to move—each limb seems weighed down by tons of lead—she can but in a hoarse faint whisper cry,—

"Help—help—help—help!"

And that one word she repeats like a person in a dream. The red glare of the fire continues. It throws up the tall gaunt figure in hideous relief against the long window. It shows, too, upon the one portrait that is in the chamber, and that portrait appears to fix its eyes upon the attempting intruder, while the flickering light from the fire makes it look fearfully life-like. A small pane of glass is broken, and the form from without introduces a long gaunt hand, which seems utterly destitute of flesh. The fastening is removed, and one-half of the window, which opens like folding doors, is swung wide open upon its hinges.

And yet now she could not scream—she could not move. "Help—help!—help!" was all she could say. But, oh, that look of terror that sat upon her face, it was dreadful—a look to haunt the memory for a life time—a look to obtrude itself upon the happiest moments, and turn them to bitterness.

The figure turns half round, and the light falls upon the face. It is perfectly white—perfectly bloodless. The eyes look like polished tin; the lips are drawn back, and the principal feature next to those dreadful eyes is the teeth—the fearful-looking teeth—projecting like those of some wild animal, hideously, glaringly white, and fang-like. It approaches the bed with a strange, gliding movement. It clashes together the long nails that literally appear to hang from the finger ends. No sound comes from its lips. Is she going mad—that young and beautiful girl exposed to so much terror? she has drawn up all her limbs; she cannot even now say help. The power of articulation is gone, but the power of movement has returned to her; she can draw herself slowly along to the other side of the bed from that towards which the hideous appearance is coming.

But her eyes are fascinated. The glance of a serpent could not have produced a greater effect upon her than did the fixed gaze of those awful, metallic-looking eyes that were bent on her face. Crouching down so that the gigantic height was lost, and the horrible, protruding, white face was the most prominent object, came on the figure. What was it?—what did it want there?—what made it look so hideous—so unlike an inhabitant of the earth, and yet to be on it?

Now she has got to the verge of the bed, and the figure pauses. It seemed as if when it paused she lost the power to proceed. The clothing of the bed was now clutched in her hands with unconscious power. She drew her breath short and thick. Her bosom heaves, and her limbs tremble, yet she cannot withdraw her eyes from that marble-looking face. He holds her with his glittering eye.

The storm has ceased—all is still. The winds are hushed; the church clock proclaims the hour of one: a hissing sound comes from the throat of the hideous being, and he raises his long, gaunt arms—the lips move. He advances. The girl places one small foot from the bed on to the floor. She is unconsciously dragging the clothing with her. The door of the room is in that direction—can she reach it? Has she power to walk?—can she withdraw her eyes from the face of the intruder, and so break the hideous charm? God of Heaven! is it real, or some dream so like reality as to nearly overturn the judgment for ever?

The figure has paused again, and half on the bed and half out of it that young girl lies trembling. Her long hair streams across the entire width of the bed. As she has slowly moved along she has left it streaming across the pillows. The pause lasted about a minute—oh, what an age of agony. That minute was, indeed, enough, for madness to do its full work in.

With a sudden rush that could not be foreseen—with a strange howling cry that was enough to awaken terror in every breast, the figure seized the long tresses of her hair, and twining them round his bony hands he held her to the bed. Then she screamed—Heaven granted her then power to scream. Shriek followed shriek in rapid succession. The bedclothes fell in a heap by the side of the bed—she was dragged by her long silken hair completely on to it again. Her beautifully rounded limbs quivered with the agony of her soul. The glassy, horrible eyes of the figure ran over that angelic form with a hideous satisfaction—horrible profanation. He drags her head to the bed's edge. He forces it back by the long hair still entwined in his grasp. With a plunge he seizes her neck in his fang-like teeth—a gush of blood, and a hideous sucking noise follows. *The girl has swooned, and the vampire is at his hideous repast!*

Chapter II

(The house is aroused by the girl's screaming. Her mother, her brothers, Henry and George, and a "stranger" in the house come running to the girl's chamber, only to find the door barred.)

To those who were engaged in forcing open the door of the antique chamber, where slept the young girl whom they named Flora, each moment was swelled into an hour of agony; but, in reality, from the first moment of the alarm to that when the loud cracking noise heralded the destruction of the fastenings of the door, there had elapsed but very few minutes indeed.

"It opens—it opens," cried the young man.

"Another moment," said the stranger, as he still plied the crowbar—"another moment, and we shall have free ingress to the chamber. Be patient."

This stranger's name was Marchdale; and even as he spoke, he succeeded in throwing the massive door wide open, and clearing the passage to the chamber.

To rush in with a light in his hand was the work of a moment to the young man named Henry; but the very rapid progress he made into the apartment prevailed him from observing accurately what it contained, for the wind that came in from the open window caught the flame of the candle, and although it did not actually extinguish it, it blew it so much on one side, that it was comparatively useless as a light.

"Flora—Flora!" he cried.

Then with a sudden bound something dashed from off the bed. The concussion against him was so sudden and so utterly unexpected, as well as so tremendously violent, that he was thrown down, and, in his fall, the light was fairly extinguished.

All was darkness, save a dull, reddish kind of light that now and then, from the nearly consumed mill in the immediate vicinity, came into the room. But by that light, dim, uncertain, and flickering as it was, some one was seen to make for the window.

Henry, although nearly stunned by his fall, saw a figure, gigantic in height, which nearly reached from the floor to the ceiling. The other young man, George, saw it, and Mr. Marchdale likewise saw it, as did the lady who had spoken to the two young men in the corridor when first the screams of the young girl awakened alarm in the breasts of all the inhabitants of that house.

The figure was about to pass out at the window which led to a kind of balcony, from whence there was an easy descent to a garden.

Before it passed out they each and all caught a glance of the side-face, and they saw that the lower part of it and the lips were dabbled in blood. They saw, too, one of those fearful-looking, shining, metallic eyes which presented so terrible an appearance of unearthly ferocity.

No wonder that for a moment a panic seized them all, which paralysed any exertions they might otherwise have made to detain that hideous form.

But Mr. Marchdale was a man of mature years; he had seen much of life, both in this and in foreign lands; and he, although astonished to the extent of being frightened, was much more likely to recover sooner than his younger companions, which, indeed, he did, and acted promptly enough.

"Don't rise, Henry," he cried. "Lie still."

Almost at the moment he uttered these words, he fired at the figure, which then occupied the window, as if it were a gigantic figure set in a frame.

The report was tremendous in that chamber, for the pistol was no toy weapon, but one made for actual service, and of sufficient length and bore of barrel to carry destruction along with the bullets that came from it.

"If that has missed its aim," said Mr. Marchdale, "I'll never pull a trigger again."

As he spoke he dashed forward, and made a clutch at the figure he felt convinced he had shot.

The tall form turned upon him, and when he got a full view of the face, which he did at that moment, from the opportune circumstance of the lady returning at the instant with a light she had been to her own chamber to procure, even he, Marchdale, with all his courage, and that was great, and all his nervous energy, recoiled a step or two, and uttered the exclamation of, "Great God!"

That face was one never to be forgotten. It was hideously flushed with colour—the colour of fresh blood; the eyes had a savage and remarkable lustre; whereas, before, they had looked like polished tin—they now wore a ten times brighter aspect, and flashes of light seemed to dart from them. The mouth was open, as if, from the natural formation of the countenance, the lips receded much from the large canine-looking teeth.

A strange, howling noise came from the throat of this monstrous figure, and it seemed upon the point of rushing upon Mr. Marchdale. Suddenly, then, as if some impulse had seized upon it, it uttered a wild terrible shrieking kind of laugh; and then turning, dashed through the window, and in one instant disappeared from before the eyes of those who felt nearly annihilated by its fearful presence.

"God help us!" ejaculated Henry.

(They give chase. Although Henry fires his pistol and hits the fleeing figure, the monster escapes, leaving no trace of bloodstains from a wound.

Henry watches all night by the bedside of Flora, whose neck displays two bloody bite marks. She sleeps only fitfully and cries out in anguish upon awakening. After hearing her confused account of the attack, he goes to take counsel with Marchdale.)

Henry proceeded at once to the chamber, which was, as he knew, occupied by Mr. Marchdale; and as he crossed the corridor, he could not but pause a moment to glance from a window at the face of nature.

As is often the case, the terrific storm of the preceding evening had cleared the air, and rendered it deliriously invigorating and lifelike. The weather had been dull, and there had been for some days a certain heaviness in the atmosphere, which was now entirely removed.

The morning sun was shining with uncommon brilliancy, birds were sieging in every tree and on every bush; so pleasant, so spirit-stirring, health-giving a morning, seldom had he seen. And the effect upon his spirits was great, although not altogether what it might have been, had all gone as it usually was in the habit of doing at that house. The ordinary little casualties of evil fortune had certainly from time to time, in the shape of illness, and one thing or another, attacked the family of the Bannerworths in common with every other family, but here suddenly had arisen a something at once terrible and inexplicable.

He found Mr. Marchdale up and dressed, and apparently in deep and anxious thought. The moment he saw Henry, he said,—

"Flora is awake, I presume."

"Yes, but her mind appears to be much disturbed."

"From bodily weakness, I dare say."

"But why should she be bodily weak? she was strong and well, ay, as we; as she could ever be in all her life. The glow of youth and health was on her cheeks. Is if possible that, in the course of one night, she should become bodily weak to such in extent?"

"Henry," said Mr. Marchdale, sadly, "sit down. I am not, as you know, a superstitious man."

"You certainly are not."

"And yet, I never in all my life was so absolutely staggered as I have been by the occurrences of to-night."

"Say on."

"There is a frightful, a hideous solution to them; one which every consideration will tend to add strength to, one which I tremble to name now, although, yesterday, at this hour, I should have laughed it to scorn."

"Indeed!"

"Yes, it is so. Tell no one that which I am about to say to you. Let the dreadful suggestion remain with ourselves alone, Henry Bannerworth."

"I—I am lost in wonder."

"You promise me?"

"What—what?"

"That you will not repeat my opinion to my one."

"I do."

"On your honour."

"On my honour, I promise."

Mr. Marchdale rose, and proceeding to the door, he looked out to see that there were no listeners near. Having ascertained then that they were quite alone, he returned, and drawing a chair close to that on which Henry sat, he said,—

"Henry, have you never heard of a strange and dreadful superstition which, in some countries, is extremely rife, by which it is supposed that there are beings who never die?"

"Never die!"

"Never. In a word, Henry, have you never heard of—of—I dread to pronounce the word."

"Speak it. God of Heaven! let me hear it."

"A vampyre!"

Henry sprung to his feet. His whole frame quivered with emotion, the drops of perspiration stood upon his brow, as, in a strange, hoarse voice, he repeated the words,—

"A vampyre!"

"Even so; one who has to renew a dreadful existence by human blood—one who lives on for ever, and must keep up such a fearful existence upon human gore—one who eats not and drinks not as other men—a vampyre."

Henry dropped into his seat, and uttered a deep groan of the most exquisite anguish.

"I could echo that groan," said Marchdale, "but that I .am so thoroughly bewildered I know not what to think."

"Good God—good God!"

Wake Not the Dead

Johann Ludwig Tieck

"WILT THOU FOR EVER sleep? Wilt thou never more awake, my beloved, but henceforth repose for ever from thy short pilgrimage on earth? O yet once again return! and bring back with thee the vivifying dawn of hope to one whose existence hath, since thy departure, been obscured by the dunnest shades. What! dumb? for ever dumb? Thy friend lamenteth, and thou heedest him not? He sheds bitter, scalding tears, and thou reposest unregarding his affliction? He is in despair, and thou no longer openest thy arms to him as an asylum from his grief? Say then, doth the paly shroud become thee better than the bridal veil? Is the chamber of the grave a warmer bed than the couch of love? Is the spectre death more welcome to thy arms than thy enamoured consort? Oh! return, my beloved, return once again to this anxious disconsolate bosom."

Such were the lamentations which Walter poured forth for his Brunhilda, the partner of his youthful passionate love; thus did he bewail over her grave at the midnight hour, what time the spirit that presides in the troublous atmosphere, sends his legions of monsters through mid-air; so that their shadows, as they flit beneath the moon and across the earth, dart as wild, agitating thoughts that chase each other o'er the sinner's bosom:—thus did he lament under the tall linden trees by her grave, while his head reclined on the cold stone.

Walter was a powerful lord in Burgundy, who, in his earliest youth, had been smitten with the charms of the fair Brunhilda, a beauty far surpassing in loveliness all her rivals; for her tresses, dark as the raven face of night, streaming over her shoulders, set off to the utmost advantage the beaming lustre of her slender form, and the rich dye of a cheek whose tint was deep and brilliant as that of the western heaven; her eyes did not resemble those burning orbs whose pale glow gems the vault of night, and whose immeasurable distance fills the soul with deep thoughts of eternity, but rather as the sober beams which cheer this nether world, and which, while they enlighten, kindle the sons of earth to joy and love. Brunhilda became the wife of Walter, and both being equally enamoured and devoted, they abandoned themselves to the enjoyment of a passion that rendered them reckless of aught besides, while it lulled them in a fascinating dream. Their sole apprehension was lest aught should awaken them from a delirium which they prayed might continue for ever. Yet how vain is the wish that would arrest the decrees of destiny! as well might it seek to divert the circling planets from their eternal course. Short was the duration of this phrenzied passion; not that it gradually decayed and subsided into apathy, but death snatched away his blooming victim, and left Walter to a widowed couch. Impetuous, however, as was his first burst of grief, he was not inconsolable, for ere long another bride became the partner of the youthful nobleman.

Swanhilda also was beautiful; although nature had formed her charms on a very different model from those of Brunhilda. Her golden locks waved bright as the beams of morn: only when excited by some emotion of her soul did a rosy hue tinge the lily paleness of her cheek: her limbs were proportioned in the nicest symmetry, yet did they not possess that luxuriant fullness of animal life: her eye beamed eloquently, but it was with the milder radiance of a star, tranquillizing to tenderness rather than exciting to warmth. Thus formed, it was not possible that she should steep him in his former delirium, although she rendered happy his waking hours—tranquil and serious, yet cheerful, studying in all things her husband's pleasure, she restored order and comfort in his family, where her presence shed a general influence all around. Her mild benevolence tended to restrain the fiery, impetuous disposition of Walter: while at the same time her prudence recalled him in some degree from his vain, turbulent wishes, and his aspirings after unattainable enjoyments, to the duties and pleasures of actual life. Swanhilda bore her husband two children, a son and a daughter; the latter was mild and patient as her mother, well contented with her solitary sports, and even in these recreations displayed the serious turn of her character. The boy possessed his father's fiery, restless disposition, tempered, however, with the solidity of his mother. Attached by his offspring more tenderly towards their mother, Walter now lived for several years very happily: his thoughts would frequently, indeed, recur to

Johann Ludwig Tieck, "Wake Not the Dead," *Popular Tales and Romances of the Northern Nations*. Copyright in the Public Domain.

Brunhilda, but without their former violence, merely as we dwell upon the memory of a friend of our earlier days, borne from us on the rapid current of time to a region where we know that he is happy.

But clouds dissolve into air, flowers fade, the sands of the hourglass run impeceptibly away, and even so, do human feelings dissolve, fade, and pass away, and with them too, human happiness. Walter's inconstant breast again sighed for the ecstatic dreams of those days which he had spent with his equally romantic, enamoured Brunhilda--again did she present herself to his ardent fancy in all the glow of her bridal charms, and he began to draw a parallel between the past and the present; nor did imagination, as it is wont, fail to array the former in her brightest hues, while it proportionably obscured the latter; so that he pictured to himself, the one much more rich in enjoyment, and the other, much less so than they really were. This change in her husband did not escape Swanhilda; whereupon, redoubling her attentions towards him, and her cares towards their children, she expected, by this means, to reunite the knot that was slackened; yet the more she endeavoured to regain his affections, the colder did he grow,—the more intolerable did her caresses seem, and the more continually did the image of Brunhilda haunt his thoughts. The children, whose endearments were now become indispensable to him, alone stood between the parents as genii eager to affect a reconciliation; and, beloved by them both, formed a uniting link between them. Yet, as evil can be plucked from the heart of man, only ere its root has yet struck deep, its fangs being afterwards too firm to be eradicated; so was Walter's diseased fancy too far affected to have its disorder stopped, for, in a short time, it completely tyrannized over him. Frequently of a night, instead of retiring to his consort's chamber, he repaired to Brunhilda's grave, where he murmured forth his discontent, saying: "Wilt thou sleep for ever?"

One night as he was reclining on the turf, indulging in his wonted sorrow, a sorcerer from the neighbouring mountains, entered into this field of death for the purpose of gathering, for his mystic spells, such herbs as grow only from the earth wherein the dead repose, and which, as if the last production of mortality, are gifted with a powerful and supernatural influence. The sorcerer perceived the mourner, and approached the spot where he was lying.

"Wherefore, fond wretch, dost thou grieve thus, for what is now a hideous mass of mortality—mere bones, and nerves, and veins? Nations have fallen unlamented; even worlds themselves, long ere this globe of ours was created, have mouldered into nothing; nor hath any one wept over them; why then should'st thou indulge this vain affliction for a child of the dust—a being as frail as thyself, and like thee the creature but of a moment?"

Walter raised himself up:—"Let yon worlds that shine in the firmament" replied he, "lament for each other as they perish. It is true, that I who am myself clay, lament for my fellow-clay: yet is this clay impregnated with a fire,—with an essence, that none of the elements of creation possess—with love: and this divine passion, I felt for her who now sleepeth beneath this sod."

"Will thy complaints awaken her: or could they do so, would she not soon upbraid thee for having disturbed that repose in which she is now hushed?"

"Avaunt, cold-hearted being: thou knowest not what is love. Oh! that my tears could wash away the earthy covering that conceals her from these eyes;—that my groan of anguish could rouse her from her slumber of death!—No, she would not again seek her earthy couch."

"Insensate that thou art, and couldst thou endure to gaze without shuddering on one disgorged from the jaws of the grave? Art thou too thyself the same from whom she parted; or hath time passed o'er thy brow and left no traces there? Would not thy love rather be converted into hate and disgust?"

"Say rather that the stars would leave yon firmament, that the sun will henceforth refuse to shed his beams through the heavens. Oh! that she stood once more before me;—that once again she reposed on this bosom!—how quickly should we then forget that death or time had ever stepped between us."

"Delusion! mere delusion of the brain, from heated blood, like to that which arises from the fumes of wine. It is not my wish to tempt thee;—to restore to thee thy dead; else wouldst thou soon feel that I have spoken truth."

"How! restore her to me," exclaimed Walter casting himself at the sorcerer's feet. "Oh! if thou art indeed able to effect that, grant it to my earnest supplication; if one throb of human feeling vibrates in thy bosom, let my tears prevail with thee; restore to me my beloved; so shalt thou hereafter bless the deed, and see that it was a good work."

"A good work! a blessed deed!"—returned the sorcerer with a smile of scorn; "for me there exists nor good nor evil; since my will is always the same. Ye alone know evil, who will that which ye would not. It is indeed in my power to restore her to thee: yet, bethink thee well, whether it will prove thy weal. Consider too, how deep the abyss between life and death; across this, my power can build a bridge, but it can never fill up the frightful chasm."

Walter would have spoken, and have sought to prevail on this powerful being by fresh entreaties, but the latter prevented him, saying: "Peace! bethink thee well! and return hither to me tomorrow at midnight. Yet once more do I warn thee, 'Wake not the dead.'"

Having uttered these words, the mysterious being disappeared. Intoxicated with fresh hope, Walter found no sleep on his couch; for fancy, prodigal of her richest stores, expanded before him the glittering web of futurity; and his eye, moistened with the dew of rapture, glanced from one vision of happiness to another. During the next day he wandered through the woods, lest wonted objects by recalling the memory of later and less happier times, might disturb the blissful idea, that he should again behold her—again fold her in his arms, gaze on her beaming brow by day, repose on her bosom at night: and, as this sole idea filled his imagination, how was it possible that the least doubt should arise; or that the warning of the mysterious old man should recur to his thoughts?

No sooner did the midnight hour approach, than he hastened before the grave-field where the sorcerer was already standing by that of Brunhilda. "Hast thou maturely considered?" inquired he.

"Oh! restore to me the object of my ardent passion," exclaimed Walter with impetuous eagerness. "Delay not thy generous action, lest I die even this night, consumed with disappointed desire; and behold her face no more."

"Well then," answered the old man, "return hither again tomorrow at the same hour. But once more do I give thee this friendly warning, 'Wake not the dead.'"

All in the despair of impatience, Walter would have prostrated himself at his feet, and supplicated him to fulfil at once a desire now increased to agony; but the sorcerer had already disappeared. Pouring forth his lamentations more wildly and impetuously than ever, he lay upon the grave of his adored one, until the grey dawn streaked the east. During the day, which seemed to him longer than any he had ever experienced, he wandered to and fro, restless and impatient, seemingly without any object, and deeply buried in his own reflections, inquest as the murderer who meditates his first deed of blood: and the stars of evening found him once more at the appointed spot. At midnight the sorcerer was there also.

"Hast thou yet maturely deliberated?" inquired he, "as on the preceding night?"

"Oh what should I deliberate?" returned Walter impatiently. "I need not to deliberate; what I demand of thee, is that which thou hast promised me—that which will prove my bliss. Or dost thou but mock me? if so, hence from my sight, lest I be tempted to lay my hand on thee."

"Once more do I warn thee," answered the old man with undisturbed composure, "'Wake not the dead'—let her rest."

"Aye, but not in the cold grave: she shall rather rest on this bosom which burns with eagerness to clasp her."

"Reflect, thou mayst not quit her until death, even though aversion and horror should seize thy heart. There would then remain only one horrible means."

"Dotard!" cried Walter, interrupting him, "how may I hate that which I love with such intensity of passion? how should I abhor that for which my every drop of blood is boiling?"

"Then be it even as thou wishest," answered the sorcerer; "step back."

The old man now drew a circle round the grave, all the while muttering words of enchantment. Immediately the storm began to howl among the tops of the trees; owls flapped their wings, and uttered their low voice of omen; the stars hid their mild, beaming aspect, that they might not behold so unholy and impious a spectacle; the stone then rolled from the grave with a hollow sound, leaving a free passage for the inhabitant of that dreadful tenement. The sorcerer scattered into the yawning earth, roots and herbs of most magic power, and of most penetrating odour, so that the worms crawling forth from the earth congregated together, and raised themselves in a fiery column over the grave: while rushing wind burst from the earth, scattering the mould before it, until at length the coffin lay uncovered. The moonbeams fell on it, and the lid burst open with a tremendous sound. Upon this the sorcerer poured upon it some blood from out of a human skull, exclaiming at the same time, "Drink, sleeper, of this warm stream, that thy heart may again beat within thy bosom." And, after a short pause, shedding on her some other mystic liquid, he cried aloud with the voice of one inspired: "Yes, thy heart beats once more with the flood of life: thine eye is again opened to sight. Arise, therefore, from the tomb."

As an island suddenly springs forth from the dark waves of the ocean, raised upwards from the deep by the force of subterraneous fires, so did Brunhilda start from her earthy couch, borne forward by some invisible power. Taking her by the hand, the sorcerer led her towards Walter, who stood at some little distance, rooted to the ground with amazement.

"Receive again," said he, "the object of thy passionate sighs: mayest thou never more require my aid; should that, however, happen, so wilt thou find me, during the full of the moon, upon the mountains in that spot and where the three roads meet."

Instantly did Walter recognize in the form that stood before him, her whom he so ardently loved; and a sudden glow shot through his frame at finding her thus restored to him: yet the night-frost had chilled his limbs and palsied his tongue. For a while he gazed upon her without either motion or speech, and during this pause, all was again become hushed and serene; and the stars shone brightly in the clear heavens.

"Walter!" exclaimed the figure; and at once the well-known sound, thrilling to his heart, broke the spell by which he was bound.

"Is it reality? Is it truth?" cried he, "or a cheating delusion?"

"No, it is no imposture; I am really living:—conduct me quickly to thy castle in the mountains."

Walter looked around: the old man had disappeared, but he perceived close by his side, a coal-black steed of fiery eye, ready equipped to conduct him thence; and on his back lay all proper attire for Brunhilda, who lost no time in arraying herself. This being done, she cried; "Haste, let us away ere the dawn breaks, for my eye is yet too weak to endure the light of day." Fully recovered from his stupor, Walter leaped into his saddle, and catching up, with a mingled feeling of delight and awe, the beloved being thus mysteriously restored from the power of the grave, he spurred on across the wild, towards the mountains, as furiously as if pursued by the shadows of the dead, hastening to recover from him their sister.

The castle to which Walter conducted his Brunhilda, was situated on a rock between other rocks rising up above it. Here they arrived, unseen by any save one aged domestic, on whom Walter imposed secrecy by the severest threats.

"Here will we tarry," said Brunhilda, "until I can endure the light, and until thou canst look upon me without trembling as if struck with a cold chill." They accordingly continued to make that place their abode: yet no one knew that Brunhilda existed, save only that aged attendant, who provided their meals. During seven entire days they had no light except that of tapers: during the next seven, the light was admitted through the lofty casements only while the rising or setting-sun faintly illumined the mountain-tops, the valley being still enveloped in shade.

Seldom did Walter quit Brunhilda's side: a nameless spell seemed to attach him to her; even the shudder which he felt in her presence, and which would not permit him to touch her, was not unmixed with pleasure, like that thrilling awful emotion felt when strains of sacred music float under the vault of some temple; he rather sought, therefore, than avoided this feeling. Often too as he had indulged in calling to mind the beauties of Brunhilda, she had never appeared so fair, so fascinating, so admirable when depicted by his imagination, as when now beheld in reality. Never till now had her voice sounded with such tones of sweetness; never before did her language possess such eloquence as it now did, when she conversed with him on the subject of the past. And this was the magic fairy-land towards which her words constantly conducted him. Ever did she dwell upon the days of their first love, those hours of delight which they had participated together when the one derived all enjoyment from the other: and so rapturous, so enchanting, so full of life did she recall to his imagination that blissful season, that he even doubted whether he had ever experienced with her so much felicity, or had been so truly happy. And, while she thus vividly portrayed their hours of past delight, she delineated in still more glowing, more enchanting colours, those hours of approaching bliss which now awaited them, richer in enjoyment than any preceding ones. In this manner did she charm her attentive auditor with enrapturing hopes for the future, and lull him into dreams of more than mortal ecstasy; so that while he listened to her siren strain, he entirely forgot how little blissful was the latter period of their union, when he had often sighed at her imperiousness, and at her harshness both to himself and all his household. Yet even had he recalled this to mind would it have disturbed him in his present delirious trance? Had she not now left behind in the grave all the frailty of mortality? Was not her whole being refined and purified by that long sleep in which neither passion nor sin had approached her even in dreams? How different now was the subject of her discourse! Only when speaking of her affection for him, did she betray anything of earthly feeling: at other times, she uniformly dwelt upon themes relating to the invisible and future world; when in descanting and declaring the mysteries of eternity, a stream of prophetic eloquence would burst from her lips.

In this manner had twice seven days elapsed, and, for the first time, Walter beheld the being now dearer to him than ever, in the full light of day. Every trace of the grave had disappeared from her countenance; a roseate tinge like the ruddy streaks of dawn again beamed on her pallid cheek; the faint, mouldering taint of the grave was changed into a delightful violet scent; the only sign of earth that never disappeared. He no longer felt either apprehension or awe, as he gazed upon her in the sunny light of day: it was not until now, that he seemed to have recovered her completely; and, glowing with all his former passion towards her, he would have pressed her to his bosom, but she gently repulsed him, saying:—"Not yet—spare your caresses until the moon has again filled her horn."

Spite of his impatience, Walter was obliged to await the lapse of another period of seven days: but, on the night when the moon was arrived at the full, he hastened to Brunhilda, whom he found more lovely than she had ever appeared before. Fearing no obstacles to his transports, he embraced with all the fervour of a deeply enamoured and successful lover. Brunhilda, however, still refused to yield to his passion. "What!" exclaimed she, "is it fitting that I who have been purified by death from the frailty of mortality, should become thy concubine, while a mere daughter of the earth bears the title of thy wife: never shall it be. No, it must be within the walls of thy palace, within that chamber where I once reigned as queen, that thou obtainest the end of thy wishes,—and of mine also," added she, imprinting a glowing kiss on the lips, and immediately disappeared.

Heated with passion, and determined to sacrifice everything to the accomplishment of his desires, Walter hastily quitted the apartment, and shortly after the castle itself. He travelled over mountain and across heath, with the rapidity of a storm, so that the turf was flung up by his horse's hoofs; nor once stopped until he arrived home.

Here, however, neither the affectionate caresses of Swanhilda, or those of his children could touch his heart, or induce him to restrain his furious desires. Alas! is the impetuous torrent to be checked in its devastating course by the beauteous flowers over which it rushes, when they exclaim:—"Destroyer, commiserate our helpless innocence and beauty, nor lay us waste?"—the stream sweeps over them unregarding, and a single moment annihilates the pride of a whole summer.

Shortly afterwards did Walter begin to hint to Swanhilda that they were ill-suited to each other; that he was anxious to taste that wild, tumultuous life, so well according with the spirit of his sex, while she, on the contrary, was satisfied with the monotonous circle of household enjoyments:—that he was eager for whatever promised novelty, while she felt most attached to what was familiarized to her by habit: and lastly, that her cold disposition, bordering upon indifference, but ill assorted with his ardent temperament: it was therefore more prudent that they should seek apart from each other that happiness which they could not find together. A sigh, and a brief acquiescence in his wishes was all the reply that Swanhilda made: and, on the following morning, upon his presenting her with a paper of separation, informing her that she was at liberty to return home to her father, she received it most submissively: yet, ere she departed, she gave him the following warning: "Too well do I conjecture to whom I am indebted for this our separation. Often have I seen thee at Brunhilda's grave, and beheld thee there even on that night when the face of the heavens was suddenly enveloped in a veil of clouds. Hast thou rashly dared to tear aside the awful veil that separates the mortality that dreams, from that which dreameth not? Oh! then woe to thee, thou wretched man, for thou hast attached to thyself that which will prove thy destruction."

She ceased: nor did Walter attempt any reply, for the similar admonition uttered by the sorcerer flashed upon his mind, all obscured as it was by passion, just as the lightning glares momentarily through the gloom of night without dispersing the obscurity.

Swanhilda then departed, in order to pronounce to her children, a bitter farewell, for they, according to national custom, belonged to the father; and, having bathed them in her tears, and consecrated them with the holy water of maternal love, she quitted her husband's residence, and departed to the home of her father's.

Thus was the kind and benevolent Swanhilda driven an exile from those halls where she had presided with grace;—from halls which were now newly decorated to receive another mistress. The day at length arrived on which Walter, for the second time, conducted Brunhilda home as a newly made bride. And he caused it to be reported among his domestics that his new consort had gained his affections by her extraordinary likeness to Brunhilda, their former mistress. How ineffably happy did he deem himself as he conducted his beloved once more into the chamber which had often witnessed their former joys, and which was now newly gilded and adorned in a most costly style: among the other decorations were figures of angels scattering roses, which served to support the purple draperies whose ample folds o'ershadowed the nuptial couch. With what impatience did he await the hour that was to put him in possession of those beauties for which he had already paid so high a price, but, whose enjoyment was to cost him most dearly yet! Unfortunate Walter! revelling in bliss, thou beholdest not the abyss that yawns beneath thy feet, intoxicated with the luscious perfume of the flower thou hast plucked, thou little deemest how deadly is the venom with which it is fraught, although, for a short season, its potent fragrance bestows new energy on all thy feelings.

Happy, however, as Walter was now, his household were far from being equally so. The strange resemblance between their new lady and the deceased Brunhilda filled them with a secret dismay,—an undefinable horror; for there was not a single difference of feature, of tone of voice, or of gesture. To add too to these mysterious circumstances, her female attendants discovered a particular mark on her back, exactly like one which Brunhilda had. A report was now soon circulated, that their lady was no other than Brunhilda herself, who had been recalled to life by the power of necromancy. How truly horrible was the idea of living under the same roof with one who had been an inhabitant of the tomb, and of being obliged to attend upon her, and acknowledge her as mistress! There was also in Brunhilda much to increase this aversion, and favour their superstition: no ornaments of gold ever decked her person; all that others were wont to wear of this metal, she had formed of silver: no richly coloured and sparkling jewels glittered upon her; pearls alone, lent their pale lustre to adorn her bosom. Most carefully did she always avoid the cheerful light of the sun, and was wont to spend the brightest days in the most retired and gloomy apartments: only during the twilight of the commencing or declining day did she ever walk abroad, but her favourite hour was when the phantom light of the moon bestowed on all objects a shadowy appearance and a sombre hue; always too at the crowing of the cock an involuntary shudder was observed to seize her limbs. Imperious as before her death, she quickly imposed her iron yoke on every one around her, while she seemed even far more terrible than ever, since a dread of some supernatural power attached to her, appalled all who approached her. A malignant withering glance seemed to shoot from her eye on the unhappy object of her wrath, as if it would annihilate its victim. In short, those halls which, in the time of Swanhilda were the residence of cheerfulness and mirth, now resembled an extensive desert tomb. With fear imprinted on their pale countenances, the domestics glided through the apartments of the castle; and in this abode of terror, the crowing of the cock caused the living to tremble, as if they were the spirits of the departed; for the sound always reminded them of their mysterious mistress. There was no one but who shuddered at meeting her in a lonely place, in the dusk of evening, or by the light of the moon, a circumstance that was deemed to be ominous of some evil: so great was the apprehension of her female attendants, they pined in continual disquietude, and, by degrees, all quitted her. In the course of time even others of the domestics fled, for an insupportal horror had seized them.

The art of the sorcerer had indeed bestowed upon Brunhilda an artificial life, and due nourishment had continued to support the restored body: yet this body was not able of itself to keep up the genial glow of vitality, and to nourish the flame whence springs all the affections and passions, whether of love or hate; for death had for ever destroyed and withered it: all that Brunhilda now possessed was a chilled existence, colder than that of the snake. It was nevertheless necessary that she should love, and return with equal ardour the warm caresses of her spell-enthralled husband, to whose passion alone she was indebted for her renewed existence. It was necessary that a magic draught should animate the dull current in her veins and awaken her to the glow of life and the flame of love—a potion of abomination—one not even to be named without a curse—human blood, imbibed whilst yet warm, from the veins of youth. This was the hellish drink for which she thirsted: possessing no sympathy with the purer feelings of humanity; deriving no enjoyment from aught that interests in life and occupies its varied hours; her existence was a mere blank, unless when in the arms of her paramour husband, and therefore was it that she craved incessantly after the horrible draught. It was even with the utmost effort that she could forbear sucking even the blood of Walter himself, reclined beside her. Whenever she beheld some innocent child whose lovely face denoted the exuberance of infantine health and vigour, she would entice it by soothing words and fond caresses into her most secret apartment, where, lulling it to sleep in her arms, she would suck from its bosom the warm, purple tide of life. Nor were youths of either sex safe from her horrid attack: having first breathed upon her unhappy victim, who never failed immediately to sink into a lengthened sleep, she would then in a similar manner drain his veins of the vital juice. Thus children, youths, and maidens quickly faded away, as flowers gnawn by the cankering worm: the fullness of their limbs disappeared; a sallow line succeeded to the rosy freshness of their cheeks, the liquid lustre of the eye was deadened, even as the sparkling stream when arrested by the touch of frost; and their locks became thin and grey, as if already ravaged by the storm of life. Parents beheld with horror this desolating pestilence devouring their offspring; nor could simple or charm, potion or amulet avail aught against it. The grave swallowed up one after the other;

or did the miserable victim survive, he became cadaverous and wrinkled even in the very morn of existence. Parents observed with horror this devastating pestilence snatch away their offspring—a pestilence which, nor herb however potent, nor charm, nor holy taper, nor exorcism could avert. They either beheld their children sink one after the other into the grave, or their youthful forms, withered by the unholy, vampire embrace of Brunhilda, assume the decrepitude of sudden age.

At length strange surmises and reports began to prevail; it was whispered that Brunhilda herself was the cause of all these horrors; although no one could pretend to tell in what manner she destroyed her victims, since no marks of violence were discernible. Yet when young children confessed that she had frequently lulled them asleep in her arms, and elder ones said that a sudden slumber had come upon them whenever she began to converse with them, suspicion became converted into certainty, and those whose offspring had hitherto escaped unharmed, quitted their hearths and home—all their little possessions—the dwellings of their fathers and the inheritance of their children, in order to rescue from so horrible a fate those who were dearer to their simple affections than aught else the world could give.

Thus daily did the castle assume a more desolate appearance; daily did its environs become more deserted; none but a few aged decrepit old women and grey-headed menials were to be seen remaining of the once numerous retinue. Such will in the latter days of the earth be the last generation of mortals, when childbearing shall have ceased, when youth shall no more be seen, nor any arise to replace those who shall await their fate in silence.

Walter alone noticed not, or heeded not, the desolation around him; he apprehended not death, lapped as he was in a glowing elysium of love. Far more happy than formerly did he now seem in the possession of Brunhilda. All those caprices and frowns which had been wont to overcloud their former union had now entirely disappeared. She even seemed to dote on him with a warmth of passion that she had never exhibited even during the happy season of bridal love; for the flame of that youthful blood, of which she drained the veins of others, rioted in her own. At night, as soon as he closed his eyes, she would breathe on him till he sank into delicious dreams, from which he awoke only to experience more rapturous enjoyments. By day she would continually discourse with him on the bliss experienced by happy spirits beyond the grave, assuring him that, as his affection had recalled her from the tomb, they were now irrevocably united. Thus fascinated by a continual spell, it was not possible that he should perceive what was taking place around him. Brunhilda, however, foresaw with savage grief that the source of her youthful ardour was daily decreasing, for, in a short time, there remained nothing gifted with youth, save Walter and his children, and these latter she resolved should be her next victims.

On her first return to the castle, she had felt an aversion towards the offspring of another, and therefore abandoned them entirely to the attendants appointed by Swanhilda. Now, however, she began to pay considerable attention to them, and caused them to be frequently admitted into her presence. The aged nurses were filled with dread at perceiving these marks of regard from her towards their young charges, yet dared they not to oppose the will of their terrible and imperious mistress. Soon did Brunhilda gain the affection of the children, who were too unsuspecting of guile to apprehend any danger from her; on the contrary, her caresses won them completely to her. Instead of ever checking their mirthful gambols, she would rather instruct them in new sports: often too did she recite to them tales of such strange and wild interest as to exceed all the stories of their nurses. Were they wearied either with play or with listening to her narratives, she would take them on her knees and lull them to slumber. Then did visions of the most surpassing magnificence attend their dreams: they would fancy themselves in some garden where flowers of every hue rose in rows one above the other, from the humble violet to the tall sunflower, forming a parti-coloured broidery of every hue, sloping upwards towards the golden clouds where little angels whose wings sparkled with azure and gold descended to bring them delicious cakes or splendid jewels; or sung to them soothing melodious hymns. So delightful did these dreams in short time become to the children that they longered for nothing so eagerly as to slumber on Brunhilda's lap, for never did they else enjoy such visions of heavenly forms. They were the most anxious for that which was to prove their destruction:—yet do we not all aspire after that which conducts us to the grave—after the enjoyment of life? These innocents stretched out their arms to approaching death because it assumed the mask of pleasure; for, which they were lapped in these ecstatic slumbers, Brunhilda sucked the life-stream from their bosoms. On waking, indeed, they felt themselves faint and exhausted, yet did no pain nor any mark betray the cause. Shortly, however, did their strength entirely fail, even as the summer brook is gradually dried up: their sports became less and less noisy; their loud, frolicsome laughter was converted into a faint smile; the full tones of their voices died away into a mere whisper. Their attendants were filled with horror and despair; too well did they conjecture the horrible truth, yet dared not to impart their suspicions to Walter, who was so devotedly attached to his horrible partner. Death had already smote his prey: the children were but the mere shadows of their former selves, and even this shadow quickly disappeared.

The anguished father deeply bemoaned their loss, for, notwithstanding his apparent neglect, he was strongly attached to them, nor until he had experienced their loss was he aware that his love was so great. His affliction could not fail to excite the displeasure of Brunhilda: "Why dost thou lament so fondly," said she, "for these little ones? What satisfaction could such unformed beings yield to thee unless thou wert still attached to their mother? Thy heart then is still hers? Or dost thou now regret her and them because thou art satiated with my fondness and weary of my endearments? Had these young ones grown up, would they not have attached thee, thy spirit and thy affections more closely to this earth of clay—to this dust and have alienated thee from that sphere to which I, who have already passed the grave, endeavour to raise thee? Say is thy spirit so heavy, or thy love so weak, or thy faith so hollow, that the hope of being mine for ever is unable to touch thee?" Thus did Brunhilda express her indignation at her consort's grief, and forbade him her presence. The fear of offending her beyond forgiveness and his anxiety to appease her soon dried up his tears; and he again abandoned himself to his fatal passion, until approaching destruction at length awakened him from his delusion.

Neither maiden, nor youth, was any longer to be seen, either within the dreary walls of the castle, or the adjoining territory:—all had disappeared; for those whom the grave had not swallowed up had fled from the region of death. Who, therefore, now remained to quench the horrible thirst of the female vampire save Walter himself? and his death she dared to contemplate unmoved; for that divine sentiment that unites two beings in one joy and one sorrow was unknown to her bosom. Was he in his tomb, so was she free to search out other victims and glut herself with destruction, until she herself should, at the last day, be consumed with the earth itself, such is the fatal law to which the dead are subject when awoke by the arts of necromancy from the sleep of the grave.

She now began to fix her blood-thirsty lips on Walter's breast, when cast into a profound sleep by the odour of her violet breath he reclined beside her quite unconscious of his impending fate: yet soon did his vital powers begin to decay; and many a grey hair peeped through his raven locks. With his strength, his passion also declined; and he now frequently left her in order to pass the whole day in the sports of the chase, hoping thereby to regain his wonted vigour. As he was reposing one day in a wood beneath the shade of an oak, he perceived, on the summit of a tree, a bird of strange appearance, and quite unknown to him; but, before he could take aim at it with his bow, it flew away into the clouds; at the same time letting fall a rose-coloured root which dropped at Walter's feet, who immediately took it up and, although he was well acquainted with almost every plant, he could not remember to have seen any at all resembling this. Its delightfully odoriferous scent induced him to try its flavour, but ten times more bitter than wormwood it was even as gall in his mouth;

upon which, impatient of the disappointment, he flung it away with violence. Had he, however, been aware of its miraculous quality and that it acted as a counter charm against the opiate perfume of Brunhilda's breath, he would have blessed it in spite of its bitterness: thus do mortals often blindly cast away in displeasure the unsavoury remedy that would otherwise work their weal.

When Walter returned home in the evening and laid him down to repose as usual by Brunhilda's side, the magic power of her breath produced no effect upon him; and for the first time during many months did he close his eyes in a natural slumber. Yet hardly had he fallen asleep, ere a pungent smarting pain disturbed him from his dreams; and. opening his eyes, he discerned, by the gloomy rays of a lamp, that glimmered in the apartment what for some moments transfixed him quite aghast, for it was Brunhilda, drawing with her lips, the warm blood from his bosom. The wild cry of horror which at length escaped him, terrified Brunhilda, whose mouth was besmeared with the warm blood. "Monster!" exclaimed he, springing from the couch, "is it thus that you love me?"

"Aye, even as the dead love," replied she, with a malignant coldness.

"Creature of blood!" continued Walter, "the delusion which has so long blinded me is at an end: thou are the fiend who hast destroyed my children—who hast murdered the offspring of my vassals." Raising herself upwards and, at the same time, casting on him a glance that froze him to the spot with dread, she replied, "It is not I who have murdered them;—I was obliged to pamper myself with warm youthful blood, in order that I might satisfy thy furious desires—thou art the murderer!"—These dreadful words summoned, before Walter's terrified conscience, the threatening shades of all those who had thus perished; while despair choked his voice.

"Why," continued she, in a tone that increased his horror, "why dost thou make mouths at me like a puppet? Thou who hadst the courage to love the dead—to take into thy bed, one who had been sleeping in the grave, the bed-fellow of the worm—who hast clasped in thy lustful arms, the corruption of the tomb—dost thou, unhallowed as thou art, now raise this hideous cry for the sacrifice of a few lives?—They are but leaves swept from their branches by a storm.—Come, chase these idiot fancies, and taste the bliss thou hast so dearly purchased." So saying, she extended her arms towards him; but this motion served only to increase his terror, and exclaiming: "Accursed Being,"—he rushed out of the apartment.

All the horrors of a guilty, upbraiding conscience became his companions, now that he was awakened from the delirium of his unholy pleasures. Frequently did he curse his own obstinate blindness, for having given no heed to the hints and admonitions of his children's nurses, but treating them as vile calumnies. But his sorrow was now too late, for, although repentance may gain pardon for the sinner, it cannot alter the immutable decrees of fate—it cannot recall the murdered from the tomb. No sooner did the first break of dawn appear, than he set out for his lonely castle in the mountains, determined no longer to abide under the same roof with so terrific a being; yet vain was his flight, for, on waking the following morning, he perceived himself in Brunhilda's arms, and quite entangled in her long raven tresses, which seemed to involve him, and bind him in the fetters of his fate; the powerful fascination of her breath held him still more captivated, so that, forgetting all that had passed, he returned her caresses, until awakening as if from a dream he recoiled in unmixed horror from her embrace. During the day he wandered through the solitary wilds of the mountains, as a culprit seeking an asylum from his pursuers; and, at night, retired to the shelter of a cave; fearing less to couch himself within such a dreary place, than to expose himself to the horror of again meeting Brunhilda; but alas! it was in vain that he endeavoured to flee her. Again, when he awoke, he found her the partner of his miserable bed. Nay, had he sought the centre of the earth as his hiding place; had he even imbedded himself beneath rocks, or formed his chamber in the recesses of the ocean, still had he found her his constant companion; for, by calling her again into existence, he had rendered himself inseparably hers; so fatal were the links that united them.

Struggling with the madness that was beginning to seize him, and brooding incessantly on the ghastly visions that presented themselves to his horror-stricken mind, he lay motionless in the gloomiest recesses of the woods, even from the rise of sun till the shades of eve. But, no sooner was the light of day extinguished in the west, and the woods buried in impenetrable darkness, than the apprehension of resigning himself to sleep drove him forth among the mountains. The storm played wildly with the fantastic clouds, and with the rattling leaves, as they were caught up into the air, as if some dread spirit was sporting with these images of transitoriness and decay: it roared among the summits of the oaks as if uttering a voice of fury, while its hollow sound rebounding among the distant hills, seemed as the moans of a departing sinner, or as the faint cry of some wretch expiring under the murderer's hand: the owl too, uttered its ghastly cry as if foreboding the wreck of nature. Walter's hair flew disorderly in the wind, like black snakes wreathing around his temples and shoulders; while each sense was awake to catch fresh horror. In the clouds he seemed to behold the forms of the murdered; in the howling wind to hear their laments and groans; in the chilling blast itself he felt the dire kiss of Brunhilda; in the cry of the screeching bird he heard her voice; in the mouldering leaves he scented the charnel-bed out of which he had awakened her. "Murderer of thy own offspring," exclaimed he in a voice making night, and the conflict of the element still more hideous, "paramour of a blood-thirsty vampire, reveller with the corruption of the tomb!" while in his despair he rent the wild locks from his head. Just then the full moon darted from beneath the bursting clouds; and the sight recalled to his remembrance the advice of the sorcerer, when he trembled at the first apparition of Brunhilda rising from her sleep of death;—namely, to seek him at the season of the full moon in the mountains, where three roads met. Scarcely had this gleam of hope broke in on his bewildered mind than he flew to the appointed spot.

On his arrival, Walter found the old man seated there upon a stone as calmly as though it had been a bright sunny day and completely regardless of the uproar around. "Art thou come then?" exclaimed he to the breathless wretch, who, flinging himself at his feet, cried in a tone of anguish:--"Oh save me—succour me—rescue me from the monster that scattereth death and desolation around her.

"Wherefore a mysterious warning? why didst thou not rather disclose to me at once all the horrors that awaited my sacrilegious profanation of the grave?"

"And wherefore a mysterious warning? why didst thou not perceivest how wholesome was the advice—'Wake not the dead.'

"Wert thou able to listen to another voice than that of thy impetuous passions? Did not thy eager impatience shut my mouth at the very moment I would have cautioned thee?"

"True, true:—thy reproof is just: but what does it avail now;—I need the promptest aid."

"Well," replied the old man, "there remains even yet a means of rescuing thyself, but it is fraught with horror and demands all thy resolution."

"Utter it then, utter it; for what can be more appalling, more hideous than the misery I now endure?"

"Know then," continued the sorcerer, "that only on the night of the new moon does she sleep the sleep of mortals; and then all the supernatural power which she inherits from the grave totally fails her. 'Tis then that thou must murder her."

"How! murder her!" echoed Walter.

"Aye," returned the old man calmly, "pierce her bosom with a sharpened dagger, which I will furnish thee with; at the same time renounce her memory for ever, swearing never to think of her intentionally, and that, if thou dost involuntarily, thou wilt repeat the curse."

"Most horrible! yet what can be more horrible than she herself is?—I'll do it."

"Keep then this resolution until the next new moon."

"What, must I wait until then?" cried Walter, "alas ere then, either her savage thirst for blood will have forced me into the night of the tomb, or horror will have driven me into the night of madness."

"Nay," replied the sorcerer, "that I can prevent;" and, so saying, he conducted him to a cavern further among the mountains. "Abide here twice seven days," said he; "so long can I protect thee against her deadly caresses. Here wilt thou find all due provision for thy wants; but take heed that nothing tempt thee to quit this place. Farewell, when the moon renews itself, then do I repair hither again." So saying, the sorcerer drew a magic circle around the cave, and then immediately disappeared.

Twice seven days did Walter continue in this solitude, where his companions were his own terrifying thoughts, and his bitter repentance. The present was all desolation and dread; the future presented the image of a horrible deed which he must perforce commit; while the past was empoisoned by the memory of his guilt. Did he think on his former happy union with Brunhilda, her horrible image presented itself to his imagination with her lips defiled with dropping blood: or, did he call to mind the peaceful days he had passed with Swanhilda, he beheld her sorrowful spirit with the shadows of her murdered children. Such were the horrors that attended him by day: those of night were still more dreadful, for then he beheld Brunhilda herself, who, wandering round the magic circle which she could not pass, called upon his name till the cavern reechoed the horrible sound. "Walter, my beloved," cried she, "wherefore dost thou avoid me? art thou not mine? for ever mine—mine here, and mine hereafter? And dost thou seek to murder me?—ah! commit not a deed which hurls us both to perdition—thyself as well as me." In this manner did the horrible visitant torment him each night, and, even when she departed, robbed him of all repose.

The night of the new moon at length arrived, dark as the deed it was doomed to bring forth. The sorcerer entered the cavern; "Come," said he to Walter, "let us depart hence, the hour is now arrived:" and he forthwith conducted him in silence from the cave to a coal-black steed, the sight of which recalled to Walter's remembrance the fatal night. He then related to the old man Brunhilda's nocturnal visits and anxiously inquired whether her apprehensions of eternal perdition would be fulfilled or not. "Mortal eye," exclaimed the sorcerer, "may not pierce the dark secrets of another world, or penetrate the deep abyss that separates earth from heaven." Walter hesitated to mount the steed. "Be resolute," exclaimed his companion, "but this once is it granted to thee to make the trial, and, should thou fail now, nought can rescue thee from her power."

"What can be more horrible than she herself?—I am determined:" and he leaped on the horse, the sorcerer mounting also behind him.

Carried with a rapidity equal to that of the storm that sweeps across the plain they in brief space arrived at Walter's castle. All the doors flew open at the bidding of his companion, and they speedily reached Brunhilda's chamber, and stood beside her couch. Reclining in a tranquil slumber; she reposed in all her native loveliness, every trace of horror had disappeared from her countenance; she looked so pure, meek and innocent that all the sweet hours of their endearments rushed to Walter's memory, like interceding angels pleading in her behalf. His unnerved hand could not take the dagger which the sorcerer presented to him. "The blow must be struck even now:" said the latter, "shouldst thou delay but an hour, she will lie at daybreak on thy bosom, sucking the warm life drops from thy heart."

"Horrible! most horrible!" faltered the trembling Walter, and turning away his face, he thrust the dagger into her bosom, exclaiming—"I curse thee for ever!"—and the cold blood gushed upon his hand. Opening her eyes once more, she cast a look of ghastly horror on her husband, and, in a hollow dying accent said—"Thou too art doomed to perdition."

"Lay now thy hand upon her corpse," said the sorcerer, "and swear the oath."—Walter did as commanded, saying, "Never will I think of her with love, never recall her to mind intentionally, and, should her image recur to my mind involuntarily, so will I exclaim to it: be thou accursed."

"Thou hast now done everything," returned the sorcerer;—"restore her therefore to the earth, from which thou didst so foolishly recall her; and be sure to recollect thy oath: for, shouldst thou forget it but once, she would return, and thou wouldst be inevitably lost. Adieu—we see each other no more." Having uttered these words he quitted the apartment, and Walter also fled from this abode of horror, having first given direction that the corpse should be speedily interred.

Again did the terrific Brunhilda repose within her grave; but her image continually haunted Walter's imagination, so that his existence was one continued martyrdom, in which he continually struggled, to dismiss from his recollection the hideous phantoms of the past; yet, the stronger his effort to banish them, so much the more frequently and the more vividly did they return; as the night-wanderer, who is enticed by a fire-wisp into quagmire or bog, sinks the deeper into his damp grave the more he struggles to escape. His imagination seemed incapable of admitting any other image than that of Brunhilda: now he fancied he beheld her expiring, the blood streaming from her beautiful bosom: at others he saw the lovely bride of his youth, who reproached him with having disturbed the slumbers of the tomb; and to both he was compelled to utter the dreadful words, "I curse thee for ever." The terrible imprecation was constantly passing his lips; yet was he in incessant terror lest he should forget it, or dream of her without being able to repeat it, and then, on awaking, find himself in her arms. Else would he recall her expiring words, and, appalled at their terrific import, imagine that the doom of his perdition was irrecoverably passed. Whence should he fly from himself? or how erase from his brain these images and forms of horror? In the din of combat, in the tumult of war and its incessant pour of victory to defeat; from the cry of anguish to the exultation of victory—in these he hoped to find at least the relief of distraction: but here too he was disappointed. The giant fang of apprehension now seized him who had never before known fear; each drop of blood that sprayed upon him seemed the cold blood that had gushed from Brunhilda's wound; each dying wretch that fell beside him looked like her, when expiring, she exclaimed,—"Thou too art doomed to perdition"; so that the aspect of death seemed more full of dread to him than aught beside, and this unconquerable terror compelled him to abandon the battle-field. At length, after many a weary and fruitless wandering, he returned to his castle. Here all was deserted and silent, as if the sword, or a still more deadly pestilence had laid everything waste: for the few inhabitants that still remained, and even those servants who had once shewn themselves the most attached, now fled from him, as though he had been branded with the mark of Cain. With horror he perceived that, by uniting himself as he had done with the dead, he had cut himself off from the living, who refused to hold any intercourse with him. Often, when he stood on the battlements of his castle, and looked down upon desolate fields, he compared their present solitude with the lively activity they were wont to exhibit, under the strict but benevolent discipline of Swanhilda. He now felt that she alone could reconcile him to life, but durst he hope that one, whom he so deeply aggrieved, could pardon him, and receive him again? Impatience at length got the better of fear; he sought Swanhilda, and, with the deepest contrition, acknowledged his complicated guilt; embracing her knees as he beseeched her to pardon him, and to return to his desolate castle, in order that it might again become the abode of contentment and peace. The pale form which she beheld at her feet, the shadow of the lately blooming youth, touched Swanhilda. "The folly," said she gently, "though it has caused me much sorrow, has never excited my resentment or my anger. But say, where are my children?" To this dreadful interrogation the agonized father could for a while frame no reply: at length he was obliged to confess the dreadful truth. "Then we are sundered for ever," returned Swanhilda; nor could all his tears or supplications prevail upon her to revoke the sentence she had given.

Stripped of his last earthly hope, bereft of his last consolation, and thereby rendered as poor as mortal can possibly be on this side of the grave. Walter returned homewards; when, as he was riding through the forest in the neighbourhood of his castle, absorbed in his gloomy meditations, the sudden sound of a horn roused him from his reverie. Shortly after he saw appear a female figure clad in black, and mounted on a steed of the same colour: her attire was like that of a huntress, but, instead of a falcon, she bore a raven in her hand; and she was attended by a gay troop of cavaliers and dames. The first salutations bring passed, he found that she was proceeding the same road as himself; and, when she found that Walter's castle was close at hand, she requested that he would lodge her for that night, the evening being far advanced. Most willingly did he comply with this request, since the appearance of the beautiful stranger had struck him greatly; so wonderfully did she resemble Swanhilda, except that her locks were brown, and her eye dark and full of fire. With a sumptous banquet did he entertain his guests, whose mirth and songs enlivened the lately silent halls. Three days did this revelry continue, and so exhilarating did it prove to Walter that he seemed to have forgotten his sorrows and his fears; nor could he prevail upon himself to dismiss his visitors, dreading lest, on their departure, the castle would seem a hundred times more desolate than beforehand his grief be proportionally increased. At his earnest request, the stranger consented to stay seven, and again another seven days. Without being requested, she took upon herself the superintendence of the household, which she regulated as discreetly and cheerfully as Swanhilda had been wont to do, so that the castle, which had so lately been the abode of melancholy and horror, became the residence of pleasure and festivity, and Walter's grief disappeared altogether in the midst of so much gaiety. Daily did his attachment to the fair unknown increase; he even made her his confidant; and, one evening as they were walking together apart from any of her train, he related to her his melancholy and frightful history. "My dear friend," returned she, as soon as he had finished his tale, "it ill beseems a man of thy discretion to afflict thyself on account of all this. Thou hast awakened the dead from the sleep of the grave and afterwards found," — "what might have been anticipated, that the dead possess no sympathy with life. What then? thou wilt not commit this error a second time."

"Thou hast however murdered the being whom thou hadst thus recalled again to existence—but it was only in appearance, for thou couldst not deprive that of life which properly had none. Thou hast, too, lost a wife and two children: but at thy years such a loss is most easily repaired. There are beauties who will gladly share thy couch, and make thee again a father. But thou dreadst the reckoning of hereafter:—go, open the graves and ask the sleepers there whether that hereafter disturbs them." In such manner would she frequently exhort and cheer him, so that, in a short time, his melancholy entirely disappeared. He now ventured to declare to the unknown the passion with which she had inspired him, nor did she refuse him her hand. Within seven days afterwards the nuptials were celebrated, and the very foundations of the castle seemed to rock from the wild tumultuous uproar of unrestrained riot. The wine streamed in abundance; the goblets circled incessantly; intemperance reached its utmost bounds, while shouts of laughter almost resembling madness burst from the numerous train belonging to the unknown. At length Walter, heated with wine and love, conducted his bride into the nuptial chamber: but, oh! horror! scarcely had he clasped her in his arms ere she transformed herself into a monstrous serpent, which entwining him in its horrid folds, crushed him to death. Flames crackled on every side of the apartment; in a few minutes after, the whole castle was enveloped in a blaze that consumed it entirely: while, as the walls fell in with a tremendous crash, a voice exclaimed aloud—"Wake not the dead!"

Murderer the Women's Hope

Oskar Kokoschka

Characters

Man
Woman
Chorus: Men and Women

Night sky. Tower with large red iron grille as door; torches the only light; black ground, rising to the tower in such a way that all the figures appear in relief.

The Man in blue armor, white face, kerchief covering a wound, with a crowd of men—savage in appearance, gray-and-red kerchiefs, white-black-and-brown clothes, signs on their clothes, bare legs, long-handled torches, bells, din—creeping up with handles of torches extended and lights; wearily, reluctantly try to hold back the adventurer, pull his horse to the ground; he walks on, they open up the circle around him, crying out in a slow crescendo.

MEN: We were the flaming wheel around him, We were the flaming wheel around you, assailant of locked fortresses!
Hesitantly follow him again in chain formation; he, with the torch bearer in front of him, heads the procession.
MEN: Lead us, pale one!
While they are about to pull his horse to the ground, women with their leader ascend steps on the left.
WOMAN, *red clothes, loose yellow hair, tall.*
WOMAN, *loud*: With my breath I fan the yellow disc of the sun, my eye collects the jubilation of the men, their stammering lust prowls around me like a beast.
FEMALE ATTENDANTS *separate themselves from her, only now catch sight of the stranger.*
FIRST FEMALE ATTENDANT: His breath attaches itself to the virgin!
FIRST MAN *to the others*: Our master is like the moon that rises in the East.
SECOND GIRL, *quiet, her face averted*: When will she be enfolded joyfully?
Listening, alert, the CHORUS walks round the whole stage, dispersed in groups; THE MAN and the WOMAN meet in front of the gate. (Pause.)

WOMAN *observes him spellbound, then to herself*: Who is the stranger that has looked on me?
GIRLS *press to the fore.*
FIRST GIRL *recognizes him, cries out*: His sister died of love.
SECOND GIRL: Oh the singing of Time, flowers never seen.
THE MAN, *astonished; his procession halts*: Am I real? What did the shadows say?
Raising his face to her.
Did you look at me, did I look at you?
WOMAN, *filled with fear and longing*: Who is the pallid man? Hold him back.
FIRST GIRL, *with a piercing scream, runs back*: Do you let him in? It is he who strangles my little sister praying in the temple.
FIRST MAN *to the girl*: We saw him stride through the fire, his feet unharmed.
SECOND MAN: He tortured animals to death, killed neighing mares by the pressure of his thighs.
THIRD MAN: Birds that ran before us he made blind, stifled red fishes in the sand.
THE MAN *angry, heated*: Who is she that like an animal proudly grazes amidst her kin?
FIRST MAN: She divines what none has understood.
SECOND MAN: She perceives what none has seen or heard.
THIRD MAN: They say shy birds approach her and let themselves be seized.
GIRLS *in time with the men.*
FIRST GIRL: Lady, let us flee. Extinguish the flares of the leader.
SECOND GIRL: Mistress, escape!
THIRD GIRL: He shall not be our guest or breathe our air. Let him not lodge with us, he frightens me.
MEN, *hesitant, walk on,* WOMEN *crowd together anxiously.*
THE WOMAN *goes up to* THE MAN, *prowling, cautious.*
FIRST GIRL: He has no luck.
FIRST MAN: She has no shame.
WOMAN: Why do you bind me, man, with your gaze? Ravening light, you confound my flame! Devouring life overpowers me.

Oskar Kokoschka, "Murderer, the Women's Hope," *The Tulane Drama Review*, trans. Michael Hamburger, vol. 2, no. 3. Copyright © 1958 by Michael Hamburger. Reprinted with permission by Johnson & Alcock Ltd.

Oh take away my terrible hope—and may torment overpower you.

THE MAN, *enraged*: My men, now brand her with my sign, hot iron into her red flesh.

MEN *carry out his order. First the* CHORUS, *with their lights, struggle with her, then the* OLD MAN *with the iron; he rips open her dress and brands her.*

WOMAN, *crying out in terrible pain*: Beat back those men, the devouring corpses.

She leaps at him with a knife and strikes a wound in his side. THE MAN *falls.*

MEN: Free this man possessed, strike down the devil. Alas for us innocents, bury the conqueror. We do not know him.

THE MAN, *in convulsions, singing with a bleeding, visible wound*: Senseless craving from horror to horror, unappeasable rotation in the void. Birth pangs without birth, hurtling down of the sun, quaking of space. The end of those who praised me. Oh, your unmerciful word.

MEN: We do not know him; spare us. Come, you singing girls, let us celebrate our nuptials on his bed of affliction.

GIRLS: He frightens us; you we loved even before you came.

Three masked men on the wall lower a coffin on ropes; the wounded man, hardly stirring now, is placed inside the tower. WOMEN *retire with the* MEN. *The* OLD MAN *rises and locks the door, all is dark, a torch, quiet, blue light above in the cage.*

WOMAN, *moaning and revengeful*: He cannot live, nor die; how white he is!

She creeps round the cage like a panther. She crawls up to the cage inquisitively, grips the bars lasciviously, inscribes a large white cross on the tower, cries out.

Open the gate; I must be with him.

Shakes the bars in despair.

MEN AND WOMEN, *enjoying themselves in the shadows, confused*: We have lost the key—we shall find it—have you got it?—haven't you seen it?—we are not guilty of your plight, we do not know you—

They go back again. A cock crows, a pale light rises in the background.

WOMAN *slides her arm through the bars and prods his wound, hissing maliciously, like an adder*: Pale one, do you recoil? Do you know fear? Are you only asleep? Are you awake? Can you hear me?

THE MAN, *inside, breathing heavily, raises his head with difficulty; later, moves one hand; then slowly rises, singing higher and higher, soaring*: Wind that wanders, time repeating time, solitude, repose and hunger confuse me. Worlds that circle past, no air, it grows long as evening.

WOMAN, *incipient fear*: So much light is flowing from the gap, so much strength from the pale as a corpse he's turned.

Once more creeps up the steps, her body trembling, triumphant once more and crying out with a high voice.

THE MAN *has slowly risen, leans against the grille, slowly grows.*

WOMAN *weakening, furious*: A wild beast I tame in this cage; is it with hunger your song barks?

THE MAN: Am I the real one, you the dead ensnared? Why are you turning pale?

Crowing of cocks.

WOMAN, *trembling*: Do you insult me, corpse?

THE MAN, *powerfully*: Stars and moon! Woman! In dream or awake, I saw a singing creature brightly shine. Breathing, dark things become clear to me. Who nourishes me?

WOMAN *covers him entirely with her body; separated by the grille, to which she clings high up in the air like a monkey.*

THE MAN: Who suckles me with blood? I devour your melting flesh.

WOMAN: I will not let you live, you vampire, piecemeal you feed on me, weaken me, woe to you, I shall kill you—you fetter me—you I caught and caged—and you are holding me—let go of me. Your love imprisons me—grips me as with iron chains—throttles me—let go—help! I lost the key that kept you prisoner.

Lets go the grille, writhes on the steps like a dying animal, her thighs and muscles convulsed.

THE MAN *stands upright now, pulls open the gate, touches the woman—who rears up stiffly, dead white—with his fingers. She feels that her end is near, highest tension, released in a slowly diminishing scream; she collapses and, as she falls, tears away the torch from the hands of the rising leader. The torch goes out and covers everything in a shower of sparks. He stands on the highest step; men and women who attempt to flee from him run into his way, screaming.*

CHORUS: The devil! Tame him, save yourselves, save yourselves if you can—all is lost!

He walks straight towards them. Kills them like mosquitoes and leaves the fire behind. From very far away, crowing of cocks.

Translated by Michael Hamburger

The Ghost Sonata (1907)

August Strindberg

Characters

THE OLD MAN, *Director Hummel*
THE STUDENT, *Arkenholz*
THE MILKMAID, *an apparition*
THE SUPERINTENDENT'S WIFE
THE SUPERINTENDENT
THE DEAD MAN, *a Consul*
THE LADY IN BLACK, *daughter of the Dead Man and the Superintendent's wife*
THE COLONEL
THE MUMMY, *the Colonel's wife*
THE YOUNG LADY, *the Colonel's daughter, but actually the Old Man's daughter*
BARON SKANSKORG, *engaged to the Lady in Black*
JOHANSSON, *Hummel's servant*
BENGTSSON, *The Colonel's footman*
THE FIANCÉE, *a white-haired old woman, formerly engaged to Hummel*
THE COOK
BEGGARS
A MAID

Scene 1

(OUTSIDE A FASHIONABLE APARTMENT building. Only a corner and the first two floors are visible. The ground floor ends in the Round Room; the floor above ends in a balcony with a flagpole.

When the curtains are drawn up in the Round Room, a white marble statue of a young woman can be seen, surrounded by palms and lit brightly by the sun. In the window to the left are potted hyacinths in blue, white, and pink.

Hanging on the railing of the balcony are a blue silk quilt and two white pillows. The windows to the left are draped with white sheets [in Sweden the indication that someone has died]. It is a clear Sunday morning.

Standing in front of the house downstage is a green bench.

Downstage right is a public fountain, downstage left a freestanding column covered with posters and announcements.

In the house façade upstage left is the entrance. The steps leading up to the door are of white marble, the railings of mahogany with brass fittings. Flanking the steps on the sidewalk are laurels in tubs.

The corner of the house with the Round Room faces a side street which runs upstage.

To the left of the entrance door a mirror is mounted outside a window [enabling the occupant of that apartment to observe, without being seen, what is happening in the street].

As the curtain rises, church bells can be heard in the distance.

All the doors visible in the house are open. A woman dressed in black stands motionless on the steps.

The SUPERINTENDENT'S WIFE *in turn sweeps the vestibule, polishes the brass on the front door, and waters the laurels.*

The OLD MAN *sits reading a newspaper in a wheelchair near the poster column. He has white hair, a beard and wears glasses.*

The MILKMAID *enters from around the corner carrying bottles in a wire basket. She is wearing a summer dress, with brown shoes, black stockings, and a white cap. She takes off her cap and hangs it on the fountain, wipes the sweat from her brow, takes a drink from a dipper in the fountain, washes her hands, and arranges her hair, using the water as a mirror.*

A steamboat's bell can be heard, and from time to time the bass notes of an organ in a nearby church penetrate the silence.

The silence continues for a few moments after the MILKMAID *has finished her toilet.* Then the STUDENT *enters left, sleepless and unshaven, and crosses directly to the fountain. Pause*)

STUDENT: Can I borrow the dipper? (*The* MILKMAID *hugs the dipper to her.*) Aren't you through using it? (*She stares at him in terror.*)
OLD MAN (*to himself*): Who is he talking to?—I don't see anyone!—Is he crazy? (*continues to stare at them in amazement*)
STUDENT (*to the* MILKMAID): Why are you staring? Do I look so frightening?—Well, I didn't sleep last night and I guess you think I've been out carousing ... (*the* MILKMAID *as before*) Think I've been drinking, huh?—Do I smell of whiskey? (*the* MILKMAID *as before*) I didn't shave, I know that ... Give me a drink of water, girl, I've earned it! (*pause*) All

---

August Strindberg, "The Ghost Sonata," *Strindberg: Five Plays*, trans. Harry G. Carlson, pp. 265–297. Copyright © 1983 by the Regents of the University of California. Reprinted with permission by the University of California Press.

right, I suppose I have to tell you. All night I've been bandaging wounds and tending injured people. I was there, you see, when the house collapsed last night ... Now you know. *(The* MILKMAID *rinses the dipper and gives him a drink.)* Thanks! *(The* MILKMAID *stands motionless. The* STUDENT *continues slowly.)* Would you do me a big favor? *(pause)* The thing is, my eyes are inflamed, as you can see. Since my hands have been touching the injured and the dead, I don't dare bring them near my eyes ... Would you take my clean handkerchief, moisten it in fresh water, and bathe my poor eyes?—Would you?—Would you be a good Samaritan? *(The* MILKMAID *hesitates but does as he asks.)* Thank you, friend! *(He takes out his wallet. She makes a gesture of refusal.)* Forgive me, that was thoughtless, but I'm not really awake ...

OLD MAN *(to the* STUDENT*)*: Excuse me, but I heard you say that you were at the accident last night ... I was just reading about it in the paper...

STUDENT: Is it already in the paper?

OLD MAN: Yes, the whole story. And your picture too. But they regret they couldn't learn the name of the very able student ...

STUDENT *(looking at the paper):* Really? Yes, that's me! Well!

OLD MAN: Whom were you talking to just now?

STUDENT: Didn't you see? (pause)

OLD MAN: Would you think me rude if I ... asked your name?

STUDENT: What for? I don't want any publicity.—First comes praise, then criticism.—Slandering people has become a fine art nowadays.—Besides, I didn't ask for any reward ...

OLD MAN: You're wealthy, eh?

STUDENT: Not at all ... on the contrary. I'm penniless.

OLD MAN: You know ... there's something familiar about your voice. I've only met one other person who pronounces things the way you do. Are you possibly related to a wholesale merchant by the name of Arkenholz?

STUDENT: He was my father.

OLD MAN: Strange are the ways of fate ... I saw you when you were little, under very painful circumstances ...

STUDENT: Yes, they say I came into the world in the middle of a bankruptcy proceedings ...

OLD MAN: That's right.

STUDENT: Can I ask what your name is?

OLD MAN: My name is Hummel.

STUDENT: Are you ... ? Yes, I remember ...

OLD MAN: You've heard my name mentioned often in your family?

STUDENT: Yes!

OLD MAN: And probably mentioned with a certain ill will? *(The* STUDENT *remains silent)* Yes, I can imagine!—I suppose you heard that I was the one who ruined your father?—People who ruin themselves through stupid speculation always blame the one person they couldn't fool for their ruin. *(pause)* The truth is that your father swindled me out of seventeen thousand crowns—my whole life savings at the time.

STUDENT: It's amazing how a story can be told in two such different ways.

OLD MAN: You don't, think I'm lying, do you?

STUDENT: What else can I think? My father never lied!

OLD MAN: That's very true. A father never lies ... but I too am a father, and consequently ...

STUDENT: What are you trying to say?

OLD MAN: I saved your father from disaster, and he repaid me with all the terrible hatred of a man who feels obliged to be grateful. He taught his family to speak ill of me.

STUDENT: Maybe you made him ungrateful by poisoning your charity with unnecessary humiliations.

OLD MAN: All charity is humiliating, young man.

STUDENT: What do you want of me?

OLD MAN: I'm not asking for money. If you would perform a few services for me, I'd be well repaid. As you can see, I'm a cripple. Some people say it's my own fault; others blame my parents. Personally, I believe life itself is to blame, waiting in ambush for us, and if you avoid one trap, you walk straight into another. However—I can't run up and down stairs or ring doorbells. And so, I'm asking you: help me!

STUDENT: What can I do?

OLD MAN: First of all, push my chair so that I can read those posters. I want to see what's playing tonight …

STUDENT *(pushing the wheelchair):* Don't you have a man to help you?

OLD MAN: Yes, but he's away on an errand … be back soon … Are you a medical student?

STUDENT: No, I'm studying languages. But I really don't know what I want to be …

OLD MAN: Aha.—How are you at mathematics?

STUDENT: Fairly good.

OLD MAN: Fine.—Would you like a job?

STUDENT: Sure, why not?

OLD MAN: Good! *(reading the posters)* They're giving a matinee of *The Valkyrie* … That means the Colonel and his daughter will be there. And since he always sits on the aisle in the sixth row, I'll put you next to them. Would you go into that telephone booth and reserve a ticket for seat number eighty-two in the sixth row?

STUDENT: You want me to go to the opera in the middle of the day?

OLD MAN: Yes. You do as I tell you, and you'll be well rewarded. I want you to be happy, rich, and respected. Your debut yesterday as a courageous rescuer will make you famous overnight. Your name will be really worth something.

STUDENT *(crossing to the booth):* What an amusing adventure …

OLD MAN: Are you a gambler?

STUDENT: Yes, unfortunately …

OLD MAN: We'll make that "fortunately!"—Make the call! *(He reads his newspaper. The* LADY IN BLACK *has come out on the sidewalk to speak to the* SUPERINTENDENT'S WIFE; *the* OLD MAN *listens to them, but the audience hears nothing. The* STUDENT *returns.)* Is it all arranged?

STUDENT: It's all arranged.

OLD MAN: Have you ever seen this house before?

STUDENT: I certainly have! … I walked by here yesterday when the sun was blazing on its windows—and could picture all the beauty and luxury there must be inside. I said to my friend: "Imagine owning an apartment there, four flights up, a beautiful young wife, two lovely little children, and an independent income of 20,000 crowns a year …"

OLD MAN: Did you say that? *Did you say that?* Well! I too love that house …

STUDENT: You speculate in houses?

OLD MAN: Mmm, yes. But not in the way you think …

STUDENT: Do you know the people who live here?

OLD MAN: All of them. At my age you know everyone, their fathers and forefathers before them, and we're all kin, in some way or another.—I just turned eighty—but no one knows me, not really.—I take an interest in people's destinies … *(The curtains in the Round Room are drawn up. The* COLONEL *can be seen inside, dressed in civilian clothes. After looking at the thermometer, he crosses away from the window to stand in front of the statue.)* Look, there's the Colonel you'll sit next to this afternoon …

STUDENT: Is that—the Colonel? I don't understand any of this. It's like a fairy tale …

OLD MAN: My whole life is like a book of fairy tales, young man. But although the tales are different, a single thread joins them together, and the same theme, the leitmotif, returns again and again, like clockwork.

STUDENT: Is that statue of someone?

OLD MAN: It's his wife, of course …

STUDENT: Was she that wonderful?

OLD MAN: Uh, yes. Yes!

STUDENT: Tell me, really!

OLD MAN: It's not for us to judge other people, my boy!—If I were to tell you that she left him, that he beat her, that she returned and remarried him and now sits in there like a mummy, worshipping her own statue, you'd think I was crazy.

STUDENT: What? I don't understand!

OLD MAN: I can well believe it.—Then we have the hyacinth window. That's his daughter's room … She's out riding, but she'll be home soon …

STUDENT: Who's the dark lady talking to the caretaker?

OLD MAN: Well, you see, that's a little complicated. It has to do with the dead man, up there, where you see the white sheets hanging ...

STUDENT: Who was he?

OLD MAN: He was a human being, like the rest of us. But the most conspicuous thing about him was his vanity ... If you were a Sunday child, you'd soon see him come out the front door to look at the consulate flag flying at half-mast in his honor.—He was a consul, you see, and adored coronets, lions, plumed hats, and colored ribbons.

STUDENT: You mentioned a Sunday child—I'm told I was born on a Sunday ...

OLD MAN: No! Were you ... ? I might have known it ... I saw it in the color of your eyes ... but then you can see what others can't see. Have you ever noticed that?

STUDENT: I don't know what others see, but sometimes ... Well, things like that you don't talk about.

OLD MAN: I was almost certain of it! But you can talk about them with me ... because I—understand such things ...

STUDENT: Yesterday, for example ... I was drawn to that secluded street where the house later collapsed ... I walked down it and stopped in front of a building I'd never seen before ... Then I noticed a crack in the wall, and heard the floorboards breaking. I ran forward and snatched up a child who was walking under the wall ... The next moment the house collapsed...I was rescued, but in my arms, where I thought I held the child, there was nothing ...

OLD MAN: Amazing ... And I thought that ... Tell me something: why were you gesturing just now by the fountain? And why were you talking to yourself?

STUDENT: Didn't you see the milkmaid I was talking to?

OLD MAN (*terrified*): Milkmaid?

STUDENT: Yes, certainly. The girl who handed me the dipper.

OLD MAN: Is that right? So, that's what it was ... Well, even if I can't see, there are other things I can do ... (*A white-haired woman sits down at the window with the mirror.*) Look at that old woman in the window! Do you see her?—Good! She was once my fiancée, sixty years ago ... I was twenty then.—Don't be alarmed, she doesn't recognize me. We see each other every day, but I feel nothing, despite that we swore to be true to each other then—forever!

STUDENT: How indiscreet your generation was! Young people don't talk like that nowadays.

OLD MAN: Forgive us, young man. We didn't know any better!—But can you see that that old woman was once young and beautiful?

STUDENT: It doesn't show. Though I like the way she looks around, I can't see her eyes. (*The* SUPERINTENDENT'S WIFE *comes out of the house and hangs up a funeral wreath on the front door.*)

OLD MAN: That's the Superintendent's Wife.—The Lady in Black over there is her daughter by the dead man upstairs. That's why her husband got the job as superintendent ... but the Lady in Black has a lover, an aristocrat with grand expectations. He's in the process of getting a divorce, and his wife is giving him a mansion to get rid of him. This aristocratic lover is son-in-law to the dead man whose bedclothes you see being aired up there on the balcony ... As I said, it's all very complicated.

STUDENT: It's damned complicated!

OLD MAN: Yes, but that's the way it is, internally and externally. Though it looks simple.

STUDENT: Yes, but then who was the dead man?

OLD MAN: You just asked me and I told you. If you could see around the corner, by the service entrance, you'd notice a crowd of poor people, whom he used to help ... when he felt like it ...

STUDENT: So he was a kind man, then?

OLD MAN: Yes ... sometimes.

STUDENT: Not always?

OLD MAN: No! ... That's the way people are. Oh, young man, push my wheelchair a little, into the sun! I'm so terribly cold. When you never get to move around, the blood congeals.—I'm going to die soon, I know that. But before I do, I have a few things to take care of.—Take my hand and feel how cold I am.

STUDENT: Yes, incredibly! (*He tries in vain to free his hand.*)

OLD MAN: Don't leave me. I'm tired, I'm lonely, but I haven't always been like this, you know. I have an infinitely long life behind me—infinitely.—I've made people unhappy, but they've made me unhappy. The one cancels out the other. Before I die, I want to see you happy … Our destinies are intertwined through your father—and in other ways too …

STUDENT: But let go of my hand! You're draining my strength, you're freezing me. What do you want of me?

OLD MAN: Patience, and you'll see and understand … Here comes the young lady …

STUDENT: The Colonel's daughter?

OLD MAN: Yes! "His daughter"! Look at her!—Have you ever seen such a masterpiece?

STUDENT: She's like the marble statue in there …

OLD MAN: Well, that is her mother!

STUDENT: You're right.—Never have I seen such a woman of woman born.—Happy the man who leads her to the altar and his home.

OLD MAN: You can see it!—Not everyone recognizes her beauty … Well, so it is written. (*The* YOUNG LADY *enters left, wearing an English riding habit. She crosses slowly, without looking at anyone, to the front door, where she stops and says a few words to the* SUPERINTENDENT'S WIFE. *She then enters the house. The* STUDENT *covers his eyes with his hand.*) Are you crying?

STUDENT: In the face of what's hopeless there can be only despair!

OLD MAN: But I can open doors and hearts if I but find a hand to do my will … Serve me and you shall prevail!

STUDENT: Is this some kind of pact? Do I have to sell my soul?

OLD MAN: Sell nothing!—You see, all my life I have *taken*. Now I have a desperate longing to be able to give! give! But no one will accept … I am rich, very rich, but I have no heirs, except for a good-for-nothing who plagues the life out of me … Be like a son to me. Be my heir while I'm still alive. Enjoy life while I'm here to see it, even if just from a distance.

STUDENT: What am I to do?

OLD MAN: First, go and listen to *The Valkyrie*.

STUDENT: As good as done. What else?

OLD MAN: Tonight you shall sit in there, in the Round Room.

STUDENT: How do I get there?

OLD MAN: By way of *The Valkyrie!*

STUDENT: Why have you chosen me as your medium? Did you know me before?

OLD MAN: Yes, of course! I've had my eyes on you for a long time … But look, up on the balcony. The maid is raising the flag to half-mast for the Consul … and she's turning the bedclothes … Do you see that blue quilt?—Once two people slept under it, but now only one … (*The* YOUNG LADY, *her clothes changed, appears at the window to water the hyacinths.*) Ah, there's my little girl. Look at her, look!—She's talking to the flowers. Isn't she like a blue hyacinth herself? … She's giving them drink, just ordinary water, and they transform the water into color and fragrance … Here comes the Colonel with a newspaper!—He's showing her the story about the house collapsing … He's pointing out your picture! She's interested … she's reading about your bravery … I think it's getting cloudy. What if it should rain? I'll be in fine fix if Johansson doesn't come back soon … (*It grows cloudy and dark. The old woman at the mirror closes her window.*) My fiancée is closing her window … seventy-nine years old … That mirror is the only mirror she uses, because she can't see herself in it, just the outside world in two different directions. But the world can see her, and that she didn't think of … A beautiful little old lady though … (*The* DEAD MAN, *in his winding-sheet, comes out the front door.*)

STUDENT: Oh my God!

OLD MAN: What's the matter?

STUDENT: Don't you see? There, in the doorway, the dead man!

OLD MAN: I see nothing, but I expected this! Go on …
STUDENT: He's going out into the street … *(pause)* Now he's turning his head to look at the flag.
OLD MAN: What did I tell you? Now he'll count the funeral wreaths and read the names on the cards … God help those who are missing!
STUDENT: Now he's turning the corner …
OLD MAN: He's gone to count the poor people at the service entrance … They'll add a nice touch to his obituary: "Accompanied to his grave by the blessings of ordinary citizens." Well, he won't have my blessing!—Just between us, he was a great scoundrel …
STUDENT: But charitable …
OLD MAN: A charitable scoundrel, who always dreamed of a beautiful funeral … When he felt that the end was near, he fleeced the government of fifty thousand crowns! … Now his daughter is having an affair with another woman's husband and wondering if she's in his will … The scoundrel can hear every word we say, and he deserves it!—Ah, here's Johansson! (JOHANSSON *enters from left.*) Report! (JOHANSSON *speaks but the audience cannot hear.*) Not at home, eh? You're an ass!—Any telegrams?—Nothing at all! … Go on, go on! … Six o'clock this evening? That's fine!—An extra edition?—And his name in full! Arkenholz, student, born … parents … splendid … I think it's starting to rain … What did he have to say? … Is that right?—He doesn't want to?—Well, he'll just have to!—Here comes the aristocratic lover!—Push me around the corner, Johansson, I want to hear what the poor people are saying … Arkenholz, you wait for me here … do you understand?—Hurry up, hurry up! (JOHANSSON *pushes the chair around the corner. The* STUDENT *remains behind, watching the* YOUNG LADY, *who is loosening the soil around the flowers.* BARON SKANSKORG *enters, wearing mourning, and speaks to the* LADY IN BLACK, *who has been walking up and down the sidewalk.*)
BARON SKANSKORG: Well, what can we do about it?—We'll simply have to wait!
LADY IN BLACK: But I can't wait!
BARON SKANSKORG: Really? Better leave town then!
LADY IN BLACK: I don't want to.
BARON SKANSKORG: Come over here, otherwise they'll hear what we're saying. (*They cross to the poster column and continue their conversation, unheard by the audience.* JOHANSSON *enters right and crosses to the* STUDENT.)
JOHANSSON: My master asks you not to forget the other matter, sir.
STUDENT (*carefully*): Listen—first tell me: who is your master?
JOHANSSON: Oh, he's a lot of things, and he's been everything.
STUDENT: Is he sane?
JOHANSSON: Yes, and what is that, eh?—He says all his life he's been looking for a Sunday child, but maybe it's not true …
STUDENT: What does he want? Money?
JOHANSSON: He wants power … All day long he rides around in his chariot, like the great god Thor … He looks at houses, tears them down, widens streets, builds over public squares. But he also breaks into houses, crawls through windows, destroys people's lives, kills his enemies, and forgives nothing.—Can you imagine that that little cripple was once a Don Juan? Although he always lost his women.
STUDENT: That doesn't make sense.
JOHANSSON: Well, you see, he was so cunning that he got the women to leave once he tired of them … However, now he's like a horse thief, only with people. He steals them, in all kinds of ways … He literally stole me out of the hands of justice … I had committed a … blunder that only he knew about. Instead of turning me in, he made me his slave, which is what I do, just for my food, which is nothing to brag about …
STUDENT: What does he want to do in this house?
JOHANSSON: Well, I wouldn't want to say. It's so complicated.
STUDENT: I think I'd better get out of here … (*The* YOUNG LADY *drops her bracelet through the window.*)

JOHANSSON: Look, the young lady's dropped her bracelet through the window … (*The* STUDENT *crosses slowly to the bracelet, picks it up, and hands it to the* YOUNG LADY, *who thanks him stiffly. The* STUDENT *crosses back to* JOHANSSON.) So, you were thinking about leaving, eh? … It's not as easy as you think, once the old man's dropped his net over your head … And he's afraid of nothing between heaven and earth … well, except for one thing, or rather one person…

STUDENT: Wait, I think I know who!

JOHANSSON: How could you know that?

STUDENT: I'm guessing!—Is it … a little milkmaid that he's afraid of?

JOHANSSON: He always turns away when he sees a milk wagon … and then he talks in his sleep. You see, he was once in Hamburg …

STUDENT: Can anyone believe this man?

JOHANSSON: You can believe him—capable of anything!

STUDENT: What is he doing around the corner?

JOHANSSON: Listening to the poor people … Planting ideas here and there, pulling out bricks, one at a time, until the house collapses … metaphorically speaking … You see, I'm an educated man; I was once a bookseller … Are you going to leave now?

STUDENT: I don't want to seem ungrateful … The man saved my father once, and now he's only asking a small favor in return …

JOHANSSON: What's that?

STUDENT: I'm going to see *The Valkyrie* …

JOHANSSON: That's beyond me … He's always coming up with a new idea … Look, now he's talking to the police. He's always close with the police. He uses them, involves them in his schemes, binds them hand and foot with false hopes and promises. All the while he pumps them for information.—You'll see—before the day is over he'll be received in the Round Room.

STUDENT: What does he want there? What is there between him and the Colonel?

JOHANSSON: Well, I have my suspicions, but I'm not sure. You'll just have to see for yourself when you get there …

STUDENT: I'll never get in there…

JOHANSSON: That depends on you.—Go to *The Valkyrie* …

STUDENT: Is that the way?

JOHANSSON: If he said it was.—Look, look at him, in his war chariot, drawn in triumph by beggars who get nothing for their pains but the vague promise of a handout at his funeral! (*The* OLD MAN *enters standing in his wheelchair, drawn by one of the* BEGGARS, *and followed by others.*)

OLD MAN: Hail the noble youth, who at the risk of his own life, rescued so many in yesterday's accident! Hail, Arkenholz! (*The* BEGGARS *bare their heads but do not cheer. At the window the* YOUNG LADY *waves her handkerchief. The* COLONEL *stares out his window. The* OLD WOMAN *rises at her window. The* MAID *on the balcony raises the flag to the top.*) Clap your hands, my fellow citizens! It's Sunday, it's true, but the ass in the well and the stalk in the field give us absolution. Even though I'm not a Sunday child, I have both the spirit of prophecy and the gift of healing, for once I brought a drowned person back to life … Yes, it was in Hamburg on a Sunday afternoon just like this one … (*The* MILKMAID *enters, seen only by the* STUDENT *and the* OLD MAN. *She reaches out with her arms, like someone drowning, and stares at the* OLD MAN, *who sits down and shrinks back in terror.*) Johansson! Push me out of here! Quickly—Arkenholz, don't forget *The Valkyrie!*

STUDENT: What is all this?

JOHANSSON: We'll have to wait and see! We'll just have to wait and see!

Scene 2

(*The Round Room. Upstage is a white porcelain tile stove, studded with mirrors and flanked by a pendulum clock and a candelabra. To the right the entrance hall, through which can be seen a green room with mahogany furniture. To the left a wallpaper-covered door leading to a closet. Further left the statue, shadowed by potted palms; it can be concealed by draperies. Upstage left is the door to the Hyacinth Room, where the*

YOUNG LADY *sits reading. The* COLONEL *is visible, his back to the audience, writing in the green room.*

BENGTSSON, *the footman, dressed in livery, enters from the hall with* JOHANSSON, *who is dressed as a waiter.*)

BENGTSSON: Johansson, you'll do the serving, and I'll take their clothes. You've done this sort of thing before, haven't you?

JOHANSSON: As you know, I push that war chariot around during the day, but in the evenings I work as a waiter at receptions. Besides, it's always been my dream to come into this house ... They're peculiar people, aren't they?

BENGTSSON: Well, yes, a little unusual, you might say.

JOHANSSON: Is it going to be a musical evening, or what?

BENGTSSON: Just the usual ghost supper, as we call it. They drink tea and never say a word, or else the Colonel does all the talking. And they nibble on cookies, all at the same time, so that it sounds like rats nibbling in an attic.

JOHANSSON: Why is it called a ghost supper?

BENGTSSON: They look like ghosts ... And this has been going on for twenty years, always the same people, saying the same things, or else too ashamed to say anything.

JOHANSSON: Isn't there a lady of the house too?

BENGTSSON: Oh yes, but she's queer in the head. She sits in a closet, because her eyes can't stand the light ... She's right in there ... *(points to the wallpaper-covered door)*

JOHANSSON: In there?

BENGTSSON: Well, I told you they were a little unusual ...

JOHANSSON: How does she look?

BENGTSSON: Like a mummy ... Do you want to see her? *(opens the door)* See, there she is!

JOHANSSON: Oh, Jesus ...

MUMMY *(like a baby):* Why did you open the door? Haven't I told you to keep it shut? ...

BENGTSSON *(using baby talk):* Ta, ta, ta, ta! Sweetums must be good, then you'll get something nice!—Pretty polly!

MUMMY *(like a parrot):* Pretty polly! Is Jacob there? Awwk!

BENGTSSON: She thinks she's a parrot, and who knows? maybe she is ... *(to the* MUMMY*)* Polly, whistle a little for us. *(She whistles.)*

JOHANSSON: I've seen lots in my life, but this beats everything!

BENGTSSON: You see, when a house gets old, it gets moldy. And when people sit around tormenting each other for so long, they get crazy. Now the madam here—quiet Polly!—this mummy has been sitting here for forty years—same husband, same furniture, same relatives, same friends ... *(closes the wallpaper-covered door)* Even I don't know everything that's gone on in this house ... Do you see this statue? ... that's the madam when she was young!

JOHANSSON: Oh, my God!—Is that the Mummy?

BENGTSSON: Yes!—It's enough to make you cry!—And somehow or other—the power of imagination, maybe—she's taken on some of the qualities of a real parrot.—For instance, she can't stand cripples or sick people ... That's why she can't stand the sight of her own daughter ...

JOHANSSON: Is the young lady sick?

BENGTSSON: Didn't you know that?

JOHANSSON: No! ... And the Colonel, who is he?

BENGTSSON: You'll have to wait and see!

JOHANSSON *(looking at the statue):* It's terrible to think that ... How old is the madam now?

BENGTSSON: No one knows ... but they say that when she was thirty-five, she looked nineteen, and convinced the Colonel that she was ... In this house ... Do you know what that black Japanese screen is for, there, next to the chaise longue?—It's called the death screen, and when someone is dying, it's put up around them, just like in a hospital ...

JOHANSSON: What a horrible place! ... And the student wants to come here because he thinks it's a paradise ...

BENGTSSON: What student? Oh, him! The one who's coming here this evening ... The Colonel and the young lady met him at the opera and were taken by him ... Hm! ... Now

it's my turn to ask questions: who is your master? the businessman in the wheelchair?
JOHANSSON: Yes. — Is he coming here too?
BENGTSSON: He's not invited.
JOHANSSON: If necessary, he'll come uninvited … (*The* OLD MAN *appears in the hallway, dressed in a frock coat. He steals forward on his crutches to eavesdrop.*)
BENGTSSON: I hear he's an old crook!
JOHANSSON: Full blown!
BENGTSSON: He looks like the devil himself!
JOHANSSON: And he must be a magician too! — for he can go through locked doors …
OLD MAN (*crosses and grabs* JOHANSSON *by the ear*): Rascal! — You watch your step! (*to* BENGTSSON) Announce me to the Colonel!
BENGTSSON: Yes, but we're expecting guests…
OLD MAN: I know that! But my visit is as good as expected, if not exactly looked forward to …
BENGTSSON: Is that so? And what was the name? Director Hummel!
OLD MAN: Precisely! (BENGTSSON *crosses to the hallway and enters the green room, closing the door behind him. The* OLD MAN *turns to* JOHANSSON.) Disappear! (JOHANSSON *hesitates.*) Disappear! (JOHANSSON *disappears into the hallway. The* OLD MAN *inspects the room, stopping in front of the statue in great astonishment.*) Amalia! … It's she! … She! (*He wanders about the room fingering things; he straightens his wig in front of the mirror, and returns to the statue.*)
MUMMY (*from within the closet*): Pretty polly!
OLD MAN (*wincing*): What was that? Is there a parrot in the room? I don't see one!
MUMMY: Is Jacob there?
OLD MAN: The place is haunted!
MUMMY: Jaaaacob!
OLD MAN: I'm scared … So, these are the secrets they've been hiding in this house! (*He looks at a painting, his back turned to the closet.*) There he is! … He! (*The* MUMMY *comes out of the closet, goes up to him from behind, and yanks on his wig.*)
MUMMY: Squir-rel! Is it Squir-rel?
OLD MAN (*badly frightened*): Oh my God! — Who are you?
MUMMY (*in a normal voice*): Is it you, Jacob?

OLD MAN: As a matter of fact, my name is Jacob …
MUMMY (*moved*): And my name is Amalia.
OLD MAN: Oh, no, no, no … Lord Je …
MUMMY: Yes, this is how I look! — And (*pointing to the statue*) that's how I *used* to look! Life teaches us so much. — I stay in the closet mostly, both to avoid seeing people, and being seen … But what do you want here, Jacob?
OLD MAN: My child! Our child …
MUMMY: She's in there.
OLD MAN: Where?
MUMMY: There, in the hyacinth room.
OLD MAN (*looking at the* YOUNG LADY): Yes, there she is. (*pause*) What does her father say? The Colonel? Your husband?
MUMMY: Once, when I was angry at him, I told him everything …
OLD MAN: And?
MUMMY: He didn't believe me. He just said: "That's what all wives say when they want to murder their husbands." — Even so, it was a terrible crime. Everything in his life is a forgery, his family tree too. Sometimes when I look at the List of the Nobility, I think to myself: "Why that woman has a false birth certificate, like a common servant girl. People get sent to prison for that."
OLD MAN: Many people do that. I seem to remember you falsified your age …
MUMMY: My mother made me … it wasn't my fault! … But in our crime you were most responsible …
OLD MAN: No, your husband provoked the crime when he stole my fiancée away from me! — I was born unable to forgive until I've punished! I saw it as a compelling duty … and still do!
MUMMY: What are you looking for in this house? What do you want? How did you get in? — Is it my daughter? If you touch her, you'll die!
OLD MAN: I want what's best for her.
MUMMY: But you must spare her father!
OLD MAN: No!
MUMMY: Then you shall die. In this room. Behind that screen …

OLD MAN: That may be … but once I sink my teeth into something, I can't let go …

MUMMY: You want to marry her off to that student. Why? He has nothing and is nothing.

OLD MAN: He'll become rich, through me!

MUMMY: Were you invited here this evening?

OLD MAN: No, but I intend to get an invitation to the ghost supper.

MUMMY: Do you know who's coming?

OLD MAN: Not exactly.

MUMMY: The Baron … who lives upstairs and whose father-in-law was buried this afternoon…

OLD MAN: The one who's getting divorced so he can marry the superintendent's daughter … The one who was once your—lover!

MUMMY: Another guest will be your former fiancée, whom my husband seduced …

OLD MAN: What an elegant gathering …

MUMMY: God, if only we could die! If *only* we could die!

OLD MAN: Then why do you associate with each other?

MUMMY: Crimes and secrets and guilt bind us together!—We've broken up and gone our separate ways an endless number of times, but we're always drawn back together again …

OLD MAN: I think the Colonel's coming …

MUMMY: Then I'll go in to Adèle … *(pause)* Jacob, mind what you do! Spare him … *(pause; she leaves.)*

COLONEL *(entering; cool reserved):* Won't you sit down? *(The* OLD MAN *sits down slowly; pause; the* COLONEL *stares at him.)* Are you the one who wrote this letter?

OLD MAN: Yes.

COLONEL: Your name is Hummel?

OLD MAN: Yes. *(pause)*

COLONEL: Since I know you bought up all my unpaid promissory notes, it follows that I am at your mercy. What is it you want?

OLD MAN: Payment of one kind or another.

COLONEL: What kind did you have in mind?

OLD MAN: A very simple one—but let's not talk about money.—Just tolerate me in your house as a guest.

COLONEL: If that's all it takes to satisfy you …

OLD MAN: Thank you.

COLONEL: Anything else?

OLD MAN: Fire Bengtsson!

COLONEL: Why should I do that? My trusted servant, who's been with me for a generation—who wears the national medal for loyal and faithful service? Why should I do that?

OLD MAN: All his beautiful virtues exist only in your imagination.—He's not the man he appears to be.

COLONEL: But who is?

OLD MAN *(winces)*: True! But Bengtsson must go!

COLONEL: Are you trying to run my house?

OLD MAN: Yes! Since I own everything here: furniture, curtains, dinner service, linen … and other things!

COLONEL: What other things?

OLD MAN: Everything! I own everything! It's all mine!

COLONEL: Very well, it's all yours. But my family's coat of arms, and my good name—they remain mine!

OLD MAN: No, not even those! *(pause)* You're not a nobleman.

COLONEL: How dare you?

OLD MAN *(taking out a paper)*: If you read this extract from the Book of Noble Families, you'll see that the name you bear died out a hundred years ago.

COLONEL *(reading)*: I've certainly heard such rumors, but the name I bear was my father's … *(reading)* It's true, you're right … I'm not a nobleman!—Not even that remains!—Then I'll take off my signet ring.—It too belongs to you … Here, take it!

OLD MAN *(pocketing the ring)*: Now we'll continue!—You're not a colonel either.

COLONEL: I'm not?

OLD MAN: No! You were a former temporary colonel in the American Volunteers, but when the army was reorganized after the Spanish-American War, all such ranks were abolished …

COLONEL: Is that true?

OLD MAN *(reaching into his pocket)*: Do you want to read about it?

COLONEL: No, it's not necessary! … Who are you, that you have the right to sit there and strip me naked like this?

The Ghost Sonata (1907)

OLD MAN: We'll see! But speaking about stripping ... do you know who you really are?
COLONEL: Have you no sense of shame?
OLD MAN Take off your wig and look at yourself in the mirror! Take out your false teeth too, and shave off your mustache! We'll have Bengtsson unlace your corset, and we'll see if a certain servant, MR. XYZ, won't recognize himself: a man who was once a great sponger in a certain kitchen ... (*The* COLONEL *reaches for the bell on the table but is stopped by the* OLD MAN.) Don't touch that bell! If you call Bengtsson in here, I'll have him arrested ... Your guests are arriving.—You keep calm and we'll continue to play our old roles awhile longer!
COLONEL: Who are you? I recognize that expression in your eyes and that tone in your voice ...
OLD MAN: No more questions! Just keep quiet and do as you're told!
STUDENT (*enters and bows to the* COLONEL): Good evening, sir!
COLONEL: Welcome to my home, young man! Everyone is talking about your heroism at that terrible accident, and it's an honor for me to greet you ...
STUDENT: Colonel, my humble origin ... Your brilliant name and noble background ...
COLONEL: Let me introduce you: Director Hummel, Mr. Arkenholz ... Would you go in and join the ladies? I have to finish my conversation with the director ... (*The* STUDENT *is shown into the Hyacinth Room, where he remains visible, engaged in shy conversation with the* YOUNG LADY.) A superb young man, musical, sings, writes poetry ... If he were a nobleman and our equal socially, I would have nothing against ... yes ...
OLD MAN: Against what?
COLONEL: My daughter ...
OLD MAN: Your daughter?—By the way, why does she always sit in there?
COLONEL: Whenever she's at home, she feels compelled to sit in the Hyacinth Room. It's a peculiar habit she has ... Ah, here comes Miss Beate von Holsteinkrona ... a charming old lady ... Very active in the church and with a modest income from a trust ...
OLD MAN (*to himself*): My old fiancée! (*The* FIANCÉE *enters; she is whitehaired and looks crazy.*)
COLONEL: Director Hummel, Miss Holsteinkrona ... (*She curtsies and sits. The* BARON *enters, dressed in mourning and looking as if he is hiding something; he sits.*) Baron Skanskorg ...
OLD MAN (*to himself, without rising*): If it isn't the jewel thief ... (*to the* COLONEL) Call in the Mummy, and the party will be complete ...
COLONEL (*at the door to the Hyacinth Room*): Polly!
MUMMY (*entering*): Squir-rel!
COLONEL: Should the young people be in here too?
OLD MAN: No! Not the young people! They'll be spared ... (*They all sit in silence in a circle.*)
COLONEL: Can we have the tea served?
OLD MAN: What for? No one here likes tea, so there's no use pretending we do. (*pause*)
COLONEL: Shall we talk then?
OLD MAN (*slowly, with long pauses*): About what: the weather, which we all know? Ask about each other's health, which we also know. I prefer silence. Then you can hear thoughts and see into the past. In silence you can't hide anything ... as you can in words. The other day I read that the reason different languages developed was because primitive tribes tried to keep secrets from each other. And so languages are codes, and whoever finds the key will understand them all. But there are certain secrets that can be exposed without a key, especially when it comes to proving paternity. But proving something in a courtroom is something else. That takes two false witnesses, providing their stories agree. But on the kinds of expeditions I'm thinking of, witnesses aren't taken along. Nature itself plants in human beings an instinct for hiding that which should be hidden. Nevertheless, we stumble into things without intending to, and sometimes the opportunity presents itself to reveal the deepest of secrets, to tear the mask off the imposter, to expose the villain ... (*pause; all watch each other without speaking.*) How quiet it's become! (*long silence*) Here, for instance, in

this honorable house, in this lovely home, where beauty, culture and wealth are united ... *(long silence)* All of us know who we are ... don't we? ... I don't have to tell you ... And you know me, although you pretend ignorance ... In there is my daughter, *mine!* You know that too ... She had lost the desire to live, without knowing why ... because she was withering away in this atmosphere of crime, deceit and falseness of every kind ... That's why I looked for a friend for her in whose company she could sense the light and warmth of a noble deed ... *(long silence)* And so my mission in this house was to pull up the weeds, expose the crimes, settle all accounts, so that those young people might start anew in a home that I had given them! *(long silence)* Now I'm going to give you a chance to leave, under safe-conduct, each of you, in your own time. Whoever stays, I'll have arrested! *(long silence)* Listen to the clock ticking, like a deathwatch beetle in the wall! Do you hear what it says? "Times-up! Times-up!—" In a few moments it'll strike and your time will be up. Then you may go, but not before. But it sounds a threat before it strikes.—Listen! There's the warning: "The clock-can-strike."—I too can strike ... (*He strikes the table with his crutch.*) Do you hear? (*silence; the* MUMMY *crosses to the clock and stops it.*)

MUMMY (*clearly and seriously*): But I can stop time in its course.—I can wipe out the past, undo what has been done. Not with bribes, not with threats—but through suffering and repentance—(*crosses to the* OLD MAN) We are only wretched human beings, we know that. We have trespassed and we have sinned, like all the rest. We are not what we seem, for deep down we are better than ourselves, since we detest our faults. But that you, Jacob Hummel, with your false name, can sit here and judge us, proves that you are worse than us miserable creatures! You too are not what you seem!—You're a thief who steals souls. You stole mine once with false promises. You murdered the Consul who was buried today; you strangled him with debts. You stole the Student by binding him to a debt you pretended was left by his father, who never owed you a penny ... (*During her speech, the* OLD MAN *has tried to rise and speak, but has fallen back in his chair, crumpling up more and more as she continues.*) But there's a dark spot in your life. I've long suspected what it is, but I'm not sure ... I think Bengtsson knows. *(rings the bell on the table)*

OLD MAN: No, not Bengtsson! Not him!

MUMMY: Ah, then he does know! (*She rings again. The little* MILKMAID *appears in the hallway door, unseen by everyone except the* OLD MAN, *who becomes terrified. The* MILKMAID *disappears as* BENGTSSON *enters.*)

MUMMY: Bengtsson, do you know this man?

BENGTSSON: Yes, I know him, and he knows me. Life has its ups and downs, as we all know. I was once in his service; another time he was in mine. For two whole years he was a sponger who used to flirt with the cook in my kitchen.—Because he had to get away by three o'clock, dinner was ready by two. And so we had to eat the warmed-over leavings of that ox!—And he also drank the soup stock, which the cook then filled up with water. He was like a vampire, sucking the marrow out of the house and turning us all into skeletons.—And he almost got us put in prison when we called the cook a thief. Later, I met him in Hamburg under another name. This time he was a usurer, a bloodsucker. And he was accused of having lured a girl out onto the ice to drown her, because she had witnessed a crime he was afraid would be discovered ... (*The* MUMMY *passes her hand across the* OLD MAN'S *face.*)

MUMMY: This is you! Now give me the notes and the will! (JOHANSSON *appears in the hallway door and watches the proceedings with great interest, knowing that he will shortly be freed from his slavery. The* OLD MAN *takes out a bundle of papers and throws them on the table. The* MUMMY *strokes him on the back.*) Polly! Is Jacob there?

OLD MAN (*like a parrot*): Ja-cob is there!—Kakadora! Dora!

MUMMY: Can the clock strike?

OLD MAN (*clucking*): The clock can strike! (*imitating a cuckoo clock*) Cuck-oo, cuck-oo, cuck-oo! …

MUMMY (*opens the closet door*): Now the clock has struck!—Get up and go into that closet, where I've spent twenty years grieving for our mistake.—There's a rope hanging in there. Let it stand for the one you used to strangle the Consul upstairs, and with which you intended to strangle your benefactor … Go! (*The* OLD MAN *goes into the closet. The* MUMMY *closes the door.*) Bengtsson! Put out the screen! The death screen! (BENGSSTON *puts the screen out in front of the door.*) It is finished!—May God have mercy on his soul!

ALL: Amen! (*long silence; in the Hyacinth Room the* YOUNG LADY *can be seen accompanying the* STUDENT *on the harp as he recites.*)

STUDENT: (*after a prelude*):

I saw the sun, and thought I saw
what was hidden.
You cannot heal with evil
deeds done in anger.
Man reaps as he sows;
blessed is the doer of good.
Comfort him you have grieved
with your goodness, and you will have
healed.
No fear has he who has done no ill;
goodness is innocence.

Scene 3

(*The Hyacinth Room. The style of the decor is somewhat bizarre, with oriental motifs. Hyacinths of every color everywhere. On top of the porcelain tiled stove is a large statue of a seated Buddha. In his lap is a bulb, out of which the stalk of a shallot has shot up, bearing its globe-shaped cluster of white, starlike flowers.*

Upstage right the door to the Round Room, where the COLONEL *and the* MUMMY *sit silently, doing nothing. A portion of the death screen is also visible. To the left the door to the pantry and the kitchen.*

The STUDENT *and the* YOUNG LADY, *Adèle, are near a table, she with the harp, he standing.*)

YOUNG LADY: Sing for my flowers!

STUDENT: Is the hyacinth the flower of your soul?

YOUNG LADY: The one and only. Do you love the hyacinth?

STUDENT: I love it above all others—its virginal figure rising so slim and straight from the bulb, floating on the water and sending its pure white roots down into the colorless fluid. I love its colors: the snow-white of innocence, the honey-gold of sweetness and pleasure, the rosy pink of youth, the scarlet of maturity, but above all the blue, the blue of deep eyes, of dew, of faithfulness … I love its colors more than gold and pearls, I have loved them since I was a child, have worshipped them because they possess all the virtues I lack … And yet …

YOUNG LADY: What?

STUDENT: My love is not returned, for these lovely blossoms hate me …

YOUNG LADY: How do you mean?

STUDENT: Their fragrance—strong and pure as the early winds of spring that have passed over melting snow—it confuses my senses, deafens me, crowds me out of the room, dazzles me, shoots me with poisoned arrows that wound my heart and set my head on fire. Don't you know the legend of this flower?

YOUNG LADY: Tell me.

STUDENT: But first its meaning. The bulb, whether floating on water or buried in soil, is our earth. The stalk shoots up, straight as the axis of the world, and above, with its six-pointed star flowers, is the globe of heaven.

YOUNG LADY: Above the earth—the stars! How wonderful! Where did you learn to see things this way?

STUDENT: Let me think!—In your eyes!—And so this flower is a replica of the universe … That's why the Buddha sits brooding over the bulb of the earth in his lap, watching it grow outwards and upwards, transforming itself into a heaven.—This wretched earth aspires to become heaven! That's what the Buddha is waiting for!

YOUNG LADY: Now I see—aren't snowflakes also six-pointed, like hyacinth lilies?

STUDENT: You're right! — Then snowflakes are falling stars ...
YOUNG LADY: And the snowdrop is a snow star...rising from the snow.
STUDENT: And the largest and most beautiful of all the stars in the firmament, the red and gold Sirius, is the narcissus, with its red and gold chalice and six white rays ...
YOUNG LADY: Have you ever seen the shallot in bloom?
STUDENT: I certainly have! — It too bears its flowers in a ball, a sphere like the globe of heaven, strewn with white stars ...
YOUNG LADY: Yes! God, how magnificent! Whose idea was this?
STUDENT: Yours!
YOUNG LADY: Yours!
STUDENT: Ours! — Together we have given birth to something. We are wed ...
YOUNG LADY: Not yet ...
STUDENT: What else remains?
YOUNG LADY: The waiting, the trials, the patience!
STUDENT: Fine! Try me! *(pause)* Tell me, why do your parents sit so silently in there, without saying a word?
YOUNG LADY: Because they have nothing to say to each other, because neither believes what the other says. As my father puts it: "What's the point of talking, when we can't fool each other?"
STUDENT: What a terrible thing to believe ...
YOUNG LADY: Here comes the Cook ... Oh, look at her, she's so big and fat ...
STUDENT: What does she want?
YOUNG LADY: She wants to ask me about dinner. I run the house, you see, while my mother is ill ...
STUDENT: Why should we bother about the kitchen?
YOUNG LADY: We have to eat ... You look at her, I can't bear to ...
STUDENT: Who is this monstrous woman?
YOUNG LADY: She belongs to the Hummel family of vampires. She's devouring us ...
STUDENT: Why don't you get rid of her?
YOUNG LADY: She won't go! We have no control over her. She is punishment for our sins ... Can't you see that we're wasting away, withering? ...
STUDENT: You mean you don't get enough to eat?
YOUNG LADY: Oh yes, we get lots to eat, but nothing nourishing. She boils the meat until there's nothing left but gristle and water, while she drinks the stock herself. And when there's a roast, she first cooks out all the goodness and drinks the gravy and broth. Everything she touches shrivels up and dries out. It's as if she can drain you with her eyes. She drinks the coffee and we get the grounds. She drinks from the wine and fills the bottles with water ...
STUDENT: Drive her out of the house!
YOUNG LADY: We can't!
STUDENT: Why not?
YOUNG LADY: We don't know! She won't go! No one has any control over her! — She's taken all our strength!
STUDENT: May I send her away?
YOUNG LADY: No! Things must be as they are! — Now she's here. She'll ask what we'll have for dinner. I'll answer this and that. She'll object and get her own way.
STUDENT: Then let her decide the meals.
YOUNG LADY: She won't do that!
STUDENT: This *is* a strange house. It's bewitched!
YOUNG LADY: Yes. — Oh, she turned away when she saw you.
COOK (*in the door*): No, that wasn't why. (*She sneers, her teeth showing.*)
STUDENT: Get out, woman!
COOK: When I'm good and ready. *(pause)* Now I'm ready. *(disappears)*
YOUNG LADY: Don't lose your temper! — You must be patient. She's one of the trials we have to endure in this house. Another is the maid — we have to clean up after her.
STUDENT: I feel myself sinking down! *Cor in aethere!* Music!
YOUNG LADY: Wait!
STUDENT: Music!
YOUNG LADY: Patience! — This room is called the room of trials. — It's beautiful to look at, but it's full of imperfections ...

STUDENT: I can't believe that! But we'll have to overlook them. It is beautiful, but it feels cold. Why don't you have a fire?
YOUNG LADY: Because it smokes.
STUDENT: Can't you have the chimney cleaned?
YOUNG LADY: It doesn't help! ... Do you see that writing table?
STUDENT: It's very beautiful.
YOUNG LADY: But it wobbles! Every day I put a piece of cork under that leg, but the maid takes it away when she sweeps, and I have to cut a new one. Every morning the penholder is covered with ink, and so is the inkstand. As sure as the sun rises, I'm always cleaning up after that woman. *(pause)* What chore do you hate most?
STUDENT: Separating dirty laundry. Ugh!
YOUNG LADY: That's what I have to do. Ugh!
STUDENT: What else?
YOUNG LADY: Be awakened from a sound sleep to lock a window ... which the maid left rattling.
STUDENT: What else?
YOUNG LADY: Climb a ladder to fix the damper on the stove after the maid pulled the cord loose.
STUDENT: What else?
YOUNG LADY: Sweep after her, dust after her, light the stove after her—she'll only put the wood in! Open the damper, wipe the glasses dry, reset the table, uncork the wine bottles, open the windows to air the rooms, remake my bed, rinse the water pitcher when it gets green with algae, buy matches and soap, which we're always out of, wipe the lamp chimneys, and trim the wicks to keep the lamps from smoking. And to be sure they won't go out when we have company, I have to fill them myself ...
STUDENT: Music!
YOUNG LADY: Wait!—First, the drudgery, the drudgery of keeping the filth of life at a distance.
STUDENT: But you're well off. You've got two servants.
YOUNG LADY: It wouldn't help if we had three. It's so difficult just to live, and sometimes I get so tired ... Imagine if there were a nursery too!
STUDENT: The greatest joy of all ...
YOUNG LADY: And the most expensive ... Is life worth this much trouble?
STUDENT: That depends on what you want in return ... I would do anything to win your hand.
YOUNG LADY: Don't talk like that!—You can never have me.
STUDENT: Why not?
YOUNG LADY: You mustn't ask. *(pause)*
STUDENT: But you dropped your bracelet out of the window ...
YOUNG LADY: Because my hand has grown so thin ... *(pause; the COOK appears carrying a bottle of Japanese soy sauce.)* It's she, who's devouring me, devouring us all.
STUDENT: What's she got in her hand?
YOUNG LADY: The Japanese bottle with the lettering like scorpions! It's soy sauce to turn water into broth. She uses it instead of gravy when she cooks cabbage and makes mock turtle soup.
STUDENT: Get out!
COOK: You suck the juices out of us, and we out of you. We take the blood and give you back water—with coloring. This is colored water!—I'm going now, but I'm staying in this house, as long as I want! *(exits)*
STUDENT: Why did Bengtsson get a medal?
YOUNG LADY: For his great merits.
STUDENT: Has he no faults?
YOUNG LADY: Oh yes, terrible ones, but you don't get medals for them. *(They smile.)*
STUDENT: You have many secrets in this house ...
YOUNG LADY: Like everyone else ... Let us keep ours! *(pause)*
STUDENT: Don't you like frankness?
YOUNG LADY: Yes, within reason.
STUDENT: Sometimes I get a raging desire to say exactly what I think. But I know that if people were really frank and honest, the world would collapse. *(pause)* I was at a funeral the other day ... in the church.—It was very solemn and beautiful.
YOUNG LADY: For Director Hummel?

STUDENT: Yes, my false benefactor!—At the head of the coffin stood an old friend of the dead man, carrying the funeral mace. I was especially impressed by the minister because of his dignified manner and moving words.— Yes, I cried, we all cried.—Afterwards we went to a restaurant ... There I learned that the man with the mace had been in love with the dead man's son ... *(The YOUNG LADY stares at him questioningly.)* And that the dead man had borrowed money from his son's ... admirer ... *(pause)* The next day the minister was arrested for embezzling church funds!—Pretty story, isn't it?

YOUNG LADY: Oh! *(pause)*

STUDENT: Do you know what I'm thinking now about you?

YOUNG LADY: Don't tell me, or I'll die!

STUDENT: I must, or I'll die! ...

YOUNG LADY: It's only in asylums that people say everything they think ...

STUDENT: Yes, exactly!—My father ended up in a madhouse ...

YOUNG LADY: Was he ill?

STUDENT: No, he was well, but he was crazy. The madness broke out one day, when things became too much for him ... Like the rest of us, he had a circle of acquaintances, which, for the sake of convenience, he called friends. Naturally, they were a miserable bunch, as most people are. But he needed them because he couldn't bear to be alone. Well, he didn't ordinarily tell people what he thought of them, any more than anyone else does. He certainly knew how false they were, what treachery they were capable of! ... However, he was a prudent man, and well brought up, and so he was always polite. But one day he gave a big party.—It was in the evening, and he was tired, tired after the day's work, and tired from the strain of wanting to keep his mouth shut and having to talk nonsense with his guests...*(The YOUNG LADY shrinks back in horror.)* Anyway, at the dinner table, he rapped for silence, raised his glass, and began to talk ... Then something loosed the trigger, and in a long speech he stripped everybody naked, one after another, exposing all their falseness! Exhausted, he sat down in the middle of the table and told them all to go to hell!

YOUNG LADY: Oh!

STUDENT: I was there, and I'll never forget what happened next! ... My father and mother fought, and the guests rushed for the door ... My father was taken to a madhouse, where he died. *(pause)* When we keep silent for too long, stagnant water starts to form, and everything rots! And that's the way it is in this house too! There's something rotting here! And I thought this was a paradise the first time I saw you enter here ... On that Sunday morning I stood outside and looked in. I saw a colonel who wasn't a colonel. I had a noble benefactor who was a bandit and had to hang himself. I saw a mummy who was not a mummy, and a maiden—which reminds me: where is virginity to be found? Where is beauty? Only in Nature or in my mind when it's dressed up in Sunday best. Where are honor and faith? In fairy tales and children's games. Where is anything that fulfills its promise? ... In my imagination!— Do you see? Your flowers have poisoned me, and now I've given the poison back to you.— I begged you to be my wife and share our home. We made poetry, sang and played, and then in came the Cook ... *Sursum Corda!* Try once more to strike fire and splendor from the golden harp ... try, I beg you, I command you on my knees! ... Very well, then I'll do it myself! *(takes the harp and plucks the strings, but there is no sound)*

It's deaf and dumb! Why is it that the most beautiful flowers are so poisonous, the most poisonous? Damnation hangs over the whole of creation ... Why wouldn't you be my bride? Because you're sick at the very source of life ... I can feel that vampire in the kitchen beginning to drain me. I think she's a Lamia who sucks the blood of children. It's always in the kitchen that a child's seed leaves are nipped, its growth stunted, if it hasn't already happened in the bedroom ... There are poisons that blind you, and poisons that open your eyes.—I must have been born with the second kind in my veins, for I can't see beauty in ugliness or call evil

good, I can't! Jesus Christ descended into hell. That was his pilgrimage on this earth: to this madhouse, this dungeon, this morgue of a world. And the madmen killed him when he tried to set them free, but they let the bandit go. It's always the bandit who gets the sympathy!—Alas! Alas for us all! Savior of the World, save us, we are perishing! *(The* YOUNG LADY, *apparently dying, lies crumpled in her chair. She rings and* BENGTSSON *enters.)*
YOUNG LADY: Bring the screen! Quickly—I'm dying! (BENGTSSON *exits and returns with the screen, which he unfolds and sets up around the* YOUNG LADY.)
STUDENT: He's coming to set you free! Welcome, you pale and gentle deliverer!—Sleep, my beautiful one, lost and innocent, blameless in your suffering. Sleep without dreaming. And when you awaken again … may you be greeted by a sun that does not burn, in a home without dust, by friends who cause no pain, by a love without flaw … You wise and gentle Buddha, sitting there waiting for a heaven to rise up out of the earth, grant us patience in the time of testing, and purity of will, so that your hope may not be in vain!

(The strings of the harp make a murmuring sound. The room is filled with white light.)

I saw the sun, and thought I saw
what was hidden.
You cannot heal with evil
deeds done in anger.
Man reaps as he sows;
blessed is the doer of good.
Comfort him you have grieved
with your goodness, and you will
have healed.
No fear has he who has done no ill;
goodness is innocence.

(A whimpering can be heard from behind the screen.) You poor little child, child of this world of illusion, guilt, suffering, and death; this world of endless change, disappointment and pain. The Lord of Heaven be merciful to you on your journey …

(The room disappears. Böcklin's painting, "The Island of the Dead," appears in the background, and from the island comes music, soft, calm, and gently melancholy.)

For the Blood Is the Life (1911)

F. Marion Crawford

WE HAD DINED AT sunset on the broad roof of the old tower, because it was cooler during the great heat of summer. Besides, the little kitchen was built at one corner of the great square platform, which made it more convenient than if the dishes had to be carried down the steep stone steps, broken in places and everywhere worn with age. The tower was one of those built all down the west coast of Calabria by the Emperor Charles V early in the sixteenth century, to keep off the Barbary pirates, when the unbelievers were allied with Francis I against the Emperor and the Church. They have gone to ruin, a few still stand intact, and mine is one of the largest. How it came into my possession ten years ago, and why I spend a part of each year in it, are matters which do not concern this tale. The tower stands in one of the loneliest spots in southern Italy, at the extremity of a curving rocky promontory, which forms a small but safe natural harbor at the southern extremity of the Gulf of Policastro, and just north of Cape Scalea, the birthplace of Judas Iscariot, according to the old local legend. The tower stands alone on this hooked spur of the rock, and there is not a house to be seen within three miles of it. When I go there I take a couple of sailors, one of whom is a fair cook, and when I am away it is in charge of a gnomelike little being who was once a miner and who attached himself to me long ago.

My friend, who sometimes visits me in my summer solitude, is an artist by profession, a Scandinavian by birth, and a cosmopolitan by force of circumstances. We had dined at sunset; the sunset glow had reddened and faded again, and the evening purple steeped the vast chain of the mountains that embrace the deep gulf to eastward and rear themselves higher and higher toward the south. It was hot, and we sat at the landward corner of the platform, waiting for the night breeze to come down from the lower hills. The color sank out of the air, there was a little interval of deep-gray twilight, and a lamp sent a yellow streak from the open door of the kitchen, where the men were getting their supper.

Then the moon rose suddenly above the crest of the promontory, flooding the platform and lighting up every little spur of rock and knoll of grass below us, down to the edge of the motionless water. My friend lighted his pipe and sat looking at a spot on the hillside. I knew that he was looking at it, and for a long time past I had wondered whether he would ever see anything there that would fix his attention. I knew that spot well. It was clear that he was interested at last, though it was a long time before he spoke. Like most painters, he trusts to his own eyesight, as a lion trusts his strength and a stag his speed, and he is always disturbed when he cannot reconcile what he sees with what he believes that he ought to see.

"It's strange," he said. "Do you see that little mound just on this side of the boulder?"

"Yes," I said, and I guessed what was coming.

"It looks like a grave," observed Holger.

"Very true. It does look like a grave."

"Yes," continued my friend, his eyes still fixed on the spot. "But the strange thing is that I see the body lying on the top of it. Of course," continued Holger, turning his head on one side as artists do, "it must be an effect of light. In the first place, it is not a grave at all. Secondly, if it were, the body would be inside and not outside. Therefore, it's an effect of the moonlight. Don't you see it?"

"Perfectly; I always see it on moonlight nights."

"It doesn't seem to interest you much," said Holger.

"On the contrary, it does interest me, though I am used to it. You're not so far wrong, either. The mound is really a grave."

"Nonsense!" cried Holger, incredulously. "I suppose you'll tell me what I see lying on it is really a corpse!"

"No," I answered, "it's not. I know, because I have taken the trouble to go down and see."

"Then what is it?" asked Holger.

"It's nothing."

"You mean that it's an effect of light, I suppose?"

"Perhaps it is. But the inexplicable part of the matter is that it makes no difference whether the moon is rising or setting, or waxing or waning. If there's any moonlight at all, from east or west or overhead, so long as it shines on the grave you can see the outline of the body on top."

F. Marion Crawford, "For the Blood Is the Life." Copyright in the Public Domain.

Holger stirred up his pipe with the point of his knife, and then used his finger for a stopper. When the tobacco burned well he rose from his chair.

"If you don't mind," he said, "I'll go down and take a look at it."

He left me, crossed the roof, and disappeared down the dark steps. I did not move, but sat looking down until he came out of the tower below. I heard him humming an old Danish song as he crossed the open space in the bright moonlight, going straight to the mysterious mound. When he was ten paces from it, Holger stopped short, made two steps forward, and then three or four backward, and then stopped again. I knew what that meant. He had reached the spot where the Thing ceased to be visible—where, as he would have said, the effect of light changed.

Then he went on till he reached the mound and stood upon it. I could see the Thing still, but it was no longer lying down; it was on its knees now, winding its white arms round Holger's body and looking up into his face. A cool breeze stirred my hair at that moment, as the night wind began to come down from the hills, but it felt like a breath from another world.

The Thing seemed to be trying to climb to its feet, helping itself up by Holger's body while he stood upright, quite unconscious of it and apparently looking toward the tower, which is very picturesque when the moonlight falls upon it on that side.

"Come along!" I shouted. "Don't stay there all night!"

It seemed to me that he moved reluctantly as he stepped from the mound, or else with difficulty. That was it. The Thing's arms were still round his waist, but its feet could not leave the grave. As he came slowly forward it was drawn and lengthened like a wreath of mist, thin and white, till I saw distinctly that Holger shook himself, as a man does who feels a chill. At the same instant a little wail of pain came to me on the breeze—it might have been the cry of the small owl that lives among the rocks—and the misty presence floated swiftly back from Holger's advancing figure and lay once more at its length upon the mound.

Again I felt the cool breeze in my hair, and this time an icy thrill of dread ran down my spine. I remembered very well that I had once gone down there alone in the moonlight; that presently, being near, I had seen nothing; that, like Holger, I had gone and had stood upon the mound; and I remembered how, when I came back, sure that there was nothing there, I had felt the sudden conviction that there was something after all if I would only look behind me. I remembered the strong temptation to look back, a temptation I had resisted as unworthy of a man of sense, until, to get rid of it, I had shaken myself just as Holger did.

And now I knew that those white, misty arms had been round me too; I knew it in a flash, and I shuddered as I remembered that I had heard the night owl then too. But it had not been the night owl. It was the cry of the Thing.

I refilled my pipe and poured out a cup of strong southern wine; in less than a minute Holger was seated beside me again.

"Of course there's nothing there," he said, "but it's creepy, all the same. Do you know, when I was coming back I was so sure that there was something behind me that I wanted to turn round and look? It was an effort not to."

He laughed a little, knocked the ashes out of his pipe, and poured himself out some wine. For a while neither of us spoke, and the moon rose higher, and we both looked at the Thing that lay on the mound.

"You might make a story about that," said Holger after a long time.

"There is one," I answered. "If you're not sleepy, I'll tell it to you."

"Go ahead," said Holger, who likes stories.

Old Alario was dying up there in the village behind the hill. You remember him, I have no doubt. They say that he made his money by selling sham jewelry in South America, and escaped with his gains when he was found out. Like all those fellows, if they bring anything back with them, he at once set to work to enlarge his house; and, as there are no masons here, he sent all the way to Paola for two workmen. They were a rough-looking pair of scoundrels—a Neapolitan who had lost one eye and a Sicilian with an old scar half an inch deep across his left cheek. I often saw them, for on Sundays they used to come down here and fish off the rocks. When Alario caught the fever that killed him the masons were still at work. As he had agreed that part of their pay should be their board and lodging, he made them sleep in the house. His wife was dead, and he had an only son called Angelo, who was a much better sort than himself. Angelo was to marry the daughter of the richest man in the village, and, strange to say, though the marriage was arranged by their parents, the young people were said to be in love with each other.

For that matter, the whole village was in love with Angelo, and among the rest a wild, good-looking creature called Cristina, who was more like a gipsy than any girl I ever saw about here. She had very red lips and very black eyes, she was built like a greyhound, and had the tongue of the devil. But Angelo did not care a straw for her. He was rather a simple-minded fellow, quite different from his old scoundrel of a father, and under what I should call normal circumstances I really believe that he would never have looked at any girl except the nice plump little creature, with a fat dowry, whom his father meant him to marry. But things turned up which were neither normal nor natural.

On the other hand, a very handsome young shepherd from the hills above Maratea was in love with Cristina, who seems to have been quite indifferent to him. Cristina had no regular means of subsistence, but she was a good girl and willing to do any work or go on errands to any distance for the sake of a loaf of bread or a mess of beans, and permission to sleep under cover. She was especially glad when she could get something to do about the house of Angelo's father. There is no doctor in the village, and when the neighbors saw that old Alario was dying they sent Cristina to Scalea to fetch one. That was late in the afternoon, and if they had waited so long, it was because the dying miser refused to allow any such extravagance while he was able to speak. But while Cristina was gone, matters grew rapidly worse, the priest was brought to the bedside, and when he had done what he could he gave it as his opinion to the bystanders that the old man was dead, and left the house.

You know these people. They have a physical horror of death. Until the priest spoke, the room had been full of people. The words were hardly out of his mouth before it was empty. It was night now. They hurried down the dark steps and out into the street.

Angelo was away, Cristina had not come back—the simple woman servant who had nursed the sick man fled with the rest, and the body was left alone in the flickering light of the earthen oil lamp.

Five minutes later two men looked in cautiously and crept forward toward the bed. They were the one-eyed Neapolitan mason and his Sicilian companion. They knew what they wanted. In a moment they had dragged from under the bed a small but heavy iron-bound box, and long before any one thought of coming back to the dead man they had left the house and the village under cover of the darkness. It was easy enough, for Alario's house is the last toward the gorge which leads down here, and the thieves merely went out by the back door, got over the stone wall, and had nothing to risk after that except the possibility of meeting some belated countryman, which was very small indeed, since few of the people use that path. They had a mattock and shovel, and they made their way here without accident.

I am telling you this story as it must have happened, for, of course, there were no witnesses to this part of it. The men brought the box down by the gorge, intending to bury it until they should be able to come back and take it away in a boat. They must have been clever enough to guess that some of the money would be in paper notes, for they would otherwise have buried it on the beach in the wet sand, where it would have been much safer. But the paper would have rotted if they had been obliged to leave it there long, so they dug their hole down there, close to that boulder. Yes, just where the mound is now.

Cristina did not find the doctor in Scalea, for he had been sent for from a place up the valley, halfway to San Domenico. If she had found him, he would have come on his mule by the upper road, which is smoother but much longer. But

Cristina took the short cut by the rocks, which passes about fifty feet above the mound, and goes round that corner. The men were digging when she passed, and she heard them at work. It would not have been like her to go by without finding out what the noise was, for she was never afraid of anything in her life, and, besides, the fishermen sometimes came ashore here at night to get a stone for an anchor or to gather sticks to make a little fire. The night was dark, and Cristina probably came close to the two men before she could see what they were doing. She knew them, of course, and they knew her, and understood instantly that they were in her power. There was only one thing to be done for their safety, and they did it. They knocked her on the head, they dug the hole deep, and they buried her quickly with the iron-bound chest. They must have understood that their only chance of escaping suspicion lay in getting back to the village before their absence was noticed, for they returned immediately, and were found half an hour later gossiping quietly with the man who was making Alario's coffin. He was a crony of theirs, and had been working at the repairs in the old man's house. So far as I have been able to make out, the only persons who were supposed to know where Alario kept his treasure were Angelo and the one woman servant I have mentioned. Angelo was away; it was the woman who discovered the theft.

It is easy enough to understand why no one else knew where the money was. The old man kept his door locked and the key in his pocket when he was out, and did not let the woman enter to clean the place unless he was there himself. The whole village knew that he had money somewhere, however, and the masons had probably discovered the whereabouts of the chest by climbing in at the window in his absence. If the old man had not been delirious until he lost consciousness he would have been in frightful agony of mind for his riches. The faithful woman servant forgot their existence only for a few moments when she fled with the rest, overcome by the horror of death. Twenty minutes had not passed before she returned with the two hideous old hags who are always called in to prepare the dead for burial. Even then she had not at first the courage to go near the bed with them, but she made a pretense of dropping something, went down on her knees as if to find it, and looked under the bedstead. The walls of the room were newly whitewashed down to the floor, and she saw at a glance that the chest was gone. It had been there in the afternoon, it had therefore been stolen in the short interval since she had left the room.

There are no carabineers stationed in the village; there is not so much as a municipal watchman, for there is no municipality. There never was such a place, I believe. Scalea is supposed to look after it in some mysterious way, and it takes a couple of hours to get anybody from there. As the old woman had lived in the village all her life, it did not even occur to her to apply to any civil authority for help. She simply set up a howl and ran through the village in the dark, screaming out that her dead master's house had been robbed. Many of the people looked out, but at first no one seemed inclined to help her. Most of them, judging her by themselves, whispered to each other that she had probably stolen the money herself. The first man to move was the father of the girl whom Angelo was to marry; having collected his household, all of whom felt a personal interest in the wealth which was to have come into the family, he declared it to be his opinion that the chest had been stolen by the two journeyman masons who lodged in the house. He headed a search for them, which naturally began in Alario's house and ended in the carpenter's workshop, where the thieves were found discussing a measure of wine with the carpenter over the half-finished coffin, by the light of one earthen lamp filed with oil and tallow. The search party at once accused the delinquents of the crime, and threatened to lock them up in the cellar till the carabineers could be fetched from Scalea. The two men looked at each other for one moment, and then without the slightest hesitation they put out the single light, seized the unfinished coffin between them, and using it as a sort of battering ram, dashed upon their assailants in the dark. In a few moments they were beyond pursuit.

That is the end of the first part of the story. The treasure had disappeared, and as no trace of it could be found the people naturally supposed that the thieves had succeeded in carrying it off. The old man was buried, and when Angelo came back at last he had to borrow money to pay for the miserable funeral, and had some difficulty in doing so. He hardly needed to be told that in losing his inheritance he had lost his bride. In this part of the world marriages are made on strictly business principles, and if the promised cash is not forthcoming on the appointed day the bride or the bridegroom whose parents have failed to produce it may as well take themselves off, for there will be no wedding. Poor Angelo knew that well enough. His father had been possessed of hardly any land, and now that the hard cash which he had brought from South America was gone, there was nothing left but debts for the building materials that were to have been used for enlarging and improving the old house. Angalo was beggared, and the nice plump little creature who was to have been his turned up her nose at him in the most approved fashion. As for Cristina, it was several days before she was missed, for no one remembered that she had been sent to Scalea for the doctor, who had never come. She often disappeared in the same way for days together, when she could find a little work here and there at the distant farms among the hills. But when she did not come back at all, people began to wonder, and at last made up their minds that she had connived with the masons and had escaped with them.

I paused and emptied my glass.

"That sort of thing could not happen anywhere else," observed Holger, filling his everlasting pipe again. "It is wonderful what a natural charm there is about murder and sudden death in a romantic country like this. Deeds that would be simply brutal and disgusting anywhere else become dramatic and mysterious because this is Italy and we are living in a genuine tower of Charles V built against genuine Barbary pirates."

"There's something in that," I admitted. Holger is the most romantic man in the world inside of himself, but he always thinks it necessary to explain why he feels anything.

"I suppose they found the poor girl's body with the box," he said presently.

"As it seems to interest you," I answered, "I'll tell you the rest of the story."

The moon had risen high by this time; the outline of the Thing on the mound was clearer to our eyes than before.

The village very soon settled down to its small, dull life. No one missed old Alario, who had been away so much on his voyages to South America that he had never been a familiar figure in his native place. Angelo lived in the half-finished house, and because he had no money to pay the old woman servant she would not stay with him, but once in a long time she would come and wash a shirt for him for old acquaintance' sake. Besides the house, he had inherited a small patch of ground at some distance from the village; he tried to cultivate it, but he had no heart in the work, for he knew he could never pay the taxes on it and on the house, which would certainly be confiscated by the Government, or seized for the debt of the building material, which the man who had supplied it refused to take back.

Angelo was very unhappy. So long as his father had been alive and rich, every girl in the village had been in love with him; but that was all changed now. It had been pleasant to be admired and courted, and invited to drink wine by fathers who had girls to marry. It was hard to be stared at coldly, and sometimes laughed at because he had been robbed of his inheritance. He cooked his miserable meals for himself, and from being sad became melancholy and morose.

At twilight, when the day's work was done, instead of hanging about in the open space before the church with young fellows of his own age, he took to wandering in lonely places on the outskirts of the village till it was quite dark. Then he slunk home and went to bed to save the expense of a light. But in those lonely twilight hours he began to have strange waking dreams. He was not always alone, for often when he sat on the stump of a tree, where the narrow path turns down the gorge, he was sure that a woman came up noiselessly over the rough stones, as if her feet were bare; and she stood under a clump of chestnut trees only half a dozen yards down the path, and beckoned to him without speaking.

Though she was in the shadow he knew that her lips were red, and that when they parted a little and smiled at him she showed two small sharp teeth. He knew this at first rather than saw it, and he knew that it was Cristina, and that she was dead. Yet he was not afraid; he only wondered whether it was a dream, for he thought that if he had been awake he should have been frightened.

Besides, the dead woman had red lips, and that could only happen in a dream. Whenever he went near the gorge after sunset she was already there waiting for him, or else she very soon appeared, and he began to be sure that she came a little nearer to him every day. At first he had only been sure of her blood-red mouth, but now each feature grew distinct, and the pale face looked at him with deep and hungry eyes.

It was the eyes that grew dim. Little by little he came to know that some day the dream would not end when he turned away to go home, but would lead him down the gorge out of which the vision rose. She was nearer now when she beckoned to him. Her cheeks were not livid like those of the dead, but pale with starvation, with the furious and unappeased physical hunger of her eyes that devoured him. They feasted on his soul and cast a spell over him, and at last they were close to his own and held them. He could not tell whether her breath was as hot as fire or as cold as ice; he could not tell whether her red lips burned his or froze them, or whether her five fingers on his wrists seared scorching scars or bit his flesh like frost; he could not tell whether he was awake or asleep, whether she was alive or dead, but he knew that she loved him, she alone of all creatures, earthly or unearthly, and her spell had power over him.

When the moon rose high that night the shadow of that Thing was not alone down there upon the mound.

Angelo awoke in the cool dawn, drenched with dew and chilled through flesh, and blood, and bone. He opened his eyes to the faint gray light, and saw the stars still shining overhead. He was very weak, and his heart was beating so slowly that he was almost like a man fainting. Slowly he turned his head on the mound, as on a pillow, but the other face was not there. Fear seized him suddenly, a fear unspeakable and unknown; he sprang to his feet and fled up the gorge, and he never looked behind him until he reached the door of the house on the outskirts of the village. Drearily he went to his work that day, and wearily the hours dragged themselves after the sun, till at last he touched the sea and sank, and the great sharp hills above Maratea turned purple against the dove-colored eastern sky.

Angelo shouldered his heavy hoe and left the field. He felt less tired now than in the morning when he had begun to work, but he promised himself that he would go home without lingering by the gorge, and eat the best supper he could get himself, and sleep all night in his bed like a Christian man. Not again would he be tempted down the narrow way by a shadow with red lips and icy breath; not again would he dream that dream of terror and delight. He was near the village now; it was half an hour since the sun had set, and the cracked church bell sent little discordant echoes across the rocks and ravines to tell all good people that the day was done. Angelo stood still a moment where the path forked, where it led toward the village on the left, and down to the gorge on the right, where a clump of chestnut trees overhung the narrow way. He stood still a minute, lifting his battered hat from his head and gazing at the fast-fading sea westward, and his lips moved as he silently repeated the familiar evening prayer. His lips moved, but the words that followed them in his brain lost their meaning and turned into others, and ended in a name that he spoke aloud—Cristina! With the name, the tension of his will relaxed suddenly, reality went out and the dream took him again and bore him on swiftly and surely like a man walking in his sleep, down, down, by the steep path in the gathering darkness. And as she glided beside him, Cristina whispered strange sweet things in his ear, which somehow, if he had been awake, he knew that he could not quite have understood; but now they were the most wonderful words he had ever heard in his life. And she kissed him also, but not upon his mouth. He felt her sharp kisses upon his white throat, and he knew that her lips were red. So the wild dream sped on through twilight and darkness and moonrise, and all the glory of the summer's night. But in the chilly dawn he lay as one half dead upon the mound down there, recalling and not recalling, drained of his blood, yet strangely longing to give those red lips more. Then came the fear, the awful nameless panic, the mortal horror that guards the confines of the world we see not, neither know of as we know of other things, but which we feel when its icy chill freezes our bones and stirs our hair with the touch of a ghostly hand. Once more Angelo sprang from the mound and fled up the gorge in the breaking day, but his step was less sure this time, and he panted for breath as he ran; and when he came to the bright spring of water that rises halfway up the hillside, he dropped upon his knees and hands and plunged his whole face in and drank as he had never drunk before—for it was the thirst of the wounded man who has lain bleeding all night long upon the battlefield.

She had him fast now, and he could not escape her, but would come to her every evening at dusk until she had drained him of his last drop of blood. It was in vain that when the day was done he tried to take another turning and to go home by a path that did not lead near the gorge. It was in vain that he made promises to himself each morning at dawn when he climbed the lonely way up from the shore to the village. It was all in vain, for when the sun sank burning into the sea, and the coolness of the evening stole out as from a hiding-place to delight the weary world, his feet turned toward the old way, and she was waiting for him in the shadow under the chestnut trees; and then all happened as before, and she fell to kissing his white throat even as she flitted lightly down the way, winding one arm about him. And as his blood failed, she grew more hungry and more thirsty every day, and every day when he awoke in the early dawn it was harder to rouse himself to the effort of climbing the steep path to the village; and when he went to his work his feet dragged painfully, and there was hardly strength in his arms to wield the heavy hoe. He scarcely spoke to any one now, but the people said he was "consuming himself" for love of the girl he was to have married when he lost his inheritance; and they laughed heartily at the thought, for this is not a very romantic country. At this time, Antonio, the man who stays here to look after the tower, returned from a visit to his people, who live near Salerno. He had been away all the time since before Alario's death and knew nothing of what had happened. He has told me that he came back late in the afternoon and shut himself up in the tower to eat and sleep, for he was very tired. It was past midnight when he awoke, and when he looked out the waning moon was rising over the shoulder of the hill. He looked out toward the mound, and he saw something, and he did not sleep again that night. When he went out again in the morning it was broad daylight, and there was nothing to be seen on the mound but loose stones and driven sand. Yet he did not go very near it; he went straight up the path to the village and directly to the house of the old priest.

"I have seen an evil thing this night," he said; "I have seen how the dead drink the blood of the living. And the blood is the life."

"Tell me what you have seen," said the priest in reply.

Antonio told him everything he had seen.

"You must bring your book and your holy water tonight," he added. "I will be here before sunset to go down with you, and if it pleases your reverence to sup with me while we wait, I will make ready."

"I will come," the priest answered, "for I have read in old books of these strange beings which are neither quick nor dead, and which lie ever fresh in their graves, stealing out in the dusk to taste life and blood."

Antonio cannot read, but he was glad to see that the priest understood the business; for, of course, the books must have instructed him as to the best means of quieting the half-living Thing forever.

So Antonio went away to his work, which consists largely in sitting on the shady side of the tower, when he is not perched upon a rock with a fishing line catching nothing. But on that day he went twice to look at the mound in the bright sunlight, and he searched round and round it for some hole through which the being might get in and out; but he found none. When the sun began to sink and the air was cooler in the shadows, he went up to fetch the old priest, carrying a little wicker basket with him; and in this they placed a bottle of holy water, and the basin, and sprinkler, and the stole which the priest would need; and they came down and waited in the door of the tower till it should be dark. But while the light still lingered very gray and faint, they saw something moving, just there, two figures, a man's that walked, and a woman's that flitted beside him, and while her head lay on his shoulder she kissed his throat. The priest has told me that, too, and that his teeth chattered and he grasped Antonio's arm. The vision passed and disappeared into the shadow. Then Antonio got the leathern flask of strong liquor, which he kept for great occasions, and poured such a draught as made the old man feel almost young again; and he got the lantern, and his pick and shovel, and gave the priest his stole to put on and the holy water to carry, and they went out together toward the spot where the work was to be done. Antonio says that in spite of the rum his own knees shook together, and the priest stumbled over his Latin. For when they were yet a few yards from the mound the flickering light of the lantern fell upon Angelo's white face, unconscious as if in sleep, and on his upturned throat, over which a very thin red line of blood trickled down into his collar; and the flickering light of the lantern played upon another face that looked up from the feast—upon two deep, dead eyes that saw in spite of death—upon parted lips redder than life itself—upon two gleaming teeth on which glistened a rosy drop. Then the priest, good old man, shut his eyes tight and showered holy water before him, and his cracked voice rose almost to a scream; and then Antonio, who is no coward after all, raised his pick in one hand and the lantern in the other, as he sprang forward, not knowing what the end should be; and then he swears that he heard a woman's cry, and the Thing was gone, and Angelo lay alone on the mound unconscious, with the red line on his throat and the beads of deathly sweat on his cold forehead. They lifted him, half-dead as he was, and laid him on the ground close by! then Antonio went to work, and the priest helped him, though he was old and could not do much; and they dug deep, and at last Antonio, standing in the grave, stooped down with his lantern to see what he might see.

His hair used to be dark brown, with grizzled streaks about the temples; in less than a month from that day he was as gray as a badger. He was a miner when he was young, and most of these fellows have seen ugly sights now and then, when accidents have happened, but he had never seen what he saw that night—that Thing which is neither alive nor dead, that Thing that will abide neither above ground nor in the grave. Antonio had brought something with him which the priest had not noticed. He had made it that afternoon—a sharp stake shaped from a piece of tough old driftwood. He had it with him now, and he had his heavy pick, and he had taken the lantern down into the grave. I don't think any power on earth could make him speak of what happened then, and the old priest was too frightened to look in. He says he heard Antonio breathing like a wild beast, and moving as if he were fighting with something almost as strong as himself; and he heard an evil sound also, with blows, as of something violently driven through flesh and bone; and then the most awful sound of all—a woman's shriek, the unearthly scream of a woman neither dead nor alive, but buried deep for many days. And he, the poor old priest, could only rock himself as he knelt there in the sand, crying aloud his prayers and exorcisms to drown these dreadful sounds. Then suddenly a small iron-bound chest was thrown up and rolled over against the old man's knee, and in a moment more Antonio was beside him, his face as white as tallow in the flickering light of the lantern, shoveling the sand and pebbles into the grave with furious haste, and looking over the edge till the pit was half full; and the priest had said that there was much fresh blood on Antonio's hands and on his clothes.

I had come to the end of my story. Holger finished his wine and leaned back in his chair.

"So Angelo got his own again," he said. "Did he marry the prim and plump young person to whom he had teen betrothed?"

"No; he had been badly frightened. He went to South America, and has not been heard of since."

"And that poor thing's body is there still, I suppose," said Holger. "Is it quite dead yet, I wonder?"

I wonder, too. But whether it is dead or alive, I should hardly care to see it, even in broad daylight.

Antonio is as gray as a badger, and he has never been quite the same man since that night.

Revelations in Black (1933)

Carl Jacobi

It was a dreary, forlorn establishment way down on Harbor Street. An old sign announced the legend: "Giovanni Larla — Antiques," and a dingy window revealed a display half masked in dust.

Even as I crossed the threshold that cheerless September afternoon, driven from the sidewalk by a gust of rain and perhaps a fascination for all antiques, the gloominess fell upon me like a material pall. Inside was half darkness, piled boxes and a monstrous tapestry, frayed with the warp showing in worn places. An Italian Renaissance wine cabinet shrank despondently in its corner and seemed to frown at me as I passed,

"Good afternoon, *Signor*, There is something you wish to buy? A picture, a ring, a vase perhaps?"

I peered at the squat bulk of the Italian proprietor there in the shadows and hesitated.

"Just looking around," I said, turning to the jumble about me. "Nothing in particular. ..."

The man's oily face moved in smile as though he had heard the remark a thousand times before. He sighed, stood there in thought a moment, the rain drumming and swishing against the outer pane. Then very deliberately he stepped to the shelves and glanced up and down them considering. At length he drew forth an object which I perceived to be a painted chalice.

"An authentic Sixteenth Century Tandart," he murmured. "A work of art, *Signor*."

I shook my head. "No pottery," I said. "Books perhaps, but no pottery."

He frowned slowly. "I have books too," he replied, "rare books which nobody sells but me, Giovanni Larla. But you must look at my other treasures too."

There was, I found, no hurrying the man. A quarter of an hour passed during which I had to see a Glycon cameo brooch, a carved chair of some indeterminate style and period, and a muddle of yellowed statuettes, small oils and one or two dreary Portland vases. Several times I glanced at my watch impatiently, wondering how I might break away from this Italian and his gloomy shop. Already the fascination of its dust and shadows had begun to wear off, and I was anxious to reach the street.

But when he had conducted me well toward the rear of the shop, something caught my fancy. I drew then from the shelf the first book of horror. If I had but known the events that were to follow, if I could only have had a foresight into the future that September day, I swear I would have avoided the book like a leprous thing, would have shunned that wretched antique store and the very street it stood on like places accursed. A thousand times I have wished my eyes had never rested on that cover in black. What writhings of the soul, what terrors, what unrest, what madness would have been spared me!

But never dreaming the secret of its pages I fondled it casually and remarked:

"An unusual book. What is it?"

Larla glanced up and scowled.

"That is not for sale," he said quietly, "I don't know how it got on these shelves. It was my poor brother's."

The volume in my hand was indeed unusual in appearance. Measuring but four inches across and five inches in length and bound in black velvet with each outside corner protected with a triangle of ivory, it was the most beautiful piece of book-binding I had ever seen. In the center of the cover was mounted a tiny piece of ivory intricately cut in the shape of a skull. But it was the title of the book that excited my interest. Embroidered in gold braid, the title read:

"*Five Unicorns* and *a Pearl*."

I looked at Larla. "How much?" I asked and reached for my wallet.

He shook his head. "No, it is not for sale. It is … it is the last work of my brother. He wrote it just before he died in the institution."

"The institution?"

Larla made no reply but stood staring at the book, his mind obviously drifting away in deep thought. A moment of silence dragged by. There was a strange gleam in his eyes when finally he spoke. And I thought I saw his fingers tremble slightly.

"My brother, Alessandro, was a fine man before he wrote that book," he said slowly. "He wrote beautifully, *Signor*, and he was strong and healthy. For hours I could sit while he read to me his poems. He was a dreamer, Alessandro;

Carl Jacobi, "Revelations in Black," *Weird Tales*. Copyright © 1933 by the Estate of Carl Jacobi.

he loved everything beautiful, and the two of us were very happy.

"All … until that terrible night. Then he … but no … a year has passed now. It is best to forget." He passed his hand before his eyes and drew in his breath sharply.

"What happened?" I asked.

"Happened, *Signor*? I do not really know. It was all so confusing. He became suddenly ill, ill without reason. The flush of sunny Italy, which was always on his cheek, faded, and he grew white and drawn. His strength left him day by day. Doctors prescribed, gave medicines, but nothing helped. He grew steadily weaker until … until that night."

I looked at him curiously, impressed by his perturbation.

"And then—?"

Hands opening and closing, Larla seemed to sway unsteadily; his liquid eyes opened wide to the brows.

"And then … oh, if I could but forget! It was horrible. Poor Alessandro came home screaming, sobbing. He was … he was stark, raving mad!

"They took him to the institution for the insane and said he needed a complete rest, that he had suffered from some terrific mental shock. He … died three weeks later with the crucifix on his lips."

For a moment I stood there in silence, staring out at the falling rain. Then I said:

"He wrote this book while confined to the institution?"

Larla nodded absently.

"Three books," he replied. "Two others exactly like the one you have in your hand. The bindings he made, of course, when he was quite well. It was his original intention, I believe, to pen in them by hand the verses of Marini. He was very clever at such work. But the wanderings of his mind which filled the pages now, I have never read. Nor do I intend to. I want to keep with me the memory of him when he was happy. This book has come on these shelves by mistake. I shall put it with his other possessions."

My desire to read the few pages bound in velvet increased a thousand-fold when I found they were unobtainable. I have always had an interest in abnormal psychology and have gone through a number of books on the subject. Here was the work of a man confined in the asylum for the insane. Here was the unexpurgated writing of an educated brain gone mad. And unless my intuition failed me, here was a suggestion of some deep mystery. My mind was made up. I must have it.

I turned to Larla and chose my words carefully.

"I can well appreciate your wish to keep the book," I said, "and since you refuse to sell, may I ask if you would consider lending it to me for just one night? If I promised to return it in the morning? …"

The Italian hesitated. He toyed undecidedly with a heavy gold watch chain.

"No, I am sorry …"

"Ten dollars and back tomorrow unharmed."

Larla studied his shoe.

"Very well, *Signor*, I will trust you. But please, I ask you, please be sure and return it."

That night in the quiet of my apartment I opened the book. Immediately my attention was drawn to three lines scrawled in a feminine hand across the inside of the front cover, lines written in a faded red solution that looked more like blood than ink. They read:

"Revelations meant to destroy but only binding without the stake. Read, fool, and enter my field, for we are chained to the spot. Oh wo unto Larla."

I mused over these undecipherable sentences for some time without solving their meaning. At last, I turned to the first page and began the last work of Alessandro Larla, the strangest story I had ever in my years of browsing through old books, come upon.

"On the evening of the fifteenth of October I turned my steps into the cold and walked until I was tired. The roar of the present was in the distance when I came to twenty-six bluejays silently contemplating the ruins. Passing in the midst of them I wandered by the skeleton trees and seated myself where I could watch the leering fish. A child worshipped. Glass threw the moon at me. Grass sang a litany at my feet And the pointed shadow moved slowly to the left.

"I walked along the silver gravel until I came to five unicorns galloping beside water of the past. Here I found a pearl, a magnificent pearl, a pearl beautiful but black. Like a flower it carried a rich perfume, and once I thought the odor was but a mask, but why should such a perfect creation need a mask?

"I sat between the leering fish and the five galloping unicorns, and I fell madly in love with the pearl. The past lost itself in drabness and—"

I laid the book down and sat watching the smoke-curls from my pipe eddy ceilingward. There was much more, but I could make no sense of any of it. All was in that strange style and completely incomprehensible. And yet it seemed the story was more than the mere wanderings of a madman. Behind it all seemed to lie a narrative cloaked in symbolism.

Something about the few sentences had cast an immediate spell of depression over me. The vague lines weighed upon my mind, and I felt myself slowly seized by a deep feeling of uneasiness.

The air of the room grew heavy and close. The open casement and the out-of-doors seemed to beckon to me. I walked to the window, thrust the curtain aside, stood there, smoking furiously. Let me say that regular habits have long been a part of my make-up. I am not addicted to nocturnal strolls or late meanderings before seeking my bed; yet now, curiously enough, with the pages of the book still in my mind I suddenly experienced an indefinable urge to leave my apartment and walk the darkened streets.

I paced the room nervously. The clock on the mantel pushed its ticks slowly through the quiet. And at length I threw my pipe to the table, reached for my hat and coat and made for the door.

Ridiculous as it may sound, upon reaching the street I found that urge had increased to a distinct attraction. I felt that under no circumstances must I turn any direction but northward, and although this way led into a district quite unknown to me, I was in a moment pacing forward, choosing streets deliberately and heading without knowing why toward the outskirts of the city. It was a brilliant moonlight night in September. Summer had passed and already there was the smell of frosted vegetation in the air. The great chimes in Capitol tower were sounding midnight, and the buildings and shops and later the private houses were dark and silent as I passed.

Try as I would to erase from my memory the queer book which I had just read, the mystery of its pages hammered at me, arousing my curiosity. "Five Unicorns and a Pearl!" What did it all mean?

More and more I realized as I went on that a power other than my own will was leading my steps. Yet once when I did momentarily come to a halt that attraction swept upon me as inexorably as the desire for a narcotic.

It was far out on Easterly Street that I came upon a high stone wall flanking the sidewalk. Over its ornamented top I could see the shadows of a dark building set well back in the grounds. A wrought-iron gate in the wall opened upon a view of wild desertion and neglect. Swathed in the light of the moon, an old courtyard strewn with fountains, stone benches and statues lay tangled in rank weeds and undergrowth. The windows of the building, which evidently had once been a private dwelling, were boarded up, all except those on a little tower or cupola rising to a point in front. And here the glass caught the blue-gray light and refracted it into the shadows.

Before that gate my feet stopped like dead things. The psychic power which had been leading me had now become a reality. Directly from the courtyard it emanated, drawing me toward it with an intensity that smothered all reluctance.

Strangely enough, the gate was unlocked; and feeling like a man in a trance I swung the creaking hinges and entered, making my way along a grass-grown path to one of the benches. It seemed that once inside the court the distant sounds of the city died away, leaving a hollow silence broken only by the wind rustling through the tall dead weeds. Rearing up before me, the building with its dark wings, cupola and facade oddly resembled a colossal hound, crouched and ready to spring.

There were several fountains, weather-beaten and ornamented with curious figures, to which at the time I paid only casual attention. Farther on, half hidden by the underbrush, was the life-size statue of a little child kneeling in position of prayer. Erosion on the soft stone had disfigured the face, and in the half-light the carved features presented an expression strangely grotesque and repelling.

How long I sat there in the quiet, I don't know. The surroundings under the moonlight blended harmoniously with my mood. But more than that I seemed physically unable to rouse myself and pass on.

It was with a suddenness that brought me electrified to my feet that I became aware of the significance of the objects about me. Held motionless, I stood there running my eyes wildly from place to place, refusing to believe. Surely I must be dreaming. In the name of all that was unusual this ... this absolutely couldn't be. And yet—

It was the fountain at my side that had caught my attention first. Across the top of the water basin were *five stone unicorns,* all identically carved, each seeming to follow the other in galloping procession. Looking farther, prompted now by a madly rising recollection, I saw that the cupola, towering high above the house, eclipsed the rays of the moon and threw *a long pointed shadow* across the ground *at my left.* The other fountain some distance away was ornamented with the figure of a stone fish, *a fish* whose empty eye-sockets *were leering* straight in my direction. And the climax of it all—the wall! At intervals of every three feet on the top of the street expanse were mounted crude carven stone shapes of birds. And counting them I saw that *those birds were twenty-six bluejays.*

Unquestionably—startling and impossible as it seemed—I was in the same setting as described in Larla's book! It was a staggering revelation, and my mind reeled at the thought of it. How strange, how odd that I should be drawn to a portion of the city I had never before frequented and thrown into the midst of a narrative written almost a year before!

I saw now that Alessandro Larla, writing as a patient in the institution for the insane, had seized isolated details but neglected to explain them. Here was a problem for the psychologist, the mad, the symbolic, the incredible story of the dead Italian. I was bewildered and I pondered for an answer.

As if to soothe my perturbation there stole into the court then a faint odor of perfume. Pleasantly it touched my nostrils, seemed to blend with the moonlight. I breathed it in deeply as I stood there by the fountain. But slowly that odor became more noticeable, grew stronger, a sickish sweet smell that began to creep down my lungs like smoke. Heliotrope! The honeyed aroma blanketed the garden, thickened the air.

And then came my second surprise of the evening. Looking about to discover the source of the fragrance I saw opposite me, seated on another stone bench, a woman. She was dressed entirely in black, and her face was hidden by a veil. She seemed unaware of my presence. Her head was slightly bowed, and her whole position suggested a person in deep contemplation.

I noticed also the thing that crouched by her side. It was a dog, a tremendous brute with a head strangely out of proportion and eyes as large as the ends of big spoons. For several moments I stood staring at the two of them. Although the air was quite chilly, the woman wore no overjacket, only the black dress relieved solely by the whiteness of her throat.

With a sigh of regret at having my pleasant solitude thus disturbed I moved across the court until I stood at her side. Still she showed no recognition of my presence, and clearing my throat I said hesitatingly:

"I suppose you are the owner here. I ... I really didn't know the place was occupied, and the gate ... well, the gate was unlocked. I'm sorry I trespassed."

She made no reply to that, and the dog merely gazed at me in dumb silence. No graceful words of polite departure came to my lips, and I moved hesitatingly toward the gate.

"Please don't go," she said suddenly, looking up. "I'm lonely. Oh, if you but knew how lonely I am!" She moved to one side on the bench and motioned that I sit beside her. The dog continued to examine me with its big eyes.

Whether it was the nearness of that odor of heliotrope, the suddenness of it all, or perhaps the moonlight, I did not know, but at her words a thrill of pleasure ran through me, and I accepted the proffered seat.

There followed an interval of silence, during which I puzzled for a means to start conversation. But abruptly she turned to the beast and said in German:

"*Fort mit dir, Johann!*"

The dog rose obediently to its feet and stole slowly off into the shadows. I watched it for a moment until it disappeared in the direction of the house. Then the woman said to me in English which was slightly stilted and marked with an accent:

"It has been ages since I have spoken to anyone ... We are strangers. I do not know you, and you do not know me. Yet ... strangers sometimes find in each other a bond of interest. Supposing ... supposing we forget customs and formality of introduction? Shall we?"

For some reason I felt my pulse quicken as she said that. "Please do," I replied. "A spot like this is enough introduction in itself. Tell me, do you live here?"

She made no answer for a moment, and I began to fear I had taken her suggestion too quickly. Then she began slowly:

"My name is Perle von Mauren, and I am really a stranger to your country, though I have been here now more than a year. My home is in Austria near what in now the Czechoslovakian frontier. You see, it was to find my only brother that I came to the United States. During the war he was a lieutenant under General Mackensen, but in 1916, in April I believe it was, he ... he was reported missing.

"War is a cruel thing. It took our money; it took our castle on the Danube, and then—my brother. Those following years were horrible. We lived always in doubt, hoping against hope that he was still living.

"Then after the Armistice a fellow officer claimed to have served next to him on grave-digging detail at a French prison camp near Monpré. And later came a thin rumor that he was in the United States. I gathered together as much money as I could and came here in search of him."

Her voice dwindled off, and she sat in silence staring at the brown weeds. When she resumed, her voice was low and wavering.

"I ... found him ... but would to God I hadn't! He ... he was no longer living."

I stared at her. "Dead?" I asked.

The veil trembled as though moved by a shudder, as though her thoughts had exhumed some terrible event of the past. Unconscious of my interruption she went on:

"Tonight I came here—I don't know why—merely because the gate was unlocked, and there was a place of quiet within. Now have I bored you with my confidences and personal history?"

"Not at all," I replied. "I came here by chance myself. Probably the beauty of the place attracted me. I dabble in amateur photography occasionally and react strongly to unusual scenes. Tonight I went for a midnight stroll to relieve my mind from the bad effect of a book I was reading."

She made a strange reply to that, a reply away from our line of thought and which seemed an interjection that escaped her involuntarily.

"Books," she said, "are powerful things. They can fetter one more than the walls of a prison."

She caught my puzzled stare at the remark and added hastily: "It is odd that we should meet here."

For a moment I didn't answer. I was thinking of her heliotrope perfume, which for a woman of her apparent culture was applied in far too great a quantity to show good taste. The impression stole upon me that the perfume cloaked some secret, that if it were removed I should find ... but what?

The hours passed, and still we sat there talking, enjoying each other's companionship. She did not remove her veil, and though I was burning with desire to see her features, I had not dared to ask her to. A strange nervousness had slowly seized me. The woman was a charming conversationalist, but there was about her an indefinable something which produced in me a distinct feeling of unease.

It was, I should judge, but a few moments before the first streaks of a dawn when it happened. As I look back now, even with mundane objects and thoughts on every side, it is not difficult to realize the significance of that vision. But at the time my brain was too much in a whirl to understand.

A thin shadow moving across the garden attracted my gaze once again into the night about me. I looked up over the spire of the deserted house and started as if struck by a blow. For a moment I thought I had seen a curious cloud formation racing low directly above me, a cloud black and impenetrable with two wing-like ends strangely in the shape of a monstrous flying bat.

I blinked my eyes hard and looked again.

"That cloud!" I exclaimed, "that strange cloud! ... Did you see—"

I stopped and stared dumbly.

The bench at my side was empty. The woman had disappeared.

During the next day I went about my professional duties in the law office with only half interest, and my business partner looked at me queerly several times when he came upon me mumbling to myself. The incidents of the evening before were rushing through my mind. Questions unanswerable hammered at me. That I should have come upon the very details described by mad Larla in his strange book: the leering fish, the praying child, the twenty-six bluejays, the pointed shadow of the cupola—it was unexplainable; it was weird.

"Five Unicorns and a Pearl." The unicorns were the stone statues ornamenting the old fountain, yes—but the pearl? With a start I suddenly recalled the name of the woman in black: *Perle* von Mauren. What did it all mean?

Dinner had little attraction for me that evening. Earlier I had gone to the antique-dealer and begged him to loan me the sequel, the second volume of his brother Alessandro. When he had refused, objected because I had not yet returned the first book, my nerves had suddenly jumped on edge. I felt like a narcotic fiend faced with the realization that he could not procure the desired drug. In desperation, yet hardly knowing why, I offered the man more money, until at length I had come away, my powers of persuasion and my pocketbook successful.

The second volume was identical in outward respects to its predecessor except that it bore no title. But if I was expecting more disclosures in symbolism I was doomed to disappointment. Vague as "Five Unicorns and a Pearl" had been, the text of the sequel was even more wandering and was obviously only the ramblings of a mad brain. By watching the sentences closely I did gather that Alessandro Larla had made a second trip to his court of the twenty-six bluejays and met there again his "pearl."

There was the paragraph toward the end that puzzled me. It read:

"Can it possibly be? I pray that it is not. And yet I have seen it and heard it snarl. Oh the loathsome creature! I will not, I will not believe it."

I closed the book and tried to divert my attention elsewhere by polishing the lens of my newest portable camera. But again, as before, that same urge stole upon me, that same desire to visit the garden. I confess that I had watched the intervening hours until I would meet the woman in black again; for strangely enough, in spite of her abrupt exit before, I never doubted that she would be there waiting for me. I wanted her to lift the veil. I wanted to talk with her. I wanted to throw myself once again into the narrative of Larla's book.

Yet the whole thing seemed preposterous, and I fought the sensation with every ounce of will-power I could call to mind. Then it suddenly occurred to me what a remarkable picture she would make, sitting there on the stone bench, clothed in black, with the classic background of the old courtyard. If I could but catch the scene on a photographic plate. ...

I halted my polishing and mused a moment. With a new electric flash-lamp, that handy invention which has supplanted the old mussy flash-powder, I could illuminate the garden and snap the picture with ease. And if the result were satisfactory it would make a worthy contribution to the International Camera Contest at Geneva next month.

The idea appealed to me, and gathering together the necessary equipment I drew on an ulster (for it was a wet, chilly night) and slipped out of my rooms and headed northward. Mad, unseeing fool that I was! If only I had stopped then and there, returned the book to the antique-dealer and closed the incident! But the strange magnetic attraction had gripped me in earnest, and I rushed headlong into the horror.

A fall rain was drumming the pavement, and the streets were deserted. Off to the east, however, the heavy blanket of clouds glowed with a soft radiance where the moon was trying to break through, and a strong wind from the south gave promise of clearing the skies before long. With my coat collar turned well up at the throat I passed once again into the older section of the town and down forgotten Easterly Street. I found the gate to the grounds unlocked as before, and the garden a dripping place masked in shadow.

The woman was not there. Still the hour was early, and I did not for a moment doubt that she would appear later. Gripped now with the enthusiasm of my plan, I set the camera carefully on the stone fountain, training the lens as well as I could on the bench where we had sat the previous evening. The flash-lamp with its battery handle I laid within easy reach.

Scarcely had I finished my arrangements when the crunch of gravel on the path caused me to turn. She was approaching the stone bench, heavily veiled as before and with the same sweeping black dress.

"You have come again," she said as I took my place beside her.

"Yes," I replied. "I could not stay away."

Our conversation that night gradually centered about her dead brother, although I thought several times that the woman tried to avoid the subject. He had been, it seemed, the black sheep of the family, had led more or less of a dissolute life and had been expelled from the University of Vienna not only because of his lack of respect for the pedagogues of the various sciences but also because of his queer unorthodox papers on philosophy. His sufferings in the war prison camp must have been intense. With a kind of grim delight she dwelt on his horrible experiences in the grave-digging detail which had been related to her by the fellow officer. But of the manner in which he had met his death she would say absolutely nothing.

Stronger than on the night before was the sweet smell of heliotrope. And again as the fumes crept nauseatingly down my lungs there came that same sense of nervousness, that same feeling that the perfume was hiding something I should know. The desire to see beneath the veil had become maddening by this time, but still I lacked the boldness to ask her to lift it.

Toward midnight the heavens cleared and the moon in splendid contrast shone high in the sky. The time had come for my picture.

"Sit where you are," I said. "I'll be back in a moment."

Stepping to the fountain I grasped the flash-lamp, held it aloft for an instant and placed my finger on the shutter lever of the camera. The woman remained motionless on the bench, evidently puzzled as to the meaning of my movements. The range was perfect. A click, and a dazzling white light enveloped the courtyard about us. For a brief second she was outlined there against the old wall. Then the blue moonlight returned, and I was smiling in satisfaction.

"It ought to make a beautiful picture," I said.

She leaped to her feet.

"Fool!" she cried hoarsely. "Blundering fool! What have you done?"

Even though the veil was there to hide her face I got the instant impression that her eyes were glaring at me, smouldering with hatred. I gazed at her curiously as she stood erect, head thrown back, body apparently taut as wire, and a slow shudder crept down my spine. Then without warning she gathered up her dress and ran down the path toward the deserted house. A moment later she had disappeared somewhere in the shadows of the giant bushes.

I stood there by the fountain, staring after her in a daze. Suddenly, off in the umbra of the house's facade there rose a low animal snarl.

And then before I could move, a huge gray shape came hurtling through the long weeds, bounding in great leaps straight toward me, It was the woman's dog, which I had seen with her the night before. But no longer was it a beast passive and silent. Its face was contorted in diabolic fury, and its jaws were dripping slaver. Even in that moment of terror as I stood frozen before it, the sight of those white nostrils and those black hyalescent eyes emblazoned itself on my mind, never to be forgotten.

Then with a lunge it was upon me. I had only time to thrust the flash-lamp upward in half protection and throw my weight to the side. My arm jumped in recoil. The bulb exploded, and I could feel those teeth clamp down hard on the handle. Backward I fell, a scream gurgling to my lips, a terrific heaviness surging upon my body.

I struck out frantically, beat my fists into that growling face. My fingers groped blindly for its throat, sank deep into the hairy flesh. I could feel its very breath mingling with my own now, but desperately I hung on.

The pressure of my hands told. The dog coughed and fell back. And seizing that instant I struggled to my feet, jumped forward and planted a terrific kick straight into the brute's middle.

"*Fort mit dir, Johann!*" I cried, remembering the woman's German command.

It leaped back and, fangs bared, glared at me motionless for a moment. Then abruptly it turned and slunk off through the weeds.

Weak and trembling, I drew myself together, picked up my camera and passed through the gate toward home.

Three days passed. Those endless hours I spent confined to my apartment suffering the tortures of the damned.

On the day following the night of my terrible experience with the dog I realized I was in no condition to go to work. I drank two cups of strong black coffee and then forced myself to sit quietly in a chair, hoping to soothe my nerves. But the sight of the camera there on the table excited me to action. Five minutes later I was in the dark room arranged as my studio, developing the picture I had taken the night before. I worked feverishly, urged on by the thought of what an unusual contribution it would make for the amateur contest next month at Geneva, should the result be successful.

An exclamation burst from my lips as I stared at the still-wet print. There was the old garden clear and sharp with the bushes, the statue of the child, the fountain and the wall in the background, but the bench—the stone bench was empty. There was no sign, not even a blur of the woman in black.

I rushed the negative through a saturated solution of mercuric chloride in water, then treated it with ferrous oxalate. But even after this intensifying process the second print was like the first, focused in every detail, the bench standing in the foreground in sharp relief, but no trace of the woman.

She had been in plain view when I snapped the shutter. Of that I was positive. And my camera was in perfect condition. What then was wrong? Not until I had looked at the print hard in the daylight would I believe my eyes. No explanation offered itself, none at all; and at length, confused, I returned to my bed and fell into a heavy sleep.

Straight through the day I slept. Hours later I seemed to wake from a vague nightmare, and had not strength to rise from my pillow. A great physical faintness had overwhelmed me. My arms, my legs, lay like dead things. My heart was fluttering weakly. All was quiet, so still that the clock on my bureau ticked distinctly each passing second. The curtain billowed in the night breeze, though I was positive I had closed the casement when I entered the room.

And then suddenly I threw back my head and screamed! For slowly, slowly creeping down my lungs was that detestable odor of heliotrope!

Morning, and I found all was not a dream. My head was ringing, my hands trembling, and I was so weak I could hardly stand. The doctor I called in looked grave as he felt my pulse.

"You are on the verge of a complete collapse," he said. "If you do not allow yourself a rest it may permanently affect your mind. Take things easy for a while. And if you don't mind, I'll cauterize those two little cuts on your neck. They're rather raw wounds. What caused them?"

I moved my fingers to my throat and drew them away again tipped with blood.

"I ... I don't know," I faltered.

He busied himself with his medicines, and a few minutes later reached for his hat.

"I advise that you don't leave your bed for a week at least," he said. "I'll give you a thorough examination then and see if there are any signs of anemia." But as he went out the door I thought I saw a puzzled look on his face.

Those subsequent hours allowed my thoughts to run wild once more. I vowed I would forget it all, go back to my work and never look upon the books again. But I knew I could not. The woman in black persisted in my mind, and each minute away from her became a torture. But more than that, if there had been a decided urge to continue my reading in the second book, the desire to see the third book, the last of the trilogy, was slowly increasing to an obsession.

At length I could stand it no longer, and on the morning of the third day I took a cab to the antique store and tried to persuade Larla to give me the third volume of his brother. But the Italian was firm. I had already taken two books, neither of which I had returned. Until I brought them back he would not listen. Vainly I tried to explain that one was of no value without the sequel and that I wanted to read the entire narrative as a unit. He merely shrugged his shoulders.

Cold perspiration broke out on my forehead as I heard my desire disregarded. I argued. I pleaded. But to no avail.

At length when Larla had turned the other way I seized the third book as I saw it lying on the shelf, slid it into my pocket and walked guiltily out. I made no apologies for my action. In the light of what developed later it may be considered a temptation inspired, for my will at the time was a conquered thing blanketed by that strange lure.

Back in my apartment I dropped into a chair and hastened to open the velvet cover. Here was the last chronicling of that strange series of events which had so completely become a part of my life during the past five days. Larla's volume three. Would all be explained in its pages? If so, what secret would be revealed?

With the light from a reading-lamp glaring full over my shoulder I opened the book, thumbed through it slowly, marveling again at the exquisite hand-printing It seemed then as I sat there that an almost palpable cloud of quiet settled over me, muffling the distant sounds of the street. Something indefinable seemed to forbid me to read farther. Curiosity, that queer urge told me to go on. Slowly, I began to turn the pages, one at a time, from back to front.

Symbolism again. Vague wanderings with no sane meaning.

But suddenly my fingers stopped! My eyes had caught sight of the last paragraph on the last page, the final pennings of Alessandro Larla. I read, re-read, and read again those blasphemous words. I traced each word in the lamplight, slowly, carefully, letter for letter. Then the horror of it burst within me.

In blood-red ink the lines read:

"What shall I do? She has drained my blood and rotted my soul. My pearl is black as all evil. The curse be upon her brother; for it is he who made her thus. I pray the truth in these pages will destroy them for ever.

"Heaven help me, Perle von Mauren and her brother, Johann, are vampires!"

I leaped to my feet.

"Vampires!"

I clutched at the edge of the table and stood there swaying. Vampires! Those horrible creatures with a lust for human blood, taking the shape of men, of bats, of dogs.

The events of the past days rose before me in all their horror now, and I could see the black significance of every detail.

The brother, Johann—some time since the war he had become a vampire. When the woman sought him out years later he had forced this terrible existence upon her too.

With the garden as their lair the two of them had entangled poor Alessandro Larla in their serpentine coils a year before. He had loved the woman, had worshipped her. And then he had found the awful truth that had sent him stumbling home, raving mad.

Mad, yes, but not mad enough to keep him from writing the fact in his three velvet-bound books. He had hoped the disclosures would dispatch the woman and her brother for ever. But it was not enough.

I whipped the first book from the table and opened the cover. There again I saw those scrawled lines which had meant nothing to me before.

"Revelations meant to destroy but only binding without the stake. Read, fool, and enter my

field, for we are chained to the spot. Oh, wo unto Larla!"

Perle von Mauren had written that. The books had not put an end to the evil life of her and her brother. No, only one thing could do that. Yet the exposures had not been written in vain. They were recorded for mortal posterity to see.

Those books bound the two vampires, Perle von Mauren, Johann, to the old garden, kept them from roaming the night streets in search of victims. Only him who had once passed through the gate could they pursue and attack.

It was the old metaphysical law: evil shrinking in the face of truth.

Yet if the books had found their power in chains they had also opened a new avenue for their attacks. Once immersed in the pages of the trilogy, the reader fell helplessly into their clutches. Those printed lines had become the outer reaches of their web. They were an entrapping net within which the power of the vampires always crouched.

That was why my life had blended so strangely with the story of Larla. The moment I had cast my eyes on the opening paragraph I had fallen into their coils to do with as they had done with Larla a year before. I had been drawn relentlessly into the tentacles of the woman in black. Once I was past the garden gate the binding spell of the books was gone, and they were free to pursue me and to—

A giddy sensation rose within me. Now I saw why the doctor had been puzzled. Now I saw the reason for my physical weakness. She had been—feasting on my blood! But if Larla had been ignorant of the one way to dispose of such a creature, I was not. I had not vacationed in south Europe without learning something of these ancient evils.

Frantically I looked about the room. A chair, a table, one of my cameras with its long tripod. I seized one of the wooden legs of the tripod in my hands, snapped it across my knee. Then, grasping the two broken pieces, both now with sharp splintered ends, I rushed hatless out of the door to the street.

A moment later I was racing northward in a cab bound for Easterly Street.

"Hurry!" I cried to the driver as I glanced at the westering sun. "Faster, do you hear?"

We shot along the cross-streets, into the old suburbs and toward the outskirts of town. Every traffic halt found me fuming at the delay. But at length we drew up before the wall of the garden.

I swung the wrought-iron gate open and with the wooden pieces of the tripod still under my arm, rushed in. The courtyard was a place of reality in the daylight, but the moldering masonry and tangled weeds were steeped in silence as before.

Straight for the house I made, climbing the rotten steps to the front entrance. The door was boarded up and locked. I retraced my steps and began to circle the south wall of the building. It was this direction I had seen the woman take when she had fled after I had tried to snap her picture. Well toward the rear of the building I reached a small half-open door leading to the cellar. Inside, cloaked in gloom, a narrow corridor stretched before me. The floor was littered with rubble and fallen masonry, the ceiling interlaced with a thousand cobwebs.

I stumbled forward, my eyes quickly accustoming themselves to the half-light from the almost opaque windows.

At the end of the corridor a second door barred my passage. I thrust it open—and stood swaying there on the sill staring inward.

Beyond was a small room, barely ten feet square, with a low-raftered ceiling. And by the light of the open door I saw side by side in the center of the floor—two white wood coffins.

How long I stood there leaning weakly against the stone wall I don't know. There was an odor drifting from out of that chamber. Heliotrope! But heliotrope defiled by the rotting smell of an ancient grave.

Then suddenly I leaped to the nearest coffin, seized its cover and ripped it open.

Would to heaven I could forget that sight that met my eyes. There lay the woman in black—unveiled.

That face—it was divinely beautiful, the hair black as sable, the cheeks a classic white. But the lips—! I grew suddenly sick as I looked upon them. They were scarlet ... and sticky with human blood.

I reached for one of the tripod stakes, seized a flagstone from the floor and with the pointed end of the wood resting directly over the woman's heart, struck a crashing blow. The stake jumped downward. A violent contortion shook the coffin. Up to my face rushed a warm, nauseating breath of decay.

I wheeled and hurled open the lid of her brother's coffin. With only a glance at the young masculine Teutonic face I raised the other stake high in the air and brought it stabbing down with all the strength in my right arm.

In the coffins now, staring up at me from eyeless sockets, were two gray and moldering skeletons.

The rest is but a vague dream. I remember rushing outside, along the path to the gate and down Easterly, away from that accursed garden of the jays.

At length, utterly exhausted, I reached my apartment. Those mundane surroundings that confronted me were like balm to my eyes. But there centered into my gaze three objects lying where I had left them, the three volumes of Larla.

I turned to the grate on the other side of the room and flung the three of them onto the still glowing coals.

There was an instant hiss, and yellow flame streaked upward and began eating into the velvet. The fire grew higher … higher … and diminished slowly.

And as the last glowing spark died into a blackened ash there swept over me a mighty feeling of quiet and relief.

Luella Miller (1903)

Mary E. Wilkins-Freeman

CLOSE TO THE VILLAGE street stood the one-story house in which Luella Miller, who had an evil name in the village, had dwelt. She had been dead for years, yet there were those in the village who, in spite of the clearer light which comes on a vantage-point from a long-past danger, half believed in the tale which they had heard from their childhood. In their hearts, although they scarcely would have owned it, was a survival of the wild horror and frenzied fear of their ancestors who had dwelt in the same age with Luella Miller. Young people even would stare with a shudder at the old house as they passed, and children never played around it as was their wont around an untenanted building. Not a window in the old Miller house was broken: the panes reflected the morning sunlight in patches of emerald and blue, and the latch of the sagging front door was never lifted, although no bolt secured it. Since Luella Miller had been carried out of it, the house had had no tenant except one friendless old soul who had no choice between that and the far-off shelter of the open sky. This old woman, who had survived her kindred and friends, lived in the house one week, then one morning no smoke came out of the chimney, and a body of neighbours, a score strong, entered and found her dead in her bed. There were dark whispers as to the cause of her death, and there were those who testified to an expression of fear so exalted that it showed forth the state of the departing soul upon the dead face. The old woman had been hale and hearty when she entered the house, and in seven days she was dead; it seemed that she had fallen a victim to some uncanny power. The minister talked in the pulpit with covert severity against the sin of superstition; still the belief prevailed. Not a soul in the village but would have chosen the almshouse rather than that dwelling. No vagrant, if he heard the tale, would seek shelter beneath that old roof, unhallowed by nearly half a century of superstitious fear.

There was only one person in the village who had actually known Luella Miller. That person was a woman well over eighty, but a marvel of vitality and unextinct youth. Straight as an arrow, with the spring of one recently let loose from the bow of life, she moved about the streets, and she always went to church, rain or shine. She had never married, and had lived alone for years in a house across the road from Luella Miller's.

This woman had none of the garrulousness of age, but never in all her life had she ever held her tongue for any will save her own, and she never spared the truth when she essayed to present it. She it was who tore testimony to the life, evil, though possibly wittingly or designedly so, of Luella Miller, and to her personal appearance. When this old woman spoke—and she had the gift of description, although her thoughts were clothed in the rude vernacular of her native village—one could seem to see Luella Miller as she had really looked. According to this woman, Lydia Anderson by name, Luella Miller had been a beauty of a type rather unusual in New England. She had been a slight, pliant sort of creature, as ready with a strong yielding to fate and as unbreakable as a willow. She had glimmering lengths of straight, fair hair, which she wore softly looped round a long, lovely face. She had blue eyes full of soft pleading, little slender, clinging hands, and a wonderful grace of motion and attitude.

"Luella Miller used to sit in a way nobody else could if they sat up and studied a week of Sundays," said Lydia Anderson, "and it was a sight to see her walk. If one of them willows over there on the edge of the brook could start up and get its roots free of the ground, and move off, it would go just the way Luella Miller used to. She had a green shot silk she used to wear, too, and a hat with green ribbon streamers, and a lace veil blowing across her face and out sideways, and a green ribbon flyin' from her waist. That was what she came out bride in when she married Erastus Miller. Her name before she was married was Hill. There was always a sight of "l's" in her name, married or single. Erastus Miller was good lookin', too, better lookin' than Luella. Sometimes I used to think that Luella wa'n't so handsome after all. Erastus just about worshiped her. I used to know him pretty well. He lived next door to me, and we went to school together. Folks used to say he was waitin' on me, but he wa'n't. I never thought he was except once or twice when he said things that some

Mary E. Wilkins-Freeman, "Luella Miller." Copyright in the Public Domain.

girls might have suspected meant something. That was before Luella came here to teach the district school. It was funny how she came to get it, for folks said she hadn't any education, and that one of the big girls, Lottie Henderson, used to do all the teachin' for her, while she sat back and did embroidery work on a cambric pocket-handkerchief. Lottie Henderson was a real smart girl, a splendid scholar, and she just set her eyes by Luella, as all the girls did. Lottie would have made a real smart woman, but she died when Luella had been here about a year—just faded away and died: nobody knew what ailed her. She dragged herself to that schoolhouse and helped Luella teach till the very last minute. The committee all knew how Luella didn't do much of the work herself, but they winked at it. It wa'n't long after Lottie died that Erastus married her. I always thought he hurried it up because she wa'n't fit to teach. One of the big boys used to help her after Lottie died, but he hadn't much government, and the school didn't do very well, and Luella might have had to give it up, for the committee couldn't have shut their eyes to things much longer. The boy that helped her was a real honest, innocent sort of fellow, and he was a good scholar, too. Folks said he overstudied, and that was the reason he was took crazy the year after Luella married, but I don't know. And I don't know what made Erastus Miller go into consumption of the blood the year after he was married: consumption wa'n't in his family. He just grew weaker and weaker, and went almost bent double when he tried to wait on Luella, and he spoke feeble, like an old man. He worked terrible hard till the last trying to save up a little to leave Luella. I've seen him out in the worst storms on a wood-sled—he used to cut and sell wood—and he was hunched up on top lookin' more dead than alive. Once I couldn't stand it: I went over and helped him pitch some wood on the cart—I was always strong in my arms. I wouldn't stop for all he told me to, and I guess he was glad enough for the help. That was only a week before he died. He fell on the kitchen floor while he was gettin' breakfast. He always got the breakfast and let Luella lay abed. He did all the sweepin' and the washin' and the ironin' and most of the cookin'. He couldn't bear to have Luella lift her finger, and she let him do for her. She lived like a queen for all the work she did. She didn't even do her sewin'. She said it made her shoulder ache to sew, and poor Erastus's sister Lily used to do all her sewin'. She wa'n't able to, either; she was never strong in her back, but she did it beautifully. She had to, to suit Luella, she was so dreadful particular. I never saw anythin' like the fagottin' and hemstitchin' that Lily Miller did for Luella. She made all Lucia's weddin' outfit, and that green silk dress, after Maria Babbit cut it. Maria she cut it for nothin', and she did a lot more cuttin' and fittin for nothin' for Luella, too. Lily Miller went to live with Luella after Erastus died. She gave up her home, though she was real attached to it and wa'n't a mite afraid to stay alone. She rented it and she went to live with Luella right away after the funeral."

Then this old woman, Lydia Anderson, who remembered Luella Miller, would go on to relate the story of Lily Miller. It seemed that in the removal of Lily Miller to the house of her dead brother, to live with his widow, the village people first began to talk. This Lily Miller had been hardly past her first youth, and a most robust and blooming woman, rosy-cheeked, with curls of strong, black hair overshadowing round, candid temples and bright dark eyes. It was not six months after she had taken up her residence with her sister-in-law that her rosy colour faded and her pretty curves become wan hollows. White shadows began to show in the black rings of her hair, and the light died out of her eyes, her features sharpened, and there were pathetic lines at her mouth, which yet wore always an expression of utter sweetness and even happiness. She was devoted to her sister; there was no doubt that she loved her with her whole heart, and was perfectly content in her service. It was her sole anxiety lest she should die and leave her alone.

"The way Lily Miller used to talk about Luella was enough to make you mad and enough to make you cry," said Lydia Anderson. "I've been in there sometimes toward the last when she was too feeble to cook and carried her some blanc-mange or custard—somethin' I thought she might relish, and she'd thank me, and when I asked her how she was, say she felt better than she did yesterday, and asked me if I didn't think she looked better, dreadful pitiful, and say poor Luella had an awful time takin' care of her and doin' the work—she wa'n't strong enough to do anythin'—when all the time Luella wa'n't liftin' her finger and poor Lily didn't get any care except what the neighbours gave her, and Luella eat up everythin' that was carried in for Lily. I had it real straight that she did. Luella used to just sit and cry and do nothin'. She did act real fond of Lily, and she pined away considerable, too. There was those that thought she'd go into a decline herself. But after Lily died, her Aunt Abby Mixter came, and then Luella picked up and grew as fat and rosy as ever. But poor Aunt Abby begun to droop just the way Lily had, and I guess somebody wrote to her married daughter, Mrs. Sam Abbot, who lived in Barre, for she wrote her mother that she must leave right away and come and make her a visit, but Aunt Abby wouldn't go. I can see her now. She was a real good-lookin' woman, tall and large, with a big, square face and a high forehead that looked of itself kind of benevolent and good. She just tended out on Luella as if she had been a baby, and when her married daughter sent for her she wouldn't stir one inch. She'd always thought a lot of her daughter, too, but she said Luella needed her and her married daughter didn't. Her daughter kept writin' and writin', but it didn't do any good. Finally she came, and when she saw how bad her mother looked, she broke down and cried and all but went on her knees to have her come away. She spoke her mind out to Luella, too. She told her that she'd killed her husband and everybody that had anythin' to do with her, and she'd thank her to leave her mother alone. Luella went into hysterics, and Aunt Abby was so frightened that she called me after her daughter went. Mrs. Sam Abbot she went away fairly cryin' out loud in the buggy, the neighbours heard her, and well she might, for she never saw her mother again alive. I went in that night when Aunt Abby called for me, standin' in the door with her little green-cheeked shawl over her head. I can see her now. 'Do come over here, Miss Anderson,' she sung out, kind of gasping for breath. I didn't stop for anythin'. I put over as fast as I could, and when I got there, there was Luella laughin' and cryin' all together, and Aunt Abby trying to hush her, and all the time she herself was white as a sheet and shakin' so she could hardly stand. 'For the land sakes, Mrs. Mixter,' says I, 'you look worse than she does. You ain't fit to be up out of your bed.'

"'Oh, there ain't anythin' the matter with me,' says she. Then she went on talkin' to Luella. 'There, there, don't, don't, poor little lamb,' says she. 'Aunt Abby is here. She ain't goin' away and leave you. Don't, poor little lamb.'

"'Do leave her with me, Mrs. Mixter, and you get back to bed,' says I, for Aunt Abby had been layin' down considerable lately, though somehow she contrived to do the work.

"'I'm well enough,' says she. 'Don't you think she had better have the doctor, Miss Anderson?'

"'The doctor,' says I, 'I think *you* had better have the doctor. I think you need him much worse than some folks I could mention.' And I looked right straight at Luella Miller laughin' and cryin' and goin' on as if she was the centre of all creation. All the time she was actin' so—seemed as if she was too sick to sense anythin'—she was keepin' a sharp lookout as to how we took it out of the corner of one eye. I see her. You could never cheat me about Luella Miller. Finally I got real mad and I run home and I got a bottle of valerian I had, and I poured some boilin' hot water on a handful of catnip, and I mixed up that catnip tea with most half a wineglass of valerian, and I went with it over to Luella's. I marched right up to Luella, a-holdin' out of that cup, all smokin'. 'Now,' says I, 'Luella Miller, *you swaller this!*'

"'What is—what is it, oh, what is it?' she sort of screeches out. Then she goes off a-laughin' enough to kill.

"'Poor lamb, poor little lamb,' says Aunt Abby, standin' over her, all kind of tottery, and tryin' to bathe her head with camphor.

"'*You swaller this right down,*' says I. And I didn't waste any ceremony. I just took hold of Luella Miller's chin and I tipped her head back, and I caught her mouth open with laughin', and I clapped that cup to her lips and I fairly hollered at her: 'Swaller, swaller, swaller!' and she gulped it right down. She had to, and I guess it did her good. Anyhow, she stopped cryin' and laughin' and let me put her to bed, and she went to sleep like a baby inside of half an hour. That was more than poor Aunt Abby did. She lay awake all that night and I stayed with her, though she tried not to have me; said she wa'n't sick enough for watchers. But I stayed, and I made some good cornmeal gruel and I fed her a teaspoon every little while all night long. It seemed to me as if she was jest dyin' from bein' all wore out. In the mornin' as soon as it was light I run over to the Bisbees and sent Johnny Bisbee for the doctor. I told him to tell the doctor to hurry, and he come pretty quick. Poor Aunt Abby didn't seem to know much of anythin' when he got there. You couldn't hardly tell she breathed, she was so used up. When the doctor had gone, Luella came into the room lookin' like a baby in her ruffled nightgown. I can see her now. Her eyes were as blue and her face all pink and white like a blossom, and she looked at Aunt Abby in the bed sort of innocent and surprised. 'Why,' says she, 'Aunt Abby ain't got up yet?'

"'No, she ain't,' says I, pretty short.

"'I thought I didn't smell the coffee,' says Luella.

"'Coffee,' says I. 'I guess if you have coffee this mornin' you'll make it yourself.'

"'I never made the coffee in all my life,' says she, dreadful astonished. 'Erastus always made the coffee as long as he lived, and then Lily she made it, and then Aunt Abby made it. I don't believe I *can* make the coffee, Miss Anderson.'

"'You can make it or go without, jest as you please,' says I.

"'Ain't Aunt Abby goin' to get up?' says she.

"'I guess she won't get up,' says I, 'sick as she is.' I was gettin' madder and madder. There was somethin' about that little pink-and-white thing standin' there and talkin' about coffee, when she had killed so many better folks than she was, and had jest killed another, that made me feel 'most as if I wished somebody would up and kill her before she had a chance to do any more harm.

"'Is Aunt Abby sick?' says Luella, as if she was sort of aggrieved and injured.

"'Yes,' says I, 'she's sick, and she's goin' to die, and then you'll be left alone, and you'll have to do for yourself and wait on yourself, or do without things.' I don't know but I was sort of hard, but it was the truth, and if I was any harder than Luella Miller had been I'll give up. I ain't never been sorry that I said it. Well, Luella, she up and had hysterics again at that, and I jest let her have 'em. All I did was to bundle her into the room on the other side of the entry where Aunt Abby couldn't hear her, if she wa'n't past it—I don't know but she was—and set her down hard in a chair and told her not to come back into the other room, and she minded. She had her hysterics in there till she got tired. When she found out that nobody was comin' to coddle her and do for her she stopped. At least I suppose she did. I had all I could do with poor Aunt Abby tryin' to keep the breath of life in her. The doctor had told me that she was dreadful low, and give me some very strong medicine to give to her in drops real often, and told me real particular about the nourishment. Well, I did as he told me real faithful till she wa'n't able to swaller any longer. Then I had her daughter sent for. I had begun to realize that she wouldn't last any time at all. I hadn't realized it before, though I spoke to Luella the way I did. The doctor he came, and Mrs. Sam Abbot, but when she got there it was too late; her mother was dead. Aunt Abby's daughter just give one look at her mother layin' there, then she turned sort of sharp and sudden and looked at me.

"'Where is she?' says she, and I knew she meant Luella.

"'She's out in the kitchen,' says I. 'She's too nervous to see folks die. She's afraid it will make her sick.'

"The Doctor he speaks up then. He was a young man. Old Doctor Park had died the year before, and this was a young fellow just out of college. 'Mrs. Miller is not strong,' says he, kind of severe, 'and she is quite right in not agitating herself.'

"'You are another, young man; she's got her pretty claw on you,' thinks I, but I didn't say anythin' to him. I just said over to Mrs. Sam Abbot that Luella was in the kitchen, and Mrs. Sam Abbot she went out there, and I went, too, and I never heard anythin' like the way she talked to Luella Miller. I felt pretty hard to Luella myself, but this was more than I ever would have dared to say. Luella she was too scared to go into hysterics. She jest flopped. She seemed to just shrink away to nothin' in that kitchen chair, with Mrs. Sam Abbot standin' over her and talkin' and tellin' her the truth. I guess the truth was most too much for her and no mistake, because Luella presently actually did faint away, and there wa'n't any sham about it, the way I always suspected there was about them hysterics. She fainted dead away and we had to lay her flat on the floor, and the Doctor he came runnin' out and he said somethin' about a weak heart dreadful fierce to Mrs. Sam Abbot, but she wa'n't a mite scared. She faced him jest as white as even Luella was layin' there lookin' like death and the Doctor feelin' of her pulse.

"'Weak heart,' says she, 'weak heart; weak fiddlesticks! There ain't nothin' weak about that woman. She's got strength enough to hang onto other folks till she kills 'em. Weak? It was my poor mother that was weak: this woman killed her as sure as if she had taken a knife to her.'

"But the Doctor he didn't pay much attention. He was bendin' over Luella layin' there with her yellow hair all streamin' and her pretty pink-and-white face all pale, and her blue eyes like stars gone out, and he was holdin' onto her hand and smoothin' her forehead, and tellin' me to get the brandy in Aunt Abby's room, and I was sure as I wanted to be that Luella had got somebody else to hang onto, now Aunt Abby was gone, and I thought of poor Erastus Miller, and I sort of pitied the poor young Doctor, led away by a pretty face, and I made up my mind I'd see what I could do.

"I waited till Aunt Abby had been dead and buried about a month, and the Doctor was goin' to see Luella steady and folks were beginnin' to talk; then one evening when I knew the Doctor had been called out of town and wouldn't be round, I went over to Luella's. I found her all dressed up in a blue muslin with white polka dots on it, and her hair curled jest as pretty, and there wa'n't a young girl in the place could compare with her. There was somethin' about Luella Miller seemed to draw the heart right out of you, but she didn't draw it out of *me*. She was settin' rocking in the chair by her sittin'-room window, and Maria Brown had gone home. Maria Brown had been in to help her, or rather to do the work, for Luella wa'n't helped when she didn't do anythin'. Maria Brown was real capable and she didn't have any ties; she wa'n't married, and lived alone, so she'd offered. I couldn't see why she should do the work any more than Luella; she wa'n't any too strong; but she seemed to think she could and Luella seemed to think so, too, so she went over and did all the work—washed, and ironed, and baked, while Luella sat and rocked. Maria didn't live long afterward. She began to fade away just the same fashion the others had. Well, she was warned, but she acted real mad when folks said anythin': said Luella was a poor, abused woman, too delicate to help herself, and they'd ought to be ashamed, and if she died helpin' them that couldn't help themselves she would—and she did.

"'I s'pose Maria has gone home,' says I to Luella, when I had gone in and sat down opposite her.

"'Yes, Maria went half an hour ago, after she had got supper and washed the dishes,' says Luella, in her pretty way.

"'I suppose she has got a lot of work to do in her own house tonight,' says I, kind of bitter, but that was all thrown away on Luella Miller. It seemed to her right that other folks that wa'n't any better able than she was herself should wait on her, and she couldn't get it through her head that anybody should think it *wa'n't* right.

"'Yes,' says Luella, real sweet and pretty, 'yes, she said she had to do her washin' to-night. She has let it go for a fortnight along of comin' over here.'

"'Why don't she stay home and do her washin' instead of comin' over here and doin' *your* work, when you are just as well able, and enough sight more so, than she is to do it?' says I.

"Then Luella she looked at me like a baby who has a rattle shook at it. She sort of laughed as innocent as you please. 'Oh, I can't do the work myself, Miss Anderson,' says she. 'I never did. Maria *has* to do it.'

"Then I spoke out: 'Has to do it!' says I. 'Has to do it! She don't have to do it, either. Maria Brown has her own home and enough to live on. She ain't beholden to you to come over here and slave for you and kill herself.'

"Luella she jest set and stared at me for all the world like a dollbaby that was so abused that it was comin' to life.

"'Yes,' says I, 'she's killin' herself. She's goin' to die just the way Erastus did, and Lily, and your Aunt Abby. You're killin' her jest as you did them. I don't know what there is about you, but you seem to bring a curse,' says I. 'You kill everybody that is fool enough to care anythin' about you and do for you.'

"She stared at me and she was pretty pale.

"'And Maria ain't the only one you're goin' to kill,' says I. 'You're goin' to kill Doctor Malcom before you're done with him.'

"Then a red colour came flamin' all over her face. 'I ain't goin' to kill him, either,' says she, and she begun to cry.

"'Yes, you *be*!' says I. Then I spoke as I had never spoke before. You see, I felt it on account of Erastus. I told her that she hadn't any business to think of another man after she'd been married to one that had died for her: that she was a dreadful woman; and she was, that's true enough, but sometimes I have wondered lately if she knew it—if she wa'n't like a baby with scissors in its hand cuttin' everybody without knowin' what it was doin'.

"Luella she kept gettin' paler and paler, and she never took her eyes off my face. There was somethin' awful about the way she looked at me and never spoke one word. After awhile I quit talkin' and I went home. I watched that night, but her lamp went out before nine o'clock, and when Doctor Malcom came drivin' past and sort of slowed up he see there wa'n't any light and he drove along. I saw her sort of shy out of meetin' the next Sunday, too, so he shouldn't go home with her, and I begun to think mebbe she did have some conscience after all. It was only a week after that that Maria Brown died—sort of sudden at the last, though everybody had seen it was comin'. Well, then there was a good deal of feelin' and pretty dark whispers. Folks said the days of witchcraft had come again, and they were pretty shy of Luella. She acted sort of offish to the Doctor and he didn't go there, and there wa'n't anybody to do anythin' for her. I don't know how she *did* get along. I wouldn't go in there and offer to help her—not because I was afraid of dyin' like the rest but I thought she was just as well able to do her own work as I was to do it for her, and I thought it was about time that she did it and stopped killin' other folks. But it wa'n't very long before folks began to say that Luella herself was goin' into a decline jest the way her husband, and Lily, and Aunt Abby and the others had, and I saw myself that she looked pretty bad. I used to see her goin' past from the store with a bundle as if she could hardly crawl, but I remembered how Erastus used to wait and 'tend when he couldn't hardly put one foot before the other, and I didn't go out to help her.

"But at last one afternoon I saw the Doctor come drivin' up like mad with his medicine chest, and Mrs. Babbit came in after supper and said that Luella was real sick.

"'I'd offer to go in and nurse her,' says she, 'but I've got my children to consider, and mebbe it ain't true what they say, but it's queer how many folks that have done for her have died.'

"I didn't say anythin', but I considered how she had been Erastus's wife and how he had set his eyes by her, and I made up my mind to go in the next mornin', unless she was better, and see what I could do; but the next mornin' I see her at the window, and pretty soon she came steppin' out as spry as you please, and a little while afterward Mrs. Babbit came in and told me that the Doctor had got a girl from out of town, a Sarah Jones, to come there, and she said she was pretty sure that the Doctor was goin' to marry Luella.

"I saw him kiss her in the door that night myself, and I knew it was true. The woman came that afternoon, and the way she flew around was a caution. I don't believe Luella had swept since Maria died. She swept and dusted, and washed and ironed; wet clothes and dusters and carpets were flyin' over there all day, and every time Luella set her foot out when the Doctor wa'n't there there was that Sarah Jones helpin' of her up and down the steps, as if she hadn't learned to walk.

"Well, everybody knew that Luella and the Doctor were goin' to be married, but it wa'n't long before they began to talk about his lookin' so poorly, jest as they had about the others; and they talked about Sarah Jones, too.

"Well, the Doctor did die, and he wanted to be married first, so as to leave what little he had to Luella, but he died before the minister could get there, and Sarah Jones died a week afterward.

"Well, that wound up everything for Luella Miller. Not another soul in the whole town would lift a finger for her. There got to be a sort of panic. Then she began to droop in good earnest. She used to have to go to the store herself, for Mrs. Babbit was afraid to let Tommy go for her, and I've seen her goin' past and stoppin' every two or three steps to rest. Well, I stood it as long as I could, but one day I see her comin' with her arms full and stoppin' to lean against the Babbit fence, and I run out and took her bundles and carried them to her house. Then I went home and never spoke one word to her though she called after me dreadful kind of pitiful. Well, that night I was taken sick with a chill, and I was sick as I wanted to be for two weeks. Mrs. Babbit had seen me run out to help Luella and she came in and told me I was goin' to die on account of it. I didn't know whether I was or not, but I considered I had done right by Erastus's wife.

"That last two weeks Luella she had a dreadful hard time, I guess. She was pretty sick, and as near as I could make out nobody dared go near her. I don't know as she was really needin' anythin' very much, for there was enough to eat in her house and it was warm weather, and she made out to cook a little flour gruel every day, I know, but I guess she had a hard time, she that had been so petted and done for all her life.

"When I got so I could go out, I went over there one morning. Mrs. Babbit had just come in to say she hadn't seen any smoke and she didn't know but what it was somebody's duty to go in, but she couldn't help thinkin' of her children, and I got right up, though I hadn't been out of the house for two weeks and I went in there, and Luella she was layin' on the bed, and she was dyin'.

"She lasted all that day and into the night. But I sat there after the new doctor had gone away. Nobody else dared to go there. It was about midnight that I left her for a minute to run home and get some medicine I had been takin', for I begun to feel rather bad.

"It was a full moon that night, and just as I started out of my door to cross the street back to Luella's, I stopped short, for I saw something."

Lydia Anderson at this juncture always said with a certain defiance that she did not expect to be believed, and then proceeded in a hushed voice:

"I saw what I saw, and I know I saw it, and I will swear on my death bed that I saw it. I saw Luella Miller and Erastus Miller, and Lily, and Aunt Abby, and Maria, and the Doctor, and Sarah, all goin' out of her door, and all but Luella shone white in the moonlight, and they were all helpin' her along till she seemed to fairly fly in the midst of them. Then it all disappeared. I stood a minute with my heart poundin', then I went over there. I thought of goin' for Mrs. Babbit, but I thought she'd be afraid. So I went alone, though I knew what had happened. Luella was layin' real peaceful, dead on her bed."

This was the story that the old woman, Lydia Anderson, told, but the sequel was told by the people who survived her, and this is the tale which has become folklore in the village.

Lydia Anderson died when she was eighty-seven. She had continued wonderfully hale and hearty for one of her years until about two weeks before her death.

One bright moonlight evening she was sitting beside a window in her parlour when she made a sudden exclamation, and was out of the house and across the street before the neighbour who was taking care of her could stop her. She followed as fast as possible and found Lydia Anderson stretched on the ground before the door of Luella Miller's deserted house, and she was quite dead.

The next night there was a red gleam of fire athwart the moonlight and the old house of Luella Miller was burned to the ground. Nothing is now left of it except a few old cellar stones and a lilac bush, and in summer a helpless trail of morning glories among the weeds, which might be considered emblematic of Luella herself.

The Girl with the Hungry Eyes

Fritz Leiber

ALL RIGHT, I'LL TELL you why the Girl gives me the creeps. Why I can't stand to go downtown and see the mob slavering up at her on the tower, with that pop bottle or pack of cigarettes or whatever it is beside her. Why I hate to look at magazines any more because I know she'll turn up somewhere in a brassière or a bubble bath. Why I don't like to think of millions of Americans drinking in that poisonous half-smile. It's quite a story—more story than you're expecting.

No, I haven't suddenly developed any long-haired indignation at the evils of advertising and the national glamor-girl complex. That'd be a laugh for a man in my racket, wouldn't it? Though I think you'll agree there's something a little perverted about trying to capitalize on sex that way. But it's okay with me. And I know we've had the Face and the Body and the Look and what not else, so why shouldn't someone come along who sums it all up so completely, that we have to call her the Girl and blazon her on all the billboards from Times Square to Telegraph Hill?

But the Girl isn't like any of the others. She's unnatural. She's morbid. She's unholy.

Oh, these are modern times, you say, and the sort of thing I'm hinting at went out with witchcraft. But you see I'm not altogether sure myself what I'm hinting at, beyond a certain point. There are vampires and vampires, and not all of them suck blood.

And there were the murders, if they were murders. Besides, let me ask you this. Why, when America is obsessed with the Girl, don't we find out more about her? Why doesn't she rate a *Time* cover with a droll biography inside? Why hasn't there been a feature in *Life* or the *Post*? A profile in The *New Yorker?* Why hasn't *Charm* or *Mademoiselle* done her career saga? Not ready for it? Nuts!

Why haven't the movies snapped her up? Why hasn't she been on "Information, Please?" Why don't we see her kissing candidates at political rallies? Why isn't she chosen queen of some sort of junk or other at a convention?

Why don't we read about her tastes and hobbies, her views of the Russian situation? Why haven't the columnists interviewed her in a kimono on the top floor of the tallest hotel in Manhattan and told us who her boyfriends are?

Finally—and this is the real killer—why hasn't she ever been drawn or painted?

Oh no she hasn't. If you knew anything about commercial art, you'd know that. Every blessed one of those pictures was worked up from a photograph. Expertly? Of course. They've got the top artists on it. But that's how it's done.

And now I'll tell you the why of all that. It's because from the top to the bottom of the whole world of advertising, news, and business, there isn't a solitary soul who knows where the Girl came from, where she lives, what she does, who she is, even what her name is.

You heard me. What's more, not a single solitary soul ever sees her—except one poor damned photographer, who's making more money off her than he ever hoped to in his life and who's scared and miserable as hell every minute of the day.

No, I haven't the faintest idea who he is or where he has his studio. But I know there has to be such a man and I'm morally certain he feels just like I said.

Yes, I might be able to find her, if I tried. I'm not sure though—by now she probably has other safeguards. Besides, I don't want to.

Oh, I'm off my rocker, am I? That sort of thing can't happen in the Era of the Atom? People can't keep out of sight that way, not even Garbo?

Well, I happen to know they can, because last year I was that poor damned photographer I was telling you about. Yes, last year, when the Girl made her first poisonous splash right here in this big little city of ours.

Yes, I know you weren't here last year and you don't know about it. Even the Girl had to start small. But if you hunted through the files of the local newspapers, you'd find some ads, and I might be able to locate you some of the old displays—I think Lovelybelt is still using one of them. I used to have a mountain of photos myself, until I burned them.

Yes, I made my cut off her. Nothing like what that other photographer must be making, but enough so it still bought this whiskey. She was funny about money. I'll tell you about that.

Fritz Leiber, Jr., from *The Girl with the Hungry Eyes: and other Stories*. Copyright © 1949 by the Estate of Fritz Leiber, Jr. Reprinted with permission by Richard Curtis Associates.

But first picture me then. I had a fourth-floor studio in that rathole the Hauser Building, not far from Ardleigh Park.

I'd been working at the Marsh-Mason studios until I'd gotten my bellyful of it and decided to start in for myself. The Hauser Building was awful—I'll never forget how the stairs creaked—but it was cheap and there was a skylight.

Business was lousy. I kept making the rounds of all the advertisers and agencies, and some of them didn't object to me too much personally, but my stuff never clicked. I was pretty near broke. I was behind on my rent. Hell, I didn't even have enough money to have a girl.

It was one of those dark gray afternoons. The building was very quiet—I'd just finished developing some pix I was doing on speculation for Lovelybelt Girdles and Budford's Pool and Playground. My model had left. A Miss Leon. She was a civics teacher at one of the high schools and modeled for me on the side, just lately on speculation, too. After one look at the prints, I decided that Miss Leon probably wasn't just what Lovelybelt was looking for—or my photography either. I was about to call it a day.

And then the street door slammed four storys down and there were steps on the stairs and she came in.

She was wearing a cheap, shiny black dress. Black pumps. No stockings. And except that she had a gray cloth coat over one of them, those skinny arms of hers were bare. Her arms are pretty skinny, you know, or can't you see things like that any more?

And then the thin neck, the slightly gaunt, almost prim face, the tumbling mass of dark hair, and looking out from under it the hungriest eyes in the world.

That's the real reason she's plastered all over the country today, you know—those eyes. Nothing vulgar, but just the same they're looking at you with a hunger that's all sex and something more than sex. That's what everybody's been looking for since the Year One—something a little more than sex.

Well, boys, there I was, alone with the Girl, in an office that was getting shadowy, in a nearly empty building. A situation that a million male Americans have undoubtedly pictured to themselves with various lush details. How was I feeling? Scared.

I know sex can be frightening. That cold heart-thumping when you're alone with a girl and feel you're going to touch her. But if it was sex this time, it was overlaid with something else.

At least I wasn't thinking about sex.

I remember that I took a backward step and that my hand jerked so that the photos I was looking at sailed to the floor.

There was the faintest dizzy feeling like something was being drawn out of me. Just a little bit.

That was all. Then she opened her mouth and everything was back to normal for a while.

"I see you're a photographer, mister," she said. "Could you use a model?"

Her voice wasn't very cultivated.

"I doubt it," I told her, picking up the pix. You see, I wasn't impressed. The commercial possibilities of her eyes hadn't registered on me yet, by a long shot. "What have you done?"

Well, she gave me a vague sort of story and I began to check her knowledge of model agencies and studios and rates and what not and pretty soon I said to her, "Look here, you never modeled for a photographer in your life. You just walked in here cold."

Well, she admitted that was more or less so.

All along through our talk I got the idea she was feeling her way, like someone in a strange place. Not that she was uncertain of herself, or of me, but just of the general situation.

"And you think anyone can model?" I asked her pityingly.

"Sure," she said.

"Look," I said, "a photographer can waste a dozen negatives trying to get one halfway human photo of an average woman. How many do you think he'd have to waste before he got a real catchy, glamorous photo of her?"

"I think I could do it," she said.

Well, I should have kicked her out right then. Maybe I admired the cool way she stuck to her dumb little guns. Maybe I was touched by her underfed look. More likely I was feeling mean on account of the way my pictures had been snubbed by everybody and I wanted to take it out on her by showing her up.

"Okay, I'm going to put you on the spot," I told her. "I'm going to try a couple of shots of you. Understand it's strictly on spec. If somebody should ever want to use a photo of you, which is about one chance in two million, I'll pay you regular rate for your time. Not otherwise."

She gave me a smile. The first. "That's swell by me," she said.

Well, I took three or four shots, close-ups of her face since I didn't fancy her cheap dress, and at least she stood up to my sarcasm. Then I remembered I still had the Lovelybelt stuff and I guess the meanness was still working in me because I handed her a girdle and told her to go behind the screen and get into it and she did, without getting flustered as I'd expected, and since we'd gone that far, I figured we might as well shoot the beach scene to round it out, and that was that.

All this time I wasn't feeling anything particular one way or the other, except every once in a while I'd get one of those faint dizzy flashes and wonder if there was something wrong with my stomach or if I could have toe a bit careless with my chemicals.

Still, you know, I think the uneasiness was in me all the while.

I tossed her a card and pencil. "Write your name and address and phone," I told her and made for the darkroom.

A little later she walked out. I didn't call any good-byes. I was irked because she hadn't fussed around or seemed anxious about her poses, or even thanked me, except for that one smile.

I finished developing the negatives, made some prints, glanced at them, decided they weren't a great deal worse than Miss Leon. On an impulse I slipped them in with the pictures I was going to take on the rounds next morning.

By now I'd worked long enough, so I was a bit fagged and nervous but I didn't dare waste enough money on liquor to help that. I wasn't very hungry. I think I went to a cheap movie.

I didn't think of the Girl at all, except maybe to wonder faintly why in my present womanless state I hadn't made a pass at her. She had seemed to belong to a—well, distinctly more approachable social strata than Miss Leon. But then, of course, there were all sorts of arguable reasons for my not doing that.

Next morning I made the rounds. My first step was Munsch's Brewery. They were looking for a "Munsch Girl." Papa Munsch had a sort of affection for me, though he razzed my photography. He had good natural judgment about that, too. Fifty years ago he might have been one of the shoestring boys who made Hollywood.

Right now he was out in the plant, pursuing his favorite occupation. He put down the beaded schooner, smacked his lips, gabbled something technical to someone about hops, wiped his fat hands on the big apron he was wearing, and grabbed my thin stack of pictures.

He was about hallway through, making noises with his tongue and teeth, when he came to her. I kicked myself for even having stuck her in.

"That's her," he said. "The photography's not so hot, but that's the girl."

It was all decided. I wonder now why Papa Munsch sensed what the Girl had right away, while I didn't. I think it was because I saw her first in the flesh, if that's the right word.

At the time I just felt faint.

"Who is she?" he asked.

"One of my new models." I tried to make it casual.

"Bring her out tomorrow morning," he told me. "And your stuff. We'll photograph her here."

"Here, don't look so sick," he added. "Have some beer."

Well, I went away telling myself it was just a fluke, so that she'd probably blow it tomorrow with her inexperience, and so on.

Just the same, when I reverently laid my next stack of pictures on Mr. Fitch, of Lovelybelt's, rose-colored blotter, I had hers on top.

Mr. Fitch went through the motions of being an art critic. He leaned over backward, squinted his eyes, waved his long fingers, and said, "Hmm. What do you think, Miss Willow? Here, in this light, of course, the photograph doesn't show the bias cut. And perhaps we should use the Lovelybelt Imp instead of the Angel, Still, the girl ... Come over here, Binns." More finger-waving. "I want a married man's reaction."

He couldn't hide the fact that he was hooked.

Exactly the same thing happened at Budford's Pool and Playground, except that Da Costa didn't need a married man's say-so.

"Hot stuff,' he said, sucking his lips. "Oh boy, you photographers!"

I hotfooted it back to the office and grabbed up the card I'd given her to put down her name and address.

It was blank.

I don't mind telling you that the next five days were about the worst I ever went through, in an ordinary way. When next morning rolled around and I still hadn't got hold of her, I had to start stalling.

"She's sick," I told Papa Munsch over the phone.

"She at a hospital?" he asked me.

"Nothing that serious," I told him.

"Get her out here then. What's a little headache?"

"Sorry, I can't."

Papa Munsch got suspicious. "You really got this girl?"

"Of course I have."

"Well, I don't know. I'd think it was some New York model, except I recognized your lousy photography."

I laughed.

"Well, look, you get her here tomorrow morning, you hear?"

"I'll try."

"Try nothing. You get her out here."

He didn't know half of what I tried. I went around to all the model and employment agencies. I did some slick detective work at the photographic and art studios. I used up some of my last dimes putting advertisements in all three papers. I looked at high school yearbooks and at employee photos in local house organs. I went to restaurants and drugstores, looking at waitresses, and to dime stores and department stores, looking at clerks. I watched the crowds coming out of movie theaters. I roamed the streets.

Evenings, I spent quite a bit of time along Pickup Row. Somehow that seemed the right place.

The fifth afternoon I knew I was licked. Papa Munsch's deadline—he'd given me several, but this was it—was due to run out at six o'clock. Mr. Fitch had already canceled.

I was at the studio window, looking out at Ardleigh Park.

She walked in.

I'd gone over this moment so often in my mind that I had no trouble putting on my act. Even the faint dizzy feeling didn't throw me off.

"Hello," I said, hardly looking at her.

"Hello," she said.

"Not discouraged yet?"

"No." It didn't sound uneasy or defiant. It was just a statement.

I snapped a look at my watch, got up and said curtly, "Look here. I'm going to give you a chance,.There's a client of mine looking for a girl your general type. If you do a real good job you might break into the modeling business."

"We can see him this afternoon if we hurry," I said. I picked up my stuff. "Come on. And next time if you expect favors, don't forget to leave your phone number."

"Uh-uh," she said, not moving.

"What do you mean?" I said.

"I'm not going out to see any client of yours."

"The hell you aren't," I said. "You little nut, I'm giving you a break."

She shook her head slowly. "You're not fooling me, baby. You're not fooling me at all. They want me." And she gave me the second smile.

At the time I thought she must have seen my newspaper ad. Now I'm not so sure.

"And now I'll tell you how we're going to work," she went on. "You aren't going to have my name or address or phone number. Nobody is. And we're going to do all the pictures right here. Just you and me."

You can imagine the roar I raised at that. I was everything—angry, sarcastic, patiently explanatory, off my nut, threatening, pleading.

I would have slapped her face off, except it was photographic capital.

In the end all I could do was phone Papa Munsch and tell him her conditions. I knew I didn't have a chance, but I had to take it.

He gave me a really angry bawling out, said "no" several times and hung up.

It didn't worry her. "We'll start shooting at ten o'clock tomorrow," she said.

It was just like her, using that corny line from the movie magazines.

About midnight Papa Munsch called me up.

"I don't know what insane asylum you're renting this girl from," he said, "but I'll take her. Come around tomorrow morning and I'll try to get it through your head just how I want the pictures. And I'm glad I got you out of bed!"

After that it was a breeze. Even Mr. Fitch reconsidered and, after taking two days to tell me it was quite impossible, he accepted the conditions too.

Of course you're all under the spell of the Girl, so you can't understand how much self-sacrifice it represented on Mr. Fitch's part when he agreed to forego supervising the photography of my model in the Lovelybelt Imp or Vixen or whatever it was we finally used.

Next morning she turned up on time according to her schedule, and we went to work. I'll say one thing for her, she never got tired and she never kicked at the way I fussed over shots. I got along okay, except I still had that feeling of something being shoved away gently. Maybe you've felt it just a little, looking at her picture.

When we finished I found out there were still more rules. It was about the middle of the afternoon. I started with her to get a sandwich and coffee.

"Uh-uh," she said, "I'm going down alone. And look, baby, if you ever try to follow me, if you ever so much as stick your head out of that window when I go, you can hire yourself another model."

You can imagine how all this crazy stuff strained my temper—and my imagination. I remember opening the window after she was gone—I waited a few minutes first—and standing there getting some fresh air and trying to figure out what could be behind it, whether she was hiding from the police, or was somebody's ruined daughter, or maybe had got the idea it was smart to be temperamental, or more likely Papa Munsch was right and she was partly nuts.

But I had my pictures to finish up.

Looking back, it's amazing to think how fast her magic began to take hold of the city after that. Remembering what came after, I'm frightened of what's happening to the whole country—and maybe the world. Yesterday I read something in *Time* about the Girl's picture turning up on billboards in Egypt.

The rest of my story will help show you why I'm frightened in that big, general way. But I have a theory, too, that helps explain, though it's one of those things that's beyond that "certain point." It's about the Girl. I'll give it to you in a few words.

You know how modern advertising gets everybody's mind set in the same direction, wanting the same things, imagining the same things. And you know the psychologists aren't so skeptical of telepathy as they used to be.

Add up the two ideas. Suppose the identical desires of millions of people focused on one telepathic person. Say a girl. Shaped her in their image.

Imagine her knowing the hiddenmost hungers of millions of men. Imagine her seeing deeper into those hungers than the people that had them, seeing the hatred and the wish for death behind the lust. Imagine her shaping herself in that complete image, keeping herself as aloof as marble. Yet imagine the hunger she might feel in answer to their hunger.

But that's getting a long way from the facts of my story. And some of those facts are darn solid. Like money. We made money.

That was the funny thing I was going to tell you. I was afraid the Girl was going to hold me up. She really had me over a barrel, you know.

But she didn't ask for anything but the regular rates. Later on I insisted on pushing more money at her, a whole lot. But she always took it with that same contemptuous look, as if she were going to toss it down the first drain when she got outside.

Maybe she did.

At any rate, I had money. For the first time in months I had money enough to get drunk, buy new clothes, take taxicabs. I could make a play for any girl I wanted to. I only had to pick.

And so of course I had to go and pick …

But first let me tell you about Papa Munsch.

Papa Munsch wasn't the first of the boys to try to meet my model but I think he was the first to really go soft on her. I could watch the change in his eyes as he looked at her pictures. They began to get sentimental, reverent. Mama Munsch had been dead for two years.

He was smart about the way he planned it. Me got me to drop some information which told him when she came to work, and then one morning he came pounding up the stairs a few minute before.

"I've got to see her, Dave," he told me.

I argued with him, I kidded him, I explained he didn't know just how serious she was about her crazy ideas. I even pointed out he was cutting both our throats. I even amazed myself by bawling him out.

He didn't take any of it in his usual way. He just kept repeating, "But, Dave, I've got to see her."

The street door slammed.

"That's her," I said, lowering my voice. "You've got to get out."

He wouldn't, so I shoved him in the darkroom, "And keep quiet," I whispered. "I'll tell her I can't work today."

I knew he'd try to look at her and probably come busting in, but there wasn't anything else I could do.

The footsteps came to the fourth floor. But she never showed at the door. I got uneasy.

"Get that bum out of there!" she yelled suddenly from beyond the door. Not very loud, but in her commonest voice.

"I'm going up to the next landing," she said. "And if that fat-bellied bum doesn't march straight down to the street, he'll never get another picture of me except spitting in his lousy beer."

Papa Munsch came out of the darkroom. He was white. He didn't look at me as he went out. He never looked at her pictures in front of me again.

That was Papa Munsch. Now it's me I'm telling about. I talked around the subject with her, I hinted, eventually I made my pass.

She lifted my hand off her as if it were a damp rag.

"No, baby," she said. "This is working time."

"But afterward …" I pressed.

"The rules still hold." And I got what I think was the fifth smile.

It's hard to believe, but she never budged an inch from that crazy line. I mustn't make a pass at her in the office, because our work was very important and she loved it and there mustn't be any distractions. And I couldn't see her anywhere else, because if I tried to, I'd never snap another picture of her—and all this with more money coming in all the time and me never so stupid as to think my photography had anything to do with it.

Of course I wouldn't have been human if I hadn't made more passes. But they always got the wet-rag treatment and there weren't any more smiles.

I changed. I went sort of crazy .and light-headed—only sometimes I felt my head was going to burst. And I started to talk to her all the time. About myself.

It was like being in a constant delirium that never interfered with business. I didn't pay any attention to the dizzy feeling. It seemed natural.

I'd walk around and for a moment the reflector would look like a sheet of white-hot steel, or the shadows would seem like armies of moths, or the camera would be a big black coal car. But the next instant they'd come all right again.

I think sometimes I was scared to death of her. She'd seem the strangest, most horrible person in the world. But other times. …

And I talked. It didn't matter what I was doing—lighting her, posing her, fussing with props, snapping my pictures—or where she was—on the platform, behind the screen, relaxing with a magazine—I kept up a steady gab.

I told her everything I knew about myself. I told her about my first girl. I told her about my brother Bob's bicycle. I told her about running away on a freight, and the licking Pa gave me when I came home. I told her about shipping to South America and the blue sky at night. I told her about Betty. I told her about my mother dying of cancer. I told her about being beaten up in a fight in an alley behind a bar. I told her about Mildred. I told her about the first picture I ever sold. I told her how Chicago looked from a sailboat. I told her about the longest drunk I was ever on. I told her about Marsh-Mason.

I told her about Gwen. I told her about how I met Papa Munsch. I told her about hunting her. I told her about how I felt now.

She never paid the slightest attention to what I said. I couldn't even tell if she heard me.

It was when we were getting our first nibble from national advertisers that I decided to follow her when she went home.

Wait, I can place it better than that. Something you'll remember from the out-of-town papers—those maybe murders I mentioned. I think there were six.

I say "maybe" because the police could never be sure they weren't heart attacks. But there's bound to be suspicion when attacks happen to people whose hearts have been okay, and always at night when they're alone and away from home and there's a question of what they were doing.

The six deaths created one of those "mystery poisoner" scares. And afterward there was a feeling that they hadn't really stopped, but were being continued in a less suspicious way.

That's one of the things that scares me now.

But at that time my only feeling was relief that I'd decided to follow her.

I made her work until dark one afternoon. I didn't need any excuses, we were snowed under with orders. I waited until the street door slammed, then I ran down. I was wearing rubber-soled shoes. I'd slipped on a dark coat she'd never seen me in, and a dark hat.

I stood in the doorway until I spotted her. She was walking by Ardleigh Park toward the heart of town. It was one of those warm fall nights. I followed her on the other side of the street. My idea for tonight was just to find out where she lived. That would give me a hold on her.

She stopped in front of a display window of Everley's department store, standing back from the flow. She stood there looking in.

I remembered we'd done a big photograph of her for Everley's, to make a flat model for a lingerie display. That was what she was looking at.

At the time it seemed all right to me that she should adore herself, if that was what she was doing.

When people passed she'd turn away a little or drift back farther into the shadows.

Then a man came by alone. I couldn't see his face very well, but he looked middle-aged. He stopped and stood looking in the window.

She came out of the shadows and stepped up beside him.

How would you boys feel if you were looking at a poster of the Girl and suddenly she was there beside you, her arm linked with yours?

This fellow's reaction showed plain as day. A crazy dream had come to life for him.

They talked for a moment. Then he waved a taxi to the curb. They got in and drove off.

I got drunk that night. It was almost as if she'd known I was following her and had picked that way to hurt me. Maybe she had. Maybe this was the finish.

But the next morning she turned up at the usual time and I was back in the delirium, only now with some new angles added.

That night when I followed her she picked a spot under a streetlight, opposite one of the Munsch Girl billboards.

Now it frightens me to think of her lurking that way.

After about twenty minutes a convertible slowed down going past her, backed up, swung into the curb.

I was closer this time. I got a good look at the fellow's face. He was a little younger, about my age.

Next morning the same face looked up at me from the front page of the paper. The convertible had been found parked on a side street. He had been in it. As in the other maybe-murders, the cause of death was uncertain.

All kinds of thoughts were spinning in my head that day, but there were only two things I knew for sure. That I'd got the first real offer from a national advertiser, and that I was going to take the Girl's arm and walk down the stairs with her when we quit work.

She didn't seem surprised. "You know what you're doing?" she said.

"I know."

She smiled. "I was wondering when you'd get around to it."

I began to feel good. I was kissing everything good-bye, but I had my arm around hers.

It was another of those warm fall evenings. We cut across into Ardleigh Park. It was dark there, but all around the sky was a sallow pink from the advertising signs.

We walked for a long time in the park. She didn't say anything and she didn't look at me, but I could see her lips twitching and after a while her hand tightened on my arm.

We stopped. We'd been walking across the grass. She dropped down and pulled me after her. She put her hands on my shoulders. I was looking down at her face. It was the faintest sallow pink from the glow in the sky. The hungry eyes were dark smudges.

I was fumbling with her blouse. She took my hand away, not like she had in the studio. "I don't want that," she said.

First I'll tell you what I did afterward. Then I'll tell you why I did it. Then I'll tell you what she said.

What I did was run away. I don't remember all of that because I was dizzy, and the pink sky was swinging against the dark trees. But after a while I staggered into the lights of the street. The next day I closed up the studio. The telephone was ringing when I locked the door and there were unopened letters on the floor. I never saw the Girl again in the flesh, if that's the right word.

I did it because I didn't want to die. I didn't want the life drawn out of me. There are vampires and vampires, and the ones that suck blood aren't the worst. If it hadn't been for the warning of those dizzy flashes, and Papa Munsch and the face in the morning paper, I'd have gone the way the others did. But I realized what I was up against while there was still time to tear myself away. I realized that wherever she came from, whatever shaped her, she's the quintessence of the horror behind the bright billboard. She's the smile that tricks you into throwing away your money and your life. She's the eyes that lead you on and on, and then show you death. She's the creature you give everything for and never really get. She's the being that takes everything you've got and gives nothing in return. When you yearn toward her face on the billboards, remember that. She's the lure. She's the bait. She's the Girl.

And this is what she said, "I want you. I want your high spots. I want everything that's made you happy and everything that's hurt you bad. I want your first girl. I want that shiny bicycle. I want that licking. I want that pinhole camera. I want Betty's legs. I want the blue sky filled with stars. I want your mother's death. I want your blood on the cobblestones. I want Mildred's mouth. I want the first picture you sold. I want the lights of Chicago. I want the gin. I want Gwen's hands. I want your wanting me. I want your life. Feed me, baby, feed me."

Love-Starved (1979)

Charles L. Grant

CHARLES L. GRANT (born 1942) is one of the foremost authors of dark fantasy in America today. A resident of New Jersey for most of his life, Grant concentrates on small-town America and the lives of fairly ordinary people, lives that become something other than ordinary when normality suddenly disappears.

Grant's residence in Connecticut while he attended Trinity College resulted in a memorable series of novels, written in Grant's personal style of "quiet" horror, about the fictional New England town of Oxrun Station. His other novels include *The Nestling* (1982), *Night Songs* (1984), *The Tea Party* (1985), and *The Pet* (1986).

Grant won his earliest reputation with his short stories, of which he has published more than a hundred. Some of his best are collected in Tales from the Nightside (1981).

Vampires are the center of attention in "The Soft Whisper of the Dead" (1982), a very traditional vampire tale told in the style of the nineteenth century. But Grant's usual method, especially in his short stories, is to employ the devices of dark fantasy to explore the inner recesses of the human mind. That is what he does in "Love-Starved," which was first published in *The Magazine of Fantasy and Science Fiction* in August 1979.

You REALLY THINK I'M that different, do you?

Oh, I know you meant it as a compliment, don't worry. But seeing as how we've known each other for so long now, I'll give you your due, and a warning at the same time that you won't believe a word of it. And I won't mind if you laugh, or raise an eyebrow or two. As a matter of fact, I'll be disappointed if you don't. I'm a fair man, I think, and you really should know what you're getting yourself into.

No, of course I'm not trying to break tomorrow's engagement.

But as I said: I'm a fair man.

Can't you see it in my eyes?

So. Where should I begin? With a woman, I suppose, though I hope you won't be jealous. It's all very pertinent. Believe me, it is.

What it comes down to, I think, is that I remember Alicia Chou, not because of the experience we shared, but because it was she who stopped me from even dreaming about marriage again. Or about love in the sense you would ordinarily consider it.

Unrequited passion? I hardly think so, though I've considered it, that's true. That sounds too much like a line from a grade B, 1940s film; though, if I were pressed, I would have to admit that in a grotesquely perverse way I may love her yet. Or part of me does, anyway. But that's the one thing I can't explain just now. I'm not even sure that I'll ever have the answer.

The attraction certainly wasn't her astonishing, almost exquisite beauty—I told you not to be jealous, be patient—though that too lingers, rather like *in* aftertaste uncommitted to being either sweet or sour. And if that sounds odd to say in this day and age, it's because she herself was a strange one, in a way only someone like myself can truly appreciate.

As of this moment, to be frank, I honestly cannot think of exactly what it was about her that affected me first, despite the apparent simplicity of the problem. But, then, perhaps I'm still too close to the situation after ten short years.

Tell you what. Let's turn this into a game of sorts. You order yourself another one of those pink things (none for me, thanks; perhaps later), and we'll pretend we're in one of those nineteenth-century country inns, whiling away the winter evenings scaring the hell out of each other with nonsensical ghost stories. I haven't much time, but I think I can give you a hint of what's happening—not that I expect that you'll take it. No one ever does. Which is odd, my dear, because it's not only happening to me.

If you'll remember, it was a remarkably short time before the photography studio had opened downtown was doing extremely well for its rather limited size. Over the first few

Charles L. Grant, "Love-Starved," *The Magazine of Fantasy and Science Fiction*. Copyright © 1979 by The Estate of Charles L. Grant. Reprinted with permission.

months I'd been commissioned to shoot cover material for just about every men's and general circulation magazine going; there were even a few location trips to Europe thrown in to sweeten the lot. But when July came around, I felt myself going stale—my head was beginning to feel groggy in the same way you feel when you've just completed two or three final exams in a row. Every model was getting that same vapid, hurry-up-you-creep-these-lights-are-hot look. Every location was flat and uninviting. I dreaded going to work, dreaded even waking up in the morning. And naturally, all this eventually surfaced in the final product. I had obviously been pushing too hard, too fast, trying to make a few bucks and a name.

Finally, when the very thought of sticking my eye anywhere near a lens made me want to gag, I said the hell with it, and I left. Oh, a few clients squealed and wrung their hot little hands; a few editors growled at me over the phone; but when I told them all in the plainest, nonadvertising language what they could do with their precious campaigns and covers, all they did was purse their lips and shake their heads and tell me I needed a vacation.

So I took one. As simple as that.

I packed a bag and fled the city without looking back. It had been some time since I'd bothered driving with the top down, and the wind cresting over the windshield felt absolutely great. Just cool enough to take the sting out of the hot sun, and strong enough to make me feel glad I still had all my hair. Everything, then, and every miserable working day was blown so far away I had to think to remember what I did for a living. Knowing me as you do, you're not going to believe this, but I was even singing out loud at the top of my voice and thinking I should have practiced for the Met.

Whim chose my direction, and I paid little attention to the odometer, gladly patching a tire or two myself simply because there was no appointment I had to make by two o'clock or we'll cancel the contract and find someone else more reliable, thank you. God, but that was a magnificent feeling! On the second morning out, in fact, I'd stuffed my watch into the glove compartment and didn't put it on again for three days. It's almost supernatural, the freedom one feels when you don't turn your wrist every ten minutes to see that ten minutes have passed since the last time you looked. Incredible. And wonderful.

But then, by hook, crook, or some other heavy-handed and cliché-scarred beck of Fate's temptation, I found myself missing a few familiar comforts and ended up back in the Cape Cod I'd bought over there on Hawthorne Street, right on the river above the bend. I guess I had it in the back of my mind all along, in spite of the fact that my conscious plan was just to keep driving until I'd refueled, you should pardon the pun. I'd picked it up already furnished, but I'd never had a chance to really enjoy the overstuffed chairs and the dusty bookcases, the stereo, the TV, and God knew what else; I'd seldom stayed there more than just to sleep, and sometimes not that, if you know what I mean. But now ... Lord, I could roam through the cool and quiet, let that old place soak out of my system everything the drive in the country hadn't banished. I turned myself into the absolute sloth, and I loved it, every minute, even fell in love with the shadows in the house.

And though I wasn't used to taking things easy, I had no problem at all falling into the slow, casual tempo of summer neighborhood life. Early evening walks really *seeing* the place where I'd chosen to live, scuffing leaves in the park and listening to bandstand music after a leisurely cooked dinner, once even stringing a hammock between two trees in the yard and humming in time to the river that marked the end of my lot.

It was ... beautiful, because, for I don't know how many champagne days, I was actually seeing things through my own eyes instead of a camera's, and I was totally convinced I couldn't have been happier.

Then, one afternoon, I was baking in a sauce of suntan oil on a small section of riverbank set aside as a beach. I spent a lot of good time watching the kids splashing around, dunking each other and really getting frustrated learning to swim in the river's moderate currents. For a while there I really got involved rooting for one little guy who was experimenting holding his breath and trying not to drown at the same time. I was timing him by counting thousands and making bets with myself, when this indescribable pair of legs blocked my view.

Now I know that some men are devotees of the decolletage, and others are—as one of my girls once put it—admirers of ass; but I prefer those anatomical delights that carry the rest of the woman around. It has always been my solemn creed that bust or buttock, nose or navel, aren't anything at all without a fine pair of legs to support them. Not that this woman didn't have the appropriate accessories, mind you … but Lord, those legs! All the Troys in history would have gladly fallen for them, would have definitely been singed by the rest of her. Curiously, she was wearing a one-piece bathing suit that would have aroused attention on any beach simply because it was so out of place it was quaint. Black, too, her hair, curled inward slightly at the ends and cut to a point between her shoulders.

I lay there quietly, waiting for her to turn around, and paradoxically hoping that she would stay facing the water.

But she turned, abruptly, and looked straight into my eyes.

(As I do now, so I can see you're not jealous.)

Disconcerted though I was, her stare wasn't at all unfriendly. She was Eurasian: so temptingly French (perhaps), so tantalizingly Oriental (perhaps), that a dozen years' concentration couldn't have discovered where one began and the other left off.

When I sat up, she knelt directly in front of me and smiled, her deep tan looking darker in the shadow of her lips. I felt a bit fuzzy, as if I'd had too much sun and beer, but I managed a weak grin in return. Obviously, I wasn't at the top of my form.

"I'm sorry," I said, thinking all the while how brilliant that sounded and how stupidly seventeenish I was feeling.

"For what?" She laughed clear into eyes perfectly framed by black bangs.

"You got me. For staring at you, I guess. It's not exactly the most polite form of introduction."

She laughed again, tossing her head from side to side, and damned if I didn't feel shocked—at myself. Right at that moment I wanted to rape that animal—there's no other word—kneeling so primly not a hand's breadth from my feet. I know you know me well enough to understand that I'm not one to get upset over an occasional erotic impulse; but the sheer force of that woman had to be felt to be believed.

And while I was smothering in this sense-overload trance, she covered her mouth with silver-painted nails and swung around on her heels until she was resting on the grass beside me. Which is how we spent the rest of the afternoon. Seduction without words.

Except…most of the time I tried to stay just a few inches behind her. To avoid her eyes.

Alicia Chou. Eyes brown-black, with a single gold fleck in each, just off-center.

And when I finally introduced myself, she said, "Carroll is an odd name for a man, isn't it?" Her voice was less a purr than a growl lurking beneath thin velvet. "Your father must have been a very handsome man."

The touch of her hand on my knee, thigh, shoulder—the gentle way she brushed my back was colder than the lotion she rubbed absently into my skin.

Cobra and mouse.

Once, she kissed the back of my neck, and I nearly grabbed a mirror from a passing woman to see if I'd been branded.

Everyone smiled at us. The adults at me, the children at her. What a handsome couple, I knew they were thinking.

It was only natural, then, that I asked her to dinner.

She wouldn't tell me where she was staying—a wise precaution for a woman alone—but promised to meet me at my place at seven. We parted and I ran—you're laughing, but I did—I ran home and stood in front of the bedroom mirror, thinking that all that had happened was far too good to be even remotely true. I scowled at my reflection: too much hair for a smallish head, eyes too blue, nose too long and too sharp, ears too close to my head. No leading man, that was for certain, and thus no physical reason why Alicia should clasp me so suddenly to her not insubstantial bosom. I laughed aloud.

By God, Carroll, I said to myself, you've been picked up! You've actually been picked up. By a raving nymphomaniac, a psychotic murderess ... I couldn't have cared less. She was elegantly available and I was on vacation.

What I hadn't planned on, of course, was falling in love.

And that is the wrong place to laugh, my dear. It was marvelous, right out of Hollywood, magnificent ... and terrifying.

If I'd listened to myself then, I wouldn't be telling you this now.

So she came, and we drove to a riverbank restaurant in a hotel in the next town. Dined and danced and stood on the balcony that faced the water. I kissed her cheek, felt giddy with the wine, kissed her lips ... and when it was over I was drained, so drained that I had to lean against the marble railing to keep from collapsing.

For one second, hardly worth mentioning then, I hated her.

Then it was over and we headed back to my home. There had been no innuendo conversation. The slight turn of her mouth, the graceful flow of her hands spoke for her. She never asked about my job, family, income or tailor. I myself had been too stunned by what I'd thought was instant love to mumble even a hello and you look wonderful and why don't we dance.

I never felt the pain that lanced my will.

Neither do I remember the drive back to the house, the opening of the door, the walk upstairs. I couldn't help but feel as if the world had wound down to slow motion, so languid her movements, in careful the display of her smile and her charm.

She sat on the edge of the bed and gestured toward the chair I kept by the nightstand. "Drink?"

Why not, I thought. Get bombed, Carroll, and let's get on with whoever is raping who.

"Of course," I said, mixed what she asked and finally, at last, she let me sit down.

We toasted each other, and I loved her again.

Then her gaze narrowed over the top of the champagne glass, and I realized with a start how I had spent most of the afternoon avoiding those eyes, all the evening losing myself in them. But when, as an experiment in masculine control, I tried to break away, I couldn't. And my palms became unaccountably moist.

"Carroll is a strange name," she said.

"You've already said that once, Alicia," I said, grinning stupidly. "It was my dear departed mother's idea, not knowing what she would have at the time and not feeling like coming up with two sets for the sexes."

"I love you, strange name," she whispered. Not a word out of place, not a change in tone. Something broke briefly through the sparkling cloud I felt over me, but I couldn't put a name to it and so shrugged it away.

Instead, I emptied the glass and set it on the floor beside me. Cleared my throat and said, "This is going to sound ... well, it's going to sound ridiculous, under the circumstances, Alicia—but, damnit, I think I love you, too." It was all so bloody serious, so intolerably solemn that I wanted to laugh. But I couldn't; I was too nervous. Not of breaking the spell that nights and champagne and mysterious women weave, but of her and those eyes with their single flecks of gold.

"For how long, strange name?"

"Shouldn't that be obvious? Forever. How else?"

It was she who laughed then. Deeply. In her throat. And as she did, I became inexplicably angry. Didn't she know, I demanded of myself, that in thirty-four goddamned years on this road I had said that only once before when I'd meant it—to a cheerleader in high school. Who had also laughed, but loudly and shrilly, with her head thrown back and her eyes rolled heavenward to total disbelief.

"Strange name, love me," Alicia said.

I hesitated. I stalled. Her request became a demand.

And I did, and am now regrettably forced to resort to the old purple-prose lines of jungle passions and animal ferocity. But that, I'm afraid, is exactly the way it was. Stripped, perspiring even before we began, stalking each other without benefit of cinematic loveplay, manual directions of foreplay and stimulation. Sheets and blankets were literally torn, glasses were shattered, bottles smashed ... again and again and again ... and again.

"Love me," she hissed.

And I did. Bleeding, drawing blood, bruised and bruising ... again and again.

"More," she crooned.

I did. God, I did.

Dawn, and I did not see it. Dusk, and I could not see it. Crying, laughing—a haze of cigarette smoke, a waste basket gushing uneaten meals one of us made downstairs in the kitchen.

It must have been her. I couldn't have moved.

We stood by the window in caftan robes and watched the river pass a beautifully bright day beneath us, beneath the willows. It was peaceful and wonderful; I held her gently against my chest and told her so, whispering in her ear all the idiot lovephrases that men think original when the loving is done.

"Then love me," she whispered back.

The radio played Brahms and Vaughan Williams. Nothing louder for this room, on this day, at this time.

"Love me," she sang.

I told her how, when I was in college up there in Hartford, I had exhausted myself during one summer vacation visiting ten European cities in less than sixteen days. I must have been drunk when I said it, I don't remember now, but I suddenly turned mawkish and sentimental, muttering "Those were the good old days" over and over again and praising their lack of tears and responsibility and extolling my love for them in dreams and bursts of unbidden nostalgia. I told her about an Irish setter I once had, how he could never go with us on vacation because he always got carsick and had to stay at the vet's. About the cheerleader. About the models. About the slices of my soul that went into my work.

"Love me," she comforted.

Everything is relative, said the speeding turtle to the snail. There must have been Time someplace, but two days were gone before I first began to think that I was losing my mind.

Alicia was sleeping at my side, peacefully, evenly. My mouth was burlap, my head cement, and, God, dear God, how everything ached! For one nauseating moment I thought of a morning a couple years back when I'd eaten tainted food in a Boston fast-food joint and they used a fool stomach pump while I was semi-conscious. I groaned and pushed myself up on my elbows, looking for a mirror to see if in fact I was really turning into an airless balloon; but a pain I knew instantly was frighteningly abnormal flattened me like a hammer, and I had to gasp for a breath. Beyond that, however, I felt ... nothing. I registered the room and what I could see through the window, but there was nothing left inside me to hang the pictures on.

That, I think, is when the terror began. As if I were suffering a malaria attack, I simultaneously grew cold and soaked the sheets with a bath of perspiration that made me tremble. And I grew still more terrified when I tried to cry out with that slow-growing pain, and my mind said there was no reason, and my mouth made no sound.

I fell asleep then, unwillingly, and I dreamt as I do now—in black and greys and splashes of sterile white. And once, in that dream, I heard someone mention food, and I heaved dryly for ten minutes before I could fall asleep again.

The last thing I recall seeing was a floating, broken camera.

I woke once more. I think it was daylight. I really don't know because Alicia was bending over me, her lips parted and smiling.

"Can you love me, strange name?" she asked, carelessly tracing a meaningless pattern from my chest to my stomach to my groin and back.

"My God, Alicia!"

"Can you love?" she insisted.

"My God, no!'

She pouted through a smile that told me she knew better.

"Alicia, please."

"You don't love me anymore."

A fleeting array of artfully shadowed images: of Alicia in her gown, the swimsuit, the robe, her nakedness atavistic in the arousal it produced, all made me smile lazily until I turned my head ... and saw the look in her eyes.

And in that final moment before she smiled again, I knew at last what I'd been trying to avoid: Alicia was still hungry, and she kissed me, hard, before I finally passed out.

So then. Before you tell me what you think, my dear, let me tell you what I think you've already decided. Let's see: maybe I'm simply crazy, right? Ah, too easy. Perhaps then it's a fantasy, cleverly manipulated to hide a disastrous affair. Or, better yet, perhaps I had become so drunk at dinner that I was physically incapable of playing the Don Juan in anything more than high-sounding words, thus striking myself low with assorted simple trauma.

I was right, wasn't I.

Well, it all sounds very intelligent, I admit; all very up-to-date and properly sophisticated. In fact, if I didn't have to hurry along right now you might even have convinced me, given enough time.

But I really must run, as I warned you at the start. And, for heaven's sakes, stop worrying about my health. I'll promise you now, if you like, that I'll dine without fail later this evening.

Ah, my darling, you *are* jealous, aren't you?

But you know me, first things first; so please don't worry, I won't forget. You see, there's this wonderfully attractive brunette named Claire who's dying to see the river from my bedroom. Look, why don't you have another drink on me, and I'll see you tomorrow. I've worked up a marvelous appetite talking with you, and Claire is waiting for me right this moment.

I think you'd like her. She's a wonderful girl. A great girl. She thinks the gold in my eyes is sexy.

She loves me. She really does.

But just so you'll know that I will keep my promise, lean over here and I'll give you a kiss.

One kiss.

That's all.

One kiss.

I'm hungry.

Man has conquered space before. You may be sure of that. Somewhere beyond the Egyptians, in that dimness out of which come echoes of half-mythical names—Atlantis, Mu—somewhere back of history's first beginnings there must have been an age when mankind, like us today, built cities of steel to house its star-roving ships and knew the names of the planets in their own native tongues—heard Venus' people call their wet world "Sha-ardol" in that soft, sweet, slurring speech and mimicked Mars' guttural "Lakkdiz" from the harsh tongues of Mars' dryland dwellers. You may be sure of it. Man has conquered Space before, and out of that conquest faint, faint echoes run still through a world that has forgotten the very fact of a civilization which must have been as mighty as our own. There have been too many myths and legends for us to doubt it. The myth of the Medusa, for instance, can never have had its roots in the soil of Earth. That tale of the snake-haired Gorgon whose gaze turned the gazer to stone never originated about any creature that Earth nourished. And those ancient Greeks who told the story must have remembered, dimly and half believing, a tale of antiquity about some strange being from one of the outlying planets their remotest ancestors once trod.

SHAMBLEAU! HA ... SHAMBLEAU!" The wild hysteria of the mob rocketed from wall to wall of Lakkdarol's narrow streets and the storming of heavy boots over the slag-red pavement made an ominous undernote to that swelling bay, "Shambleau! Shambleau!"

Northwest Smith heard it coming and stepped into the nearest doorway, laying a wary hand on his heat-gun's grip, and his colorless eyes narrowed. Strange sounds were common enough in the streets of Earth's latest colony on Mars—a raw, red little town where anything might happen, and very often did. But Northwest Smith, whose name is known and respected in every dive and wild outpost on a dozen wild planets, was a cautious man, despite his reputation. He set his back against the wall and gripped his pistol, and heard the rising shout come nearer and nearer.

Then into his range of vision flashed a red running figure, dodging like a hunted hare from shelter to shelter in the narrow street. It was a girl—a berry-brown girl in a single tattered garment whose scarlet burnt the eyes with its brilliance. She ran wearily, and he could hear her gasping breath from where he stood. As she came into view he saw her hesitate and lean one hand against the wall for support, and glance wildly around for shelter. She must not have seen him in the depths of the doorway, for as the bay of the mob grew louder and the pounding of feet sounded almost at the corner she gave a despairing little moan and dodged into the recess at his very side.

When she saw him standing there, tall and leather-brown, hand on his heat-gun, she sobbed once, inarticulately, and collapsed at his feet, a huddle of burning scarlet and bare, brown limbs.

Smith had not seen her face, but she was a girl, and sweetly made and in danger; and though he had not the reputation of a chivalrous man, something in her hopeless huddle at his feet touched that chord of sympathy for the underdog that stirs in every Earthman, and he pushed her gently into the corner behind him and jerked out his gun, just as the first of the running mob rounded the corner.

It was a motley crowd, Earthmen and Martians and a sprinkling of Venusian swampmen and strange, nameless denizens of unnamed planets—a typical Lakkdarol mob. When the first of them turned the corner and saw the empty street before them there was a faltering in the rush and the foremost spread out and began to search the doorways on both sides of the street.

"Looking for something?" Smith's sardonic call sounded clever above the clamor of the mob.

They turned. The shouting died for a moment as the took in the scene before them—tall Earthman in the space-explorer's leathern garb,

C. L. Moore, "Shambleau," *Shambleau and Others*. Copyright © 1953 by the Estate of C. L. Moore.

all one color from the burning of savage suns save for the sinister pallor of his no-colored eyes in a scarred and resolute face, gun in his steady hand and the scarlet girl crouched behind him, panting.

The foremost of the crowd—a burly Earthman in tattered leather from which the Patrol insignia had been ripped away—stared for a moment with a strange expression of incredulity on his face overspreading the savage exultation of the chase. Then he let loose a deep-throated bellow, "Shambleau!" and lunged forward. Behind him the mob took up the cry again, "Shambleau! Shambleau! Shambleau!" and surged after.

Smith lounging negligently against the wall, arms folded and gun-hand draped over his left forearm, looked incapable of swift motion, but at the leader's first forward step the pistol swept in a practiced half-circle and the dazzle of blue-white heat leaping from its muzzle seared an arc in the slag pavement at his feet. It was an old gesture, and not a man in the crowd but understood it. The foremost recoiled swiftly against the surge of those in the rear, and for a moment there was confusion as the two tides met and struggled. Smith's mouth curled into a grim curve as he watched. The man in the mutilated Patrol uniform lifted a threatening fist and stepped to the very edge of the deadline, while the crowd rocked to and fro behind him.

"Are you crossing that line?" queried Smith in an ominously gentle voice.

"We want that girl!"

"Come and get her!" Recklessly Smith grinned into his face. He saw danger there, but his defiance was not the foolhardy gesture it seemed. An expert psychologist of mobs from long experience, he sensed no murder here. Not a gun had appeared in any hand in the crowd. They desired the girl with an inexplicable bloodthirstiness he was at a loss to understand, but toward himself he sensed no such fury. A mauling he might expect, but his life was in no danger. Guns would have appeared before now if they were coming out at all. So he grinned in the man's angry face and leaned lazily against the wall.

Behind their self-appointed leader the crowd milled impatiently, and threatening voices began to rise again. Smith heard the girl moan at his feet.

"What do you want with her?" he demanded.

"She's Shambleau! Shambleau, you fool! Kick her out of there—we'll take care of her!"

"I'm taking care of her," drawled Smith.

"She's Shambleau, I tell you! Damn your hide, man, we never let those things live! Kick her out here!"

The repeated name had no meaning to him, but Smith's innate stubbornness rose defiantly as the crowd surged forward to the very edge of the arc, their clamor growing louder. "Shambleau! Kick her out here! Give us Shambleau! Shambleau!"

Smith dropped his indolent pose like a cloak and planted both feet wide, swinging up his gun threateningly. "Keep back!" he yelled. "She's mine! Keep back!"

He had no intention of using that heat-beam. He knew by now that they would not kill him unless he started the gunplay himself, and he did not mean to give up his life for any girl alive. But a severe mauling he expected, and he braced himself instinctively as the mob heaved within itself.

To his astonishment a thing happened then that he had never known to happen before. At his shouted defiance the foremost of the mob—those who had heard him clearly—drew back a little, not in alarm but evidently surprised. The ex-Patrolman said, "Yours! She's *yours*?" in a voice from which puzzlement crowded out the anger.

Smith spread his booted legs wide before the crouching figure and flourished his gun.

"Yes," he said. "And I'm keeping her! Stand back there!"

The man stared at him wordlessly, and horror, disgust and incredulity mingled on his weather-beaten face. The incredulity triumphed for a moment and he said again,

"*Yours!*"

Smith nodded defiance.

The man stepped back suddenly, unutterable contempt in his very pose. He waved an arm to the crowd and said loudly, "It's—his!" and the press melted away, gone silent, too, and the look of contempt spread from face to face.

The ex-Patrolman spat on the slag-paved street and turned his back indifferently. "Keep her, then," he advised briefly over one shoulder. "But don't let her out again in this town!"

Smith stared in perplexity almost open-mouthed as the suddenly scornful mob began to break up. His mind was in a whirl. That such bloodthirsty animosity should vanish in a breath he could not believe. And the curious mingling of contempt and disgust on the faces he saw baffled him even more. Lakkdarol was anything but a puritan town—it did not enter his head for a moment that his claiming the brown girl as his own had caused that strangely shocked revulsion to spread through the crowd. No, it was something more deeply-rooted than that. Instinctive, instant disgust had been in the faces he saw—they would have looked less so if he had admitted cannibalism or *Pharol*-worship.

And they were leaving his vicinity as swiftly as if whatever unknowing sin he had committed were contagious. The street was emptying as rapidly as it had filled. He saw a sleek Venusian glance back over his shoulder as he turned the corner and sneer, "Shambleau!" and the word awoke a new line of speculation in Smith's mind. Shambleau! Vaguely of French origin, it must be. And strange enough to hear it from the lip of Venusians and Martian drylanders, but it was their use of it that puzzled him more. "We never let these things live," the ex-Patrolman had said. It reminded him dimly of something ... an ancient line from some writing in his own tongue ... "Thou shall not suffer a witch to live." He smiled to himself at the similarity, and simultaneously was aware of the girl at his elbow.

She had risen soundlessly. He turned to face her, sheathing his gun, and stared at first with curiosity and then in the entirely frank openness with which men regard that which is not wholly human. For she was not. He knew it at a glance, though the brown, sweet body was shaped like a woman's and she wore the garment of scarlet—he saw it was leather—with an ease that few unhuman beings achieve toward clothing. He knew it from the moment he looked into her eyes, and a shiver of unrest went over him as he met them. They were frankly green as young grass, with slit-like, feline pupils that pulsed unceasingly, and there was a look of dark, animal wisdom in their depths—that look of the beast which sees more than man.

There was no hair upon her face—neither brows nor lashes, and he would have sworn that the tight scarlet turban bound around her head covered baldness. She had three fingers and a thumb, and her feat had four digits apiece too, and all sixteen of them were tipped with round claws that sheathed back into the flesh like a cat's. She ran her tongue over her lips—a thin, pink, flat tongue as feline as her eyes—and spoke with difficulty. He felt that that throat and tongue had never been shaped for human speech.

"Not—afraid now," she said softly, and her little teeth were white and pointed as a kitten's.

"What did they want you for?" he asked her curiously. "What had you done? Shambleau ... is that your name?"

"I—not talk your—speech," she demurred hesitantly.

"Well, try to—I want to know. Why were they chasing you? Will you be safe on the street now, or hadn't you better get indoors somewhere? They looked dangerous."

"I—go with you." She brought it out with difficulty.

"Say you!" Smith grinned. "What are you, anyhow? You look like a kitten to me."

"Shambleau." She said it somberly.

"Where d'you live? Are you a Martian?"

"I come from—from far—from long ago—far country—"

"Wait!" laughed Smith. "You're getting your wires crossed. You're not a Martian?"

She drew herself up very straight beside him, lifting the turbaned head, and there was something queenly in the poise of her.

"Martian?" she said scornfully. "My people—are—are—you have no word. Your speech—hard for me."

"What's yours? I might know it—try me."

She lifted her head and met his eyes squarely, and there was in hers a subtle amusement—he could have sworn it.

"Some day I—speak to you in—my own language," she promised, and the pink tongue flicked out over her lips, swiftly, hungrily.

Approaching footsteps on the red pavement interrupted Smith's reply. A dryland Martian came past, reeling a little and exuding an aroma of *segir*-whisky, the Venusian brand. When he caught the red flash of the girl's tatters he turned his head sharply, and as his *segir*-steeped brain took in the fact of her presence he lurched toward the recess unsteadily, bawling, "Shambleau, by *Pharol*! Shambleau!" and reached out a clutching hand.

Smith struck it aside contemptuously.

"On your way, drylander," he advised.

The man drew back and stared, blear-eyed.

"Yours, eh?" he croaked. *"Zut!* You're welcome to it!" And like the ex-Patrolman before him he spat on the pavement and turned away, muttering harshly in the blasphemous tongue of the drylands.

Smith watched him shuffle off, and there was a crease between his colorless eyes, a nameless unease rising within him.

"Come on," he said abruptly to the girl. "If this sort of thing is going to happen we'd better get indoors. Where shall I take you?"

"With—you," she murmured.

He stared down into the flat green eyes. Those ceaselessly pulsing pupils disturbed him, but it seemed to him, vaguely, that behind the animal shallows of her gaze was a shutter—a closed barrier that might at any moment open to reveal the very deeps of that dark knowledge he sensed there.

Roughly he said again, "Come on, then," and stepped down into the street.

She pattered along a pace or two behind him, making no effort to keep up with his long strides, and though Smith—as men know from Venus to Jupiter's moons—walks as softly as a cat, even in spacemen's boots, the girl at his heels slid like a shadow over the rough pavement, making so little sound that even the lightness of his footsteps was loud in the empty street.

Smith chose the less frequented ways of Lakkdarol, and somewhat shamefacedly thanked his nameless gods that his lodgings were not far away, for the few pedestrians he met turned and stared after the two with that by now familiar mingling of horror and contempt which he was as far as ever from understanding.

The room he had engaged was a single cubicle in a lodging-house on the edge of the city. Lakkdarol, raw camp-town that it was in those days, could have furnished little better anywhere within its limits, and Smith's errand there was not one he wished to advertise. He had slept in worse places than this before, and knew that he would do so again.

There was no one in sight when he entered, and the girl slipped up the stairs at his heels and vanished through the door, shadowy, unseen by anyone in the house. Smith closed the door and leaned his broad shoulders against the panels, regarding her speculatively.

She took in what little the room had to offer in a glance—frowsy bed, rickety table, mirror hanging unevenly and cracked against the wall, unpainted chairs—a typical camp-town room in an Earth settlement abroad. She accepted its poverty in that single glance, dismissed it, then crossed to the window and leaned out for a moment, gazing across the low roof-tops toward the barren countryside beyond, red slag under the late afternoon sun.

"You can stay here," said Smith abruptly, "until I leave town. I'm waiting here for a friend to come in from Venus. Have you eaten?"

"Yes," said the girl quickly. "I shall—need no—food for—a while."

"Well—" Smith glanced around the room. "I'll be in sometime tonight. You can go or stay just as you please. Better lock the door behind me."

With no more formality than that he left her. The door closed and he heard the key turn, and smiled to himself. He did not expect, then, ever to see her again.

He went down the steps and out into the late-slanting sunlight with a mind so full of other matters that the brown girl receded very quickly into the background. Smith's errand in Lakkdarol, like most of his errands, is better not spoken of. Man lives as he must, and Smith's living was a perilous affair outside the law and ruled by the ray-gun only. It is enough to say that the shipping-port and its cargoes outbound interested him deeply just now, and that the friend he awaited was Yarol the Venusian, in that swift little Edsel ship the *Maid* that can flash from world to world with a derisive speed that laughs at Patrol boats and leaves pursuers floundering in the ether far behind. Smith and Yarol and the *Maid* were a trinity that had caused the Patrol leaders much worry and many gray hairs in the past, and the future looked very bright to Smith himself that evening as he left his lodging-house.

Lakkdarol roars by night, as Earthmen's camp-towns have a way of doing on every planet where Earth's outposts are, and it was beginning lustily as Smith went down among the awakening lights toward the center of town. His business there does not concern us. He mingled with the crowds where the lights were brightest, and there was the click of ivory counters and the jingle of silver, and red *segir* gurgled invitingly from black Venusian bottles, and much later Smith strolled homeward under the moving moons of Mars, and if the street wavered a little under his feet now and then—why, that is only understandable. Not even Smith could drink red *segir* at every bar from the *Martian Lamb* to the *New Chicago* and remain entirely steady on his feet. But he found his way back with very little difficulty—considering—and spent a good five minutes hunting for his key before he remembered he had left it in the inner lock for the girl.

He knocked then, and there was no sound of footsteps from within, but in a few moments the latch clicked and the door swung open. She retreated soundlessly before him as he entered, and took up her favorite place against the window, leaning back on the sill and outlined against the starry sky beyond. The room was in darkness.

Smith flipped the switch by the door and then leaned back against the panels, steadying himself. The cool night air had sobered him a little, and his head was clear enough—liquor went to Smith's feet, not his head, or he would never have come this far along the lawless way he had chosen. He lounged against the door now and regarded the girl in the sudden glare of the bulbs, blinded a little as much at the scarlet of her clothing as at the light.

"So you stayed," he said.

"I—waited," she answered softly, leaning farther back against the sill and clasping the rough wood with slim, three-fingered hands, pale brown against the darkness.

"Why?"

She did not answer that, but her mouth curved into a slow smile. On a woman it would have been reply enough—provocative, daring. On Shambleau there was something pitiful and horrible in it—so human on the face of one half-animal And yet ... that sweet brown body curving so softly from the tatters of scarlet leather—the velvety texture of that brownness—the white-flashing smile. ... Smith was aware of a stirring excitement within him. After all—time would be hanging heavy now until Yarol came. ... Speculatively he allowed the steel-pale eyes to wander over her, with a slow regard that missed nothing. And when he spoke he was aware that his voice had deepened a little. ...

"Come here," he said.

She came forward slowly, on bare clawed feet that made no sound on the floor, and stood before him with downcast eyes and mouth trembling in that pitifully human smile. He took her by the shoulders—velvety soft shoulders, of a creamy smoothness that was not the texture of human flesh. A little tremor went over her, perceptibly, at the contact of his hands. Northwest Smith caught his breath suddenly and dragged her to him ... sweet yielding brownness in the circle of his arms ... heard her own breath catch and quicken as her velvety arms closed about his neck. And then he was looking down into her face, very near, and the green animal eyes met his with the pulsing pupils and the flicker of—something—deep behind their shallows—and through the rising clamor of his blood, even as he stooped his lips to hers, Smith felt something deep within him shudder away—inexplicable, instinctive, revolted. What it might be he had no words to tell, but the very touch of her was suddenly loathsome—so soft and velvet and unhuman—and it might have been an animal's face that lifted itself to his mouth—the dark knowledge looked hungrily from the darkness of those slit pupils—and for a mad instant he knew that same wild, feverish revulsion he had seen in the faces of the mob. ...

"God!" he gasped, a far more ancient invocation against evil than he realized, then or ever, and he ripped her arms from his neck, swung her away with such a force that she reeled half across the room. Smith fell back against the door, breathing heavily, and stared at her while the wild revolt died slowly within him.

She had fallen to the floor beneath the window, and as she lay there against the wall with bent head he saw, curiously, that her turban had slipped—the turban that he had been so sure covered baldness—and a lock of scarlet hair fell below the binding leather, hair as scarlet as her garment, as unhumanly red as her eyes were unhumanly green. He stared, and shook his head dizzily and stared again, for it seemed to him that the thick lock of crimson had moved, *squirmed* of itself against her cheek.

At the contact of it her hands flew up and she tucked it away with a very human gesture and then dropped her head again into her hands. And from the deep shadow of her fingers he thought she was staring up at him covertly.

Smith drew a deep breath and passed a hand across his forehead. The inexplicable moment had gone as quickly as it came—too swiftly for him to understand or analyze it. "Got to lay off the *segir*," he told himself unsteadily. Had he imagined that scarlet hair? After all, she was no more than a pretty brown girl-creature from one of the many half-human races peopling the planets. No more than that, after all. A pretty little thing, but animal. ... He laughed a little shakily.

"No more of that," he said. "God knows I'm no angel, but there's got to be a limit somewhere. Here." He crossed to the bed and sorted out a pair of blankets from the untidy heap, tossing them to the far corner of the room. "You can sleep there."

Wordlessly she rose from the floor and began to rearrange the blankets, the uncomprehending resignation of the animal eloquent in every line of her.

Smith had a strange dream that night. He thought he had awakened to a room full of darkness and moonlight and moving shadows, for the nearer moon of Mars was racing through the sky and everything on the planet below her was endued with a restless life in the dark. And something ... some nameless, unthinkable *thing* ... was coiled about his throat ... something like a soft snake, wet and warm. It lay loose and light about his neck ... and it was moving gently, very gently, with a soft, caressive pressure that sent little thrills of delight through every nerve and fiber of him, a perilous delight—beyond physical pleasure, deeper than joy of the mind. That warm softness was caressing the very roots of his soul with a terrible intimacy. The ecstasy of it left him weak, and yet he knew—in a flash of knowledge born of this impossible dream—that the soul should not be handled. ... And with that knowledge a horror broke upon him, turning the pleasure into a rapture of revulsion, hateful, horrible—but still most foully sweet. He tried to lift his hands and tear the dream-monstrosity from his throat—tried but half-heartedly; for though his soul was revolted to its very deeps, yet the delight of his body was so great that his hands all but refused the attempt. But when at last he tried to lift his arms a cold shock went over him and he found that he could not stir ... his body lay stony as marble beneath the blankets, a living marble that shuddered with a dreadful delight through every rigid vein.

The revulsion grew strong upon him as he struggled against the paralyzing dream—a struggle of soul against sluggish body—titanically, until the moving dark was streaked with blankness that clouded and closed about him at last and he sank back into the oblivion from which he had awakened.

Next morning, when the bright sunlight shining through Mars' clear thin air awakened him, Smith lay for a while trying to remember. The dream had been more vivid than reality, but he could not now quite recall ... only that it had been more sweet and horrible than anything else in life. He lay puzzling for a while, until a soft sound from the corner aroused him from his thoughts and he sat up to see the girl lying in a catlike coil on her blankets, watching him with round, grave eyes. He regarded her somewhat ruefully.

"Morning," he said. "I've just had the devil of a dream. ... Well, hungry?"

She shook her head silently, and he could have sworn there was a covert gleam of strange amusement in her eyes.

He stretched and yawned, dismissing the nightmare temporarily from his mind.

"What am I going to do with you?" he inquired, turning to more immediate matters. "I'm leaving here in a day or two and I can't take you along, you know. Where'd you come from in the first place?"

Again she shook her head.

"Not telling? Well, it's your own business. You can stay here until I give up the room. From then on you'll have to do your own worrying."

He swung his feet to the floor and reached for his clothes.

Ten minutes later, slipping the heat-gun into its holster at his thigh, Smith turned to the girl. "There's food-concentrate in that box on the table. It ought to hold you until I get back. And you'd better lock the door again after I've gone."

Her wide, unwavering stare was his only answer, and he was not sure she had understood, but at any rate the lock clicked after him as before, and he went down the steps with a faint grin on his lips.

The memory of last night's extraordinary dream was slipping from him, as such memories do, and by the time he had reached the street the girl and the dream and all of yesterday's happenings were blotted out by the sharp necessities of the present.

Again the intricate business that had brought him here claimed his attention. He went about it to the exclusion of all else, and there was a good reason behind everything he did from the moment he stepped out into the street until the time when he turned back again at evening; though had one chosen to follow him during the day his apparently aimless rambling through Lakkdarol would have seemed very pointless.

He must have spent two hours at the least idling by the space-port, watching with sleepy, colorless eyes the ships that came and went, the passengers, the vessels lying at wait, the cargoes—particularly the cargoes. He made the rounds of the town's saloons once more, consuming many glasses of varied liquors in the course of the day and engaging in idle conversation with men of all races and worlds, usually in their own languages, for Smith was a linguist of repute among his contemporaries. He heard the gossip of the spaceways, news from a dozen planets of a thousand different events. He heard the latest joke about the Venusian Emperor and the latest report on the Chino-Aryan war and the latest song hot from the lips of Rose Robertson, whom every man on the civilized planets adored as "the Georgia Rose." He passed the day quite profitably, for his own purposes, which do not concern us now, and it was not until late evening, when he turned homeward again, that the thought of the brown girl in his room took definite shape in his mind, though it had been lurking there, formless and submerged, all day.

He had no idea what comprised her usual diet, but he bought a can of New York roast beef and one of Venusian frog-broth and a dozen fresh canal-apples and two pounds of that Earth lettuce that grows so vigorously in the fertile canal-soil of Mars. He felt that she must surely find something to her liking in this broad variety of edibles, and—for his day had been very satisfactory—he hummed *The Green Mills of Earth* to himself in a surprisingly good baritone as he climbed the stairs.

The door was locked, as before, and he was reduced to kicking the lower panels gently with his boot, for his arms were full. She opened the door with that softness that was characteristic of her and stood regarding him in the semi-darkness as he stumbled to the table with his load. The room was unlit again.

"Why don't you turn on the lights?" he demanded irritably after he had barked his shin on the chair by the table in an effort to deposit his burden there.

"Light and—dark—they are alike—to me," she murmured.

"Cat eyes, eh? Well, you look the part. Here, I've brought you some dinner. Take your choice. Fond of roast beef? Or how about a little frog-broth?"

She shook her head and backed away a step.

"No," she said. "I can not—eat your food."

Smith's brows wrinkled. "Didn't you have any of the food tablets?"

Again the red turban shook negatively.

"Then you haven't had anything for—why, more than twenty-four hours! You must be starved."

"Not hungry," she denied.

"What can I find for you to eat, then? There's time yet if I hurry. You've got to eat, child."

"I shall—eat," she said softly. "Before long—I shall—feed. Have no—worry."

She turned away then and stood at the window, looking out over the moonlit landscape as if to end the conversation. Smith cast her a puzzled glance as he opened the can of roast beef. There had been an odd undernote in that assurance that, undefinably, he did not like. And the girl had teeth and tongue and presumably a fairly human digestive system, to judge from her human form. It was nonsense for her to pretend that he could find nothing that she could eat. She must have had some of the food concentrate after all, he decided, prying up the thermos lid of the inner container to release the long-sealed savor of the hot meal inside.

"Well, if you won't eat you won't," he observed philosophically as he poured hot broth and diced beef into the dishlike lid of the thermos can and extracted the spoon from its hiding-place between the inner and outer receptacles. She turned a little to watch him as he pulled up a rickety chair and sat down to the food, and after a while the realization that her green gaze was fixed so unwinkingly upon him made the man nervous, and he said between bites of creamy canal-apple, "Why don't you try a little of this? It's good."

"The food—I eat is—better," her soft voice told him in its hesitant murmur, and again he felt rather than heard a faint undernote of unpleasantness in the words. A sudden suspicion struck him as he pondered on that last remark—some vague memory of horror-tales told about campfires in the past—and he swung round in the chair to look at her, a tiny, creeping fear unaccountably arising. There had been that in her words—in her unspoken words, that menaced. ...

She stood up beneath his gaze demurely, wide green eyes with their pulsing pupils meeting his without a falter. But her mouth was scarlet and her teeth were sharp. ...

"What food do you eat?" he demanded. And then, after a pause, very softly, "Blood?"

She stared at him for a moment, uncomprehending; then something like amusement curled her lips and she said scornfully, "You think me—vampire, eh? No—I am Shambleau!"

Unmistakably there were scorn and amusement in her voice at the suggestion, but as unmistakably she knew what he meant—accepted it as a logical suspicion—vampires! Fairy tales—but fairy tales this unhuman, outland creature was most familiar with. Smith was not a credulous man, nor a superstitious one, but he had seen too many strange things himself to doubt that the wildest legend might have a basis of fact. And there was something namelessly strange about her. ...

He puzzled over it for a while between deep bites of the canal-apple. And though he wanted to question her about a great many things, he did not, for he knew how futile it would be.

He said nothing more until the meat was finished and another canal-apple had followed the first, and he had cleared away the meal by the simple expedient of tossing the empty can out of the window. Then he lay back in the chair and surveyed her from half-closed eyes, colorless in a face tanned like saddle-leather. And again he was conscious of the brown, soft curves of her, velvety—subtle arcs and planes of smooth flesh under the tatters of scarlet leather. Vampire she might be, unhuman she certainly was, but desirable beyond words as she sat submissive beneath his low regard, her red-turbaned head bent, her clawed fingers lying in her lap. They sat very still for a while, and the silence throbbed between them.

She was so like a woman—an Earth woman—sweet and submissive and demure, and softer than soft fur, if he could forget the three-fingered claws and the pulsing eyes—and that deeper strangeness beyond words. ... (Had he dreamed that red lock of hair that moved?

Had it been *segir* that woke the wild revulsion he knew when he held her in his arms? Why had the mob so thirsted for her?) He sat and stared, and despite the mystery of her and the half-suspicions that thronged his mind—for she was so beautifully soft and curved under those revealing tatters—he slowly realized that his pulses were mounting, became aware of a kindling within ... brown girl-creature with downcast eyes ... and then the lids lifted and the green flatness of a cat's gaze met his, and last night's revulsion woke swiftly again, like a warning bell that clanged as their eyes met—animal, after all, too sleek and soft for humanity, and that inner strangeness. ...

Smith shrugged and sat up. His failings were legion, but the weakness of the flesh was not among the major ones. He motioned the girl to her pallet of blankets in the corner and turned to his own bed.

From deeps of sound sleep he awoke much later. He awoke suddenly and completely, and with that inner excitement that presages something momentous. He awoke to brilliant moonlight, turning the room so bright that he could see the scarlet of the girl's rags as she sat up on her pallet. She was awake, she was sitting with her shoulder half turned to him and her head bent, and some warning instinct crawled coldly up his spine as he watched what she was doing. And yet it was a very ordinary thing for a girl to do—any girl, anywhere. She was unbinding her turban. ...

He watched, not breathing, a presentiment of something horrible stirring in his brain, inexplicably. ...The red folds loosened, and—he knew then that he had not dreamed—again a scarlet lock swung down against her cheek ... a hair, was it? a lock of hair? ... thick as a thick worm it fell, plumply, against that smooth cheek ... more scarlet than blood and thick as a crawling worm ... and like a worm it crawled.

Smith rose on an elbow, not realizing the motion, and fixed an unwinking stare, with a sort of sick, fascinated incredulity, on that—that lock of hair. He had not dreamed. Until now he had taken it for granted that it was the *segir* which had made it seem to move on that evening before. But now ... it was lengthening, stretching, moving of itself. It must be hair, but it *crawled;* with a sickening life of its own it squirmed down against her cheek, caressingly, revoltingly, impossibly. ... Wet, it was, and round and thick and shining. ...

She unfastened the last fold and whipped the turban off. From what he saw then Smith would have turned his eyes away—and he had looked on dreadful things before, without flinching—but he could not stir. He could only lie there on his elbow staring at the mass of scarlet, squirming—worms, hairs, what?—that writhed over her head in a dreadful mockery of ringlets. And it was lengthening, falling, somehow growing before his eyes, down over her shoulders in a spilling cascade, a mass that even at the beginning could never have been hidden under the skull-tight turban she had worn. He was beyond wondering, but he realized that. And still it squirmed and lengthened and fell, and she shook it out in a horrible travesty of a woman shaking out her unbound hair—until the unspeakable tangle of it—twisting, writhing, obscenely scarlet—hung to her waist and beyond, and still lengthened, an endless mass of crawling horror that until now, somehow impossibly, had been hidden under the tight-bound turban. It was like a nest of blind, restless red worms ... it was—it was like naked entrails endowed with an unnatural aliveness, terrible beyond words.

Smith lay in the shadows, frozen without and within in a sick numbness that came of utter shock and revulsion.

She shook out the obscene, unspeakable tangle over her shoulders, and somehow he knew that she was going to turn in a moment and that he must meet her eyes. The thought of that meeting stopped his heart with dread, more awfully than anything else in this nightmare horror; for nightmare it must be, surely. But he knew without trying that he could not wrench his eyes away—the sickened fascination of that sight held him motionless, and somehow there was a certain beauty. ...

Her head was turning. The crawling awfulnesses rippled and squirmed at the motion, writhing thick and wet and shining over the soft brown shoulders about which they fell now in obscene cascades that all but hid her body. Her head was turning. Smith lay numb. And very slowly he saw the round of her cheek foreshorten and her profile come into view, all the scarlet horrors twisting ominously, and the profile shortened in turn and her full face came slowly round toward the bed—moonlight shining brilliantly as day on the pretty girl-face, demure and sweet, framed in tangled obscenity that crawled. ...

The green eyes met his. He felt a perceptible shock, and a shudder rippled down his paralyzed spine, leaving an icy numbness in its wake. He felt the goose-flesh rising. But that numbness and cold horror he scarcely realized, for the green eyes were locked with his in a long, long look that somehow presaged nameless things—not altogether unpleasant things—the voiceless voice of-her mind assailing him with little murmurous promises. ...

For a moment he went down into a blind abyss of submission; and then somehow the very sight of that obscenity in eyes that did not then realize they saw it, was dreadful enough to draw him out of the seductive darkness ... the sight of her crawling and alive with unnamable horror.

She rose, and down about her in a cascade fell the squirming scarlet of—of what grew upon her head. It fell in a long, alive cloak to her bare feet on the floor, hiding her in-a wave of dreadful, wet, writhing life. She put up her hands and like a swimmer she parted the waterfall of it, tossing the masses back over her shoulders to reveal her own brown body, sweetly curved. She smiled exquisitely, and in starting waves back from her forehead and down about her in a hideous background writhed the snaky wetness of her living tresses. And Smith knew that he looked upon Medusa.

The knowledge of that—the realization of vast backgrounds reaching into misted history—shook him out of his frozen horror for a moment, and in that moment he met her eyes again, smiling, green as glass in the moonlight, half hooded under drooping lids. Through the twisting scarlet she held out her arms. And there was something soul-shakingly desirable about tier, so that all the blood surged to his head suddenly and he stumbled to his feet like a sleeper in a dream as she swayed toward him, infinitely graceful, infinitely sweet in her cloak of living horror.

And somehow there was beauty in it, the wet scarlet writhings with moonlight sliding and shining along the thick, worm-round tresses and losing itself in the masses only to glint again and move silvery along writhing tendrils—an awful, shuddering beauty more dreadful than any ugliness could be.

But all this, again, he but half realized, for the insidious murmur was coiling again through his brain, promising, caressing, alluring, sweeter than honey; and the green eyes that held his were clear and burning like the depths of a jewel, and behind the pulsing slits of darkness he was staring into a greater dark that held all things. ... He had known—dimly he had known when he first gazed into those flat animal shallows that behind them lay this—all beauty and terror, all horror and delight, in the infinite darkness upon which her eyes opened like windows, paned with emerald glass.

Her lips moved, and in a murmur that blended indistinguishably with the silence and the sway of her body and the dreadful sway of her—her hair—she whispered—very softly, very passionately, "I shall—speak to you now—in my own tongue—oh, beloved!"

And in her living cloak she swayed to him, the murmur swelling seductive and caressing in his innermost brain—promising, compelling, sweeter than sweet. His flesh crawled to the horror of her, but it was a perverted revulsion that clasped what it loathed. His arms slid round her under the sliding cloak, wet, wet and warm and hideously alive—and the sweet velvet body was clinging to his, her arms locked about his neck—and with a whisper and a rush the unspeakable horror closed about them both.

In nightmares until he died he remembered that moment when the living tresses of Shambleau first folded him in their embrace. A nauseous, smothering odor as the wetness shut around him—thick, pulsing worms clasping every inch of his body, sliding, writhing, their wetness and warmth striking through his garments as if he stood naked to their embrace.

All this in a graven instant—and after that a tangled flash of conflicting sensation before oblivion closed over him. For he remembered the dream—and knew it for nightmare reality now, and the sliding, gently moving caresses of those wet, warm worms upon his flesh was an ecstasy above words—that deeper ecstasy that strikes beyond the body and beyond the mind and tickles the very roots of the soul with unnatural delight. So he stood, rigid as marble, as helplessly stony as any of Medusa's victims in ancient legends were, while the terrible pleasure of Shambleau thrilled and shuddered through every fiber of him; through every atom of his body and the intangible atoms of what men call the soul, through all that was Smith the dreadful pleasure ran. And it was truly dreadful. Dimly he knew it, even as his body answered to the root-deep ecstasy, a foul and dreadful wooing from which his very soul shuddered away—and yet in the innermost depths of that soul some grinning traitor shivered with delight. But deeply, behind all this, he knew horror and revulsion and despair beyond telling, while the intimate caresses crawled obscenely in the secret places of his soul—knew that the soul should not be handled—and shook with the perilous pleasure through it all.

And this conflict and knowledge, this mingling of rapture and revulsion all took place in the flashing of a moment while the scarlet worms coiled and crawled upon him, sending deep, obscene tremors of that infinite pleasure into every atom that made up Smith. And he could not stir in that slimy, ecstatic embrace—and a weakness was flooding that grew deeper after each succeeding wave of intense delight, and the traitor in his soul strengthened and drowned out the revulsion—and something within him ceased to struggle as he sank wholly into a blazing darkness that was oblivion to all else but that devouring rapture. ...

The young Venusian climbing the stairs to his friend's lodging-room pulled out his key absent-mindedly, a pucker forming between his fine brows. He was slim, as all Venusians are, as fair and sleek as any of them, and as with most of his countrymen the look of cherubic innocence on his face was wholly deceptive. He had the face of a fallen angel, without Lucifer's majesty to redeem it; for a black devil grinned in his eyes and there were faint lines of ruthlessness and dissipation about his mouth to tell of the long years behind him that had run the gamut of experiences and made his name, next to Smith's, the most hated and the most respected in the records of the Patrol.

He mounted the stairs now with a puzzled frown between his eyes. He had come into Lakkdarol on the noon liner—the *Maid* in her hold very skillfully disguised with paint and otherwise—to find in lamentable disorder the affairs he had expected to be settled. And cautious inquiry elicited the information that Smith had not been seen for three days. That was not like his friend—he had never failed before, and the two stood to lose not only a large sum of money but also their personal safety by the inexplicable lapse on the part of Smith. Yarol could think of one solution only: fate had at last caught up with his friend. Nothing but physical disability could explain it.

Still puzzling, he fitted his key in the lock and swung the door open.

In that first moment, as the door opened, he sensed something very wrong. ...The room was darkened, and for a while he could see nothing, but at the first breath he scented a strange, unnamable odor, half sickening, half sweet. And deep stirrings of ancestral memory awoke within him—ancient swamp-born memories from Venusian ancestors far away and long ago....

Yarol laid his hand on his gun, lightly, and opened the door wider. In the dimness all he could see at first was a curious mound in the far corner. ...Then his eyes grew accustomed to the dark, and he saw it more clearly, a mound that somehow heaved and stirred within itself. ...A mound of—he caught his breath sharply—a mound like a mass of entrails, living, moving, writhing with an unspeakable aliveness. Then a hot Venusian oath broke from his lips and he cleared the doorsill in a swift stride, slammed the door and set his back against it, gun ready in his hand, although his flesh crawled—for he knew. ...

"Smith!" he said softly, in a voice thick with horror. "Northwest!"

The moving mass stirred—shuddered—sank back into crawling quiescence again.

"Smith! Smith!" The Venusian's voice was gentle and insistent, and it quivered a little with terror.

An impatient ripple went over the whole mass of aliveness in the corner. It stirred again, reluctantly, and then tendril by writhing tendril it began to part itself and fall aside, and very slowly the brown of a spaceman's leather appeared beneath it, all slimed and shining.

"Smith! Northwest!" Yarol's persistent whisper came again, urgently, and with a dreamlike slowness the leather garments moved ... a man sat up in the midst of the writhing worms, a man who once, long ago, might have been Northwest Smith. From head to foot he was slimy from the embrace of the crawling horror about him. His face was that of some creature beyond humanity—dead-alive, fixed in a gray stare, and the look of terrible ecstasy that overspread it seemed to come from somewhere far within, a faint reflection from immeasurable distances beyond the flesh. And as there is mystery and magic in the moonlight which is after all but a reflection of the everyday sun, so in that gray face turned to the door was a terror unnamable and sweet, a reflection of ecstasy beyond the understanding of any who have known only earthly ecstasy themselves. And as he sat there turning a blank, eyeless face to Yarol the red worms writhed ceaselessly about him, very gently, with a soft, caressive motion that never slacked.

"Smith ... come here! Smith...get up ... Smith, Smith!" Yard's whisper hissed in the silence, commanding, urgent—but he made no move to leave the door.

And with a dreadful slowness, like a dead man rising, Smith stood up in the nest of slimy scarlet. He swayed drunkenly on his feet, and two or three crimson tendrils came writhing up his legs to the knees and wound themselves there, supportingly, moving with a ceaseless caress, that seemed to give him some hidden strength, for he said then, without inflection,

"Go away. Go away. Leave me alone." And the dead ecstatic face never changed.

"Smith!" Yarol's voice was desperate. "Smith, listen! Smith, can't you hear me?"

"Go away," the monotonous voice said. "Go away. Go away. Go—"

"Not unless you come too. Can't you hear? Smith! Smith! I'll—"

He hushed in mid-phrase, and once more the ancestral prickle of race-memory shivered down his back, for the scarlet mass was moving again, violently, rising. ...

Yarol pressed back against the door and gripped his gun, and the name of a god he had forgotten years ago rose to his lips unbidden. For he knew what was coming next, and the knowledge was more dreadful than any ignorance could have been.

The red, writhing mass rose higher, and the tendrils parted and a human face looked out—no, half human, with green cat-eyes that shone in that dimness like lighted jewels, compellingly....

Yarol breathed "Shar!" again, and flung up an arm across his face, and the tingle of meeting that green gaze for even an instant went thrilling through him perilously.

"Smith!" he called in despair. "Smith, can't you hear me?"

"Go away," said that voice that was not Smith's. "Go away."

And somehow, although he dared not look, Yarol knew that the—the other—had parted those worm-thick tresses and stood there in all the human sweetness of the brown, curved woman's body, cloaked in living horror. And he felt the eyes upon him, and something was crying insistently in his brain to lower that shielding arm. ... He was lost—he knew it, and the knowledge gave him that courage which comes from despair. The voice in his brain was growing, swelling, deafening him with a roaring command that all but swept him before it—command to lower that arm—to meet the eyes that opened upon darkness—to submit—and a promise, murmurous and sweet and evil beyond words, of pleasure to come. ...

But somehow he kept his head—somehow, dizzily, he was gripping his gun in his upflung hand—somehow, incredibly, crossing the narrow room with averted face, groping for Smith's

Shambleau (1933)

shoulder. There was a moment of blind fumbling in emptiness, and then he found it, and gripped the leather that was slimy and dreadful and wet—and simultaneously he felt something loop gently about his ankle and a shock of repulsive pleasure went through him, and then another coil, and another, wound about his feet. ...

Yarol set his teeth and gripped the shoulder hard, and his hand shuddered of itself, for the feel of that leather was slimy as the worms about his ankles, and a faint tingle of obscene delight went through him from the contact.

That caressive pressure on his legs was all he could feel, and the voice in his brain drowned out all other sounds, and his body obeyed him reluctantly—but somehow he gave one heave of tremendous effort and swung Smith, stumbling, out of that nest of horror. The twining tendrils ripped loose with a little sucking sound, and the whole mass quivered and reached after, and then Yarol forgot his friend utterly and turned his whole being to the hopeless task of freeing himself. For only a part of him was fighting, now—only a part of him struggled against the twining obscenities, and in his innermost brain the sweet, seductive murmur sounded, and his body clamored to surrender. ...

"Shar! Shar y'danis ... Shar mor'la-rol—" prayed Yarol, gasping and half unconscious that he spoke, boy's prayers that he had forgotten years ago, and with his back half turned to the central mass he kicked desperately with his heavy boots at the red, writhing worms about him. They gave back before him, quivering and curling themselves out of reach, and though he knew that more were reaching for his throat from behind, at least he could go on struggling until he was forced to meet those eyes. ...

He stamped and kicked and stamped again, and for one instant he was free of the slimy grip as the bruised worms curled back from his heavy feet, and he lurched away dizzily, sick with revulsion and despair as he fought off the coils, and then he lifted his eyes and saw the cracked mirror on the wall. Dimly in its reflection he could see the writhing scarlet horror behind him, cat face peering out with its demure girl-smile, dreadfully human, and all the red tendrils reaching after him. And remembrance of something he had read long ago swept incongruously over him, and the gasp of relief and hope that he gave shook for a moment the grip of the command in his brain.

Without pausing for a breath he swung the gun over his shoulder, the reflected barrel in line with the reflected horror in the mirror, and flicked the catch.

In the mirror he saw its blue flame leap in a dazzling spate across the dimness, full into the midst of that squirming, reaching mass behind him. There was a hiss and a blaze and a high, thin scream of inhuman malice and despair—the flame cut a wide arc and went out as the gun fell from his hand, and Yarol pitched forward to the floor.

Northwest Smith opened his eyes to Martian sunlight streaming thinly through the dingy window. Something wet and cold was slapping his face, and the familiar fiery sting of *segir*-whisky burnt his throat.

"Smith!" Yarol's voice was saying from far away. "N. W.! Wake up, damn you! Wake up!"

"I'm—awake," Smith managed to articulate thickly. "Wha's matter?"

Then a cup-rim was thrust against his teeth and Yarol said irritably, "Drink it, you fool!"

Smith swallowed obediently and more of the fire-hot *segir* flowed down his grateful throat. It spread a warmth through his body that awakened him from the numbness that had gripped him until now, and helped a little toward driving out the all-devouring weakness he was becoming aware of slowly. He lay still for a few minutes while the warmth of the whisky went through him, and memory sluggishly began to permeate his brain with the spread of the *segir*. Nightmare memories ... sweet and terrible ... memories of—

"God!" gasped Smith suddenly, and tried to sit up. Weakness smote him like a blow, and for an instant the room wheeled as he fell back against something firm and warm—Yarol's shoulder. The Venusian's arm supported him while the room steadied, and after a while he twisted a little and stared into the other's black gaze.

Yarol was holding him with one arm and finishing the mug of *segir* himself, and the black eyes met his over the rim and crinkled into sudden laughter, half hysterical after that terror that was passed.

"By *Pharol!*" gasped Yarol, choking into his mug. "By *Pharol*, N.W.! I'm never gonna let you forget this! Next time you have to drag me out of a mess I'll say—"

"Let it go," said Smith. "What's been going on? How—"

"Shambleau." Yarol's laughter died. "Shambleau! What were you doing with a thing like that?"

"What was it?" Smith asked soberly.

"Mean to say you didn't know? But where'd you find it? How—"

"Suppose you tell me first what you know," said Smith firmly. "And another swig of that *segir* too, please. I need it."

"Can you hold the mug now? Feel better?"

"Yeah—some. I can hold it—thanks. Now go on."

"Well—I don't know just where to start. They call them Shambleau—"

"Good God, is there more than one?"

"It's a—a sort of race, I think, one of the very oldest. Where they come from nobody knows. The name sounds a little French, doesn't it? But it goes back beyond the start of history. There have always been Shambleau."

"I never heard of 'em."

"Not many people have. And those who know don't care to talk about it much."

"Well, half this town knows. I hadn't any idea what they were talking about, then. And I still don't understand, but—"

"Yes, it happens like this, sometimes. They'll appear, and the news will spread and the town will get together and hunt them down, and after that—well, the story doesn't get around very far. It's too—too unbelievable."

"But—my God, Yarol!—what was it? Where'd it come from? How—"

"Nobody knows just where they come from. Another planet—maybe some undiscovered one. Some say Venus—I know there are some rather awful legends of them handed down in our family—that's how I've heard about it. And the minute I opened that door, awhile back—I—I think I knew that smell. ..."

"But—what *are* they?"

"God knows. Not human, though they have the human form. Or that may be only an illusion ... or maybe I'm crazy. I don't know. They're a species of the vampire—or maybe the vampire is a species of—of them. Their normal form must be that—that mass, and in that form they draw nourishment from the—I suppose the life-forces of men. And they take some form—usually a woman form, I think, and key you up to the highest pitch of emotion before they—begin. That's to work the life-force up to intensity so it'll be easier. ... And they give, always, that horrible, foul pleasure as they—feed. There are some men who, if they survive the first experience, take to it like a drug—can't give it up—keep the thing with them all their lives—which isn't long—feeding it for that ghastly satisfaction. Worse than smoking *ming* or—or 'praying to *Pharol.*'"

"Yes," said Smith. "I'm beginning to understand why that crowd was so surprised and—and disgusted when I said—well, never mind. Go on."

"Did you get to talk to—to it?" asked Yarol.

"I tried to. It couldn't speak very well. I asked it where it came from and it said—'from far away and long ago'—something like that."

"I wonder. Possibly some unknown planet—but I think not. You know there are so many wild stories with some basis of fact to start from, that I've sometimes wondered—mightn't there be a lot more of even worse and wilder superstitions we've never even heard of? Things like this, blasphemous and foul, that those who know have to keep still about? Awful, fantastic things running around loose that we never hear rumors of at all!

"These things—they've been in .existence for countless ages. No one knows when or where they first appeared. Those who've seen them, as we saw this one, don't talk about it. It's just one of those vague, misty rumors you find half hinted at in old books sometimes. ... I believe they are an older race than man, spawned from ancient seed in times before ours, perhaps on planets that have gone to dust, and so horrible to man that when they are discovered the discoverers keep still about it—forget them again as quickly as they can.

"And they go back to time immemorial. I suppose you recognized the legend of Medusa? There isn't any question that the ancient Greeks knew of them. Does it mean that there have been civilizations before yours that set out from Earth and explored other planets? Or did one of the Shambleau somehow make its way into Greece three thousand years ago? If you think about it long enough you'll go off your head! I wonder how many other legends are based on things like this—things we don't suspect, things we'll never know.

"The Gorgon, Medusa, a beautiful woman with—with snakes for hair, and a gaze that turned men to stone, and Perseus finally killed her—I remembered this just by accident, N. W., and it saved your life and mine—Perseus killed her by using a mirror as he fought to reflect what he dared not look at directly. I wonder what the old Greek who first started that legend would have thought if he'd known that three thousand years later his story would save the lives of two men on another planet. I wonder what that Greek's own story was, and how he met the thing, and what happened. ...

"Well, there's a lot we'll never know. Wouldn't the records of that race of—of *things*, whatever they are, be worth reading! Records of other planets and other ages and all the beginnings of mankind! But I don't suppose they've kept any records. I don't suppose they've even any place to keep them—from what little I know, or anyone knows about it, they're like the Wandering Jew, just bobbing up here and there at long intervals, and where they stay in the meantime I'd give my eyes to know! But I don't believe that terribly hypnotic power they have indicates any superhuman intelligence. It's their means of getting food—just like a frog's long tongue or a carnivorous flower's odor. Those are physical because the frog and the flower eat physical food. The Shambleau uses a—a mental reach to get mental food. I don't quite know how to put it. And just as a beast that eats the bodies of other animals acquires with each meal greater power over the bodies of the rest, so the Shambleau, stoking itself up with the life-forces of men, increases its power over the minds and the souls of other men. But I'm talking about things I can't define—things I'm not sure exist.

"I only know that when I felt—when those tentacles closed around my legs—I didn't want to pull loose, I felt sensations that—that—oh, I'm fouled and filthy to the very deepest part of me by that—pleasure—and yet—"

"I know," said Smith slowly. The effect of the *segir* was beginning to wear off, and weakness was washing back over him in waves, and when he spoke he was half meditating in a low voice, scarcely realizing that Yarol listened. "I know it—much better than you do—and there's something so indescribably awful that the thing emanates, something so utterly at odds with everything human—there aren't any words to say it. For a while I was a part of it, literally, sharing its thoughts and memories and emotions and hungers, and—well, it's over now and I don't remember very clearly, but the only part left free was that part of me that was but insane from the—the obscenity of the thing. And yet it was a pleasure so sweet—I think there must be some nucleus of utter evil in me—in everyone—that needs only the proper stimulus to get complete control; because even while I was sick all through from the touch of those—things—there was something in me that was—was simply gibbering with delight. ... Because of that I saw things—and knew things—horrible, wild things I can't quite remember—visited unbelievable places, looked backward through the memory of that—creature—I was one with, and saw—God, I wish I could remember!"

"You ought to thank your God you can't," said Yarol soberly.

His voice roused Smith from the half-trance he had fallen into, and he rose on his elbow, swaying a little from weakness. The room was wavering before him, and he closed his eyes, not to see it, but he asked, "You say they—they don't turn up again? No way of finding—another?"

Yarol did not answer for a moment. He laid his hands on the other man's shoulders and pressed him back, and then sat staring down into the dark, ravaged face with a new, strange, undefinable look upon it that he had never seen there before—whose meaning he knew, too well.

"Smith," he said finally, and his black eyes for once were steady and serious, and the little grinning devil had vanished from behind them, "Smith, I've never asked your word on anything before, but I've—I've earned the right to do it now, and I'm asking you to promise me one thing."

Smith's colorless eyes met the black gaze unsteadily. Irresolution was in them, and a little fear of what that promise might be. And for just a moment Yarol was looking, not into his friend's familiar eyes, but into a wide gray blankness that held all horror and delight—a pale sea with unspeakable pleasures sunk beneath it. Then the wide stare focused again and Smith's eyes met his squarely and Smith's voice said, "Go ahead. I'll promise."

"That if you ever should meet a Shambleau again—ever, anywhere—you'll draw your gun and burn it to hell the instant you realize what it is. Will you promise me that?"

There was a long silence. Yarol's somber black eyes bored relentlessly into the colorless ones of Smith, not wavering. And the veins stood out on Smith's tanned forehead. He never broke his word—he had given it perhaps half a dozen times in his life, but once he had given it, he was incapable of breaking it. And once more the gray seas flooded in a dim tide of memories, sweet and horrible beyond dreams. Once more Yarol was staring into blankness that hid nameless things. The room was very still.

The gray tide ebbed. Smith's eyes, pale and resolute as steel, met Yarol's levelly.

"I'll—try," he said. And his voice wavered.